Rowing Science

Volker Nolte, PhD

Editor

HUMAN KINETICS

Library of Congress Cataloging-in-Publication Data

Names: Nolte, Volker, 1952- editor.
Title: Rowing science / Volker Nolte, editor.
Description: Champaign, IL : Human Kinetics, [2024] | Includes
  bibliographical references and index.
Identifiers: LCCN 2022057191 (print) | LCCN 2022057192 (ebook) | ISBN
  9781492594383 (paperback) | ISBN 9781492594390 (epub) | ISBN
  9781492594406 (pdf)
Subjects: LCSH: Rowing--Training. | Rowing--Physiological aspects.
Classification: LCC GV791 .R686 2024 (print) | LCC GV791 (ebook) | DDC
  797.12/3071--dc23/eng/20221219
LC record available at https://lccn.loc.gov/2022057191
LC ebook record available at https://lccn.loc.gov/2022057192

ISBN: 978-1-4925-9438-3 (print)

The web addresses cited in this text were current as of December, 2022, unless otherwise noted.

Acquisitions Editor: Diana Vincer; **Developmental Editor:** Anne Hall; **Managing Editor:** Kevin Matz; **Copyeditor:** Heather Gauen Hutches; **Proofreader:** Kiezha Ferrell; **Indexer:** Nancy Ball; **Permissions Manager:** Laurel Mitchell; **Graphic Designer:** Denise Lowry; **Cover Designer:** Keri Evans; **Cover Design Specialist:** Susan Rothermel Allen; **Photograph (cover):** Jamie Squire/Getty Images; **Photographs (interior):** © Human Kinetics, unless otherwise noted; **Photo Asset Manager:** Laura Fitch; **Photo Production Manager:** Jason Allen; **Senior Art Manager:** Kelly Hendren; **Illustrations:** © Human Kinetics, unless otherwise noted; **Printer:** Versa Press

Human Kinetics books are available at special discounts for bulk purchase. Special editions or book excerpts can also be created to specification. For details, contact the Special Sales Manager at Human Kinetics.

Printed in the United States of America   10 9 8 7 6 5 4 3 2 1

The paper in this book is certified under a sustainable forestry program.

Human Kinetics
1607 N. Market Street
Champaign, IL 61820
USA

United States and International
Website: **US.HumanKinetics.com**
Email: info@hkusa.com
Phone: 1-800-747-4457

Canada
Website: **Canada.HumanKinetics.com**
Email: info@hkcanada.com

E7978

In the best memory of my father, Herbert. As a young son I took his support for granted far too often, but experience has shown that he always paved the right way for me, never refused me care, and always loved me with pride, although it was not easy for him to show it.

Contents

Introduction

The Study and Knowledge of Rowing

It all started when I was 13 years old. Resting at the riverbanks during a bicycle trip in my hometown, a single rower happened to stop right in front of me, turn his boat around, and row back the other way. I watched him intensely, intrigued by the boat he was using that was so very long from the side, but so very narrow when you looked at it straight ahead. Immediately, I wanted to learn how to handle such equipment and did not stop bothering my parents until they enlisted me in the rowing club. From this day on, I went to the club every day, looking for any opportunity to get coaching on the water or to learn about boat maintenance by stopping at the work bay where the elderly boatman did the equipment repairs and asking him endless questions.

Coaches were not exempt from my curiosity; I always needed to know why we would do things one way and not another. At age 14 I started to write down my first strength training program, and the most exciting factor for me was to notice the improvements that were carefully marked down in my training diary. Progress was graphed.

A few years later, I convinced my civic engineering professors to allow me to do some of my year-end projects about rowing-related topics instead of studying buildings or bridges. In one of these projects I measured the effects of different rudder types in the flume down in the basement of the faculty building. In another, I learned how to measure forces with strain gauges. In this way I acquired the basics to design the first-ever measurement oarlock that could be fitted on any of the then-common boats and weighed only a few grams more than a usual oarlock. This invention became the centerpiece of measurement equipment that I used for my doctoral thesis (Nolte 1984).

It seems as if I have been on the path of rowing science right from my first contacts with the sport, understanding "science as a collective institution [that] aims to produce more and more accurate natural explanations of how the natural world works, what its components are, and how the world got to be the way it is now" (UC Berkley, 2019). It has always been of special interest to me to find explanations for why things were done in a certain way—though now I know all too well that they could never be the final explanations. Helfand (2017) stated this so nicely: "I define science as a system designed to search for falsifiable models of Nature" (19). This I had to learn the hard way.

As was the trend in the late 1980s, some internationally successful crews like the Norwegians or the East Germans rowed using longer oars than their competition. The explanation given to me made sense: a longer outboard would have a larger arc, assuming a rower covers the same oar angle and is strong enough to do so. On first view, one could argue that this longer arc should improve propulsion. Equipped with this logic, I tried to convince some of the crews I was coaching to use longer oars. Specifically, the two best crews that I ever coached resisted, insisting that we even cut their oars down before the most important races. In those days, we did not have interchangeable handles, so it was necessary to physically cut the wooden oars. Luckily, the crews were persistent enough to win their argument, and we ended up having the most success with cut-down oars. I now know that these top-class rowers' instincts were indeed correct, proof that shorter oars are better (see Nolte 2009), which will be discussed in detail later on.

It is all too often the way in sport science that practitioners have a certain "feel" or idea that they implement in their training and competition. This idea, because it turns out to be successful, will then be studied by scientists who formulate the idea into a hypothesis that allows the design of a measurement method that helps to prove or refute the correctness of the idea. However, this bears some scientific challenges. One has to design a test that measures the outcomes of different pieces of equipment, training methods, or interventions, and those differences have to be measured under circumstances that are close to the real performance situation, so that coaches and athletes have to agree to perform them. This costs time and effort that may affect the planned training.

Another obstacle also arises when a study proves the advantage of a certain method: It is often hard to convince coaches and athletes about scientific findings that do not fit in their particular way of thinking. I had this experience a number of times.

I finished my PhD in 1984 and was extremely proud to present the main findings that year to an audience of international coaches during their annual conference hosted by the international rowing federation, FISA (now called World Rowing). One of the cornerstones in my thesis was the discovery that hydrodynamic lift is responsible for a large portion of the propulsion in rowing (Nolte 1984). After presenting this conclusion to the conference, I found to my surprise the room split into two groups: One that was excited about the findings and discussing how to use it in their training, and the other that would not accept the conclusions, insisting that the theory was flawed and could not be used in practice.

The resistance to accept scientific findings is obviously frustrating for sincere sport scientists, because their intention is to help coaches and athletes to perform better, at a lower cost in time or money, or with reduced risk of injury. But where does this resistance come from? For one, it may be that new findings contradict previously accepted ones or ones that are not directly insightful and a person who is not specifically educated in the particular field may be at a loss to decide what to believe. Then, if scientists cannot convincingly prove the proper conclusions, practitioners are left to make subjective decisions.

Secondly, scientific findings may be presented in a very complicated way, or the conclusion is so difficult to understand that laypeople basically cannot follow it. A third explanation may be that some people simply resist change and only want to hear arguments that support their own theory, but refuse to accept that another person may have better arguments or understandings. This is especially difficult in current times, when it is possible to widely share opinions or misinformation as if they were true or important.

Contradicting reports of the same topic are often based on misinformation, as Helfand (2017) points out so eloquently in his book *A Survival Guide to the Misinformation Age*. Especially with the inexpensive possibilities that the Internet and self-publishing offer, it is easy to present theories that sound superficially compelling so that a reader is inclined to accept them, especially if they somewhat confirm the reader's own opinion. However, science does not present the "absolute truth" but stands on solid ground when it is carried out with scientific methods and scrutinized by accepted experts in their fields. Scientists have to make sure that they present their findings in a comprehensible way that practitioners can understand and follow. Also, studies need to be presented in a way that is accessible to coaches. Peer-reviewed papers in international journals are presented for a scientific audience and are not easy for everyone to find.

Individual Innovations in Rowing

The study and knowledge of rowing—what we could also call the *science of rowing*—has a long history. Coaches and engineers were the first to study the sport in an effort to gain an advantage in high-profile, prestigious competitions like the famous Oxford–Cambridge Boat Race and the Henley Royal Regatta, as well as the professional races that were very popular at that time, for which there was considerable money involved. The spike in rowing-related patents in the late 1800s and book publications in the early 1900s are evidence of these scientific endeavors. Some of these patents were so far ahead of their time that they could only be fully realized many years later. For example, George Isaacs patented a sliding rigger concept in 1876 that was not possible to convert into a practically usable construction with the technology and materials available at the time (figure 1*a*). Although several attempts were made over time to implement the principle into a usable model, it took until 1981 (figure 1*b*) to be finally translated into a race-worthy boat design using modern technology and materials (Nolte 1981). Likewise, Michael Davis patented an asymmetric blade shape in 1880 that only in 1991 was transformed into a successful design by the oar manufacturer Concept2 and then built using composite materials.

A similar development can be observed in the progress of measuring devices. The rowing boat and oars are well suited to accommodate devices that enable the measurement of physical quantities such as speed or forces, which sparked the interest of early engineers and researchers. Atkinson (1896; 1898) presented a force and angle measurement oarlock, and Lefeuvre and Paillotte (1904) developed a more complete measurement system for oarlock and footstretcher forces, boat velocity, and seat position. These exclusively mechanical measurement tools gave the sport its first real data about the physical quantities of rowing and preliminary insight into the functioning of the rowing stroke. Although from today's perspective there were limitations regarding accuracy, weight, practical applicability, and the number of strokes that could be measured, the information recorded was quite amazing compared with a modern data set (figure 2).

There have been many attempts over the years to develop measurement instruments that could be used in the rowers' own boats and that allowed for racelike conditions. However, those efforts remained only partly successful because measurement was limited to singular variables until Schneider and Morell (1977) and Nolte (1984) compiled measurement equipment for the first time, which allowed complex biomechanical measurements under racing conditions and using rowers' own familiar equipment (figure 3). These systems were successful to advance basic research in rowing, but were not applicable for general use because of the technical complexity involved. With rapid technology development, however, it is now possible to measure even more variables using increasingly compact, lighter, and more accurate measuring devices, which can also store much more data.

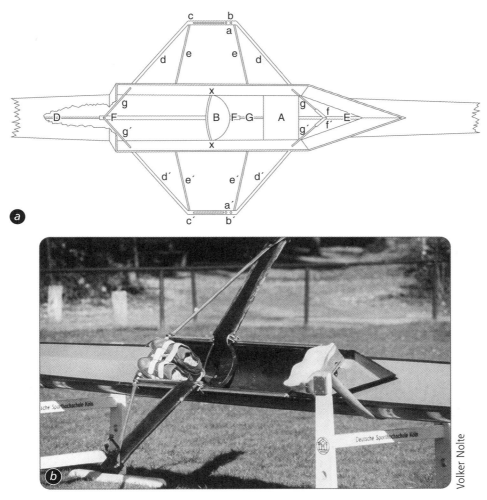

▶ **Figure 1** Comparison of *(a)* the original concept of the sliding rigger (U.S. Patent No. 182023, 1876, George Isaacs) with *(b)* the first model that was successfully used in competition (Nolte 1981).

Volker Nolte

The development of rowing equipment and measuring devices will inevitably progress. The miniaturization of electronics and wireless data transformation allow the measurement of more variables directly in the athletes' competition boats without any impediment of movement or performance. This has led to a larger variety of measurement equipment, from heart rate monitors to devices for measuring stroke frequency, boat speed, and oarlock force. These devices are now so compact and user-friendly that they can be operated by any rower without the support of specifically qualified staff. They are primarily used to provide direct feedback to the rower and the coach in training and competition, but can also be implemented in broader scientific research. However, in order to make good use of such devices, a certain amount of knowledge is required so that correct conclusions can be drawn. For example, one must know how to interpret heart rate data correctly so that training can be controlled in a meaningful way.

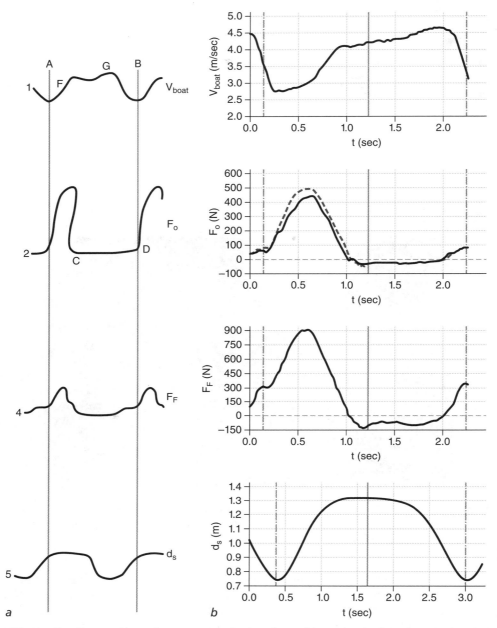

▶ **Figure 2** Comparison of measurement data from *(a)* mechanical equipment in 1904 (Lefeuvre and Paillotte 1904) and *(b)* modern equipment (PowerLine) in 2022. V_{boat} = boat velocity; F_o = oarlock force; F_F = footstretcher force; d_s = seat displacement relative to the boat.

In addition to the field of biomechanics, developments have been made in the fields of boat building, physiology, and psychology. It should also be remembered that a wide range of blade shapes and shaft types are available today, which, together with the length adjustability of the oars, offers a huge number of conceivable rigging variations that must be carefully considered in order to find the best possible setting for the individual rower.

▶ **Figure 3** Comparison of oar angle and oarlock force measurement systems *(a)* in 1984 (the amplifier and storage devices are circled; no direct feedback for rower was possible; all equipment was connected by wires) and *(b)* in 2022 (wireless with monitors that store data and provide real-time feedback; NK EmPower Oarlock with SpeedCoach shown here).

Photos courtesy Volker Nolte.

All of this innovation has led to a tremendous increase in rowing-related publications, which in turn supported the steady performance improvements in rowing that, with few interruptions, still continue today (Kleshnev 2020; Kleshnev 2021). These developments are of course very interesting for scientists and always spur further studies.

Wading Through the Research

This trend of innovation is more likely to progress than to slow, leaving rowers and coaches with even more options. Therefore, they must either learn the basics, follow relevant scientific publications, and keep up with developments, or rely on the judgements and suggestions of experts. The former is certainly the more arduous path, but comes with the advantage of greater autonomy, conviction, and motivation, as well as the possibility of further discoveries by practitioners. There are, of course, limits to how much knowledge a person can accumulate in all scientific fields. Therefore, at a certain point one must rely on experts, which enables faster and easier decisions, but is more expensive and requires the user to place trust in expert judgement.

The challenge arises in this case to identify the proper experts. At a time when anyone can claim to have expertise and publish their opinion, one can find numerous myths and misinformation about rowing science on the Internet and in poorly reviewed prints. It is therefore even more important that rowers and coaches master basic knowledge and are trained in critical thinking.

As with every discovery in science, as soon as some questions are answered new ones arise. We have, for example, a very good understanding of boat movement, such as horizontal velocity and pitch, because there are very good tools available to accurately measure all aspects of it. On the other hand, though theoretically well understood, we are still in the process of finding methods to carry out identification of the position and measurement of the movement of the overall center of gravity with a high enough precision that would validate theories regarding its propulsion during the drive and best conservation of its energy during the recovery.

Similarly, a lot of information has been collected about training and the human body's adaptation to it, but there are still answers to be found about the influence of specific training intensities on individual athletes and therefore how to best guide them. As the duration of training increases, it seems that there is a limit to the overall amount of work that can be done before the athlete's progress is inhibited. It is conceivable—but not proven—that there are more efficient combinations of training intensities and duration for the individual athlete. In addition, there is still no consistent understanding of how certain injuries occur, how training impacts them, and how they can best be prevented. For example, rowers still experience rib stress fractures and low back pain too often.

The influence of mental health on personal development and performance has come to the forefront in recent years, but studies in this field are still needed, especially with regard to its effect on individuals and their unique coping mechanisms. The formation of the circumstances that cause such problems and the manifestation of their effects are often discovered too late.

All these examples show that there are numerous questions related to rowing performance that need further scientific investigations. The resulting knowledge will help to continuously improve rowing performance, which will subsequently lead to a further reduction in the world best times in racing.

Interpreting the Data

What does all this mean now for the athlete and coach who want to do their best? It means that science cannot give a final answer. It can give a lot of very good information and certainly identify a lot of errors to avoid. An individual has leeway to tailor their technique and training to their specific needs; however, one should not use this leeway to follow the misunderstandings, myths, and incorrect interpretations that are still quite prevalent in the sport.

There is not one single best way to prepare athletes for high performance—rather, this book brings together proven scientific understandings with present best practices to form the bases of many effective methods of preparation. All this is intended to be presented in a language that all rowers and coaches can understand. All contributors are scientists, but also have tremendous practical experience. They speak—as you might say—the rowing lingo, but will do so on a scientific basis.

The Role of Biological Attributes vs Practice in Rowing Success

Drake Nolte

The Genetics of Performance

Paula Jardine

To be an elite Olympic rower, an individual needs to be tall, be strong, and have good cardiopulmonary endurance. Of these core characteristics, height, which is the most strongly determined by genetics, is the easiest to select for. Although elite performance is complex and multifactorial, height has become the characteristic most favored over the last 30 years by Olympic rowing coaches in search of a competitive advantage when selecting from athletes with similar physiological and technical capabilities. This selection strategy first emerged as a response to the German Democratic Republic's (GDR) almost total dominance of the sport between 1968 and 1988, and it has continued since without critical evaluation. As a result, many contemporary Olympic rowers are now drawn from the 99th percentile of the population for height and push the outer genetic limits for size.

Application to Talent Identification

In practice, the primary interest in genetics from the perspective of sport is its application to talent identification. Despite advances in the field of genetics, little of practical utility for this purpose has been forthcoming. Australian scientists have identified only two genes that appear to contribute to sport performance. These genes, called ACE and ACTN3, are found with greater frequency in elite athletes, suggesting they confer some as-yet unquantifiable advantage. ACTN3 codes for a muscle protein and is thought to contribute to sprinting ability. ACE regulates an enzyme found primarily in the capil-

Key Point

A genetic test for the ACE gene is available commercially in some countries for parents interested in directing their children toward sports where, in theory, they might have a greater genetic predisposition for success. Although the ACE and ACTN3 genes have been found in some studies to occur in greater frequency in elite athletes, they are more likely to make a contribution at the margins of elite performance than to be predictive of it. The utility of such testing is therefore dubious and arguably even counterproductive if it encourages early specialization.

laries of the lungs and lining of blood vessels, which can raise blood pressure by causing these vessels to constrict. By comparison, 697 gene alleles have been identified and linked to height, none of which have been directly linked to performance or potential.

Height and Epigenetics

In 1990, the U.S. National Institutes of Health (NIH) initiated a collaborative international scientific project to identify, sequence, and map all human genes, called the Human Genome Project (HGP). When it was completed in 2003, the researchers had determined that humans have approximately 20,500 genes. These genes control inherited traits such as height, skin color, or eye color. A gene will code for hair, whereas the specific variation of the gene an individual has, called an allele, determines whether the hair is colored red, blond, brown, or so forth. Alleles are estimated to number in the millions and can be either inherited or occur as a result of random mutations.

A total of 697 alleles are believed to influence height. With up to 90% of the variation in height thought to be due to genetics, it is the most heritable of the three primary physical characteristics of rowers. Although tall parents tend to have tall children, significant differences can arise between siblings in the same family.

Between 1896 and 1996, the global mean height for both men and women increased by 5%, with men increasing from 162.5 cm to 171.3 cm and women from 151.5 cm to 159.5 cm. Because of the high number of gene variants, average heights in populations around the world can be very different, and some regions have seen more pronounced changes than others. North American women increased from 155.6 cm to 162.7 cm, whereas European and central Asian women showed the greatest increase, from 153.19 cm to 164.1 cm (Roser et al. 2013). This phenomenon is not due to alterations in the genetic code but is driven instead by epigenetics—environmental factors that influence the activation of genes (e.g., diet, toxins, and hormones). Childhood health and nutrition improved during the 20th century as public sanitation and living standards rose, activating gene variants that enabled individuals to achieve their full genetic potential for height.

Key Point

Although the use of genetics to identify sport talent has not proven effective thus far, there are tantalizing hints that epigenetics, the effect of environmental factors on gene expression, may be more significant in the development of elite athletes. One underresearched and poorly understood phenomenon is that elite athletes often grow up in rural environments, on farms, or in small villages: Among Olympic medal winning rowers, Anna Bebbington, Victoria Thornley, Pertti Karppinen, Kjetil Borch, Olaf Tufte, Rob Waddell, Mahé Drysdale, Hamish Bond, Eric Murray, and Sverri Nielsen all have this in common.

Rowers and Height

As a subset of the population, rowers are taller than the global average. Even lightweight rowers, at an average height of 182.7 cm (85th percentile) for men and 173 cm (92nd percentile) for women, are much taller than the global mean. The dominant trend for most of the last 50 years was for male (figure 1.1) and female (figure 1.2) Olympic finalists to be getting taller and heavier. Between Mexico City 1968 and Rio 2016, the average height of male Olympic rowing finalists increased 3.2%, from 188 cm to 194 cm, whereas the average weight increased by 10.7%, from 86 kg to 95 kg. Modern Olympic openweight finalists now average 194 cm in height for men and 180 cm for women, both inside the 99th percentile. A third of the men's height increase—a jump of 2 cm—took place between 1984 and 1988. This is not a product of epigenetic change but selection preferences of coaches.

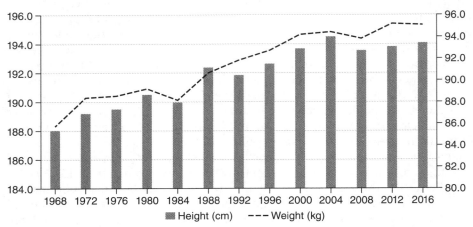

▶ **Figure 1.1** Body height and weight of male openweight Olympic finalists, 1968-2016. All the anthropometric data cited in this chapter was compiled from www.sports-reference.com/Olympics. Further analysis of this data was used to produce the tables and graphs.

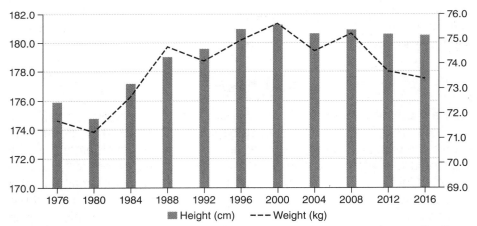

▶ **Figure 1.2** Body height and weight of female openweight Olympic finalists, 1976-2016.

Height in the GDR Era

Through the 1970s and 1980s the German Democratic Republic (GDR), with its highly sophisticated, professionally organized sport development system, dominated the sport of rowing. East German sport scientists determined the optimal average weight and height range for rowers. The system selected athletes who possessed the necessary strength and cardiopulmonary capacities while remaining within this optimal range. The preference was for crews to be made up of athletes within one standard deviation of optimal height while average weight of the crew also remained close to a targeted optimum (see tables 1.1 and 1.2).

Table 1.1 GDR Olympic Men's Crews and Current World Best Time Crews: Average Height and Weight

TOURNAMENT		MEXICO CITY 1968	
Event	Athlete	Height (cm)	Weight (kg)
1x	A Hill	184	78
2x	U Schmied	187	84
	M Haake	186	86
	Crew average	**186.5**	**85**
2-	J Lucke	193	91
	H-J Bothe	195	91
	Crew average	**194**	**91**
2+	H Wollmann	197	83
	W Gunkel	192	92
	Crew average	**194.5**	**87.5**
4-	F Forberger	190	87
	D Grahn	189	86
	F Ruehle	192	93
	D Schubert	187	83
	Crew average	**189.5**	**87.3**
4+	P Kremtz	188	87
	R Goehler	191	84
	M Glepke	188	84
	K Jakob	185	82
	Crew average	**188**	**84.3**
8+	G Bergau	185	87
	K-D Bahr	187	85
	C Wilke	193	100
	P Gorny	189	84
	R Zerfowski	187	82
	P Hein	182	81
	M Schneider	196	93
	P Pompe	189	86
	Crew average	**188.5**	**87.3**
	Team average	**189.2**	**86.5**
	Min	**182.0**	**78.0**
	Max	**197.0**	**100.0**
	VAR	**15.3**	**24.3**
	STDEV	**3.9**	**4.9**

(continued)

Table 1.1 *(continued)*

TOURNAMENT		MUNICH 1972	
Event	Athlete	Height (cm)	Weight (kg)
1x	W Gueldenpfennig	182	82
2x	H-J Boehmer	182	82
	H-U Schmied	187	84
	Crew average	**184.5**	**83**
2-	S Brietzke	192	90
	W Mager	190	87
	Crew average	**191**	**88.5**
2+	W Gunkel	192	92
	J Lucke	193	91
	Crew average	**192.5**	**91.5**
4-	F Forberger	190	87
	D Grahn	189	86
	F Ruehle	192	93
	D Schubert	187	83
	Crew average	**189.5**	**87.3**
4+	D Zander	193	95
	R Gust	190	92
	E Martens	191	94
	R Jobst	190	83
	Crew average	**190**	**91**
8+	H-J Borzym	188	92
	J Langvoigt	190	85
	H Dimke	197	87
	M Schneider	196	93
	H Schreiber	190	90
	M Schmorde	192	88
	B Langvoigt	188	88
	H Mederow	186	84
	Crew average	**190.9**	**88.4**
	Team average	**189.9**	**88.2**
	Min	**182.0**	**82.0**
	Max	**197.0**	**95.0**
	VAR	**13.2**	**16.8**
	STDEV	**3.6**	**4.1**
TOURNAMENT		MONTREAL 1976	
Event	Athlete	Height (cm)	Weight (kg)
1x	J Dreifke	192	95
2x	H-U Schmied	187	84
	J Bertow	184	79
	Crew average	**185.5**	**81.5**

TOURNAMENT	MONTREAL 1976		
Event	Athlete	Height (cm)	Weight (kg)
2-	J Langvoigt	190	85
	B Langvoigt	188	88
	Crew average	**189**	**86.5**
2+	H Jaehrling	198	94
	F-W Ulrich	194	103
	Crew average	**196**	**98.5**
4x	W Gueldenpfennig	182	82
	R Reiche	198	96
	K-H Bussert	194	84
	M wolfgramm	180	85
	Crew average	**188.5**	**86.8**
4-	S Brietzke	192	90
	A Decker	195	96
	S Semmler	190	94
	W Mager	190	87
	Crew average	**191.8**	**91.8**
4+	A Schulz	188	86
	R Kunze	188	95
	W Diessner	188	84
	U Diessner	189	83
	Crew average	**188.25**	**87**
8+	B Baumgart	190	84
	G Doehn	196	96
	W Klatt	190	98
	H-J Lueck	191	88
	D Wendisch	192	91
	R Kostulski	192	82
	U Karnatz	192	91
	K-H Prudoehl	185	89
	Crew average	**190.1**	**89.1**
	Team average	**190.2**	**89.2**
	Min	**180.0**	**79.0**
	Max	**198.0**	**103.0**
	VAR	**18.9**	**35.9**
	STDEV	**4.4**	**6.0**
TOURNAMENT	MOSCOW 1980		
Event	Athlete	Height (cm)	Weight (kg)
1x	P Kersten	187	78
2x	J Dreifke	192	95
	K Kroeppelien	189	90
	Crew average	**190.5**	**92.5**

(continued)

Table 1.1 *(continued)*

Event	Athlete	Height (cm)	Weight (kg)
TOURNAMENT		**MOSCOW 1980**	
2-	J Langvoigt	190	85
	B Langvoigt	188	88
	Crew average	**189**	**86.5**
2+	H Jaehrling	198	94
	F-W Ulrich	194	103
	Crew average	**196**	**98.5**
4x	F Dundr	186	89
	C Bunk	189	76
	U Heppner	196	91
	M Winter	194	91
	Crew average	**191.3**	**86.8**
4-	S Brietzke	192	90
	A Decker	195	96
	S Semmler	190	94
	J Thiele	185	80
	Crew average	**190.5**	**90**
4+	D Wendisch	192	91
	U Diessner	189	83
	W Diessner	188	84
	G Doehn	196	96
	Crew average	**191.25**	**88.5**
8+	B Krauss	192	89
	H-P Koppe	187	75
	U Kons	195	95
	J Friedrich	193	93
	J Doberschuetz	190	81
	U Karnatz	192	91
	U Duehring	186	86
	B Hoeing	192	88
	Crew average	**190.9**	**87.3**
	Team average	**191.0**	**88.6**
	Min	**185.0**	**75.0**
	Max	**198.0**	**103.0**
	VAR	**11.9**	**44.8**
	STDEV	**3.5**	**6.7**
TOURNAMENT		**DUISBERG 1983 WORLDS**	
Event	**Athlete**	**Height (cm)**	**Weight (kg)**
1x	U Mund	190	89
2x	T Lange	189	89
	U Heppner	196	91
	Crew average	**192.5**	**90**

TOURNAMENT	DUISBERG 1983 WORLDS		
Event	Athlete	Height (cm)	Weight (kg)
2-	C Ertel	194	90
	U Sauerbrey	192	91
	Crew average	**193**	**90.5**
2+	T Greiner	193	90
	U Diessner	189	83
	Crew average	**191**	**86.5**
4x	K-H Bussert		
	M Winter	194	91
	R Reiche	198	96
	J Dreifke		
	Crew average	**196**	**93.5**
4-	J Thiele	185	80
	H-P Koppe	187	75
	J Doberschuetz	190	81
	U Heinke		
	Crew average	**187.3**	**78.7**
4+	D Schiller		
	J Friedrich	193	93
	B Niesecke	190	89
	B Eichwurzel	196	91
	Crew average	**193**	**91**
8+	K Buettner	192	89
	U Gasch	190	89
	G Uebeler	189	95
	K Schmeling	196	91
	R Brudel	192	90
	H Jaehrling	198	94
	J Seyfarth		
	B Hoeing	**192**	**88**
	Crew average	**192.8**	**91.2**
	Team average	**191.2**	**89.2**
	Min	**185.0**	**75.0**
	Max	**198.0**	**96.0**
	VAR	**12.5**	**25.8**
	STDEV	**3.5**	**5.1**
TOURNAMENT	SEOUL 1988		
Event	Athlete	Height (cm)	Weight (kg)
1x	T Lange	189	89
2x	U Mund	190	89
	U Heppner	196	91
	Crew average	**193**	**90**

(continued)

Table 1.1 *(continued)*

TOURNAMENT		SEOUL 1988	
Event	Athlete	Height (cm)	Weight (kg)
2-	C Ertel	194	90
	U Gasch	190	89
	Crew average	192	89.5
2+	M Streit	200	92
	D Kirchhoff	208	106
	Crew average	204	99
4x	S Bogs	189	89
	S Zuehlke	198	92
	H Habermann	194	87
	J Koeppen	194	87
	Crew average	193.8	88.8
4-	R Schroeder	192	90
	T Greiner	193	90
	R Brudel	192	90
	O Foerster	190	89
	Crew average	191.8	89.8
4+	F Klawonn	196	91
	B Eichwurzel	196	91
	B Niesecke	190	89
	K Schmeling	196	91
	Crew average	193.0	90.1
	Team average	194.1	90.6
	Min	189.0	87.0
	Max	208.0	106.0
	VAR	21.5	15.8
	STDEV	4.6	4.0
WORLD BEST TIME: CREWS			
Event	Athlete	Height (cm)	Weight (kg)
1x	Robert Manson (NZL)	188	89
2x	M Sinkovic (CRO)	188	95
	V Sinkovic (CRO)	187	93
	Crew average	187.5	94
2-	E Murray (NZL)	195	98
	H Bond (NZL)	189	89
	Crew average	192	93.5
2+	E Murray (NZL)	195	98
	H Bond (NZL)	189	89
	Crew average	192	93.5

WORLD BEST TIME: CREWS			
Event	Athlete	Height (cm)	Weight (kg)
4x	A Mikhay (UKR)	195	96
	O Morozov (UKR)	195	100
	D Nadtoka (UKR)	195	95
	I Dovhodko (UKR)	196	100
	Crew average	**195.25**	**97.75**
4-	A Gregory (GBR)	199	90
	P Reed (GBR)	198	100
	T James (GBR)	190	85
	A Triggs Hodge (GBR)	192	97
	Crew average	**194.8**	**93**
8+	J Weisenfeld (GER)	199	90
	F Wimberger (GER)	190	92
	M Planer (GER)	198	94
	T Johannesen (GER)	187	89
	J Schneider (GER)	196	93
	M Jakschik (GER)	193	88
	R Schmidt (GER)	186	74
	H Ocik (GER)	190	91
	Crew average	**192.4**	**88.9**
	Team average	**193.9**	**92.6**
	Min	**186.0**	**74.0**
	Max	**199.0**	**100.0**
	VAR	**18.3**	**52.6**
	STDEV	**4.2**	**5.9**

Table 1.2 GDR Olympic Women's Crews and Current World Best Time Crews: Average Height and Weight

TOURNAMENT		MONTREAL 1976	
Event	Athlete	Height (cm)	Weight (kg)
1x (gold)	Hahn-Scheiblich	172	68
2x Silver	Jahn	174	69
	Wach-Boesler	174	69
	Crew average	**174**	**69**
2- Silver	Noack	177	83
	Dahne	177	73
	Crew average	**177**	**78**
4+ Gold	Metze-Ullbricht	180	82
	Borrmann-Schwede	174	77
	Kuehn-Lohs	184	86
	Sredzki-Kurth	178	77
	Crew average	**179**	**77**

(continued)

Table 1.2 *(continued)*

Event	Athlete	Height (cm)	Weight (kg)
TOURNAMENT	**MONTREAL 1976**		
4x (+) Gold	Zobelt	188	83
	Lau	175	65
	Kowalschek-Poley	169	68
	Borchmann-Gruenberg	176	65
	Crew average	**177**	**70.25**
8+ Gold	Landvoigt-Goretzki	182	77
	Koepke-Knetsch	181	72
	Richter-Doerfel	172	80
	Ahrenholz	178	85
	Leschhorn-Kallies	185	88
	Dobler-Ebert	177	83
	Lehmann	183	75
	Weise-Mueller	176	84
	Crew average	**178.9**	**81**
	Team average	**177.7**	**76.6**
	Min	**169**	**65**
	Max	**188**	**88**
	VAR	**21.8**	**53.8**
	STDEV	**4.8**	**7.3**
TOURNAMENT	**MOSCOW 1980**		
Event	Athlete	Height (cm)	Weight (kg)
1x (bronze)	Schroeter	181	71
2x Silver	Linse	184	78
	Westphal	175	70
	Crew average	**179.5**	**74**
2- Gold	Steindorf	176	72
	Klier-Buegel	175	66
	Crew average	**175.5**	**69**
4+ Gold	Kapheim-Jahnke	177	68
	Froehlich-Arndt	182	74
	Noack	177	83
	Topf-Saalfeld	176	63
	Crew average	**178**	**72**
4x (+) Gold	Schenk-Ploch	178	73
	Lau	175	65
	Reinhardt-Tietze	176	65
	Reichel-Zobelt	188	83
	Crew average	**179.25**	**71.5**
8+ Gold	Kirchner-Boesler	175	70
	Koepke-Neisser	175	70
	Koepke-Knetsch	181	72
	Schuetz	179	76

TOURNAMENT	MOSCOW 1980		
Event	Athlete	Height (cm)	Weight (kg)
	Kuehn-Lohs	184	86
	Richter-Doerfel	172	80
	Sandig-Gasch	175	68
	Metze-Ullbricht	180	82
	Crew average	178	76.3
	Team average	178.1	73.1
	Min	172	63
	Max	188	86
	VAR	15.7	44.7
	STDEV	4.0	6.7
TOURNAMENT	SEOUL 1988		
Event	Athlete	Height (cm)	Weight (kg)
1x (gold)	Hampe-Behrendt	181	75
2x Gold	Peter	185	78
	Schroeter	181	71
	Crew average	183	74.5
2- 4th	Spittler	183	78
	Schroeder	184	79
	Crew average	183.5	78.5
4+ Gold	Walther	187	85
	Dorberschuetz-Mey	183	76
	Hornig-Mieseler	186	82
	Seich	180	75
	Crew average	184	79.5
4x Gold	Foerster-Pieloth	177	69
	Mundt-Richter	178	78
	Schramm	188	77
	Rau-Sorgers	181	77
	Crew average	181	75.25
8+ Gold	Balthasar	177	71
	Haacker	181	72
	Kluge	186	82
	Schroder-Lehman	186	75
	Schell-Stange	180	80
	Strauch	184	77
	Noetzel-Wild	180	81
	Ungemach-Zeidler	182	81
	Crew average	182.7	78.3
	Team average	182.4	77.1
	Min	177	69
	Max	188	85
	VAR	10.3	16.8
	STDEV	3.2	4.1

(continued)

Table 1.2 *(continued)*

WORLD BEST TIME: CREWS			
Event	Athlete	Height (cm)	Weight (kg)
1x	R Neykova (BUL)	177	80
2x	Aldesey (AUS)	183	75
	Kehoe (AUS)	172	75
	Crew average	**177.5**	**75**
2-	Prendergast (NZL)	183	73
	Gowler (NZL)	182	76
	Crew average	**182.5**	**74.5**
4-	Pratt (NZL)	179	73
	Bevan (NZL)	174	70
	Prendergast (NZL)	183	73
	Gowler (NZL)	182	76
	Crew average	**182**	**76**
4x	Thiele (GER)	173	68
	Baer (GER)	185	75
	Lier (GER)	183	78
	Schmidla (GER)	173	76
	Crew average	**178.5**	**74.25**
8+	Polk (USA)	180	79
	Simmonds (USA)	183	82
	Regan (USA)	188	81
	Schmetterling (USA)	180	77
	Luczak (USA)	191	77
	Lind (USA)	183	80
	Opitz (USA)	180	69
	Robbins (USA)	188	80.7
	Crew average	**184.1**	**78.2**
	Team average	**181.0**	**75.9**
	Min	**172.0**	**68.0**
	Max	**191.0**	**82.0**
	VAR	**26.0**	**15.4**
	STDEV	**5.1**	**3.9**

Rivalry of the Genetic Cousins

Perhaps the fiercest rivalry of the era was between the two Germanys. It was a lopsided battle, with East Germany (population 17 million) winning 46 Olympic medals—half of them gold, whereas West Germany (Federal Republic of Germany, or FRG), drawing from a population of 70 million, won only four Olympic medals in the 1970s. These performance differences cannot be attributed to genetics; they are a product of differing development systems.

At Munich 1972, West Germany's sole victory on the rowing course came when their coxed four (4+) defeated the GDR by half a length. Dubbed "the Bulls of Konstanz" in tribute to their size and the lake they trained on, the West Germans were by far the biggest crew at the Games. At an average height of 192 cm, they were within the average height range. Their nickname alluded to their 99 kg average weight—8 kg more than their vanquished cousins from East Germany, who were themselves the size of super heavyweight boxers. The Bulls of Konstanz were rowing's first super-sized openweight crew, and in Munich they were in a class of their own.

Then came Montreal 1976 and its most famous race, the men's single scull (1x). The Finnish giant Pertti Karppinen (201 cm, 103 kg) overhauled Peter-Michael Kolbe (194 cm, 84 kg), the world champion from West Germany, in the final 10 strokes to win by 2.7 seconds. Before Karppinen's shock win, it was rare for a finalist in the 1x to be over 190 cm in height—in the previous decade, there had only been two, the American scullers Jon Van Blom (194 cm, 84 kg), who was fourth in Mexico City, and Jim Dietz (201 cm, 91 kg), fifth in Munich. Although the Finn towered over his rivals in the final, height was no guarantee of success. The two other scullers of comparable size, Dietz and the 199 cm Swede Hans Svensson, both failed to advance. Previously, the tallest rowers were ectomorphic in build and within the normative range for weight; now here was a champion who broke the mold. Karppinen was the original standout specimen of a super-sized rower. .He won three consecutive Olympic titles and, perhaps more than any other rower, embodied the idea that bigger might be better.

West Germany absorbed these lessons: the first, their success by the biggest crew on the water, and the second, their defeat by the biggest man on the water. They adopted a new approach in the 1980s, preferentially selecting crews of male rowers who were over 195 cm tall—outside the normative range for Olympic rowers. Size became a form of arms race in the battle against the East Germans. Summed up: When all else fails, bring a bigger dog to the fight.

The Soviet, Romanian, and British coaches also began selecting taller and bigger crews throughout the 1980s. The GDR responded conservatively; athletes from the lower half of the standard range for male rowers, under 190 cm tall, began to disappear, replaced by athletes who were taller while average crew weight remained close to the optimal target of 90 kg (see table 1.1). By Seoul 1988, only two athletes shorter than 190 cm remained: Lange in the single scull (1x) and Bogs in the quad scull (4x). Although the GDR remained the most successful team in Seoul, their results showed a slight decline from the pre-1984 period as the double scull (2x) and coxless pair (2–) finished fifth. The Italian Abbagnale brothers (182 cm, 90 kg and 187 cm, 97 kg) beat the much larger GDR duo of Kirchhoff and Streit (208 cm, 106 kg and 200 cm, 92 kg) in the coxed pair (2+), and Italy kept the GDR off the top of the podium in the 4x with another Abbagnale brother on board. None of the Italian scullers exceeded 190 cm in height. Narrowing the selection pool by excluding marginally smaller athletes perhaps made it harder for the GDR to develop enough athletes of the required physiological standard to contest all the events, and for the first time there was no men's eight (8+).

In November 1989, the Berlin Wall fell, and not long after the 1990 World Rowing Championships the GDR disappeared as a nation-state, leaving a vacuum to be filled at the top of the sport. The yardstick against which success in the sport was measured disappeared overnight. The end of the GDR era marks the start of a new one and an informal experiment with size that began as a 1980s solution to a 1970s problem continued without the GDR as a control group and without critical evaluation.

Height in the Post-GDR Era

Notwithstanding the success of the Italians in Seoul against much larger GDR opposition, a confirmation bias effect occurred. Super-sized crews and individual rowers the size of Karppinen became common. In Barcelona 1992, the first post-GDR Olympics, Great Britain—with former GDR women's coach Jürgen Gröbler as head men's coach— is a case in point, winning both pair events with athletes in the same mold: brothers Greg and Jonny Searle (198 cm, 99 kg and 196 cm, 100 kg) in the 2+ and Steven Redgrave and Matthew Pinsent (193 cm, 103 kg and 196 cm, 108 kg) in the 2–. (Newspaper reports from 1992 put Pinsent's weight before Barcelona at 97 kg.)

It is impossible to know how any of these super-sized crews would have fared against GDR crews, or indeed what the response of the GDR would have been to the ever-increasing size of the opposition. It is conceivable that in the interests of maintaining the size of the selection pool, the collective wisdom would have returned to the optimal-range strategy that served them so well for 20 years, despite the evident preference of at least one former GDR coach (Gröbler) for the largest athletes possible. It is no small irony that the remaining men's sculling events in Barcelona produced a second consecutive win in the 1x by Karppinen's successor Thomas Lange (189 cm, 89 kg), one of the two smaller East Germans from Seoul, and an extraordinary win by the Australian lightweights Stephen Hawkins (approx. 178cm) and Peter Antonie (approx. 182 cm, 76 kg) racing in the openweight 2x.

Genetics and Weight Class

If the disappearance of the East Germans removed the original yardstick for success, the introduction of lightweight coxless four (4–) and double scull (2x) in Atlanta 1996 provided another, allowing insight into the relative value of height when weight is constrained and crews evenly matched for average weight (70kg). The average height of the lightweight sweep rowers settled at 184.3 cm, with a normative range of 181 to 187 cm. Approximately 20% of medalists fell outside this range in recent years. At 176 cm, Italian Catello Amarante was the shortest medalist (bronze in Athens 2004), and only once since the lightweight category was added did the tallest crew win the Olympic final—South Africa, averaging 186.3 cm, in 2012. Racing for South Africa was John Smith, the tallest medalist at 190 cm. The evidence suggests that excess height generally doesn't confer an advantage: The tallest crews usually found themselves in fourth and fifth place.

Table 1.3 Lightweight Male Olympic Finalists, 1996-2016: Average Height and Weight

Class	FINALISTS		MEDALISTS		GOLD MEDALISTS	
	Height (cm)	Weight (kg)	Height (cm)	Weight (kg)	Height (cm)	Weight (kg)
Men's LM 4–	184.3	72.2	183.6	72.3	183.9	72.7
Min-max	176-199	68-78	176-190	70-76	178-190	70-76
Men's LM 2x	181.1	72.1	181.0	72.3	181.0	73.3
Min-max	170-193	69-78	173-191	70-78	173-184	71-75
Average	**182.7**	**72.2**	**182.3**	**72.3**	**182.5**	**73.0**

The lightweight 2x is more remarkable for its uniformity. The scullers average 181 cm, with a normative range of 178 to 184 cm for gold medalists and 176 to 187 cm for medalists. Only one gold medalist, the 173 cm Dane Rasmus Quist, has been outside the normal range; Quist and his partner Mads Rasmussen (183 cm) set a world best time in 2007.

In the openweight 2x, small stature is not a disadvantage. The aggregated data (table 1.4) can be misleading. It is not unusual over the last 30 years for the gold medalists to be the shortest crew in the race (although their size puts them within the GDR's original normative range). For example, the 2016 Olympic champions from Croatia, Martin (188 cm, 95 kg) and Valentin Sinković (187 cm, 93 kg) are shorter than the mean, while the 2012 champions from New Zealand, Nathan Cohen (184 cm, 87 kg) and Joseph Sullivan (182 cm, 82 kg) are similar in height to lightweights (table 1.5). The Sinkovićs recorded a world best time of 5:59.72 for the 2x in 2014. The following day, the South Africans Smith (190 cm, 72 kg) and Thompson (182 cm, 70 kg) set a lightweight world best of 6:05.26, a time only 1.5% slower. At Lucerne in 2012, racing in a quad scull (4x) with David Šain (185 cm, 91 kg) and Damir Martin (187 cm, 95 kg), the Sinkovićs set a fleeting world best time of 5:35.10. The Australian, British, and Canadian talent identification programs set minimum height requirements between 190 and 193 cm; all four of the Croatians would have been screened out.

Table 1.4 Openweight Male Olympic Sculling Finalists, 1968-1988: Average Height and Weight

Class	FINALISTS		MEDALISTS		GOLD MEDALISTS	
	Height (cm)	Weight (kg)	Height (cm)	Weight (kg)	Height (cm)	Weight (kg)
Men's 4x	188.2	86.7	189.4	87.3	189.8	87.5
Min-max	175-201	71-100	178-201	76-100	180-198	76-96
Men's 2x	189.0	86.8	190.2	87.6	191.7	90.5
Min-max	170-201	72-97	182-198	77-97	184-198	84-96
Men's 1x	189.9	87.8	189.6	84.9	191.5	92.5
Min-max	178-201	79-103	179-201	79-102	178-201	78-102
Average	**189.0**	**87.1**	**189.7**	**86.6**	**191.0**	**90.2**

Table 1.5 Openweight Male Sculling Olympic Finalists, 1992-2016: Average Height and Weight

Class	FINALISTS		MEDALISTS		GOLD MEDALISTS	
	Height (cm)	Weight (kg)	Height (cm)	Weight (kg)	Height (cm)	Weight (kg)
Men's 4x	193.3	94.0	193.7	94.9	195.0	96.6
Min-max	178-206	63-114	181-202	79-105	185-202	89-105
Men's 2x	190.5	92.3	188.7	92.3	189.2	89.5
Min-max	176-202	76-110	182-202	82-110	182-197	82-96
Men's 1x	192.6	96.5	194.0	98.0	194.3	97.7
Min-max	185-201	83-108	187-200	92-105	189-200	89-103
Average	**192.1**	**94.3**	**192.1**	**95.1**	**192.8**	**94.6**

In the lightest of boats—the 1x—the additional power and mass, when correctly harnessed, appeared to offer super-sized rowers an advantage. The Karppinen-like New Zealanders Rob Waddell (200 cm, 103 kg) and Mahé Drysdale (200 cm, 102 kg) have won three of the Olympic titles contested so far this century. In Tokyo 2021, the 1x title was won by Stefanos Ntouskos (186cm, 73 kg) from Greece, who competed in Rio as a lightweight.

The 4x event has had more super-sized rowers than any other. The Germans, Russians, Ukrainians, Bulgarians, Italians, and Australians at various times all selected boats filled with them. All of the gold-medal-winning teams from 1988 to 2000 contained them (table 1.6). In Athens 2004, half of all the finalists in the 4x were super sized.

Table 1.6 Openweight Male Olympic Sweep Finalists, 1968-1988: Average Height and Weight

	FINALISTS		MEDALISTS		GOLD MEDALISTS	
Class	**Height (cm)**	**Weight (kg)**	**Height (cm)**	**Weight (kg)**	**Height (cm)**	**Weight (kg)**
Men's 8+	191.6	89.6	191.2	89.1	191.5	89.6
Min-max	182-205	75-102	182-204	75-99	183-204	75-98
Men's 4+	191.1	90.7	191.6	91.4	192	92.7
Min-max	178-206	77-105	179-206	77-105	179-200	82-109
Men's 4−	190	88.1	190	88.6	191	90.4
Min-max	170-203	72-105	170-203	75-98	185-203	80-96
Men's 2+	191.7	92.3	192	93	189.6	93
Min-max	179-208	76-109	182-208	76-109	182-198	76-103
Men's 2−	189.1	86.3	190.4	88.7	191	90
Min-max	178-203	72-104	180-203	72-104	187-195	85-103
Average	**190.5**	**89.4**	**191**	**90.1**	**191**	**91**

Table 1.7 Openweight Male Olympic Sweep Finalists, 1992-2016: Average Height and Weight

	FINALISTS		MEDALISTS		GOLD MEDALISTS	
Class	**Height (cm)**	**Weight (kg)**	**Height (cm)**	**Weight (kg)**	**Height (cm)**	**Weight (kg)**
Men's 8+	194.8	93.9	195.4	94.7	195.0	94.2
Min-max	173-209	68-110	180-208	70-110	185-208	83-102
Men's 4+ (1992 only)	192.8	93.2	195.6	96.1	195.7	94.7
Min-max	187-204	85-104	190-204	93-104	192-198	93-97
Men's 4−	193.2	92.2	193.4	93.1	193.8	95.7
Min-max	180-205	79-110	182-202	79-110	188-202	85-110
Men's 2+ (1992 only)	191.0	92.0	192.0	95.5	197.0	99.5
Min-max	182-198	82-100	182-198	90-100	n/a	n/a
Men's 2−	193.6	92.7	193.7	93.5	193.8	96.5
Min-max	184-202	84-108	184-200	85-108	189-200	85-108
Average	**193.1**	**92.8**	**194.0**	**94.6**	**195.0**	**96.1**

Men's 4+ and 2+ were only contested in 1992.

It's possible that the theoretical advantage of greater height equating to longer stroke length is, to some extent, illusory. Some shorter rowers compensate by rowing at unusually high stroke rates per minute, turning a 2 km race into an all-out sprint. Another technical adaptation common among quads scull crews is to row with very upright posture and little layback, an adaptation that may have arisen to accommodate their great height and to regulate the effort expended. In fact, since 2004, 4x athletes have been getting shorter once again (table 1.7).

Strength and Weight Class

Although flexibility and limb proportions can make the actual arc rowed shorter than desired, the idea that taller athletes might have an advantage is a seductively simplistic one. Some of the increase in muscle mass evident in the long-term trend data (figures 1.1 and 1.2) is probably explained by the professionalization of Olympic sport systems around the world since 1988. Most athletes are now in full-time training under specialist strength coaches. The logic behind athletes being so much heavier, which places additional demands on the cardiopulmonary system, is less apparent because strength can be increased without increasing muscle mass. It is perhaps an extension of the logic behind the anabolic steroid programs once used in the Eastern Bloc, with absolute strength being prioritised but using naturally bigger and more powerful athletes instead.

In Mexico City, the only Summer Olympics held at altitude, the crews averaged between 84 and 86 kg, with few individuals breaking the 90 kg mark. The heaviest medalist not in an 8+ was Frank Ruehle (192 cm, 93 kg), the 3 seat of the GDR 4-, and the only 100 kg athlete was Clause Wilke (193 cm) in the GDR 8+, which finished seventh. The GDR prioritized high relative strength within the optimal weight range rather than absolute strength. This represents a cost–benefit equation: Muscle is metabolically expensive. The more muscle an athlete has, the more oxygen is required, and there is a point at which supply cannot meet demand, limited by the body's ability to extract and deliver oxygen to the muscles. Therefore, the biggest athletes are most commonly found in the quad scull (4x) and the eight (8+), both faster boats in which effort doesn't need to be sustained for as long.

Women's Crews

When female rowers first competed in Montreal 1976, crews from the GDR, USSR, Romania, and Bulgaria divided the medals among themselves, with the United States and West Germany capturing just three minor medals. The Eastern Bloc crews were the tallest and heaviest, with the biggest women found in the 8+ and 4+. Only two finalists exceeded 185 cm in height: the East German Roswietha Zobelt (188 cm, 83 kg) at 2 seat in the 4x and American Carie Graves (186 cm, 77 kg) at 3 seat in the 8+. In an era associated with the abuse of anabolic steroids, many of the Eastern Bloc women were notable for their bulk. The 1976 silver medal Soviet 8+ averaged 182.7 cm and 85 kg; the women in the middle of the boat, each weighing 92 kg, were 3 kg heavier than the average male finalist.

Since 1988, the average openweight female Olympic rowing finalist is similar in build to a lightweight male sculler, slightly shorter at an average of 180 cm and a little heavier at an average of 74.5 kg. Like the openweight men, women this tall are in the 99th percentile for height. (See tables 1.8 and 1.9.)

Table 1.8   Female Olympic Sculling Finalists, 1988-2016: Average Height and Weight

	FINALISTS		MEDALISTS		GOLD MEDALISTS	
Class	**Height (cm)**	**Weight (kg)**	**Height (cm)**	**Weight (kg)**	**Height (cm)**	**Weight (kg)**
Women's 4x	180.4	74.5	180.2	74.4	181.6	74.9
Min-max	165-196	47-90	165-193	60-82	173-188	65-80
Women's 2x	180.5	73.1	180.2	74.1	180.2	74.6
Min-max	165-193	47-89	165-193	47-84	178-185	68-78
Women's 1x	179.1	74.1	180.6	76.2	182.5	77.6
Min-max	170-188	65-85	170-188	68-80	177-188	72-82
Average	**180.0**	**73.9**	**180.3**	**74.9**	**181.4**	**75.7**

Table 1.9   Female Olympic Sweep Finalists, 1988-2016: Average Height and Weight

	FINALISTS		MEDALISTS		GOLD MEDALISTS	
Class	**Height (cm)**	**Weight (kg)**	**Height (cm)**	**Weight (kg)**	**Height (cm)**	**Weight (kg)**
Women's 8+	181.3	75.1	181.7	75.5	181.8	77.7
Min-max	168-195	64-97	170-195	64-91	173-193	66-86
Women's 4–	178.8	73.3	178.9	73.5	175.8	72.0
Min-max	170-188	66-85	170-188	66-82	173-178	66-75
Women's 2–	180.2	74.0	180.2	74.6	179.7	73.6
Min-max	155-191	60-86	172-190	64-86	174-186	67-77
Average	**180.1**	**74.1**	**180.3**	**74.5**	**179.1**	**74.4**

Great size is not a prerequisite for success. For example, the Canadian women's team that dominated in Barcelona were among the shortest and lightest Olympic champions, at an average of 177.5 cm and 72.6 kg. However, the Americans revived the Eastern bloc experiment in size when Hartmut Buschbacher, the coach of the 1988 GDR women's 8+, was hired as the U.S. women's coach in 1991. Like Grobler, with whom he had worked, he preferred athletes taller than normal. Buschbacher also placed a heavy emphasis on ergometer scores. Because height is an advantage on the Concept2 rowing ergometer, which was still relatively new technology in the early 1990s, he possibly favored the tallest women because they were producing better test scores (Mallory 2011), although this does not always translate into boat moving ability.

Excessive size is more obviously limiting for women than men. Women taller than 185 cm are within the pre-1988 normative height range for openweight male finalists but are incapable of producing the same power as males (table 1.10). The women's Concept2 indoor world record for the 2,000 m is 6:22.8 and is held by Olena Buryak (196 cm, 90 kg) of Ukraine, who finished last in the 2x in London 2012 and fourth in the 4x in Rio 2016 with smaller teammates who brought the average weight down to 80 kg.

In the lightweight women's 2x, medalists are usually slightly taller than non-medalists. Over the last three Olympics, fewer tall lightweight women like Romania's Angela Alupei (181 cm) and Germany's Claudia Blasberg (182 cm) were selected, and rowers in this category are now shorter and more muscular than they used to be.

Table 1.10 Lightweight Women's 2x Olympic Finalists, 1996-2016: Average Height and Weight

	FINALISTS		MEDALISTS		GOLD MEDALISTS	
Class	Height (cm)	Weight (kg)	Height (cm)	Weight (kg)	Height (cm)	Weight (kg)
Women's LW 2x	173.1	58.9	173.9	59.2	174.3	59.0
Min-max	165-182	55-64	165-182	55-64	165-181	55-64

Key Point

In 1998, in an effort to create a national women's rowing team, the Australian Institute of Sport (AIS) started a talent identification program. It was loosely based on the East German talent selection program, but the starting premise, one that was rejected by the GDR, was that talent was innate and innate abilities can be tested for. Athletes were selected using physiological testing for $\dot{V}O_2$max and strength. Megan Still (182 cm, 75 kg), an athlete almost not selected by the talent search program, became the 1996 Olympic 2- champion. In 2002 Great Britain started a talent identification program, World Class Start (WCS), which was modeled on the AIS program. The height criteria for selection was 180 cm for women and 190 cm tall for men, with wingspans greater than their height. The mantra was "you can't train them tall," while an assumption was made that athletes with heights above the mean were more likely to be successful. It had limited success.

An incremental step test on a Schwinn arm–leg bike was used as a substitute for a laboratory maximal aerobic power test, and three-repetition maximum leg and arm strength was tested on a Concept2 DYNO.

In 2003, two Cambridge University rowers, Anna Bebbington (183 cm, 78 kg) and Annie Vernon (178 cm, 75 kg), who were already pulling sub-7-min 2 km ergometer scores, were recruited to WCS and fast-tracked onto the British team. They won medals in Beijing 2008, securing the future of the project. UK Sport ran additional talent identification campaigns branded under the names Sporting Giants, Tall and Talented, and Girls for Gold in an effort to maximize medal prospects at the London 2012 Olympic Games. In 2012, four female athletes recruited through this campaign competed: Lindsey Maguire (187 cm, 76 kg), Victoria Thornley (193 cm, 76 kg), Heather Stanning (181 cm, 72 kg), and Helen Glover (177 cm, 67 kg). Together, Stanning and Glover won the 2012 and 2016 Olympic titles in 2− and Thornley went on to win a silver in the 2x in Rio. However, Stanning was not a standout during the preliminary assessments and progressed via her university team into WCS, and Glover lied about her height on the application and avoided detection on the assessment day by standing on tiptoes to meet the minimum height requirement of 180 cm (https://harryeverettsportsjournalism 2016).

Five of the London 2012 men's team also came up through the WCS system. All were recruited between 2002 and 2004. Moe Sbihi (202 cm, 110kg) and Alex Gregory (198 cm, 97 kg) won medals; the other three, Sam Townsend (199 cm, 102 kg), Bill Lucas (199 cm, 100 kg), and Charles Cousins (198 cm, 100 kg) were in sculling boats that came fifth behind smaller, lighter rivals.

Conclusion

The search for athletic genes is a manifestation of the ideological construct of talent as a product of giftedness. The concept of giftedness fits poorly with the GDR construct of talent, which Ekkart Arbeit, head coach of the GDR Track and Field team, explained thus:

> *To acknowledge the dominance of athletes on genetic and geographic grounds a priori and to take it for granted, is a non-scientific and counter-productive point of view. Of course, we each have this or that genetic advantage or disadvantage—be that anatomical, physiological, psychological, emotional and so on. The fact is however, that such advantage or giftedness—or lack of it—is only one factor in achievement of top performance. Of at least equal, but almost certainly greater importance in producing top performance is the athlete's commitment to and pursuit of a training process designed to meet his or her development needs. (Arbeit 1997)*

Although it's possible the GDR may have embraced the irrational exuberance for both height and muscularity as Grobler and Buschbacher did, it seems more likely that the inherent conservatism within the system would have prevailed. They were, after all, already struggling to find enough athletes of the right quality to fill all the boats. It's even conceivable that a reversion to including athletes from the lower part of the normative range would have occurred, resulting from a collective realization that arbitrarily restricting the athlete pool excludes individuals with other physiological or psychological advantages who might potentially be better rowers despite their shorter stature.

Anatomical gifts of genetic origin such as height are just one possible advantage. The lesson of the Abbagnales, the Sinković brothers, Hawkins and Antonie, and the Canadian women of 1992, among others, is that other things matter too. New Zealand, with a population of less than 5 million, has produced Olympic medalists from both ends of the size spectrum. It deliberately avoids talent identification testing to prevent any such artificial restriction of its talent pool, enabling athletes of shorter stature with other physiological or psychological capabilities, or even advantages, to progress through its development system.

It is evident that smaller athletes with superior technique can prevail over the biggest competitors. The trend now is that male and female openweight rowers are getting lighter once again, and though the biggest crews may have an advantage in certain racing conditions, as is evident from an analysis of the attributes of world best time holders, the fastest crews in ideal conditions are usually within the normative range as identified in the 1960s by the GDR. We should remember the old adage: "It's not the size of the dog in the fight but the size of the fight in the dog"—or, one might say, the bull.

CHAPTER 2

Biological Maturation

Paula Jardine

Biological maturation, or progress toward a mature state, varies in timing and tempo among individuals and between different bodily systems (Beunen 2008). Individuals can be classified during adolescence as early, average, or late biological maturers as determined by when they achieve their maximum rate of growth in stature, which is termed *peak height velocity*. Its importance is well established in the sport science literature, because individual athletes of the same chronological age can have differing developmental needs depending on their relative maturation.

Key Point

Peak height velocity (PHV) is the point during puberty at which height is gained at the fastest rate. It is the primary marker used to identify whether someone is early, average, or late biologically maturing. Average maturing girls reach PHV at age 12, whereas average maturing boys reach PHV at age 14. The age of peak performance for both male and female rowers is 26.

Maturational differences in strength and size can influence subjective perceptions of athletic abilities during adolescence, especially in male athletes. This has significant implications for talent selection, because care must be taken to prevent late biologically maturing males, who show greater increases in performance in young adulthood (between the ages of 18 and 30) than early or average maturers, from being selected out of competitive sport prematurely. Frameworks such as Long Term Athlete Development (LTAD) have attempted to incorporate the principles of biological maturation into coaching practice in order to optimize development of athletic abilities during childhood and adolescence.

Our understanding of the elite rowing population from the perspective of biological maturation is constrained by the limitations of the research literature. Because knowledge of its importance first came from coaches and sport scientists in the Eastern Bloc, the research conducted on elite athletes remains unpublished and inaccessible. As an anecdotal rule, those from the Eastern Bloc preferred late biological maturers.

In the absence of sport-specific longitudinal research to further our understanding, biological maturation remains something of a black box. The difficulty of identifying future elite athletes during adolescence significantly limits the availability of quality longitudinal performance and anthropometric data on early entry elite rowers. Additionally, many rowers enter the sport in postadolescence, when it is impossible to determine an individual's maturation classification retrospectively in the absence of reliable anthropometric data.

Most of the longitudinal research into biological maturation that does exist is medical in nature and largely unconcerned with athletic development. The Leuven Longitudinal Study on Belgian boys is perhaps the most useful in understanding the relationship between maturation classification and physical abilities (Beunen et al. 1997). It is one of the few that grouped participants by maturation classification and included physiological tests such as the vertical jump. It clearly demonstrated that although early maturing boys performed better on physical tests during adolescence, late maturers had an advantage in functional and explosive strength that only became apparent when they entered adulthood (Beunen et al. 1997). The Leuven study on girls detected no similar maturation-related trends, although retrospective studies of female rowers suggest that many are average or late maturers based on age of onset of menarche (Beunen and Malina 2008).

More importantly for rowing, relative $\dot{V}O_2$max, expressed per kg of body mass, is higher in both male and female late maturers (Beunen and Malina 2008). Two longitudinal studies of individual male Olympic scullers (one Dane and one Belgian) found that $\dot{V}O_2$max continues to increase as a function of adaptation to training until the mid-20s, peaking at age 24 for the Danish rower (Nybo et al. 2014) and between 26 and 27 for the Belgian rower (Bourgois, Steyaert, and Boone 2014). These two studies suggest an association with biological maturation, although the maturation classification of the two rowers is unstated or unknown.

Key Point

As a rule, talent selection based on longitudinal testing data is superior to testing for purportedly innate abilities. Rowing talent identification programs select athletes based on one-off performances on strength and endurance tests. A small number of successful athletes have been identified this way, and there is a better track record in identifying successful female rowers than male rowers. Testing-based talent identification programs usually target adolescents between the age of 15 and 20 for recruitment. At this age, early and average biologically maturing males still have physical advantages over late maturing males, particularly in strength; thus, late maturers can be overlooked. Although maturation classification would improve interpretation of test data, it cannot be accurately determined after PHV has passed.

Biological Maturation of the Nervous System

Knowing that late biological maturation is advantageous for competitive rowers, especially male rowers, is one thing, but understanding why is another. Recent research into the development of the central nervous system, the last system in the body to fully mature, provides some insights that contribute to understanding.

Diversified physical activity is a stimulus that influences the development of the brain and the central nervous system. Although the human brain reaches 95% of its adult size by age 6, it does not fully mature until well into the third decade of life. The physical and sensory stimulus it receives in the first two decades are profoundly important because they are necessary stimuli to facilitate its maturation and organization. To use a computer analogy, physical activity and motor learning help to wire up the body's operating system (the brain and nervous system), which runs in the background, interfacing between the hardware (the body) and the software (the ability to play an instrument or a sport).

Neurons making up the grey matter in the brain are overproduced and peak in volume just before puberty. They are then subject to a process of competitive elimination whereby the connections between neurons that are stimulated are strengthened while redundant neurons are eliminated. The sex steroids that puberty unleashes about 18 months after PHV, particularly testosterone, affect brain organization as they terminate neural pruning in the grey matter and stimulate the maturation of the white matter tracts that facilitate the functional integration of the two hemispheres of the brain and its disparate structures. These steroids accelerate the maturation of glial cells, which are specialized nerve cells that produce myelin, a fatty insulation sheath that wraps around nerve axons and improves the transmission of electrical impulses along the neural pathways.

Informal physical play peaks in adolescence and then wanes. Because juveniles of all species of mammals engage in play, it suggests that this activity must serve a purpose; biologists have linked it to the development of the cerebellum, or "little brain," where it appears to stimulate neural pruning (Byers 1998). The cerebellum, which is not very genetically controlled and is highly susceptible to environmental stimulation, is involved in motor learning and in the fluidity of movement execution. It is also involved in the transfer of learning into new skills (Seidler 2010). Neuroimaging studies have found that once a motor task ceases to be novel, there is less activity in the cerebellum (Diamond 2000). A prolonged period of abundant diversified development helps because it keeps providing novel stimuli.

The early physical strength and power that comes with early biological maturation may have had evolutionary benefits to survival, but it comes with a trade-off (Kaiser and Gruzelier 1996). Pruning goes on longer in late maturers than it does in early maturers, resulting in brains with simpler neural structures that conduct information more efficiently than those of early maturers (Saugstad 1989). Because the window during which physical activity stimulates neural pruning closes earlier for early maturing males, a greater volume of activity needs to be packed into a shorter period of time to compensate. In sport performance terms, their age of peak performance comes earlier.

Key Point

In many European countries that are still influenced by the GDR system, it remains common for rowers to take up the sport between the ages of 13 and 15. The importance of diversified multisport training through adolescence is recognized and incorporated into training programs. The volume of low-intensity distance training is carefully increased through adolescence in order to let hearts and lungs adapt, enlarging and strengthening in response to endurance training before being stressed with high-intensity speed work.

Late Entry to the Sport

Rowing is an ideal sport for postadolescent entry, even after the age of 20. However, sport administrators concerned with development pathways often focus their attention on junior athletes and progression through the international age group competition system, in the belief that starting younger produces more technically skillful athletes. This approach can result in the concentration of resources on athletes who fail to continue to make progress through their 20s. Early specialization in the sport can also be detrimental to long-term results.

Athletes entering from other sports are among the best candidates for rowing. These athletes can progress rapidly, overtaking others who have been journeymen since the junior age groups. In the last decade, there are two high-profile examples of this. Kim Crow, the 2016 Olympic sculling champion, was a 2001 World Youth Championship medalist in the 400 m hurdles who took up rowing at age 20, winning her first World Rowing Championship medal a year later. The sculler Oliver Zeidler was a German junior national champion in swimming who began rowing in 2016 at age 20, winning the World Rowing Championship at his second attempt in 2019. In evaluating and structuring national systems underpinning national teams, it would be wise to ensure that club- and university-based development programs allow the opportunity for such athletes to flourish.

Special Considerations for Male Athletes

A major challenge for talent selection purposes is how to account for the influence of biological maturation in male athletes. Late biological maturers do not reach the same levels of strength as early and average maturers until their early 20s, and thereafter they have an advantage in both explosive and static strength (Beunen and Malina 2008). This problem was even recognized in medieval England when the age of majority was first raised from 15 to 21: At a time when knights in heavy armor began to fight on horseback rather than dismounting to fight on foot, it was apparent that many younger males didn't have the necessary strength or skill to be sent into combat (James 1960).

Let us consider a real-world example of biological maturation from the sport of athletics involving two sprinters, Asafa Powell and Mark Lewis-Francis. They were born 3 months apart in 1982 and share Jamaican heritage. In 2000, when Lewis-Francis, the junior world champion, was being lauded as a future superstar, no one would have suspected that Powell would be the one to become a sprinting legend, recording 97 sub-10-s 100 m times. Powell, who played soccer as a teenager, began sprinting in his final year of high school. His best time was 11.45 s into a headwind, a time Lewis-Francis eclipsed as a 15-year-old (http://www.cfpitiming.com/class_1_boys_results.htm). In 2000, Powell failed to make the final at the Jamaican Interschool Athletics Championship, but by 2003, he was the Jamaican Mens National Champion. He ran his first sub-10-s 100 m in June 2004, ending the season with a total of nine sub-10-s performances and a fifth-place finish in the Olympic 100 m final. He set a world record of 9.77 s a year later.

Rowing has a more significant endurance component, but like sprinters, rowers need power. In males, power comes when puberty unleashes testosterone. The vertical jump is a good proxy test for this. Lewis-Francis's performance profile points to him being an early biological maturer who likely went through puberty around age 13. Powell's performance profile suggests he went through puberty 3 years later. Their performances intersect between the age of 21 and 22 years, mirroring both the trend and the intersection point seen in the vertical jump data from the Leuven study (Beunen et al. 1997).

Conclusion

Although there is still much to learn, biological maturation is clearly a significant consideration for both optimizing athletic development and for the selection of talent. For males in particular, the relationship between power and the timing of PHV is the best prognostic indicator of future performance as it is possible to have. It is likely to remain difficult to examine its true impact on the elite rowing population, but its importance should not be underestimated.

3 CHAPTER

Neurobiology of Rowing

Paula Jardine

Australian Steve Fairbairn (1862-1938) is arguably considered history's most influential rowing coach. Once called "The Socrates of the towpath" by the *London Standard* newspaper, Fairbairn was famous in his lifetime as the originator of training methods based on insights garnered from his own experience as an athlete as well as observations of the athletes he coached. His methodology was empirically validated through the results he achieved and is still used by coaches in the modern era. Ignoring the dictate of his orthodox contemporaries that rowers should keep their eyes in the boat—one that remains common today—he encouraged his pupils to learn by watching their blade move in the water. His method involved rowers learning to identify the movement by feel, first by not looking, then by rowing with their eyes shut, and finally alternating the three until they had internalized the feel of a good stroke and could recognize one without looking. He believed that this allowed the subconscious mind to control the movements of the body, freeing it to move naturally and efficiently. Many decades later, neuroscientists have begun to reveal how the biology of how the brain works subconsciously, and their discoveries have implications for how we teach and train rowers.

The Mirror Neuron System

In 1992, Italian neuroscientists Giacomo Rizzolatti and Vittorio Gallese were experimenting on a macaque monkey by using electrodes implanted in its brain to locate the specific neurons that fired when it raised its arm. Having taken a lunch break during which the monkey remained connected to the electrodes, one of the team returned to the lab with an ice cream. When the monkey saw him raise his arm to eat the ice cream, the same neurons in its brain activated as when the monkey raised its own arm during the experiment—only this time the monkey made no movement. It was an important discovery, because for the first time there was evidence of a previously unknown type of neuron that fired not only when an action was performed, but when the same action was observed. These specialized neurons form part of the sensory motor system and are especially concentrated in the premotor cortex. They are called *mirror neurons.*

Humans learn by imitation, and mirror neurons are involved in all aspects of motor learning (Buccino and Riggio 2006). We learn first with our eyes, which is why we use expert performers to demonstrate to a beginner how a movement should be performed. Mirror neurons activate subconsciously, allowing the observer of a physical action to instantaneously create a simulation in their own brain. The better the exemplar, the better the internal simulation is likely to be.

Observing an action and then performing it creates a mutually reinforcing feedback loop, with mirror neurons matching the executed actions with the visual observation (Urgesi et al. 2012). They help us to understand the intent in actions. An observer who has prior experience of performing the movement will subconsciously perceive the feeling in their own body (Buccino and Riggio 2006). This explains why experts discern subtle differences that casual observers, who have no internal model to compare it to, do not. For instance, an expert rower observing another rower who is rowing short will sense it physically but subconsciously via the mirror neuron system, whereas a casual observer with no experience of rowing would perceive no difference. Expert performers also perceive and react to actions more rapidly than novices do (Royal et al. 2006).

This ability to subconsciously perceive intent in movement appears to be a part of the body's evolutionary survival network. It's a rapid cognition system, developed experientially, that facilitates the ability to react defensively. A right-handed player facing a left hander doesn't see a mirror image of their action. The image is flipped, altering their perception of their opponent's actions and slowing their ability to correctly identify intent. It may explain why left handers, though only comprising about 10% of the general population, are overrepresented at elite levels in oppositional sports. A left hander also sees a flipped image when they observe a right-handed player, but they become better adapted to playing right handers because they encounter them more often. As they progress through the sport, this small advantage accumulates. Peruse a list of famous left-handed athletes and you will encounter names like Wayne Gretzky, Bobby Orr, Martina Navratilova, Jimmy Connors, John McEnroe, Ferenc Puskás, Pelé, Diego Maradona, Johan Cruyff, Larry Bird, LeBron James, Manny Pacquiao, and Joe Frazier, to name but a few. The caliber of the athletes on this list suggests that the advantage is considerable.

Key Point

The specificity of the mirror neuron system has implications for how coaches use video, one of the most common teaching tools, to show rowers models of good technical rowing. To activate the mirror neuron system appropriately, rowers need to see models that are specific to their discipline and, for sweep rowers, their side.

Amygdala Mediated Responses

The work of another neuroscientist, Joseph LeDoux, also has implications for how we develop and train rowers. By seeking "a biological rather than psychological understanding of our emotions" (LeDoux 1997), he pioneered the study of the biology of emotions and how they are hardwired into the brain. LeDoux's work "explores the differences between emotional memories (implicit–unconscious–memories) processed in pathways that take information into the amygdala, and memories of emotion (explicit–conscious–memories) processed at the level of the hippocampus and neocortex" (LeDoux 1997).

The amygdala comprises two small almond-shaped structures that are involved in emotional processing. There is one in each hemisphere of the brain. It is the amygdala that perceives and stores information, learning what to do in response to stimuli and functioning as a surveillance system in order to activate in ambiguous learning situations (Pessoa 2010). As sensory information is taken in from the environment, the amygdala directs attention to positive or negative stimuli and facilitates instinctive reactions based on subconscious memories. For example, if the boat rocks suddenly, you might instinctively lift your hand off the oar handle to avoid the pain of smashing your fingers on the gunwale, or if your blade catches the water and you lose your grip on the handle altogether, you will try to catch it again to stabilize the boat.

When the amygdala is activated in defense, it prepares the body for fight or flight via the autonomic nervous system. It stimulates the release of adrenaline, elevates heart and respiration rates, and raises blood pressure by constricting blood vessels. Prolonged activation in a sustained effort such as a rowing race, which already places high demands on the cardiorespiratory system, would be deleterious to performance.

The Amygdala and Decision Making

Cognitive neuroscientists use dual process theory to explore the dynamics of decision making, differentiating between two complementary but separate processes. System 1 decisions are rapid, instinctive responses to sensory input from the environment. They draw on subconscious emotions and memories to make reactive decisions. For a rower, it could be perceiving a subtle faltering in an opponent's boat speed that presents the opportunity for a surprise attacking push. The advantage of system 1 decision making is that it is not inherently fatiguing.

System 2 decisions are conscious, deliberate decisions made in the frontal cortex. In a race situation, you might decide to raise the rate or put an extra push in as a response to a move from a rival crew. These decisions do cause fatigue. This is one of the reasons that side-by-side, one-on-one match racing like the Oxford–Cambridge Boat Race or Henley Royal Regatta can be so uniquely grueling. In a closely fought contest, it's not simply a case of sticking to your own race plan—constant vigilance is required to detect, defend, and counterattack moves from the other crew.

In one study, it was shown that there is a trade-off between mental and physical output, with mental output being prioritized over physical output. The rowers participated in three tests: a 3 min erg test; a memory recall test in which rowers were shown 75 words and had to remember as many as possible; and a final test that combined the two. In the final test, performance declined in both, but the decline in power output was 25% greater than the decline in memory recall (Longman, Stock, and Wells 2017). However, the study didn't include a biomechanical evaluation of the rowers' technique and how it might have contributed to the drop in power, only that it occurred and that mental output was conserved over physical output.

Another experiment that looked at the relationship between skill execution, fatigue, and decision making was conducted on water polo players who completed two test batteries, one cognitive and one physical, under increasing levels of fatigue (Royal et al. 2006). While in the water and with a ball in their shooting hand, video-based decision-making prediction tests were conducted by showing the players video clips from international games and obscuring their vision when a tactical decision was required; players then called out what they thought the correct decision was. A second test battery examined shooting technique, accuracy, and speed under cumulative fatigue. The researchers found that as fatigue increased, decision-making prediction accuracy improved. However, although the players could shoot at the target with the same speed and accuracy as they fatigued, biomechanical analysis showed they couldn't raise their bodies as far out of the water to do it, which would make it more difficult to evade defenders to score in a game situation. In effect, to compensate, they did what rowers do when they fatigue—they shortened up.

Both experiments highlight the prioritization of cognitive tasks under fatigue—in the context of the brain's survival systems, survival may depend to a greater extent on making the right decision. In a sport setting, then, coaches might be better off focusing on the decision-making elements—for example, a side-by-side exercise simulating tactical moves—instead of focusing too much on technical corrections toward the end of a training session when athletes are fatigued and less able to absorb information. Fairbairn himself saw too much instruction from the coach as an intrusion into the rowers' consciousness, which prevented them from grooving in the movements. He advocated making most individual technical corrections outside the boat, rather than during an on-water session, during which he preferred to speak to the whole crew—an approach that is perfectly suited to using modern video technology.

Expert decision makers in sports are good at making conscious decisions, but the very best are even better at making instinctive ones. This has implications for crew selections in coxless boats. The person at bow can be tasked with steering and calling the race tactically because they have the best view and are best heard by all crew members. This rower needs to be a good decision maker in order to balance the competing cognitive and physical demands. Some coaches prefer to divide the workload, perhaps asking the 2 seat to make the tactical calls while bow or stroke steers.

Applying Dual Process Theory to Training

So what implications does dual process theory have for coaching rowing in light of the fact that increasing cognitive demands can compromise physiological output? There are two possible solutions: Reduce the demands on system 2 decision making to the greatest extent possible or make the training environment more cognitively challenging to stimulate adaptation.

The simplest means of reducing system 2 demands for rowers is to put a coxswain in the boat. Coxswains take on the conscious decision-making responsibilities, thereby lowering the cognitive demands placed on the rowers. This approach is not unique to rowing. Professional cycling teams use team radios, enabling directors to communicate race tactics from the support car. The five-time winner of the cycling ultradistance Race Across America (RAAM), Jure Robič, pushed himself to physical extremes by deploying his support team as his "second brain." As effective a strategy as this approach is, it has one significant drawback: It limits the rower's ability to adapt to working hard while dealing with cognitive challenges.

The best way to create a cognitively enriched training environment for rowing is to train in small boats, because rowers must remain engaged with and stimulated by their environment. Many top coaches, including Steve Fairbairn, Karl Adam, Al Morrow, and Mike Spracklen, have done exactly this. Rowing in packs of small boats outside the confines of artificial lanes develops the capabilities of both decision-making systems. Athletes become better at perceiving where they are in relation to other boats, determining how close they can get without clashing blades or bumping into one another, and detecting subtle changes in the speed of the boats around them as they jostle for position.

It is useful for athletes to learn to adapt to stressful environments and calm the amygdala so that it does not activate unnecessarily, causing a chronic release of adrenaline that makes the body feel tired or short of breath. They learn to cope with changing wind and water conditions, subconsciously making subtle compensatory adjustments. With no coxswain to reduce the cognitive demands, rowers learn to deal with them, and come race day, confined by lanes, the environment becomes significantly less complex and the reduction in cognitive demands means the rower has a greater capacity to physically exert themselves.

Key Point

The East Germans understood the benefits of cognitively enriched training environments and utilized them extensively. These included occasional training sessions in the dark, which makes the neurons associated with hearing more sensitive and alters the way speed and effort are perceived. Deprived of visual input, a rower enhances their internal feedback mechanisms, learning to detect the sound of a good catch and the feel of the vibration traveling up the oar. They embraced cross-training, favoring cross-country running or skiing, which not only contributes to the volume of fitness training, but also develops the athletes' perceptual skills, requiring them to pay attention to subtle changes in terrain or obstacles in the environment while also teaching them to have greater awareness of where others are and how they are moving in relation to one another. Ball game sessions were incorporated in all weekly training programs, giving everyone the opportunity to develop decision-making skills, which, like all other skills, improve with experience. In fact, coach Jürgen Gröbler still incorporates game sessions into his training program today, just as he learned to decades ago in the GDR.

Conclusion

When Fairbairn talked about the role of the subconscious mind in rowing, he was describing the automation of movements that occurs as rowers become more skilled. A century later, neuroscientists have begun to uncover the biological workings of the unconscious mind and confirm the validity of long-established coaching practices, such as using video models or challenging athletes by increasing the cognitive demands placed upon them. The mirror neuron system is a powerful tool that can be used to develop good technique. Manipulating the training environment to stimulate the sensory systems and form subconscious emotional memories in the amygdala enhances rowers' ability to perform. As neuroscience research advances, new insights will further enhance the tool kit available to coaches.

CHAPTER 4

Mileage Makes Champions

Paula Jardine

Mileage makes champions. Every rower instantly associates these three words with the sport's high-volume, low-intensity training paradigm (see Chapter 15). It's a methodology that has been used to great effect for decades. Successful Olympic coaches like Karl Adam and Frank Read used these methods in the 1950s and 1960s. It was integral to the GDR system, whose sport scientists' rigorous studies advanced understanding of the training technique. But the methodology itself was devised by Steve Fairbairn, mentioned previously in chapter 3 as an innovator in the area of coaching who stood out by teaching his students to row kinesthetically and by observation. Fairbairn himself called "mileage makes champions" his main slogan. Surprisingly, however, little of his prolific writing on rowing addresses the topic directly, and where it does, the subject is not limited to mileage in the boat. This perspective is a useful starting point for consideration.

Key Point

Exercise physiology did not yet exist as a scientific discipline when Fairbairn began coaching. Knowledge gained from scientific enquiry has enabled refinements to be made to his methodology, while advances in fields such as neuroscience have added further insights into the underlying mechanisms.

Validation has been made through experimental studies conducted in the Eastern Bloc, observational studies, and more recently retrospective analysis of the training histories of elite Olympic endurance athletes. This research has consistently found an 80/20 distribution of volume versus intensity in their training. This 80/20 distribution is now referred to in the sport science literature as *polarized training* (Seiler and Kjerland 2006).

Diversified Development

As a coach, Fairbairn lamented the lack of athleticism in many rowers, saying: "Oarsmen are not drawn from the highest class of athletes; cricket, football etc., take the best athletes and so we get many men in the rowing world whose athletic sense is dormant" (Fairbairn 1990, 344). Presciently, he recognized the importance of general athleticism as a necessary base from which rowing skill could be developed, saying, "The true view of rowing is that it consists of the cultivation of the sense of touch, timing, control and balance which is the secret of success in every form of athletics and the main principle is: there must be no effort; if you can't do it easily you can't do it at all"(Fairbairn 1990, 118).

Fairbairn was himself an accomplished rower in the pre-Olympic era, racing twice in winning Boat Race crews for Cambridge in the 1880s, as well as winning the Grand Challenge Cup, the Stewards, and the Wyfold at Henley Royal Regatta. There was no research on athletic development in the 19th century to guide him, but having been an accomplished multisport athlete in his youth, he was his own experiment of one. He attributed his achievements in cricket, Australian Rules Football, athletics, and swimming to "regular long work."

Embracing the idea that other activities could remedy the absence of athleticism in many rowers, he encouraged cross-training, recommending long power walks, weightlifting, and especially skipping—twice a day for 30 minutes—saying, "Skipping synchronizes the movement of all the limbs, and makes a man a better athlete, because the capacity for athletics is proportionate to one's ability to move one's limbs in harmony" (Fairbairn 1990, 448).

Fairbairn's belief in the need for large volumes of varied activity to develop general athleticism was correct and is now well supported in the sport science literature. What was called *multilateral development* was integral to the Cold War–era state-sponsored sport systems of the Eastern Bloc. The Soviets and East Germans both conducted longitudinal studies in the 1960s and 1970s that clearly identified the benefits of early diversification and late specialization for most sports (Bompa 2000).

The GDR rowing handbook states: "With few exceptions, the best oarsmen also have a wide array of sporting skills in other disciplines and generally master them very well. Rowing capacity and athletic versatility go hand in hand" (Herberger et al. 2004 178). Training activities and volumes were carefully planned and tracked, and programs included flexibility and agility training using gymnastics (sometimes set to music to develop rhythm), cross-country skiing, cross-country running, swimming, and team ball sports—there's even mention of Fairbairn's favorite, skipping.

Research suggests that athletes engaged in true early specialization sports like gymnastics often suffer from burnout, compromised social development, injury, and premature plateauing of results. However, such sports are especially beneficial for developing general athleticism because children are constantly challenged to learn new motor skills. Diversification of activity continually stimulates learning, which results in structural changes in the gray matter of the developing brain as new links called synapses form between neurons. Early diversification with later specialization is a particularly beneficial approach for sports like rowing.

In the first decade of life there is an overproduction of neurons in the grey matter followed by an extended period of competitive elimination. Motor learning wires together nerves in the cerebral cortex, which contains the sensory and motor areas of the human brain (Black et al. 1990). As previously discussed in chapter 2, by learning multiple unrelated motor skills, athletes become more adaptable; they learn how to learn new motor skills and in the process to learn them faster (Seidler et al. 2002). Repetitive exercise like running is insufficient because it only stimulates the growth of new blood vessels rather than the formation of new synapses.

Key Point

Contemporary sport researchers investigating the relationship between training hours and elite performance through retrospective studies found that the number of hours of deliberate practice needed to produce expert performances (M = 3,939 hours) is inversely related to the number of other sport activities and accumulated training volume prior to specialization (Abernethy, Farrow, and Berry 2003). In late specialization sports like rowing, where the age of peak performance comes after 20, world and Olympic medals have been won by athletes with as few as 3,000 to 4,000 hours of sport-specific training. The former swimmer Oliver Zeidler, who became world champion in the men's 1x in 2019, three years after he first stepped in a boat, is only one prominent example.

Motor Learning

The second observation to which Fairbairn applied his famous adage about mileage was that, among rowers who took up the sport in adolescence, those with the best watermanship skills were the ones who learned first in single sculls before progressing to row in pairs. Fairbairn extended his recommendation for small boat work to all rowers as the best way to improve boat feel, with a further suggestion that sweep rowers learn to row both sides and alternate sides every other day so as to balance the development of musculature.

A recent neuroscience study provides new insight into why learning to scull first is beneficial to long-term skill development and is particularly relevant to those who take up the sport during adolescence. A longitudinal brain imaging study of adolescent pianists documented practice-related changes in the thickness of myelin, a white fatty insulating material that builds up around the neural fiber tracts that functionally connect disparate areas of the brain and enable nerve impulses to be transmitted faster—a process called *myelination* (Bengtsonn et al. 2005). The production of myelin is stimulated each time an electrical signal passes along a neural pathway, consolidating the pathway as it thickens. More practice equates to more myelin and faster transmission speeds.

The study results reflect the sequence of brain maturation. Up until the age of 16, it is the corpus callosum, the main fiber tract linking the two hemispheres of the brain, that thickens most in response to practice (Bengtsonn et al. 2005). Sculling, the coordination of which involves both hemispheres of the brain, is a more complicated movement than sweep rowing. Sculling therefore provides optimal stimulation for the early adolescent brain during this developmental phase when the functions of the two hemispheres are being integrated. After the age of 16, practice stimulates myelination of fiber tracts within each hemisphere, linking the instinctive areas at the back of the brain, which mature earliest, with the executive function areas of the frontal cortex, which mature last.

The GDR development system was designed to maximize the benefit from both early and late entry to sport. Depending upon the age at which learning a new sport began, different training priorities applied. Fairbairn's methodology was refined in line with the principles outlined in Kurt Meinel's theory of motor learning (Meinel 1962).

The optimal age for sport motor learning was identified by Meinel as being between 10 and 12, which is before puberty for boys and before the onset of menarche (the end stage of puberty) for girls. The emphasis for children this age was on learning to perfectly coordinate movements with minimal application of power. Basic movements could be perfected and patterned in the nervous system before sex hormones unleashed by puberty began to influence the consolidation of motor learning by accelerating the process of myelination. There was an important caveat, however: Children under 12 only began sculling if special lighter boats and shorter oars were available, and only in optimal conditions combining warm weather, knee-deep water, and perfect still conditions. They did not specialize, instead maintaining a broad activity base incorporating play-based learning. A few Olympians, such as Thomas Lange, began rowing at this age, but most began later.

Although Fairbairn was the first to advocate the art of coaching the blade and not the body, the East Germans turned it into a science, coaching to perfect the shape of the force curve in order to move the boat with the greatest efficiency (Mallory 2011). GDR novices learned first with their eyes by watching a live or film demonstration before attempting to scull one at a time in rowing tanks or, more commonly, in two or four-person rowing gigs with an experienced rower to copy in the stroke seat. Once the sculling technique could be performed correctly in crew boats, they moved to heavy U-bottomed clinker-built singles, which were less stable than gigs but more stable than racing singles. Fairbairn also advocated using singles that were heavier than racing singles as a tool for learning watermanship because they provide better sensory feedback to the rower, who can feel a more pronounced difference between how the boat responds to a stroke that is well executed and one that is not.

The use of heavier equipment in the intermediate learning stage when a rower is learning to apply power likely has another important benefit: It facilitates the incorporation of a larger number of motor units into the neural pathways in the peripheral nervous system that enable the movements to be executed. During the earliest learning stages, before myelination shapes neural pathways, more muscles are recruited than are required. If more motor units need to be recruited to move a heavier object, more become wired into the neural pathways as they myelinate (in accordance with the principle that cells that fire together, wire together). Another potential benefit arises later—to conserve energy under conditions of fatigue, there is a cycling of motor units. If more have been recruited into the neural pathways when they are first established, there are more to cycle through.

It was more common for GDR rowers to begin later, between the ages of 13 and 15. The method for teaching them to row was the same, but the training programs remained diversified, with the volume of low-intensity long distance training carefully increased over time in order to let the heart and lungs adapt before being stressed with high-intensity work. Older entrants, usually aged between 16 and 20, resembled Zeidler; they were athletes of demonstrable quality in other sports who, having exhausted their potential or finding themselves surplus to requirements, were given the opportunity to try something new. Their existing training base permitted an accelerated development program, and the successful ones would progress into senior national team programs within 12 to 24 months.

Key Point

Myelination is an important process underpinning motor learning. It is just as capable of consolidating poor movement patterns as it is good movement patterns. Once myelin has been laid down, it becomes difficult to integrate new neurons into a pathway, which is why it is important to learn movement patterns correctly from the outset.

Movement Economy

Fairbairn had another reason for recommending mileage: He wanted rowers to learn to automate their movement in a natural and efficient way, thereby eliminating unnecessary effort. An important GDR refinement to his methods was to reduce the stroke rate per minute to between 16 and 18 for long distance rows, during which strength is built as muscles spend more time under tension. Moderate effort can also be sustained for longer without elevating levels of lactate in the blood. Lactate, which was once believed to be a metabolic waste product, is now recognized as a neuroprotectant that acts as a fuel source for neurons when oxygen is in short supply (Proia et al. 2016).

Rowing at lower stroke rates also develops the technical finesse—timing, control, balance, touch—required to row well. The training distances were carefully increased in line with the training age of the adolescent rower, further tailoring programs to address individual deficiencies in either strength or endurance. The rule was volume before intensity, allowing the still-developing juvenile heart and lungs to strengthen and adapt before the stress of high-intensity work was added (Herberger et al. 2004). In the first year, young rowers built up to distances of 10 km in individual training sessions. Longer distance rows of between 15 and 20 km were occasionally added. As the athlete's boat speed improved, the distance was increased to stimulate adaptation. By year 3, the average distance covered in a long row was 16 km but could sometimes be extended up to 20 or 25 km.

Physiological Adaptation

The athlete's body adapts physiologically to aerobic training in a number of ways, but the primary objective is to increase the amount of blood pumped with each heartbeat while raising the oxygen pulse, which is the amount of oxygen consumed by the body with each heartbeat (figure 4.1). To increase the volume of blood in the body, the bone marrow must produce more red blood cells to provide more hemoglobin for oxygen to attach to and increase the watery plasma portion of the blood so the strengthened and enlarged heart is able to pump more blood around the body with each heartbeat. The increase in blood volume allows the body to produce more power without overheating.

Lung capacity also enlarges, allowing more air to enter the body, and oxygen extraction becomes more efficient as the number of alveoli and blood capillaries in the lungs increase, resulting in a greater surface area across which oxygen can diffuse into the blood and carbon dioxide can be expelled from the body. The number of blood capillaries in the working muscles increases, as does the density of mitochondria in the muscle cells, increasing the capacity to generate energy within the cells. These are

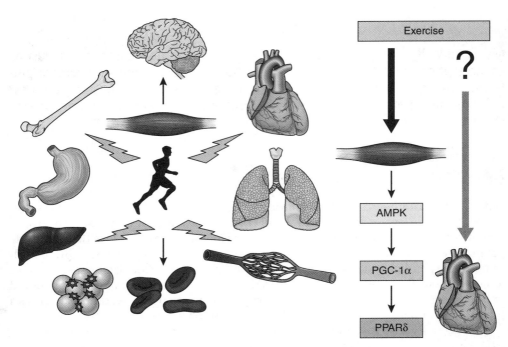

▶ **Figure 4.1** The body's primary physiological objective is to increase the amount of blood pumped with each heartbeat while raising the oxygen pulse.

enduring changes that support the body's ability to continue to generate power when the intensity of the work goes up.

The training load of athletes entering the sport in late adolescence or as adults with a diverse and high-volume training base can be increased faster because they should already be well conditioned, flexible, and agile, and the cardiopulmonary adaptations necessary for high performance will have already been made.

Conclusion

"Mileage makes champions" may have been a product of Fairbairn's intuition and astute observations, but later scientific researchers have validated his methodology in each of the three contexts that he used it: a large volume of diversified developmental experiences to develop general athleticism, small boat rowing to develop athleticism, and long distance rowing to develop the physiological engine. His favorite catchphrase remains as true now as when he first used it and will continue to be valuable for many generations to come.

Rowing Mechanics for Efficiency and Effective Technique

Jeremy Ivey

Biomechanical Principles for Stroke Efficiency

Volker Nolte, PhD

Rowing is a complex movement of many interconnected parts, many details of which are still not completely understood. With the development of new technology, however, more details of the rowing movement can now be measured and studied. For example, the miniaturization of measurement equipment now allows us to collect data in race-like situations or even during races. These tools, which are so small and light that they do not affect the rower's movement or performance in any way, have provided new insights that we are only beginning to understand. In fact, biomechanical analysis from research institutions now offer so many data that most practitioners and even some biomechanists are overstrained to interpret it all properly.

However, some hard-to-eradicate misconceptions still prevail in the rowing community. For instance, many coaches dispute that lift forces are exerted on the rowing blade at all, let alone accept the importance of these forces or think about how best to use them. Another example is that some coaches believe that a rower can move from the finish to the full reach position without pulling on the footstretcher (Hamilton 2016).

Biomechanics of sport is the science that uses mechanical concepts to explain the interactions of movements and forces of humans in the sport context. This chapter will provide an update on the basic research of rowing biomechanics and project best applications of this knowledge into practice. We will develop criteria by which we can evaluate the interaction between the rower and the system and the resulting mechanical efficiency. To achieve these goals, we first have to dive into the basics of biomechanics.

We will discuss the biomechanical foundations of rowing, which we then will use to develop the understanding for an ideal rowing technique and how performance can be improved. This will also allow us to understand how to best use rowing equipment and adjust it to the individual athlete.

Biomechanical Foundations

One can look at the rowing motion as a transfer of energy (see figure 5.1). The metabolic system of a rower uses the energy of ingested nutrients to produce mechanical energy through the muscles to pull on the oar handles. This energy is then transformed by the oars and the blade into propulsive energy, which is needed to offset the energy that it costs to overcome the air and water resistance that rowers, boat, and oars generate while

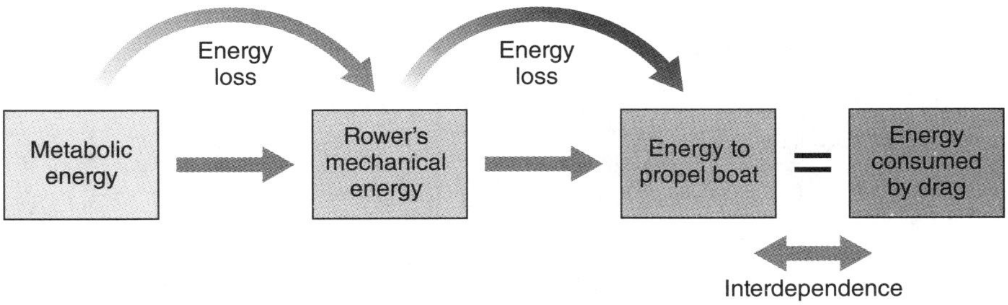

▶ **Figure 5.1** Energy transfer to propel a rowing boat.

moving through these fluids. It is a natural law that some amount of energy is necessarily lost in each of these transfers. The trick will be to keep the energy loss at each step of the process as small as possible, so that more energy is available in the next step.

Transferring metabolic to mechanical energy is a physiological mechanism and is presented later in this book. The step from mechanical energy of the rower to propulsion is influenced by biomechanics, which we will discuss now. There is a direct connection between propulsion and overall drag. Propulsion has to offset the energy caused by drag if the rower wants to maintain a certain velocity. Rowers can move faster if they can generate more propulsion, so they will always be attempting to transfer as much of their mechanical energy into propulsion as possible. This is achieved through proper rowing technique, which will be examined in this chapter and the next, as well as through proper setup of the individual rower's equipment, which will be further analyzed in chapter 9.

If propulsion is larger than the drag, the whole rowing system will increase in velocity, which in turn generates more drag until both measures are back in a state of equilibrium. Conversely, if drag is larger than the propulsion, the system will slow down until propulsion and drag are again equal in magnitude.

Defining Biomechanical Terms

To clarify biomechanical terms, concepts, and principles, we will now define the mechanical concepts to be used. We will then apply these mechanical concepts specifically to the biomechanics of rowing, which will allow the statement of the *biomechanical principles of rowing* and form the basis of an optimized rowing technique.

Coordinate System

Figure 5.2 presents the coordinate system in rowing, with the longitudinal axis of the boat along the x-axis and the x-direction pointing in direction of travel. The horizontal direction perpendicular to the boat is represented by the y-axis and the vertical direction is represented by the z-axis. The centers of mass (CoM) and the horizontal oar angle θ_O are also shown.

Centers of Mass

There are three main independent parts that make up the *overall rowing system* (CoM_{total}): the rower (CoM_{rower}), the boat (CoM_{boat}), and the oars CoM_{oar}. The positions of these centers are presented with the relative mass in the size of the symbol indicated in figure 5.2. A typical mass of a single sculler varies between 59 kg (130 lb) for lightweight

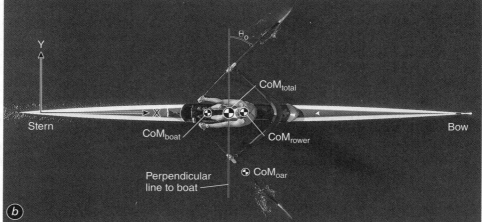

▶ **Figure 5.2** The coordinate system in rowing with the centers of mass in a single scull (including the oar angle θ_o).

Photos courtesy Volker Nolte.

women and 110 kg (242 lb) for men. A single scull boat usually has a mass of 14 kg (31 lb), which is the minimum mass such a boat must have according to the international rules of racing; most racing shells are built to this size. A scull has a mass of about 1.3 kg (2.9 lb). Because the oar mass is so small compared to the mass of the rower, one can simplify further discussions by assuming that the oar is a rigid object of a specific dimension and shape with a mass of 0 kg (0 lb) without introducing serious error.

Key Point

Each physical object has a center of mass (CoM), which is the point around which its entire mass could be assumed to be concentrated. This construct makes it easier to study the motion of objects by simplifying the body to one single point. The CoM reacts to all external forces in the same way as the system that it represents. The force of gravity, which is the weight (W) of the object, acts downward precisely through this point.

Positions and Phases of the Stroke

To discuss and describe the rowing motion properly, important positions and phases need to be identified. *Position* is the configuration of the body parts at one particular time, whereas a *phase* is a series of events over a length of time. To describe the main parts of the rowing stroke, two positions and four phases are distinguished in table 5.1.

Table 5.1 Definitions of the Positions and Phases of the Rowing Stroke

POSITIONS	
Full reach	The hands reach the most aftward point (closest to the stern of the boat) during the stroke; hands have the smallest x-coordinate relative to the boat and oar angle μ_o has the largest negative value.
Finish	The hands reach the most forward point (closest to the bow of the boat) during the stroke; hands have the largest x-coordinate relative to the boat and oar angle μ_o has the largest positive value.
PHASES	
Drive	The movement of the rower from the full reach to the finish position. All propulsion occurs during this phase. The hands move in a circle around the pin. The entry and the release phases are part of the drive phase.
Entry	The movement from the full reach position until the blade is completely submerged in the water. The hands move simultaneously in a horizontal and upward vertical direction relative to the boat.
Release	The movement starting when the upper edge of the blade first rises through the water line until the finish position. The hands move simultaneously in a horizontal and downward vertical direction relative to the boat.
Recovery	The movement from the finish to the next full reach position.

Forces in Rowing and the Equations of Motion

The basis to describe the motions of the different parts of the rowing system in space over time is now possible with these definitions. The next step is to lay the foundation for the study of the forces that are responsible for the motions of all rowing parts. For this, mechanical models of the main rowing systems with all their respective external forces need to be developed, which will then be used to express the equations of motion of these systems and allow the analysis of the movements of the different centers of mass.

The equation of motion is based on Newton's second law, which states that the sum of all external forces on an object (O) causes it to accelerate—or, in other words, to change its motion (equation 5.1).

$$\Sigma F_{\text{ext}} = m_o \times a_o \qquad (5.1)$$

An *external force* is thus acting between the object and the environment surrounding it and causing the object to move relative to the environment. Water resistance, as an example, is an external force on the overall system, slowing it down.

Each object also has numerous *internal forces*, which are forces that act between parts of the object, but not with the environment. Internal forces are important to hold certain parts of the object in place or move parts within an object—for example, there are numerous forces within the human body to keep its shape without causing any motion of the body in the environment—but only external forces can move a system within the environment. The arm and leg muscles of a rower generate forces that cause the body to move, but without the connections of the rower with the handles or the footstretcher, there would be no movement of the rower possible in the environment. Similarly, there are numerous internal forces within the overall system (pin, footstretcher, or seat forces, for example), but only the external water forces on the blades allow the rower to move the overall system relative to the environment.

In addition, according to Newton's third law, each force comes as an interaction of two objects—generally known as "for every action, there is an equal and opposite reaction." One object generates a force on the second object that has the same magnitude and the same line of action, but acts in the opposite direction. For example, the rower pushes on the footstretcher and generates the so-called *footstretcher force*. The footstretcher, as part of the boat, absorbs this force and transfers it to the boat, which causes some movement of the boat. At the same time, the footstretcher pushes back on the feet of the rower with the same magnitude, but in the opposite direction, causing movement of the rower.

Figure 5.3 presents the mechanical model of the overall rowing system (CoM_{total}) with all its external forces. It is important to realize that a rower has to move the whole system over a certain distance, not only their body or the boat alone. As one can see, there are actually only a small number of external forces on this system. Based on this model, the respective equations of motion shown in equations 5.2 and 5.3 indicate the effect of all forces acting on the system.

▶ **Figure 5.3** Mechanical model of the overall rowing system (CoM_{total}) with all external forces.

The equations of motion of the overall rowing system in x- and z-directions are:

$$\Sigma F_x = F_{propel} - F_{boat} - F_{air} = m_{total} \times a_{x\text{-}total} \tag{5.2}$$

where F_{propel} is propulsion on the blades; F_{boat} is water resistance on the boat; F_{air} is air resistance on the overall rowing system; m_{total} is the mass of the overall system; and $a_{x\text{-}total}$ is acceleration of the overall system in x-direction.

$$\Sigma F_z = B - W = m_{total} \times a_{z\text{-}total} \tag{5.3}$$

where B is buoyancy; W is the weight of the overall system; and $a_{z\text{-total}}$ is acceleration of the overall system in z-direction.

This means that the only forces that can accelerate the overall system in the desired direction of travel are the propulsion forces on the blades (F_{propel}). Water and wind resistance act opposite to the propulsive forces and slow the system down. Figure 5.4 provides a visual example from a women's single of how F_{boat} and F_{propel} act as the main external forces in x-direction on the overall system.

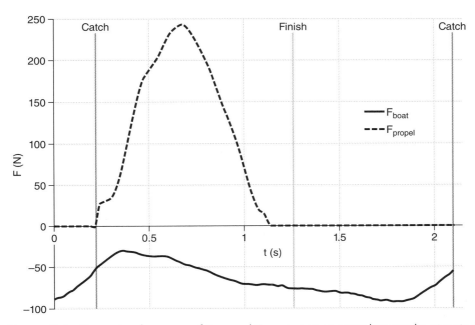

▶ **Figure 5.4** Example of courses of F_{boat} and F_{propel} over one complete stroke at a stroke rate of 31.9 strokes per min (spm).

Key Point

Only the water forces on the blade can propel the overall system in the desired direction of travel.

It is important to realize that the rower and the boat move within the overall system, so the instantaneous velocities of these three systems ($v_{CoMtotal}$, $v_{CoMrower}$, and v_{boat}) are all different over the course of one stroke. However, the average velocities taken for a complete stroke are the same for all three systems, meaning that each system covers the same distance during one complete stroke.

Water resistance is the external force on CoM_{total} that slows the system down. Because this force acts on the boat, its magnitude is directly influenced by boat velocity, not by the velocity of the overall system. This fact is often misunderstood, but has very important implications, as we will explore later in this chapter.

The rower and the boat are part of the overall system. Movement of these two parts within the system is possible through internal forces, which do not directly affect the motion of the overall system in the environment. For instance, the rower pushes with their feet on the footstretcher. At the same time, the footstretcher, as part of the boat, pushes back on the rower. These two forces are opposite and cancel each other out, because the footstretcher and rower are part of the whole system.

Let's verify this phenomenon with two thought experiments: If we tied the two blades together with a rope in the full reach position so that the blades could not move, the rower could pull on the handle—and indeed, we could measure handle, oarlock, and footstretcher forces—but the whole system would not move. Similarly, if a single rower in the middle of a calm lake with no wind simulated the rowing stroke without the blades touching the water, we could measure the forces on the footstretcher that are necessary to move the rower and the boat within the overall system. We could even build a braking system onto the pin like some rowing ergometers have, so that the rower would need increased forces to move the sculls. However, the overall system would not move in either of these scenarios!

Key Point

According to Archimedes' principle, buoyancy, or the force acting in a positive z-direction (upward) on a body immersed in a fluid, has the same magnitude as the weight of the volume of the fluid that the body displaces. When a crew steps into a boat, it sinks into the water until it displaces an amount that is equal in weight to that of the total system. This is why modern boats are exactly designed for the weight of the crew.

The mass of a specific volume of water, or density, varies mainly depending on its temperature and salinity. Density increases with decreasing temperature and its salt content. This means, for example, that a boat will not sink as much into cold salt water as in warm fresh water.

Equation 5.2 also clarifies the intermittent structure of the rowing motion. F_{propel} is, of course, only active during the propulsion phase, and the velocity of CoM_{total} in x-direction ($v_{x\text{-total}}$) increases as long as it is larger than the resistance forces. During the recovery, when there is no propulsion, $v_{x\text{-total}}$ will decrease.

Equation 5.3 indicates that changes in buoyancy result in vertical movements of the overall center of mass. Changes of buoyancy are the results of interactions between the rower's mass and the boat. For example, when the rower raises their center of mass, the boat first gets pushed into the water, which increases buoyancy and results in a positive acceleration of the overall center of mass in the vertical direction.

Forces on the Individual Centers of Mass

It is important to study the individual rower system for further inquiries. For this, the rower is cut off, so to speak, from all contact points with the environment. In turn, all external forces on the rower are placed at these contact points. There are five external forces acting on the rower: the weight of the rower, the handle force generated by the rower through the pull on the oar, the footstretcher force, the seat force, and the air resistance on the rower (see figure 5.6).

The weight of the rower is distributed to the seat and the footstretcher, depending on where the rower's center of mass is located horizontally. The rower pulls on the handle with a force directed slightly upward, which generates the external reaction force of the handle on the hands. This force has a large horizontal and a small downward vertical component.

The rower pushes on the angled footstretcher and generates the reaction force, which is the external footstretcher force acting on the rower.

The rowing seat slides on ball bearings and straight tracks that normally have a small 2° incline toward the bow, which gives the rower minor assistance approaching the full reach position during the recovery. This costs a small amount of energy during the drive, but the horizontal force is negligible.

The air resistance is dependent on the size and shape of the rower and their clothing, as well as on the velocity of the rower relative to the air. This is a drag force that only acts in x-direction, because the rower mainly moves horizontally.

The sum of all external forces causes the CoM of the rower to accelerate in the indicated direction. Figure 5.6 shows the mechanical model of the rower system with its external forces during the drive.

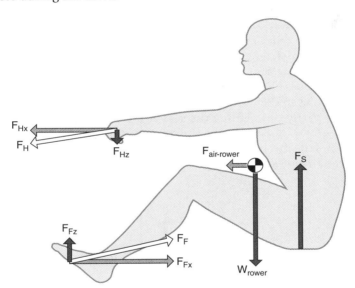

▶ **Figure 5.5** Mechanical model of the individual rower system with all its external forces.

The equations of motion for the rower system in x- and z-directions are as follows:

$$\Sigma F_x = F_{Fx} - F_{Hx} - F_{air\text{-}rower} = m_{rower} \times a_{x\text{-}rower} \tag{5.4}$$

where F_{Fx} is footstretcher force in x-direction; F_{Hx} is handle or pulling force in x-direction; $F_{air\text{-}rower}$ is the air resistance on the rower; m_{rower} is the mass of the rower; and $a_{x\text{-}rower}$ is the acceleration of the rower in x-direction.

$$\Sigma F_z = F_{Fz} - F_{Hz} + F_S - W_{rower} = m_{rower} \times a_{z\text{-}rower} \tag{5.5}$$

where F_{Fz} is footstretcher force in z-direction; F_{Hz} is the handle or pulling force in z-direction; F_s is seat force; W_{rower} is the weight of the rower; and $a_{z\text{-}rower}$ is the acceleration of the rower in z-direction.

Because horizontal footstretcher force F_{Fx} over the drive is larger than the horizontal handle force F_{Hx} and air resistance $F_{air\text{-}rower}$ together, the rower accelerates in positive x-direction.

The rower has to move from the finish position to the full reach position during the recovery and therefore has to accelerate in a negative direction. This can only be done by the rower pulling on the footstretcher, which means that the horizontal component of the footstretcher force F_{Fx} becomes negative during the first part of the recovery. There is no other way, because the footstretcher provides the only possible support that would allow a force in negative x-direction when the blades are out of the water. If the rower tried to generate this negative force with the oar handles, the oars would be pulled out of the oarlock. The larger the mass of the boat and the faster the rower moves out of the finish position, the larger the negative footstretcher force.

Rowers will always try to keep the movement of their center of mass in the z-direction small, because it costs energy that in turn reduces their available power to produce propulsion. The vertical movement that is unavoidable through the rotation of the trunk around the hip and the straightening and bending of the knees causes only small accelerations when executed properly, so that the inertial force $m_{rower} \times a_{z\text{-}rower}$ in equation 5.5 remains small. This means that the sum of the two downward-oriented forces, weight of the rower W and vertical component of the handle force F_{Hz}, need to be absorbed by the seat and the footstretcher during the drive. If one would try to unload the seat completely, the whole load would rest on the footstretcher with the same effect regarding buoyancy on the boat. During the entry phase, when the rower's center of mass is close to the footstretcher and the hands are moving upward to immerse the blades in the water, a large portion of the vertical forces are placed on the footstretcher, partly unweighing the seat at the same time. The majority of load eventually moves onto the seat during the course of the drive.

Figure 5.7 shows the mechanical model of the boat system. Note there are a number of external forces already seen in the previous models now acting on the boat as reaction forces.

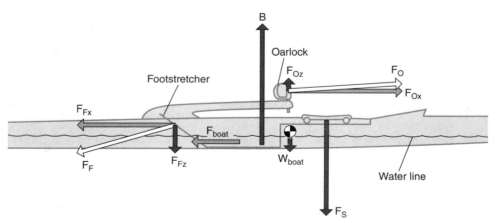

▶ **Figure 5.6** Mechanical model of the system boat with all its external forces.

The equations of motion for the boat system in x- and z-directions are as follows:

$$\Sigma F_x = F_{Ox} - F_{Fx} - F_{boat} = m_{boat} \times a_{x\text{-}boat} \tag{5.6}$$

where F_{Fx} is footstretcher force in x-direction; F_{Ox} is oarlock force in x-direction; F_{water} is water resistance on the boat; m_{boat} is the mass of the boat, and $a_{x\text{-boat}}$ is the acceleration of the boat in x-direction.

$$\Sigma F_z = B + F_{Oz} - F_{Fz} - F_S - W_{boat} = m_{boat} \times a_{z\text{-boat}} \qquad (5.7)$$

where B is buoyancy; F_{Oz} is oarlock force in z-direction; F_{Fz} is footstretcher force in z-direction; F_S is seat force; W_{boat} is the weight of the boat; m_{boat} is the mass of the boat, and $a_{z\text{-boat}}$ is the acceleration of the boat in z-direction.

The horizontal acceleration of the boat $a_{x\text{-boat}}$ is relatively easy to measure and is used extensively in biomechanical counseling of crews. Some characteristics of the course of $a_{x\text{-boat}}$ are known to have a positive effect on performance, which we will see in the next chapter.

Equation 5.6 presents the connection between boat acceleration and the horizontal forces on the boat. This will help us understand why the boat velocity reaches its maximum during the recovery even though there is no propulsion during that phase, as well as why boat velocity slows down during the first part of the drive even though propulsion has already occurred. Velocity v_{boat} and acceleration a_{boat} are standard measurements in many biomechanical analyses of the boat. Figure 5.7 is an example data of a women's single.

At the finish position, all parts of the overall rowing system do not move relative to each other by definition (see table 5.1) and therefore have the same horizontal velocity relative to the environment. The rower, however, is in a transition motion from the drive to the recovery, which means that the velocity of the rower relative to the boat

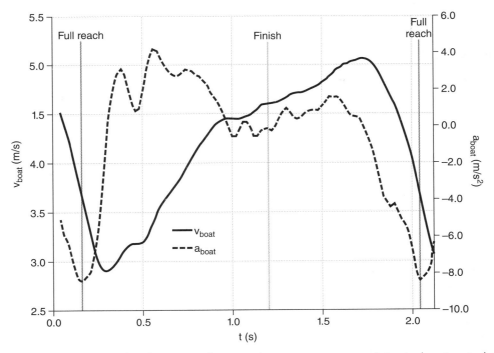

▶ **Figure 5.7** Example of courses of v_{boat} and a_{boat} over one complete stroke at a stroke rate of 31.9 spm.

is changing direction. As a consequence, the boat experiences a positive acceleration that increases its velocity without the presence of propulsion. This acceleration is based on pulling forces on the footstretcher as the rower moves their body from the finish position toward the next full reach. The footstretcher is the only contact point for the rower that allows the application of such forces. F_{Fx} is positive during this part of the recovery, and as long as its magnitude is larger than F_{boat}, acceleration of the boat relative to the environment is positive. This is the case from the first part of the recovery until the rower's CoM has reached its maximum velocity relative to the boat. Boat velocity relative to the environment increases during this phase, which is why the boat reaches its highest velocity during the recovery. The shorter the recovery time, the more pronounced this phenomenon becomes.

After the CoM_{rower} reaches maximum velocity relative to the boat, the rower has then to decelerate their CoM toward the full reach position, where velocity between the two masses will reach again zero. The rower accomplishes this deceleration by pushing on the footstretcher, generating a negative footstretcher force. This force adds to the water resistance F_{water}, which leads to a sharp decline in boat velocity starting during the last part of the recovery.

As we will see later, the blades must be off the water at the full reach position and must gain some velocity relative to the boat to enter the water at the correct velocity to be able to generate propulsion. In fact, the rower not only has to accelerate their CoM toward the bow of the boat during the entry phase, but also steadily increase the pull on the oar handles, which is only accomplished by a strong push on the footstretcher that continues from the end of the recovery. Footstretcher force and boat resistance are larger than the oarlock force for the first part of the drive, which means that the sum of these forces continue to decelerate the boat even though there is already some propulsion at the blades.

Rowing Efficiency

As described earlier, rowing is an energy transfer system, and rowers are aiming to produce the largest amount of propulsive energy out of their overall mechanical energy to perform one stroke. This means wasting the least amount of energy on any other task than propelling the overall system. The degree to which this task is accomplished is called *efficiency* η and measures how much of the overall generated energy that is put into a system is transferred out as useful energy. We observe this energy exchange in rowing over the time of one complete stroke t_{st}. The general formula for efficiency is

$$\eta = \frac{U_{out}}{U_{in}} = \frac{U_{out}/t_{st}}{U_{in}/t_{st}} = \frac{P_{out}}{P_{in}} \tag{5.8}$$

where U_{out} is energy output; U_{in} is energy input; t_{st} is time to complete one stroke; P_{out} is power output; and P_{in} is power input.

A rower can only produce a certain maximum amount of mechanical power P_{rower} for a given length of time, depending on training, age, muscle mass, and so forth. This total amount of power must cover not only the generation of the pulling power on the handle P_{handle}, but also the movement of the mass of the rower within the overall system in x- (P_{CoMx}) and in z-direction (P_{CoMz}). In other words, P_{CoMx} and P_{CoMz} are the power necessary to move, accelerate, or elevate the COM. This can be summarized in equation 5.9:

$$P_{rower} = P_{handle} + P_{CoMx} + P_{CoMz} \tag{5.9}$$

The part of the power that is used to move the rower's CoM is consequently not available to produce any more handle power. Although the goal of a rower will always be to get the most out of their mechanical power, every mechanical system will incur some power loss, so that η always will be smaller than 1. This is inevitable, because rowers must move their body parts in order to perform the rowing motion and generate P_{rower}. Efficient rowing technique and the most specifically designed and adjusted equipment can be used to minimize the amount of lost power.

Contingent on the rowing technique and the equipment used, the power applied to the handle P_{handle} will be transformed into propulsive power P_{propel} that accelerates the overall system (see equation 5.2) during the drive. Inevitably, there will be some more power lost in the water in this process. The connection is shown in equation 5.10:

$$P_{handle} = P_{propel} + P_{loss} \tag{5.10}$$

The overall stroke efficiency η_{stroke} can then be defined in equation 5.11:

$$\eta_{stroke} = \left. P_{propel} \middle/ P_{rower} \right. = \left. (P_{handle} - P_{loss}) \middle/ (P_{handle} + P_{CoM_x} + P_{CoM_z}) \right. \tag{5.11}$$

As we can see, stroke efficiency is influenced by a number of factors and increases as power loss decreases. Nolte (1984) found stroke efficiency η_{stroke} for a world-class rower to be 0.64 at a stroke rate of 32.6 spm and 0.66 at a stroke rate of 35.5 spm.

So far in this section we discussed the generation of power P_{propel}, which propels the overall system during the drive. We could call this power "positive," because it leads to the acceleration of the overall system in direction of travel. However, the overall system loses power over the whole stroke through water resistance P_{resist}, which is defined in equation 5.12:

$$P_{resist} = F_{water} \times v_{boat} \tag{5.12}$$

As well as getting the largest amount of propulsion out of their power production, rowers also can affect their overall rowing performance by minimizing P_{resist}. We will discuss this topic in more detail later.

To examine all possible power losses in the rowing system, we also must note some friction between sliding seat and slides, as well as between oarlock and pin, which the rower has to overcome. However, these forces are extremely small and equipment dependent, so we can disregard them for the purposes of this chapter.

Now that we have established that rowers must use a technique that allows them to generate the largest possible P_{rower}, move relative to the boat to produce the largest amount of P_{propel}, and accept some power losses during these processes, an efficient rowing technique therefore includes the following goals:

- Reduce P_{loss} during propulsion.
- Avoid large movements of the CoM_{rower} in z-direction.
- Optimize movement of the CoM_{rower} in x-direction.

Blade Efficiency

Efficiency of the blade η_{blade} is a measure of how much of the handle power is transformed into propulsion. This leads us to the definition of blade efficiency in equation 5.13:

$$\eta_{blade} = \left. P_{propel} \middle/ P_{handle} \right. \tag{5.13}$$

This equation is similar to equation 5.11, except that the focus is only on the transfer of the power on the handle into propulsion.

Movement of the Blade in the Water

In order to row, the rower must generate forces on the blade to create propulsion. This is only possible by moving the blade relative to the water—if you placed a rowing blade in the water and did not move it relative to the water, no resultant force on the blade would occur and no propulsion would happen.

To study the force generation on the blade, we need to identify the actual velocity of the blade relative to the water v_{res} (figure 5.8a), which is the result of the blade's movement relative to the boat v_{turn} and the movement of the boat relative to the water v_{boat}. This results in the path of the blade in the water, as shown in figures 5.8b and 5.9. The blade movement relative to the water creates a flow of water relative to the blade. This velocity v_w has the same magnitude as v_{res}, but in the opposite direction.

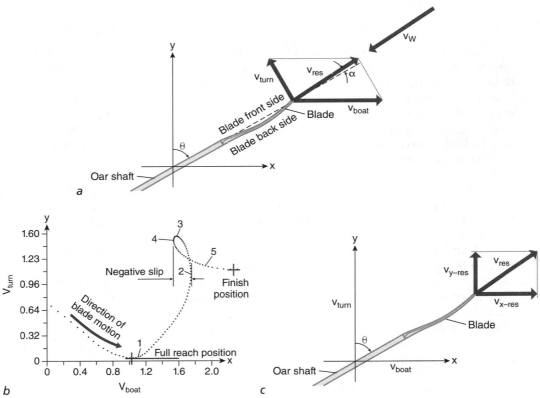

▶ **Figure 5.8** Movement of the rowing blade in the water and the resultant water flow generated by the velocity of the boat v_{boat} and the velocity of the blade relative to the boat v_{turn}. (a) v_{res} is the summation of v_{turn} and v_{boat} and results in the flow v_w relative to the blade. θ_o = oar angle; v_{boat} = boat velocity; v_{turn} = tangential velocity of the blade around the pin; v_{res} = vector addition of $v_{boat} \oplus v_{Turn}$; v_w = velocity of the water relative to the blade, resulting from v_{res}; α = angle of attack (angle of v_w with chord of the rowing blade). (b) Dots show the position of the tip of the blade in the x-y-plane during the last part of the recovery and the whole propulsion; dots are measured every 0.02 s: (1) first point just after full reach, at which propulsion occurs and blade moves in positive x-direction; (2) point at which blade starts moving in negative x-direction; (3) perpendicular oar position; (4) point at which blade starts moving again in positive x-direction; (5) last point at which propulsion acts (based on Nolte 1984, 191). (c) v_{x-res} and v_{y-res} are the components of v_{res}.

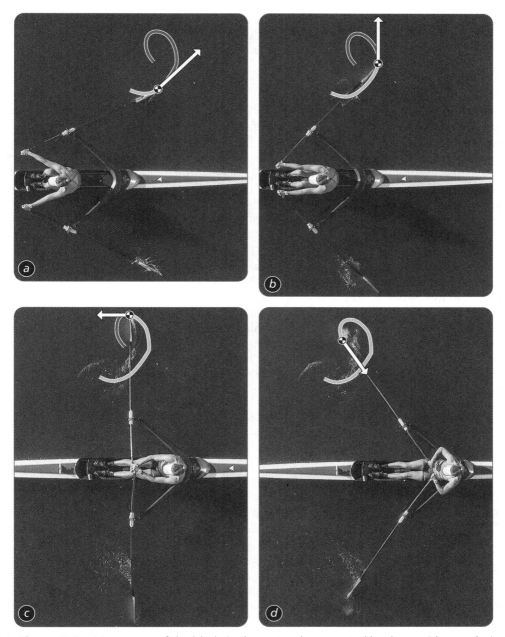

▶ **Figure 5.9** Movement of the blade in the water documented by drone video analysis. An ☯ indicates the position, the white arrow is the velocity, and the curved light gray line is the path of the tip of the blade in the water.

Photos courtesy Volker Nolte.

It is important to realize how the blade actually moves through the water. For most of the time that the blade is in the water, it moves in the direction of travel of the boat. See, for example, figure 5.8b—the blade moves about 1.0 m in positive x-direction (0.65 m from point 1 to point 2, plus 0.35 m from point 4 to point 5), 1.9 m in y-direction (1.5 m in positive y-direction from point 1 to point 3 and 0.4 m in negative y-direction from point 3 to point 5) and only about 0.2 m in negative x-direction (from point 2 to point 3). All these distances represent the slip of the blade in the water; the movement in negative x-direction is often called *negative slip*. The movement of the blade is simultaneously affected by the rotation of the oar around the pin, which the rower generates by pulling on the handle, and the velocity of the boat, with which the blade is connected through the oarlock.

The overlapping of v_{boat} and v_{turn} results in the actual blade velocity relative to the water v_{res}, which is the same as the water flow relative to the blade v_{w}. This resultant velocity of the blade can be split into its x- and y-components, as shown in figure 5.8c.

The flow oncoming to blade v_{w} builds an angle α with the chord of the blade, which is the line joining the leading and trailing edges of the blade. This angle α is called *angle of attack*, and propulsion can only occur when this angle is positive, meaning the vector of v_{w} points to the concave side of the blade.

In order to understand the complexity of the entry motion, it is important to study the whole process in detail. The velocity of the hand relative to the boat is 0 m/s at the full reach position where the entry starts. This implies that the oar and the blade also have—at that moment—no velocity relative to the boat, and all these parts are moving relative to the water with the velocity of the boat. If the blade touched the water in this position, water would attack the back side of the blade with the velocity of the boat and produce a large backsplash, which is a sign of a braking force on the blade.

The blade therefore needs a certain turning velocity v_{turn} before it touches the water during the entry. This also means that the rower has to start rotating the oar around the pin after the full reach position without the blade touching the water, called an *air stroke* (note in figure 5.8b that the blade moves slightly from full reach position to point 1). This air stroke is part of the entry, and rowers should try to keep it as small as possible, because it reduces the overall propulsive length of the drive. Rowers need to coordinate this complex movement of starting the oar rotation in the horizontal direction with the exact timing of the vertical hand motion to bury the blade in the water. Athletes also have to build their handle force, because the force on the blade starts to increase during this action.

The overall movement of the blade in the water is not readily understandable. In the past, many authors have described the course of the blade in water as nearly circular, with the blade only moving in negative x-direction (Herberger 1970; Klavora 1982; Körner and Schwanitz 1985; Williams and Scott 1967). These theories neglected that the pin, with which the blade is connected to the boat, simultaneously moves with the boat and that propulsion can not be generated only by drag forces.

Figure 5.9 gives a better visual impression of the actual path of a blade in the water. The tip of the port-side blade is marked in each picture and the respective velocity of the blade relative to the water is indicated by an arrow with its direction and magnitude. The curved light gray line represents the path of the blade in the water.

Drag and Lift

Any object that moves relative to a fluid—in our case, the rowing blade relative to water—experiences a hydrodynamic force that has two components: drag and lift. Drag is a form of friction that depends on the velocity difference between the object and the fluid. Lift forces are generated by a combination of pressure differences caused by the fluid on one side of the object moving faster than the other side (Bernoulli effect) and fluid particles being deflected perpendicular to the object pushing the object in the opposite direction (Newton's third law). It is important to point out that lift can act in any direction and has nothing to do with "lifting up"! Depending on the object's shape, its positioning, and its movement relative to the fluid, lift can be directed in any possible orientation. The name comes from the study of aerodynamic forces on flying objects, where, of course, the lift component predominantly acts in positive z-direction. In rowing, lift acts in the horizontal plane and has a major influence on propulsion.

Key Point

An object subjected to a flow of water experiences a force that has two components: drag and lift. Drag is the part of the water force that acts parallel and opposite to the oncoming flow. Lift is the component that acts perpendicular to the oncoming flow.

When the rowing blade moves through water, the flow of the water generates the force F_{blade}. This resultant force has both lift and drag, which depend on the angle with which the water approaches the blade during the drive. This angle of attack α changes at every oar angle. Figure 5.10 shows the three main flow scenarios that occur during the drive and the resulting magnitude and direction of drag and lift.

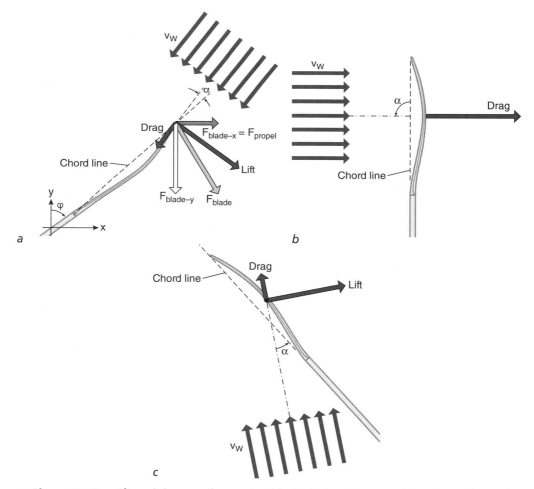

▶ **Figure 5.10** Lift and drag on the rowing blade during the propulsion phase depending on the angle of attack α *(a)* at the beginning of the drive; *(b)* at the perpendicular position of the blade to the boat; and *(c)* just before the release.

It is important to realize several particulars shown in figure 5.10. The force F_{blade} (the resultant force of drag and lift on the blade) depicted in figure 5.10*a* is also broken down into its x- and y-components $F_{blade-x}$ and $F_{blade-y}$. Its x-component $F_{blade-x}$ is the force F_{propel} that propels the overall system. It is remarkable to observe that we actually have propulsion at times when the blade moves in direction of travel. This phenomenon is similar to the way a sailboat is able to propel forward when sailing into the wind. The hydrodynamic force components drag and lift are dependent on several factors that can be expressed through the following drag and lift equations (equations 5.14 and 5.15):

$$F_{drag} = \frac{1}{2} \times c_d \times \rho \times A \times v^2 \tag{5.14}$$

where F_{drag} is drag resistance on the object moving relative to the water; c_d is the drag coefficient; ρ is the density of water; A is the cross-sectional area of the object; and v is the velocity of the object relative to the water.

$$F_{lift} = \frac{1}{2} \times c_l \times \rho \times A \times v^2 \tag{5.15}$$

where F_{lift} is lift force on the object moving relative to the water; c_l is the lift coefficient; ρ is the density of water; A is the cross-sectional area of the object; and v is the velocity of the object relative to the water.

The density of the water is influenced by temperature as well as substances that are dissolved in it. The drag and lift coefficients are dependent on the shape, design, and surface of the object. The cross-sectional area is the largest area that faces the oncoming flow. The velocity of the object in the water has a large effect on the hydrodynamic forces—they increase with the square of the velocity!

The blade experiences drag and lift forces during the drive. In fact, lift forces play a very important role in the propulsion in rowing. As shown in figure 5.8*b*, the blade moves at race pace for most of its time in the direction of travel (from point 1 to 2 and from point 4 to 5), during which only lift can provide propulsion. During that time, the drag on the blade actually generates water resistance that costs the rower energy. While the blade moves in this direction, however, the water attacks the chord of the blade at a steep angle, which maximizes the conditions for lift and minimizes the conditions for drag. The blade is in a streamlined position to the oncoming flow, so that the drag coefficient and cross-sectional area are small and only small amounts of energy are lost. After point 2 in figure 5.8*b*, the blade moves against the direction of travel and the angle of attack increases dramatically, expanding drag coefficient and cross-sectional area of the blade, so that propulsion can be generated through drag. Lift is still produced through the lateral movement of the blade, but diminishes toward point 3, where only drag forces apply to the blade (see figure 5.10*b*). The drag force generated during this phase is very favorable for propulsion. This is why this phase of the propulsion is very important, and it occurs when the large muscle groups in the rower's legs and back are active. However, kinetic energy is transferred into the water by setting it into motion. This is lost energy for the rower, so that this part of the drive is not very efficient (Affeld, Schichl, and Ziemann 1993; Kleshnev 2016; Sliasas and Tullis 2009). After point 4 in figure 5.8*c*, the blade once more starts moving in the direction of travel and lift forces take over again.

The design of the blade supports how the different forces are generated. When the angle of attack is shallow, the blade acts more like an airplane wing, thus the curvature of the blade and the winglike shape. To improve conditions for lift, features like the Concept2 Vortex Edge have been added and the rib in the middle of the concave blade side that was typical of older blades has been removed to smooth the surface. When the angle of attack increases and drag becomes the main propelling component, the blade presents its large area perpendicular to the oncoming flow, thus the development of the asymmetric blades with larger blade surfaces and the spoonlike curvature across the width.

Lift in contrary—and this must be emphasized—does not consume energy, because of the very nature of its definition. Lift forces are directed perpendicular to the movement of the blade, which means that the force is generated, but there is no movement in the direction of this force, thus energy cannot be generated and lost. However, this highly effective lift force only occurs simultaneously to some drag force whereby the lift forces are larger at shallow angles of attack, thus why the highest blade efficiencies occur at the beginning and the end of the drive.

Boat Efficiency

Boat movement in the water generates the largest amount of lost energy that the rower has to overcome. Some of this energy loss is unavoidable, but any measures that can reduce the resistance of the boat in the water will increase the overall efficiency of the rowing system. By definition of the international racing rules, "rowing is the propulsion of a displacement boat" (World Rowing 2021, 43). This regulation limits the shape designs of rowing boats.

Displacement boats only experience drag resistance (see figure 5.6). Four independent variables affect this force, according to equation 5.14. The first, drag coefficient of the boat c_d, is influenced by boat design. Like the second variable, density ρ of the water, this cannot be affected by rowing technique.

The third variable, the cross-sectional area A of the boat, hinges on the weight of the overall system and the vertical movement of the rower. The weight of the overall system, again, is a fixed measure, and though some of the rower's vertical movements are unavoidable because the rower must bend, stretch, and rotate the body to execute the stroke, they can be minimized. Nolte (1984) showed that rowers must spend about 15% of their total energy on the vertical movement, which indicates that this factor is considerable and therefore warrants attention. Each 0.01 m extra vertical movement of a rower with a mass of 80 kg at a stroke rate of 34 spm requires 4.4 W of added power, which is about 1% of the overall mechanical power of an international-level rower at race pace. Unnecessary movement can occur either in the middle of the drive or during the release, as shown in figure 5.11.

The fourth variable, boat velocity v_{boat}, has a tremendous influence on the drag force F_{water} (see equation 5.14). Of course, the rower strives to move with the highest average velocity per stroke, but variations in boat velocity over one stroke are the problem: Because of the quadratic nature of velocity's influence, the increase in drag when boat velocity is above average is larger than the decrease in drag when boat velocity is below average.

Obviously, it would be ideal if the velocity of a rowing boat were constant, but this is impossible, because of the intermittent propulsion and the additional movement of the boat relative to the overall system based on the movement of the rower in the boat. Boat velocity can only be constant if propulsion is continuously applied and the rower sits still in the boat, similar to when a motorboat travels with the throttle set to a fixed position. The intermittent propulsion in rowing is clearly seen in the velocity of the overall system, while the velocity variations of the boat based on the movement of the rowers in the boat are indicated by the difference between the velocity of the overall system and the boat velocity (= Δv_{boat}), as shown in figure 5.14.

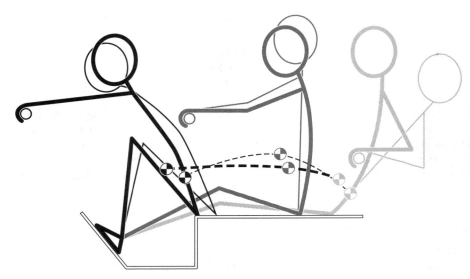

▶ **Figure 5.11** Comparison of two different body movements with the path of the CoM$_{ower}$ to achieve the same stroke length: Thick lines indicate optimized motion; thin lines indicate less efficient motion.

Key Point

Let's assume the drag on a single could be calculated by the following formula:

$$F_{drag} = 4 \times v_{boat}^2$$

The value 4 is a good estimate for a single and includes the drag coefficient c_d, density ρ, and cross-sectional area A.

Boat A moves with a constant velocity of 4 m/s, whereas boat B moves half of the time at 3 m/s and half of the time at 5 m/s. Both boats are moving with the same average velocity of 4 m/s. The drag for these boats is:

$$F_{drag} \text{ Boat A} = 4 \times 4^2 = 64 \text{ N}$$

$$F_{drag} \text{ Boat B} = (4 \times 3^2 + 4 \times 5^2) / 2 = 68 \text{ N}$$

The difference in drag is 4 N, or 6.25%, although both boats cover the same distance in a given time.

Instantaneous boat velocity v_{boat} varies substantially from 3.5 m/s to 5.9 m/s in the example in figure 5.14. The lowest velocities occur during the early part of the propulsion phase, when rowers push the boat away from them while the velocity of the overall system is low. Conversely, the highest velocity is measured during the recovery, when rowers pull the boat toward themselves and increase the already high velocity of the overall system.

The analysis of an international-level single sculler (Nolte 1984) revealed that only 36.2% of the overall energy that the boat drag consumes during a stroke is observed during the propulsion phase. In contrast, 62.8% of the boat drag energy is expended during the recovery. Boat velocity during the drive is lower than the overall system's velocity, which is why such a low magnitude of boat drag is observed during that phase. These numbers are confirmed by Kleshnev (2019) and point to the fact that the rower's movement relative to the boat during the recovery has an enormous impact on boat velocity, along with energy consumption through boat drag.

Kleshnev (2016, 32) estimates that at race pace "70-80 percent of the boat velocity variation depends on the rower's movements," so it is warranted to try to find ways to reduce these movements through technique. This is not possible during the drive, because the main focus of the rower from full reach to finish is to propel the boat, so the rower's motion relative to the boat is therefore strictly dedicated to this goal.

The purpose of the recovery, on the other hand, is to move the oar handles from the finish position to the full reach position. This leaves a number of options open to optimize the execution of the body's movement. The velocity of the overall system v_{total} decreases continuously during the recovery, because F_{water} is the only external force acting during this phase of the stroke (see equation 5.2). The amount with which v_{total} drops therefore depends mainly on boat velocity v_{boat}. The rower's mass moves in negative x-direction relative to CoM_{total} pulling the boat at the same time in positive x-direction, so that v_{boat} is higher than v_{total}. Both velocities become equal again at the full reach position. Because v_{boat} affects F_{water} in the square, the rower needs to try to keep this negative influence as small as possible.

Biomechanical Principles

With these preparatory thoughts, we now can develop biomechanical principles for rowing, which are fundamental rules based on biomechanics that explain rowing technique. The starting point for these considerations is the *ultimate goal of rowing*, which is to cover a certain distance in the shortest time possible. In other words, the rower strives to reach the highest average velocity for the whole distance that is covered. Boats are aligned by their bow balls at the start of a race and the time is recorded when the bow ball crosses the finish line. According to racing rules, therefore, the bow ball is the measurement point that needs to cover the distance. It is therefore conceivable that most people focus on the velocity of the boat v_{boat}.

Over a complete rowing stroke, however, the displacements of the CoMs of all individual parts of the system are the same. This means that the average velocities for all these parts are the same, and achieving the maximum average velocity for the rower, the boat, and the overall system applies as the ultimate goal of rowing. This overarching objective becomes the top level of biomechanical priorities that we need to employ.

The velocity of the overall system is affected by the propulsion produced by the rower and the resistance on the system according to our model in figure 5.3 and equation 5.2. The higher the propulsion and the lower the resistance, the faster the system moves. This means that rowers need to apply a technique that both produces maximum propulsion and minimizes the resistance that is generated by moving in the environment. These two main tasks of proper rowing technique form the next level of biomechanical priorities that need to be respected.

Figure 5.12 links the previous biomechanical considerations and the main tasks of rowing technique, so that we can now formulate the biomechanical principles of rowing.

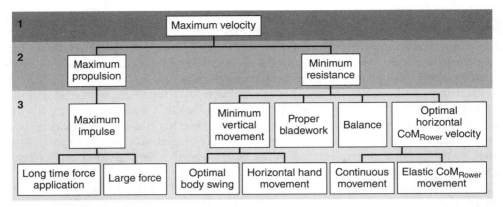

▶ **Figure 5.12** The ultimate goal of rowing (level 1), the main tasks of rowing technique (level 2), and the biomechanical principles of rowing (level 3).

The effect of propulsion shows in the increase of the overall system's velocity (Δv_{total}) during the drive. It is achieved by generating propelling impulse I during the drive, which is equal to the momentum M of the overall system gained during that phase of the stroke. This connection is expressed in equation 5.16:

$$M = m_{total} \times \Delta v_{total} = F_{Propel} \times \Delta t = I \qquad (5.16)$$

A large impulse is accomplished by applying a large propelling force over a long duration; we will discuss how this translates into rowing technique in chapters 6 and 7. It is important to emphasize here again that propulsion can only be achieved by the blade in the water during the drive.

Key Point

The effect of propulsion is apparent in the increase of the overall system's velocity during the drive, which in physical terms is called the increase of momentum M. This means that the increase in velocity is a function of the propelling force applied over the time of its application.

The other main task of rowing technique is to minimize resistance. Rowers can achieve this goal in four main ways (discussed further in chapter 7): by minimizing vertical movement, optimizing horizontal velocity of their center of mass, optimizing balance, and using proper bladework.

As stated earlier, some vertical movement of the rower's body mass during the stroke is necessary and cannot be eliminated. Trunk movement causes vertical displacement not only of its own mass, but also of the head and arms; these masses together account for about 60% of the rower's overall mass. The movement of the trunk contributes about one-third to the overall stroke length by rotating around the hip. The rower realizes this movement through a so-called lean forward at the full reach and a lean back at the finish. These leans can be measured as angles between the hip and shoulder and the z-axis (figure 5.13). Lean forward is limited by the bend of the knees, but lean back can be increased. However, a lean that is greater than about 25° from the vertical at the full

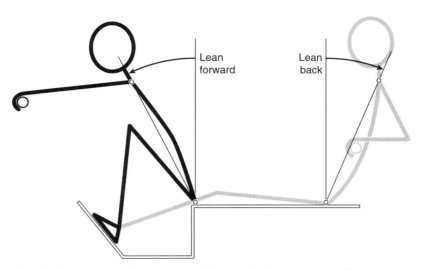

▶ **Figure 5.13** Rowers use the rotation of the trunk for the stroke. The lean is measured by the angle between the line through hip and shoulder and the vertical.

reach or the finish increases the stroke length only marginally but adds considerable vertical movements and is therefore not beneficial.

Any vertical movements of the rower's mass during the stroke not only costs energy but also causes a vertical movement of the boat that generates additional energy loss. This can be seen in the production of side waves parallel to the longitudinal axis of the boat. Although some vertical movement is unavoidable, rowers can reduce their vertical movements through skillful technique, as we will see in the following chapter.

Because the rowing system has to move with a certain horizontal velocity relative to the water and the air, it will always experience resistant forces throughout the whole rowing stroke. According to Filter (2004), the boat (including the riggers) experiences 15%, the rowers' bodies 35%, and the oars 50% of the overall wind resistance. There is very little rowers can do about their influence on the wind resistance, assuming they wear tight clothing, because their body shapes are fixed and any possible changes in movements that the rower could influence are too small to have a noteworthy impact on resistance. The riggers are the largest factor on the wind resistance of the boat, and boat builders therefore account for this as much as possible. Wind resistance of the oars can be minimized through the design of the shafts and with proper feathering and squaring of the blades, which we will encapsulate here as a component of *blade-work*. Proper oar handling has a notable impact on resistance, hence why bladework is included in the biomechanical principles to reduce resistance (level 3 of figure 5.12).

Similarly, balance has an effect on resistance. Balance is achieved when the boat has a stable position around the longitudinal axis and does not experience any rolling motion around this axis during the stroke. A rolling boat has a larger water resistance through the sideways movement of the fin and the change in shape of the submerged area of the boat. Additionally, an unbalanced boat changes the height of the oarlocks above the water, which moves the oars with them and can cause the blades to hit the water during recovery. This again creates considerable water resistance, which creates even more balance problems and interference with the rowers' motions and can even cause yawing of the boat.

Lastly, the horizontal movement of the rower in the boat has an influence on resistance. As mentioned above, intermittent propulsion in rowing causes v_{total} to increase

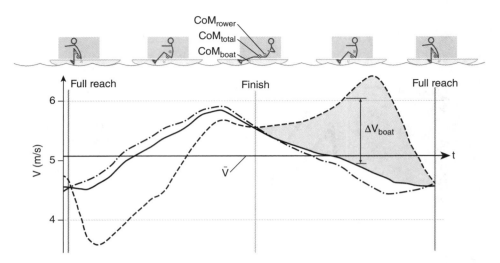

▶ **Figure 5.14** Velocity of CoM$_{total}$ (solid line), CoM$_{rower}$ (dash-dot), and CoM$_{boat}$ (dash) in the absolute coordinate system. Stick figures on top show the corresponding rowing motion and the positions of the CoMs relative to each other. In the stick figure, the gray box with its center of mass symbolizes CoM$_{total}$ and the movements of the rower and the boat relative to CoM$_{total}$ are indicated. $\bar{v}$ = average boat velocity of the whole stroke; Δv_{boat} = difference between v_{total} and v_{boat}; and area between v_{boat} and v_{total} (shaded) indicates the distance that the boat travels relative to the overall CoM.

Based on Nolte 1984, data from lightweight men's s 1x world champion at stroke rate 36 spm.

during the drive and decrease during recovery (see equation 5.2), but v_{boat} and v_{total} have quite different courses, as is shown in figure 5.14.

At the full reach position, all three CoMs (total, rower, and boat) have the same magnitude of velocity in x-direction and 0 velocity relative to each other. The rower has then to accelerate their CoM during the entry and the first part of the drive, increasing the footstretcher force F_{Fx} (see equation 5.4), which in turn slows the boat down (see equation 5.6). Only when the oarlock force F_{Ox} is large enough to offset F_{Fx} and F_{water} will boat velocity increase. The overall CoM slows down during the release at the end of the drive when the blade force is smaller than boat resistance. All velocities of the three CoMs have the same magnitude again at the finish.

The figures in figure 5.14 indicate the movements of the three centers of mass relative to each other. One can see that, relative to the overall CoM, the boat moves backward during the drive and forward during the recovery. This means that the boat travels during the recovery a longer distance than CoM$_{otal}$ and has therefore a higher velocity, because the rower moves in a negative direction relative to CoM$_{total}$, pulling the boat forward. In fact, when the rower starts moving their trunk and legs relative to CoM$_{total}$, the positive force on the footstretcher becomes so large that the boat accelerates, which leads to a spike in boat velocity. The rower then has to slow down their motion relative to the boat toward the full reach position, so that the footstretcher force F_{Fx} increases considerably in negative x-direction and combines with the resistance on the boat F_{water} to cause the large dip in boat velocity v_{boat}. These explanations show how much influence the rower's movement within the boat has on v_{boat}.

As discussed above, drag coefficient, immersed cross-sectional area of the boat, and density of the water cannot be influenced by rowing technique (or in only very limited way), but boat velocity can. As we can see in figure 5.14, v_{boat} has considerable fluctuations, and because the velocity affects F_{water} in the square and costs extra energy, the rower needs to keep these fluctuations small.

This means that rowers need to optimize horizontal velocity changes during the recovery so as to not raise v_{boat} to unnecessarily high levels. Rowers must meet two demands during the recovery: move their CoM a defined distance from finish to full reach position and do so in the time available at a given stroke rate. When CoM_{rower} moves in negative x-direction relative to CoM_{total}, CoM_{boat} moves in positive x-direction relative to CoM_{total}, so that v_{boat} becomes larger than v_{total} (shown in figure 5.14). The phenomenon that CoM_{boat} accelerates during recovery confuses many people, because only resistance forces exist during that phase and one would expect v_{boat} to decline.

One other misconception occurs when the increase in v_{boat} is interpreted as a gain. Because F_{water} increases with the square of v_{boat}, high values of v_{boat} are particularly costly. Of course, the boat has to travel a larger distance in x-direction during the recovery because of the rower's movement in the opposite direction. This necessary distance is equivalent to the area between the velocity curves of the boat and the overall CoM during the recovery (see shaded area in figure 5.14). This means that the boat velocity must be higher than the velocity of the overall CoM but it is less energy consuming if this is achieved at the end of the recovery when the velocity of the overall CoM is lowest, so that the necessary increase in boat velocity results in relative lower values of v_{boat}. This means that the inevitable spike in boat velocity should occur as late as possible during the recovery. Rowers can achieve this through their technique.

Conclusion

This chapter provides the basics of biomechanics of rowing. The whole system has to cover the race distance, but because external forces apply to individual parts of the system (e.g., propulsion in the blades, resistance on the boat), it was necessary to study each in more detail. The energy comes from the rower, who moves the oars to generate propulsion. Proper placement of the blades in the water and smart utilization of lift and drag forces are important in order to be as efficient as possible. The movement of the rower influences fluctuations in boat velocity, which increases water resistance. The challenge is to optimize these intertwining effects so that they produce the largest gains while costing the smallest losses. Understanding how the three main mechanical systems of rowing (the overall system, the rower, and the boat) interact with all these external forces builds the starting point for the biomechanical principles of rowing, which will guide the presentation of rowing technique in the following chapters.

Optimal Rowing Technique

Volker Nolte, PhD

It was 1960—the first time in modern Olympic history that the American men's eight did not win Olympic gold. The crew that defeated that team was the German men's eight, trained under the guidance of coach Karl Adam, who became famous for his successful coaching and the many innovations that he brought to rowing. He has been credited with the statement "physiology delivers lengths, technique achieves meters," which neatly summarizes his training philosophy: He clearly emphasized physiology over technique, which showed in his coaching methods. A few of his innovations in the sport include year-round training, emphasis on intensive interval training, inclusion of specific on-land strength workout sessions, high-altitude training, and physiological testing as part of the crew selection.

In contrast to Adam's approach is the common rowing adage "ergometers don't float"—a dismissal (at least in part) of the fact that high physiological power, measured by an ergometer, is one of the most important criteria of on-water performance. Critics of his approach question the informative value of ergometer test results for the prediction of on-water performance even within homogeneous groups, such as top varsity or national team athletes, because results achieved on these land-based testing and training devices are mainly based on the athletes' physical abilities and little technical rowing skill is required.

As mentioned in the previous chapter, the speed that a crew can achieve over a 2,000 m race is directly connected to the power the crew can produce. Between two athletes of the same physical ability, however, the technically more skilled one will row faster. This shows that both physiology and technique are essential for success—high performance in rowing is not possible without both. Additionally, one needs to remember that athletes in their development phase can improve tremendously from year to year, but accomplished rowers will no longer be able to increase their physical or technical abilities by wide margins and need to seek small improvements in any way possible.

The importance of rowing technique and the evaluation of its quality is widely debated, although simple comparisons underline the effect of small performance differences. There are many examples in international racing that can be used to prove this. For example, the difference between the winner and the second place crew in all the 14 Olympic boat classes at the 2019 World Championships was an average 0.5% or 1.9 s. The closest finish results occurred in the men's single, in which the second place rower was 0.03 s, the third place rower was 0.29 s, and the fourth place rower 0.69 s behind the winner. These differences could be easily contributed to either technique or physical abilities, although these athletes are highly qualified in both.

Improvements in rowing technique provide other benefits besides performance outcome—namely, safety. Proper technique protects athletes from injuries. Technically proficient crews also can maneuver their boat more capably in case of an emergency such as sudden weather changes. Furthermore, comfort and pleasure in the act of rowing increase with the quality of the rower's skill. For these reasons, rowers should always strive to better their technique.

Definition of Rowing Technique

To guide a science-based discussion about this topic, the term *rowing technique* needs to be defined. Although commonly used, it is important to lay the basis for further discussions and also distinguish it from the term *rowing style*.

Sport technique is a proven, functional, and effective sequence of movements to solve a defined task in sport (Martin 1991). In addition, McGinnis (2013) points out that technique has to comply with the rules of the sport, which is often a very important and limiting criterion. Finally, proper technique should protect the athlete from injury.

Meinel (1961, 242) adds a qualifying dimension to the concept of technique as a "procedure, developed and tested in practice, for the *best* possible solution of a specific athletic task." Grosser and Neumaier (1982, 8) do the same, describing sport technique as "the *ideal* model of a movement" to accomplish a sport goal, as well as "the realization of the intended '*ideal* movement'" by the athlete (8, emphasis in original). This means that technique in itself is optimal and ideal based on the underlying science.

The main goal of rowing is, of course, to cover a certain distance in the shortest time. Rowing technique on the basis of biomechanics is therefore the ideal movement that can solve this task in a practical manner.

Key Point

Sport technique includes the following factors:

- Is a proven, functional, and effective sequence of movements
- Solves a defined task in sport
- Complies with the sport's rules
- Reduces the risk of injury
- Is developed and tested in practice
- Is an ideal model of movement

The practical application of rowing technique is a very important criterion, because certain movement patterns may have theoretical advantages but fail miserably in practice. One example of such a failed movement is the syncopated or centipede rowing technique, in which groups of athletes in the boat row out of sync, each performing a different part of the stroke. The organization of the rowers is such that the movements of the center of masses of all individual rowers relative to the boat cancel each other out (i.e., equal 0) and that half of the rowers are always providing propulsion in the drive phase (see figure 6.1). On first view, it seems logical that this kind of rowing provides some theoretical advantages, mainly that boat velocity would be more consistent and therefore lower the water resistance of the boat at a given average velocity. There have been attempts to use this technique, including using special boats built to accommodate such rowing. Athletes were able to use this technique at low and fixed stroke rates, but consistently failed at higher stroke rates and intensities. Kleshnev (2015) showed that the centipede technique caused the rowers to apply much higher additional inertial energy, which outweighs the theoretical decrease in resistance. In addition, it is hard to imagine that recreational rowers would ever want to introduce such complications. This technique is therefore not practical.

If rowing technique is to allow rowers to "solve the task"—that is, to cover the race distance in the shortest time—it must not only let them generate the highest possible power for the duration of the race but also transfer this power into the largest possible propulsion to reach the highest possible average velocity of the overall system. Rowers

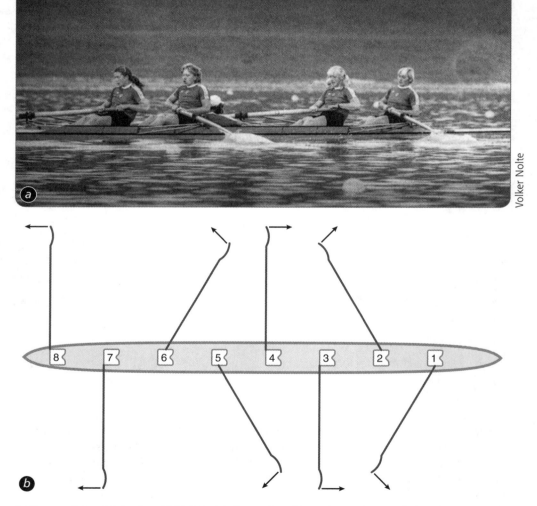

Volker Nolte

▶ **Figure 6.1** *(a)* At the 1981 World Championships, the USSR used a coxswain in the middle of the boat to attempt syncopated rowing, but in the end they decided to row conventionally. *(b)* A diagram illustrating syncopated rowing (Herberger 1970).

must be able to use all body joints to produce high power and at the same time maximize the hydrodynamic forces and minimize resistance forces on the blades. Fixed-seat rowing technique is therefore not advisable, because it excludes the strong leg muscles from providing power. Similarly, the technique used by Brian Shaw, who once held the world record over 100 m on the ergometer, would not meet these criteria either—although he can generate extremely high power values, his short strokes at rates over 50 spm are too short to be efficient enough for a 2,000 m distance.

Rowing technique must also comply with the rules of the sport. For example, the rowing technique used by Venetian gondoliers is highly efficient. They propel their boats standing up and facing the direction of travel, which has the advantage of continuously generating propulsion, and the stroke cycles of their sculling motion follow each other without recovery phases, which create a constant boat velocity. However, this technique is not allowed in international rowing, because official rules state that rowers must be "sitting with their backs to the direction of movement of the boat" (World Rowing 2020, 43).

Key Point

The model technique is based on biomechanical principles, lets coaches and athletes develop a solid perception of the proper rowing movement pattern, and provides biomechanical parameters to identify proper rowing movements. Because rowing technique must always be geared toward the practical goal of the sport, it can be influenced by successful movement patterns to improve.

Additionally, rowing technique must consider the prevention of injury as much as possible. Although numerous factors can cause injuries (which will be discussed in part VI in more detail), a technique that entails unnecessary risk of injury would not meet the criteria of the given definition. For example, it may seem advantageous for a beginner to hold the oar handle with their proximal metacarpals tightly wrapped around it to maintain strong contact and more securely direct the blade, but this technique leads to tendon injuries in the forearm and is therefore not ideal.

Toward an Ideal Model of Rowing Technique

In search of the best or most favorable rowing technique, often called *optimal technique*, one must realize that such a standard of perfection can only exist as a theoretical construct. It is in fact impossible to define in minute detail a movement pattern that would best fit every rower with their individual anthropometrics and physiology in all possible conditions and situations. Depending on the size and fitness of the rower, the weather conditions, the boat class, and the speed targets—whether it is a recreational row, long distance training, or a race—different criteria come into play to formulate a model rowing technique.

Instead of trying to define fixed numbers of angles, displacements, velocities, and accelerations to describe the ideal rowing movement, we will specify criteria to create a framework for developing an effective and efficient rowing technique. Coaches and rowers may use these criteria as a model to evaluate practically executed movements, then develop goals to be pursued as technical improvements. This part of working with a biomechanics-based rowing technique is called a *qualitative approach*. Instead of using numbers and measurement tools, coaches and athletes use descriptions like *stronger* or *lighter, faster* or *slower,* and so forth. Of course, progress toward the intended goal, how the newly acquired movement pattern performs in different conditions, and how these changes affect the athlete should then be evaluated. Figure 6.2 puts these explanations into context.

The *quantitative approach* of applying technique describes the movement with numbers that are measured with specific tools. This approach is naturally more objective but requires more effort, expense, and expertise. Because problems can occur when concepts are used that are not completely understood, biomechanics professionals are often called in to provide consultations.

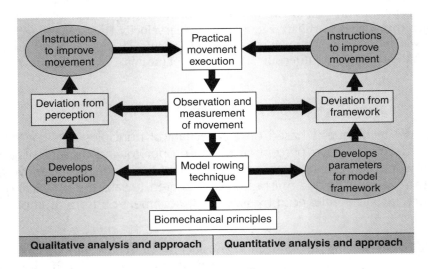

▶ **Figure 6.2** The model technique helps rowers and coaches develop the perception of the movement pattern, as well as provides biomechanical parameters by which to evaluate practical execution.

The presented proper rowing technique includes fundamental elements of the biomechanically correct execution of the rowing movement. These biomechanical criteria are of general nature and must be adapted to the specific athlete and current environmental conditions. The positions and phases of the rowing stroke are outlined in table 5.1 in the previous chapter and are defined by biomechanical parameters presented in figures 6.3 and 6.4; table 6.1 below describes the proper execution of the respective parts of the stroke. The presented technique respects the biomechanical principles outlined in level 3 of figure 5.12 in the previous chapter.

Table 6.1 presents three parts of information for each position and phase of the stroke:

1. Name and pictures of the position or phase. The pictures show a highly qualified national team athlete executing the proper rowing technique for both sculling and sweeping.

2. Biomechanical parameters that clearly define the position or phase and are identified with in figure 6.3.

3. Descriptions of the correct execution of the position or phase, specifically the body and blade positions and movements, as well as force pattern. Biomechanical parameters coincide with figure 6.3. The definitions of body angles that describe the execution of the proper technique are presented in figure 6.4.

Table 6.1 Positions and Phases of the Rowing Stroke

Position or phase of stroke	Biomechanical parameter to identify position or phase of stroke	Correct execution
Full reach	Tangential handle velocity $v_H = 0$ m/s	**Body** • Arms are straight (θ_A ~180°) with flat wrists; shoulders are stretched out. • Shins are maximally vertical; $\theta_S \geq 0°$. • Lean forward; θ_B ~25°. • Knee angle; $\theta_K >45°$. • Heels are off the footstretcher. • The spine presents a neutral curvature. • The back starts to brace, getting ready to transfer forces between handle and footstretcher. **Blades** • Blades are squared and close, but off the water. **Forces** • The rower pushes on the footstretcher to continue reversing the direction of motion of their CoM and the oars relative to the boat. • Hands experience small handle forces that are generated by the inertia of oars that also reverse their motion relative to the boat.
Entry	The phase starts with tangential handle velocity $v_H = 0$ m/s and ends when slope of v_H changes from steep to flat (this point coincides with the start of the steep increase in oarlock force F_O)	The entry is one of the two most complex and difficult parts of the rowing stroke; horizontal and vertical movements need to be coordinated while forces on the footstretcher and handle increase at the same time. This movement demands quick, precise, and very coordinated actions, because handle velocity relative to the boat must be tailored to the boat velocity as the blades enter the water. **Body** • All horizontal movement comes from the rapid knee angle extension. • Arms are kept straight with flat wrists; θ_A ~180°. • The vertical movement of the handle originates from the shoulder lifting the arms; at the same time, shoulders tense to transfer the increasing handle forces to the footstretcher. • Rower is still leaning forward and the back is kept solid in its neutral position. • Quick leg movement is generated through push off from the front of the foot. • Heels are still off the footstretcher. **Blades** • Horizontal and vertical movement of the handles are coordinated, so that blades enter the water with the least resistance while starting to generate propulsion. • Velocity of the handle v_H increases very quickly. **Forces** • Forces on the footstretcher and handle increase steadily; the rower's mass is accelerated horizontally toward the bow and tangential handle velocity increases. • Blade force increases steadily as more blade area immerses into the water and the velocity of the blade around the pin grows. • The rower reaches at the end of the phase, what is called the "the blade lock on to the water," which means that a distinct load is felt by the rower that indicates the start of the drive.

(continued)

Table 6.1 *(continued)*

Position or phase of stroke	Biomechanical parameter to identify position or phase of stroke	Correct execution
Drive 	The phase starts when the slope of v_H changes from steep to flat and ends when the slope of boat velocity v_{boat} changes from steep to flat (a_{boat} ~0 m/s²).	The drive is the main part of the propulsive phase, during which the highest forces are measured and the most propulsive work is done. The propulsive force is larger than the resistive force on the overall system, so that it accelerates. **Body** • Extension of the legs, rotation of the trunk around the hips, and bending of arms together with the pulling back of the shoulders occur in sequence with some overlap to generate a large handle velocity over a long time. • Knee angle θ_K reaches its maximum ~180° at the end of the phase. • Lean back of θ_B ~20° is reached at the end of the phase. • Heels are planted onto the footstretcher during this phase and stay connected until the finish position. **Blades** • Blades are completely submerged in water. **Forces** • Rowers strive to produce a large propulsive impulse during this phase, keeping a high blade force for a long time. • The first part of the drive is particularly important, because the blade efficiency is high—the rower strives to reach the maximum handle force early in the drive. • The middle part is also important, because the rower can produce the highest forces with the engagement of the legs and the trunk at the same time. • During the end of the drive, the rower tries to maintain a high force once the blade efficiency increases again.
Release  	The phase starts when the slope of v_{boat} changes and ends when handle velocity $v_H = 0$ m/s.	The release is the other of the two most complex and difficult parts of the rowing stroke. Horizontal and vertical movements of the handle need to be coordinated in connection with the timing of the declining handle force. As long as the blade has contact with the water, it needs to move relative to the boat, so that it does not generate resistance in the water. This means that the handle velocity must still be high enough to generate a propulsive force until the last contact of the blade with the water. Not enough handle velocity would cause drag. This means that the blade is extracted from the water well before the hands reach the finish position and the handle velocity still has a positive magnitude. After the blade is out of the water, it needs to be slowed down to 0 m/s relative to the boat. This braking motion on the handle with the blade out of the water is why the handle force becomes negative. The blades are feathered so that the blade can be more easily kept off the water during this braking motion, and the wind resistance is reduced. **Body** • Knees are extended ~180°. • Rower reaches lean back of θ_B ~20° early in this phase and holds this position. • Arms and shoulders finish the movement. • Heels are kept in contact with the footstretcher.

Position or phase of stroke	Biomechanical parameter to identify position or phase of stroke	Correct execution
Release *(continued)*	The phase starts when the slope of v_{boat} chnages And ends when handle velocity $v_H = 0$ m/s	**Blades** • Blades are rowed out of the water and then feathered. • Handle velocity must be kept up for the entire time the blades are extracted from the water, so that they do not produce resistance. **Forces** • There is a small negative handle force necessary at the last part of the phase to decelerate the handle velocity, which will be 0 m/s at the end of the phase. • At the moment when the blades lose contact with the water, the rower starts to pull on the footstretcher to decelerate the horizontal velocity of their CoM and the oars relative to the boat.
Finish	Handle velocity $v_H = 0$ m/s	**Body** • Arms are maximally bent with the forearms in horizontal position • Hands are ~20 cm apart in sculling, still in front of the body and just touching the body • Lean back of θ_B ~25° • Knees are extended ~180° **Blades** • Blades are feathered and close to (but off) the water. • Horizontal oar angle is ~45° for sculling and ~35° for sweep rowing. **Forces** • Toes are pulling on the footstretcher to continue reversing the direction of motion of the rower's CoM relative to the boat. • Feet are generating a torque on the footstretcher (toes pull and heels push) that counters the torque of the rower's weight of the upper body leaning past the seat. • The handle force is small and negative, which is caused by the inertia of oars to reverse their motion relative to the boat.

(continued)

Table 6.1 *(continued)*

Position or phase of stroke	Biomechanical parameter to identify position or phase of stroke	Correct execution
Early recovery 	The phase starts with handle velocity $v_H = 0$ m/s And ends when maximal negative tangential handle velocity v_H is reached.	**Body** • The return movement of the handles to the next full reach is accomplished through the sequence of stretching the arms, rotating the torso in the hips, and bending the legs. The start of the joint movements happens in succession in the mentioned order and the sequencing depends on the stroke rate—at lower stroke rates, there is more time to perform the joint movements in sequence, whereas at higher stroke rates, all joints start moving together. • Acceleration of oars' and rower's CoM toward the stern generates an increase in boat velocity; therefore, the rower tries moving lighter body parts first or delaying the acceleration of their CoM toward the end of this phase, so that the boat velocity is least affected. **Blades** • Blades are kept feathered about 15 cm off the water; this distance is usually sufficient to keep the blades clear of wind waves, but may be increased in more severe wind conditions or in case of motorboat waves. **Forces** • The rower pulls on the footstretcher to accelerate their CoM and the oars relative to the boat—this pull can only be executed by the front foot, which has the only connection to the boat to transfer these forces. • The negative acceleration of the rower's body is finished at the end of the phase, so that all parts of the rower's body and the handle reach their maximum negative velocity relative to the boat. • The horizontal handle force is very small, and the hands keep a vertical force on the handle to balance the oars in the oar lock.

Position or phase of stroke	Biomechanical parameter to identify position or phase of stroke	Correct execution
Final recovery 	This phase starts when the negative tangential handle velocity v_H reaches its maximum Until handle velocity v_H = 0 m/s	This phase has to be carried out in the shortest time possible. Boat velocity reaches the largest deceleration of the whole stroke (around 1 g at race pace). The magnitude of the negative acceleration of the boat is not as important for the quality of the execution of this phase than the shortness of the time for the phase. The rower needs to stay relaxed and let the bending of the knees and the pretension in the muscles happen. Athletes get ready for a quick and fluent entry with this approach. **Body** • The stretching of the arms is practically finished at the beginning of this phase so that the arms are almost at $\theta_A = 180°$ and very little further stretching happens • The final lean forward of $\theta_B \sim 20°$ is reached at the beginning of this phase so that no further swing of the back occurs. • Knee angle velocity is highest at the beginning of the phase so that considerable additional bending of the knees occurs. • Heels are starting to move away from the footstretcher and the rower maintains a solid contact on the footstretcher with the front of their feet. **Blades** • The blades are still feathered at the beginning of the phase, but have to be completely squared at the end of the phase—the squaring motion is processed toward the end of the phase and its speed depends on the skill of the rower and the stroke rate. The goal is to have the blade securely squared as late as possible to reduce the wind drag on the blade. • Blades are carried far enough off the water so that their squaring can be performed without pushing the handle down into the boat. **Forces** • The momentum that the rower generated during the early recovery by pulling on the footstretcher reached its maximum at the beginning of this phase and carries the rower through the phase. • The foot-stretcher force increases steadily during this phase because the rower needs to reverse the direction of motion of their CoM relative to the boat; this puts the rower in an advantageous position to initiate a quick and powerful entry. • Leg muscles are put into pretension state as rower gets ready for a quick and efficient entry movement. • There are small handle forces generated by the inertia of oars that also reverse their motion relative to the boat.

Photos courtesy Volker Nolte.

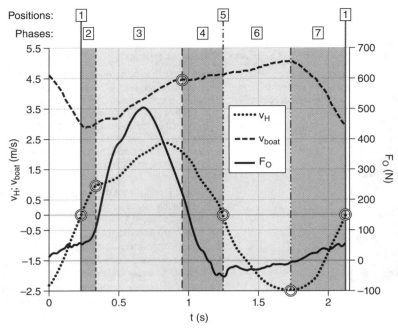

▶ **Figure 6.3** Tangential handle velocity v_H, boat velocity v_{boat}, and oarlock force F_O provide the biomechanical parameters to identify the positions (1 and 5) and the phases of the stroke (2, 3, 4, 6, and 7) that are described in table 6.1. (Data from a women's single at a stroke rate of 31.9 spm identify the specific parameters that define the positions and phases.)

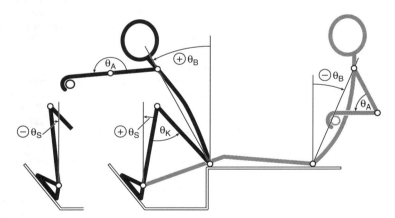

▶ **Figure 6.4** Definition of the body angles: θ_S = shin angle and θ_B = back angle relative to the z-axis; θ_K = knee angle; θ_A = arm angle. The positive and negative angles of the shin and the back angles are important to identify the proper position.

Rowing Styles

As stated, proper rowing technique presents parameters for coaches and rowers to develop a framework for the practical execution of the rowing motion. This leaves some room for individual adaptations. It is important to realize that rowing movements, like all sport movements, are executed by humans in varying conditions and with ever-improving equipment. The human body is a very complex mechanism that varies with regards to limb dimensions, muscle structures, strength distributions, and nervous systems. Each athlete has their own individual anatomical and physiological intricacies that will affect the execution of the biomechanical principles. Each athlete will therefore implement the proper rowing technique by varying some parts of the movements to best fit their individual body and condition. In this way, these athletes still execute proper technique and display their personal rowing style.

Key Point

Rowing style is the individual execution of rowing technique. A style modifies the technique in a specific way to enhance the individual rower's strengths. The main features of the technique are followed, but certain parts are emphasized or changed, which characterizes the style as such.

One method of biomechanical research is to study pictures or video recordings of highly skilled crews to identify the execution of specific movements that makes these athletes so successful. Besides displaying the biomechanical principles (e.g., long strokes, sequencing, or hand curve), such individual performances often show very specific patterns that are clearly associated with that crew. Rather than trying to generalize the technique of successful crews as ideal, then, it is important to realize that these individual displays only show how a particular crew's technique is ideal *for them*. Pictures do not show why this crew executes their technique the way they do, how the individuals' strengths are specifically used, how they got to this point in their development, how it feels for these athletes, and how other aspects like physiology or motivation factor in.

Such individual executions of rowing technique are called *styles*. The main features of the technique are followed, but certain parts are emphasized or changed by the individual. These particularities may be based on anatomical peculiarities (e.g., especially tall athletes may row with a larger knee angle at the full reach position), may emphasize an element of movement that is believed to be particularly important (e.g., the very fast movement out of the finish at the beginning of recovery was believed to diminish the vertical dip of the boat at this part of the stroke), or may have developed by chance (e.g., the larger lean back that a number of Canadian crews practiced around the year 2000 apparently developed through the country's preferred type of training at very low stroke rates).

Each athlete must strive to reach their own highly effective functionality within the framework of proper technique. It is then the task of the coach together with the athletes to combine these individual differences to create the best performance in a crew. Figure 6.5 shows one example in the New Zealand men's pair of Hamish Bond and Eric Murray, undoubtedly one of the world's best functioning crews. Together they won 69 races in an 8 year unbeaten streak, including six world titles and two Olympic gold medals, and set several world best times between 2009 and 2016.

Volker Nolte

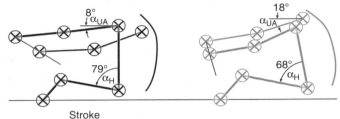

▶ **Figure 6.5** The extremely successful New Zealand men's 2– combine individual styles into a highly functioning unit at the beginning of the drive just after the entry. *(a)* Photo taken during training at World Cup Lucerne/Switzerland. *(b)* Illustration based upon the photo: Black line = left side of the body; gray line = right side of the body; a_{UA} = angle of the outside upper arm of the rower to the horizontal; a_H = hip angle of the left side of the rower; curved line = curvature of the spine.

As shown in the kinematic analysis in figure 6.5b, the New Zealand pair did not execute every movement in exactly the same way. Some body positions were different, the heights at which the handles were moved during the drive were different, and each athlete maintained his individual posture, as indicated by the curvature of their spines. However, they managed to combine these individual features into an extremely efficient technique. This means that each of these athletes had his own rowing style based on proper rowing technique (as outlined in table 6.1) that they fit together into an extremely successful unit.

Besides fitting individual style differences together, rowers need to be able to adapt their stroke execution to specific race situations or weather conditions. For example, in the middle of a race in tailwind conditions, when the rower needs to focus on reaching high blade efficiency while boat velocity is relatively high, it would be advisable to increase oar angles by few degrees at full reach and apply the maximum handle force earlier in the drive. On the other hand, at the end of a race in a strong headwind, when a rower needs to focus on producing the highest power possible while boat velocity is relatively low because of the conditions, it would be advisable to increase the stroke rate, reduce the oar angles at the full reach position, and apply the highest handle force a little later in the drive. Overall, an ideal technique cannot be reduced to a strict sequence of fixed movements; it must be adapted to the individual rower and the environmental circumstances.

Discussing Rowing Styles

Figure 6.6 shows examples of multiple rowing styles. All rowers shown are internationally experienced Canadian national team members, and all display proper rowing technique, but each has their own personal style. For example, rower A is a smaller person than rower B and therefore uses more upper body swing to reach proper stroke length.

Conclusion

It is impossible to define one movement pattern as the optimal technique for all rowers. Rather, the biomechanical principles were used here as the basis for a framework for proper rowing technique, which can be used to develop a personal style that is most effective and efficient for each individual rower. The measures for effectiveness and efficiency mean the technique lets the rower achieve their personal goals. For a masters rower, such goals might be to stay healthy and enjoy rowing in varying crews with likeminded friends, while the competitive rower might be to achieve the highest velocity of the overall system over a specific distance in different environmental conditions.

This framework can be used by athletes and coaches to achieve the following goals:

- Recognize the main indicators of an effective and efficient rowing technique, including standard biomechanical measures
- Develop the perception of a movement pattern for a complete stroke cycle of the proper rowing technique
- Identify examples of rowing styles that are based on proper technique

Equipped with this framework and a good conception of proper technique, coaches can compare the given indicators to the body positions, movements, and biomechanical measures of their own rowers so that they can work together with athletes to improve technique.

At the end of the technique improvement process, coaches and athletes need to decide if their interventions were successful. This is best done through practical testing of the main goal: Does the rower move the overall system faster, either by being able to generate more power or by using their existing power more efficiently? Can the crew row longer distances with more ease or feel more comfortable at a certain pace? Can they cover a certain distance faster given different wind and water conditions?

The challenge for successful improvement does not stop with finding deviations from proper technique and deciding which to address in training. It is also important to realize that some interventions may affect athletes or a crew in different ways and that technique has to be adapted to the conditions. The next chapter will discuss principles that can be used to optimize this process. Additionally, technique deviations are often caused by the equipment and its rigging. These aspects will also be studied in the following chapters.

▶ **Figure 6.6** Examples of rowing styles of experienced rowers: *(a)* lightweight single sculler; *(b)* openweight single sculler; *(c)* sweep rower.

Photos courtesy Jeremy Ivey.

CHAPTER 7

Biomechanical Principles to Optimize Rowing Performance

Volker Nolte, PhD

After learning about the scientific basis of the biomechanics of rowing and the presentation of proper technique in the previous two chapters, this chapter will discuss how to optimize rowing performance through technique. The biomechanical principles outlined in chapter 5 are the basis for this discussion, and their influence on performance will be presented through practical examples. Descriptions of how to recognize proper technique and which deviations can occur will provide coaches, athletes, and researchers with indicators to focus on when teaching technique.

Assess Performance

It should be noted at this point that suggestions to improve performance need to be selected carefully. After identifying a deviation from the prescribed technique, one needs to decide the importance of the technical fault and the possible influence of a technical change on other factors. If the rower shows several technical faults—and most rowers do—it is important to carefully consider which is the most important and would have the largest impact, as well as which is easiest to fix. A rower can normally only focus on changing one technical factor at a time. An easy fix, such as the position of the hand on the oar handle, can be addressed immediately. A more difficult or complex fault needs more attention and often multiple approaches to change. It is therefore prudent to choose the fault that has presumably the most impact on the speed of rowing or the coordination of the crew.

Eliminate Extenuating Factors

In the attempt to make technical improvements, one needs to eliminate the possibility that the fault is based on factors other than incorrect movements by the rower. It is frequently the case that some technical faults are based on other factors, like poor rigging, physical circumstances of the rower, the influence of crewmembers' movements, or even psychological factors. Consider a single sculler whose full reach oar angle is

---

Key Point

Use the following strategy to identify the most important error to focus on:

- ◆ Assess impact on performance.
- ◆ Exclude possible limitations, such as rigging, rower physiology, injury, or psychology.
- ◆ Consider possible interference with other parts of the movement.
- ◆ Choose feedback (verbal, visual, tactile).
- ◆ Develop a progression of feedback or exercises that build toward improvement.
- ◆ Select possible exercises or drills.
- ◆ Decide how to measure success.

---

measured at −45°. It is safe to say that this angle is too small for an effective full reach position and the athlete could row faster when reaching a larger negative oar angle. Before making any further decisions, however, the coach needs to investigate if this lack of reach is based on rigging measurements (footstretcher positioned too far in the bow; too high or too steep; too large inboard or span), or on the rower's physique (the athlete is very small, overweight, handicapped by injury, or inflexible), crew members' mistiming cues, or physiological ability (the sculler has poor fitness and cannot perform a longer stroke without getting overly fatigued). Finally, could it even be that the rower is afraid to reach farther and risk disrupting the balance of the boat?

Evaluate Performance Impact

The next step to establish the proper intervention to improve technique is to consider the influence that this technical element has on rowing performance. Continuing our previous example, although a larger oar angle at the full reach position would undoubtedly increase propulsion, it has to be considered if a different movement fault has a larger influence on performance or would need to be addressed first in order to successfully work on improving stroke length.

These examples should make it evident that there is no simple one-step, black-and-white process to address a technique error. Careful considerations based on solid biomechanical principles and the possible impact of other influencing factors must be made. More details of these principles, and which measurements can be used to verify their proper application, will be discussed next.

Maximize Propulsion

Generally speaking, rowing is a sport with intermittent propulsion but consistently acting resisting forces. This means that velocity of the overall system fluctuates and needs to be accelerated during the time of propulsion to maintain a certain average velocity over one rowing cycle. This is shown in figure 5.14 in chapter 5. There are two criteria that need to be met to maintain an average velocity of the overall system:

1. The propulsive force during the drive must be larger than the resistive force.

2. The velocity of the overall system gained through propulsion during the drive must offset the velocity lost during entry and release (when resistance is larger than propulsion) and during the recovery (when only the resistive forces are acting).

The rower must strive to achieve a large propulsive force in the most effective and efficient manner. The size of the impulse is of course dependent on the time that propulsion acts and the magnitude of the propulsive force on the blade. A larger impulse can be achieved by either increasing the duration of force application (figure 7.1a), applying a higher maximum force (figure 7.1b), or a combination of both.

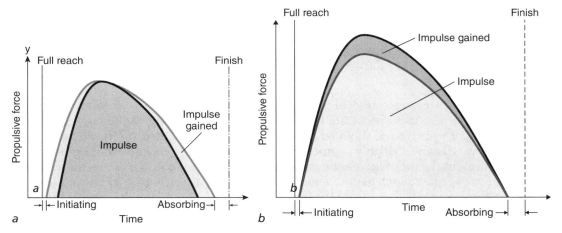

▶ **Figure 7.1** Schematic representation of the propulsive impulse and its possible gain through (a) increased duration of application and (b) increased force.

Increase Duration of Force Application

The time that the propulsive force acts on the blades can be influenced by following factors:

- The arc of the oar
- The angle of the oar at full reach position
- Air strokes (the time that the blade is moving without water contact during entry and release phases)

Large Arc of the Oar

Rowers can increase the arc of the oar by achieving larger oar angles at the full reach and the finish positions. The length of the stroke increases, as does the length of the path of the blade in the water, which automatically leads to a longer time of force application—assuming that all other factors (e.g., effort, rigging) stay the same.

However, the stroke length that a rower can effectively achieve at the finish is limited. Given the proper lean back (see table 6.1), the rower needs to be able to produce a high handle force F_H, ideally at a 90° angle to the oar's longitudinal axis, to maximize the effect on the rotation of the oar around the pin. Figure 7.2 shows examples of oar angles that still allow the rowers to generate high handle forces. Any further movement of the handles would put the rowers in a position where the magnitude or the direction of their handle force cannot be applied effectively anymore.

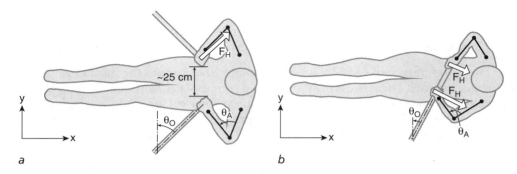

▶ **Figure 7.2** The maximum oar angles θ_O at the finish position for *(a)* sculling and *(b)* sweep are limited by the rower's trunk and the arm angles θ_A at which the rower still can generate enough handle force F_H to finish the drive.

Kleshnev (2016) suggests ideal oar angles at the finish to be 44° in sculling and 33° in sweep. These angles may be adjusted by –1° to –4° depending on the rower's individual height and arm and shoulder strength. These recommended angles can be used by all rowers, from the highly competitive to recreational rowers and even beginners.

The deciding factor to choose the proper finish oar angle is one that allows the rower to generate a large enough handle velocity and handle force during the release phase to keep the angle of attack α toward the front of the blade (<180°) for as long as the blade has contact with the water. This implies that the rower still applies a certain velocity to the handle at the last water contact. The rower then must absorb this velocity in a follow-through motion before reaching the finish position.

A simple indicator that the finish oar angle is too large is that the blade cannot be retracted cleanly out of the water. If the rower is not able to move the handle quickly and strongly enough, the angle of attack of the water exceeds 180°, which means that the water attacks the back side of the blade, causing undesired resistance (see figure 7.3a).

Large Full Reach Angle of the Oar

Although the finish position leaves limited room to increase the arc of the oar, the oar angle at the full reach position can vary widely. For international-level rowers, Kleshnev (2016) suggests a range from –63° to –70° for sculling and –58° to –59° for sweep, with smaller angles intended for women and lightweight rowers and larger angles for the open men's category. Beyond that, masters, recreational rowers, or beginners will probably reach even smaller magnitudes of oar angles at the full reach position, which increases the possible range of the oar angle even more.

Table 7.1 summarizes the considerations for choosing the proper oar angle.

The advantage of large oar angles at the full reach position is paramount, but there are still some reservations from practitioners who question

1. whether propulsive forces are possible at these angles, and
2. whether there is waste of effort from the rower by what is often called "pinching the boat" through the y-component of the blade force.

Objection 1 is already refuted in chapter 5 of this book. Kleshnev (2016; 2019) presented arguments to disprove objection 2. A comparison with cross-country skiing provides another explanation for this phenomenon.

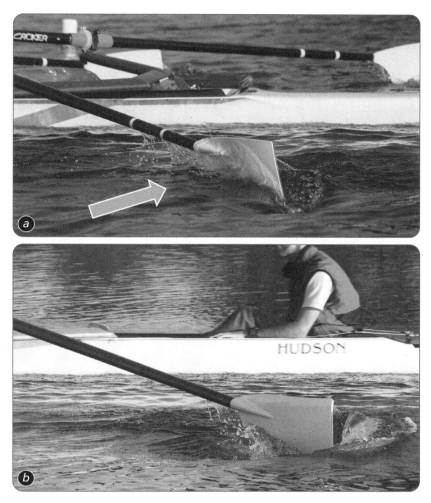

▶ **Figure 7.3** *(a)* Typical manifestation of water attacking the back side of the blade when the release is not executed properly; very often, this is an indication that the oar angle at the finish is too large. *(b)* Properly executed release in which the blade is extracted cleanly.
Photos courtesy Volker Nolte.

In the classic cross-country skiing technique, called *diagonal stride*, the athlete pushes straight back to propel, generating the foot force directly in direction of travel. The ski is always pointed in direction of travel and the propulsive force is generated by the friction of the still-standing waxed ski with the snow. This technique could be compared to rowing, in which only the drag component of the blade force is used for propulsion—for example, when rowing with a very small oar arc around the perpendicular oar position.

Using the *skating technique of skiing*, propulsive foot force is generated by the edge of the tilted ski carving in the snow and producing a force component in direction of travel. Realizing that the skating technique lets the skier move at a higher speed than with the classic technique, the advantage is achieved since propulsion is produced with the ski moving in direction of travel. Placing the blade in the water at a large oar angle

Table 7.1 Advantages and Disadvantages of Large Oar Angles at the Full Reach Position

Advantages	Disadvantages
Larger propulsive impulse	Increased dynamic gearing
Higher blade efficiency	Limited possible stroke rate
Lower tangential handle velocity necessary to reach positive angle of attack of the water on the blade, making smaller initiating air stroke necessary during entry	More skill and "feel" necessary from the rower to generate the appropriate oar angle acceleration
Increased opportunity to produce higher maximal blade force	Increased challenge to balance the boat
Higher rowing velocity at a given stroke rate	Increased challenge to handle the necessary power

at full reach position has a similar effect by allowing the rower to generate propulsion while the blade is moving in direction of travel.

The oar angle at the full reach position is the main contributor to the length of the arc that the oar covers and therefore determines the magnitude of the propulsive impulse.

There are limitations to a large oar angle at the full reach position. One is the necessity of the rower to adjust their force application to the speed of the boat, which takes some increased skill. Secondly, the greater the oar angle, the greater the magnitude of power the rower must physiologically generate to fully utilize the advantageous effects of the larger oar angle. It is no wonder that tall and powerful athletes row with astonishing large full reach positions, as illustrated in figure 7.4.

Overall, however, the advantages of using large oar angles at the full reach position outweigh these limitations by far (see table 7.1). Concerns regarding increased dynamic gearing leading to a higher load during the first part of the drive, as well as the limitation of the stroke rate, can be mitigated by changes in the rigging measurements of the oar (discussed in chapter 9).

Large oar angles at the first part of the drive are also advantageous to utilize hydrodynamic lift on the blade for a longer time, which makes the whole drive more efficient.

▶ **Figure 7.4** (a) Three-time Olympic champion Pertti Karppinen (Finland) and (b) World Cup gold medalist Carling Zeeman (Canada) demonstrating large oar angles at the full reach position.

Photos courtesy Volker Nolte.

This, again, involves specific skill and feel from the rower, who must gauge velocity and force production to make this process as efficient as possible. Using the lift component of the blade force allows the rower to move the blade with comparatively low velocity relative to the boat and still generate propulsion, which keeps the velocity of the rower compared to the boat low and in turn is physiologically more efficient for the athlete.

Air Strokes

The time that the blade can generate propulsion lengthens as the initiating and absorbing angles become smaller. These are angles where the blade is out of the water during the drive (see figures 7.1 and 7.5). Before the blade touches the water after the full reach position, it needs to be accelerated relative to the boat so that the angle of attack of the water can become >0° when the blade is entered into the water. Also, the blade must still have some rotational velocity relative to the boat until it is extracted from the water at the end of the drive. The remaining rotational velocity of the oar relative to the boat after the last water contact needs to be absorbed by the athlete before the finish position is reached. These initiating and absorbing motions as the blade moves relative to the boat outside of the water are called *air strokes* and must be kept as small as possible.

The air strokes at the beginning and the end of the drive are necessary to achieve the proper angle of attack, which is the decisive factor for efficient movement of the blade in the water. The lengths of the initiating and absorbing air strokes are affected by the velocity of the boat and the skill of the rower. A higher boat velocity requires larger angular velocity of the oar so that the angle of attack can generate propulsive force once the blade makes contact with the water. This means that as boat velocity increases, the rower requires more skill to proficiently coordinate the higher horizontal and vertical acceleration of the oar handle.

The phenomenon of air stroke is not very well studied, perhaps because it is difficult to detect and measure blade movement when the blade is not in contact with the water. No known research paper discusses the air stroke during the release, although every handle or oarlock force measurement indicates its existence. As can be seen in figure 6.3 in the previous chapter, the oarlock force F_O crosses the 0 line at about the 1-s mark and about 0.12 s before the finish position is reached, whereas the handle velocity is still about 0.7 m/s at that moment. This means that the blade moves outside of the water relative to the boat for about 0.06 m horizontally toward the stern and covers an angle of about 4° before the athlete reaches the finish position. This movement of the blade outside of the water represents the air stroke at the end of the release.

Only a few sparse studies have quantified air strokes during the entry. Handle or oarlock force measurements cannot identify the first water contact of the blade, because the inertial force of the oar generates positive magnitudes of these forces. Probably the most accurate measurements were presented by Bogucki (2008), who filmed three different boats (1x, 2–, 4x) of national team caliber athletes with a frame rate of 500 fps. He found air stroke distances d_{AS} of +0.010 m to −0.016 m relative to the boat, which lasted up to 0.05 s. The positive air stroke distance (blade moved toward the bow of the boat) occurred in the 4x with the athlete generating a backsplash on the blade, indicating resistance. These results suggest two findings: The air stroke at the entry of the blade is very small for high-caliber athletes, and it can vary even within one crew quite substantially.

It is therefore understandable that other attempts to measure the air stroke at the entry were limited in their findings. Video analyses with normal frame rates of 30 fps will maximally show two frames for the time of an air stroke (Wegschneider 2012), and measurements of the vertical and horizontal oar angle within the boat are affected by the rolling of the boat (Macrossan and Macrossan 2006).

Although they are quite difficult to measure, however, it is clear that rowers need to keep air strokes as small as possible, and proper performance is relatively simple to identify by the splashes on the blade.

Increase Magnitude of Force

The second technique to increase the propulsive force is by increasing the magnitude of force on the blade in direction of travel. It is not only the maximal propulsive force at one point of the drive that is important, but the magnitude of the force over the whole drive. It is quite a complex process for a rower to achieve both parameters. Table 7.1 outlines the factors that come into play; they are illustrated in figure 7.5.

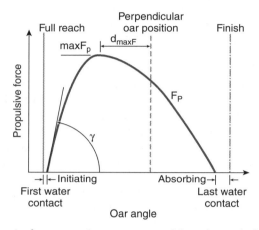

▶ **Figure 7.5**   The main factors to increase propulsion through force on the blade are gradient γ of the force after first water contact; maximum force $maxF_p$; distance d_{maxF} of maximum force from perpendicular position of the oar; "belly" shaped curve toward the last water contact. The initiating and absorbing air stroke angles during entry and release are indicated.

After the blade touches the water, the gradient γ of the propulsive force needs to be held steep until the maximum force is achieved. This requires a lot of skill, because the delicate entry of the blade has to be realized through coordination of vertical and horizontal movements of the blade followed without transition by vast increases in speed of motion and force. This complex interaction has to be adjusted depending on boat velocity, stroke rate, oar dimensions (blade type and lever lengths), oar angle, and environmental conditions. Additionally, it has to match the physical strength of the rower.

Reaching maximum force early in the drive before the perpendicular position (i.e., large d_{maxF}) is advantageous, because this force generation utilizes the hydrodynamic lift component of the blade force for propulsion and adds efficiency. At the perpendicular position, only drag forces can generate the blade force, which—although acting in the proper direction—are very costly in energy. Here, the blade must completely overcome the velocity of the boat, so that the rower has to move the handle fastest during the drive, which requires high power generation.

After the oar passes through the perpendicular position, the rower needs to maintain large propulsive forces, which generates the so-called "belly" shape of the force curve. The challenge here is the coordination of the three body joints (knees, hips, arms) that produce the handle velocity. The goal is to keep the handle velocity up in order to generate propulsion, which becomes more difficult at the end of drive when the predominantly smaller and weaker arm muscles get involved while the boat velocity increases.

Speed of Movements

Hill (1938) showed that a muscle produces its highest power when it moves at a speed that is in the middle of its physiological range. In addition, fast movements require the activation of fast-twitch muscle fibers—a process that produces lactate, which rowers should carefully limit. Thus, rowers must control the speed of motion, so that it remains in this optimal range—quick, but not maximally fast. Correct sequencing (discussed later in this chapter) puts the rower in the position to achieve this, and proper gearing will help keep control.

The entry motion of the blade into the water must be performed quickly, without generating a resistive force. When the blade is fully submerged, the rower realizes a distinct onset of the blade force—a so-called "lock on" of the blade with the water—followed by a solid horizontal handle force as if the rower "hangs" off the handle. All of this must be done delicately, quickly, and firmly, all at the same time. It cannot be felt as hard or hasty. If the movement is properly executed, the rower experiences it as light and fluent.

The magnitude of the blade velocity relative to the boat in negative x-direction must be larger than that of the boat velocity when the blade enters the phase of the drive where drag contributes to propulsion. This motion is caused by the rower moving the oar handle in positive x-direction relative to the boat. The higher handle velocities—which reach more than 2 m/s for an international women's single sculler (see figure 6.3) and more than 3 m/s for the outside hand of an international men's eight rower—are realized by the coordination of the main body joints. This larger handle velocity requires the simultaneous activation of two or even all three joints (knees, hips, and arms). These very complex movements require enormous motor control from rowers, who must adjust constantly to various boating situations and conditions (training, race, start, sprint, weather conditions), oar angles, and rigging influences.

Blade Depth in the Water

The depth of the blade in the water during the drive influences the propulsive force that the blade can generate. Ideally, the blade should be just completely submerged in water (figure 7.6b). Placing the blade at the proper depth not only maximizes the utilization of the hydrodynamic design of the blade, it also minimizes the vertical distance that the blade has to travel during the entry and release, which reduces the energy that the rower has to produce for these movements that do not directly help with propulsion.

If the blade is not placed deeply enough in the water, air pockets develop behind the blade and the water surface is scraped (figure 7.6a). The blade does not find the proper resistance and cannot benefit from the hydrodynamics of the water. Conversely, placing the blade too deep in the water (figure 7.6c) costs the rower extra time and effort, loses the hydrodynamic benefit of the specific blade shape, and generates additional resistance.

▶ **Figure 7.6** Rowing blades at different depths in the water: *(a)* too shallow; *(b)* correct depth; *(c)* too deep.

Photos courtesy Volker Nolte.

Use of Efficient Blade Force

Rowers must make an effort to use their energy output wisely and therefore should focus on three specific factors of force production:

1. Start generating the propulsive force as early as possible after passing through the full reach position.
2. Produce the respective movement speeds and forces when in the best position to do so.
3. Effectively use blade forces when they are most efficient in order to lose the least amount of energy.

The first factor has already been discussed; a large oar angle at the full reach position and a quick entry motion are key aspects to achieve the best results. The second factor will be further studied later. To examine the third factor, some more insight into blade efficiency needs to be gained.

The basics of blade efficiency are defined and discussed in chapter 5, with the angle of attack α playing the most decisive role. Figure 7.7*a* demonstrates the large changes in angle of attack during the drive, whereas figure 7.7*b* depicts the measurements of angles of attack for both blades of an international-level women's single sculler.

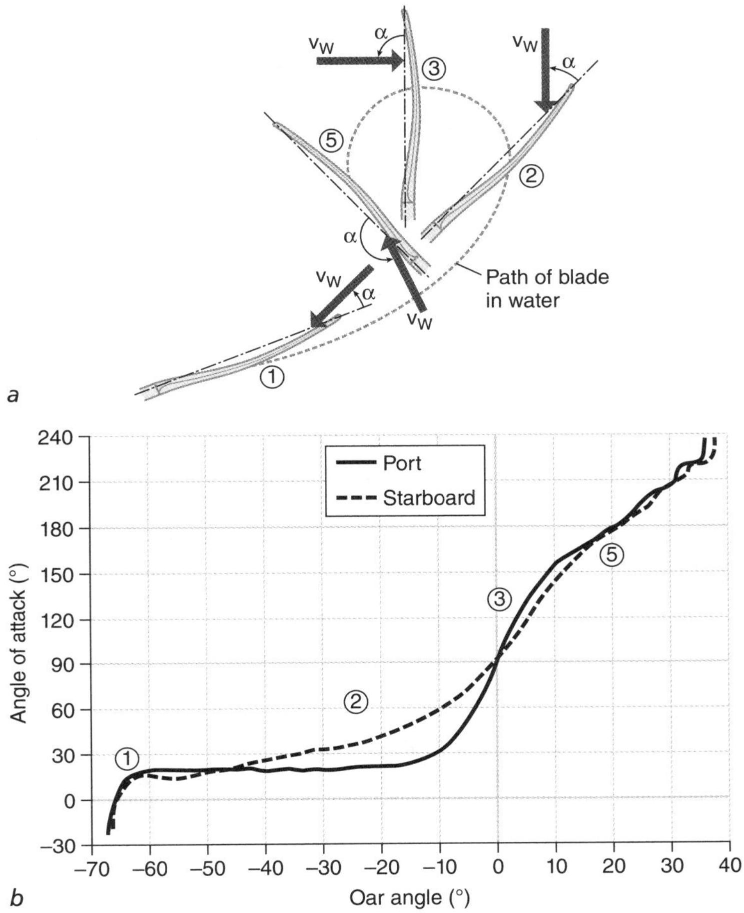

a

b

▶ **Figure 7.7**   *(a)* Schematic representation of how the angle of attack α (angle of the water flow relative to the chore of the blade) measured at the tip of the blade changes during the drive: α is very small during the entry (1) and reaches 90° at the perpendicular position (3) (oar angle = 0°); the flow of the water on to the blade v_w approaches the blade during the release (5) from the shaft end of the blade until α reaches 180°. *(b)* Example of the angle of attack for both blades of a single (31.9 spm) with the different positions 1-5 from part *a* indicated. Port and starboard (Stb) are the blades on the respective sides of the boat.

Positions 1-5 also correspond to the model and the numbering in figure 5.8*b*. Both positions 2 and 4 indicate when the blade movement changes direction relative to the water: transition from lift to drag (2) and drag to lift (4). These changes are not seen in the angle of attack.

The course of the angle of attack over a complete drive has some significant markers. The blade is at the full reach position outside of the water, so that a calculated angle of attack is only of imaginary value. It has a negative magnitude at this position, which would cause backsplash (meaning resistance) if the blade were touching the water. This is why the rower needs to start moving the handle toward the bow first, only inserting the blade in the water when α becomes ≥0°. The angle of attack increases rapidly until the blade is completely covered in water and the full hydrodynamic force starts applying (position 1 in figure 7.7). The rower should try to control the handle speed, so that α remains close to its most efficient magnitude—which is around 15°, according to Föppl (1912)—for as long as possible (see figure 7.9a). Figure 7.7b shows that the rower accomplished this task very well, especially with her port scull in position 2. When the oar approaches the perpendicular position, the angle of attack becomes 90° (position 3 in figure 7.7), and for one instant the blade generates propulsion only through drag. The direction of the force is ideal, but because the blade moves in negative x-direction, it costs a lot of energy. The blade efficiency is the lowest at that moment, although the force is still very high. The blade starts moving in the direction of travel again shortly after the perpendicular oar position (position 4), the angle of attack closes in on the blade from the shaft side, and only the lift component of the blade force can generate propulsion. Rowers must now bend their arms to maintain the necessary handle speed and force to keep the angle of attack in front of the blade, which becomes increasingly difficult.

Research about blade efficiency is ongoing and includes multiple conceptual approaches. For example, Affeld and Schichl (1985) took a purely theoretical approach and calculated a so-called optimal blade efficiency assuming the ideal blade shape. Cabrera and Ruina (2006) presented two very similar courses of blade efficiencies (model based and data based), whereas Kleshnev (1998) measured the blade efficiency for different boat classes based on his mechanical model. These four examples of blade efficiency are presented in figure 7.8.

Although the magnitudes of the efficiency curves in figure 7.8 cannot not be compared directly, some major resemblances are striking. All four examples show the highest efficiency at the beginning and the end of the drive, and efficiency is low or even lowest around the perpendicular position.

Another approach to blade efficiency could be taken by studying the lift and drag coefficients. There are no known laboratory tests of current rowing blades that could be used for the presented model. Such tests are normally done in flumes or towing tanks where the velocity of the oncoming water is constant over the whole blade. However, rowing blades do not move solely in a linear fashion—because translation and rotation are overlapping, different water velocities are found at the tip and the shaft end of the

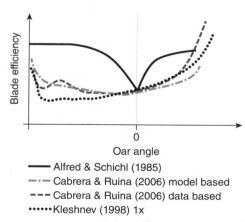

▶ **Figure 7.8** General representation of blade efficiency curves over oar angle from different researchers. Because the authors used different scales and units, comparison only shows their general paths.

blade. On the other hand, lift and drag are studied intensely relative to the angle of attack, especially in the aviation industry, so the general course of their coefficients can be accepted with great certainty.

Föppl (1912) did some measurements with curved plates that resemble the shape of current rowing blades very well. Although he conducted his experiments only up to 45°, the further course of the curve up to 90° can be extrapolated based on general knowledge, and the data from 90° to 180° mirror them from 0° to 90°. The result of this thought process is shown in figure 7.9a. Very similar connections have also been shown by other researchers, including Abbott and Von Doenhoff (1959) and Spera (2008).

Having these data will then allow to calculate the relation c_l/c_d, which can be interpreted as a general course of blade efficiency (see figure 7.9b). The rowing blade has a high efficiency if the oncoming water generates a large lift and a small drag force component and vice versa. The blade efficiency curve found in this way largely coincides with the results shown in figure 7.8.

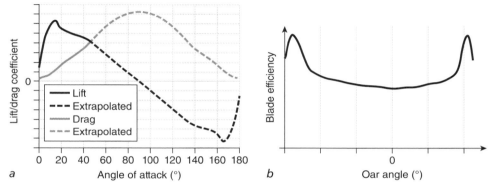

▶ **Figure 7.9** *(a)* Lift and drag coefficients (c_l and c_d) depending on the angle of attack based on Föppl (1912); Föppl only published data up to 45° angle of attack; the data for angles larger than 45° were extrapolated based on general knowledge. *(b)* Blade efficiency based on the relation lift divided by drag coefficients (c_l/c_d) from part *a*.

It is thus clear that the blade force at the beginning and the end of the drive is very efficient because of its large lift component, but there is still considerable debate about how to maximize propulsive force through clever usage of this lift component on the blade.

The blade movement through the water can be divided into three distinct parts based on how the blade force is generated. The blade moves in direction of travel during phases 1 to 2 and 4 to 5, as shown in figure 5.8b ($v_{x\text{-res}}$ is positive), so that only the lift component of the blade force can contribute to propulsion. Conversely, the blade moves mainly in negative x-direction between 10° before and 10° after the perpendicular position 3. This means that only drag acts on the blade for this part of the drive, so that we can identify this short phase as the *drag phase*. This phase is similar to the propulsion in the classic style of cross-country skiing. During the rest of the drive (from 2 to 4) the blade velocity has a component in negative x-direction and a considerable component in y-direction. This means that both drag and lift components of the blade force contribute to propulsion. This phase can therefore be called *drag–lift phase*.

As shown in chapter 5, the time for the lift phases is almost two-thirds of the total duration of the drive, which underlines their importance. The significance of the first part of the lift–drag phase (from points 2-3) comes from the fact that rowers can produce their highest handle force at this part of the drive.

All this means that hydrodynamic lift plays an enormous part in propulsion. It is therefore extremely vital to think about how this phenomenon can be maximally utilized. The first part of the drive (positions 1-3) is the most important part. Entering the water and "locking on" quickly, then increasing the handle force steadily to its maximum secures the use of hydrodynamic lift to its fullest.

Figure 7.10 illustrates the three propulsion phases of the drive based on the velocity of the blade relative to the water with its components in x- and y-directions.

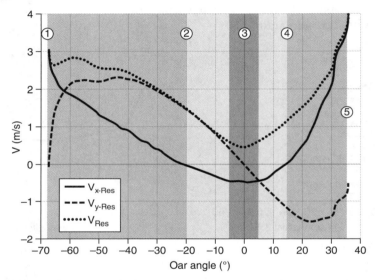

▶ **Figure 7.10** Blade velocity (v_{res}) relative to the water with its x- and y-components. Positions 1-5 are shown as in figure 5.8*b* and 7.7. Shading indicates the different propulsion phases: medium gray are the lift phases, light gray are the drag–lift phases, and dark gray is the drag phase.

Suspension

Suspension is often misunderstood in rowing, because horizontal and vertical forces are mixed when rowers are told to "suspend their weight" (Hamilton 2016; Thompson 2005). Based on the understanding developed in engineering, suspension is a system of mobile linkages that absorbs forces to secure the proper function of the apparatus. The suspension system must be flexible and strong at the same time. For example, if the axle of a car's suspension is too stiff, the sudden drop of the wheel into a pothole and the sudden push up again would cause tremendous peak forces, and this part would be prone to breaking. If the car suspension is too soft, the wheels would bounce at every small bump in the road and lose contact with the road. A proper suspension easily compensates for both scenarios, transferring the weight and the vertical inertial forces of the car onto the road so that the car can be controlled securely and the passengers have a comfortable ride.

The vertical forces in rowing are well supported by the seat and the footstretcher; it is not conceivable that the vertical forces on the footstretcher and seat could have a positive influence on horizontal forces. Therefore, the suspension must handle the main forces in the horizontal direction. These horizontal footstretcher forces need to be transferred to the oar handles, ideally without energy loss (see figure 7.11). This is achieved through joint movements along with controlled blade depth and balance. Note that unloading the seat immediately transfers the load onto the footstretcher (Nolte 2010).

Volker Nolte

▶ **Figure 7.11** Suspension in rowing is the efficient transfer of horizontal forces from the footstretcher to the handle.

Proper suspension allows the generation of a large handle force during the drive and is characterized by a strong push with the legs, straight arms during the first part of the drive, and a consistent application of handle force throughout the whole drive. Suspension is lost when a joint moves without generating handle velocity and force. For example, "shooting the seat (i.e., the seat moves faster than the hands towards the bow)," starting the drive with bent arms, or stretching the shoulders during any part of the drive leads to loss of handle velocity and therefore to a loss of power, which automatically reduces the propulsion.

Crew Synchronization

Crew synchronization, or the precise coordination of the movements of the individual crew members, is important to achieve high propulsive force in crew boats. Although there is a theoretical advantage to spreading out the force application of a crew over a longer time by staggering the movements of the individuals, all practical trials of this technique failed miserably, as described in chapter 6. The main reason is what Kleshnev (2006) calls the "trampoline effect."

If a crew is not synchronized, inertial forces of individual rowers applied to their footstretchers affect the forces that other rowers apply to their footstretchers, similar to when two people jump together on a trampoline. If they are not synchronized, they touch down on the trampoline at different times so that the elastic surface is stretched in a way that neither can fully apply their jumping forces, and they will not reach the heights that they could achieve if they were in sync. This is the same in rowing. Movements of crew members out of sync cost extra energy and do not let the individual rower develop their full potential force.

Sequencing

Proper sequencing of the rower's working joints is also very important. The change in joint angle leads to a translatory movement of the joint's endpoint, which contributes to the overall movement of the handle. Figure 7.12 illustrates this relation for the knee joint.

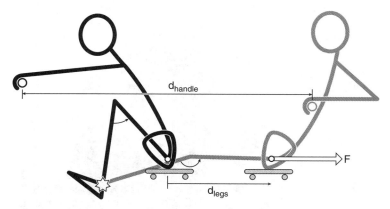

▶ **Figure 7.12** The leg movement is achieved by stretching the knee joint. The rower moves the hips the distance d_{legs} relative to the foot (*) and generates the force F. The legs' movement is one part of the total handle movement d_{handle}.

The rowing movement is accomplished by movement of the three main joints: knee (hip movement relative to the footstretcher), hip (shoulder movement relative to the hip), and arms (hand movement relative to the shoulder). The rower has to coordinate these three joint movements to generate the most propulsion. Each joint contributes a certain part of the whole handle movement and the overall power exerted on the handle. If all joints act together at the same time, it would generate a large handle velocity, which would lead to a very short drive time and extremely large handle force that not all joints, especially the arms, could transfer (see figure 7.13*a*). If the joints work one after the other without overlapping (see figure 7.13*b*), the handle velocity would oscillate. These options are therefore not practical.

To find the best sequencing, several factors need to be observed:

1. Handle velocity must steadily increase from the full reach position until the perpendicular position, from which it will progressively decrease to the finish. This means that joints need to work together in an organized way.

2. A longer duration of force application is accomplished through a targeted succession of joint movements.

3. Humans' joints achieve different movement speeds and maximum forces depending on the angle of the joint, the muscles involved, and their levers. This means that the joints must be used strategically to meet the respective requirements.

Figure 7.13*c* shows an ideal sequencing of the three main body joints.

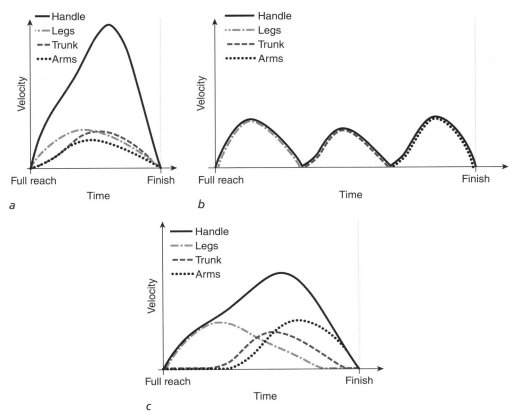

▶ **Figure 7.13** Sequencing of the body joints and the resultant handle velocity: *(a)* All joints working together at the same time. *(b)* Joints working one after the other without overlap. *(c)* Ideal sequencing of legs, trunk, and arms with overlap.

Minimize Resistance

Although the rowing motion inevitably generates resistance that increases with velocity and that additionally rises through the velocity fluctuations of the boat, it is possible to minimize certain negative effects with proper rowing technique. Reducing resistance saves energy that the rower can then use to increase propulsion and therefore increase the average velocity.

Optimize Horizontal Velocity of the Rower's Center of Mass

The rower's horizontal movement relative to the boat causes extra fluctuations in boat velocity that influence the resistance forces on the boat. As discussed previously, this movement is dictated by the necessity to generate force on the handle during the drive and therefore cannot be changed. During the recovery, however, the rower can vary sequencing and speed of motion to get back to the full reach position. The following discussion is therefore only focused on the recovery.

Sliding-rigger boats, in which the rower sits on a fixed seat and the footstretcher rigger moves, dramatically reduced the displacement of the rower's mass relative to the boat (Nolte 1984). Thus, the boat showed a distinctively different velocity curve over one drive, with considerably fewer fluctuations, and consequently was significantly faster — 6 to 12 s for a 2,000 m race according to Nolte (1981), or 2.1 to 3.6 s according to Hill and Fahrig (2009). This example shows that reducing velocity fluctuations of the boat can have a large influence on the water resistance. It is therefore theoretically possible that altering the rower's movement patterns also could reduce the resistance.

The shaded area in figure 5.14 corresponds to the distance that the boat moves relative to the total CoM. Although this distance cannot be changed for a given stroke length of a rower in a sliding-seat boat, the athlete has theoretically some freedom to vary the kinematics of their recovery through the sequencing and the speed of the joint movements and with those the course of the boat velocity.

Closer investigation into this topic, however, indicates limitations of these efforts. First, sequencing must account for the fact that the knee movement must be restricted until the hands pass the knees on their way to the full reach position. Raising the knees too early and too quickly may inhibit the path of the hands. Secondly, Hill and Fahrig (2009) found that under race pace conditions "velocity fluctuations cannot be reduced substantially in the sliding-seat boat" (593). Kleshnev (2021) added to Hill and Fahrig's argument and showed that, at race stroke rates, the duration for the recovery comes close to the minimal time necessary for rowers to execute the movement, which means that rowers simply have minimal leeway to effectively vary their sequencing in the limited time available for the recovery. Based on these arguments, there is little to no gain possible by manipulating rowing movements to influence the variations in boat velocity under race conditions (see figure 7.14b).

However, rowers do have opportunities to vary sequencing and speed of movements during training, when low stroke rates allow a recovery time three to four times longer than at race pace. Under these conditions, it is possible to delay or speed up certain movements with the goal of keeping boat velocity as low as possible and delaying the velocity spike initiated by the acceleration of the rower's larger body parts. This can be achieved by moving very slowly at the beginning of the recovery—or only moving the arms—so that these actions do not add to the already high velocity of the boat. The acceleration of the trunk and legs should be delayed to later in the recovery, when the velocity of the total CoM has slowed down.

For this reason, the so-called *micropause* at the finish position has become popular among international crews in recent years. This rowing style is characterized by a very slow movement of the handle in the very first part of the recovery —or even by pausing the whole rowing movement in the finish position—, followed by a somewhat accelerated movement into the full reach position (see figure 7.14a).

Minimize Vertical Movement

As discussed in chapter 5, a certain amount of vertical movement is necessary to perform the overall task of rowing. However, rowers have some, albeit limited, freedom to influence the sequence and the range of motion of their body joints (see figure 5.11). The CoM of the legs is highest at the full reach position and lowest when the knees are fully extended toward the finish position. This movement cannot be avoided, because the two endpoints of the legs (feet and hips) are directly connected to the boat. The CoM of the trunk rotates around the hip and therefore, also moves up and down during the rowing motion, from a relatively low point at the full reach up to its highest point when the trunk is in its perpendicular position to its lowest point in the finish position. (see figure 5.11) The effect of these vertical

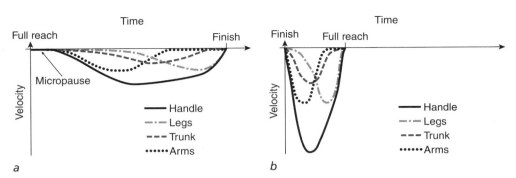

▶ **Figure 7.14** Ideal movement of the main body joints during (a) training and (b) race stroke rates. Time and velocity scales are comparable in the two graphs.

movements can be reduced by limiting the lean forward (positive θ_B in figure 6.4) or the lean back (negative θ_B in figure 6.4) and by coordinating the movements of the legs and the trunk so that the individual vertical movements cancel each other out. An example for a poor coordination of movements is the early hip extension at the beginning of drive, which was already shown to have a negative effect on force application, and additionally would increase the vertical position of the total CoM at a time that it is already high. It is therefore advisable to extend the legs first and then start extending the trunk when the CoM of the legs is already in the downward motion (see figure 5.11).

The rotation of the trunk around the hip contributes to the stroke length and is necessary to generate power. However, as shown in figure 5.13, the negative effects of vertical movement overtake the positive effects of reaching a longer stroke if a rower leans more than the proposed ±25°. The final choice of proper back angles at the full reach and finish positions depends on the anthropometrics and muscle strength of the rower.

Although the masses of the arms are relatively small, their vertical movements also affect vertical oar movement. This process costs energy, and therefore the hands should move as horizontally as possible, except for the necessary execution of proper bladework during entry and release. Additionally, horizontal hand movement is important to maintain proper blade depth during the drive and to help with balance during the recovery.

Finally, a rower needs to avoid added vertical inertial movements, which not only cost extra energy, but also increase the resistance of the boat through pitching and heaving. Accelerated vertical movements of the trunk ("lunging" towards the full reach position, "dumping" into the finish position) or extreme vertical movements with the hands and shoulders during entry or release phases are examples of such unnecessary movements that have only negative effects.

Proper Bladework

Proper bladework has significant influence on resistance. Clean placement of the blade into the water during the entry, moving it at a correct and constant depth through the water, releasing it cleanly out of the water, and carrying it with the least air resistance in the recovery ensure the lowest negative forces. Big splashes in any direction, particularly backsplashes and water attacking the shaft (see figure 7.6c) or the blade (see figure 7.3a) from the back side, are signs of unnecessary water resistance during the drive. Facing a large blade area to the oncoming air during the recovery (not fully feathering the blade, late feathering after the release, and early squaring before the full reach position) increase the air resistance.

Key Point

Bladework is the primary term for all movements of the blade in and out of the water. Generating propulsion and avoiding negative resistance during the drive is achieved when the blade is positioned so that the water's angle of attack is always positive. Additionally, maintaining proper blade depth during the drive is part of bladework.

During the recovery, the blade needs to be feathered as quickly and squared as late as possible so that air resistance is minimal. Any water contact or unnecessary vertical movement during the recovery diminishes bladework.

Finally, perfect synchronization of all blade movements within a crew is considered good bladework.

Balance

A balanced boat is characterized by a constant and stable roll angle of 0°. Although every boat observes some roll movement, Nolte and McLaughlin (2005) demonstrated that highly qualified crews have a more balanced boat compared to crews of lower performance levels. This increased stability not only gives the crew a better platform to physically perform, costs them less energy to maintain equilibrium, and improves the confidence of the athletes, it also decreases resistance.

Rowers in an unbalanced boat tend to hit their blades on the water more often during the recovery, causing more splashing and dragging during the entry and the release. All of this creates greater resistance on the oars. In addition, rolling movements of the boat increase the water resistance of the boat, including the fin. Also, a rolling boat is less stable to direct, making additional course corrections necessary that also cost energy. Finally, unbalanced boats increase the probability of injuries. Rowers can bruise their hands on the gunwales or the rigger if the boat rolls unexpectedly, and force application in an unbalanced boat can lead to knee, hip, or back injuries.

Conclusion

There are number of factors that influence propulsion and resistance. Improving propulsion and decreasing resistance is often a matter of optimizing rather than maximizing. For example, although increasing the full reach oar angle offers several advantages, there are also possible negative effects (see table 7.1).

Simply maximizing one technical factor does not necessarily lead to the expected improvements. Instead, one must analyze all possible effects of such technique changes and weigh their influence on the individual rower. After deciding which factor needs attention and how the improvement is going to be achieved, the rower must have time to get used to the change in rowing technique, with the coach providing feedback, video, or biomechanical measurements for the learning process. A final assessment is then used to determine whether the changes are leading to the intended goal. This can only be validated through on-water testing, for which the rower should collect comparable data.

It is impossible to determine and set specific technique parameters for all rowers. The biomechanical principles set forth in these chapters give clear directions about proper technique, but anthropometry, physical ability, skill level, and also the goals of the rower need to be taken into account. In addition, rowers should be prepared to alter their technique for various situations, such as changing weather conditions (e.g., from head to tailwind), race tactics (e.g., during the start or final sprint) or boat types (e.g., moving from a single into a quad). Having athletes experience as many of these situations as possible in training and work through various adaptations guided by biomechanical principles will help them to be prepared for technique changes that become necessary in varying conditions. It is also possible to optimize propulsion and resistance through boat adjustments, which will be discussed more detail in chapters 8 and 9.

Shell Design

Glen Burston and Daniel Bechard

The design and construction of rowing shells are steeped in tradition and history. For equipment manufacturers, it is a difficult task to honor those traditions and their rules while taking advantage of the advancements in research and technology that surround the sport. However, through modern history, the expansion of knowledge has resulted in significant advancements in performance. One such example can be found in the nonfiction novel *The Boys in the Boat* by Daniel James Brown (2013), which describes the shapability, strength, weight, and durability of western red cedar versus other types of wood commonly used to build boats in the early 1900s. Decades later, the advancement in materials and further research has led to a significant industry shift to composites. A greater understanding of materials such as carbon fiber as well as newer construction methods and hull design have led to an increase in design options and customizations not possible generations before.

Today we can quantify the return to equilibrium stability, stiffness, and drag of a shell based on its shape, design, and proposed purpose. We also know that small changes in design can affect what the athlete feels and how the boat responds to applied forces. It is clear that one hull size does not fit all, and the same boat will elicit different feedback from various crews based on factors such as anthropometrics, skill level, and force inputs. Shapes and adjustability must still be balanced with tradition. Shells must continue to conform to regulations defined by World Rowing, including length and weight standards, flotation requirements, innovation restrictions, and the "natural flow of water rule" (World Rowing 2020). Despite these restrictions, and regardless of the design priority being stability or performance, advancements in materials and design technology have allowed hulls and components to be increasingly constructed around the athlete rather than requiring the athlete to conform to the geometry of the shell. As a result, the number of possible hull shapes, component designs, and adjustable features to address a range of athlete anthropometrics has increased dramatically. This chapter will focus on the overall system impact of advancements in our understanding of hull and component design and how these variations can impact performance.

Key Point

Advancements in materials and design technology have allowed hulls and components to be increasingly constructed around the athlete rather than requiring the athlete to conform to the geometry of the shell.

Design and Construction Considerations

The great truth of rowing shell design and construction that no rower wants to hear—and no builder wants to accept—is that it is a series of compromises. Designing a hull with the lowest drag scientifically possible is a matter of only moderately complex mathematics. However, such a shape would not provide the necessary seakeeping or stability, nor would it allow for the physical space required by the athletes to use the shell. Likewise, the construction of the shell is also bound by practical considerations, including longevity, manufacturability, weight, and of course cost.

To understand the intersection of athlete and equipment, it is valuable to understand the competing constraints that affect the design and construction of these craft.

Seakeeping

Seakeeping ability is often called *seaworthiness* and represents a broad topic of a boat's suitability for a specific application. In rowing terms, we consider seakeeping the ability of a rowing shell to prevent water from entering the cockpit or lapping in any significant volume onto the bow or stern decks. The cockpit is the open portion of the shell where the rowers sit and is of particular importance because it can allow a significant mass of water to be retained onboard.

Virtually every rower has experienced water sloshing around the cockpit of their shell and can appreciate the performance degradation that results. When the shell takes on water, this additional mass results in the shell sinking deeper into the water to displace a matching volume. The end effect of this is an increase in drag, a decrease in stability, and a decreased freeboard, making the shell more prone to taking on additional water.

Most incidents of any significant amount of water entering the cockpit of a rowing shell occur due to wave action, either caused by a regular pattern of wind-induced waves or less predictable rogue waves or wake from other boats. Additionally, waves interacting with other waves can create a constructive interference phenomenon whereby the wave amplitude rises to the sum of the combined amplitude of the two waves.

As a boat builder, it is necessary to consider the conditions of use for the rowing shell and design accordingly. The primary variable influencing seakeeping is a measure called the *freeboard*. Freeboard is defined as the distance from the waterline to the top of the gunwale in the cockpit area and is illustrated in figure 8.1. It can also be considered as the distance between the waterline and deck to hull seam in the bow and stern deck area.

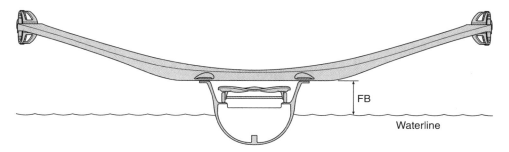

▶ **Figure 8.1**   Freeboard (FB) measurement location.

Manufacturers all have their own standards based on their experience and markets served, but table 8.1 presents typical freeboard measurements of the various boat classes.

Table 8.1 Typical Rowing Shell Freeboard (FB) Measurements

Boat class	Freeboard (cm)
1x	12.5
2–, 2x	14.0
4–, 4x	15.0
8+	16.5

Higher freeboard results in a drier boat, but comes at the cost of a heavier boat with more exposed hull and therefore more aerodynamic effects and wind drag. This is one of the conflicting parameters designers find themselves facing. Additionally, with most current racing shells being of the gunwale-mounted wing-rigger variety, the freeboard is limited to ensure adequate clearance between the rower's hands and the rigger frame as it crosses the hull.

Consider that racing shells are made for use over a range of crew weights before stepping up or down to the next hull size. For a single (1x) designed for a sculler of 79 kg (174 lb) and a recommended range of ±6 kg (13 lb), the nominal freeboard listed in table 8.1 is 12.5 cm. As a point of reference, table 8.2 provides weight-to-immerse coefficients typical of each boat class. Although these numbers change specific to each hull model, weight class, and actual immersion, they illustrate the weight required to increase or decrease the shell immersion in the water by 1 mm.

Table 8.2 Typical Rowing Shell Immersion Coefficients

Boat class	Weight to immerse (kg/mm)
1x	1.4
2–, 2x	2.1
4–, 4x	3.4
8+	6.7

Using the freeboard measurements from table 8.1 and the immersion coefficients from table 8.2, we can calculate the freeboard change for this shell over its recommended athlete weight range.

$$\text{Nominal freeboard } (FB_{nominal}) = 125 \text{ mm}$$

$$\text{Weight to immerse } (W_{immerse}) = 1.4 \text{ kg/mm}$$

$$\text{Change in rower weight } (\Delta W_{rower}) = \pm 6 \text{ kg}$$

$$FB_{85} = FB_{nominal} - \Delta W_{rower} / WI$$

$$FB_{85} = 125 - 6/1.4 = 121 \text{ mm}$$

Repeating for the minimum suggested athlete weight in the shell,

$$FB_{73} = 125 - (-6)/1.4 = 129 \text{ mm}$$

We can see from this example that the freeboard changes inversely to the crew weight by a total of 8 mm for this hull—from 129 mm with a 73 kg (161 lb) athlete to 121 mm with an 85 kg (187 lb) athlete (figure 8.2).

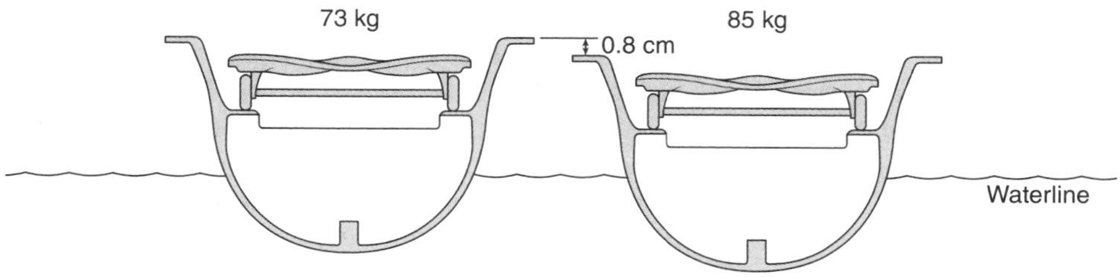

▶ **Figure 8.2** Reduction in freeboard related to rower's weight.

Consider that additional unit of water entering the cockpit has the same freeboard reduction effect. Every kilogram of water lowers the freeboard and reduces the shell's ability to prevent more water from entering. This reduces seakeeping ability, especially with crews beyond the recommended weight range in rough conditions, has often manifested itself in the form of a swamped shell.

Having made this caution, it is important to note that the suitability of a particular hull does not immediately cease at the boundaries of a published weight range. Rather, there is a gradual transition into a series of compromises. In this example, an athlete slightly heavier than the recommended range would sink the hull deeper and decrease its seakeeping correspondingly. Depending on the conditions where the shell is used and the athlete's capabilities, this 8 mm difference may be a trivial concern or a substantial one, and the seakeeping, stability, and therefore feedback an athlete would experience would greatly differ.

Key Point

Boats are designed for specified weights. However, the suitability of a particular hull does not immediately cease at the boundaries of a published weight range. Rather, there is a gradual transition into a series of compromises.

Stability

In a rowing context, we refer to *stability* as the lateral set or balance of the shell. It can also be described as the resistance to rolling about the long axis of the boat. Clearly, the ease of rowing is highly affected by the stability of the shell.

Assessing the stability of an empty rowing shell is a straightforward calculation (with the appropriate computer software) because the boat is a rigid body and nothing moves as the boat heels. This permits the designer to compare the stability of various hull shapes. But our interest is not in the stability of the shell when empty, but with a rower on board—and that is where the assessment gets challenging.

If the rower were a rigid department store mannequin strapped into the cockpit, stability would be once again easy to assess. However, with a theoretically rigid or inflexible rower, all racing shells would capsize, even before they left the dock. With a rower in the boat, whether human or plastic, the center of mass (CoM) is high enough that any unintentional heel results in an overturning moment rather than a righting moment. All rowers know that if you hold your body rigid in a rowing shell and lift the oars off the water without making the necessary adjustments, the rower and boat will quickly capsize.

Understanding why this happens requires an understanding of how the buoyancy and gravitational forces applied to the shell relate to each other. The center of buoyancy (CoB) is the geometric center of the water that is displaced by the hull. This is equivalent to the center of volume of the immersed portion of the hull. Although the buoyancy is distributed along the length and width of the immersed hull, from a mathematical perspective the upward force can be treated as a point force acting at the center of buoyancy. The center of buoyancy will change slightly with fore–aft pitching and rolling of the shell throughout the dynamic rowing stroke. It will always correspond with the center of volume of water displaced by the hull.

The center of gravity (CoG) is different from the center of buoyancy and represents the center of the downward gravitational force. If the structure and crew are rigid as described above, this force acts directly through the combined CoM of the shell, crew, and oars. It should be noted that, much like the center of buoyancy, the center of gravity of the seated athlete changes throughout the stroke and relative to the technique and anthropometrics of the crew. It can also change based on the height of individual components such as footstretchers, seat, and even the inclusion of a seat pad.

Still assuming the absolutely rigid crew, when the shell is displaced even slightly from a perfectly balanced condition, the horizontal distance from the center of gravity to the center of buoyancy is termed the *righting arm* (RA). In the case of a heeled rowing shell, the center of gravity is outboard of the center of buoyancy and therefore this distance is negative. The resulting moment is an overturning moment rather than a righting moment, as illustrated in figure 8.3.

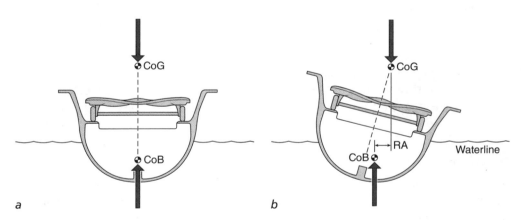

▶ **Figure 8.3** *(a)* Center of buoyancy (CoB) and center of gravity (CoG) in a level rowing shell. *(b)* Overturning moment of a heeled rowing shell.

This unstable condition is the direct result of rowing shells being very narrow craft designed specifically for minimal drag and therefore having a cross-sectional shape approaching a semicircle. From this we can see that a rowing shell with no correcting influence applied will capsize. This rigid body model is necessary for understanding the mechanics of stability, but fortunately it falls far short of the very complicated reality of rowing. Numerous influences are applied to correct the balance of the shell, keeping it upright. Most importantly, the crew is not a rigid body and can use both their bodies and the inertia of the oars to stabilize the hull. The oars are also in the water for a considerable period of the stroke cycle, enabling the rower to maintain balance in an otherwise unstable system.

Shell designers determine the hull stability that they feel is appropriate for each weight class of boat. Too much stability and the associated width of the hull will reduce top end speed, too little stability and the rower will not be able to apply maximum power and keep the boat upright. When rowing at race pace, the roll or heel angle typically varies by 1.5° either side of upright (Nolte and McLaughlin 2005). This is simply due to the imperfections of the athlete's rowing stroke, slight variations in the sideways movement of the body, and the action of waves on the hull. When something more unexpected happens the heel angle may momentarily rise to 5°, which we will use in our following analysis.

As described above, combination of rower and shell is a dynamic system as far as stability is concerned. Even though the rower's contribution cannot be determined precisely, the following example will illustrate one way to assess stability by considering the effect of matching the rower to the correct weight class of shell. To illustrate this effect, it is valuable to look at some extreme situations. For instance, how is stability affected by having a heavyweight 104 kg (229 lb) rower or a lightweight 59 kg (130 lb) rower in a single shell designed for an approximate rower weight of 82 kg (181 lb)?

Because the rower is capable of shifting their upper body sideways, these movements can have a similar effect to lowering their CoM from near the navel to somewhere around hip height. Figure 8.4 illustrates both the rower's center of gravity and the combined center of gravity for the overall rower and shell system. The overturning arm is once again the horizontal distance between the downward force through the CoM and the upward buoyant force through the center of buoyancy. As we load the boat more heavily, the stability is successively reduced. In addition, the larger rower's center of gravity would likely be higher based on their specific build. Conversely, if a lightweight rower is in a heavyweight boat the stability is increased. There are, however, more factors to consider for overall performance, including freeboard (already discussed) and, of course, rigging geometry.

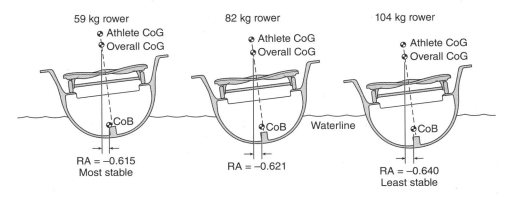

▶ **Figure 8.4** Influence of rower's weight on stability.

Key Point

Although it is possible for the same hull to be used across wide range of athlete anthropometrics, larger athletes must be more skillful, whereas lighter athletes using the same hull can be less skilled in their ability to balance the shell. To put it another way, coaches may want to reserve larger boats in their fleet for less skilled or novice athletes and smaller hulls for more skilled or advanced rowers.

Speed

By nature, competitive rowing shells are designed to have the lowest drag that is practical and therefore be capable of the highest speed with a given force input. The trade-off between stability, seakeeping, and performance has been explored; next, the critical question for a coach or athlete should be: What can I do to influence the performance of my equipment and select the right equipment for myself or my crew?

One important factor is to understand the relationship between speed and resistance, as previously discussed in chapter 5. The resistance of a rowing shell increases approximately as the square of the velocity through the water. Figure 8.5 shows an example of a midweight single where the constant force required to propel the boat at 2 m/s is 12.0 N. If we double the speed to 4 m/s the force required almost quadruples—to 46.6 N. The lesson here is that it becomes increasingly difficult to incrementally add to the shell's speed.

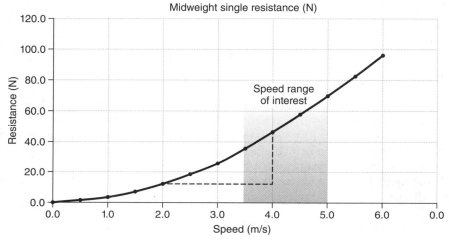

▶ **Figure 8.5** Speed versus resistance for typical midweight single.

Courtesy of Steve Killing Yacht Design.

Achieving higher speeds and overcoming the resulting increased resistance requires higher metabolic cost. There are physiological, psychological, and strategic reasons to sprint in a rowing race (discussed later in this text); however, they all come with a significant metabolic cost due to the exponential increase in drag.

Hull Shape Selection

When considering hull shape, it is important to note that shape is altered as soon as the athlete steps into the boat. Figure 8.6 illustrates that no matter how stiff the boat, there will always be some deflection caused by the centralized weight of the rower being supported by the distributed buoyancy of the hull. The magnitude of this deflection can be as much as 15 mm in a typical midweight single. Shell designers will anticipate this deflection and incorporate a "prebend" in hull shapes. The purpose of the prebend is to ensure that the intended shape of the hull is experienced when rowing and not when the shell is sitting on the boathouse rack. Not accounting for the correct magnitudes of buoyancy and weight of the crew can introduce too much or not enough rocker and have a detrimental effect on performance. For this reason, the hull will look straighter on the boat rack than in use on the water.

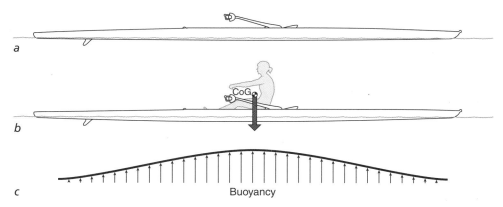

▶ **Figure 8.6** An illustration of *(a)* the shape of a pre-bent single, *(b)* the shape of a single with load, and *(c)* the corresponding buoyancy created by sections of the single. Magnitudes are exaggerated for purposes of illustration.

As a rower or a coach, it is important to select a rowing shell based on the conditions of its intended use. The best way to assess a shell is simple: test it. Just like seat racing an athlete, equipment can be tested with the same systematic methodology. In many cases, the difference between shells that appear to differ greatly in shape may actually be quite small in terms of drag, so multiple repeats of the test protocol will be needed to establish the best boat for your crew.

Key Point

The rowing shell is designed to have an optimal shape when the weight of the overall system is supported by the distributed buoyancy of the hull while on the water. Shell manufacturers will anticipate this deflection when designing the unloaded shell.

Choosing a shell based on a single factor may have less effect on speed than one might think. For example, let's consider choosing a shell based on hull length. Figure 8.7 is from an optimum length study for a midweight single. The study compared systematic variations in hull shape that each maintained a constant velocity, displacement (overall weight), and stability. The drag of each shell was plotted against its length. For this particular design, the optimum length for minimum resistance is 7.20 m. The penalty, however, for having a longer (7.5 m) or shorter (6.9 m) boat is only 0.1% in resistance (see the straight horizontal line in figure 8.7). This equates to only a 0.06% change in speed, which would result in a difference of 1.2 m at the finish of a 2,000 m race. Although that is not a distance that an advanced rower would want to give away, it illustrates that a change in length of ±0.3 m can have a very small effect on overall theoretical speed.

However, different length rowing shells exist for a reason. Longer shells will generally pitch less and can be better suited to athletes with larger upper bodies or rowing styles that tend to pitch the boat more. Shorter shells provide a little more dynamic feedback from the additional rhythmic pitching and, assuming it is not excessive, can still have competitive drag profiles.

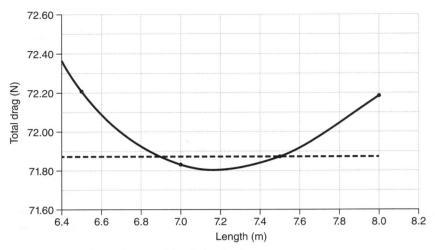

▶ **Figure 8.7** Length study on midweight single.

Courtesy of Steve Killing Yacht Design.

Footstretcher

Performance in rowing is mainly dependent upon the generation of large forces to sustain the highest boat velocity possible. Many variations in equipment design specifically focus on points of force application—namely the seat, oar handles, oarlock, rigger, and footstretcher. Boat and oar manufacturers have focused on these areas to improve compatibility with a range of athlete anthropometrics, skill levels, and personal preferences (discussed further in chapter 8). The footstretcher has been of interest for both off-water (Buckeridge, Bull, and McGregor 2015; Buckeridge et al. 2016) and on-water (Liu et al. 2018) performance because of its need to endure high magnitudes of cyclic loading and its integrated adjustability. It is common practice for the geometry of the footstretcher to be altered for height, angle, heel wedging, and splay (angle of foot turnout). In addition, advancements in hull construction have allowed for stance width to become adapted as well. A once-static component over generations of design improvements is now adjustable to within the allowed space of the rowing shell's cockpit. Although the geometry of the footstretcher is typically set by coaches and athletes based on comfort rather than mechanical advantages, this positioning has been shown to alter performance (Buckeridge et al. 2015; Buckeridge et al. 2016; Soper and Hume 2005).

Footstretcher Geometry

The most common methods of altering footstretcher geometry is through height and angle. The height is defined as the vertical distance between the lowest point of the seat to the bottom of the shoe's heel cup and typically ranges from 16 to 20 cm (Nolte 2011). Footstretcher angle is defined as the mechanism's sagittal plane orientation, with horizontal being 0° and vertical representing 90° (figure 8.8). Measurements typically range from 37° to 41° from the horizontal (Nolte 2011). Footstretchers are usually designed by manufacturers to reach measurements that are beyond these ranges so that athletes can use wide ranges of adjustability to maximize their comfort and performance, particularly at the high-performance level. For example, a 2017 World Rowing measurement survey found a range of 13.5 cm to 24 cm and 37° to 45° respectively in the men's openweight 1x category. The women's openweight 1x ranged from 14 cm to

18.5 cm and 39° to 46.6° at the same event. For lesser skilled athletes, footstretchers tend to be set lower in the hull and at a shallower angle to assist hip range of motion and stroke length at full reach. It should also be noted that changing foot-stretcher height alters the location of the athlete's CoM, affecting stability of the boat.

Physical Outcomes of Footstretcher Design

Force directed onto the footstretcher by the athlete can be separated into its x-, y-, and z-components. Ideally for the majority of the drive, the athlete maximizes the horizontal component of force (x) along the direction of travel. The vertical component of force (z), however, acts to pitch the shell. Previous work in computational fluid dynamics has suggested that pitching can have a significant effect on viscous and wave-making drag. Mediolateral forces (y) also occur due to asymmetrical force application by the athlete but are small in magnitude compared to horizontal and vertical components (figure 8.8). Asymmetrical force application is more likely in sweep rowing, but becomes more symmetrical among advanced rowers.

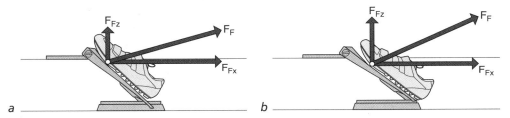

▶ **Figure 8.8** Theoretical effect of footstretchers set with *(a)* high and steep geometry vs. *(b)* low and shallow geometry. Forces are displayed in the vertical (F_{Fz}) and horizontal (F_{Fx}) direction as well as the resultant force (F_F).

A higher footstretcher has been suggested to maximize a rower's power output (Herberger 1987). Caplan and Gardner (2005) investigated the effects of varying footstretcher height on the mechanical effectiveness of rowing during a 3.5 min maximal-intensity trial on stationary rowing machines. They determined that higher foot positions resulted in increased power per stroke, mean handle force, and mean handle velocity on the ergometer. Buckeridge and colleagues (2016) found that increasing footstretcher height resulted in reduced stroke length, reduced horizontal foot force, and reduced anterior rotation of the pelvis during ergometer rowing when comparing four different heights. However, the authors argue that despite these negative impacts on factors commonly associated with good performance, peak handle force and power were unchanged. This may suggest that the rower's overall efficiency improves with higher footstretchers. Soper and Hume (2005) investigated the effects of three footstretcher angles (36°, 41°, and 46°) on mean power output during 2,000 m maximal effort. The authors found a 0.8% (women) and 2.4% (men) increase in mean power output with a steeper footstretcher.

Trial Outcomes on Footstretcher Geometry

It should be noted that all these studies were performed on Concept2 stationary rowing ergometers, as opposed to on water. Although a global standard for the replication of the rowing movement, differences between ergometer and on-water rowing have been noted in both kinetics (Torres-Moreno, Tanaka, and Penney 2000) and kinematics (Lamb 1989).

In one on-water study, Liu and colleagues (2018) investigated the effects of foot-stretcher height during a 200 m rowing trial at stroke rates similar to racing conditions. They determined a fast deceleration, a lower boat speed fluctuation, faster leg drive speed, and larger oarlock forces in 10 national team athletes when increasing footstretcher height.

Although increased footstretcher height and angle may appear advantageous, it should be recognized that most studies are performed over short distances, and therefore they do not consider the effects of the large cumulative distances that are typically required by the sport or the associated implications for injuries. For example, potential changes in body mechanics should be considered before deciding on rigging geometry (Barret and Manning 2004; Buckeridge et al. 2016; Caplan and Gardner 2005; Caplan and Garner 2008; Liu et al. 2018). As an athlete approaches the full reach position, they should have a slightly anteriorly tilted pelvis and relatively neutral spine (Thornton et al. 2017). However, this can be limited by the range of motion of the ankle and the hip and be further limited by a high footstretcher (Buckeridge et al. 2016) or steep footstretcher angle. It is possible that injury may occur in athletes who do not have the required flexibility to attain these positions and attempt to adapt their technique. Although more research is needed to fully understand best practices, there is a growing understanding that skill level, development age, anthropometrics, and flexibility can have significant implications on recommended rigging geometry for best performance (figure 8.9).

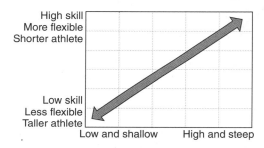

▶ **Figure 8.9** General trend graph showing the tendency of footstretcher geometry considering various athlete traits.

Design advancement in footstretcher adjustability as well as surrounding structures has led to additional opportunities for customization. Although limited peer-reviewed research exists regarding heel shims, stance width, and splay as it relates specifically to rowing performance, research in related areas as well as internal studies suggest these factors can play an important role in maximizing performance. Each of these strategies attempt to give the athlete a greater ability to engage the gluteal muscle group earlier in the drive, generating more force and improving stability. In any case, increased ability to customize allows the coach and athlete to adjust the boat to the athlete rather than the athlete to the boat.

Seat Design and Fit

Boat manufacturers focus on the seat as a key area that influences comfort and kinesthetic feel. The distribution of pressure—defined as the amount of force applied per unit of area—has been linked to perceived comfort (Navy 2011). Because peak vertical forces on the seat can range from 0.3 to 1.2 times body weight during the same stroke at maximal effort (Jensen 2007), the seat shape plays an important role on the distribution of pressure and perceived comfort. The seat in rowing is unique in that it is a static structure that must accommodate a dynamic movement. The height of the seat also plays a role in the location of the center of mass and therefore the boat's overall stability, as noted earlier.

Athlete Anatomy and Seat Design

The design of the seat must accommodate several anatomical structures of the athlete during the rowing movement, including the bony structures of the pelvis and the surrounding pressure-sensitive soft tissues, with muscular structures such as the gluteal muscle group also playing a role. Manufacturers typically focus efforts on accommodating the ischial tuberosities and the coccyx, leading to a multitude of design options (figure 8.10).

These anatomical structures are typically most important in seat design because their relatively flat and wide shape make them ideal for weight bearing and are associated with higher pressure tolerances than the surrounding soft tissue. A top-down view of the ischial tuberosities and adjoining structures would show that they are set at an oblique angle, closest together anteriorly and further apart in the posterior. Throughout the stroke cycle, pressure is typically the highest at and around these areas. At the full reach position, the pelvis is typically rotated anteriorly where the ischial tuberosities are narrowest. Knee and hip flexion create areas of high pressure around the tuberosities by lifting the athlete's legs away from the front of the seat. As the athlete continues through the drive, the pelvis typically rotates to neutral, then posteriorly at the finish. Posterior rotation of the pelvis moves the ischial tuberosities where spacing is wider. At this point of the stroke, legs make contact with the seat, progressively expanding the area of contact.

Connecting the area of high pressure at the full reach position to the finish defines the ischial tuberosity's gliding path. Boat builders and seat designers have typically compensated for areas of high pressure around the tuberosities with two holes or deep impressions for the purpose of creating a larger surface area of the seat in contact with rower's buttocks, decreasing magnitudes of pressure as a result. Pressure pattern and comfort can differ among rowers for several reasons, including gender, anthropometrics, technique, and hip range of motion. For example, women tend to have wider set ischia with greater angle than men (figure 8.11). However, both sexes display various techniques, anthropometrics, and pelvic mobility, resulting in a variety of pressure patterns—all of which are factors to consider when selecting a seat.

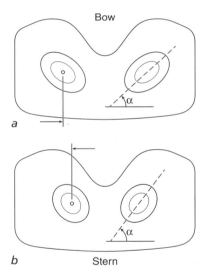

▶ **Figure 8.10** Two rowing seats with different design concepts. *(a)* A seat designed for female rowers with wider and more oblique ischial tuberosity impressions. *(b)* A seat designed for male rowers with narrower and steeply angled (α) ischial tuberosity impressions. Impressions follow the anticipated "gliding path" of the ischial tuberosity.

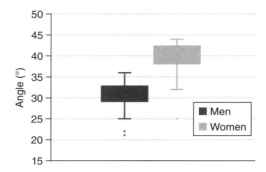

▶ **Figure 8.11** Boxplot illustrating the ischial tuberosity gliding path in a population of male vs female rowers from pressure-mapping data.

Orthopedic Influence on Seat Design

Pressure mapping, commonly used in orthopedics and health care research, has filtered into equipment fitting in many sports, including saddle fit in cycling, cockpit fit in driving, and seat fit in rowing. Although this system is typically only available through select companies or researchers, a more accessible (albeit less accurate) method is to use memory foam or corrugated cardboard to map areas of high pressure and then consult a builder. Because of the number of seat designs in use and the lack of mapping systems available, however, the most common method is still trial and error.

Consequences of Improper Seat Design

It is difficult for rowers to use a custom seat outside of personal singles. Differing track and wheel widths and designs, as well as the shared use of boats at many clubs, make this largely impractical. It should be recognized, however, that the use of a poorly fitted seat could lead to suboptimal biofeedback and possible injury. Injury at this level is multifactorial and can be a result of pressure, tissue deformation and loading, shear stress, tissue tolerances, temperature, and moisture combined with seat characteristics (Navy 2011). Cyclic loading—such as the type experienced when rowing—is enough to cause lack of blood flow to the area and resulting injury. It is suggested that compromised comfort in this area may cause athletes to change their movement patterns to accommodate the seat, which could trigger evasive movements that could lead to injury or reduce overall training time. For example, posterior rotation of the pelvis during the rowing stroke can bring the coccyx in contact with the hard surface of the seat. High localized pressure can lead to shear and abrasions of the soft tissue in that area (Thornton et al. 2017). As a result, rowing seats typically have posterior cutouts and smooth contours to reduce or eliminate this contact point.

In some cases, rowers can report leg cramping and numbness due to a poorly fitted seat. This is typically due to irritation of the sciatic nerve, which travels closely to the pelvis and gluteal muscle group. Athletes who experience these symptoms should first consult a primary care physician to rule out the possibility of a more serious medical issue. Once this is addressed, an athlete can consult a company with pressure-mapping capabilities or try different seat designs. If the issue persists, the athlete may want to try seat pads of various foam densities to help alleviate irritation of the sciatic nerve. In any case, dispersing pressure and reducing pressure gradients can improve comfort and reduce rates of injury. This can be achieved with ischial tuberosity impressions rather than holes, smoothly contoured edges, and the elimination of prominent crests.

Key Point

The following are the four most important factors in seat design:

1. Ischial tuberosity impression angle
2. Ischial tuberosity impression spacing
3. Coccyx cutout
4. Contouring and edging

Conclusion

Like other equipment-dependent sports such as cycling or downhill skiing, rowing performance is highly reliant on the athlete's relationship to their equipment. Unlike these sports, however, it would be fair to say that rowing has lagged in terms of athlete customization. Perhaps this is primarily a cost challenge, or possibly an attempt to remain compliant with our sport's tradition. In any case, seismic shifts are occurring in both our knowledge of shell performance and manufacturing capabilities.

The artistry and tradition instilled in us from generations past still exist; however, technological advancements have unveiled an unprecedented understanding of the sport. The advent of *in situ* force measurement equipment has added greatly to the knowledge base. Coupled with incredible advancements in analysis tools, computational software, and integrated manufacturing technology, we can finally see a future where equipment customization transitions from elite rowing to all levels of the sport at ever-decreasing costs. Imagine a future where customized hull and cockpit dimensions, seat tops, footstretchers, foot shims, and other aids can be produced at costs comparable to standard components.

In the meantime, builders will continue learning, researching, and growing their knowledge base with an eye to making the sport more athlete focused and accessible.

9 CHAPTER

Adjusting Equipment and Rigging to Individual Anthropometry

Volker Nolte, PhD

The ultimate end product of performance in rowing is the achieved velocity of the overall center of mass (CoM), which is highly dependent on equipment. In fact, many of the performance increases in the sport over the years are based on the technological development of boats and oars, as well as their better adjustment to the individual rower's skill, anthropometry, and physical ability. Lighter and stiffer materials, hydrodynamically advanced shell and blade designs, and small positional improvements like moving the boat's rudder from the stern end of the hull to right behind the fin have allowed substantial increases in rowing velocities (see Kleshnev and Nolte 2011; Secher 1993; Volianitis and Secher 2007).

Technological advancements have also led to technique improvements. For example, the installment of swivel oarlocks, longer slides, and adapted athletic shoes affixed to the footstretchers have allowed larger oar angles at the full reach position. There are myriad opportunities to individualize material setups and rigging measurements; the goal is to identify the biomechanical principles involved so that rowers and coaches can use them to their advantage.

Although these advancements are exciting to curious coaches and athletes, they can be overwhelming to some. Although there is plenty of research to help make decisions about individual equipment choices and rigging measurements (e.g., Davenport 2002; Kleshnev 2016a; Nolte 2005; Nolte 2011), it remains challenging to state generally valid assertions for all possible equipment selections—there are a multitude of influences that need to be taken into consideration, and some may even contradict each other. Because boat and oar setups must be used in various weather and race conditions, compromises are often made. It is therefore important to understand the biomechanical concepts that underlie rigging and identify those that are the most critical. Additionally, it is also important to understand the influences that equipment choices have on rowing technique in order to avoid technique errors based on incorrect setups.

Oar

Oar technology has advanced dramatically in recent years, including developments of the shaft, blade, and handle components. Oar manufacturers have almost complete freedom to shape shaft and blade designs with the usage of carbon fiber composite materials. It is therefore no surprise that there are more than 20 different blade shapes currently on the market. However, international results show no clear advantage to using any particular blade shape. For example, each gold medal crew at the 2021 European Championships in the women's single, men's single, men's double, and men's pair used a different blade shape. There are several possible reasons for this: The different blade shapes may have had no or only minimal performance variances; the individual oar measurements may have been more important than blade design; the different blade designs may have suited individual rowing styles; or possibly the winners were so dominant that they would have succeeded with any blade design.

Whatever the reason, rowers and coaches should understand the possible advantages of the different designs and how to find their best equipment and measurements. The following discussion examines the features of an oar and how they can be assessed. Some necessary definitions are shown in figure 9.1.

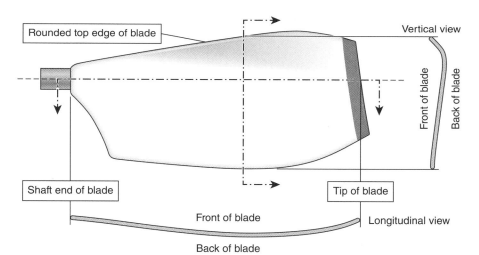

▶ **Figure 9.1** View of the front of a modern rowing blade with parts and general design features labeled. Note the asymmetric shape, mostly flat front surface, curvatures in the vertical and longitudinal cross sections, rounded top edge, and tip angled to the longitudinal axis of the oar.

Courtesy of Concept2.

Oar Measurements

The dimensions of the oar lengths and the levers of the three forces that act on the oar are of utmost importance to transfer the rower's power into propulsion, as shown in figure 9.2. Handle force F_H is applied by the rower's hand, and handle lever d_{HL} is the distance from the resultant force vector to the rotation point of the oar, which is the center of the pin. Blade force F_B is the total sum of all pressure forces that are distributed over the entire blade surface, and its point of application is the so-called

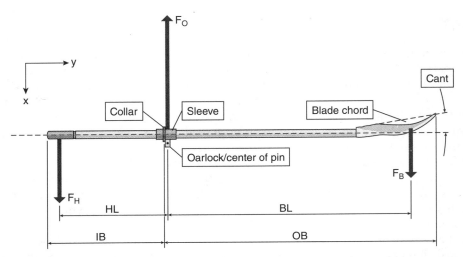

▶ **Figure 9.2** Simplified mechanical model and the main definitions of the rowing oar. Inboard (IB) is the distance from the oarlock side of the collar to the end of handle. Outboard (OB) is the distance from the oarlock side of the collar to tip of blade. Cant is the angle between oar centerline and blade chord (tilt of the blade relative to the longitudinal axis of the oar).

center of pressure (McGinnis 2013). The blade lever d_{BL} is the distance from the center of pressure to the center of the oarlock pin.

The equation of motion for an oar is shown in equation 9.1:

$$\Sigma T_P = F_H \times d_{HL} - F_B \times d_{BL} = I_O \times \alpha_O \qquad (9.1)$$

where T_P is torque around the pin; I_O is moment of inertia of the oar; and α_O is angular acceleration of the oar.

Assuming that $I_O \times \alpha_O$ is very small relative to the other components, it can be neglected, so that the handle force and blade force are related as shown in equation 9.2:

$$F_H \times d_{HL} = F_B \times d_{BL} \qquad (9.2)$$

When the rower applies force on the handle, the hands follow a circular path around the oarlock (figure 9.3). The ability of the rower to generate power depends on several measurements: the inboard IB, or the distance from the oarlock side of the collar to the end of the handle; span, or the distance between the center of the pins of the oarlocks (for sculling); and spread, or the perpendicular distance from the centerline of the boat to the center of the pin (for sweep rowing). In order to allow the rower to generate the highest power on the handle that can be best transferred into propulsion, these dimensions need to meet the following criteria:

• The rower should be able to achieve a large oar arc.

• Handle force should be mainly perpendicular to the oar, so that the best torque around the pin can be achieved, especially during the phases of the drive when the rower exerts maximal effort.

• The path of the hands should minimize the strain on the rower's body as they apply handle forces.

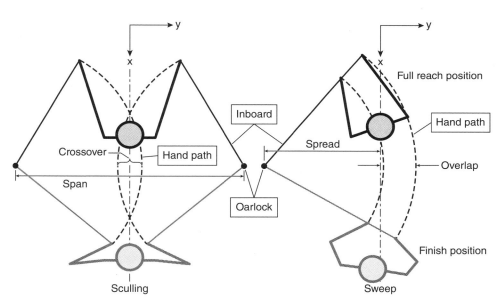

▶ **Figure 9.3** The movements of the rower's hands from the full reach to the finish position in sculling and sweep. The hands cross over each other when sculling, whereas the outside hand (hand furthest away from the oarlock) overlaps the boat's centerline when sweep rowing.

- The rower should be able to execute proper entry and release movements.
- The rower's hands must be able to move past each other when sculling.

The selection of inboard and span or spread dimensions is an optimized compromise designed to meet these objectives. Table 9.1 summarizes the implications of any rigging measurement changes, assuming overall oar length and blade type is kept consistent.

Considerations for choosing "normal" inboard and span or spread are mainly driven to meeting the geometry of the hand movement in the boat, assuming that gearing is accomplished by choosing proper outboard measures and blade types. This means that there are only small variances of ±0.01 m possible if targeted oar angles and hand positions relative to the body are to be achieved, and they depend on athletes' range of motion and their planed rowing velocity (Nolte 2011). It is therefore only logical that the following dimensions for inboard measurements have become standard in practice and can be used as a baseline:

- 0.88 m for singles
- 0.87 m for doubles and quads
- 1.14 m for eights
- 1.15 m for fours
- 1.16 m for pairs

Small acceptable variations of these baselines should be considered to meet specific qualities of the athlete (e.g., increase if the athlete is tall) or their goals (e.g., recreational athletes who row at a lower velocity can choose a larger inboard because their oar arc can be smaller). In addition, the previous criteria need to be considered.

Table 9.1 Implications of Changes in Inboard, Span, or Spread Measurements

Rigging measurement	If extended	Set normally	If reduced
Inboard only	• Lighter gearing (reduced handle force and smaller oar arc) • Footstretcher needs to be set toward bow, which leads to smaller full reach oar angle • Increased crossover or overlap, which can lead to technical problems and may increase chance of injury • Hand path farther away from and not as parallel to boat centerline	• Normal gearing • Normal oar arc • Athlete can easily and safely operate crossover or overlap • Hand path close and mostly parallel to boat centerline	• Heavier gearing (increased handle force) • Footstretcher needs to be set toward stern, which leads to smaller finish oar angle • Smaller crossover or overlap, which requires footstretcher adjustment and may lead to unfavorable direction of handle force • Hand path farther away from and not as parallel to boat centerline
Span or spread only	• No change in handle force, but smaller oar arc may feel like reduced load • Footstretcher needs to be set toward stern, which leads to smaller finish oar angle • Smaller crossover or overlap, which requires footstretcher adjustment and may lead to unfavorable direction of handle force • Hand path farther away from and not as parallel to boat centerline	• Normal gearing • Normal oar arc • Rower can easily and safely operate crossover or overlap • Hand path close and parallel to boat centerline	• No change in handle force, but larger oar arc may feel like heavier load • Footstretcher needs to be set toward bow, which leads to smaller full reach oar angle • Increased crossover or overlap, which can lead to technical problems and may increase chance of injury • Hand path farther away from and not as parallel to boat centerline
Inboard *and* span or spread	• Lighter gearing (reduced handle force and smaller oar arc) • Smaller full reach and finish oar angle • No change in crossover or overlap • Hand path more parallel to boat centerline	• Normal gearing • Normal oar arc • Rower can easily and safely operate crossover or overlap • Hand path close and parallel to boat centerline	• Heavier gearing (increased handle force and larger oar arc) • Larger full reach and finish oar angle • No change in crossover or overlap • Hand path farther away from and not as parallel to boat centerline

Because inboard and span or spread should ideally match, both measurements need to be adjusted together and in the same order of magnitude if changes are considered. Inboard and span or spread are related, as shown in equations 9.3 and 9.4 (Nolte 2021a; 2021b):

$$\text{IB}_{\text{scull}} = \text{Span}/2 + 8 \text{ cm} \pm 1 \text{ cm} \tag{9.3}$$

$$\text{IB}_{\text{sweep}} = \text{Spread} + 30 \text{ cm} \pm 1 \text{ cm} \tag{9.4}$$

After setting inboard and spread or span, the outboard length must be identified. This needs to correspond to blade type as well as to the physical and technical abilities of the rowers.

Outboard Length

The outboard length of an oar has a relatively large range of possible variations, which can have considerable influence on rowing performance. It is a measure to maximize performance that is currently not used to its full extent. The outboard length in rowing can be compared with the radii of the sprockets on a bicycle, through which the torque generated by the bicyclist on the crank is transferred to the propulsive force on the rear wheel.

Because the goal of rowing is to maximize propulsion, the blade force over the whole drive—the only source to accelerate the overall system—becomes the main focus. The following conceptual model explains why, contrary to assumption, a shorter outboard increases the blade force (Nolte 2009).

A rower exerts a specific magnitude of handle force F_H on a defined handle lever length d_{HL} to produce a certain torque on the handle. Let's assume the athlete tries two oars with different outboard lengths with blade levers d_{BL1} and d_{BL2}. In this case, d_{BL1} is longer than d_{BL2}. Using equation 9.2 and assuming that the rower applies the same effort means the same torque $F_H \times d_{HL}$ is applied to the two different oars. This leads to the following situation (equation 9.5):

$$F_H \times d_{HL} = F_{B1} \times d_{BL1} = F_{B2} \times d_{BL2} \tag{9.5}$$

Further calculations then reveal (equation 9.6):

$$F_{B2} = F_{B1} \times \frac{d_{BL1}}{d_{BL2}} \tag{9.6}$$

Because d_{BL1} is larger than d_{BL2}, F_{B1} must be smaller than F_{B2} to keep the equation correct. This implies that blade force increases if the outboard is shortened while handle force and inboard are maintained (see figure 9.4, Dreissigacker and Dreissigacker 1992; Nolte 2011).

Because the blade force is a hydrodynamic force, an increase can only be achieved by enlarging the blade surface, improving the drag and lift coefficients through specific design features (discussed later), or by moving the blade faster through the water (see equations 5.14 and 5.15). This means that rowers can indeed achieve a larger blade force by shortening the outboard without exerting more handle force, but they must either use a better blade design or move the handle faster.

Moving the handle faster can be used to improve performance in two ways: Rowers can increase the stroke rate while maintaining the same stroke length, or they can increase stroke length to increase stroke efficiency. Both measures increase propul-

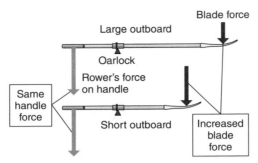

▶ **Figure 9.4**   Applying the same handle force on a fixed inboard to an oar with a shorter outboard generates a larger blade force.

Nolte 2011, 135

sion, which leads to higher rowing velocity. The challenge with these two approaches is that both require increased skill. This is why highly skilled athletes benefit more from shortening the outboard to improve rowing speed. Theoretically, one can expect considerable performance gains from shortening the outboard, but practically, the agility and skill of the rower limits the range of variation and actual advantages.

The possible changes to the outboard are much larger in magnitude than one can apply to any other rigging measure. For example, typical outboard measures for sculls with Macon blades are 2.12 m (3.00 m total length; 0.88 m inboard) and 2.00 m with Smoothie or Slick blades (2.88 m total length; 0.88 m inboard). Some masters rowers successfully use FatBlades with an outboard length of 1.83 m (2.70 m total length; 0.87 m inboard). This presents a range of outboard variations of maximally 0.29 m (almost 1 ft)!

Outboard changes are used in practice very sparsely and only in a very small range. Coaches and athletes, for example, adapt gearing to expected wind directions in races, but normally limit such variations to ±1 cm. To get a better handle on the size of possible outboard length variations, Nolte and Kleshnev (2011) conducted a study in which they changed outboard length twice by increments of 0.05 m while keeping all other rigging measures constant. They found that the participating rowers could successfully handle these changes, indicating that larger outboard adjustments should be considered, trained, and tested to find the best gearing for crews. They further concluded that "Shorter outboards allow faster handle velocity, which leads to shorter drive time even at slightly longer rowing angles and, hence, allow higher stroke rate and rowing power"—however, "optimal gearing is a balance between rower's and blade efficiencies and depends on rower's dimensions and boat speed" (1). Table 9.2 offers recommendations for how to determine the best outboard length.

Key Point

Outboards can be changed within a wide range and therefore offer rowers great possibilities to influence their performance. This measure to maximize performance is currently not used to its full extent.

Table 9.2 Considerations for Varying the Length of the Outboard of an Oar

Lengthen	Shorten
Athlete likes to row at low stroke rate or with large handle force	Athlete likes to row at higher stroke rate and less handle force
Athlete plans to reduce stroke length while maintaining stroke rate	Athlete plans to increase stroke length while maintaining stroke rate
Athlete is very strong	Athlete is not very strong
Athlete lacks skill (e.g., novice)	Skilled athlete
Blade has small surface area	Blade has large surface area
Blade has small drag or lift coefficient	Blade has large drag or lift coefficient

Unlike in cycling, in which bicyclists can easily respond to changing conditions by shifting between gears without interrupting their ride, oar lengths cannot be adjusted so easily when the crew is on the water. Currently, the only quickly executable influence on gearing in rowing are clip-on spacers that can be slipped onto or removed from the sleeve, which can only be applied when the crew stops rowing. Adding such a spacer to the sleeve automatically lengthens the inboard and shortens the outboard the same amount and changes the swivel point of the oar around the pin. Although this method is successful for changing the gearing, it also influences the position of the handle relative to the pin and alters the kinematics of the rower's hands, because the span or spread cannot be altered on the water. The unusual hand path may be the reason why this method of quick adjustments is not often used.

Blade Design

The blade itself is offered in a variety of extensive design options. These are made possible through the use of modern materials, especially carbon composites. As for design limitations, they are subject to a single rule in international rowing (World Rowing 2021): The blade thickness must be at least 3 mm for sculls and 5 mm for sweep oars. This means that blade manufacturers are free to design the blade's edge, shape, and surface size as long as a minimum thickness is maintained. It is beyond this publication to discuss all blade types that are currently on the market; therefore, the main design characteristics are discussed in general terms to help coaches and athletes choose the best oars.

Tip of the Blade Design

The importance of the tip of the blade was realized once the actual path of the blade in the water was correctly described and the influence of the lift component of the blade force on propulsion was recognized (Nolte 1984). If it is assumed that the water always attacks a blade at 90° over the whole drive (Körner and Schwanitz 1985; Thompson 2005), then the tip of the blade would have no influence on the propulsion and no additional features would need to be considered.

As it is known now, the water attacks the tip of the blade from the first water contact to the perpendicular position of the blade (points 1-3 in figure 5.8*b*), which is the main part of the drive during which about 80% of the propulsive work is done. The tip has first contact with the undisturbed water and influences the further flow of the water around the blade. It is therefore understandable that the tip has a special significance in blade design.

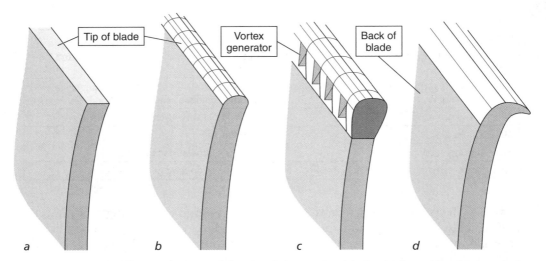

▶ **Figure 9.5** Different designs of the tip of the rowing blade: *(a)* flat edge; *(b)* rounded edge; *(c)* Vortex edge (Concept2, 2021a); *(d)* experimental edge.

Three main types of blade tips are currently in use: flat, rounded, and Vortex edges (see figure 9.5).

The flat edge is the easiest to manufacture because it is a simple cut. The rounded edge requires either extra finishing or a special mold. The Vortex tip is a separate prefabricated part that is glued to the tip of the blade. The experimental edge would either need a special mold or could be manufactured as a prefabricated piece like the Vortex edge.

The tip edge contributes to the water resistance of the blade, which only consumes energy. Therefore, it makes sense to streamline the edge, which is why a rounded shape is better than the flat shape. The Vortex edge takes an additional step to improve the performance of the blade by incorporating vortex generators (Concept2 2021a). This design not only makes the blade edge more streamlined, but also improves the water flow around the back of the blade.

Several other attempts have been made to further improve the performance of the tip of the blade. The experimental edge in figure 9.5*d* has already been tested once by using automotive filler attached to a standard blade. The design showed promise, but the filler broke off when blades hit docks or other obstacles. Other ideas included leading-edge slats similar to airplanes and various forms of holes or zigzag shapes, but none of the trials made it to general use.

One other development in blade tip design was the introduction of tapered edges or cutouts. These are often produced by cutting out triangular shapes at the two corners of the tip (see figure 9.6). Concept2 (2021a) describes these cutouts as similar to the delta wings of airplanes: "These tapered leading edges affect the airflow over the wing in a way that decreases drag and increases lift." Nørstrud and Meese (2013) supported this theory with a simulation of a blade with a tapered tip. The improvements of the water flow are particularly focused on the first lift phase of the drive, which is defined in figure 7.10.

As mentioned previously, it is difficult to test the full effects of rowing blades in laboratory settings. Attempts to perform these tests in a flume have been made several times (e.g., Caplan and Gardner 2007). However, they yield only limited results, because the flow around a rowing blade in open water is more complex than can be replicated

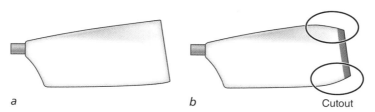

a   *b*   Cutout

▶ **Figure 9.6** *(a)* Standard asymmetric rowing blade. *(b)* Standard asymmetric blade with cutouts at the tip and Vortex edge.

Courtesy of Concept2.

with a constant flow. An improved laboratory testing method would be to simulate the actual flow of the water with a guiding mechanism that directs a blade's horizontal movement paths simultaneously with the rotations of the blade around its vertical axis, like Affeld and Schichl (1985) first attempted to reproduce. With the development of more powerful computers and sophisticated computer programs, researchers will be able to more effectively simulate the effect of certain blade designs (Ashbourne 2008; Sliasas and Tullis 2010). Conclusive findings, however, are still pending.

Nevertheless, laboratory tests help us to learn more about and understand specific hydrodynamic effects on rowing blades. A previously unpublished wind tunnel test at the University of Western Ontario gives some insight on the differences between a standard asymmetric rowing blade and a blade with cutouts and Vortex edge (Haines et al. 2004; see figure 9.7*b* and *d*). Fumes were used to visualize areas of higher velocities or turbulences of the fluid. These tests supported the speculated effects of the tip designs: The cutout blade revealed a significant improvement of the so-called corner vortexes, which generate very high fluid velocities that lead to areas of low pressure at the back of the blade and create the desired blade force (Nolte and Ashbourne 2006). The Vortex edge also showed a more concentrated area of low pressure. Under specific light and water conditions, it is possible to see these effects during actual rowing (see figure 9.7*a* and *c*). Although these visualizations help explain the effects of certain design features on lift and drag, they do not provide measurements that allow direct comparisons or final judgements of blade designs.

It is interesting to note that practical experiences of qualified rowers support the findings from the wind tunnel test. Because of the lack of final testing methods and measurements, oar manufacturers like Durham Boat Company or Concept2 often must rely on the feedback of highly skilled and experienced rowers. On their website, for example, the Durham Boat Company (2021) suggests that their APEX-R blade—an asymmetric blade with cutouts—"provides slightly better hydrodynamic performance from the catch through the first part of the drive." Similarly, regarding the cutouts and Vortex edge, Concept2 (2021b) claims that "both of these enhancements are designed to enhance efficiency during the early part of the drive. The result is a loading profile with a firmer feel at the beginning of the drive."

There is one more indication that the cutout blade is indeed more efficient than the standard blade. Concept2 (2021b) instructs their customers that "the Smoothie2 Vortex Edge is generally used with a 1–2 cm shorter overall oar length than the Smoothie2 Plain Edge." (These two blades are shown in figure 9.6.) This means that the cutout blade, with its smaller overall surface area, must generate a higher blade force than the standard blade shape, which is only possible if the two tip features provide significant increases in the lift coefficient.

▶ **Figure 9.7** Vortex formation in the water (*a* and *c*) and in the wind tunnel (*b* and *d*) of a standard asymmetric blade (*a* and *b*) and a blade with cutouts and Vortex edge (*c* and *d*). Both blades show corner vortexes and a front vortex. However, the blade with cutouts and Vortex edge presents intensified vortex creation, which indicates larger blade force.

Pictures B and D: Haines et al. 2004. Pictures A and C courtesy Volker Nolte.

Blade Shape and Size

Blade shape and size have sparked the interest of engineers, researchers, coaches, and athletes since the beginning of the sport. Woodgate (1888) mentioned that a sculler named Cox "used very small blades" (149), which indicates that different blade sizes were used in racing as early as the late 19th century. Bourne (1925) went a step further and analyzed the influence of the path of different blade types in the water, again proof that rowers were already tinkering with blade shapes to gain some advantage. The German oar manufacturer Empacher showcases in their factory numerous wooden blades that were used as templates from the 1960s to 1980s (see figure 9.8). What all these blades had in common was that they were symmetrical relative to the longitudinal axis of the oar, but their sizes and shapes were all different. Now that composite materials are used, oar manufacturers are even more unrestricted when designing new blade types.

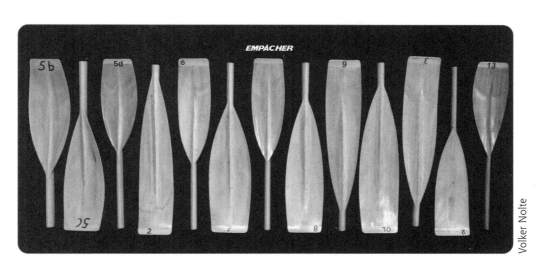

Volker Nolte

▶ **Figure 9.8**   A show board at manufacturer Empacher demonstrates the variations of sculling blade shapes and sizes that were used from the 1960s to 1980s.

Although asymmetric blade shapes were mentioned by Borrmann in 1941, they were too unstable to be used in practice until Concept2 introduced the first successful asymmetric rowing blade 50 years later. Because of its shape it was called a hatchet blade and became the template for all asymmetrical blade shapes that followed. It is also sometimes called a Big Blade because its surface area was considerably larger than those of the blades before.

The asymmetric blade type proved to be advantageous compared to the symmetric blade. Rowers loved the feel and increased rowing speed of the new blade type. The hatchet blade was swiftly adopted by all oar manufacturers and underwent further development. New introductions had smaller or larger surface areas (Durham Boat Company's Little Big Blade; Croker Oars' Slick), as well as shape modifications such as cutouts (Concept2's Smoothie2 Vortex Edge) or changes to the line at the shaft end of the blade (Croker Oars' Arrow).

Figure 9.9 signifies the advantage of the new blade type. The asymmetrical shape is designed so that the main water flow across the blade moves unimpeded in a straight line. The top and bottom edges are parallel to the water plane and the blade face offers no obstacles so that the pressure gradient between front and back of the blade increases. If the blade is submerged too deeply, the flow of water is interrupted and unnecessary turbulences are generated, which cost energy and diminish the pressure gradient between front and back of the blade. The same can be observed with the old-fashioned blade, which, because of its symmetrical design and the additional rib at the shaft end of the blade, aligns at an angle to the direction of water flow and thus causes additional resistance that costs energy.

Blade efficiency can be improved either by increasing the area of the blade surface or its lift coefficient (see equation 5.15). It is therefore only logical that attempts were made to increase the area from the typical symmetrical blade to the Big Blade and then to the FatBlade. The improvements in lift coefficient will be discussed in the curvature section later in this chapter. The increase in surface area, however, is worth a closer look.

This concept is best discussed by comparing two rowing blades that are identical in all features except the surface area. We will focus on the Smoothie2 Vortex Edge blade

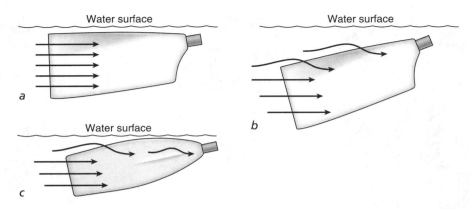

▶ **Figure 9.9** Main water flow across the front of the blade from entry to the perpendicular position with *(a)* asymmetric blade at proper depth in the water; *(b)* asymmetric blade too deep in the water; and *(c)* symmetric blade with middle rib.

Courtesy of Concept2.

and the Fat2 blade, the latter of which is 0.015 m wider (see figure 9.10*a*). Sliasas (2012) compared these two blades and found that the Fat2 blade presented a higher efficiency, especially during the first part of the drive (figure 9.10*b*). A difference in the path of the blade in the water was also observed (see figure 9.10*c*). Assuming that the drives start with both blades at 0/0 position in the water, that the rower enters and releases the blade from the water at the same oar angle, and that the drives take the same amount of time, the last position of the Fat2 blade is about 0.03 m further in x-direction. This means that the total system gained 0.03 m distance in direction of travel. The velocity of all centers of mass at the finish position is also higher. This shows that an increase in blade surface area has a positive effect on propulsion.

It is also to be expected that the blade force is higher when performing the same drive with the Fat2 blade compared to the Smoothie2 Vortex Edge blade. This means that the outboard of the oar with the Fat2 blade should be shortened to achieve a larger blade force without having to increase the handle force (as explained above).

All these measures together are good arguments for Fat2 blades being preferable to Smoothie2 blades. Tests conducted by Concept2 (2021b) confirm this advantage, with Fat2 blades showing a 1.2% increase in rowing velocity. Despite these positive results, the Fat2 blades do not enjoy great popularity in international rowing, and very few of the top teams have used them. The so-called Great Eight, a selected group of the best scullers in the world, came together at the Head of the Charles Regatta and won the Championship Eights several times using Fat2 blades. The only gold medal at World Championships won with this blade type was by the German men's 8+ in 2006. Although it was a decisive victory, the Germans abandoned their Fat2 blades after coming second in the World Championships the following year. Arguably the biggest surprise victory by a rower using the FatBlade was achieved by Greek rower Stefanos Ntouskos in the 1x at the 2020 Tokyo Olympics, where he won the gold medal.

Fat2 blades are more often used on the university level, such as Oxford Brookes University in Great Britain and University of Western Ontario in Canada, who have logged tremendous success using this type of blade. Cambridge also won the 2010 Boat Race using Fat2 blades.

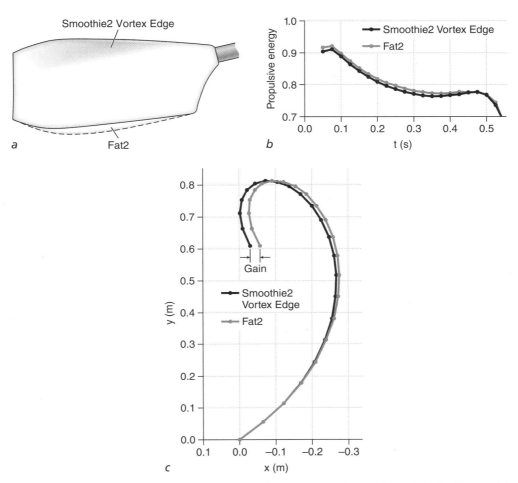

▶ **Figure 9.10** Comparison between Smoothie2 Vortex Edge and Fat2 blade shapes. *(a)* The blades are identical except for the additional surface area at the lower edge of the blade. *(b)* The Fat2 blade presents a higher efficiency. *(c)* The rower gains about 0.03 m per stroke because the Fat2 blade has less negative slip, which is shown in the path of the blade in the water during the drive.

Courtesy of Concept2.

Despite the theoretical advantage and these successes, the blades with the largest surface area never really caught on. There are probably two reasons why this is the case. First, more skill is required to handle these blades properly. Because they are larger at the widest point of the blade, they have to be carried a little higher off the water to be squared properly at the full reach position, the entry and the release require more effort and time, they are more vulnerable to wind, and the shorter outboards make balancing the boat more difficult. (Before winning the 1x with the FatBlade in 2020, Stefanos Ntouskos competed in the lightweight 4– in Rio 2016; because lightweight rowers are said to have excellent dexterity and skill, this could be a clue as to why he might have used the FatBlade to his advantage.)

Secondly, these blades are often paired with too large an outboard, so that crews struggle to perform with the higher load. Fat2 blades should be used with 0.08 to 0.15

m shorter outboard than, for example, Smoothie or Slick blade oars to bring them to a comparable gearing. Because interchangeable oars normally only allow a variation of 0.05 m, this is often not possible. For these reasons coaches and rowers may report negative experiences with the Fat2 blades and put them aside rather quickly.

Curvature

As shown in figure 9.1, a rowing blade is curved in both the vertical and longitudinal directions. Similar to the profile of an airplane wing, the blade's curvature in the longitudinal direction facilitates the generation of lift. The curvature in the vertical direction helps to keep the blade at the proper depth in the water. Both curvatures increase the drag coefficient that is particularly needed during the part of the drive when drag generates propulsion. A blade with a simple, flat surface would not be efficient in any of these areas.

Designing these curvatures is a compromise to achieve these specific characteristics while minimizing negative effects. For example, more curvature in both directions would benefit the drag coefficient when producing propulsion but would negatively affect lift forces and the ability to make a quick entry and release. Similarly, extra curvature at the top edge of blade generates some vertical forces that help to stabilize the depth of the blade in the water, and a nice side effect is that it helps to keep the blade from bouncing off the water during the recovery if the blade hits the water when the boat is unbalanced. Too much of this curvature, however, increases energy-consuming drag during the lift phase of the drive and air resistance of the blade during the recovery.

Athletes may also have individual preferences regarding a specific curvature that they feel benefits their personal rowing style. For this reason, oar manufacturers offer several blade options, although they must compromise to produce blade shapes that benefit larger groups of rowers.

Cant Angle

Cant (shown in figure 9.2) is the angle between the blade chord and the oar shaft, "with positive cant being defined as having the blade chord angled toward the bow of the shell" (Sliasas and Tullis 2009, 2861). Although oar manufacturers have tried different cant angles and collected empirical feedback from rowers, Sliasas and Tullis (2009) presented the only peer-reviewed study investigating cant that could be found, which shows that research has not paid a lot of attention to this characteristic of the blade.

Standard blades first featured a typical cant angle of −6°, which has since changed to −3° (Sliasas and Tullis 2009). Sliasas and Tullis (2009) studied various cant angles with a computational fluid dynamics model and support the change that was based on practical feedback, stating "The −3° cant angle blade features the highest overall efficiency. . .. It was found that by adding blade cant, lift force is generated earlier in the drive, resulting in a higher overall efficiency through the drive" (2861-2862). As a standard practice, manufacturers now apply the −3° angle to their blades.

Coaches and rowers must be aware that the earlier onset of lift forces during the drive increases the gearing for this part of the drive, so technique needs to be adapted or the outboard of the oar shortened. Rowers need to adjust the handle speed right after the entry when using the newer blade designs compared to the older Big Blade oars. This also means that recreational rowers who are not aiming to row with maximum velocity could either continue using Big Blade oars or pay special attention to their gearing when using more advanced types of blades.

Shaft Design

The main task of the shaft is to securely absorb the forces that are applied to it, which includes maintaining the position of the blade relative to the shaft's longitudinal axis. A shaft also must be light, aerodynamic, and suitable for everyday usage. An improvement of one of these tasks sometimes negatively influences performance in another area, so, again, compromises must be made.

The shaft must be stiff to absorb and transfer the forces, as well as possess torsional strength to hold the blade in place. These qualities are determined by the shape and size of the cross section and the strength of its material. Even the stiffest structure deforms under load, which means that there will always be some bending when exposed to the handle, oarlock, and blade forces. The amount of deflection is proportional to the applied handle force. Although the bend recoils when handle force declines toward the end of the drive, some energy is lost in this process. The softer the shaft, the larger the bend under a given load and ultimately the more energy lost.

The oar rotates around the pin on the rigger, accelerating horizontally in positive and negative directions. These movement changes cost the rower energy. Rowers talk in this context about feeling the "swing weight" of the oar, which has an impact on stroke rate when athletes get fatigued. It can be reduced by keeping its mass small and the center of mass of the oar close to its point of rotation (i.e., the pin).

The shaft is always exposed to wind resistance, especially during the recovery when the outboard accelerates in the direction of travel relative to the boat, adding to the already existing velocity of the boat. For example, a men's eight travels at 6.25 m/s at race pace, and the shaft closest to the blade moves 5.5 m/s relative to the boat. These two components together produce a speed of approximately 11.6 m/s—more than 26 mph—that the outer part of the shaft is exposed to relative to the surrounding air in calm conditions. It is therefore not surprising that the oars are responsible for 50% of the air resistance acting on the total rowing system in wind-still conditions and even more in headwind conditions (Filter 2009). Although the blade is included in this calculation, it is clear that the shaft has a substantial impact on the total wind resistance and thus efforts to consider the shaft's aerodynamics are appropriate.

Shafts must also be able to sustain normal rowing wear and tear without suffering structural damage. Oars are unintentionally hit during transportation, on docks, or on unforeseen obstacles on the water, and they must withstand such incidents without their function being impaired.

Shaft Characteristics

Shaft diameters changed dramatically with the introduction of composite material into oar manufacturing. Carbon fiber reinforced polymer (CFRP), with its high structural strength and its very low specific mass, became the perfect material for the task. The hollow circular cross section turned out to be the ideal shape for all the challenges posed to the shaft. This profile offers excellent opportunities to design a stiff shaft that also absorbs torsion very well. In addition, a relatively simple manufacturing process guarantees a consistently high production quality.

 Because the mass of a rowing shaft depends on several interdependent factors, oar manufacturers need to find design compromises. The mass of the shaft depends on the material used, its shape and diameter, and the wall thickness of the profile. For example, Ritchie (2007) reports that CFRP oar shafts are up to 60% lighter compared to previously used wooden oar shafts. The diameter of a CFRP circular tube and its wall thickness influences the stiffness of the shaft. Oar manufacturers that use a larger diameter can reduce the wall thickness (and accordingly reduce mass) to keep the strength of the shaft. Additional layers of carbon fibers on the outside of the profile will increase shaft stiffness. In fact, Laschowski and colleagues (2016) showed that designers place such additional layers strategically to produce specific deformation patterns along the shaft and influence the deflection angle at the blade end of the oar shaft, which may affect the oar "feel" for the rower. Additionally, manufacturers need to cover the very fragile and brittle carbon fiber with some extra material to protect it from catastrophic damage.

On the one hand, rowers would like to have light oars whose center of mass is situated close to the oarlock, which would reduce the necessary energy to move these oars and more easily help to achieve higher stroke rates. On the other hand, more mass away from the oarlock improves the comfort and balance. This means again that oar manufactures need to find a compromise that satisfies their customers. The oar designers can vary how much the shaft diameter decreases from the largest measure at the sleeve to the smallest at the point where it attaches to the blade. A larger taper moves the CoM towards the oarlock. The change of thickness over the length of the shaft and the placement of the additional layers of carbon fibers also affects the CoM of the shaft, respectively.

The CoM of an oar lies between the oarlock and the blade. Therefore, the masses of the inboard part of the shaft and the handle will influence its position, too. More material closer to the handle end of the shaft will move the CoM of the oar closer to the oarlock and will affect the rower's feel of the oar as described above.

As long as wood was the only material used for oar manufacturing, the development of smaller shaft diameters to minimize air resistance was limited. Since the introduction of CFRPs in boat building, however, it has become an engineering task to discover just how small the diameter of the shaft can be. The latest developments include Croker's S39 and S40 models, as well as the Skinny shaft from Concept2. Concept2 (2019) claims that their "lab tests reveal that the Skinny shaft reduces wind drag of the shaft by 25% for sculls and 50% for sweeps compared to a standard Ultralight shaft" (15). These are, of course, large improvements in drag reduction that become even more pronounced when rowing in headwind conditions. Performance rowers inevitably must take advantage of such developments.

It is relatively simple to influence shaft stiffness with the usage of carbon fiber reinforced polymers, and oar manufacturers offer shafts of varying stiffness in their product line. These shafts have exactly the same dimensions but a slightly larger mass because more material is needed to reach a higher stiffness. Laschowski and colleagues (2015) measured a mass difference of 0.1 kg between the softest (1.3 kg) and the stiffest (1.4 kg) scull in their test series.

Many rowers and coaches are adamant when it comes to a preference in oar stiffness, claiming large differences between shaft types and therefore insisting on using each stiffness only for specific groups of rowers. Recommendations of some oar manufacturers point in the same direction—for example, the softest oar shafts are often suggested for lightweight women. The following discussion will put these convictions into question.

The difference in the deflections between the softest and stiffest versions of the same type of shaft is in fact very small. Oar manufacturers have identified the difference in deflection of their softest and stiffest shafts as ≤0.01 m when exposed to 10 kg (22 lb) at the end of the shaft (Braca Sport 2021; Concept2 2021b; Empacher Bootswerft 2021).

Laschowski and colleagues (2016) confirmed these small differences in a laboratory test comparing the softest and stiffest Concept2 Skinny sculling shafts. Affixing a 201 N (24 lb) weight at the connection between shaft and blade, they measured a difference in deflection between the shafts of only about 0.01 m, expressed as a deflection angle "at most 1.18 ± 0.01°" (Laschowski et al. 2016, 1).

The practical effects of shaft stiffness were also examined in a field study in which highly qualified lightweight women single scullers repeated race pace distances with randomly assigned sculls of varied shaft stiffness (Laschowski et al. 2015). It was found that "there were small differences in the (boat) acceleration curves between the different sculls" and that the softest "oar shafts showed slightly lower rates of development to maximum force." Half of the rowers achieved a higher rowing velocity with the one set of sculls, whereas the other half of participants did so with the other; however, all "differences were on the same order of magnitude as the rower's inter-stroke inconsistencies" (Laschowski et al. 2015, 242-243). The results of these practical tests seem to refute an often-expressed assumption; namely that a softer shaft could be used to produce propulsion at the end of the drive by releasing the energy through the recoil of the larger bend of the oars (Laschowski et al. 2015).

It is interesting to note that the athletes were asked about their subjective feedback and if "they could 'feel' a difference between (the oars). However, they were unable to correctly identify the stiffness classification of each oar configuration" (Laschowski et al. 2015, 243). Also, the author did an informal test with two internationally successful male scullers. When the athletes alternated using otherwise identical pairs of sculls of the softest and the stiffest type, they claimed to be able to feel differences, but when given one scull of each stiffness to row at the same time, they were not able to identify their stiffness correctly.

It seems that the difference in stiffness that manufacturers offer is so small that general assessments are not possible. Rowers therefore do not need to worry about significant performance differences between the shaft types; individual rowing styles and preferences of athletes play a larger role in the selection of oar stiffness than objective qualifications.

Special Features

Because rowing shafts have such a large influence on the resistance of the overall rowing system, it is understandable that other measures were taken into consideration to reduce wind resistance. Leo Wolloner, the former plant manager of Empacher Bootswerft and an innovator in the field of boat manufacturing, suggested an aerodynamic cover in which oar shafts could freely turn while being held in place by the oarlock (Wolloner 1983). Filter (2009) confirmed the theorized improvement in wind tunnel testing to be a 20% reduction in wind resistance. However, the additional weight of the contraption, as well as problems associated with the different deformations of the shaft and its cover, made the design technically not feasible.

Dreher (2021) tried to improve the wind resistance of oars with what the boat company describes as an elliptical aerodynamic shaft. The shaft is designed in a way that it exposes the more aerodynamic, flat shape during the recovery, when air velocity relative to the shaft is much higher, so that air resistance is reduced during that phase of the stroke. However, this means the much larger diameter of the shaft faces the oncoming air during the drive, increasing air resistance during this phase. Additionally, the positioning of the shaft profile during the drive is not favorable for the stiffness of the oar. No studies are known to establish a final assessment of the performance of such oars.

Another way to reduce air resistance is through the installation of vortex generators on the shaft that aim to keep airflow closer to its surface and thus decrease the size of the wake behind it, resulting in a smaller drag coefficient of the shaft. Kuyt, Greidanus, and Westerweel (2016) presented calculations that suggest improvements of 0.1% to 0.4% in overall performance under specific circumstances (shaft diameter, vortex generator positioning, etc.). Although such an advantage would be considerable in international rowing, they are less relevant at all other rowing levels. In addition, questions remain about the validity of the assumptions made in the study. First, the study is based on wind tunnel tests with a constant air velocity along the shaft. Second, the advantage of the vortex generators shrinks with the size of the shaft diameter, such that newer, thinner shafts appear to benefit much less from this feature. Finally, practical considerations, such as increased weight of the oar and higher fragility during transport, make the device unusable.

The presented special features all make good theoretical sense, but seem to fail in practical applications. The vortex generators are the only features that made it into international racing, but lost influence when the thin shafts were introduced. Although there are still some improvements possible to reduce the air resistance of shafts, they are likely to be small and must pass practical tests.

Handle Design

The handle is a very important part of the oar, because it is the only contact between the rower and the propulsion-producing blade. Rowers must be able to safely and precisely apply force to it under a multitude of conditions. Temperature, humidity, rain, sweat, and dirt all influence the contact between oar and the rower. Finally, the handle needs to keep the wear and tear on the rower's hands at a minimum for many hours of use.

The handle diameter is the first parameter that needs to be investigated. Rowers need to be able to feather and square the oar easily, and a smaller force is required with a larger diameter oar. However, the rower also needs to apply high forces while keeping the handle securely and comfortably in their hand. A study by Kong and Lowe (2005) on handle diameter explains the diameters that oar manufacturers offer (see figure 9.11) and can help rowers make a good selection.

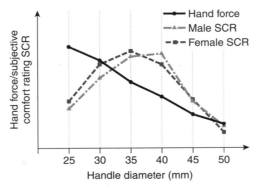

▶ **Figure 9.11** Total finger force and subjective comfort rating (SCR) depending on handle diameters.

Adapted from Kong and Lowe (2005).

Small diameters increase the pressure on the contact area of the hand and make it more difficult to feather and square the oar, whereas large diameters make the grip less secure and reduce the force that can be applied. It is therefore not surprising that handle diameters in the middle of the acceptable size range score highest in a subjective rating, and that the data given by Kong and Lowe (2005) point exactly to the range of handle diameter that are offered by oar manufacturers. Croker Oars (2021) offer handle diameters between 31 and 39 mm and Concept2 (2021b) between 32 and 37 mm for their sculls.

Oar manufacturers also offer a variety of handle materials. Older-style wooden handles are still offered, but plastic materials of various densities and porosities are becoming increasingly popular and even include contours with specific placements for each finger.

The rower's hand size and skin sensitivity should be considered when choosing the proper type of handle. Because grips are relatively inexpensive and easy to exchange, rowers should simply try certain types to select their own preferred diameter and material. Some rowers even choose to wrap their existing grip with tape or grip material similar to that used in tennis or badminton. The disadvantage of these extra materials is that they need frequent replacement, whereas the standard rowing grips are made to last much longer. There are no objective performance differences between handle designs that are offered on the market. However, comfort and reduction of injury can play a significant role in the overall well-being of a rower.

Oar Selection Guidelines

Oars offer a number of opportunities to improve performance. Blade design and oar length have the largest impact on transferring the rowers' work efficiently into propulsion. There are some general guidelines for choosing a blade, but rowers are well advised to try out which type works best for them, because once this decision is made, the blade is affixed to the shaft and can no longer be changed. More efficient blade designs often require more skill and involve a commitment from the rower to gain such skill over time. Each blade design also has its most efficient range of oar length, which needs to be taken into consideration. Modern oars allow rowers to easily manipulate inboard and outboard lengths within their construction range. This allows the rower to set their best fit lengths, which may require some experimentation. Oar length most likely has the largest impact on performance and therefore needs to be chosen very carefully.

Shaft diameter is a simple choice—the advantage of a thinner shaft on an otherwise identical oar is theoretically so evident that it will be applicable to all crews. Shaft stiffness is a personal decision in the broadest sense because differences are negligible and have been shown to have very little influence on the performance. The choice of a specific handle grip, in contrast, is entirely personal and must be tailored to the individual athlete.

Understandably, the large number of options to consider can make it difficult or even overwhelming for a rower to select the best oar. Regardless of these challenges, athletes should be encouraged to try out different oars and determine the effects on rowing performance. These hands-on experiences will help rowers become more knowledgeable and more comfortable with testing regimens.

Practical Testing

Although research over the last 150 years has delivered tremendous understanding about the biomechanical impact of boats and oars, not all equipment questions can be answered on a purely academic level. The practical use of rowing equipment is dependent on many factors that vary with the individual crew and the surrounding environment. Athletes not only differ in their anthropometrics and skills, but also in their physiological and mental abilities, and they must be able to continue rowing without being able to adjust their rigging in constantly changing environmental conditions.

It is therefore essential that practical tests are conducted to verify the value of theoretical considerations, and all coaches and rowers are encouraged to execute such tests within their abilities. It is important that anyone who runs such tests organizes them in such a way that their results are meaningful and usable. For this purpose, such tests must be objective, reliable, valid, and practical.

Objectivity

An objective test should be free from any bias. This means that the execution of the test must not be affected by any subjective influence and that anyone who interpreted the results would come to the same conclusion. If, for example, a crew wants to compare two different shells to see which fits them better, they must value each boat in the same way, use the same rigging, and have enough training time in each boat that they feel equally comfortable in both. If a coach or athlete favors a boat because of features (such as seat comfort or adjustments to footstretcher position), color or price, it will most likely affect the test results. Announcement or information about any outcome results during the tests and before all trials are finished may influence the rowers' effort and should therefore be avoided. If an outcome parameter (e.g., boat velocity or power output) is displayed on the same monitor that rowers use to receive stroke rate feedback, these fields on the monitor must be covered.

Reliability

The degree to which a test produces the same results when repeated gives an indication how reliable it is. If, for example, the effect of two different blade types is compared, test procedures are more reliable and trustworthy when several crews participate in the test and reach the same conclusion or the same crew repeats the test several times with matching results. Trials must be performed on the same stretch of water, at the same air and water temperature (e.g., same time of the day), using clear directional and distance markers, and ideally in a wind-still environment. Measurement equipment (e.g., stopwatches or force transducers) must be accurate, correctly calibrated, and properly used so that the same data is continuously measured for the same performance. Moving buoys as distance markers, random motorboat waves, and ever-changing wind will reduce reliability of the results. Test procedures should be developed to make sure athletes maintain the same physiological and technical effort in each test run. Therefore, measurement equipment should be used that helps control parameters that need to be kept constant for all test trials.

Validity

Test procedures also must be valid, which means that they actually measure what they are intending to measure. If the goal of a test procedure is to identify which of two boat designs performs better on a winding 5 km head race course, tests on a straight 500 m course are not very meaningful. Similarly, when comparing the performance of two different outboard lengths in a 2,000 m race, test procedures need to mimic rowing speeds and stroke rates that are used in such a race. Testing the two oar options at 20 spm during an endurance training session will not produce a valid result.

Practicality

Of course, such tests must also fit the whole club and training environment. Although equipment tests are highly encouraged, they must be planned thoroughly and should support the overall training plan. The fundamental basis of the test must be first be considered, then the timing, wind and weather conditions, and other logistics need to be organized. Instead of interrupting the training process, tests can serve as exciting highlights that invigorate training and lead to performance improvements.

Sample Testing Procedures

As discussed in chapter 7, it is imperative that only one variable is changed and compared at a time. Head-style trialing is also recommended so that every run is performed consistently over the whole distance without influence of other crews. Side-by-side races may affect the effort of a crew, depending on how the racing unfolds.

The following sections describe some examples of testing procedures that have already been used successfully.

1,000 to 2,000 m Races With Control Crews

These tests can be done in the actual boat class that the crew intends to race. To account for changes in wind conditions and for the increasing fatigue, one or more other crews perform the same time trials without any changes in equipment. These crews are used as a control group and are often called constants. At least two time trials should be conducted with a long rest in between, but still performed as close together as possible to maintain the same initial conditions (e.g. water temperature, wind direction, etc.). If possible, the trials could be repeated on another day. The order in which the configurations A (e.g., certain oar length or blade type) and B (e.g., shorter oars or different blade type) are trialed should be random and then reversed, if repeated. If control crews are used, they need to row as close as possible to the trial crew without interfering with the other crews to make sure that conditions are the same. Ideally, the crews should perform each trial with a consistent effort or stroke rate, beginning the trial with a so-called flying start so that the effort can be kept consistent over the full trial distance and the start performance will not influence the results. Time trials need to be done in head-style format, so that crews' performances do not affect each other. If the start or sprints are considered to be important for the evaluation of the configurations, they must be repeated exactly the same way for all trials.

If the outcome measure is the time used for the test distance, the configuration with which the shortest time was achieved would be considered the preferred one. The outcome measure could also be the subjective stress perception by the crew. In this case, the preferred configuration would be the one with which the crew feels to be able to maintain a certain stroke rate or boat speed more easily.

6 × 1,000 m (or Up to 10 × 500 m) Trials

The test configurations are performed in the following order: A, B, B, A, A, B, B, A. If a second crew is available, they should perform these in the opposite order. Careful consideration must be given to the effort with which the crew need to perform the trials. Of course, the effort must be controlled and as consistent as possible. Stroke rate or power output could serve as control measure for effort, and rowers need to be instructed accordingly. Figure 9.12 shows example data from a test of two different boat types to find the one that best performed for this particular crew.

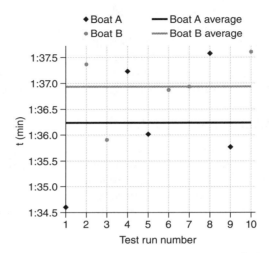

▶ **Figure 9.12** Results from a 10 × 500 m women's 8+ test of two different boat types executed by one crew. Boat A performed an average of 0.7 s better over the 500 m course.

It is important that the wind influence is minimized, which means that all trials should be performed in the same direction and wind speeds should be monitored. Some wind fluctuations must always be expected and should balance out over many test runs, but if wind changes become too large, tests should be halted and repeated at a better time. It may be the goal of the test to find which oar length is the best in a headwind, in which case tests can be run rowing into the wind. However, one needs to be aware that headwind conditions affect race times more than tailwind.

The outcome measure is the average time for all trials with the respective test configuration. The individual rowers' personal feedback could also be used as additional information. If subjective information is used, athletes must submit feedback individually, independent of other influences and before any test results are announced. Such assessments may explain or support certain observations or circumstances, but should not be used as main or sole decision-making factors.

Step Test

For a step test, the rower needs to row as consistently as possible for 30 s at a set velocity, which increases in predetermined increments for 10 intervals with 90 s of rest between each. For this purpose, the rower uses the last 30 s of the rest time to bring the boat up to the desired speed, which is then maintained for the time of the interval. After the 10 intervals, sufficient rest is taken. The rower then performs the same intervals in the opposite direction while stepping down from the highest velocity in the same increments as before to ensure that the respective boat speed is executed in the same part of the water. This test should only be conducted in ideal conditions with no or only very little wind, although wind influences should balance each other out. The second test configuration then needs to be repeated on the same stretch of water. A well-trained athlete can perform both step tests directly one after the other to take advantage of the environmental conditions.

The actual boat velocity and the handle power of the rower need to be measured and recorded for further analysis. The averages of all the two corresponding steps are calculated and can then be graphed (see figure 9.13) or subjected to further statistical analysis.

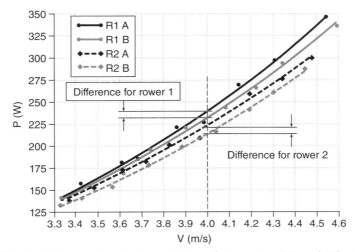

▶ **Figure 9.13** Data from a step test, consisting of two series (S1 and S2) at various, predetermined velocities with two different blade types A and B, executed by two single scullers R1 and R2 who were using the blades alternatively. For each blade type, the scullers rowed S1 in one direction, while S2 was run immediately after a turn in the opposite direction. The results of each predetermined velocity in the two directions were then averaged to account for wind, water depth, etc. and show in the graph as points. Differences in power output at boat velocity 4 m/s for both rowers are indicated as an example, and both rowers needed less power with blade type B, which would therefore be considered preferable. (Tests were performed with Nielsen-Kellerman EmPower Oarlocks and SpeedCoach systems.)

The goal is to identify how much handle power a rower has to generate for a specific boat velocity. The test configuration that allows the rower to achieve the same boat velocity with a lower handle power is, of course, the preferred one.

Conclusion

Oars and their dimensions play an enormous role in the sporting performance of a rower. Rowers today have a wide selection of oars consisting of the various choices of handles, shafts, and blades. The selection must of course accommodate the comfort and rowing style of the athletes, but should be influenced above all by performance criteria which of course is even more important at higher levels of competition, where success in international races often depends on fractions of seconds.

Making the right choice of oars can be difficult, because the variety of dimensions, blades, and shafts is enormous. Scientific research has provided essential guidance, but the ultimate fine-tuning must be done through the athlete's own experiences and with accurate testing. Of course, it can be helpful to learn what successful rowers use, but simply adopting their oar choices and dimensions often does not lead to success. It is indispensable to have one's own experience.

PART

III

Physiology
of Rowing

Jeremy Ivey

Overview of Rowing Physiology

Gunnar Treff, PhD

The fastest openweight class rowers cover the 2,000 m race distance in times ranging from 5:18 to 7:07. Depending on the crew and the environment, the duration may be considerably longer, but the intensity is still very high. To generate the corresponding pace, rowers must be able to generate forces equivalent to approximately 450 N per stroke (Secher 1993), peaking at about 900 N (Volianitis et al. 2020). This combination of high-intensity, full-body endurance exercise with the generation of relatively high forces determines the physiological demands of successful competitive rowers (Steinacker et al. 1998).

Aerobic Capacity

The race duration necessitates a high aerobic contribution to the total energy turnover. Aerobic contribution depends on a metabolic pathway that requires oxygen. During high-intensity exercise like racing, carbohydrates are the main energy source of this metabolic pathway, but during lower intensity training, fat is an important energy source, too. The total aerobic capacity quantifies the volume of oxygen that an athlete can extract per minute from the inspired air and is a measure of the capacity for aerobic energy production. The key variable is called *maximum oxygen uptake* or $\dot{V}O_2max$, and it is typically very high in rowers, up to 7 L/min in elite male rowers (Nielsen and Christensen 2020) or above 4 L/min in elite female rowers (Bourdin et al. 2017).

Any $\dot{V}O_2$ value is the result of a simple equation (equation 10.1):

$$\dot{V}O_2 = \dot{Q} \times avDO_2 \tag{10.1}$$

where $\dot{Q}$ is cardiac output, or the volume of blood that the heart circulates within the body per minute; and $avDO_2$ is the arteriovenous oxygen (O_2) difference, or the difference (D) between the arterial blood (a), which is oxygenated after passing the lungs, and the oxygen content of the venous blood (v), which is partly deoxygenated after passing the muscles, brain, and other tissues that utilize oxygen to various degrees. Maximum $avDO_2$ is not very different between trained and untrained humans (Hagberg et al. 1985), although it tends to be higher in athletes.

Cardiac output ($\dot{Q}$) is very adaptable and clearly different between trained and untrained persons (Ekblom and Hermansen 1968; Schierbauer et al. 2021). To understand how to modify $\dot{V}O_2$max we need to have a closer look at $\dot{Q}$, which is the product of the following equation (equation 10.2):

$$\dot{Q} = HR \times SV \tag{10.2}$$

Here, cardiac output ($\dot{Q}$) is the result of heart rate (HR) multiplied by stroke volume (SV), or the volume of blood that is ejected per heartbeat.

Maximum heart rate is not different between trained and untrained persons—if anything, it is lower in those who are endurance trained (Rowell 1986). But cardiac stroke volume is much higher in athletes (Ekblom and Hermansen 1968), because the chambers of the heart increase in response to endurance training. This cardiac remodeling is the consequence of two stimuli: cardiac volume stress and cardiac pressure stress. Cardiac volume stress is dominant in endurance disciplines like running, whereas cardiac pressure stress dominates in strength sports (Baggish et al. 2008). In rowing, which is a mixture of strength and endurance exercise, the interplay of both stimuli causes a homogenous enlargement of all four chambers (Baggish et al. 2010).

This homogenous enlargement is not self-evident, because the exerted pressures in these chambers are very different, ranging from approximately 5 to 140 mmHg depending on the phase of the pulse. In addition, the cardiac compliance (the ability of the heart chambers to respond to increases in transmural pressure) of a healthy rower's heart is not reduced, because the physiological cardiac hypertrophy is normally not accompanied by a disadvantageously enlarged wall thickness (Wasfy et al. 2015). Conversely, a high degree of cardiac hypertrophy has been reported in strength athletes, resulting in impaired diastolic function that reduces the heart's ability to sufficiently fill with blood (Baggish et al. 2008).

Cardiac Stroke Volume and Blood Volume

Hence, a rower's heart is large, strong, and very compliant—all adaptations that are necessary to generate a high stroke volume (Levine 2008). The functional and morphological adaptations facilitating the high cardiac stroke volumes of rowers are mediated through several mechanisms. One of them is the sitting position, where the large and synchronous working muscles of the legs are not far below the heart. Consequently, the blood must be circulated over a shorter distance against the force of gravity and therefore venous return to the heart is facilitated (Volianitis et al. 2020). Moreover, rowers have a very high total blood volume (Treff et al. 2013). Both of these characteristics support the increase in stroke volume via the so-called Frank–Starling mechanism, where a high cardiac preload leads to a fibrillar stretch of the myocardium, which, in turn, allows for a higher stroke volume than without prestretching (Levine et al. 1991).

Body Mass and Skeletal Muscle

The high blood volume of elite rowers is partly a result of high body mass of rowers (approximately 93.0 kg in males or 73.5 kg in females) (Kerr et al. 2007) and an expansion of the plasma volume (i.e. the liquid part of the blood) (Treff et al. 2013). The increase in plasma volume is also seen in other endurance athletes such as runners or cyclists, in whom it frequently leads to a lower hemoglobin concentration (i.e. the amount of hemoglobin per volume of blood in grams per liter) compared to untrained persons. This is noteworthy because hemoglobin transports the majority of oxygen in the blood and is therefore essential for the aerobic metabolism. The lowered concentration is mainly a result of a dilution effect caused by the disproportionate increase in plasma volume relative to the increase in absolute hemoglobin mass (i.e. the absolute amount of hemoglobin in the body in grams). In contrast, in rowers the increase in hemoglobin mass is approximately proportional, so that their hemoglobin concentration is not different from untrained persons (Telford et al. 1994).

This phenomenon occurs because hemoglobin mass is closely related to muscle mass, which is high in rowers. In contrast to "pure" strength athletes, skeletal muscle of rowers has a very high percentage (approximately 80%) of oxidative type I fibers (Larsson and Forsberg 1980; Roth et al. 1993). These fibers are relatively slow, but their mitochondria are able to produce energy through oxidative processes, so they can utilize the oxygen from hemoglobin to produce aerobic energy for muscle contraction, leading to deoxygenation in the blood. This oxidative capacity, which could roughly be described as the oxygen consumption capacity of the muscle, closes the link to the previously mentioned $avDO_2$.

Pulmonary Function

The lung is where the blood (or more specifically mainly the hemoglobin) is reoxygenated with O_2 from ambient air that was inhaled into the lungs. Despite the lungs being a vital component in the supply of oxygen, this important organ is not adaptive to endurance training. Combined with several other mechanical, hematological, and cardiovascular factors, this lack of adaptation contributes to the phenomenon of exercise-induced arterial hypoxemia, which is frequently observed in highly trained rowers. Arterial hypoxemia is characterized by a substantially low level of oxygen (i.e., hypo-oxygenation) in the arterial blood after passing the lung—that is, the deoxygenated blood returning from the active tissues is not sufficiently reoxygenated before being circulated back to supply oxygen to the muscle and brain (Dempsey and Wagner 1999). However, even without specific adaptation in the lung, the pulmonary function of rowers is generally high, with vital capacities of 7 to 9 L, which is above the predicted values for their body size (Volianitis et al. 2020). These high values may be interpreted as a mixture of a physiological prerequisite, anatomy, and functional adaptation of the respiratory muscles in competitive rowers.

However, aerobic metabolism does not provide more than approximately 80% of the required energy in a rowing race (Pripstein et al. 1999; Roth et al. 1983; Volianitis et al., 2020) and therefore does not cover the energy demand completely. Further, the relative and absolute contribution of aerobic metabolism changes throughout the race, as illustrated in figure 10.1 (Hartmann and Mader 2005; Roth et al. 1983). In addition, the aerobic system is relatively slow. This is partly because all the oxygen supply mechanisms just described need time to function at the necessary level. Hence, there must be additional metabolic pathways. These are the anaerobic or nonoxidative pathways, which are much faster and can provide a relatively high amount of energy instantaneously or nearly instantaneously.

Anaerobic Metabolism

At the start of a 2,000 m rowing race the energy required to accelerate the boat is very high. The demand exceeds what the relatively slow aerobic metabolism can generate at this moment. At this earliest stage of the race, the so-called anaerobic alactic metabolism generates the highest percentage of energy, mainly derived from immediately available

▶ **Figure 10.1** Schematic representation of the percentage energy contribution during a six-minute rowing race.

Adapted by permission from U. Hartmann and A. Mader, "Rowing Physiology," in *Rowing Faster*, 1st ed., edited by V. Nolte (Champaign, IL: Human Kinetics, 2005).

stores of adenosine triphosphate (ATP) and phosphocreatine (PCr) in the muscles. It is worth mentioning that the timely "delay" in the provision of energy from the aerobic system might be reduced by an effective warm-up, but there is insufficient evidence to provide accurate guidelines in this area (Sousa et al. 2014).

After a few seconds of the race, the anaerobic lactic metabolism provides more and more energy in order to maintain the high demand and lactate is produced. The lactate accumulates in the blood, and it should be noted that the aerobic metabolism keeps the blood lactate concentration within reasonable limits by oxidizing it and using it as a fuel. Hence, aerobic and anaerobic pathways work hand in hand as their relative contribution changes during the race (figure 10.1).

Even though the anaerobic lactic system provides only a relatively small amount of the energy required during a 2,000 m rowing race, it is essential to facilitate the very high energy flow rate. The high blood lactate concentrations associated with this metabolic pathway have been used for many decades with the intent of providing information on the level of anaerobic contribution. However, a given lactate concentration is not only the result of its production, but also of its oxidation or consumption, and this is why postrace or training blood lactate concentrations are a very limited quantitative measure of anaerobic contribution. Nevertheless, postrace blood lactate concentrations of 23 mmol/L or more and the extreme acidosis, with pH values reported as low as 6.74, clearly indicate that anaerobic lactic metabolism is very important for competitive rowing (Nielsen 1999). We will have a more detailed look on the aspects of exercise metabolism in the next chapter and will also learn why a high aerobic capacity is indispensable for a good end-of-race sprint.

Anthropometry

Aside from these physiological and metabolic aspects, anthropometry is another determinant of rowing performance. The magnitude of several variables that characterize successful rowers (e.g. very high $\dot{V}O_2$max) is partly mediated by their body dimensions. As discussed in chapter 9, anthropometry has factored heavily in elite competitive rowing over the past several decades. Successful rowers are relatively tall—which is a prerequisite for optimal leverage over extended work distances, because physical work is distance multiplied by force—and are usually relatively heavy as a result of their height and large muscle mass (Treff et al. 2013). It is worth mentioning that these anthropometric traits are useful in predicting career success already in junior rowers. Body heights of 190 cm to 196 cm for male or 178 cm to 184 cm for female U19 rowers and a body mass of 84 kg to 93 kg or 68 kg to 73 kg, respectively, have been proposed as normative values for this group (Winkert et al. 2019).

Conclusion

Successful elite rowers are highly trained endurance athletes with a high aerobic capacity. They have a large muscle mass that is well adapted for aerobic metabolism, together with a high cardiac output, expanded blood volume, and a high oxygen transport capacity. However, the energetic demand in competitive rowing is near maximum and stresses all metabolic pathways, which is why anaerobic metabolism is also essential for racing fast. The percentage contribution of the metabolic pathways alternates throughout the race, but each metabolic pathway is essential and active to varying extents.

CHAPTER 11

Rowing Metabolism

Gunnar Treff, PhD

Exercise metabolism describes the process of converting potential energy taken into the body into physical energy via chemical reactions. The nutrients that provide energy are carbohydrates, fat, and protein, which are available in tissues and blood. During any physical activity, most of the energy demand comes from contracting skeletal muscle. That is certainly true for rowing, where energy use is enormously high during racing and relatively high even during low-intensity training (Winkert et al., 2022).

Water, proteins, and electrolytes are indispensable for proper metabolic functioning. Proteins are complex molecules that form the basis of the cell structure (e.g., membranes) and act as biocatalysts (e.g., enzymes). Water and the dissolved electrolytes shape the cellular and extracellular environments, between which a connection across cell membranes is possible via osmosis and active transport. However, when we talk about muscle contraction, we will inevitably come across the molecule adenosine triphosphate (ATP), which is the universal fuel for any muscle contraction.

Adenosine triphosphate is an energy-rich molecule with three phosphoryl groups, which can be broken down to adenosine diphosphate (ADP) or adenosine monophosphate (AMP). The breakdown of ATP releases energy that is used for muscle contraction, resulting in a lower energetic level of the leftover. In return, ADP and AMP can be resynthesized to ATP. There are different pathways for ATP (re)synthesis, and these pathways differentiate between aerobic and anaerobic metabolism. However, the fuel for muscle contraction is always ATP, regardless of the metabolic pathway it is provided by.

Muscle Contraction

According to the sliding filament model (Huxley 1974), physiological muscle contraction is a process where the muscle shortens and relaxes. For this purpose, the filaments actin and myosin (figure 11.1) slide past each other without altering their length.

The process is similar to the change of the oar from recovery to the catch in rowing. At the catch, the oar has an angle that allows propulsion, and the rower is energy rich and under tension. Similarly, the myosin head changes from its recovery (or finish) position (45°) to its catch position (90°). In the 90° position, the myosin head will connect to an actin filament (the so-called cross-binding). During the drive phase the swinging of the myosin head then moves the actin filament until the myosin head achieves the recovery (or finish) position (i.e., energy-low 45° position). This sliding

The collegial discussion and critical review of this chapter by Dr. Hugo Maciejewski and Dr. Sebastian Gehlert is gratefully acknowledged.

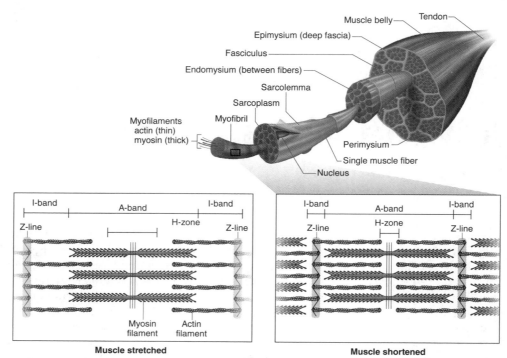

▶ **Figure 11.1** Gross and subcellular microscopic organization of skeletal muscle.

phase of the various myosin heads from 90° to 45° throughout the muscle filaments causes the shortening of the sarcomere and ultimately results in muscle contraction. However, at the end of this molecular drive phase, myosin is still connected to the actin filament and energy is required to release the connection. Note that this complex process occurs in several myosin heads at the same time and in an alternating order—that is, when one connection between myosin head and actin is released, the connection persists elsewhere at the same moment. This alternating order maintains the tension in the muscle fiber and prevents the filaments from slipping back.

The motor for this drive is sometimes termed a *molecular engine* that is fed by ATP. This engine does not work without neuronal excitation from the central nervous system (i.e., brain and spinal cord), where efferent motor neurons initiate muscular contraction in response to various feedback loops.

The basics of muscular contraction are well described in several textbooks of work physiology. However, to highlight the role of ATP, we will have a very brief look at its role during muscular contraction. ATP that is bound to the myosin heads in the 45° position is hydrolyzed as a result of ATPase activity and broken down to ADP and one phosphate ion (Pi, see equation 11.1). ATPase is an enzyme that resides in the head of the myosin. When ATP binds to this enzyme, it releases energy and brings the myosin head to its energy-rich 90° ("catch") position. Due to the free junction sites, the myosin head will now connect to the actin filament in the 90° position and release the phosphoryl group (i.e., Pi) that is left from the ATP breakdown. The release of the phosphate ion causes the "drive" of the myosin head, or an active swing back into its relaxed (finish) 45° position. Now, resynthesized ATP (if available) will bind to the myosin head, which initiates the release of myosin from actin. If calcium ion (Ca^{2+}) concentration is high due to ongoing neural activation, the process will repeat.

In this way ATP provides the energy for muscular contraction, but because stores are very limited, it must be resynthesized to provide energy for ongoing physical activity. Depending on the required rate of energy flow, the total energy demand, and substrate availability, different pathways contribute to a certain percentage to the metabolism. We will now explore these different pathways, which take place in mitochondria (aerobic metabolism) and in the cytosol (anaerobic metabolism).

Metabolic Pathways for ATP (Re)synthesis

A rowing race is a suitable model to illustrate the different metabolic pathways in a schematic way. We will introduce the pathways step by step according to their dominance during the race. We will also discuss the metabolic particularities of racing versus training, because even if racing is more spectacular, athletes spend the overwhelming proportion of their time in the boat training. However, we have to be aware that those different metabolic pathways are tightly linked and share the purpose of maintaining the required rates of ATP resynthesis for the whole organism. It is never one pathway or the other; rather, it is always one pathway dominating, with the others acting in changing percentages.

Key Point

Anaerobic alactic, anaerobic lactic, and aerobic pathways contribute to ATP resynthesis in energy metabolism.

Anaerobic Alactic Metabolism

At the start of a race, the mass of the crew, boat, and oars have to be immediately accelerated. The necessary instantaneous energy is mainly provided by the anaerobic alactic system through ATP—and phosphocreatine (PCr), as we will see below—that is stored in the muscle. This energy is directly available, and as described before, contraction occurs.

$$ATP + H_2O \rightarrow ADP + Pi + H^+ \tag{11.1}$$

This is a hydrolytic reaction, where ATP is split in a chemical reaction with water to ADP and phosphate. It is a super quick reaction without oxygen consumption—that is why it is *anaerobic* or *nonoxidative*. However, ATP stores are very small and the directly available ATP would be depleted after approximately 2 s (Hargreaves and Spriet 2020). If this were the only energetic pathway, muscle contraction would theoretically stop after the second rowing stroke of the race and ATP concentration would then be decreased to zero. It is important to understand that ATP concentration is only very transiently lowered in the exercising muscle under normal exercise situations, because ATP is rapidly resynthesized.

Such immediate ATP resynthesis is a result of phosphorylation of ADP utilizing phosphocreatine (PCr), which is another energy-rich phosphate that is directly available in the muscle. This reaction is shown in equation 11.2.

$$PCr + ADP + H^+ \rightarrow Creatine + ATP \tag{11.2}$$

PCr is cleaved when ADP increases within the cell. This reaction is catalyzed by the enzyme creatine kinase, which is sometimes used in rowing as a marker of muscular stress or more specifically myofibrillar destruction (Mougios 2007). PCr enables the resynthesis of ATP via phosphorylation so that once again ATP is available for muscle contraction without oxygen consumption. Please note that lactate is not produced by this reaction, which is why it is categorized as *anaerobic alactic*.

However, even though the PCr stores within the muscle are approximately 10 times higher than those of ATP, the PCr would theoretically be consumed after a few seconds of such an extreme activity like a rowing race (Hargreaves and Spriet 2020). Indeed, experiments have shown a 57% decrease in PCr after a 6 s sprint (Gaitanos et al. 1993). The involvement of another system of the anaerobic alactic metabolism, the adenylate system, does not change that considerably (equation 11.3).

$$2\ ADP \rightarrow ATP + AMP \tag{11.3}$$

Anaerobic Lactic Metabolism

But a rowing race is not finished after 6 s. There is obviously another dynamically responding and powerful system to provide the ATP to maintain race pace. This leads us directly to the second anaerobic pathway, which is anaerobic glycolysis, whereby glycogen is broken down to generate ATP during a reaction called *phosphorylation* (i.e., attachment of a phosphoryl group). Glycogen is a form of sugar, more specifically a polysaccharide, that is stored in the muscle, liver, and other mammalian cells. It is worth mentioning that the ATP yield is higher for glycogen than for pure glucose, which underlines the importance of ensuring glycogen stores are well loaded before endurance training. Again, oxygen is not utilized during this anaerobic or nonoxidative reaction, but lactate is produced (equation 11.4). That is why it is sometimes categorized as *anaerobic lactic*.

$$Glycogen_n + 3\ ADP + 3\ Pi \rightarrow Glycogen_{n-1} + 2\ Lactate + 3\ ATP \tag{11.4}$$

Anaerobic glycolysis starts so rapidly that after approximately 6 s of intense exercise, both anaerobic glycolysis and PCr breakdown contribute energy to exercise to a similar extent (Gaitanos et al. 1993). Moreover, this reaction allows for a higher energetic flow. Note that the lactate produced during this reaction is also an energy-rich molecule. We will return to this important fact later.

Aerobic Metabolism

Despite its favorable energy flow rate, anaerobic glycolysis alone or even in combination with the anaerobic alactic pathway would not allow rowers to row 2,000 m as fast as they actually do, because the total capacity for ATP production over the duration of a race would not be high enough. Furthermore, intramuscular homeostasis would be impaired too quickly. Therefore, an additional energy system must provide a greater total amount of energy. This system has to be efficient in terms of the energy provided per given amount of substrate, be fast enough to deliver energy several seconds after the initiation of an activity, and should ideally reuse some of the energy-rich "leftovers" produced by anaerobic glycolysis (i.e., lactate). All of these specifications are met by the aerobic metabolism, which contributes roughly 80% of the total energy demand of a rowing race (Pripstein et al. 1999; Roth et al. 1983; Secher, Espersen, and Binkhorst 1982; Steinacker 1993; Volianitis et al. 2020).

Oxidative Phosphorylation via Carbohydrates

Aerobic metabolism is based on a chemical reaction termed *oxidative phosphorylation*. Here, ATP is produced while oxygen, carbohydrates (glycogen and to a lesser extent glucose), and eventually fat are utilized to attach the desired phosphoryl group to ADP to resynthesize ATP. It is important to note that even at very low intensities, where fat is the major substrate, carbohydrates are necessary for energy production in healthy humans who are on a mixed diet. The reaction is summarized in equation 11.5.

$$\text{Glucose} + 6\ O_2 + 36\ \text{ADP} \rightarrow 6\ CO_2 + 6\ H_2O + 36\ \text{ATP} \qquad (11.5)$$

You will notice that the amount of ATP produced in equation 11.5 is considerably larger than in the previous equations, indicating a far higher efficiency of oxidative phosphorylation than the nonoxidative variant summarized in equation 11.4. The price to pay is that oxidative phosphorylation requires a longer time to reach full production rate, because oxygen delivery through increases in ventilation and cardiac output needs time to occur and the energy flow rate is lower. However, the advantage is that the total amount of energy is high and the lactate produced during nonoxidative phosphorylation (equation 11.4) can be oxidized. In this way, the previously and simultaneously produced lactate can be utilized as fuel during the race, thereby regulating the arterial lactate concentration and sparing glucose. Even though this capability of aerobic metabolism is nothing new in the scientific world, it is often missed in the practical world of rowing, thus we will dedicate a brief passage to this area.

Oxidation of Lactate

Endurance training reduces arterial lactate concentration for a given work rate, which becomes apparent in the right-shifted blood lactate-to-power curve (i.e., reduced blood lactate concentration at a given power output) after a period of predominantly aerobic training. However, it is not correct to interpret this lower blood lactate concentration at submaximum intensities as reduced lactate production per se, because the blood lactate concentration during or after exercise lasting longer than approximately 20 s is not equal to the lactate production. Rather, it is the difference of lactate produced and lactate removed (i.e., net lactate). A lowered blood lactate concentration at a given absolute workload in an individual therefore might theoretically be a result of diminished appearance or reduced production of a higher rate of oxidation through the aerobic metabolism (Bergman et al. 1999a, MacRae et al. 1992). In classic experimental studies, where oxidation of lactate was validly quantified via tracer labeling (Bergman et al. 1999a, Bergman et al. 1999b), it has been demonstrated that lactate oxidation was markedly increased after a 9 wk training, thereby leading to a decreased arterial blood lactate concentration in combination with lowered production at a given absolute submaximum mechanical power output (see figure 11.2). It is worth mentioning that at a high relative intensity, participants were still able to release lactate even at a higher rate than before, but their ability to remove or oxidize the lactate disproportionately increased (Bergman et al. 1999a, Bergman et al. 1999b).

Key Point

Blood lactate concentration is always the result of lactate appearance and removal, mainly via oxidation.

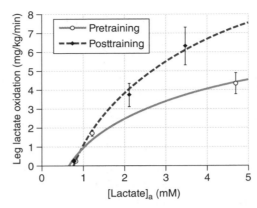

▶ **Figure 11.2** Relationship between tracer-measured leg lactate oxidation rate and arterial lactate concentration ([Lactate]$_a$) before and after 9 weeks of training. Values are means ± standard error for 7 to 9 subjects.

Reprinted by permission from B.C. Bergman, E.E. Wolfel, G.E. Butterfield, et al., "Active Muscle and Whole Body Lactate Kinetics After Endurance Training in Men," Journal of Applied Physiology 87, no. 5 (1999a): 1684-1696.

The proportion of lactate oxidation is substantial. At rest, about 50% of the lactate disposal is oxidized. But during low to moderate intensity (i.e., 50%-75% of $\dot{V}O_2$max), about 75% to 80% is oxidized, as apparent in figure 11.3 (Mazzeo et al. 1986).

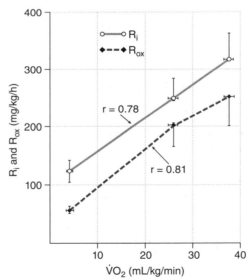

▶ **Figure 11.3** Lactate disposal (Ri) and oxidation (R$_{ox}$) rates plotted as functions of oxygen consumption rate ($\dot{V}O_2$) in 6 men at rest and exercise power outputs eliciting 50% and 75% of $\dot{V}O_2$max. Values are arithmetic means ± standard error of measurement.

Reprinted by permission from R.S. Mazzeo, G.A. Brooks, D.A. Schoeller, and T.F. Budinger, "Disposal of Blood [1-13c] Lactate in Humans During Rest and Exercise," Journal of Applied Physiology 60, no. 1 (1986): 232-241.

These few examples, selected from a large body of evidence, illustrate how lactate links nonoxidative glycolytic metabolism to oxidative metabolism, in which substantial amounts of lactate are oxidized, or in other words, used as fuel to drive ATP synthesis.

As shown in figure 11.3, lactate oxidation increases with exercise intensity. This helps to spare glucose, because the rate of lactate appearance clearly surpasses glucose rate of disappearance (Bergman et al. 1999a, Bergman et al. 1999b). At 55% of $\dot{V}O_2$max the rate of lactate oxidation already exceeds that of glucose and a marked increase in lactate oxidation is paralleled by a decrease in blood glucose oxidation. Noteworthy, if exogeneous lactate is experimentally added, even more blood glucose will be spared (Miller et al. 2002). This experiment and others clearly indicate that lactate is also an important fuel in quantitative terms, especially during exercise.

Lactate oxidation occurs in a variety of tissues like active skeletal muscle (Stanley et al. 1986), the heart (Gertz et al. 1988), and the brain (Pellerin et al. 1998). Apparently, not all lactate is immediately oxidized at its origin, therefore it accumulates in the active muscle, then in the blood, before it is distributed to distant tissues. But the fate of lactate is not limited to oxidation—it is also an important gluconeogenetic precursor for the liver or in resting muscle, so that substantial proportions of lactate are finally transformed to glucose. This process is augmented by endurance training, and though it is hard to determine at what intensity this halts, it has been shown to increase to at least 65% of $\dot{V}O_2$max in endurance-trained individuals (Bergman et al. 2000). This led to the statement that "lactate is the most important gluconeogenic precursor during rest and exercise" (Brooks et al. 2021, 4).

The intra- and intercellular shuttling of lactate between cells of an exercising skeletal muscle, between distant skeletal muscles working at different intensities, between skeletal muscle and the heart, or to and from other tissues that express lactate that is finally oxidized or utilized for gluconeogenesis is known as *lactate shuttle theory* (Brooks 1985). Lactate shuttling is enabled by an active form of membrane-bound lactate transport via monocarboxylate transport proteins (MCTs). MCTs make it possible to transport lactate across membranes independently. Several isoforms of these transporters have been described and details would surpass the scope of this chapter. Nevertheless, it should be noted that in particular the MCT1 transporter is augmented following endurance training, thereby facilitating the availability of oxidizable substances for susceptible tissues and supporting intracellular lactate shuttling (Dubouchaud et al. 2000). Of note, lactate (and therefore exercise) contributes to the increase in MCT1 via changes of the cellular redox state and increased oxidative stress (i.e., increased reactive oxygen species production). Moreover, these lactate-signaling pathways appear to play an important role in increasing mitochondrial mass in response to exercise by working with other signaling pathways to increase the levels of proteins such as PGC-1α, which are themselves essential for promoting mitochondrial biogenesis (see Brooks 2020a for review). This led to the finding that lactate serves as a *signal molecule* for aerobic adaptation (Brooks, Brooks, and Brooks 2008). Thus, exercise-induced lactate helps improve aerobic performance, and certain levels of lactate are beneficial during training to improve oxidative capacity of skeletal muscle.

Oxidative Phosphorylation via Fat

Oxidative phosphorylation or aerobic metabolism does not solely depend on carbohydrates (i.e., glucose, glycogen, and lactate). It is also possible to synthesize ATP via beta-oxidation, whereby fatty acids stored in the adipose tissue or muscle are utilized to resynthesize ATP. This is summarized in equation 11.6.

$$\text{Palmitate} + 23\ O_2 + 130\ \text{ADP} \rightarrow 16\ CO_2 + 16\ H_2O + 130\ \text{ATP} \qquad (11.6)$$

The advantage of the utilization of fat is that even in a lean rower, the amount of energy stored as fat is huge (approximately 76,000 kcal) and the limited stores of glycogen and glucose are less stressed. However, even though the amount of ATP per unit of substrate is immense, this pathway is approximately 7% less efficient in terms of ATP per unit of oxygen compared to the aerobic ATP synthesis via carbohydrates (Hargreaves and Spriet 2020; Spriet 2014). Furthermore, this pathway is slower and needs more time to be effective.

Fat is metabolized in a process called *lipolysis* and is obtained from adipose tissue or from intramuscular triglycerides. Studies have shown that lipolysis in peripheral adipose tissue is at its maximum at very low-intensity exercise of about 25% of $\dot{V}O_2$max and declines above that, but lipolysis of intramuscular triglycerides is regulated differently and peaks at 65% of $\dot{V}O_2$max. When intensity further increases to 85% of $\dot{V}O_2$max, lipolysis of intramuscular triglycerides also stops rising and total fat oxidation decreases (Romijn et al. 1993).

The fact that oxidative metabolism provides the option to use fat and carbohydrates as a fuel and the finding that fat oxidation obviously increases leads us directly to the question: When do we utilize which nutrient?

The Crossover Concept: Metabolism Depends on Exercise Intensity and Duration

The evidence of this concept is illustrated in figure 11.4, where energy flux mediates substrate utilization as a function of exercise intensity. Following this concept, fat metabolism dominates at low intensities through biochemical adaptations that allow for sparing glycogen when glycolysis is properly matched to the turnover in the so-called tricarboxylic acid cycle (TCA), a chemical process in the mitochondria that is essential for aerobic respiration. With intensified exercise, muscle contraction and force increase, a higher proportion of "fast" glycolytic muscle fibers is utilized, and the activity of the sympathetic nervous system increases. According to Brooks and Mercier (1994), "The crossover point is the power output at which energy from carbohydrate-derived fuels predominates over energy from lipids" (2253).

Figure 11.4 illustrates that fat flux peaks at about 50% of $\dot{V}O_2$max, then decreases in absolute and relative terms (probably because of the lower efficiency) and reaches its minimum when $\dot{V}O_2$ is maximum. Hence, the energy needed for racing—where $\dot{V}O_2$ typically exceeds 90% of $\dot{V}O_2$max (Pripstein et al. 1999)—is derived almost exclusively from carbohydrate and not from fat metabolism. Fat metabolism is crucial for low-intensity training of about 60% of $\dot{V}O_2$max, whereas oxidative phosphorylation from carbohydrates is of utmost importance during racing.

At a certain point of exercise intensity, the blood lactate concentration increases. According to the crossover concept, this is the result of a shift in metabolism toward glycolysis due to the increased energy demand and not the result of an oxygen deficiency. This contrasts the traditional concept of the anaerobic threshold, where the accumulation of blood lactate is thought to be a result of a lack of cellular oxygen that limits oxidative phosphorylation (Wasserman et al. 1973). Current evidence fundamentally contradicts this traditional view (for details refer to the following excellent reviews: Clanton, Hogan, and Gladden 2013; Ferguson et al. 2018; Poole et al. 2021). Lactate formation is not caused by oxygen limitation in healthy, exercising humans—however, from a teleological point of view, it seems very reasonable to shift metabolism to glycolysis when O_2 is scarce (e.g., when exercising at $\dot{V}O_2$max or in hypoxia), because the efficiency in terms of oxygen is higher.

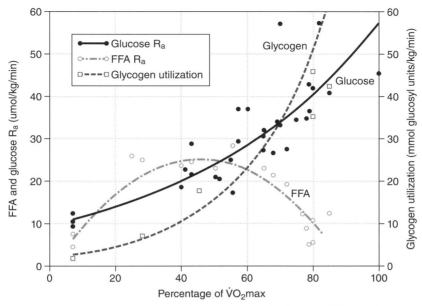

▶ **Figure 11.4**   Results of an extensive literature search showing blood glucose and free fatty acid flux rates (R_a) and net muscle glycogenolysis as functions of relative exercise intensity as given by % $\dot{V}O_2$max in humans. This form of analysis indicates exponential increments in muscle glycogenolysis and glucose R_as as functions of relative exercise intensity. In contrast, the analysis shows multicomponent polynomial response of plasma FFA flux, with easy to moderate intensity exercise eliciting a large rise in flux, but crossover and decreasing flux at approximately 55% $\dot{V}O_2$max. Note that plasma FFA flux is predicted to reach minimal values as $\dot{V}O_2$max is approached.

Reprinted by permission of G.A. Brooks and J.K. Trimmer, "Glucose Kinetics During High-Intensity Exercise and the Crossover Concept," Journal of Applied Physiology 80, no. 3 (1996): 1073-1075.

The oxygen dependence without oxygen limitation is nicely illustrated in figure 11.5 by Clanton, Hogan, and Gladden (2013), who integrated data from different studies on intracellular partial pressure of oxygen (PiO_2) in regard to work rate. These data show that PiO_2 decreases with increasing exercise intensity. However, at approximately 50% of $\dot{V}O_2$max (which is a very low exercise intensity), PiO_2 reaches a low and further increases in intensity do not lower it considerably anymore. It is apparent that we cannot assume any limitation in oxygen delivery at such a low intensity. Nevertheless, blood lactate concentration will increase in an exponential manner, as does lactate rate of appearance (R_a), but this increase is obviously not related to a lack of oxygen causing a functional limitation of the mitochondrial oxidative phosphorylation.

Lactate accumulation also happens under fully oxygenated conditions when glycolysis is accelerated due to a rapidly increasing or absolutely high energy demand, when lactate removal is lower than lactate production (Brooks 1985), or due to the recruitment of glycolytic, fast-twitch muscle fibers (Armstrong 1988). However, the question remains how glycolysis, and hence the rate of appearance of lactate, is regulated in the exercising human, if not by dysoxia. Current models propose that at higher intensities, the intracellular ratio of [ADP] × [Pi]/[ATP] (note: square brackets indicate concentrations) becomes greater, which in turn increases glycolysis (Ferguson et al. 2018).

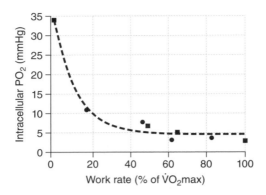

▶ **Figure 11.5** Measurements of intracellular oxygen pressure (PiO₂) versus work rate with data from several studies. Note that the reported PiO₂ value at 100% of V̇O₂max was the same in the studies considered; therefore, the square is overlying the circle at this point.

Reprinted by permission of T.L. Clanton, M.C. Hogan, and L.B. Gladden, "Regulation of Cellular Gas Exchange, Oxygen Sensing, and Metabolic Control," Comprehensive Physiology 3 (2013): 1135-1190.

Lactate, Acidosis, and Fatigue

Muscle fatigue has been defined as the decrease in force or power production in response to contractile activity (Kent-Braun, Fitts, and Christie 2012). There is a long tradition in deeming lactate and acidosis as causative factors of muscle fatigue (see, e.g., Fabiato and Fabiato 1978 as an exemplary classical study and Fitts 1994 and Fitts 2016 for additional references). This viewpoint has been heavily challenged by a substantial body of research (e.g., Hogan et al. 1995), indicating that lactate (i.e., the La⁻ anion) and concomitant acidosis (which is also due to the cellular CO_2) will likely have some negative effect on exercise performance but should not be considered to represent the major cause of fatigue (Ferguson et al. 2018). As an example, Olsson and colleagues (2020) recently demonstrated that increased intracellular acidosis only moderately affected (isolated) human muscle performance, suggesting that acidosis has a limited effect for fatigue, at least in that particular noteworthy experiment (Allen 2020; Olsson et al. 2020). Research also indicates that the beneficial effects of lactate and acidosis, like facilitated O_2 unloading in the working muscle (i.e., "Bohr effect") and increased muscle blood flow through vasodilatation, have been overlooked or at least been underestimated (Allen, Lamb, and Westerblad 2008; Maassen and Böning 2008).

Despite many complex (and often controversial) theories, the role of lactate and acidosis on fatigue has not been resolved. The scientific discussion about whether lactate is a fatigue agent or even a performance enhancer is complex and controversial (Bangsbo and Juel 2006; Fitts 2016; Lamb and Stephenson 2006; Westerblad 2016). As recently highlighted (Allen 2020), there is still a lack of detailed causalities of muscular fatigue. A comprehensive review of this topic is far beyond the scope of this chapter and thus, interested readers are referred to several review papers and special issues (Allen, Lamb, and Westerblad 2008; Ferguson et al. 2018; Fitts 1994; Gladden 2016; Kent-Braun, Fitts, and Christie 2012).

Nevertheless, it seems appropriate to briefly describe the reasons for this debate: In sport, the terms *lactate* and *acidosis* are frequently related to high blood lactate concentrations and often used interchangeably with *fatigue*. Though correlated, however, they are not the same. Secondly, the answer to whether lactate causes fatigue or acts as a performance enhancer (Allen and Westerblad 2004) depends on the type, duration, and intensity of exercise (e.g., moderate rowing training compared to an all-out race). Finally, the transferability of findings obtained on experimentally isolated animal muscles to exercising humans is often questioned, because differences in temperature heavily influence the results and important dynamic variables like changes in blood flow are often inadequately mirrored in isolated experiments. Even if data are generated *in vivo*, it makes a difference whether lactic acid was infused or produced by the muscle of interest itself, or by another muscle, and whether the muscle consists of predominantly fast glycolytic or slow oxidative fibers.

The bottom line is that exercise-induced fatigue causing the cessation of a rowing race is a multifactorial and complex process that involves peripheral and central mechanisms. In the end, there is a "failure of the intracellular contractile machinery" (Kent-Braun, Fitts and Christie 2012, 1035). Research at the molecular, cellular, and whole-muscle level identified several contributors to fatigue, including membrane depolarization, extracellular accumulation of K^+, failure of Ca^{2+} kinetics, and impaired sarcoplasmic reticulum release of Ca^{2+}, as well as metabolic deficiency, possibly promoted by oxidative stress. It is self-evident that such perturbations interact with acidosis and metabolic processing within the cell (Allen, Lamb, and Westerblad 2008). However, it seems clear that blood lactate accumulation and acidosis have several benefits and are surely not the exclusive cause of exercise fatigue. Anything else does not seem very reasonable because, as we have discussed, lactate is neither a dead end nor a waste product of anaerobic metabolism but an omnipresent metabolic intermediate.

Implications for Training and Racing

The substantial energy requirements during both training and racing are a physiological challenge for high-performance rowers. This challenge is met primarily by aerobic metabolism. However, as outlined previously, all metabolic pathways are stressed severely during a 2,000 m race. The energy demands of this relatively short duration will not deplete the glycogen and surely not the lipid stores; therefore, from a metabolic perspective, the rate of energy (ATP) synthesis, rather than limited stores, will limit 2,000 m rowing performance.

In contrast to 2,000 m racing, the energy demand per unit of time during training is not extremely high, but several sessions each of 60 to 100 min (Treff et al. 2021) can accumulate in a high total volume and metabolic load. Based on our research data, we calculated that during high-volume training weeks (1,605 min/wk, 23 sessions, of which 13 were rowing sessions) with 97.5% low-intensity endurance training (i.e., intensity below the first so-called lactate threshold), the total energy need will amount to 6,775 kcal/day, where approximately 2,899 kcal/day are due to rowing related-energy expenditure (figure 11.6, Winkert et al. 2022). This very high energy need is at the upper limit of sustainable nutritional energy intake, indicating that there is an energetic limitation for training volumes above approximately 26 h/wk. Of note, these numbers fit well to the theoretical calculations conducted by Mader and Hollmann (1977), who quantified a maximum rowing volume of approximately 3 h/day (i.e., 18-21 h/wk).

During low-intensity rowing training, fat metabolism provides substantial amounts of energy, but again, fat cannot be considered the main energy source. To illustrate this phenomenon, we will use some familiar numbers: To row with 200 W mechanical power output per rowing cycle, a heavy male rower with a $\dot{V}O_2max$ of 6.5 L/min will consume approximately 3.5 L/min of oxygen, corresponding to roughly 54% of his $\dot{V}O_2max$ with approximately maximum energy contribution from lipid metabolism

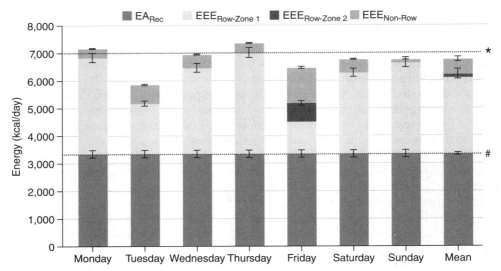

▶ **Figure 11.6** Total energy requirement by exercise energy expenditure (EEE) and recommended energy availability (EA$_{Rec}$) for an exemplary high-volume rowing training week (mean [95% confidence interval]). Calculation of exercise energy expenditure for rowing training in intensity zone 1(EEE$_{Row-Zone 1}$) and zone 2 (EEE$_{Row-Zone 2}$) based on a non-protein table and corrected for resting metabolic rate (RMR) and anaerobic energy contribution. EEE for other training (EEE$_{Non-Row}$) is approximated using corrected metabolic equivalent of task (MET) data. EA$_{Rec}$ (dashed line #) is given as 40 kcal/kg^{-1} fat free mass per day. A total energy expenditure of three times the RMR (7,011 kcal • day^{-1}, dashed line *) was assumed to reflect the upper limit of the manageable total energy expenditure. See Winkert et al. (2022) for details.

Adapted from Winkert, Steinacker, Koehler, et al. (2022). Distributed under the terms of the Creative Commons Attribution 4.0 International License (http://creativecommons.org/licenses/by/4.0/).

(see figure 11.4). If the rower increases the mechanical power output to 250 W, this will hypothetically correspond to an oxygen consumption of 4.0 L/min, or 62% of our rower's $\dot{V}O_2$max. Such an intensity is categorized as "moderate" at the upper end of training zone 1, but contribution of lipid metabolism now clearly decreases. The ability to metabolize fat at a given percentage of $\dot{V}O_2$ is higher in endurance-trained athletes (and therefore possibly higher than for those participants who contributed data to figure 11.4), and substrate utilization is linked to substrate availability, individual fitness, training intensity and duration. However, the message is clear: Rowers largely depend on carbohydrates during training, and the availability of carbohydrates can dictate the duration and intensity distribution of a rowing session.

Hence, the consumption of carbohydrates is important to fuel rowing training. This provision is even more important with higher exercise intensities that rely on proportionally greater amounts of carbohydrates (figure 11.4), which are the only fuel that can be utilized for aerobic and anaerobic metabolism (Hargreaves and Spriet 2020). Another lesson learned by successful coaches and athletes is scientifically explained by these details: if you want high volumes, decrease intensity!

Completing only low-intensity training is surely not sufficient to develop a fast rower, and we can conclude from the literature that all successful rowers integrate some percentages of high-intensity training that is associated with higher blood lactate concentrations (Fiskerstrand and Seiler 2004; Treff et al. 2017; Treff et al. 2021). There are good reasons for this even besides metabolic aspects, such as race-specific coordination and psychological resilience to pain. Interestingly, blood lactate will also generate a number of beneficial physiological adaptations for the aerobic pathways and endurance performance, because it serves as a signal molecule that promotes enhancements such as mitochondrial biogenesis (for further reading we refer you to Brooks 2018; Brooks 2020a, Brooks 2020b). Lactate is therefore not only an energy-rich substrate of carbohydrate metabolism, it also mediates a variety of important training adaptations.

Key Point

Blood lactate concentration is the result of lactate production and uptake, not a measure of force or mechanical power output.

Absolute blood lactate concentration is often used to determine training intensity and those rowers with measures below the recommended training thresholds may be deemed to be "not working hard enough." However, blood lactate concentration is the result of production and removal and it is therefore not an accurate indicator of lactate disposal and oxidation (Mazzeo et al. 1986; Maciejewski et al. 2020). Measuring lactate concentrations during training is nevertheless useful for interpreting performance if we consider the physiological principles outlined previously, consider the characteristics of the individual athlete, and include additional, ideally biomechanical variables such as mechanical power output.

Conclusion

As we have seen in this chapter, the different metabolic pathways are part of one energy system and contribute in different percentages depending on intensity and duration of exercise. At the start of a rowing race, stored ATP is utilized, then the PCr system activates almost immediately to avoid a substantial fall in ATP concentration. As early as 6 s into the race, the glycolytic pathway provides about 50% of the energy, and blood lactate concentration increases. The time elapsed so far is sufficient for the aerobic metabolism to provide substantial and dominant amounts of energy by oxidizing the glycogen, glucose, and lactate that originates from the nonoxidative metabolism Nevertheless, the contribution of the nonoxidative metabolism is indispensable in order to race in the high-intensity domain above 90% of $\dot{V}O_2$max. The contribution of lipids is minor in view of the high intensity.

When it comes to the final sprint of the race, a high aerobic energy supply has allowed the successful athletes to oxidize relatively high amounts of lactate, save carbohydrates, and keep cellular homeostasis within tolerable limits. With these preconditions, a further increase in the proportion of anaerobic energy provision is then possible. In turn, a high anaerobic capacity without high aerobic capacity will not allow a rower to reach the final sprint of a race in a promising position.

Substantial information on the metabolism for rowing was published in the 1970s and has informed much of our current physiology knowledge and practices. Over time, researchers developed a more detailed understanding of physiology—for example, the role and function of lactate—but this knowledge has not always found its way into practical training and updated rowing programs. Some aspects of this chapter and its recommended readings may therefore encourage readers to reconsider traditional views of rowing training.

Physiology of Rowing Strength, Speed, and Power

Ed McNeely

Rowers occupy a unique place in the sporting world. Competing in what would be considered in other sports a middle distance event, rowers are typically taller and heavier than other endurance athletes. They also develop and express power in a unique fashion compared to other middle distance athletes. Compared to cyclists who pedal at 90+ rpm, runners who often perform 60+ strides per min, and swimmers who perform around 70 strokes per minute, most rowers performing at race pace will only reach a stroke rate in the high 30s or low 40s. Compared to other endurance sport athletes, power in rowers requires more of a strength component than a speed component.

Relationship Between Strength, Power, and Performance

Power is the product of strength and speed, and all three are critical to success in rowing. Stronger rowers are more likely to be selected to crews (Lawton, Cornin, and Maguigan 2013) and rowing-specific strength and power correlate well to 2,000 m ergometer performance. Secher (1975) found that maximal isometric rowing strength is significantly higher in international rowers than in both national and club rowers. Using Dutch Olympic, national, and club heavyweight rowers of similar stature and age, the researchers found that in an isometric rowing simulation, international rowers generated an average of 1,999 N of force (92.6 lb), national rowers 1,793 N (83 lbs), and club rowers 1,587 N (73.5 lbs). Using other nonspecific rowing tests—isometric arm pull, back extension, trunk flexion, and leg extension—on the same groups of athletes, it was found that the higher the competition level of the rower, the greater the strength in all tests. There was also an increase in strength-to-weight ratio—from 2.07 in the club rowers to 2.20 in the national and 2.30 in the Olympic rowers. Russell, Rossignol, and Sparrow (1998) found a significant correlation ($r = -0.40$) between knee extensor strength and 2,000 m rowing time in elite 16- to 23-year-old male rowers. In another study of young rowers, Yoshiga and Higuchi (2003) found 2,000 m ergometer performance to significantly correlate ($r = 0.62$) with bilateral leg extension power. In a recent meta-analysis Thiele and colleagues (2020) found that improvements in lower body strength resulted in significant small effect size changes in rowing ergometer performance in recreational and subelite rowers.

Through its relationship to strength endurance, strength plays a critical role in rowing performance by increasing an athlete's functional reserve. During a race rowers will row at a force level equivalent to about 40% of their max strength (Secher 1975). An increase in strength allows them to either row at a faster rate using 40% of their max strength or row with a lower percentage of their max strength, which results in less fatigue during the race.

The start of the race, when the rower must accelerate the boat from zero velocity to race pace as quickly as possible, is most influenced by strength levels. The highest forces produced during a race occur during the first stroke and have been measured at 1,352 N for men and 1,019 N for women (Hartmann et al. 1993). The forces generated during the initial 10 s of a men's single scull race range from 1,000 to 1,500 N (Steinacker 1993).

Strength may also enhance rowing performance by increasing peak rowing power. Riechman and colleagues (2002) found that peak power in a 30 s rowing Wingate test was the best predictor of 2,000 m rowing ergometer performance, accounting for 75.7% of the variation in 2,000 m rowing time. In a study of international rowers, Ingham and colleagues (2002) found that the maximal power and force produced during five maximal strokes on a rowing ergometer were highly correlated with 2,000 m ergometer performance ($r = 0.95$). McNeely (2012) found that among international rowers there was a significant correlation between 2,000 m ergometer performance and peak power from a 60 s rowing Wingate test, but the relationship did not carry over to on-water performance in pairs or single sculls.

Adaptations to Strength, Speed, and Power Training

Strength, speed, and power are outcomes that result from the adaptations that occur as a result of strength training. Although strength training can induce adaptations in many body systems (discussed in part IV), the neural and muscular adaptations are of primary interest to rowers.

Muscles are made up of individual fibers, which are bundled into fascicles (see figure 12.1). The functional unit of the neuromuscular system is the motor unit, which is made up of individual fibers and the motor nerve that connects them. All our movements are patterns of motor unit activation and deactivation, which generally follow Henneman's (1957) size principle whereby the smallest motor units are recruited first, and larger motor units are activated as the intensity of the signal from the brain increases. Untrained individuals or those not accustomed to resistance training are often not able to fully activate all their motor units (Sale et al. 1983).

The strength increases seen during the first 4 to 6 weeks of strength training are predominantly the result of neural adaptations (Moritani and DeVries 1979). These adaptations usually consist of improved motor unit activation through recruitment of more motor units, more frequent activation of motor units, and greater synchronization of the firing patterns of the motor units (Sale 1992). Nervous system adaptations allow a rower to use all the musculature that they possess, but the adaptations are somewhat transient, developing and detraining in relatively short periods of time.

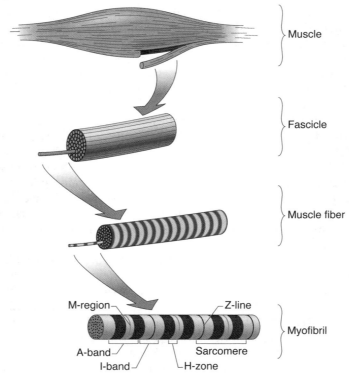

▶ **Figure 12.1** Individual fibers are bundled into fascicles to form muscles.

Rutherford and Jones (1986) have suggested that the neural adaptations occur because the muscle is not capable of generating sufficient force to act as a stimulus for hypertrophy until a certain degree of coordination has been established and enough tension can be developed in the muscle to force it to hypertrophy. This is a plausible explanation, because the rate of neural adaptation decreases throughout the strength training process as the rate of hypertrophy increases Hakkinen and Komi 1983; Hakkinen, Komi, and Alen 1985; Moritani and DeVries 1979).

Once capable of producing enough tension to stimulate hypertrophy, the initial response of the muscle is to increase the fiber size and decrease the extracellular space (see figure 12.2a, b). This results in an increased cross-sectional area of the muscle

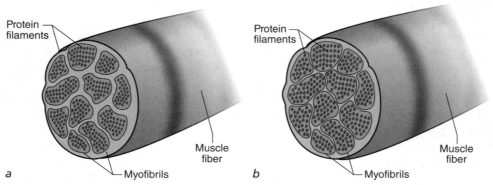

▶ **Figure 12.2** Muscle fiber before training for hypertrophy (a) and after (b).

fiber without an increase in the cross-sectional area of the whole muscle (Goldspink 1992). Muscle cross-sectional area is ultimately the limiting factor in the expression of muscular strength (Sale 1992) and has been shown to impact rowing performance.

Muscle Size and Rowing

The goals of a strength training program for rowing are to improve performance and prevent injury. Recent research on rowing is bringing to light another very important role that strength training plays in a rowing program: increasing muscle size. Yashiro and colleagues (2003) found a correlation of $r = 0.80$ between knee extensor cross-sectional area and 2,000 m ergometer performance. This is as high a correlation as is typically seen between 2,000 m performance and $\dot{V}O_2$max or anaerobic threshold, suggesting that cross-sectional area of the thigh muscles is a good predictor of rowing performance. In a study of international male heavyweight rowers, Mikulic (2009) found significant correlations between arm girth, chest girth, and gluteal thigh girth and 6,000 m rowing performance. Interestingly, all three girth measurements were more closely correlated to 6,000 m performance than arm span or lung volume. In this study, lean body mass was the most highly correlated variable to 6,000 m performance—more highly correlated than power output at ventilatory threshold or power output at $\dot{V}O_2$max. Not only is muscle mass related to overall rowing performance, but it is correlated to the power output at various phases of the stroke. Using MRI technology to measure muscle mass, Tachinaba and colleagues (2007) found significant correlations between muscle mass in the quadriceps muscle and leg drive power and between the muscles in the hamstrings and lower back and trunk swing power.

It may seem obvious that muscle mass and performance in heavyweight rowers would go hand in hand. What is less obvious and possibly of greater significance is that the same relationship holds true in lightweight rowers. Slater and colleagues (2005) in a study of Australian lightweights competing at the National Championships found that on-water times were 10.2 s faster per kg of muscle mass difference between competitors. This highlights the importance of proper weight management and strength training in lightweight training programs and has implications for the long-term development and selection of lightweight athletes. Very tall, lean athletes with smaller muscle mass who need to cut weight to be a lightweight rower will have a more difficult time developing over the long term because they cannot afford to gain muscle mass to improve power and performance.

Key Point

Many potential lightweights reach performance plateaus because they continuously have to shed muscle mass in order to reach the limits of their weight category. Natural lightweights have an advantage because they can increase muscle mass throughout their careers, improving their power production.

Training to Increase Muscle Mass

Although an increase in cross-sectional area of a whole muscle or muscle fibers is the first thing that comes to mind when contemplating increased muscle mass, an increase in overall muscle mass can be accomplished by increasing the length of the fascicles. As mentioned earlier, fascicles are bundles of muscle fibers arranged in parallel; their length is related to speed of contraction and is important in speed performances (Abe et al. 2001). In a study of 18 Olympic rowers, van der Zwaard and colleagues (2018) found that fascicle length, not physiological cross-sectional area, was most related to power.

Historically, fascicle length has been difficult to study, with most research relying on cadaver studies and animal models. Animal studies have shown that stretching can induce significant changes in fascicle length (Kearns, Brechue, and Abe 1998). The use of stretching to increase fascicle length in humans is less clear, with some studies showing it can enhance fascicle length (Panidi et al. 2021) and other studies showing no change (Konrad and Tilp 2014). Although the methods used in animal studies would be unacceptable to use in human studies, it does suggest that stretching the lower body musculature beyond what is done in a typical warm-up or cool-down may help improve speed and power by contributing to increased fascicle length. Daily static stretching for 30 min or more while holding each stretch for 45 s or more over a period of at least 6 weeks may enhance muscle architecture (Pandini et al. 2021).

Technological advances and the development of tools like 3D ultrasound imaging have recently made the measurement of fascicle length much easier and more accurate, allowing the effects of various modes of training on fascicle length to be examined. Resistance training has been shown to increase fascicle length in a contraction-specific manner, with eccentric contractions increasing the length of the fascicle and concentric muscle actions increasing cross-sectional area (Franchi et al. 2016).

Eccentric Training

Eccentric loading is not a significant part of the rowing stroke, occurring primarily in the final phase of the recovery to enhance the stretch–shortening cycle contribution to the leg drive. However, eccentric training can still contribute to rowing performance by increasing fascicle length and braking strength. Eccentric contractions occur during the lowering phase of a strength training exercise when the muscle is lengthening. Loads up to 40% heavier than a concentric max can and should be used in eccentric training. Eccentric exercise should only be done by athletes who have several years of strength training experience.

The following example of an eccentric exercise can be done on an angled leg press machine with the safety blocks in place and spotters on each side of the machine (figure 12.3). After a warm-up that includes several progressive sets of both concentric and eccentric movements, load the leg press to a load equivalent to 100% to 120% 1RM. Slowly lower the weight under control, using a 4 to 6 s count. When the weight reaches the bottom position, the spotters will push the weight back to the top and the weight is lowered again. If the eccentric lowering of the weight cannot be controlled for 4 to 6 s, decrease the weight. Perform 2 to 3 sets of 3 to 5 repetitions no more than once per week.

Eccentric workouts can cause significant soreness and muscle damage, so they should only be done during the preparation phase of the year when other forms of training are going to be done at lower volume and intensity. Eccentric training performed at other times of the year is likely to negatively impact rowing workouts.

▶ **Figure 12.3** Leg press start *(a)* and finish *(b)*.

Plyometric Training

Plyometric training, a commonly used method that involves repeated jumps and land-ings, uses eccentric loading to contribute to an increase in fascicle length (Timmins et al. 2016). van der Zwaard and colleagues (2021) examined the effects of preparation phase and competitive phase training on muscle architecture in elite female rowers. They found that there was a 5% decrease in fascicle length during the preparation phase when traditional heavy load resistance training was used, compared to a 13% increase in fascicle length during the preparation period when plyometric training was added to the program. During the preparation phase there was a 2% increase in rowing power output compared to a 5% increase during the competitive phase.

Concurrent Training

Training for both strength and endurance at the same time is known as *concurrent training*. Larger muscle size increases the force production capability of a muscle and is therefore an important part of increasing strength and power. Endurance training, on the other hand, increases oxidative capacity and tends to decrease muscle size, because a smaller muscle has a shorter oxygen diffusion distance to get to the mitochondria (van Wessel et al. 2010). This creates a conundrum for rowers who need high levels of strength, power, and endurance to perform.

The first research examining the effects of concurrent strength and aerobic training was published by Hickson in 1980. His work showed an interference effect, whereby the effects of strength and endurance development when training concurrently were diminished compared to training for strength and endurance separately. Since then, it has been shown that concurrent training potentially limits the gains in strength, mass, and power, whereas endurance is not affected or may even be positively affected (Wilson et al. 2012). The extent of the effect is related to the type of training, intensity, frequency, and volume used. Surprisingly, because many athletes are required to train for strength and aerobic fitness concurrently, there is very little concurrent training research using athletes as subjects, forcing coaches and sport scientists to rely on their own experience. The following sections go into more depth about how training vari-ables can interfere with each other during training.

Type of Training

There is not a lot of research on interference effects on different types of activity and unfortunately none using rowing as a training modality. In the research that has been done, running has been shown to increase the risk of and extent of interference effects for rowers more greatly than cycling (Lundberg 2019). The reason this occurs is unclear but may be related to the higher forces and eccentric contractions experienced during the ground contact phase of each running stride. Rowers who do large volumes of cross-training may want to consider lower impact activities with less eccentric loading, such as cycling or swimming.

Intensity

Intensity is an important consideration when performing strength and endurance training concurrently. Higher intensity exercise—that is, above the anaerobic threshold—creates more fatigue than lower intensity, aerobic base work, and has been shown to decrease force production for at least 6 hours following training (Bentley et al. 2000; Bentley, Zhou, and Davie 1998).

Frequency and Volume

Frequency and volume are also important factors to consider when using concurrent training methods. Performing aerobic training more than 3 times per week attenuates strength training adaptations (Lundberg 2019). For recreationally competitive and developing rowers, increasing the recovery time between aerobic and strength sessions by performing them on alternate days may decrease the negative effects of concurrent training (Sale 1992).

Concurrent training research examining the effects of volume of aerobic training using a similar volume to that used by competitive or recreationally competitive rowers has never been done. The closest is the original concurrent training study by Hickson (1980), which used an aerobic volume of 30 to 40 min 6 days per week, substantially below what a competitive rower performs (see table 12.1). Even at these modest volumes, any volume of aerobic training above 3 hours per week seemed to interfere with strength development.

Table 12.1 Progression of Total Training and Strength Training Volume

	Year 1	Year 2	Year 3	Year 4	Year 5	Year 6	Year 7	Year 8	Year 9	Year 10 (Olympic year)
Age	17	18	19	20	21	22	23	24	25	26
Volume (total hours)	614	645	677	711	782	860	946	975	1,023	1,100
Volume (h/wk)	13.3	14.0	14.7	15.5	17.0	18.7	20.6	21.2	22.2	23.9
Strength training (h/wk)	5.0	5.0	5.0	5.0	5.0	5.0	5.0	5.0	5.0	5.0
Strength training (% of total volume)	37%	36%	34%	32%	29%	27%	24%	24%	22%	21%

Table 12.1 breaks down the typical progression of training hours for 10 years, up through the athlete's first Olympic Games. The ages in this table are approximate and will vary depending on when the athlete entered competitive rowing and was identified as being on a high-performance path.

There is a gradual increase in training volume year over year with a similar total number of hours per week dedicated to strength training. Prioritizing the development of muscle mass in younger athletes using a higher volume of strength training as a percentage of total training volume is more conducive to building muscle during the early years of training when the overall aerobic volume is lower. As the need for aerobic training volume increases it becomes more difficult to increase muscle mass.

Decreasing Interference Effects

Based on the current research, it seems inevitable that competitive rowers will experience some degree of interference effect when performing aerobic and strength training concurrently. Because there is so little research on the effects of training variables on concurrent training, it is important to consider the potential mechanisms behind the interference to better understand how these effects can be decreased.

Metabolic stress is the most likely cause of the interference effect. Increased metabolic activity through endurance training can result in carbohydrate depletions, which in turn alter the molecular signaling mechanisms in the muscle that play a significant role in protein synthesis, limiting the amount of new proteins that are built and the amount of muscle mass increase (Ellefsen and Baar 2019). The high-volume, high-intensity training typical of rowing results in significant depletion of carbohydrate.

Nutritional interventions, particularly during the recovery period, may help reduce the extent of the interference effect, particularly if there are several hours between the aerobic and strength session. Plan to bring adequate carbohydrate sources to provide at least 30-60 g/h of CHO before and during training. Consuming 20 to 40 g of protein every 3 to 4 hours throughout the day increases muscle protein synthesis and may help negate some of the negative effects of concurrent training (Thomas, Erdman, and Burke 2016). More discussion of refueling for training can be found in part VII.

Timing of Training Sessions

Two hypotheses exist around concurrent training. One suggests that interference effects are chronic and occur when the muscle is attempting to adapt to conflicting stimuli during a longitudinal training program (Leveritt and Abernethy 1999). The other suggests they are acute and the inhibition of strength development is the result of performing endurance training immediately before strength training, which results in a decreased volume, intensity, and quality of strength training as a result of residual fatigue (Craig et al. 1991). In fact, it is likely that interference effects are the result of a combination of both acute and chronic factors.

Reduced strength performance is most pronounced when there is less than 60 min between sessions, but strength has been shown to be affected with recovery periods of 2, 4, 6, and 8 hours (Bentley et al. 2000; Bentley, Zhou, and Davie 2000; Sporer and Wenger 2003). Strength levels may be affected for as much as 72 hours following exhaustive exercise (Latorre-Román et al. 2014).

Distributing training sessions at the start and end of the day helps decrease the interference effect. An early morning row followed by a late afternoon or early evening strength session is ideal, as long as there is a good nutritional support plan in place. Long periods between sessions allow more time for glycogen recovery and have been shown to result in greater strength increases than more compressed recovery times (García-Pallarés et al. 2009). There should be a couple of hours between the end of the evening strength session and bedtime so that the exercise stimulus does not interfere with sleep.

It is common in club settings for younger, developing rowers to perform their endurance and strength sessions consecutively with little rest between the sessions. This is often done to overcome logistical challenges like facility scheduling and parental transport to and from the club. Although this is the worst-case scenario for interference effects on strength development, a little creativity can decrease the impact by keeping athletes productive and increase the time between the row and strength session. Here are a few suggestions:

1. Have a nutritional recovery plan in place. The athlete should have a smoothie or other form of energy and protein drink as soon as they are off the water.

2. Take some time to wash and put away boats and oars.

3. Debrief the session with the coach to get feedback, set goals, and focus for the next session.

4. Stretch. Although high volumes of static stretching may interfere with power output in the weight room, holding stretches for 15 to 20 s each is unlikely to have a negative impact.

5. Do some video work. Video analysis and discussion of technique is a great way to be productive and increase the time between the row and strength session.

6. Brief the strength session by discussing goals and objectives of the session with a coach.

During periods when the development of strength and power are a priority, doing the resistance training session before a row may be more beneficial for strength development but may have a negative impact on the rowing session (Arsoniadis et al. 2022). Aerobic base work following the strength session minimizes the impact of the strength session on the row.

Focus of the Strength Session

Although it is likely that a rowing session will interfere with strength development, resistance training sessions that focus on developing the technique of strength exercises are less likely to be impacted by the row. The load and volume of this type of strength session are typically lower and do not create much fatigue. During the season, strength maintenance sessions are also less likely to be affected by prior aerobic training.

Cross-Training

The muscle groups used in an endurance session influence the interference effect. Lower body endurance activities like running, cycling, and using an elliptical have less effect on upper body strength (Reed, Schilling, and Murlastis 2013; Tan et al. 2014). Planning strength and aerobic cross-training sessions so that upper body strength is done on a lower body cross-training day and vice versa may negate the acute fatigue that interferes with strength development.

Although doing both strength and endurance training simultaneously does decrease the amount of strength gained, it does not eliminate the benefits of a strength program (Arsoniadis et al. 2022). Research on concurrent training typically involves relatively short training programs of 8 to 12 weeks, with rare longer studies only getting to about 24 weeks (Küüsmaa et al. 2016). This is much shorter than the 10- to 11-month training and competitive year for most rowers, and a drop in the bucket compared to the length of a rower's career. A reduction in strength improvement of 10%, 15%, or even 20% as a result of concurrent training is likely made up with a little patience and time, emphasizing the need for long-term planning and goal setting.

Conclusion

Speed, strength, and power are key elements of rowing performance. Compared to other middle distance endurance sports, rowers develop power at a relatively low turnover rate (typically reaching a stroke rate in the high 30s to low 40s), making their power development more strength based than speed based. As a result, strength and the development of muscle mass take on greater importance. The high volumes of aerobic training needed to develop rowing fitness result in an attenuation of strength and muscle mass development compared to performing strength training only. Carefully planning for periods of the year when strength development can be a priority, as well as having a recovery and nutritional plan that supports the development of strength and muscle mass, will decrease the negative effects concurrent training has on strength development.

Environmental Stress

Stephen S. Cheung, PhD

A beauty of rowing is that, ergometers aside, it remains an outdoor sport that takes place across many regions of the world. Part and parcel of outdoor sports is a wide variability in environmental conditions to challenge athletes, adding a layer of complexity to optimizing training and race-day performance. These environmental stressors can include temperature extremes, humidity, wind, and solar load. Pollution as a result of increasing urbanization and the concentration of international competitions around larger metropolises forms another challenge for modern athletes. Unfortunately, in the coming decades climate change will likely increase the challenges from thermal extremes and pollution to both overall health and athletic capacity. Finally, although competitions at altitude may be relatively infrequent, advances in technology have made altitude or hypoxic training increasingly accessible and popular for both elite and recreational athletes.

This chapter will survey the underlying physiology by which heat and cold, pollution, and altitude stress impacts human physiology and performance potential. The majority of surveyed literature is drawn from studies using cycling or running as the exercise modality, but the similar aerobic dominance of rowing allows for high transferability. Chapter 21 will focus on countermeasures to optimize performance in heat and pollution environments, along with current consensus on best practices for hypoxic training for sea-level competitions.

Heat Balance

Heat storage is a dynamic function of heat production within the body along with heat exchange between the body and environment. In situations where heat storage is positive, there is a net heat gain and eventually body temperature will rise—for example, the combination of exercise and a temperate or hot environment typically overwhelms the cooling capacity of an ice vest, and heat storage will remain positive, though at a lower value than without the use of an ice vest. In contrast, if heat storage is negative, heat loss to the environment is greater than the amount of heat produced at rest or during exercise, and body temperature will eventually decrease. This can be seen when training on cold winter days, when higher exercise intensity or additional clothing may be needed to prevent the body from cooling.

The basic heat balance equation shown in equation 13.1 incorporates four heat exchange pathways along with metabolic heat production to model the rate of heat storage ($\dot{S}$ in W/m²).

$$\dot{S} = (\dot{M} - \dot{W}) - (\dot{R} + \dot{C} + \dot{K} + \dot{E}) + (\dot{C}_{res} + \dot{E}_{res}) \tag{13.1}$$

where $\dot{S}$ is heat storage, $\dot{M}$ is metabolic energy, $\dot{W}$ is mechanical work, $\dot{R}$ is radiation, $\dot{C}$ is conduction, $\dot{K}$ is convection, $\dot{E}$ is evaporation, and $\dot{E}_{res}$ and $\dot{C}_{res}$ are evaporation and conduction through the respiratory tract. Note that the dot above each letter in the equation indicates a rate of change in that variable. A positive *heat storage* value represents a heat gain that could eventually lead to hyperthermia, whereas a negative value represents heat loss that could eventually lead to hypothermia.

Metabolic energy is the total amount of energy conversion, and *mechanical work* is the amount of actual mechanical work being performed (e.g., a reading of 200 W from a rowing ergometer). The difference $(\dot{M} - \dot{W})$ represents the metabolic heat energy from the body at rest or during exercise. Remember that the body is highly inefficient at energy conversion, such that only about 20% of energy is converted to mechanical energy and the remainder is converted to heat. Therefore, when exercising at a power output of 200 W, a total of approximately 1,000 W of energy conversion occurs, with about 800 W of it in the form of heat.

Radiation includes the combination of the sun's direct radiation and the ground or water's reflected radiation. Radiative heat gain is why it may be comfortable sitting at an outside café on a spring day as long as the sun is out but feel much cooler if the sun goes behind a cloud. The high solar heat load from the sun and its reflection off ice and snow also explains why mountaineers can be comfortable with minimal clothing despite low air temperatures.

Conduction involves direct heat transfer between the body and the environment, such as sitting on a block of ice or immersed in a hot tub. It is dependent on the temperature gradient between the skin and your surroundings and the thermal qualities of that environment. For example, air conducts heat much more slowly than water, which explains why 15 °C water is much more uncomfortable and a higher risk for hypothermia than 15 °C air. Conduction is generally not relevant for most rowing situations, because air has low thermal conductivity and there are limited contact points between the rower and the boat. However, conduction is the primary method of heat exchange for cooling methods such as ice vests.

Convection refers to heat exchange from the movement of a fluid such as air or water over the body, and it explains why a cold and windy day causes heat loss much faster than a cold but windless day. As long as ambient temperature is lower than body temperature of 37 to 39 °C, the high rate of convective flow over a rower moving at speed can still contribute to significant heat dissipation. However, in larger boats, drafting may reduce convective heat exchange for crew in back positions.

Evaporation is the body's main heat loss mechanism in high temperatures because as air temperature increases, the thermal gradient between the body and environment decreases, reducing the effectiveness of radiation, conduction, and convection as heat loss mechanisms. Instead, the potential for evaporative heat loss is determined primarily by the water vapor pressure gradient between the body surface and the environment, allowing for sweat on the skin to evaporate and draw heat away from the body. This also means that a warm but humid environment can lead to much higher heat storage than a hotter but dry environment, because high water vapor content of the environment impairs evaporative heat loss.

Finally, *conductive and evaporative heat exchange* also occur through the respiratory tract. Especially in cold conditions, significant heat and water loss can occur when the respiratory tract heats and humidifies cold and dry air before it reaches the sensitive lung tissues, with this heat and moisture then lost when breathing out.

These multiple pathways for heat exchange all contribute to the overall thermal stress on an athlete. To ease comparison across a range of environmental conditions, one standardized value that attempts to integrate radiation, conduction, convection, and evaporation together is the wet bulb globe temperature (WBGT). Other such integrated thermal scales exist and are commonly used in different regions, including the Universal Thermal Climate Index (UTCI), the humidex in Canada, and the heat index in the United States. During colder seasons, the use of a wind chill index is common, integrating both absolute air temperature (conduction) and local wind speed (convection).

As detailed in the previous discussion on heat balance, heat stress is not solely dependent on absolute ambient temperature, and humidity, solar heat load, and wind must be factored in when assessing heat stress and potential impact on performance. When relative humidity levels were increased from 24% to 80%, rise in core temperature progressively increased, and voluntary tolerance to cycling at 70% $\dot{V}O_2$peak in a 30 °C environment progressively decreased (Maughan, Otani, and Watson 2012). High solar radiation can also negatively affect thermal perception and performance, with participants pacing at a lower power output to achieve a similar rating of perceived exertion (RPE) of 13 (6-20 scale) at moderate and high solar loads compared to low (Otani, Kaya, and Tamaki 2019). Finally, wind speed during training and competition must be considered when assessing thermal stress. Even with low ambient wind and relatively warm temperatures, rowing speeds of 15 to 20 km/h can still provide significant convective cooling. This is contrasted with stationary rowing, where the combination of room temperature, high metabolic heat production, and minimal airflow (most indoor fans are far below 10 km/h) can greatly increase thermal strain. We will return to the issue of different environmental conditions in chapter 21 and discuss different modes of heat adaptation.

Key Point

Wet bulb globe temperature (WBGT) was developed in the 1950s and combines three separate temperature readings into a single value in either °C or °F, as illustrated in figure 13.1.

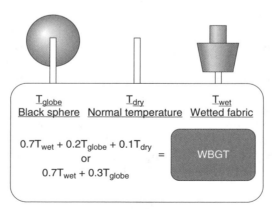

▶ **Figure 13.1** WBGT is a common index used to assess thermal stress that integrates the four main pathways for heat exchange into a single value.

Normal or "dry bulb" temperature T_{dry} is measured with a thermometer shielded from moisture or radiation. "Wet bulb" temperature T_{wet} is measured with a thermometer that remains moist because it is wrapped in fabric kept wet with water, which gives an indication of humidity and evaporative heat exchange. At relative humidity levels <100%, evaporation will occur, such that the wet bulb temperature will be less than T_{dry}. "Globe" temperature T_{globe} is measured with a thermometer housed inside a black globe to ensure full absorbance of radiation and constant exposed surface area regardless of the location of the radiative heat source.

The three temperature readings are then converted to an overall WBGT value according to a weighting of the three, as shown in equation 13.2:

$$WBGT = 0.7T_{wet} + 0.2T_{globe} + 0.1T_{dry} \tag{13.2}$$

In situations without a significant radiant load, the equation is modified to include only wet bulb and globe temperatures (equation 13.3):

$$WBGT = 0.7T_{wet} + 0.3T_{globe} \tag{13.3}$$

Heat Impact on Performance

A consensus of scientific evidence—analyzing performance across different climatic conditions in both laboratory and field settings—has clearly demonstrated that human exercise capacity decreases in the heat. In the laboratory, Galloway and Maughan (1997) had subjects cycle to voluntary exhaustion at 70% $\dot{V}O_2$peak in 4, 10, 20, and 30 °C, and reported that peak tolerance time occurred at 10 °C, with similar and shorter durations at both 4 and 20 °C and a further decrease at 30 °C. Such decrements with increasing temperatures are supported by retrospective field studies. For example, Ely and colleagues (2007) analyzed marathon running times across a range of finishing placings and race-day temperatures, reporting a progressive worsening of race times with higher ambient temperatures. Interestingly, the magnitude of impairment was exponentially greater among slower runners, suggesting that higher fitness provides a slight protective effect. Similar magnitudes of impairment and benefits of fitness were observed in both men and women. When extrapolating these findings to rowing, one thing to consider is that the optimal temperature range may be broader and also shift toward slightly higher ambient temperatures due to the typically shorter duration of rowing competitions compared to running.

Heat-related exercise impairment encompasses a wide range of physiological mechanisms, highlighted in figure 13.2 (Cheung and Sleivert 2004). Traditionally, physiological impairment from heat stress has been focused on systemic cardiovascular issues, such as maintaining adequate blood pressure in the face of reduced blood volume or increasing competition for blood flow between active muscles and the skin for thermoregulation. However, over the past two decades, research has focused on the direct impacts of hyperthermia itself, including potential reductions in cerebral blood flow, decrements in neuromuscular activation within the brain, decreases in mental arousal, changes in neurochemistry, and reduced gut blood flow leading to bacterial leakage from the gut and inflammatory response. Notably, these potential mechanisms do not act in isolation, but rather as a highly interrelated and integrated web of factors that ultimately reduce neuromuscular and exercise capacity.

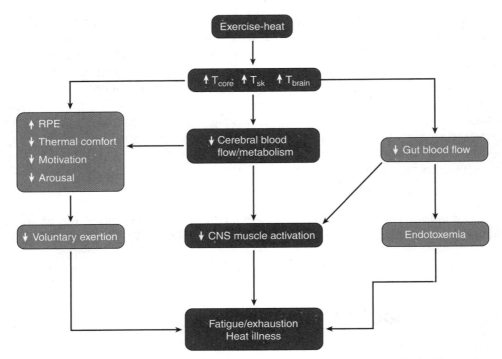

▶ **Figure 13.2** Elevated core, brain, and skin temperature during exercise heat stress can cause fatigue through a variety of interrelated physiological and psychological factors. T_{core}: core temperature, T_{sk}: skin temperature, T_{brain}: brain temperature, RPE: ratings of perceived exertion, CNS: central nervous system.

Heat Stress and Psychology

Heat stress can also affect exercise capacity via psychological mechanisms. In this psychophysiological paradigm of exercise regulation, the added discomfort from heat stress serves as a signal to the brain of a higher-than-typical rate of heat storage and potential greater risk of exertional heat illness. To compensate, it is argued that the brain reduces its willingness to work as hard in order to decrease the risk of extreme heat storage, heat illness, and catastrophic collapse. When tasked to adjust power output to maintain a constant perceived effort similar to that needed for a 20 km to 40 km cycling time trial pace, the rate of decline in voluntary power output, even early in the trial before significant core temperature rise, was higher in hotter (35 °C) compared with cooler (15 and 25 °C) environments (Tucker et al. 2006). Another variation of psychophysiological regulation argues that fatigue is a dynamic balance between perceived effort and motivation, and that heat stress and thermal discomfort can both increase perceived effort and reduce motivation.

Given that hyperthermia clearly impairs physiological function and exercise capacity, the main question for athletes is just how hot is too hot, whether ambient temperature or actual body temperature. This question is difficult to answer, because a slight or even significant rise in body temperature is not always an indication of problems during exercise, especially in fit or elite athletes. Ultramarathoners can exercise at maximal capacity for hours in moderate ambient temperatures with only minor elevations in core temperature, suggesting a strong ability to thermoregulate even under conditions of high metabolic heat production. At the same time, some endurance athletes can sustain elevated core temperatures of greater than 40 °C throughout a marathon or triathlon without major issues. Conversely, although exertional heat illnesses occur most frequently in hot and humid conditions, such problems can occur even in cool conditions with intense or prolonged exercise. Such a wide range in responses highlight the high degree of individual variability in response to heat stress, making it very difficult for coaches and sport scientists to individualize training programs, protect athletes from heat illness, or predict performance outcomes.

Heat Impact on Strength and Power

Although heat stress clearly reduces endurance capacity and performance, its impact on strength and power efforts may differ. Here, a clear distinction needs to be made between core temperature and local muscle temperature. Although high core temperatures can cause systemic reductions in performance, including a reduction in central neural activation of muscle, an elevation in local muscle temperature is essential for both aerobic and anaerobic performance. This is seen as a linear relationship between jump height from a drop jump and local thigh temperature (Racinais and Oksa 2010). This distinction highlights the importance of considering cooling options before and during competitions that balance the need for adequate warm-up while reducing overall thermal strain. Thus, whole-body immersion in cold water prior to competing may be counterproductive compared to the use of ice vests and other torso-focused cooling strategies during warm-up. In contrast, cold water immersion between racing heats may be ideal to reduce the thermal strain from competition.

Equally important as optimizing performance, athletes and especially support staff must be aware of the risk factors and symptoms of exertional heat illnesses when competing in hot environments. Apart from acute danger, extended hyperthermia can lead to long-term health issues. Table 13.1 surveys the spectrum of exertional heat illnesses along with treatment strategies.

Table 13.1 Heat Illness Diagnosis and Treatment

Heat illness	Primary symptoms	Predisposing factors	Treatment
Exertional heatstroke[a]	Central nervous system (CNS) dysfunction (disorientation, convulsions, coma) Severe (>40 °C; 104 °F) hyperthermia Nausea, vomiting, diarrhea Severe dizziness and weakness Hot and wet or dry skin Increased heart rate and respiratory rate Decreased blood pressure Extreme thirst and dehydration	Obesity Low physical fitness level Dehydration Lack of heat acclimatization Previous history of heat illness Sleep deprivation Sweat gland dysfunction Sunburn Viral illness Diarrhea Medications (i.e., stimulants, anticholinergic and cardiovascular drugs, cocaine)[b] Extremes of age[c] Uncontrolled diabetes or hypertension, cardiac disease	Institute aggressive and immediate whole-body cooling within minutes of diagnosis with water as cold as practical until temperature <38.3 °C (101 °F). Remove equipment and monitor rectal temperature. Monitor vital medical signs (airway, breathing, circulation, CNS status) continuously. Perform IV saline infusion if feasible.

(continued)

Table 13.1 *(continued)*

Heat illness	Primary symptoms	Predisposing factors	Treatment
Exertional heat exhaustion[d]	Fatigue and inability to continue exercise Ataxia, dizziness, and coordination problems Profuse sweating Headache, nausea, vomiting, diarrhea	Dehydration High body mass	Remove athlete from practice or competition and move to a shaded or air-conditioned area. Remove excess clothing and equipment. Lay victim down with legs above heart level. Rehydrate using chilled fluids or normal saline IV. Cool athlete to <38.3 °C—aggressive cold water immersion may not be required. Monitor status and transport to emergency facility if needed.
Exertional heat cramps	Intense pain Persistent muscle contractions in working muscles during prolonged exercise	Dehydration Exercise-induced muscle fatigue Large sweat sodium loss	Rehydrate and provide sodium replenishment. Prevent by sodium loading (e.g., 0.5 g in 1 L of sports drink) in cases of heavy or "salty" sweaters. Use light stretching and massage.

[a]Exertional heatstroke: Hyperthermia (core body temperature 40 °C) associated with central nervous system disturbances and multiple organ system failure.

[b]Stimulants (e.g., amphetamines, Ritalin, ephedra, alpha agonists) increase heat production; anticholinergic drugs (e.g., antidepressants, antipsychotics, and antihistamines) inhibit sweating; cardiovascular drugs (e.g., calcium channel blockers, beta blockers, diuretics, monoamine oxidase inhibitors) alter the cardiovascular response to heat storage; cocaine increases heat production and reduces heat loss by decreasing cutaneous blood flow.

[c]Children and elderly persons are particularly susceptible to heat accumulation due to decreased sweating ability, increased metabolic heat production, greater surface area–to–body mass ratio, decreased thirst response, decreased mobility, decreased vasodilatory response, and chronic medical conditions or medication effects (or both).

[d]Exertional heat exhaustion: Inability to continue to exercise; may or may not be associated with physical collapse. Generally, this does not involve severe hyperthermia >40 °C or severe CNS dysfunction.

Exercise in the Cold

Although the body can tolerate and accommodate moderate increases in core or muscle temperature quite readily during exercise, the tolerance for reduced body temperature is minimal. Ferguson and colleagues (2018) were among the first to directly test performance with mild hypothermia of –0.5 °C from baseline, reporting an approximate 5% reduction in mean power output over a 15 km cycling time trial. Coincident with core cooling is the competing muscular demands of shivering to increase internal heat generation and muscular movements for muscle recruitment, oxygen uptake, and coordination. For example, at a muscular level, more actual motor units were recruited for a longer time in order to achieve a desired force with forearm cooling (Mallette et al. 2018). Overall, such studies emphasize the importance of adequate clothing and warm-up during cold weather training.

Regardless of core temperature effects, one direct effect of exercise in the cold is the breathing of cold and dry air. Because alveolar tissue is thin, moist, and fragile, the inhaled air must be warmed and humidified prior to its entry into the lungs. Therefore, one potential hazard is hyperresponsiveness of the respiratory tract, leading to bronchoconstriction or asthmatic attacks; note that bronchoconstriction can be exacerbated by cold air even among individuals without a clinical asthma diagnosis. In either case, the breathing of cold air can trigger dyspnea and reduced exercise capacity. When exercising in +20 °C versus –18 °C environments, individuals with exercise-induced bronchoconstriction experienced a 6.5% decrease in maximum oxygen uptake and had lower running speeds in the cold. These findings were supported by greater impairments in spirometric values following exercise in the cold. The exact mechanism for the triggering of dyspnea with cold air remains unclear. Desiccation of the respiratory tract does not appear to be the primary mechanism, as no changes in the quantity or hypertonicity of the airway surface fluid were observed with bronchoconstriction elicited by hyperventilation of cold air in persons with asthma. Beyond any direct physiological impact, dyspnea and increased perception of respiratory distress can also form a signal to the brain to reduce voluntary effort.

In asymptomatic individuals, exercising in cold temperatures does not appear to pose a significant physiological or clinical risk. Hartung, Myhre, and Nunneley (1980) had participants engage in moderate exercise while breathing ambient or cold (–35 °C) air and concluded that there were minimal differences in physiological responses. Shave and colleagues (2004) investigated the risk to the cardiovascular system from prolonged exercise in the cold by having very fit athletic participants perform a 160 km (100 mi) cycling test in 0 °C and 19 °C environments. Extensive echocardiographic imaging of the heart revealed no changes in ventricular filling or contractility before or following exercise in the two environments and no differences in either systolic or diastolic blood pressure. Creatine kinase and cardiac troponin T, blood markers for cardiac muscle damage, also did not differ across temperatures, suggesting that high-intensity exercise in either temperature did not appear to elevate the risk for exercise-induced cardiac damage.

For all athletes, another issue with inspiring cold and dry air may be that, unlike what occurs in other systems such as the kidneys, which conserve water and electrolytes, there is minimal recovery of water and heat from the respiratory system. Therefore, continued expiration in cold temperatures at high ventilation rates during exercise can result in significant heat loss and potential dehydration. Cain and colleagues (1990) found that maximal expired air temperature varied only very slightly regardless of inspired temperature ranging from –40 °C to +20 °C. Thus respiratory heat loss can range up to 25% to 30% of resting and 15% to 20% of exercise metabolism, and adequate hydration remains an issue during exercise in the cold. Overall, one potential countermeasure for enhancing exercise tolerance and capacity for both symptomatic and asymptomatic individuals may be the use of a mask to assist in heat and water recovery; at present, some athlete-specific masks are commercially available. However, the design challenge is that the mask must enable adequate ventilation without adding to the resistance and work of breathing, as well as resist moisture and ice buildup.

Pollution and Exercise

Increasing population, urbanization, and development has unfortunately led to an increasing level of pollution in most regions of the world. In addition, major sporting competitions such as World Cups and the Olympics are increasingly based in major urban centers. Together, athletes are increasingly exposed to high pollution during both training and competitions, which may impact training adaptations, performance capacity, and overall health. Some of the challenges with determining the physiological effects of pollution are the vast range of pollutants and their high spatial and temporal heterogeneity. Therefore, the dominant pollutants and impact may change by the hour and over a small region, in addition to daily or seasonally. This makes even replication in the lab difficult, let alone accurate modeling and generalization of findings from a particular situation or locale to others.

Table 13.2 briefly outlines the major air pollutants currently of interest in urban environments. Keep in mind that this is limited to major airborne pollutants, which is only a very small subset of the total range of compounds to which humans are currently exposed through air, water, and food. The focus is on known major physiological effects and their potential impact on exercise performance.

Table 13.2 Major Categories of Airborne Pollutants

Pollutant	Source and size of particles	Limits for danger to human health*	Primary effects
Particulate matter	Solid particles from a wide variety of human and natural sources High regional and temporal variability due to weather and geography Dust, wood smoke, pollen Tobacco smoke, fossil fuel combustion Large (PM_{10}, 2.5-10 μm) Deposition in nasopharyngeal tract: inflammation, congestion Fine ($PM_{2.5}$, 1-2.5 μm) Deposition in trachea and bronchi: bronchospasms, congestion, bronchitis Ultrafine ($PM_{1.0}$, <1 μm) Deposition in alveoli: inflammation	1,000 mg/m³, 24 h average	Effects dependent on particle size, mass, and composition, along with individual factors (e.g., mouth vs. nasal breathing, allergies) Minimal to no controlled studies on exercise effects in humans
Sulfur oxides (SO_x)	Fossil fuel combustion Sulfur dioxide (SO_2) most common	2,620 mg/m³ (1.0 ppm), 24 h average	Highly soluble gas Respiratory irritation, bronchoconstriction, and spasms Heightened sensitivity in asthmatics, especially with cold, dry air
Nitrogen oxides (NO_x)	Fossil fuel combustion, cigarettes Nitrogen dioxide (NO_2) most common	938 mg/m³ (0.5 ppm), 24 h average 3,750 mg/m³ (2.0 ppm), 1 h average	Soluble gas that can be absorbed by nasopharyngeal tract Pulmonary dysfunction, respiratory irritation Minimal evidence for major exercise impairment at low levels Acute high doses can induce prolonged pulmonary deficits

Pollutant	Source and size of particles	Limits for danger to human health*	Primary effects
Carbon monoxide (CO)	Fossil fuel combustion	57.5 mg/m³ (50 ppm), 8 h average 86.3 mg/m³ (75 ppm), 4 h average 144 mg/m³ (125 ppm), 1 h average	High affinity (~230 times greater than that of O_2) for binding with hemoglobin, resulting in impaired oxygen-carrying capacity and cardiovascular function Permanent cardiac and neural damage; ultimately fatal in high doses
Aerosols	Suspension of primary pollutants (e.g., fine particulates) in air or other gases (e.g., smoke, mist); broad category of secondary pollutants from reactions of nitrogen oxides and sulfur oxides	800 mg/m³ (0.4 ppm), 4 h average 1,200 mg/m³ (0.6 ppm), 2 h average 1,400 mg/m³ (0.7 ppm), 1 h average	Potentially wide range and variability of cardiovascular and respiratory responses, based on pollutant and allergy or asthma history
Ozone (O_3)	Main component of smog Secondary pollutant from interaction of automobile exhaust, hydrocarbons, and nitrogen oxides with sunlight and ultraviolet radiation Highly susceptible to spikes during summers due to increased sunlight, heat, and local geography and weather	120 mg/m³, 8 h average (World Health Organization) 0.075 ppm, 8 h average (EPA)	Wide range of respiratory symptoms including irritation, bronchospasms, inflammation, dyspnea, and reduced pulmonary function Intensity of impairment during exercise dependent on concentration and effective dosage from ventilation rate Proposed threshold of 0.20-0.40 ppm for significant exercise impairment

*Environmental Protection Agency (EPA) of the United States unless noted.

Ozone (O_3) is a gaseous pollutant formed from the photochemical reaction between sunlight and volatile organic compounds and nitrogen oxides. Ozone is a respiratory irritant that can reduce pulmonary capacity during passive exposure. Along with irritation and bronchospasms, one of the most common symptoms of O_3 exposure is tightness in the chest when breathing. Currently, one major theory is that the underlying mechanism behind O_3 impairment is through a stimulation of airway receptors or nerve endings, which in turn elicit a reflex central neural inhibition of inspiration and expiration. Another potential mechanism is oxidative damage and an inflammatory response within the lung tissue, with elevation in the level of neutrophil release and immune response upon exposure. Of the major air pollutants, O_3 may be the one that is the most susceptible to high levels of variability due to its interaction with local environmental conditions like temperature, such that it can spike to extremely high levels on sunny summer days. This is further exacerbated by increased automobile traffic, which generates more pollutants to react with sunlight, as well as the greater risks of a temperature inversion in warm air, which traps the pollution and keeps it close to ground level.

Particulate matter (PM) spans a wide spectrum of pollutants. This can include seasonal pollens with potential for high sensitivity in some individuals, and which can make exercise all but impossible for them due to allergic reactions. In urban environments, PM can include by-products of fossil-fuel burning from vehicular traffic and coal-fired electrical plants. Rural environments with low population density may still experience high PM concentrations through agriculture (e.g., soil particles being blown into the air), brush burning, or forest fires. Particulate matter is categorized into several categories based on size—including large (2.5-10 μm), fine (1.0-2.5 μm), and ultrafine (<1.0 μm)—rather than by source, as seen in table 13.2. In general, the smaller the particle, the greater the potential for penetration and deposition deeper within the respiratory tract. Modeling PM concentration patterns can be challenging. For example, the dispersal rate of different sizes and types of PM may differ based on local wind patterns and the aerodynamic nature of the particles.

As can be seen from table 13.2, different air pollutants can have a multitude of effects, eliciting a range of symptoms from inflammation and bronchospasms (ozone, sulfur dioxide) to direct binding to hemoglobin and impaired oxygen-carrying capacity (carbon monoxide). This makes it difficult to generalize about the effects of air pollutants as a whole on human health and performance. However, when we study air pollutants, many consistent themes emerge, from the concept of quantifying exposure levels and dose–response to the risk from long-term exposure and the potential countermeasures.

Key Point

Air pollution concerns are not the sole domain of outdoor rowing. With indoor rowing and cross-training common, athletes may also be at risk for significant indoor pollutant exposure. First and foremost, air in indoor venues comes from the outside ambient environment and therefore may pose the same risks as training outdoors without adequate filtering. Secondly, indoor athletic venues such as sport complexes, gyms, and swimming facilities may also be susceptible to molds and fungi due to the combination of sweat, humidity, poor ventilation, and lack of thorough sanitization of facilities and equipment. Furthermore, off-gassing from building materials (e.g., paint, plastic) may be an additional risk. Given the knowledge gained from the COVID-19 pandemic, appropriate air treatment and ventilation are of primary importance to ensure a safe training environment.

Effective Dose

One of the difficulties with understanding the health and exercise effects of pollutants is quantifying and modeling the actual magnitude or pattern of exposure. Most pollutants seem to have a dose–response effect, with higher doses eliciting greater levels of physiological response and clinical symptoms. Without a standardized methodology of quantifying and reporting, however, it can be very difficult to compare findings and consequently to generalize research. Two environmental parameters common to all pollutants would appear to be ambient concentration and the duration of exposure. Because we are ultimately dealing with humans living and exercising in such environments, a third parameter would logically be the actual amount breathed in by an individual, or the ventilation rate. One basic model of quantifying this effective dose (ED), therefore, is an unweighted product of these three parameters (equation 13.4):

$$\text{Effective dose (ppm/L)} = \text{Concentration (ppm)}$$
$$\times \text{Duration (min)} \times \text{Ventilation (L/min)} \quad (13.4)$$

Beyond this simple product, modeling can become much more complex. Adams and colleagues (1981) systematically investigated the relationship between the effective dosage of O_3 and pulmonary impairment by altering concentrations, durations, and ventilation rates (using mild to moderate continuous exercise) over 18 experimental trials. At the same time, the relative importance of each of these three input parameters in modeling effective dose was tested. This research design achieved similar ED values (e.g., five conditions had ED = 800 ppm/L) with different input values, and also tested a range of effective doses, from 0 to 1200 ppm/L. Greater decreases in spirometric measures such as forced vital capacity (FVC), forced expiratory volume over 1 s (FEV_1), and maximal midexpiratory flow rate were reported with increasing ED exposure. Of the three components modeled in effective dose (concentration, duration, and ventilation), the authors proposed that O_3 concentration remained the primary determinant of toxicity and pulmonary impairment, with ventilation rate in turn playing a more important role than exposure time. The general threshold for decreases in spirometric values compared to baseline values was between 0.20 and 0.30 ppm, although no finer resolution was possible because 0.10 ppm intervals were employed for the concentration manipulation.

Finer resolution of pollutant concentration levels may be important, including factors such as temporary or local spikes in concentration rather than overall average values. During intermittent moderate exercise with prolonged 8 h exposure to 0.12 ppm O_3, differences in pulmonary impairment have been demonstrated between a square wave (i.e., constant 0.12 ppm) and a triangular (i.e., gradually increasing from 0 to 0.24 ppm over the first 4 h, decreasing back to 0 ppm over the final 4 h) exposure pattern (Hazucha et al. 1992). Specifically, greater impairment was observed during the later stages of a triangular exposure than during a square wave exposure.

In addition to absolute levels of pollutants, the relative negative "quality" of exposure to pollutants within a given dosage is also likely higher in athletes than in others. This is mainly a result of both the higher ventilation rates inherent with high-intensity exercise and the different breathing patterns that may result from higher ventilation rates. Above approximately 35 L/min, breathing patterns may become dominated by oral breathing, reducing the filtering capacity of the nasal passages. It is also possible that highly fit athletes may have deeper inspiratory force at the same ventilation, drawing pollutants deeper into the respiratory tract. Variations in breathing patterns even at the same average ventilation rate, such as those that occur with intermittent versus continuous exercise, may also affect the deposition pattern of pollutants in the body.

Pollution Effects on Exercise

Even if athletes exercise in a relatively clean environment, the commute to such venues is often through a polluted environment. Therefore, one question is whether preexposure to pollutants can affect subsequent exercise, even if performed under less polluted conditions. When exposed to diesel exhaust with 300 μg/m³ concentration of $PM_{2.5}$ (fine particulate matter between 1-2.5 μm, see table 13.2) for 60 min, impairment in pulmonary spirometry and a higher exercise heart rate were observed compared to preexposure to filtered air, but no impairment was seen in arterial saturation of oxygen or in 20 km cycling time trial performance (Giles et al. 2012). Although performance was maintained, the 6 bpm increase in heart rate in these endurance-trained individuals may mean higher potential health risks for less-fit individuals or those with preexisting cardiovascular conditions. Interestingly, this study and others from the same research group overcame the typical limitations of single pollutant research by utilizing whole diesel exhaust, including carbon monoxide and various nitrogen oxides. Specifically, a diesel generator was used to provide pollution that was diluted to realistic ambient levels, then run through a filter to achieve the desired $PM_{2.5}$ concentration.

A comprehensive consensus concerning exercise in polluted environments is difficult due to the wide range of both potential pollutants and types of exercise, compounded by the relatively limited research compared to other environmental stressors such as oxygen availability. Because carbon monoxide directly reduces oxygen transport through hemoglobin, it should theoretically have the most direct effect on exercise capacity and performance. Existing data support this idea, although a minimal threshold in carbon monoxide concentration or exercise intensity may be required before significant impairment can be discerned. Interestingly, nonsmokers may be at greater risk of impaired performance than smokers. This may be because smokers have already adapted to a higher exposure to carbon monoxide, or because they are generally at lower levels of fitness and therefore have less potential for performance impairment.

The physiological responses to ozone were first noted in the mid-19th century, and initial studies on exercising rats were performed in the 1950s. In terms of humans and exercise performance, the initial scientific reports first appeared in the 1960s; these included observations of an inverse relationship between ozone levels and race performance (i.e., worse run completion times) in high school runners. In general, research with ozone suggests a dose-dependent impairment in maximal exercise capacity, task completion rate, and overall exercise (e.g., marathon) performance. In turn, the direct data on exercise performance with the other main air pollutants (SO_2, NO_2) are relatively scarce.

Altitude and Exercise

The ultimate challenge of altitude is the reduced oxygen availability stemming from the reduction in barometric pressure (with constant 20.93% oxygen, regardless of altitude), which leads to an overall lower partial pressure of oxygen and a reduction in the gradient of oxygen reaching into the lungs, blood, and ultimately to the muscles. Not surprisingly, aerobic capacity decreases roughly curvilinearly with acute exposure to higher altitudes. For an aerobic-dominant sport such as rowing, it is thus highly likely that altitude will have a detrimental impact on performance and training capacity, both over an individual workout and also over a training cycle. If competing at altitude, this aerobic decrement requires adjustment to pacing and race strategy. If preparing an altitude camp, training volume and especially intensity need to be initially reduced and then gradually phased in over time as the body adapts to the hypoxic environment to avoid overtraining; a further emphasis on optimizing recovery might also be required. Further, although beyond the scope of this chapter, nutritional adaptations may need to be made both prior to and over the course of altitude camps, such as ensuring adequate iron intake to support hematopoiesis (Stellingwerff et al. 2019).

Key Point

The challenges posed by reduced oxygen availability are balanced against the potential ergogenic benefits of reduced air resistance due to the lower barometric pressure. This balance has been especially targeted by athletes performing power events such as discus, javelin, high jump, and long jump. Indeed, the dominant athletic memory of the 1968 Mexico City Games is Bob Beamon's shattering of the long jump record by over 55 cm, a mark that stood for 23 years. With such power sports, the minimal reliance on aerobic capacity heavily skews the cost–benefit of low oxygen versus aerodynamics toward competing at altitude. With endurance sports, cyclists have also targeted world records, such as the 1 h cycling time trial, at moderate altitudes. Even at sea level, cyclists have tried to minimize air resistance by planning record attempts around days with low atmospheric pressure and also by heating up the velodrome as much as possible (higher temperatures equals lower atmospheric pressure). Rowing, however, is performed at much lower speeds than cycling and also much more dominated by water resistance, such that the potential aerodynamic gains are likely heavily offset by the impairment from reduced oxygen availability. Therefore, when training at altitude, decrements in workload and interval targets need to be accommodated within training programs, including both a sharp acute decrement followed by partial but not full adaptation over time.

Altitude Training Efficacy

The 1968 Mexico City Olympics was the first major competition held at altitude, sparking scientific interest into the capacity for human performance with reduced oxygen availability. Since that time, elite endurance and team sport athletes have increasingly adopted some form of hypoxic training into their yearly training schedule, with the idea that passive or active exposure to hypoxia provides additional physiological stimulus. Altitude training has also evolved from its original format of living and training for extended periods at moderate altitudes of 2,000+ m. Currently, variations include living at high and training at low altitudes, training at sea level in hypoxic environments, and the use of hypoxic tents and rooms for sleep. At the opposite extreme, hyperoxic exposure has been explored to maximize training capacity and stimulus.

Although the general efficacy of hypoxic training is compelling, the benefits are far from universal. In a randomized control trial where trained cyclists were exposed to 4 weeks of either normoxia or hypoxia (simulated ~3,000 m), both groups experienced similar patterns and magnitudes of changes to total hemoglobin mass, maximal aerobic capacity, and 26 km time trial performance (Siebenmann et al. 2012). Importantly, this was a blind study, so that the participants in both groups stayed in the same simulated environments for 16 h/day and were unsuccessful in guessing whether they were in the normoxic or hypoxic condition. This study suggests that the combination of dedicated training along with a placebo effect may also be important contributors to hypoxic training camps and also supports data suggesting a significant percentage of nonresponders to hypoxic training (Chapman et al. 1998). Such findings highlight that hypoxic training remains an evolving science, along with the need to individualize protocols rather than using a generic training template.

Altitude Training Mechanisms

Oxygen availability forms a systemic stressor with impact across a wide range of physiological systems. Therefore, multiple mechanisms of benefit from hypoxic training are possible, with some of the major pathways outlined in figure 13.3.

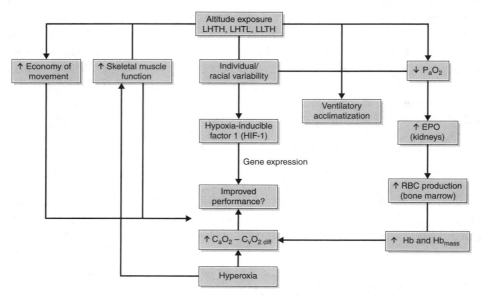

▶ **Figure 13.3**   Summary schematic of major potential hematological and nonhematological pathways that may result in performance improvement from exposure to hypoxia or hyperoxia. Elevations in skeletal muscle function are inclusive of factors such as improved muscle buffering capacity, increased glycolytic enzyme activity, enhanced capillary density, muscle mitochondrial volume, and myoglobin concentration.

One of the primary physiological adaptations underlying the concept of altitude training is an elevation in hemoglobin and red blood cell mass. At a theoretical level, the decreased oxygen availability due to lower partial pressure of oxygen (PO_2) at altitude results in local arterial hypoxia within the kidneys and stimulates an elevated secretion of erythropoietin (EPO). In turn, EPO acts on the marrow within the long bones to increase erythrocyte production. This hematopoiesis or polycythemia (i.e., increase in hemoglobin or red blood cell mass, respectively) should therefore contribute to an increase in blood volume and oxygen-carrying capacity, ultimately producing an increase in aerobic capacity. Acute exposure to hypoxia results in a rise in blood erythropoietin concentration that is detectable within hours, reaching a maximum after ~48 hours, and then declines to reach sea level values after about 3 weeks. The link between hypoxia and erythropoietin secretion involves hypoxia-inducible factor-1 alpha (HIF-1α), a protein that is rapidly degraded by normoxia but accumulates during hypoxia. It has many different effects, but importantly, it binds to the promoter region of the erythropoietin gene and upregulates transcription.

Endurance performance is not solely a function of hemoglobin changes or maximal aerobic capacity as embodied by $\dot{V}O_2$max. Rather, two other primary determinants exist. The first is the fraction of $\dot{V}O_2$max that can be sustained for prolonged periods of time. This intensity, pace, or power output has been variously quantified as lactate threshold (e.g., the work intensity at which blood lactate begins to accumulate and rise) or maximal lactate at steady state (e.g., the highest workload that can be sustained without a continued rise in blood lactate). The second, often-overlooked factor is the economy of movement, typically quantified as the amount of oxygen required to perform a set workload. In turn, economy of movement can be improved by two methods: (1) technical improvements, such as perfecting the rowing stroke, resulting in overall reduction in net cost of movement; and (2) improved cellular efficiency, resulting in less metabolic cost in adenosine triphosphate (ATP) production.

Intriguingly, hypoxic exposure appears to elicit a marked improvement in economy of movement, with reductions in submaximal oxygen requirements of 3% to 10% having been reported, though contradictory conclusions of no change in economy have also been reported (Gore et al. 2001). Breaking down cellular efficiency further, improvements in economy can be achieved via a greater production of ATP per oxygen utilization or else reduced ATP costs of muscular contraction. One potential mechanism for enhanced cellular efficiency is via improvements in the electron transport chain—for example, minimizing the amount of H^+ leakage through the mitochondrial membranes during oxidative phosphorylation. A number of uncoupling proteins (UCP) have been identified as increasing the rate of membrane H^+ leakage (thereby reducing mitochondrial efficiency); and UCP3, present in human skeletal muscle, is reported to decrease with physical training. Because the process of cellular metabolism is complex, it appears highly possible that other molecular factors within the skeletal muscles themselves may also serve to modulate metabolic efficiency and that hypoxic stress may alter the relative activity or sensitivity of these factors.

The ability of the body and the skeletal muscles to tolerate and buffer against lactate may be another nonhematological mechanism for altitude training benefits. One of the acute and chronic responses to hypoxia is hyperventilation, which occurs in an attempt to maintain alveolar PO_2 levels. At the same time, hyperventilation potentiates the removal of alveolar CO_2, resulting in a state of respiratory alkalosis. Ultimately, this can lead to enhanced muscle buffering capacity from a lowered pH and additional renal excretion of bicarbonate. Studies on athlete acclimatization to moderate altitude levels appear to support the enhanced buffering capacity model, with 2 to 3 weeks of altitude exposure above 2,000 m (6,560 ft) resulting in enhanced muscle buffering in trained individuals (Gore et al. 2001).

Conclusion

Environmental factors such as temperature extremes, pollution, and altitude form a potent stressor to training capacity and racing performance. The mechanisms at play are systemic and span multiple physiological systems, including psychological regulation of exercise. Ultimately, extremes in ambient temperature along with humidity, solar radiation, and wind can dramatically alter the thermal load. This makes it critical for athletes and support staff to develop cooling and heating strategies to ensure that the body and muscles remain at optimal temperatures over the course of training and competition. Pollution levels should be monitored and ideally modeled to ensure both short-term athletic performance and also long-term athlete health. The highly aerobic nature of rowing also means that performance will be reduced at even low to moderate altitude due to the reduced oxygen availability. This has implications for optimizing race-day pacing strategies.

The goal of this chapter was to lay out the basic underlying physiology of these environmental stressors. In chapter 21, we will focus on countermeasures to optimize training and competing in environmental extremes and potentially use environmental stressors such as altitude to advantage.

PART IV

Practical Issues
and Components
of Rowing Training

Principles of Exercise

Brett Smith, PhD

Rowing is a physically demanding sport, and to succeed, rowers need to be close to optimal levels of conditioning, which requires constant, focused training. To develop an effective training program, a coach requires a rudimentary knowledge of biomechanics, health, management, nutrition, pedagogy, physiology, psychology, and training theory. There is no single training approach that will be successful for every crew, but successful coaches can benefit from understanding the basics of training theory to develop their training templates and shape their program details. This chapter aims to introduce the reader to the fundamental principles of training relevant to the development of a rowing program and to provide background and context for the various areas of training covered in subsequent chapters. For the sake of convenience, some examples shown may draw on a single training method rather than detailing the various other options available.

The Theory of Training Adaptation

The development of an effective rowing training program requires an understanding of general adaptation syndrome (GAS), a theory that describes the human body's innate adaptive capabilities in response to stress (Selye 1973)—in this case, the stress of exercise (see figure 14.1). There is some debate over the efficacy of GAS for developing periodized training programs (Matveyev 1964), but it is commonly promoted as the principal framework for guiding coaches in designing training programs (Cunanan et al. 2018). The theory posits that if a training stress is of sufficient intensity and volume, it will elicit a biological overload specific to that stress, which will be followed by an acute fatigue phase (see figure 14.2). After a sufficient recovery period—the length of which is dictated by the individual's biological response to the stress—the fatigue dissipates, and a supercompensatory anabolic adaptation occurs. This supercompensation response leads to a period of improved conditioning, within which there is a point of optimal conditioning, during which the next training session should ideally occur (see figure 14.3a). If not, then this next session should occur during the period of enhanced conditioning to ensure continued improvements.

The anabolic response to the stress of training is reversible, so if the recovery period between subsequent training sessions is too long—that is, it falls outside the period of improved conditioning—then the athlete's conditioning will likely remain unchanged (see figure 14.3c). Conditioning can also decline if the next training session occurs before the period of improved conditioning—that is, when the athlete has not appropriately recovered and is still fatigued (see figure 14.3b). If this practice continues, the

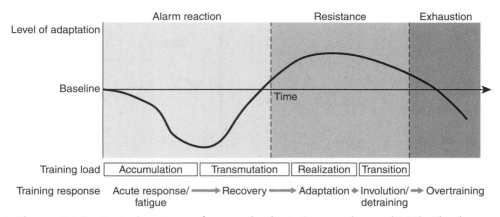

▶ **Figure 14.1** Typical pattern of general adaptation syndrome (GAS). The human body's level of adaptation to stress initially declines, followed by an increase. The level of adaptation depends on the size of the stress and recovery time.

Reprinted by permission from A.J. Cunanan, B.H. DeWeese, J.P. Wagle, et al., "The General Adaptation Syndrome: A Foundation for the Concept of Periodization," Sports Medicine 48, no. 4 (2018): 787-797. Reproduced with permission from Springer Nature.

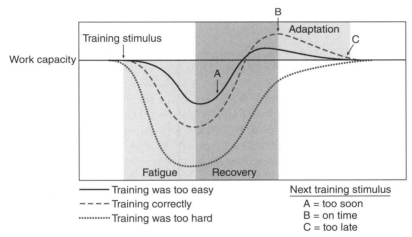

▶ **Figure 14.2** Application of the GAS principle to training and development of performance over time depending on training stimulus and recovery. A, B, and C represent the possible timing of next training stimulus.

Reprinted by permission from T. Bompa, Periodization: Theory and Methodology of Training, 4th ed. (Champaign, IL: Human Kinetics, 1999).

athlete not only risks a decline in performance, but also increases the risk of injury and illness from prolonged fatigue.

Cotter (2013) developed a model, adapted here, that expands on the GAS principle, which takes into account the various nontraining stressors that can influence the stress of training, thereby altering fatigue, recovery, and adaptation (see figure 14.4). In his model, Cotter describes how these stressors combine with the direct workload stress of training to modify both the level of overall stress on the body (which he calls *strain*) and the required recovery duration to achieve a positive adaptation. Cotter (2013) and Seyle (1973) both posit that the stress that promotes adaptation to training is more than

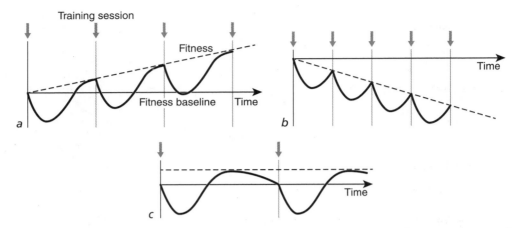

▶ **Figure 14.3** Timing of consecutive training stimuli. *(a)* Positive adaptation, stress of session matched by recovery, resulting in a continuous positive adaptation. *(b)* Negative adaptation, maladaptation, stress of session not matched by recovery (i.e., stress is too great and/or recovery is insufficient). *(c)* No supercompensation, recovery time between training sessions is too long or training is not stressful enough.

just the training session's workload. However, Cotter suggests that these other stressors can affect both the training load and recovery rate, and in turn, possibly affect the magnitude of the adaptation (or maladaptation). A fit, healthy, confident, hydrated, fueled, and resilient rower who is training at sea level in the cold and who trusts the coach and believes in the program is likely to complete a hard training session and to recover quickly afterward. On the other hand, a rower without these traits who is training at altitude in the heat while dehydrated and poorly fueled may not be able to complete the same training load or might require a prolonged recovery period to adapt positively. Psychosocial stress inside and outside the training environment can also amplify the stress response to training, which can inhibit training load, recovery, and adaptation.

Key Point

The body's adaptation to training is influenced by training and nontraining factors. A coach must be aware of the other factors that could be influencing the rower's response to training (and general well-being), because addressing these factors may help facilitate improved recovery and conditioning.

Although genetics cannot be modified, the coach and rower can take steps to modify many of the other nontraining stressors to help optimize the rowing-specific adaptations to a given training load. Identifying these stressors and exploring strategies to mitigate their effects requires expertise, accurate tools, and effective strategies, plus time and effort from coaches and support staff. One strategy to optimize recovery is to provide a stable, safe, efficacious, motivational, and inclusive environment to reduce psychosocial stress. Although much research focuses on optimizing recovery, coaches may at times deliberately amplify the total stress of training by including specific non-

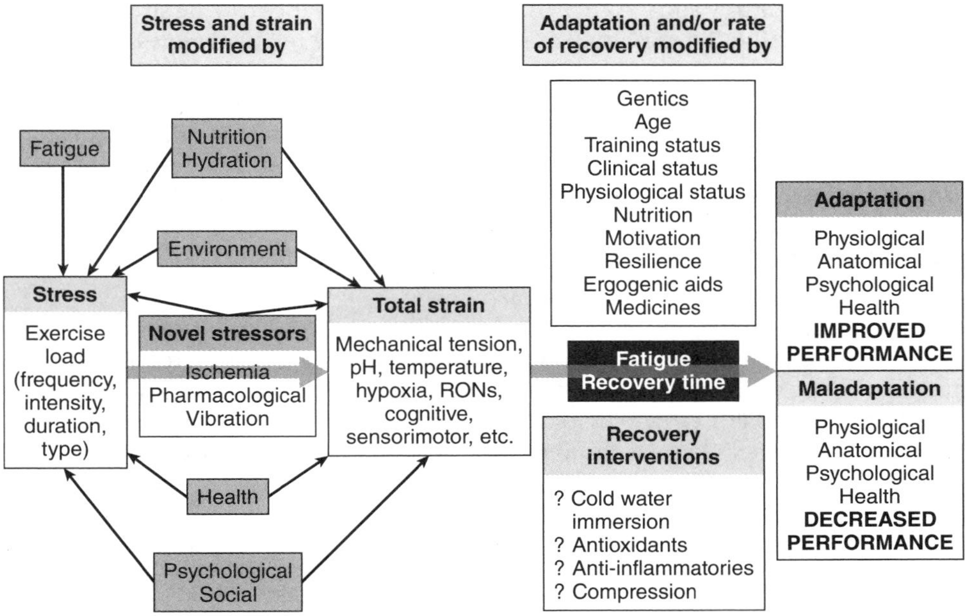

▶ **Figure 14.4**   Training and adaptation model.

Reprinted as modified by Brett Smith from J.D. Cotter, "Novel Stress Conditioning for Health and Performance," Paper presented at the 15th International Conference on Environmental Ergonomics, Queenstown, NZ, February 11-15 (2013).

training stressors, such as altitude training to enhance hemoglobin levels, at the cost of high fatigue and some reduced rowing-specific adaptations.

Key Point

High levels of training stress can lead to both high levels of adaptation and increased risk of maladaptation. An effective rowing training program therefore needs to balance the high levels of training load required for success with the requisite periods of recovery.

Selye (1973) proposed that the nature of the stress will influence the direction of the adaptive processes—that is, the acute cell-signaling and hormonal responses to a training bout leads to specific protein and functional adaptations (Cunanan et al. 2018). This response is generally termed *the specificity principle*, and it posits that the adaptions to training stress are specific to the type of training (e.g., rowing, cycling, running) and components involved (e.g., aerobic training improves aerobic fitness, strength training improves strength). Adaptations to rowing may benefit other sports and vice versa (e.g., cardiorespiratory adaptations improving rowing may also improve running and cycling), but rowing is more likely to optimize rowing-specific metabolic, neuromuscular, skeletal, and circulatory adaptations. Thus, rowing is the best conditioning for rowers, although novices who lack the technical ability to generate the required rowing intensity may benefit from cross-training. Other types of endurance exercise may also be employed to alleviate monotony or when injury limits the ability to row.

Rowers also typically add weight lifting exercises to enhance rowing strength, speed, and power. Although the maximal and average forces are relatively low during 2,000 m races across the spectrum of boat classes, the power generated through the extensive range of motion of the knee and hip are unique to rowing and arguably need to be enhanced to optimize performance. Although weight training may not be specific to rowing and therefore suffers limitations as a means of optimizing rowing-specific power, it does provide other significant benefits, which will be described in later chapters.

The FITT Principles of Training

There are general guidelines on the frequency, intensity, type, and time (duration) of exercise required to develop each of the conditioning components (aerobic endurance, anaerobic capacity, strength, power, etc.). These are termed the *FITT principles* (table 14.1). The specifics of the FITT principles for the various aspects of rowing training are covered in more detail in later chapters; however, the general aspects are introduced below.

Table 14.1 Frequency, Intensity, Type, and Time (Duration) of Exercise for Rowing Training

| | FREQUENCY | | | | Time (Volume | |
| | Sessions | Session | | | or duration in | |
Descriptors	per week	recovery	Intensity	Type	training zone)	Example methods
Active recovery	n/a	n/a	Zone 1 Easy-moderate RPE 8-9	Row Erg Other	n/a	8-12 km at 16-18 spm Warm-up, cool-down, recovery between intervals
LSD Aerobic base Zone 1	6-12	4-12 hrs	Aerobic threshold 60%-70% HRR 1.5-2.0 mM [La] ≤ LT1 or ≤ VT1 Moderate-hard RPE 10-12	Row Erg	10-120 min per interval 45-120 min per session 12-30 km per session 60-240 km per week	12-30 km steady state 6-12 × 2 km or 8 min at 18-20 spm, 1-2 min off 5-15 × 1-2 km at 16, 18, 20, 22 spm, 1-2 min off Pyramids, steps, ladders Work-to-rest ratio: ≤1:0.25
Anaerobic threshold Zone 2	3	36-48 hrs	Aerobic-anaerobic threshold 70%-85% HRR 2.0-4.0 mM [La] LT1-LT2 VT1-VT2 Moderate-hard RPE 13-16	Row Erg	5-60 min per interval 20-60 min per session 5-20 km per session 10-50 km per week	1 × 6-12 km at max sustainable SR (MSR) 2-3 × 4-5 km at MSR, 5 min off 3-4 × 10-15 min at 28-34 spm, 3-10 min off 4-8 × 500 m at 26, 28, 30, 32 spm (2,000 m total), 3-5 min off Pyramids, steps, ladders Work-to-rest ratio: 1:1 to 1:0.5

| Descriptors | FREQUENCY | | Intensity | Type | Time (Volume or duration in training zone) | Example methods |
	Sessions per week	Session recovery				
Anaerobic $\dot{V}O_2$max Zone 3	2-3	48-72 hrs	Anaerobic threshold– $\dot{V}O_2$max + 90%-100% HRR > 6.0 mM [La] > LT2 & VT2 Very hard– maximal RPE 18-20	Row Erg	15 sec to 6 min per interval 10-15 minutes per session 2-4 km per session 20-40 minutes per week 6-12 km per week	8 × 250 m at max SR, 5 min off (LaP) 6 × 500 m at race pace, 8 min off (LaP) 3-5 × 1 min at race pace, 1 min off (LaT) 4-6 × 30 s on at max SR, 1.5 min off (LaT) Work-to-rest ratio: 1:5 to 1:0.5
Strength	2-3	48-72 hrs	≥ 85% 1 RM Maximal intensity	Weight training	1-6 repetitions ≥ 3 sets per exercise 2-5 mins rest interval between sets	Back squats: 2 × 10 warm-up, 3 × 4-6 (85%-90% 1RM), 3 min rest Leg press: 10 (60% 1RM), 8 (70% 1RM) 2 × 6 (85% 1RM), 3 min rest Bench pulls 10 (2RR), 6 (1RR), 2 × 4 (1RM) Deadlift: 8, 6, 4, 2 warm-up, 2 × 1 (0.17-0.2 m/s), 5 min rest
Hypertrophy	2-3	48-72 hrs	67%-85% 1 RM Moderate-hard intensity To failure	Weight training	6-12 repetitions ≥ 3 sets per exercise 30-90 sec rest interval between sets	Single-arm dumbbell row: 6 × 10/12 (65%-75% 1RM), 30-60 s rest Romanian deadlift/ front squat: 3 × 10 (75%-80% 1RM), 1 min rest Pendlay row: 10, 9, 8, 7, 6 (75% 1RM), 1 min rest Alternating dumbbell lunge: 10 × 6 per leg, repeat at 2 min
Power	1-3	48-72 hrs	30%-70% 1 RM Maximal intensity Intention to move explosively	Gym training Erg Row	5-20 second per interval (or 1-6 repetitions) 3-6 sets per exercise 2-5 mins rest interval between sets	Power clean: 10, 8 warmup, 3 × 6 (60% 1RM), 3 min rest Box CMJ: 3 × 6, max height, body weight, 2-3 min rest Deep barbell squats: 3 × 6 (>1.5 m/s, ~30% 1RM), 2-3 min rest Row or row erg: 4-6 × 50-150 m, max SR, 2-3 min rest

1RM = maximal weight lifted for one repetition; CMJ = counter movement jump; HRR = heart rate reserve; [La] = blood lactate concentration; LT = lactate threshold; LT1 = lactate threshold 1; LT2 = lactate threshold 2; LSD = long slow distance; RPE = rate of perceived exertion (20 point scale); session recovery = time between sessions; VT1 = ventilatory threshold 1; VT2 = ventilatory threshold 2; LaP = lactate production; LaT = lactate tolerance; RR = reps in reserve e.g., 2RR means that two more weightlifting repetitions could be completed to achieve 1RM; SR = stroke rate measured in spm = strokes per minute.

Frequency

Frequency refers to the recommended number of sessions per week, and each conditioning component has its own frequency. Each component's frequency guidelines are based on their recommended recovery time, which is only an estimate of the time required after a training session for a full recovery and the optimal anabolic adaptation to occur. Ideally, however, the specific recovery time would be more useful than frequency. For example, it requires 48 to 72 hours for the exercised muscles and nerves to fully recover from an intensive strength session, yet the recommended strength training frequency of 2 to 3 times per week could be interpreted as repeating the same session on Monday, Tuesday, and Wednesday. Recovery time can therefore be modified by various factors described previously. Other factors should also be considered, such as whether the training session achieved the requisite workload (volume and intensity) and whether other forms of exercise could interfere with recovery.

Intensity

Intensity is how hard an athlete is required to train during a session to meet the requirements to develop specific exercise components, and this can be described in different ways. Exercise intensity is typically a zone or band between two threshold levels; for example, strength might be measured as 80% to 100% one-repetition maximum (1RM). Some intensities may also be described by more than one measure; for example, the aerobic base can be defined as 70% to 80% heart rate reserve (HRR), 1.5 to 2.0 mmol/L blood lactate concentration, or a rate of perceived exertion (RPE) of 14 to 16. There are various methods of monitoring intensity specific to each component. For example, heart rate is one way to gauge intensity during endurance training; however, it is of little relevance during strength training and has no applicability for flexibility training. Measuring boat speed during training is a standard measure of intensity in rowing, and though it provides crucial information to the coach on the performance of the boat and crew, it provides little information on the intensity and the associated stress on each rower required to achieve that boat speed.

The intensity level recommended for each exercise component is also individualized to some extent, depending on factors such as the rower's level of conditioning, genetic capacity, presession fatigue, and so forth. A challenge for the coach is to individualize the intensity zones for the level of the crew and each individual and ensure the availability of tools to accurately measure intensity according to what is affordable and able to be logistically worked into the training schedule.

Type

The commonly used descriptions of the type (or mode) of training are sometimes confused with the components of training. Arguably, the type of training is the mode of training, such as rowing, running, stretching, or lifting weights. The components of training better describe the specific physiological adaptations the training session is trying to enhance, which include "cardiorespiratory fitness, muscular strength and endurance (muscular fitness), body composition, flexibility, and neuromotor fitness" (Garber et al. 2011, 1336). To provide a more rowing-specific description within this textbook, we describe the components as strength, hypertrophy, power, speed, flexibility, balance (agility), technique (skill), body composition, aerobic fitness, anaerobic endurance, and anaerobic capacity. Most of these are self-explanatory apart from perhaps anaerobic endurance and anaerobic capacity. Anaerobic endurance is the ability to repeatedly perform anaerobic intensity exercise (e.g., team sports such as rugby, hockey, or basketball). Anaerobic capacity is the ability to complete a one-off maximal anaerobic effort generating maximal levels of blood lactate (e.g., a race over 500 m rowing, 400 m running, or 1,000 m cycling). It is common to combine types and components of training to achieve a more general goal (e.g., bungees or power strokes to improve both power and endurance).

Key Point

The FITT principles provide a road map for understanding the interaction between the volume, intensity, and recovery for each training session that is required to effectively develop the various conditioning components. Understanding these principles is an important step toward effective programming.

Time

Time is typically the recommended duration of each training session and the total weekly duration, and it varies with the component being trained (see table 14.1). It is common in rowing to calculate duration using distance rowed rather than time, but throughout this explanation, we will continue to use time, although the reader may wish to replace time with distance. The total session time may hide other essential aspects such as the total work time, which may be of more relevance given that total session time could include aspects such as the warm-up, cool-down, and rest time (e.g., in an interval session or when boats have to turn around). An interval session may run for 60 to 90 min, yet the actual work time could be as small as 5 to 10 min. For these types of sessions, the total session time may not provide as much relevant information as total work time and work-to-rest ratio.

For some components, such as weight training, the training volume is better described by repetitions and sets. Repetitions are the number of times an exercise is performed, and a set is a continuous block of repetitions, with the rest interval being the recovery time between sets. For example, a power training session may consist of 4 sets of 6 repetitions with a 2 min rest interval between sets. The notation for describing exercise sessions will be described in more detail in the specific training chapters, but a simple example is exercise name: sets × repetitions (intensity), rest interval. For example, squats: 4 × 10 (100 kg), 90 s rest, is 4 sets of 10 repetitions squatting 100 kg with a 90 s rest between sets. It is not uncommon to combine various descriptors such as total duration, work duration, rest interval, sets, and repetitions. For example, a 70 min lactate tolerance (LaT) session consisting of 20 min of work contains a warm-up and cool-down of 15 min each, 4 working sets consisting of 5 repetitions of 1 min work and 30 s rest, and a 5 min rest interval between each set. This session could be notated as 5 × 1 min (>90% HRR), 30 s rest, repeat 4x at race stroke rate with 5 min rest.

As mentioned previously, it is important to program the daily and weekly volume (time) of training for each specific component. Thus, an effective program requires a duration within a specific intensity band that will develop the component, which requires the coach to understand how to match the volume with the intensity for each training component. As an example, a weekly training program may consist of 10 h of on-water rowing, which breaks down into 2 h of active recovery (<70% HRR), 7 h of aerobic base (70%-80% HRR), and 1 h of anaerobic threshold (80%-85% HRR) training. The coach's challenge is ensuring that the programmed volume is being completed within the correct intensity band for each rower and, if this is not occurring, determining whether volume or intensity needs to be manipulated to achieve the required outcome.

Key Point

The FITT principles apply to all levels of rowers, although the intensity and volume will undoubtedly be reduced for nonelite rowers. For this latter group coaches need to be aware of the extra stresses created by work, home life, and other physical activities that may influence strain, recovery, and adaptation to rowing training. On the other hand, the coach also needs to be aware that elite rowers are subjected to many extraneous stressors related to selection, media coverage, competition, maintaining income, overuse injuries, etc. There are also the psychosocial costs of a lifestyle associated with heavy full-time training, competition, and regular travel to consider, too.

Unfortunately, the FITT principles are not an exact science, and a range of different principles may be promoted to achieve the same conditioning goal. Furthermore, the principles are typically modified depending on the sport, the athlete's conditioning level, training history, personal preferences, injury status, logistics, and so on. The capacities of elite rowers are so advanced that the FITT principles for this group bear little resemblance to the principles applied to lower levels of rowers, so care must be taken in applying general FITT principles to multiple levels of athletes. Despite these limitations, understanding the FITT principles provides important guidance for writing effective training programs for rowers.

Progressive Overload

An effective program should adhere to the principle of progressive overload (Kraemer and Ratamess 2004), whereby the training workload increases over time to keep in step with conditioning improvements so that the magnitude of the stress provides the required overload to stimulate continued positive adaptations. As described previously, it is ideal for the rower to recover fully between sessions so that each successive session elicits the maximal anabolic response (see figure 14.3a), whereas less successful scenarios occur when recovery is insufficient relative to the training stress such that no improvement occurs (see figure 14.3c) or repeated insufficient recovery leads to injury, overreaching, or overtraining (see figure 14.3b).

In practice, the ability to achieve full recovery between each session so that progressive overload can be maximized is extremely difficult. Thus, the typical method of achieving progressive overload is to systematically increase the microcycle training load rather than increasing the training load on a session-by-session basis. A microcycle can be defined as the shortest block of training developed to achieve a specific training goal (e.g., a specified volume or intensity of training) and is typically a week in duration. Suggestions on how to structure a microcycle to achieve specific training goals will be discussed later, but to aid clarity, we will refer to a training "week" instead of "microcycle" throughout this chapter.

Structure of the Overload

Training overload is typically progressed on a week-by-week basis rather than on a session-by-session or day-by-day basis. It is important that the appropriate FITT principles are applied to each session in a manner that allows adequate recovery between sessions to ensure the rower's conditioning improves over the week. The simplest method is for each session within the first week to be identical and then to increase the session load for the subsequent weeks. An example of this would be a 15 km aerobic base rowing session every day of the week, which is then progressed to a 17.5 km aerobic base session every day for the next week, with similar continuous weekly increases. This approach is sometimes used in rowing, but typically the session workloads vary throughout the week, enabling a wider range of components to be developed within the week and reducing monotony and boredom. For example, a week may consist of 2 strength sessions, 4 aerobic base rows, 2 anaerobic threshold rows, and 1 power session. The easiest method is to increase the workload of every session by increasing the volume or intensity; other methods include only increasing the workload in some sessions and leaving others unchanged or to increase the volume of some sessions and the intensity of others.

Key Point

Rapid increase in weekly training workload (i.e., workload spikes) are more likely to result in severe fatigue, illness, or injury. Therefore, a gradual and progressive increase in training workload interspersed with unloading or recovery periods should be employed to achieve the high levels of workload required to optimize rowing conditioning.

The training load is often increased each week in a stepwise manner for 3 to 6 weeks, followed by a week of reduced loading that acts as a regeneration week. This grouping of step-loaded weeks is typically termed a *mesocycle*. The structure of the mesocycle helps alleviate the stagnation of the hormonal and immune system responses to the continued stress of a consistent block of training. A training program is often constructed as a series of mesocycles, with each mesocycle constructed to achieve a different goal. Within the training program, the mesocycles are sequenced so that the required components are developed to achieve the optimal response. A simple example of the order of mesocycle goals for weight training might be introductory weight training, hypertrophy, strength, general power, and rowing-specific power. An example of the order of mesocycle goals for aerobic fitness might be non-specific aerobic base (addition of cross-training), aerobic base, anaerobic threshold, and maximal oxygen uptake. More than one mesocycle may be dedicated to developing a vital component; for example, it is common to repeat the same aerobic base mesocycle with a slight change in focus. This pattern of mesocycle sequencing is typically termed *block periodization*, and the reader should be aware that there is a fair amount of debate about the effectiveness of this method (Issurin 2010; Kiely 2012).

Magnitude of the Overload

There are few evidence-based empirical rules for determining the magnitude of the weekly increase in training load. Typical recommendations are to individualize the weekly load increase by taking into account the sport, athletes, training history, levels of fatigue, conditioning levels, health and injury status, environment, stage of the season, motivation, and effectiveness of previous training. Making decisions about how much to change training load is an important decision—too little may not provide an adequate stimulus to optimize conditioning improvements, whereas too much may increase the risk of injury or overreaching. For many components of training the "methods for optimal progression are not known" (Kraemer et al. 2009, 1335) or recommendations are generalized and call for a gradual increase in frequency, intensity, and/or duration until the desired goal is achieved (Garber et al. 2011). For strength training, the ACSM recommends that a "2-10% increase in load be applied when the individual can perform the current workload for one to two repetitions over the desired number" (Kraemer et al. 2009, 690). A popular guideline for endurance sports promotes no more than a 10% increase per week (the 10% rule), which has little evidential support (Gabbett 2020).

One commonly used strategy to guide weekly workload changes that has created much debate is the acute-to-chronic ratio (Maupin et al. 2020), which can provide a recommended target for the upcoming training week based on the athlete's recent training load. The acute load is the target training workload for the upcoming week, whereas the chronic workload is the training workload over the previous weeks, typically calculated by a rolling average (e.g., average from the previous 3-4 weeks), or an exponentially weighted moving average formula (EWMA). Calculation of the acute-to-chronic ratio indicates the athlete's preparedness or capacity to handle the upcoming training load, with the recommended ratio being between 0.8 and 1.5 (Gabbett 2020). The goal of this strategy is to reduce the risk of injury associated with large increases (spikes) in training load. Noticeable increases in injury rates have been found when acute-to-chronic ratio is greater than 1.5; large decreases (troughs) in training workload may also increase injury risk (Gabbett 2020). Fundamentally, Gabbett (2020) promotes the importance of well-planned graduated weekly workload modifications with high levels of chronic workload (i.e., good conditioning levels), where large spikes and troughs in weekly training load are only used sparingly. One important caveat is that the acute-to-chronic ratio is used to manage the risk of injury; it does not determine the optimal increase in weekly training load. There are several challenges to using this method, including determining which metrics to use, deciding whether to manipulate volume or intensity, and individualizing the load for each rower in a crew.

A potential danger exists using this method during a heavy training session: A rower nearing the end of the mesocycle who is averaging 220 km per week would have a maximum weekly safe distance of 330 km. This number is arguably far too high to be safe (i.e., 1.5 acute-to-chronic ratio multiplied by the chronic distance of 220 km equals a 330 km maximal weekly safe distance). Anecdotally, international crews often average 220 km per week throughout a heavy mesocycle, but it is doubtful that any international rowing program would complete a 330 km training week. Arguably a better strategy for establishing the magnitude of the maximal safe weekly increase in training load would be to use a 1.5 acute-to-chronic ratio at some minimal weekly load, which changes linearly (or exponentially) to a ratio of approximately 1.2 at some predetermined maximal training load. For example, a 120 km chronic weekly load would generate a maximal safe week of 180 km (i.e., 1.5 acute-to-chronic × 120 km chronic = 180 km maximum safe weekly load), while a 220 km chronic weekly load would generate a maximal safe week of 265 km (i.e., 1.2 acute-to-chronic × 220 km chronic = 265 km maximum safe weekly load). Current experiments are underway using such a progressive overload model that seeks to account for these factors, but a few challenges remain unsolved.

Key Point

The acute-to-chronic ratio is a useful tool for managing progressive increases in planned training workload. There are several strengths and weaknesses to this method; readers are recommended to stay up to date with research in this field.

Risking High Stress to Optimize Gains

The law of diminishing returns must also be considered with progressive overload, in that the closer a rower gets to their genetically determined ceiling for each conditioning component, the more difficult it is to gain even small positive adaptations. However, the small differences in finish times in elite rowing races often make those small improvements in conditioning necessary to achieve success and are therefore worth striving for (Smith and Hopkins 2011). In this instance, the challenge is balancing the large amount of stress required to elicit a continued positive response with the requisite recovery period. A training program with an effective progressive overload should produce improved conditioning so that the rower perceives the high absolute levels of stress as relatively normal. Despite this, as the rower gets closer to their optimal conditioning, the required training stress becomes so large and close to the rower's maximal capacity that tolerances between sufficient and excessive training load become very small and hard to manage (Smith et al. 2011).

Coaches sometimes employ one or more heavy workload weeks to facilitate further development. These so-called shock microcycles involve workload increases beyond those previously experienced, such that the rower is unable to recover sufficiently, resulting in severe fatigue. Bompa and Buzzichelli (2018) promote the use of this strategy to "break the ceiling of adaptation achieved in a previous phase so the athlete pushes to a superior homeostasis" (174). This strategy is risky and requires a longer than normal recovery phase and is therefore used sparingly, typically away from important races. Shock microcycles are not uncommon, especially in elite programs where conditioning gains are difficult to achieve, because many coaches believe the benefits outweigh the risk.

Managing Training Load and Fatigue

An effective rowing training program requires the concurrent development of multiple components. For example, developing aerobic base and hypertrophy may be the initial focus, followed by more intensive aerobic rowing with strength development, with the final focus being the addition of anaerobic rowing with power training. Therefore, each mesocycle may contain weekly step-loaded increases of two components with the maintenance of one or more other components. In the previous example, the final focus may be anaerobic rowing, but aerobic rowing will also be maintained. Likewise, gym training may focus on power but also include strength maintenance. The interference effect, discussed in chapter 12, describes the physiological effects of training different components concurrently. The exact nature and magnitude of this interference is not clearly understood (Coffey and Hawley 2017), but a straightforward strategy to deal with interference is to accept that not all components will be optimally developed and therefore prioritize the most important component to develop in a mesocycle.

Because elite rowers require large aerobic and anaerobic capacities (Hagerman 1984), they must often train very hard to develop the highest levels of conditioning required for success. Large training workloads will result in high fatigue levels, which must be managed in order to avoid increased rates of injury, overreaching, and possible overtraining caused by prolonged periods of extensive fatigue. The effective coach needs to develop a training program that balances the reward of optimized anabolic response with the associated risk of high levels of fatigue. It is important to note that at specific times the high levels of fatigue should not necessarily be viewed as a negative response to training—in fact, some successful elite rowing coaches welcome this response as a sign that their program can generate high levels of conditioning (Pope, Penney, and Smith 2018).

Key Point

This process of managing fatigue becomes very challenging with rowers close to their peak. At such high workloads, relatively small increases can greatly enhance the risk of severe fatigue, illness, or injury. Coaches need to develop a range of methods to aid their understanding of how individual rowers are responding to training.

The Challenge of Individualizing Recovery Within a Crew

Although these principles guide the development of an overall rowing training program, each rower's fundamental requirement is adherence to the GAS principle, which ensures that the stress of training is balanced by the recovery period. Unfortunately, the ability of each rower in a crew to recover appropriately between sessions or over a prolonged period cannot be guaranteed, and steps are therefore required to manage this process. Although individualizing an athlete's training load and recovery is common in most team sports, many argue that rowing is unique in that "there is hardly any other sport in which athletes depend on and affect each other to such an extent as they do in rowing" (Kellmann et al. 2006, 481). Rowing is considered the ultimate team sport in that the boat will only reach its best performance with the completely synchronized, focused, intensive, and technically correct effort of every member of the crew. These factors have led some coaches to believe that putting all crew members on the same training program is crucial to developing a good crew dynamic and, most importantly, engendering trust, which is an essential ingredient in crew rowing (Brown 2014).

It is therefore difficult to modify recovery time within rowing programs. For logistical reasons, rowing schedules are typically locked into set times of the day throughout the week. Therefore, the rower struggling to recover typically has the option of either missing training or reducing the intensity or volume of training until they have recovered, both of which are complicated options in a rowing crew. In some instances, training intensities are individualized; however, this can lead to the complaint that the crew is starting to achieve good boat run when a heart rate monitor or some other measure signals for a decrease in intensity. Boat run is measured by the distance the boat travels between strokes; when everything comes together and good run is achieved with hard work and perfect synchronization, it can generate a unique feeling of rhythm, swing, and speed. At this stage, many rowers perceive the boat as light, fast, responsive, and alive to every stroke. This state is akin to the notion of flow (Swann 2016), a psychological construct used by many athletes to describe being "in the zone" (Pineau et al. 2014), which is the goal for both training and competition.

Given the sometimes extreme difficulty in achieving good boat run, it is not always easy for coaches to balance against the need to develop optimal conditioning. If boat run is the priority, then individual differences in physiologies, capacities, and conditioning can result in some crew members working too hard to achieve the required boat run and speed. Those rowers will not be adapting positively to the training program due to inadequate recovery time. Even if a crew breaks down into smaller boats for training, all rowers typically perform the same training program, and a rower struggling to recover is arguably more likely to find it challenging to keep up even in a smaller boat.

Therefore, the challenge with a rower who is struggling to recover over a prolonged period is to find ways to support the required level of recovery. At one end of the spectrum, the rower who is not recovering between sessions may eventually end up sick or injured, removing them from the crew, whereas individualizing their training load and recovery may negatively affect boat run and crew dynamic. A coach who can engender a positive culture within a crew so that they accept reduced workloads or longer recovery for some rowers has a definite advantage, but the author contends that this is difficult to achieve, given the culture of rowing. It should be noted that individualizing a training program for a single sculler does not usually suffer from these problems.

Improving Recovery Rate

Given the challenges of individualizing training load and recovery, perhaps the most effective strategy to manage excessive fatigue in some crew members is improving their recovery rate. There are recovery interventions that may be effective in reducing recovery time by diminishing the stress of the training session, thereby reducing fatigue. Although there is much debate around the effectiveness of these interventions, the commonly recommended strategies include active recovery, anti-inflammatory analgesics, antioxidants, compression garments, cryotherapy, and hydrotherapy, including cold water immersion and massage (Barnett 2006; Bishop, Jones, and Woods 2008). Recovery interventions can be a double-edged sword: Because training stress is required for adaptation, a recovery intervention that reduces stress and enhances recovery may also inhibit the magnitude of the training adaption (Kellmann, Bertollo, et al. 2018). In simple terms, a recovery intervention may reduce both recovery time and conditioning gains, so perhaps an individual athlete struggling to adapt may be better served by reducing the training load than by implementing a recovery intervention. However, if a coach wishes all rowers to be on the same program to create a good crew dynamic, this potential risk may be outweighed by having the rower ready for the next training session. It should be noted that rowers can suffer mental fatigue from training, which also inhibits recovery. Various techniques such as cognitive self-regulation and psychological relaxation can help accelerate psychological recovery (Kellmann, Pelka, et al. 2018).

Monitoring Training Effectiveness

Before an intervention to improve recovery can be employed, accurate measurement strategies need to be implemented to inform the coach whether rowers are improving, remaining stagnant, or losing ground. Typical approaches to monitoring a training program's effectiveness include measurements of external load, internal load, changes in conditioning, and changes in performance. Training load indicators (external and internal load) are commonly employed in rowing, but little scientific evidence supports their practical effectiveness (Kellmann, Bertollo, et al. 2018). External load is simply the work completed by the rower and is typically expressed in volume and time (e.g., 2 min pace per 500 m for 60 min), whereas internal load is the stress placed on the athlete to achieve the work output (i.e., external load). Although the external load is important for understanding the workload completed and capability of the athlete, internal load provides a better insight into the stress of training, which is the crucial factor for facilitating adaptation (Halson 2014). Internal load measures include rate of perceived exertion (RPE), heart rate (HR), training impulse (TRIMP), lactate concentration (La), heart rate variability (HRV), endocrine measures, immune function, metabolic measures, cognitive tests, wellness questionnaires (including fatigue and soreness), mood state, and quality of sleep (Halson 2014).

If a motivated rower's external workload is unable to be maintained, then arguably the training load is too hard. However, monitoring only one measure can often lead to errors—for example, an athlete may decrease the weights they are lifting over time solely because they see no benefit to their rowing performance in their current weightlifting program. Also, if only RPE or HR are measured, these may increase from session to session because the rowers are making the boat go faster each session rather than because their bodies are working harder to maintain consistent boat speed. Perhaps the most effective monitoring strategies are a combination of external and internal measures that provide better insight into the level of stress generated from a specific training workload. For example, suppose an athlete records a lactate concentration of 1.5 mmol/L, HR of 175, and RPE of 16 from a 60 min aerobic base rowing ergometer session performed at a 1:50 split per 500 m at a stroke rate of 20 spm. This enables the coach to determine whether the external workload is generating the appropriate levels of stress—that is, that the aerobic base workout (ergometer split, duration, and stroke rate) is generating the correct lactate concentration, HR, and RPE. Repeating this ergometer session at the same day and time each week can provide beneficial information on either improved conditioning or poor recovery. For example, if in subsequent sessions the lactate concentration, HR, and RPE increases but workload decreases (either in reduced volume or intensity) then arguably conditioning is deteriorating due to insufficient recovery. If managed appropriately, monitoring internal and external measures in repeated training sessions can provide the coach with good rowing-specific information on the athlete's progress.

Monitoring on-water training has limitations: Unlike the rowing ergometer and single scull, which provide individual workload measures, boat speed is the sole measure of external workload for every rower in the crew, and this can be hugely affected by environmental variables (Smith and Hopkins 2011). With time, technology should improve to the level where it is financially feasible to accurately measure and display each rower's external workload during on-water rowing, similar to a Concept2 rowing ergometer. Discussions with rowing coaches about this type of development have met with mixed responses, because some worry that rowers will become obsessed with generating a specific work level rather than focusing on working together with good technique to optimize boat run and speed.

Key Point

It is important that coaches establish effective communication with their rowers to help understand factors such as boredom and monotony when building and adapting their training programs.

One caveat should be noted around best practice strategies for monitoring rowers. A group of very successful elite New Zealand rowing coaches was interviewed about how they monitored their rowers to ensure optimal conditioning and reduce the risk of overtraining. The coaches monitored their athletes using observation, communication, and training workload measures, eschewing the recommended internal workload measurement tools (Pope, Penney, and Smith 2018). The coaches chose this approach because they trusted their intuitions and cues from regularly observing and communicating with rowers before, during, and after every training session.

Conclusion

The fundamentals of developing a good rowing program are a knowledge of how the body recovers and adapts to the various stressors associated with rowing, and the ability to implement the relevant FITT principles and progressive overload to develop the required conditioning components. However, individual rowers within a crew will often recover and adapt differently in response to the same training program as a result of factors that are unrelated to the physical aspect of training or competition. The challenge for the coach is finding methods to individualize training to ensure adequate recovery and ongoing positive adaptations for all members within a crew when, by its very nature, rowing requires everyone to do the same training. Rowing coaches who wish to be innovative in their training methods and their athlete management will benefit from understanding the fundamentals of exercise prescription and the associated scientific principles. Such knowledge can provide a framework for what areas can be improved and how.

Many coaches argue that the ultimate proof of the effectiveness of a training program is whether or not it generates success. Arguably, race performance is the definitive measure of success, and as such regular racing should be included within the program to help monitor progress toward the ultimate goal. However, unless the rower is competing in the single scull, racing does not necessarily provide information on the physical capacity or progress of the individual rowers in the crew. Racing also does not indicate whether all the components required to optimize rowing performance are at the requisite levels or have improved. Thus, a common strategy for determining the effectiveness of training is to employ regular monitoring of the various components required for rowing success, a topic that will be covered in chapter 20.

15 CHAPTER

Aerobic and Anaerobic Rowing Conditioning

Brett Smith, PhD

So, what is the process for a coach or sport scientist to build a training program to develop aerobic and anaerobic conditioning in a crew? For many, the process of creating a rowing training program is probably as much an art as it is a science, with experience, observation, and intuition playing just as important a part as the scientific principles of exercise prescription. Some coaches argue that rowing has a reputation for hard training, so as long as their rowers train hard, then it doesn't matter which training methods they use. Although there may be some truth to this, we all should use best practice methods to help athletes achieve their just rewards for their hard work. The question is: What is best practice for rowing training? Unfortunately, there is still a lot of debate about that very question among elite rowing coaches and the sport science community. This chapter will critically explore some common strategies for improving the aerobic and anaerobic lactic aspects of conditioning (*anaerobic* from this point forward will by default mean anaerobic lactic) and include examples of the strategies one could use to apply theory into practice to generate an on-water rowing training program.

Determining the effectiveness of a training program can be difficult and often involves two different metrics. The first is whether the program produces successful outcomes, and the second is whether the program employs current best practice principles. Ideally, an effective training program achieves success by using best practices, but constant debate about what best practice training methods are and how success is measured make this problematic.

Strengths and Weaknesses of Copying Successful Rowing Programs

Seiler and Tønnessen (2009) make a strong case in support of following successful rowing coaches' training methods. Although a range of nonscientific factors may influence the training methods employed by successful elite rowing coaches, training strategies that show consistent long-term success are likely to be repeated. This repetition leads to other coaches becoming exposed to these methods, and they, in turn, copy those training strategies; further success will lead to these methods spreading throughout the rowing community. Likewise, coaches and rowers will avoid training methods that have proven unsuccessful, resulting in their eventual demise. Seiler and Tønnessen (2009) argue that a consistent pattern of training intensity distribution therefore evolves as "a result of a successful self-organization (evolution) towards a population optimum" (35).

There are numerous limitations to following successful coaches' training methods, however. Success may come from elements unrelated to the coach's ability to optimize the crew's physical conditioning—that is, effective recruitment, technical development, athlete management, motivation, training and recovery balance, and so forth. Even if a successful coach has employed an effective training regime, it is always challenging to be confident that the programmed training intensities match those typically achieved by all crew members. The biggest issue is that an effective training program is individualized to achieve the best result for that specific crew; therefore copying a successful coach's program may only work if your crew is identical in every way to theirs.

Constructing a Training Program Using Scientific Principles of Training

Following a successful rowing coach's program may not be feasible for various reasons (e.g., the training group differs a lot or the training environment does not allow for the same training volumes). In this case, a coach may decide to base their training program solely on current best practice scientific principles. Unfortunately, there is still vigorous debate regarding the effectiveness of various training models. This debate is complex and hinges around arguments over the physiological benefits of different training intensity zones and durations. Initially, the discussion was about the importance of one specific type of training over others—for example, the effectiveness of low-intensity long slow distance training versus high-intensity interval training. The current debate is much more nuanced and focuses more on the optimal mix of training intensity distribution (TID), with the polarized training distribution model being presently in vogue in sport science circles.

Key Point

When writing an effective rowing program, coaches should understand the polarized and pyramidal TID models and how these two models differ in the portions of long slow distance training, lactate threshold training, and high-intensity interval training.

Various training methods have been employed since rowing became a competitive sport. What has changed is the subsequent systematization and classification of these different approaches into various training concepts and models by sport scientists and coaches. A detailed examination of every successful training method combined with the various scientific theories of rowing training would exceed the scope of this book, so what follows is an overview of some key issues.

There is currently a spirited debate over which TID model is ideal for rowing conditioning. This chapter aims to introduce and critically discuss the standard TID models currently recommended for rowing and, in the process, describes their three conditioning concepts: namely, long slow distance (LSD) training, lactate threshold

(LT) training, and high-intensity interval training (HIIT) (Arne, Stephen, and Eike 2009; Seiler 2010; Stöggl and Sperlich 2014; Treff et al. 2019).

These three conditioning concepts each focus on one of three intensity zones (see table 14.1). The table also shows that most of these overarching intensity zones have two further training zone descriptors. LSD is split into training intensity 1 (T1) and utilization 2 (U2), LT is split into utilization 1 (U1) and anaerobic threshold (AT), and HIIT is split into lactate tolerance (LaT) and lactate production (LaP). These descriptors are a mixture of various names from other programs that best describe the training zones utilized in our example program. Please note that AR and T1 are sometimes the same zone, but for many programs AR is added to facilitate recovery or for technique sessions while T1 sessions seek to provide a small amount of aerobic conditioning.

Zone 1 relates to LSD training and typically incorporates exercise intensities between 60% $\dot{V}O_2$max and the aerobic threshold. The upper limit of the zone 1 training intensity, the aerobic threshold, can be identified in one of the following ways:

- The first lactate threshold
- The first ventilatory threshold
- 2 mmol/L blood lactate concentration
- 70% heart rate reserve (HRR)
- 12 rate of perceived exertion (RPE)

As mentioned previously, Zone 1 is often divided into two subcategories: T1, derived from the Australian Rowing program to describe the lower intensity range; and U2, derived from the East German rowing program to describe the upper intensity range. The U2 training intensity was employed extensively within the successful East German rowing program as a means of optimally enhancing aerobic conditioning; with time this method became the foundation of many other successful rowing programs. Given the difficulty in consistently maintaining U2 training intensities across multiple daily sessions throughout the week, at times the Australian and New Zealand rowing programs reverted to replacing some U2 training with T1 to ensure adequate recovery while maintaining some small aerobic enhancements. Lactate threshold 1 (LT1) is considered the lowest intensity that generates an increased blood lactate above resting levels, while the first ventilatory threshold (VT1) is the lowest exercise intensity where ventilation first increases at a faster rate than oxygen consumption (Svedahl and MacIntosh 2003).

Zone 2 intensity is linked to LT training and incorporates exercise between the aerobic and anaerobic thresholds. The anaerobic threshold is estimated as the second lactate or ventilatory threshold, or 4 mmol/L blood lactate concentration, and is often called the *onset of blood lactate accumulation* (OBLA). The training intensities for zone 2 typically use the same measurement techniques presented for zone 1 and can be identified as follows:

- Between first and second lactate thresholds
- Between first and second ventilatory thresholds
- 2-4 mmol/L blood lactate concentration
- 70%-85% HRR
- 14-17 RPE

Zone 2 is often divided into two subcategories: U1, derived from the old East German rowing program to describe for the lower intensity range of zone 2; and AT, from the

New Zealand rowing program to describe the upper intensity range of zone 2. The differences between these two training intensities are quite subtle; arguably AT is maximal sustainable intensity for 30-90 minutes, while U1 is any training that sits between U2 and AT intensities. Lactate threshold 2 (LT2), or maximal lactate steady state, is the highest steady state exercise intensity where a constant blood lactate value can be maintained, while the second ventilatory threshold 2 (VT2) is the second disproportionate increase in ventilation relative to oxygen consumption (Svedahl and MacIntosh 2003).

Training within zone 3 involves HIIT and includes exercise intensities above the anaerobic threshold, and at or around $\dot{V}O_2$max intensity. Zone 3 is often divided into many subcategories, but only two are used here: lactate tolerance (LaT) and lactate production (LaP), both derived from the New Zealand rowing program. As the term implies, the goal of lactate production training is to maximize lactate production. Thus, the sessions consist of maximal intensity workloads of approximately 30 seconds to 3 minutes with long rest periods to facilitate recovery for consistent maximal work and lactate concentrations. On the other hand, lactate tolerance training often involves the same work durations but with shorter rest periods. Shorter rests inhibit full recovery, thereby generating submaximal anaerobic workloads and a steady raise in submaximal lactate levels. Maximal oxygen consumption ($\dot{V}O_2$max) is considered the highest rate of oxygen consumption that occurs during maximal intensity exercise (Saltin and Anstrad 1967).

Please note some of these measurement estimates of the aerobic and anaerobic thresholds are often considered inaccurate within the science community. Although the measures are all in practical use, some researchers argue that they don't represent the actual aerobic or anaerobic thresholds. Thus, onset of blood lactate (OBLA) and lactate threshold are considered separate measures of the anaerobic threshold, even though the initial reason for developing these measures was to estimate the anaerobic threshold.

There is also a fourth training intensity zone, called active recovery (AR), which is often arbitrarily described as any low-intensity exercise that facilitates recovery. Some training systems incorporate AR within Zone 1, whereas its intensity falls below Zone 1 in others. Rowers train at AR intensity during warm-up, cool-down, and between interval training sets; thus, although specific AR intensity sessions may play a small part of the training program, the actual AR volume in a week can be pretty high.

Training Concepts and Distribution Models

Although each of these conditioning concepts focuses on training within their specific intensity zone, in reality, an effective training program involves a mixture of training intensity zones. For example, even if a rower trained exclusively within zone 1 LSD training, they would still race 2,000 m in zone 3; thus, a portion of their monthly in-season workload will likely include zone 3. Likewise, a rower focused on zone 3 HIIT would probably only manage 2 to 3 sessions per week at this high intensity and would likely undertake some zone 1 training between their HIIT sessions. Therefore, all training systems typically involve a distribution of different intensities, which often change at different phases of the season. For this reason, discussions about current rowing programs focus more on determining which combinations of the three training zones (i.e., training zone distributions) optimize rowing conditioning. This chapter will therefore now describe the three training concepts (LSD, LT, and HIIT) before discussing and critiquing the two common training intensity distribution models in rowing, polarized, and pyramidal training.

Long Slow Distance (LSD) Training Model

Up until the early 1960s, rowing—like most Olympic endurance sports—involved little if any systematic scientifically based planning in its training (Ingham et al. 2008). During this period, the GDR instituted a training approach focused on extensive long slow distance (LSD) steady-state aerobic training. Dr. Theo Körner, one of the architects of this system, stated that his PhD research helped inform his training method. It promoted the development of the aerobic energy system through extensive long-distance training around the aerobic threshold, which he proposed to be the 2 mmol/L blood lactate concentration (Körner, pers. comm.). Beyond this, Körner declared that the critical enzymatic changes required to optimize anaerobic conditioning needed minimal specific anaerobic training. Also, good aerobic conditioning supported anaerobic performance through various factors such as enhanced lactic acid clearance. In response to further questioning about the importance of specific anaerobic conditioning, Körner stated that he believed large volumes of anaerobic conditioning inhibited the development of the essential aerobic system. As an aside, Körner also said that he thought that tough athletes could handle pain and that improvement in anaerobic conditioning was more related to athletes developing resilience to the pain of lactic acidosis rather than specific metabolic changes. Thus, selecting tough athletes with the required genetic capabilities and optimizing their aerobic conditioning via extensive LSD training was his recipe for success. Superficially viewed, it was hard to argue against 48 Olympic medals (33 gold) from 1965 to 1991.

Key Point

Long slow distance training was one of the first systematic scientifically based training approaches employed in rowing. This concept was developed in the GDR and later spread throughout the rowing world, generating much success.

Körner described his training philosophy during a presentation at the 1993 FISA Coaches Conference (Körner 1993), which is summarized here. The heart rate associated with 2 mmol/L blood lactate concentration was monitored during all training sessions, and rowers were required to maintain this heart rate even if it resulted in fatigue and a reduction in boat speed. This practice helped ensure fatigue management, and if a rest period of 4 to 5 h could be implemented, then two 20 to 25 km (90 to 120 min) sessions per day could be achieved. Körner stated that it was important that the required intensity was maintained throughout to ensure both optimal aerobic adaptations and an efficient rowing technique. He suggested that "impressive" race performances could occur on the back of extensive LSD training, and for this reason, about 90% of the on-water training was at LSD intensity, whereas only 4% was anaerobic (Körner 1993).

There have been numerous critiques of the GDR's extensive LSD endurance training model, perhaps the strongest being related to the well-documented use of illegal performance-enhancing drugs throughout this program. A greater understanding of exercise physiology and biochemistry has also refuted a number of the physiological mechanisms used to promote the efficacy of extensive LSD for optimizing rowing conditioning. Perhaps the most significant contradictory scientific finding has been evidence that anaerobic exercise can significantly enhance anaerobic and aerobic conditioning (Buchheit and Laursen 2013). From a physiological perspective, it is difficult to reconcile the need to perform many kilometers at aerobic threshold pace to optimize conditioning for a race that is essentially 5 to 7 min at approximately $\dot{V}O_2$max pace.

Another critique is that, although the East Germans may have predominantly used LSD training, they often raced 2,000 m; hence the athletes were exposed to regular bouts of very intensive anaerobic racing loads. It is possible that the focus of extensive LSD aerobic training worked because regular intensive anaerobic racing was enough to facilitate good anaerobic development. In any case, it is important to note that the success of the GDR's rowing program was not solely due to extensive LSD training: The program also instituted innovative best practices across all areas of crew preparation, including technical modeling, talent identification, nutrition, biomechanics, boat building, and sports medicine.

The description of the GDR training model as LSD is perhaps a misnomer; in the Rowing New Zealand (RNZ) program, world and Olympic champion rowers were unable to maintain workloads at 2 mmol/L blood lactate concentration or at correlating heart rates. After much research, the LSD training intensity measure dropped to 1.5 mmol/L blood lactate. Perhaps this correction reflects a more profound concern, which is whether a set blood lactate concentration is an accurate measure of aerobic threshold in the first place. It is also unclear whether the GDR program meant 2 mmol/L blood lactate to reflect the aerobic threshold; it is challenging to get clarity about this (and many other related questions) because the GDR's scientific research was not generally disseminated to the West.

Like all training models, LSD involves training for specific durations at set intensities; in this case, the duration is extensive, and the intensity is the approximate aerobic threshold (i.e., 2 mmol/L blood lactate). The practicalities of ensuring each individual within a crew consistently rows at the required intensity are challenging. For LSD training, the biggest challenge is that it is logistically and technically impractical to measure blood lactate throughout each training session. Thus, other measurable predictors of aerobic threshold intensity are used, with heart rate being the preferred method, although RPE, boat speed at set stroke rates, and power production are also used. However, each of these predictor measures has its own set of practical, logistical, technical, and physiological constraints, which limit their effectiveness and are further discussed in chapters 12 and 19. Because it is common for highly successful rowers in the same crew to have different intensity distributions, it is therefore possible that despite the GDR programming workloads involving extensive durations at 2 mmol/L blood lactate intensities, the rowers may not have consistently achieved these programmed intensities (Plews and Laursen 2017).

Key Point

In addition to the extensive on-water training time to achieve good aerobic conditioning, technical development, crew coherence, and feel for the water that shorter, more intensive training sessions don't allow, LSD training may provide multiple nonconditioning-related benefits that are more difficult to achieve with the other training concepts.

Although the GDR dominated international rowing from the mid-1960s to early 1990s, other rowing nations enjoyed some success with different training methods. In fact, Coach Karl Adam gained success employing an interval training system over the border in West Germany. However, before and during the breakup of the GDR, their LSD training method was exported to many nations through various conduits, including the coaching manuals from World Rowing, becoming a popular training method in many countries for decades. Whatever the critiques, the LSD training model proved very successful in not only rowing but many other middle distance sports (Ingham et al. 2008). The Australian rowing program also achieved success with an LSD-focused training program at the 2020 Tokyo Olympics.

Lactate Threshold (LT) Training Model

Although there are studies examining the efficacy of LT training in rowing or sports of similar physiological requirements (Mejuto et al. 2012; Stöggl and Sperlich 2014), there is no published evidence of modern elite rowing teams employing LT training methods. Lactate threshold training has been shown to improve endurance performance primarily in untrained subjects. The scientific evidence around the efficacy of LT training for rowing or sports of similar physiological requirements has been equivocal, with either some limited benefits, no benefit, or even negative effects (Mejuto et al. 2012; Stöggl and Sperlich 2014). Anecdotally, there is probably only one modern-day elite program that successfully employs LT training, and that is the elite Italian program. I was fortunate to observe members of the Italian rowing team training between 2016 and 2019 while I was with the Australian rowing team based at Lake Varese in Italy. Watching training sessions of the Italian rowing squad, it seemed that the regular sessions of reasonable volumes of moderate- to high-intensity interval training fitted more into the LT training classification than HIIT. It is important to note that this anecdotal evidence and my short-term subjective observations are in no way empirical evidence, although copies of the Italian training program from as long ago as 1990 show a relatively high proportion of LT training (Jensen, Secher, and Smith 1990).

High-Intensity Interval Training (HIIT) Model

There is an extensive and growing body of scientific evidence describing the benefits of HIIT in various sports, including rowing, and as a consequence, there is a concerted push from members of the sport science community to include more HIIT (Driller et al. 2009; Ní Chéilleachair, Harrison, and Warrington 2017). It is perhaps a little ironic that the highly successful GDR program was founded on the notion that LSD optimized rowing performance and that too much anaerobic training would blunt aerobic development, yet modern-day sports scientists are pushing HIIT anaerobic conditioning to develop both aerobic and anaerobic conditioning (Buchheit and Laursen 2013). Although many teams have shown success with LSD training, 2,000 m rowing performance is at approximately $\dot{V}O_2$max pace, therefore the specificity principle alone would support HIIT. The physiology mechanisms supporting HIIT are beyond the scope of this chapter; for more in this area, see Buchheit and Laursen (2013).

A challenge for many older coaches is reconciling their skepticism over how an anaerobic HIIT session can improve the important aerobic component for rowing, given the traditional belief that the associated high levels of blood lactate increase muscle damage, extend recovery time, and reduce training (Gullstrand 1996). Under the LSD training methods, HIIT-type sessions were often sparingly employed to improve anaerobic conditioning and not aerobic conditioning. HIIT is zone 3 intensity (above anaerobic threshold around $\dot{V}O_2$max intensity), which will lead to lactate accumulation at a rate commensurate with the exercise intensity and, if maintained, will force exercise cessation. At this training intensity, the aerobic system is heavily if not fully engaged with the anaerobic system, thus should elicit a potent stimulus for both aerobic and anaerobic adaptations according to the specificity principle.

There are still many detractors of high levels of HIIT within the rowing community. One concern is the ability to generate positive aerobic adaptations with such a small volume of training combined with high levels of catabolic by-products of anaerobic metabolism such as lactic acid. However, there is evidence that aerobic metabolic adaptations occur to the same degree or better in response to HIIT, and these by-products are often stimulants for positive aerobic and anaerobic anabolic adaptations. There is still debate on the benefits of HIIT over LSD for improving skeletal muscle capillary density, cardiovascular function, and blood volume (MacInnis and Gibala, 2017).

One indisputable limitation to HIIT is that it generates a considerable amount of fatigue and pain, and it typically requires 2 to 3 days of recovery before another full HIIT session can be repeated. This limits rowers to 2 to 3 HIIT sessions per week consisting of about 10 to 15 min of work per session. Thus, although HIIT may be the conditioning focus, the reality is that other training sessions at lesser intensities are required to ensure the required technical and crew adaptations occur as well. From personal experience, rowers are often attracted to changing from LSD to HIIT solely because the training volume reduces significantly. However, the reality of having to do 2 to 3 sessions per week at close to maximum anaerobic intensity (RPE 18-20) soon takes the gloss off that attraction. After extended periods of this training, it is not uncommon for rowers to reduce the session intensity. Hence, an HIIT session will eventually resemble more of an LT intensity, which compromises physiological adaptations. Rowers who maintain the required intensity will often struggle with motivation due to the regular instances of intense pain and fatigue. Therefore, it is important that coaches modify interval durations and rest intervals and, if possible, slightly modulate the intensity within the zone 3 sector to help maintain motivation. Buchheit and Laursen (2013) provide more specific information on the broad range of HIIT intensity, duration, and rest intervals.

Key Point

There is a body of scientific evidence to support the implementation of HIIT sessions to improve endurance conditioning. Despite this, many successful international rowing programs opt to continue to focus large portions of the season on LSD training. There are many unanswered questions and opportunities for innovation in this space.

My personal experience with HIIT within various elite rowing programs from Atlanta 1996 to Tokyo 2021 suggests that although HIIT is an important training element, it is typically used sparingly near the end of the season to develop anaerobic conditioning. When I view the training programs for each of these Olympics, it is clear that there are defined patterns to the distribution of the intensity zones occurring at different stages of the season. In simplistic terms, LSD training predominates in the early season but remains a significant component throughout. At the same time, the portion of LT training increases midseason but is increasingly replaced by HIIT sessions through the latter part of the competitive season. Thus, I believe a good rowing program uses set distributions of AR, LSD, LT, and HIIT. The pattern of these distributions is altered at different stages of the season, which may be further modified based on the crew's needs. Today, it is more common to talk about training intensity distribution (TID) models rather than pushing the benefit of one single training concept over another.

Key Point

The time available to train may help the coach decide whether to employ LSD, LT, or HIIT concepts. HIIT takes the least time but arguably generates the most pain. Although this method may be a useful conditioning tool for many rowers with limited time, the constant high-intensity training sessions may enhance the dropout rate, especially among young rowers.

Polarized Training Intensity Distribution Model

Arguably the most well-known TID model is the polarized training model, which was developed by Seiler and colleagues to determine which combinations of volume and intensity best enhanced measures of endurance conditioning and performance (Esteve-Lanao et al. 2007; Fiskerstrand and Seiler 2004; Seiler 2010; Seiler and Kjerland 2006; Seiler and Tønnessen 2009). The authors examined the published training methods employed by the coaches of successful endurance athletes to develop their polarized training model. Seiler and Tønnessen (2009) hypothesized that the reason that this "polarized" training pattern emerged from their analysis was that this distribution created the best mix of adaptations required to optimize endurance performance. The polarized TID model (figure 15.1) consists of higher percentages of training time spent in zone 1 (75%-80%), followed by zone 3 (15%-20%) with minimal time spent in zone 2 (5%).

Several research articles have promoted the effectiveness of polarized training based on rowing observation studies (Arne et al., 2009; Fiskerstrand and Seiler 2004; Plews and Laursen 2017; Steinacker et al. 1998; Tran et al. 2015b) and results of experimental rowing training studies (Driller et al. 2009; Ní Chéilleachair et al. 2017). Other research has also promoted polarized training practices for endurance sports with similar physiological requirements to rowing (Seiler 2010; Stöggl and Sperlich 2014).

Anecdotally, there are concerns that the large volume of training in zone 1 may not be intensive enough to optimize the various aerobic adaptations required to improve anaerobic threshold, which is an important aspect of rowing conditioning. This concern is typically held by coaches used to the LSD method, which promotes large training volumes at aerobic threshold (zone 1 is defined as below aerobic threshold, specifically at or below first lactate or first ventilatory threshold). The difference between training at aerobic threshold versus training at or below aerobic threshold is subtle, but often considered important to adherents of the LSD training model. Likewise, the relatively small, but still significant, regular amounts of zone 3 (anaerobic) training, often employing high-intensity intervals at approximately $\dot{V}O_2$max pace, can be mentally taxing and difficult to maintain over the many months and years a rower trains. Despite these anecdotal concerns there is scientific evidence that a polarized TID model can provide greater improvements in $\dot{V}O_2$max, time to exhaustion, power at OBLA, and peak power and velocity compared to other TID models (Stöggl and Sperlich, 2014).

Polarized TID
- %Zone 3 > %Zone 2 ^ %Zone 1 > %Zone 3 ^ %Zone 1 > %Zone 2
- Small proportion of Zone 2

Pyramidal TID
- %Zone 1 > %Zone 2 > %Zone 3
- %Zone 1 may be very high (i.e., "High Volume Low Intensity")

Lactate threshold TID
- Emphasizes Zone 2 training
- May be pyramidal structure

High-intensity TID
- Emphasizes Zone 3 training
- %Zone 3 > %Zone 1 ^ %Zone 3 > %Zone 2
- May be inverse pyramidal structure or %Zone 1 ≥ %Zone 2

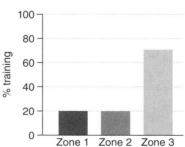

▶ **Figure 15.1** Various training intensity distributions (TID), their schematic proportions, and key characteristics (indicated by black bars). Zone 1 (basic endurance): Between 50% $\dot{V}O_2$max and first lactate or ventilatory threshold; zone 2 (lactate threshold): between first and second lactate or ventilatory threshold; zone 3 (high intensity): above second lactate or ventilatory threshold.

Pyramidal Training Intensity Distribution Model

The pyramidal TID model involves a high percentage of training volume spent in zone 1 and proportionally less in zones 2 and 3 (e.g., 70% in zone 1, 20% in zone 2, and 10% in zone 3) (Treff et al. 2019). Pyramidal training is similar to polarized training in that the vast majority of training is performed in zone 1; however, there is a greater portion of zone 2 training rather than zone 3. The pyramidal model was arguably discovered in studies of actual training distribution patterns rather than being developed around theoretical physiological notions that an increase portion of zone 2 training will develop better conditioning for rowers. Furthermore, the differences between polarized and pyramidal training may be more related to differences in the methods employed to measure and interpret the training zone intensities than to actual differences between the models.

Polarized Versus Pyramidal TID Models

Tran and colleagues (2015b) and Plews and Laursen (2017) actually recorded a pyramidal TID pattern with elite Australian and New Zealand rowers respectively, as did Stöggl and Sperlich (2014) with internationally competitive endurance athletes. Some of the rowers in these studies (Plews et al. 2014; Tran et al. 2015a) won Olympic medals after using a pyramidal TID model during the respective study periods. Despite this success, however, Plews and Laursen (2017) and Tran and colleagues (2015b) promoted polarized TID as the more effective training method. Given the extreme difficulty in achieving this level of success, it's arguably problematic to promote polarized TID based on a theoretical rationale over the pyramidal TID that was actually employed.

In a review of Olympic rowing, Treff, Winkert, and Steinacker (2021) explored the TID models across nine published studies of elite rowers encompassing seven different national rowing programs. From their findings these authors state "To the best of our knowledge, there are no data available indicating that a polarized intensity distribution is superior to a pyramidal on the long term in elite rowing" (Treff, Winkert, and Steinacker 2021, 207). However, these authors do speculate that polarized TID may be superior for some individuals and is likely applied "during certain phases of a competitive season" in most rowing programs (Treff, Winkert, and Steinacker 2021, 207). The key message from these authors emphasizes the importance of large volumes of low-intensity training (i.e., LSD) to facilitate the physiological adaptations required to optimize race performance and enhance rowing technique and crew efficiency.

Key Point

Polarized TID has been promoted as the ideal training intensity distribution model for rowing, yet a number of studies have shown the effectiveness of a pyramidal rather than polarized TID model in rowing. It is possible that an effective training program employs different TIDs at different phases of the season.

One of the challenges with the TID research in rowing and related sports is the lack of consistency in how the different training intensities and their distributions are measured and classified, which has resulted in the development of a "polarisation index" (Treff et al. 2019). For example, Plews and Laursen (2017) reported that in the 4 year period leading to the Rio Olympics, the most famous New Zealand men's pair implemented two different TID models (polarized as well as pyramidal). This study was criticized by other authors who suggested that if another TID classification system were used, the training of the two rowers would have fit into the polarized TID category (Treff et al. 2019).

Selecting a TID and Associated FITT Principles to Develop a Rowing Training Program

When it comes to selecting a TID for a rowing training program, there are significant implications to calculating by session, time, or distance. For example, a TID focusing on HIIT may include a total distance of 120 km per week of on-water rowing consisting of 3 HIIT sessions each of 3 km of work within an overall 10 km distance, 3 LSD sessions of 20 km each, and 3 AR sessions of 10 km each. If the AR trainings were removed from the TID calculation, it would result that 50% of the sessions were performed in zones 3 and 1 respectively, but if TID were calculated by distance, 85% of the training would be performed in zone 1 and 14% in zone 3. If AR is included in zone 1 (which often occurs), then 67% of the sessions would be performed at an intensity of zone 1 and 33% at zone 3, but calculated by distance, 93% would be at zone 1 and 7% at zone 3. Unfortunately, the scientific literature tends to focus on measuring TID rather than providing guidelines on generating a polarized or pyramidal training program.

The focus of the chapter has been on discussing which TID produces the best conditioning and physiological adaptations. Still, there is more to effective programming than which intensity zones should be utilized. An effective program must address all the elements of the FITT principles (frequency, intensity, time, and type of training) and employ an effective progressive overload strategy. However, deciding which TID method to use is typically the first and most important part of the planning process, then the other elements are built into the various phases of the season, blocks (mesocycles), weeks (microcycles), and sessions.

The process of using the TID, FITT, and progressive overload principles to construct a successful rowing training program is covered in chapter 19. Like Figure 15.1, which gives an overview of long-term planning, table 15.1 explains the individual steps for the planning of training sessions.

If the reader is interested in the process of applying theory to practice in this area, then it is highly recommended that they turn directly to chapter 19.

Conclusion

Developing an effective training program is the combination of an art and a science. Although copying other successful rowing programs that have similar rowers and goals may be useful, the program should also employ the requisite FITT and progressive overload principles. An effective rowing program consists of changes in the training intensity distribution and associated methods at specific times throughout the season to achieve different conditioning goals. There is much debate over the TID models and training methods that help optimize rowing conditioning, and it is important that coaches continue to critically evaluate these discussions. Coaches should not be afraid to be innovative with their training programs as long as they can monitor their rowers' progress. Regular and accurate monitoring allows the coach to modify the training program if the rowers are failing to progress or going backwards; this important area will be covered in chapter 19.

Table 15.1 Example of Steps to Develop a Long-term Training Plan

Seasons	Season 1: Constant evolution of training philosophy and methods		Season 2: Constant evolution of training philosophy and methods		Season 3: Constant evolution of training philosophy and methods		Etc.			
Season strategy	Overall season plan: Conditioning goals, periodization strategy, training intensity distribution model, training methods									
Phases	PREPARATORY				COMPETITION				TRANSITION	
Subphases	General preparation General overall foundation conditioning		Specific preparation Rowing specific foundation conditioning		Pre-competition Preparatory conditioning for racing		Major competition Optimizing race specific conditioning		Rest Recover Rehab and prehab	Restart Rehab and prehab
Mesocycles	3-6 weeks	3-6 weeks	3-6 weeks	3-6 weeks	3-6 weeks	3-6 weeks	3-6 weeks	3-6 weeks	3-6 weeks	3-6 weeks
Mesocycle strategy	For each specific mesocycle, determine the priority components to be developed. Implement the pre-determined TID model and associated training methods to generate a training plan to develop the priority physical components across the microcycles while maintaining conditioning in any other important components									
Microcycle	Set training workload goal from prior testing and assessments Typically 1-week duration		Implement progressive overload plan and monitor Typically 1-week duration		Implement progressive overload plan and monitor Typically 1-week duration		Implement progressive overload plan and monitor Typically 1-week duration		Implement progressive overload plan and monitor Typically 1-week duration	
Microcycle strategy	For each specific microcycle, utilize the predetermined TID model and training methods to apply the requisite FITT principles across the sessions within the microcycle to develop a training program to improve the priority training components while maintaining conditioning in any other important components									
Day	Monitor fatigue and recovery		Monitor fatigue and recovery		Monitor fatigue and recovery		Monitor fatigue and recovery		Monitor fatigue and recovery	
Session	a.m.	p.m.	a.m.	p.m.	a.m.	p.m.	a.m.	p.m.	a.m.	p.m.
Session strategy	Follow the intensity, duration, type, and details (e.g., steady state, interval, fartlek, sets, reps, rest intervals, etc.) of the session plan prescribed in the microcycle training program. Ensure appropriate session preparation and recovery, and ideally monitor both external performance measures (power, speed, load, etc. and duration) and internal load (HR, RPE, etc.) responses to each session									

CHAPTER 16

Resistance Training

Ed McNeely

Strength training can be a valuable part of a rowing program. Not only has it been shown to improve measures of strength with no negative impact on aerobic performance (Lawton, Cronin, and McGuigan 2013), but stronger rowers are more likely to be selected to a crew for competition (Lawton, Cronin, and McGuigan 2013a, b). Strength training typically accounts for 20% to 25% of total training time for rowers, a significant investment that needs to be well planned.

There are two primary goals for a strength program for rowers: (1) to develop the underlying physiological systems responsible for neural and muscular abilities and (2) to transfer those abilities to rowing performance. Increased strength and power are the intended results of these adaptations. These goals are accomplished with a combination of weight room training and rowing-specific activities.

In the Weight Room

Weight training has become a common part of rowing preparation. Many boathouses have built weight rooms into their facilities to make access easier for athletes, and many clubs are hiring strength coaches or supplying continuing education for rowing coaches who want to learn to design strength programs.

Selecting Exercises

The most obvious variable in a strength program is the exercises used. Which exercises are chosen will depend on availability of equipment and time of the year as well as the individual rower's resistance training experience, age, gender, level of competition, and injury history. Rowing coaches and strength coaches tend to use a relatively small set of exercises in their programs. The power clean and squat are the two most recommended exercises, with 87% of coaches and strength coaches recommending them (Gee et al. 2011), followed by the leg press, bench pull, deadlift, bent row, and bench press (figures 16.1 to 16.7). For rowers with limited resistance training experience, changing exercises results in greater increases in strength than changing loading schemes (Fonseca et al. 2014).

▶ **Figure 16.1** Power clean.

▶ **Figure 16.2** Squat.

 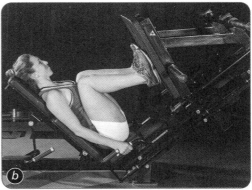

▶ **Figure 16.3** Leg press.

▶ **Figure 16.4** Bench pull.

▶ **Figure 16.5** Deadlift.

▶ **Figure 16.6** Bent row.

▶ **Figure 16.7** Bench press.

Key Point

Changing strength exercises creates a different stimulus and helps break up monotony in training. However, changing too frequently does not allow an athlete to develop the nervous system adaptations that allow them to use enough load to force the muscles to adapt. Changing 2 to 3 exercises every month strikes a good balance between consistency and variety.

One way of deciding which exercises are most useful for rowers is to examine the relationship between the exercise and rowing performance, either on an ergometer or on water. One study of female collegiate rowers (Folk et al. 2020) found the 1RM squat to be a predictor of 2,000 m ergometer time, whereas 1RM hang clean was not found to be a predictor. Lawton, Cronin, and McGuigan (2013b) found weight room exercises to be good predictors of 2,000 m and peak rowing power performance, with bench pull (in which a barbell is pulled into the bottom of a high bench from a prone position) and 1RM power clean being the best predictors of peak rowing stroke power and 5RM leg press and 6RM bench pull the best predictors of 2,000 m performance in elite heavyweight male rowers.

Although they provide valuable information for adjusting programs in the weight room, weight lifting tests and exercises do not necessarily reflect the true strength demands of the sport (McMaster et al. 2014). The concept of movement pattern specificity in strength training has been generally supported in the literature, with the greatest improvements in performance occurring in the movement pattern and range of motion trained (Morrissey, Harmon, and Johnson 1995). Weight training exercises, though using similar muscle groups, do not closely simulate the rowing stroke or key positions and may not contribute to improved rowing technique. Figure 16.8 shows a series of force curves from a female rower in an eight. Despite approximately 30% increases in squat and deadlift 1RM during this time, there is little change in the shape of the stroke, particularly around the catch, and only a 6.5% increase in peak stroke force.

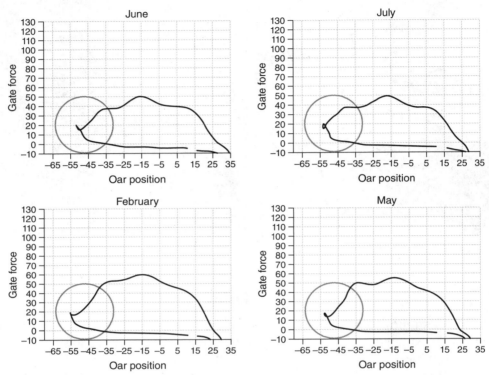

▶ **Figure 16.8** Changes in gate forces with substantial weight room–based strength training gains.

Load

Once an athlete has a basic technical competence in the fundamental strength training movements and exercises, the load that they use is a primary determining factor in the outcome of the program, particularly the development of strength. A load below 60% 1RM is considered suboptimal for the development of strength (ACSM 2002; Kraemer and Ratames 2004), although there is some research emerging suggesting that a lower load may be enough to stimulate muscle hypertrophy (Mitchell et al. 2012; Morton et al. 2016; Schoenfeld et al. 2015).

High volumes of aerobic training may interfere with adaptations to a strength program, as discussed in chapter 11. High-load, low-repetition training at 85% to 95% 1RM has been suggested to be best for increasing rowing strength in more experienced elite rowers (McNeely, Sandler, and Bamel 2005). This is similar to the recommended 85% 1RM that Peterson, Rhea, and Alvar (2004) recommend in their meta-analysis of the dose–response relationship to strength training in athletes.

Optimal loading parameters may be affected by the level of rower and their strength training experience. Gallagher and colleagues (2010) compared high-load, low-repetition training to low-load, high-repetition training in collegiate male rowers and found no statistical difference between either the trial group or the control group. There was a trend toward greater improvement in the strength training groups, with the high-load, low-volume group exhibiting the larger improvement. Ebben and colleagues (2004) compared high-load (6RM-12RM) and low-load (15RM-32RM) training in varsity and novice collegiate female rowers, finding that high-load training produced superior results in varsity athletes, whereas low-load training produced better results in novice athletes. This may be due to improved anaerobic energy system fitness induced by low-load training in novice rowers, who are likely to have lower metabolic fitness than varsity athletes.

Key Point

Most research studies on strength training are less than 24 weeks in duration, far shorter than a typical sport training year. Although studies are often designed to isolate specific aspects of training, the periodized nature of most training programs means that rowers are likely to use both high-load, low-volume and low-load, high-volume training during the year.

Factors Affecting Loading Ability

The ability to self-regulate and choose an appropriate weight and progression on any given day is an important skill that ensures optimal progression in a strength program. It involves self-awareness, goal setting, and the ability to look forward to the demands of the rest of the training week.

Most people will not select a high enough intensity on their own. Glass and Stanton (2004) found that novice lifters self-selected an intensity in the 42% to 57% 1RM range, and Cotter and colleagues (2017) found the average self-selected intensity for resistance exercises was 57% in a group of young women who had been resistance training at least 3 times per week for a year prior to the study. Although choosing an intensity that is too low will impact the outcome of the program, there are some athletes who are too aggressive, choosing loads that are beyond their physical or technical abilities.

Fear of Injury   An overabundance of caution on the part of coaches working with teenage athletes often limits the loading that these athletes experience prior to college. Some coaches have a fear that loading or progressing the athletes will cause injuries. Strength training is a safe activity with injury rates lower than most high school sports (2-4 injuries per 1,000 h). Even competitive lifting sports have low injury rates, with bodybuilding training resulting in 0.24 to 1 injury per 1,000 h, strongman competitors experiencing 4.5 to 6.1 injuries per 1,000 h (Winwood et al. 2014), and powerlifters having 3.6 to 5.8 injuries per 1,000 h (Keogh, Hume, and Pearson 2006). Overall, high school and middle school sports have an injury rate of 8.5 per 1,000 h, with middle school soccer and volleyball having injury rates of 13.4 and 20.7 per 1,000 h, respectively (Barber Foss et al. 2018). When strength training injuries do occur, the majority—up to almost 80% for some age groups—occur from dropped weights (Kerr, Collins, and Comstock 2010). Once an athlete has acceptable technique, load progression becomes the cornerstone of strength development both for performance and preparation for a higher level of competition and the increased training load it requires.

Load and Anxiety The selection of inadequate intensity during resistance training contrasts with aerobic training studies, where self-selected intensity is more in line with typical training recommendations (Dias et al. 2018). The reasons for this are unknown, but state anxiety is decreased with strength training in the 40% to 60% 1RM range and increases above 70% 1RM (Bartholomew and Linder 1998; Focht 2002). A strength coach who creates a safe training environment (e.g., competent spotters and safety bars in rack) and a culture where athletes feel confident in their abilities and are encouraged to challenge themselves will help athletes to overcome the anxiety associated with higher loads.

Key Point

Anxiety and fear are common when an activity is new or unfamiliar, but athletes will get over this quickly as their skill and confidence improve. It is important that coaches who are unfamiliar with strength training do not let their fear and anxiety create a culture that negatively affects their rowers' desire to challenge themselves.

Loading Methods

There are a variety of ways to determine and monitor training load.

RM Loading Method There is an inverse relationship between the amount of weight lifted and the number of repetitions performed: As the weight increases the number of reps performed to muscular failure (the point where you cannot do another rep on your own) decreases. You will often see this written as 3RM or 10RM, meaning 3 or 10 reps to muscular failure. This was a very popular method for describing load for strength exercises and was used extensively in strength training research because it sets a defined finish point for each set. More recent research suggesting that training to failure is not necessary has decreased the popularity of this method of describing loading (Davies et al. 2016). The loading used directly affects the training outcome, with different loading schemes needed to optimize strength, power and hypertrophy, and muscular endurance. Figure 16.9 shows the relationship between RM load and training outcome.

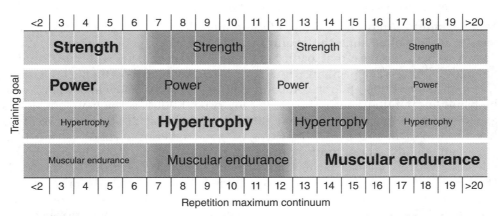

▶ **Figure 16.9** This continuum shows how RM ranges are associated with various training goals.

Percent 1RM Method   Basing training on percentages of 1RM is another common methodology used in strength program design. The mathematical nature of this method makes it ideal for long-term planning of training load across a season. It is particularly useful for athletes in strength and power sports (e.g., powerlifting and weightlifting) who know and test their 1RM on a regular basis.

For athletes with little strength training experience and those who do not regularly test their 1RM, percentage-based training is less useful. These athletes often do not have the technical skills to do a 1RM that represents their true strength, making any load prescription based on their test less accurate. Periods of rapid strength increase or getting back into a program following time off also make it difficult to use percentages of 1RM unless testing is done very frequently. For example, if an athlete had a 1RM of 100 kg and was expected to work at 80% 1RM, they would be lifting 80 kg. If their strength increased by 20% over the next month but their 1RM was not reevaluated, the 80 kg that they believe to be 80% 1RM would now be only 67% 1RM, resulting in a different training outcome. To overcome the disruption caused by frequent 1RM testing, several formulae have been developed to estimate a 1RM from repetitions to failure. (table 16.1).

Table 16.1   Estimating 1RM From Number of Repetitions (reps) Achieved With a Certain Weight (wt) to Failure

Brzycki (1993)	1RM = 100 × rep wt / (102.78 − 2.78 × reps)
Epley (1985)	1RM = (1 + 0.0333 × reps) × rep wt
Lander (1985)	1RM = 100 × rep wt / (101.3 − 2.67123 × reps)
Lombardi (1989)	1RM = rep wt × reps$^{0.1}$
Mayhew et al. (1992)	1RM = 100 × rep wt / (52.2 + 41.9 × exponent [−0.55 × reps])
O'Conner, Simmons, and O'Shea (1989)	1RM = rep wt × (1 + 0.25 reps)

As with the RM loading method, there is a relationship between training outcomes and the percentage of 1RM used in training. Table 16.2 shows the relationship between 1RM and training outcomes.

Table 16.2   Load and Repetition Assignments Based on the Training Goal

Training goal	Load (% 1RM)	Goal repetitions
Strength	≥85	≤6

Power
  Single-effort event
  Multiple-effort event
	
	80-90
	75-85
		
		1-2
		3-5

Hypertrophy	67-85	6-12
Muscular endurance	≤67	≥12

Reps in Reserve Method   The reps in reserve (RIR) method is a modified perceived exertion rating where the athlete is asked to estimate how many extra reps they could have done with a given weight (Zourdos et al. 2016). For instance, if an athlete did 6 reps but felt they could have done 8 they would have had 2 RIR. This method is easy to use and seems to be valid and reliable for a variety of skill and experience levels. Because the RIR method is based on the athlete's perception, it allows them to self-regulate and adjust for the fatigue they are experiencing at that point in time, overcoming the weaknesses associated with 1RM or RM loading that is based on a test that may or may not reflect current strength levels (Helms et al. 2016). RIR is most effective when the range is 1 to 3 RIR; more than this makes it difficult to accurately estimate the load to lift.

Key Point

Using the reps in reserve method provides a margin of safety for less experienced athletes. Variation in movement increases as the set gets closer to failure, resulting in poor body mechanics and the need for competent spotters. Spotting an exercise is as much a skill as performing the exercise, and poor spotting can injure both the lifter and the spotter. Leaving 1 or 2 reps in reserve decreases the likelihood that a spot will be needed.

Overall, the loading method used depends on the age, maturity, mathematical ability of the athlete, and their interest in strength training. It is best to begin with the RIR method because it is the easiest to understand and leaving a couple of RIR also provides a margin of safety if technique breaks down toward the end of a set. Many athletes will stick with the RIR method, but those who have an aptitude for math can estimate 1RM from a formula and use percentages.

Teaching loading does not happen overnight. There needs to be a plan, time, and effort for the athlete to understand and practice the skill. Eventually they will learn to self-regulate and selecting loads and progressions will become second nature. For progression through a long-term training plan, this is an essential skill that coaches and athletes should work to develop.

Frequency and Volume

Rowers typically strength train 2 to 3 times per week during both the in-season and off-season (Gee et al. 2011). This is in line with the optimal dose–response relationship of 2 days per week per muscle group with up to 8 sets per muscle group suggested by Peterson, Rhea, and Alvar (2004) for trained athletes. Younger athletes or those just starting a training program may need to train 3 times per week (Rhea et al. 2003).

Methods for Transferring Weight Room Strength to the Water

Resistance training does not necessarily need to be done using conventional weight room exercises. Isometric and plyometric exercises are also common in rowing. About half of the rowing coaches and strength coaches surveyed by Gee and colleagues (2011) included some form of jump training in their programs. This author has found higher correlations between various catch-specific isometric force–time parameters and 2,000 m and peak rowing power performance than between traditional weight room exercises and rowing performance (table 16.3).

Table 16.3 Correlation Matrix for Selected Weight Room and Isometric Force Variables and Rowing Ergometer Performance.

Exercise and force variable	Peak erg power	2,000 m erg (W)
Squat	0.176	−0.013
Bench Pull	0.599	0.301
Deadlift	0.353	0.123
Isometric peak force	0.783	0.718
Isometric force at 50 ms	0.554	0.352
Isometric force at 100 ms	0.618	0.554
Isometric force at 150 ms	0.629	0.645
Isometric force at 200 ms	0.705	0.746
Isometric force at 250 ms	0.704	0.596
Isometric force at 300 ms	0.721	0.692
Isometric force at 350 ms	0.744	0.642
Isometric force at 400 ms	0.718	0.664
Isometric force at 450 ms	0.695	0.672
Isometric force at 500 ms	0.714	0.678
Peak erg power	1	0.672
2,000 m erg power	0.672	1

The shaded cells denote the significance of correlations at the $p < 0.05$ level.

Key Point

Increases in strength and power in the weight room are great, but ultimately not very useful to a rower unless they translate to improved on-water performance. These changes in weight room strength primarily improve rowing performance early in a rower's career, but with more experience and at higher levels of performance, further increases are limited in their ability to improve performance.

Plyometrics

As mentioned in chapter 12, plyometrics increase power and contribute to an increase in fascicle length, which is important for speed. Although commonly used, research on the effects of plyometric training on rowing performance is scarce. Kramer, Morrow, and Leger (1993) found no effect on performance in a 2,500 m ergometer test when plyometrics were added. Egan-Shuttler and colleagues (2017) found that the addition of plyometrics 3 times per week improved time over 500 m and rowing economy, which is the energy cost to perform 500 m of rowing.

Plyometrics use the stretch–shortening cycle or stretch reflex, where a rapid stretch of a muscle immediately before a contraction takes advantage of the elastic components of the muscle, like a rubber band, to enhance power production. Although plyometrics can be done using either upper or lower body muscles, jumping is the most common form of plyometrics for rowers. Plyometric jumping exercises follow a specific sequence:

- *Landing.* The landing phase starts as soon as the muscles start to experience an eccentric contraction. The rapid eccentric contraction serves to stretch the elastic component of the muscle and activate the stretch reflex. A high level of eccentric strength is needed during the landing phase. Inadequate strength will result in a slow rate of stretch and less activation of the stretch reflex.
- *Amortization.* The amortization phase, the time on the ground, is the most important part of a plyometric exercise. It represents the turnaround time from landing to takeoff and is crucial for power development. If the amortization phase is too long, the stretch reflex is lost and there is no plyometric effect.
- *Takeoff.* The takeoff is the concentric contraction that follows the landing. During this phase the stored elastic energy is used to increase jump height.

Most plyometric jumps involve a relatively short range of motion with only a small amount of bend in the knee. Because the most important part of the rowing stroke for power development is the catch, rowers should use a full range of motion, getting to the depth of knee angle on the landing that they would achieve at the catch position. The amortization phase would be the rapid turnaround from this deep position.

Plyometric volume is determined by foot contacts; note that a landing on both feet counts as two contacts. Rowers aim for 40-to-100-foot contacts per training session 1 to 3 times per week. Plyometrics are a power development tool, and as such the jumps per set are low—1 to 5 with long rest periods of 2 to 4 minutes. Continuous jumping for high numbers of reps or even minutes at a time, as practiced by some rowers, may develop some energy system properties but is not effective for increasing power and speed.

Isometrics

With the development of lower cost force platforms, there has been a renewed interest in the use of isometric contractions as both a training and testing tool. Isometrics involve the contraction of a muscle or group of muscles without any external movement. Isometrics have been shown to have positive effects on dynamic strength and jump performances (Lum and Barbosa 2019) as well club head speed in golf (Leary et al. 2012) and sprint and change-of-direction speed in soccer (Mason et al. 2020; West et al. 2011).

Key Point

Isometric testing and training has gained popularity over the past decade, ultimately spiking as a result of pandemic lockdowns that forced people to find at-home alternatives to gym-based strength programs. Although this type of training may feel new and cutting edge, isometric training has been around for thousands of years, having been a part of many martial arts disciplines. Isometrics also became popular in the 1950s and 1960s following some research that showed improvements in isometric strength following only 4 weeks of training.

Isometrics are particularly useful for training positions where the muscles are at a biomechanical disadvantage or positions that are hard to achieve with traditional weight room exercises (Lum and Barbosa 2019). Rowing-specific isometric exercises have the potential to improve force and power development as well as the way forces are developed in the boat, particularly if the isometric pulls are done in the catch position. Be sure to pull in the same way as in the boat so that good posture is maintained and risk of injury is reduced. Figure 16.10 shows a rowing-specific isometric device that was instrumented with a force plate.

Ed McNeely

▶ **Figure 16.10**   Rowing-specific isometric device instrumented with a force plate.

Figure 16.11 shows three examples of how changes in isometric force and rate of force development, as measured by the force produced at 200 ms, relate to changes in the oarlock forces in the boat. Note that in the second example there is no change in gate forces or isometric forces, strengthening the idea that changes in isometric force impact the rowing stroke.

The energy requirements of isometrics are less than those of traditional weight room exercises (Lum and Barbosa 2019), making them a great tool during the competitive phase of the year when high-intensity rowing and the need for recovery become priorities over fatiguing weight training sessions.

To increase strength, use maximum-effort isometric pulls of 1 to 5 s, for a total of 30 to 90 s per session (Lum and Barbosa 2019). Very short pulses of less than 1 s seem to help increase rate of force development and force in the first 200 ms of the stroke. Catch position isometrics are affected by the frequency of training sessions per week, with 3 sessions per week providing the best results.

You don't need an isometric device to perform isometric pulls. Loop a boat strap through the handle of an ergometer and around the frame and tighten it so that the strap is tight when at the catch (figure 16.12). When doing an isometric catch, ensure that the pull is done in the same way that a rowing stroke would be done. Drive through the feet and keep your rear end in contact with the seat. The most common errors when doing an isometric catch pull are to trying to open with the upper body first, shooting the slide, or lifting completely off the seat.

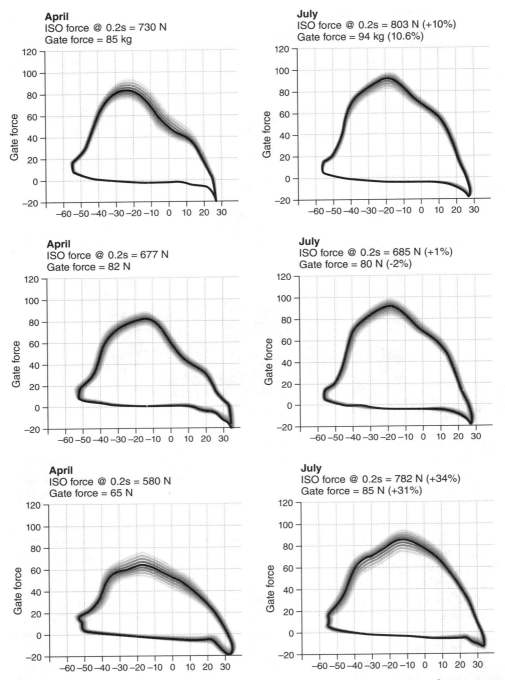

▶ **Figure 16.11** The effects of adding rowing-specific isometric training on force curves in the boat. There is a high degree of transfer, with positive changes in on water force production occurring when force at 0.2 s increases and no changes when force at 0.2 s does not change.

▶ **Figure 16.12** Ergometer prepared for isokinetic training.

Isometrics can be included as part of a strength session as the first or second exercise after warm-up. Because they can be done using an ergometer they can also be done prior to rowing-specific training, particularly higher intensity efforts. Feros and colleagues (2012) found that a series of 5 isometric contractions of 5 s each prior to a 1,000 m ergometer performance improved mean power output by 6.6% and reduced time by 0.8% with the majority of the improvements in the first 500 m, making them a good addition to a warm-up prior to ergometer peak power training.

Peak Power: High-Load Ergometer Sprints

Because the importance of aerobic fitness for rowing performance is well known, the aerobic system is generally quite well trained in competitive rowers. As the level of competition increases, the difference in aerobic fitness between competitors decreases. By the international level the difference in aerobic fitness between first and last place crews is often less than the error in the machines used to measure aerobic fitness.

Because this difference is so small among crews of similar competitive level, there are other factors that give winning crews an edge. Outside of technique, the physical factor that has emerged as a good predictor of rowing performance is peak power. There have been several studies in the past few years that have shown peak power is more strongly correlated to rowing performance in both elite and subelite rowers than $\dot{V}O_2$max or anaerobic threshold (Riechman et al. 2002; da Silva et al. 2021).

Peak power (i.e., the highest wattage one is capable of pulling) limits race ability by setting a power ceiling for performance. For instance, a rower achieving 2,000 m on the Concept2 ergometer in 6 min would need to pull approximately 475 W for the entire duration. If the rower's peak power is only 500 W, it is going to be very difficult to hold the 475 W pace for very long. In fact, if their target pace is more than 55% of their peak power, the rower will have a very difficult time holding that pace.

If peak power is higher, athletes will be able to work at a lower percentage of peak power and still hit target paces. This makes the race feel a little easier and provides a performance buffer in order to make a hard sprint in the final 500 m.

Development of peak power can be done using high-resistance ergometer work as an adjunct to strength training. Performing 10 sets of 10 strokes capped at 40 spm increases peak power but only when done in small doses. Figure 16.13 shows the changes in peak power after various numbers of training sessions. The largest gains were in the first 10 sessions, followed by slower improvements or a plateau in performance; this plateau seemed to occur whether the frequency was 2 or 3 sessions per week. The pattern could be repeated from a higher baseline following 6 to 8 weeks away from the peak power training as long as weight room strength development continued.

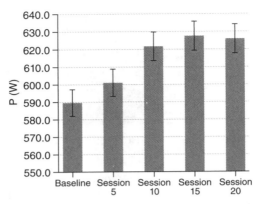

▶ **Figure 16.13** Changes in peak power following ergometer power training.

Resisted Rowing

Resisted rowing is common in many rowing programs, particularly during the racing season, but there has only been one study that has examined the effects of resisted rowing. Lawton, Cronin, and McGuigan (2013a) examined the effects of resisted rowing on lower body strength over 14 weeks measured using the Concept2 Dyno and a standing isometric pull with the bar set just below the knee. They found that on-water rowing alone was enough to maintain lower body strength, but that the addition of weight training twice per week increased lower body strength. If an athlete has adequate strength, they may not need weight room work for short periods of time during the competitive season. If the competitive season is long (14 weeks or more) or the athlete still needs to develop strength, a session or two in the weight room will help maintain muscle mass that is critical for longer term strength and power production.

Key Point

When using resisted rows for rowing-specific strength development, treat them like strength exercises, using short sets of 8 to 20 strokes with longer 2 to 3 min rest periods between sets and a resistance that is high enough to be challenging but not high enough to affect rowing technique. The longer sets of resisted rowing that are often used may produce metabolic changes but are less likely to result in strength and power improvements.

Conclusion

Strength training has become a significant part of rowing preparation, comprising 20% to 25% of most rowing programs. Strength development can occur both in the weight room, where underlying physiological changes in the nervous system and muscular system will occur, and in rowing-specific activities that translate to on-water improvements in stroke mechanics, force, and power production. Weight room activities are most important for younger, less experienced rowers, where an emphasis on multijoint exercises like squats, deadlifts, and bench pulls make up the bulk of the program. For more experienced rowers approaching the competitive season, on-water or ergometer strength development plays a greater role. Integration of strength training into a program of high-volume aerobic training can be a balancing act, as discussed in chapter 12, but it is worth the effort for the performance gains that come with greater strength.

Cross-Training

Ed McNeely

Rowing is a power endurance sport that requires large volumes of training to be successful, with top-level rowers typically training in excess of 1,000 hours per year (Fiskerstrand and Seiler 2004). Analysis of the distribution of training across intensity categories shows a common pattern of high-volume, low-intensity aerobic training making up the bulk of a rower's training time, accounting for up to 90% of training volume in certain periods of the year (Mäestu, Jürimäe, and Jürimäe 2005). Training for rowing is typically made up of sport-specific on- and off-water training, strength training, and endurance-based cross-training.

Cross-training is any training activity outside of the main sport activity or very close approximations of the sport activity. Common forms of cross-training for rowing include strength training and other forms of land-based aerobic conditioning like cycling, running, and cross-country skiing.

Benefits of Cross-Training

Cross-training has been proposed as a means of reducing overuse injuries, alleviating boredom and monotony to prevent staleness and burnout (Raglin and Morgan 1989), and maintaining fitness when returning from injury (Krause 2009). Although commonly used in rowing programs, there is no research on the benefits of endurance-based cross-training for rowers; much of the evidence is anecdotal and based on best practices of top coaches and athletes. Among runners, cross-training is often used to alleviate the impact of running while keeping overall training volume high (Paquette et al. 2018). Although rowing does not have the same impact as running, it is a higher force endurance sport than running, cycling, or swimming as a result of the high power output at relatively low turnover rates. The repetitive nature of the rowing stroke predisposes rowers to overuse injuries of the lower back, knee, and wrist (Hosea and Hannafin 2012), which may be decreased with cross-training.

Key Point

Cross-training provides a physical and psychological break from the repetitive nature of rowing, which improves motivation and decreases the risk of overuse injuries.

Volume of Cross-Training

There needs to be a balance between cross-training and rowing-specific training. Finding this balance depends on the level and age of the rower and environmental conditions. Rowers in warmer climates with year-round access to on-water facilities will have an easier time doing on-water training than those in colder climates where, for significant portions of the year, on-water rowing is inaccessible.

Mäestu, Jürimäe, and Jürimäe (2005) have suggested that up to 70% to 80% of endurance training time may be spent on the water for some rowers, with typical amounts ranging from 52% to 55% of total training volume for an 18-year-old to 55% to 60% for a 21-year-old and up to 65% for a senior rower. They have also suggested that the amount of time dedicated to specific rowing training should increase as the level of the rower increases. Table 17.1 shows a progression of training volume and training mode based on age for a competitive rower starting 9 years from their first Olympic games.

Table 17.1   Training Hours and Training Mode Progression

	Year 1	Year 2	Year 3	Year 4	Year 5	Year 6	Year 7	Year 8	Year 9	Year 10 (Olympic year)
Age	17	18	19	20	21	22	23	24	25	26
Volume (total hours)	614	645	677	711	782	860	946	975	1,023	1,100
Volume (h/wk)	13.3	14.0	14.7	15.5	17.0	18.7	20.6	21.2	22.2	23.9
Strength training (h/wk)	5.0	5.0	5.0	5.0	5.0	5.0	5.0	5.0	5.0	5.0
Strength training (% of total volume)	37%	36%	34%	32%	29%	27%	24%	24%	22%	21%
On-water training (% time)	40%	40%	41%	43%	45%	45%	42%	45%	50%	55%
Ergometer	15%	15%	15%	14%	14%	14%	14%	12%	11%	9%
Cross-training	15%	13%	13%	11%	12%	14%	20%	19%	17%	15%
Strength training (total hours)	184	207	207	230	230	230	230	230	230	230
On-water training (total hours)	246	258	278	306	352	387	397	439	512	605
Ergometer (total hours)	92	97	102	100	109	120	132	117	113	99
Cross-training (total hours)	92	84	88	78	94	120	189	185	174	165

Strength training is one of the most common forms of cross-training. It is a key component of training for rowing and accounts for about 20% to 25% of total training volume depending on the experience, fitness, and competitive level of the rower (Mäestu, Jürimäe, and Jürimäe 2005). Practical experience suggests that the volume of strength training may be higher for younger athletes. The increasing volume of aerobic training that rowers need to excel as they age makes it more difficult to increase muscle mass, so it is an advantage to a young rower if they can build the muscle mass needed to compete successfully at higher levels. More discussion of incorporating strength training into rowing programs can be found in chapter 16.

The amount of cross-training can vary significantly across the year, with up to about 50% of training volume in the off-season (McNeely 2014). Table 17.2 shows a breakdown of different training modes across the year. There is some ergometer and cross-training work included in the plan year-round to allow individualized training sessions to address athlete-specific needs, which cannot be met rowing a crew boat.

Table 17.2 Sample Breakdown of Training Phases Over One Year

Training phase	General preparation	Specific preparation	Precompetition	Competition	Transition
No. of weeks	12	12	10	12	6
Volume (h/phase)	300	300	230	200	60
Strength training (h/phase)	80	63	48	25	10
On-water training (h/phase)	85	137	145	153	0
Ergometer (h/phase)	45	30	25	12	0
Cross-training (h/phase)	90	70	11.5	10	50
Strength training (% of total volume)	27%	21%	21%	13%	17%
On-water training (% of total volume)	28%	46%	63%	77%	0%
Ergometer (% of total volume)	15%	10%	11%	6%	0%
Cross-training (% of total volume)	30%	23%	5%	5%	83%

During the general preparation phase, cross-training is used to gradually build training volume and prevent overuse injuries. The volume of cross-training is highest at the start of the phase and decreases closer to the specific preparation phase. Athletes who are unable to row on water for extended periods should increase the volume of cross-training as part of their transition to the water to help prevent wrist injuries from feathering the blade after having been away from that skill.

Mode of Exercise

Adaptations to training are specific to the type of training. This includes energy system training, mode of exercise, range of motion, and speed of movement. Specificity is a key component of transfer of training. According to Issurin (2013), transfer of training, or the proportion of improvement in one exercise that translates to another, ultimately determines how useful or useless each given exercise is for a targeted population.

Improvement in sport performance is often the result of improving underlying physiological systems and then converting those adaptations to sport-specific movements. Aerobic training affects a multitude of bodily systems and creates a variety of training adaptations, including increased cardiac output via increased left ventricle filling and increased ejection fraction leading to improvements in $\dot{V}O_2$max, increased oxygen-carrying capacity through higher blood volume and hemoglobin, increased capillarization of muscle fibers and interaction with myoglobin (van der Zwaard et al. 2018), and changes in fiber type. Many of these adaptations represent changes in underlying physical structures that are not specific to any movement or skill.

Cross-training can improve general motor abilities like strength and flexibility as well as fitness parameters like $\dot{V}O_2$max, but it does little to enhance specific movement skills. In untrained people the amount of improvement in muscularly similar activities does not seem to differ between specific and nonspecific exercises (Loy et al. 1993). Foster and colleagues (1995) suggested that cycle cross-training can create positive muscular changes to aid running performance but not to the same degree as increasing one's specific training.

Tanaka (1994) has suggested that cycling and running may be better modes of improving $\dot{V}O_2$max than swimming. Although this may be true for ground-based sports, the use of upper body musculature in swimming may benefit rowers, who require both upper and lower body endurance. Other activities like cross-country skiing and the VersaClimber also involve both upper and lower body musculature. In the event of a lower body injury, arm crank ergometers can be a useful tool for maintaining cardiovascular fitness while improving upper body aerobic performance (figure 17.1).

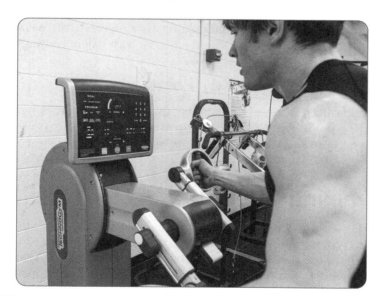

▶ **Figure 17.1**   Crank ergometer.

An often-overlooked form of cross-training is participation in team sports, particularly soccer. Small-sided games common to team sport practices have been shown to be as effective as high-intensity interval training for increasing $\dot{V}O_2$max (Kunz et al. 2019), as has recreational soccer (Milanović et al. 2015). Team sports expose the player to a variety of intensities and durations of activity. The continuous nature of soccer makes it a better cross-training modality for rowing than discontinuous team sports like baseball, softball, or volleyball. Team sports are also a great way for younger rowers to improve their physical literacy, which may enhance their ability to learn rowing skills. Rowers who have not participated in team or racket sports need to prepare with a few weeks of change-of-direction drills and submaximal sprinting before jumping into a game situation.

Key Point

Team sports are a great change of pace as a cross-training tool for rowers and provide a bit of a competitive environment, team building, and fitness—as long as they are not so competitive that injuries result.

Although cross-training is often viewed as a means of decreasing overuse injuries caused by the primary sport, too much cross-training leads to rowers developing overuse injuries common to other endurance sports, such as knee pain from cycling and shin splints from running. Ensure that any equipment used in cross-training (bikes, skis, poles, running shoes, etc.) fit properly and are well maintained. Understand the basic skills of any new cross-training activity and introduce new modes of exercise gradually over a period of several weeks—a weekend of cross-country skiing or other novel activity can quickly lead to overuse injuries for unaccustomed participants.

Rowers have a wide variety of cross-training options to choose from, ranging from traditional lower-body cross-training modes like running and cycling, to more upper-body exercises like swimming and Nordic skiing. Using several different cross-training options likely provides the greatest benefit with the least risk of causing injuries.

Key Point

Trying new and different types of exercises or workouts for cross-training can be fun and exciting if you don't overdo it. When taking up a new mode of training, gradually increase the volume of activity over a couple of weeks.

Cross-Training Intensity

Intensity during aerobic activities is typically built around training zones. Although there are a variety of naming conventions that vary from sport to sport and by country, most zone systems are derived from an assessment of aerobic threshold, anaerobic threshold, and $\dot{V}O_2$max. There is no research examining the relationship between training intensity zones created from on-water rowing or rowing ergometer data compared to other modalities. In some rowers the relationship between heart rate, lactate, and workload can be very different when cross-training compared to rowing or ergometer training (Tran et al. 2014). There are several means of determining training zones and training load for cross-training, ranging from mathematical calculations to physiological measures of heart rate, lactate, and oxygen consumption.

T2Minute Method

Another method of monitoring and tracking training load and intensity during cross-training is the T2minute method used by Australian high-performance rowers. Tran and colleagues (2014) developed a set of weighting factors to convert various training intensity zones and modes of exercise to an equivalent of T2minutes (T2 being a training zone around the aerobic threshold). Their system is based on the theory that the nature of the stress placed on the athlete is a function of not only volume and intensity but also mode of exercise. It attempts to account for posture, muscles used, task familiarity, training history, skill, and perceptual demands of various training modes.

Various modes of exercise were compared to how hard they were compared to on-water training at a T2 intensity. Their weighting factors of training load compared to on-water rowing were 0.8 for road cycling, 0.95 for stationary cycling, 1.4 for running, 1.2 for swimming, and 0.5 for walking. This means that that each walking minute only counts for half a minute of training time compared to on-water training. The T2minute method provides an excellent framework for conceptualizing the differences in response that occur as a result of cross-training, but it does not account for individual differences between athletes, which can be measured through physiological testing.

Physiological Monitoring

Figure 17.2 shows the results of a progressive incremental lactate step test on both a rowing ergometer and bike ergometer in two international rowers. In both cases the bike test was stopped once the athlete reached an intensity around anaerobic threshold.

Athlete 2 was a very experienced cyclist, having competed in some cycling events at various times in their career, whereas Athlete 1 used to cycle as one of several cross-

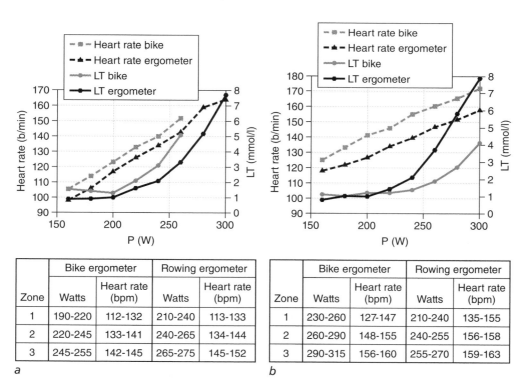

▶ **Figure 17.2** Comparison of heart rate (HR), lactate (La), and power data between cycling and rowing, as well as the determination of the training zones for athlete 1 (a) and athlete 2 (b), who prioritize different cross-training sports.

training modalities. In athlete 1 the heart rate zones are comparable between the bike and rowing ergometers, but in athlete 2 the differences between zones on the bike and ergometer are too great to use the two interchangeably. Why this happens in some athletes and not others is unclear, but it may be a result of experience and technical proficiency with different types of training and whether the cross-training is focused around one or more modalities. Generally, athletes who use a greater number of cross-training modalities for modest volumes can make use of rowing heart rate zones more effectively than those who specialize in one type of cross-training activity.

If you do not have access to blood lactate and heart rate measures to establish training zones it is possible to use a rating of perceived exertion (RPE) scale to monitor cross-training intensity (table 17.3). The RPE scale been widely used to measure exertion during acute exercise as well as session RPE after training sessions (Boutcher et al. 1989).

Table 17.3   Sample Rating of Perceived Exertion (RPE) Scale

Rating	Description
1	Nothing at all (lying down)
2	Extremely little
3	Very easy
4	Easy (could do this all day)
5	Moderate
6	Somewhat hard (starting to feel it)
7	Hard
8	Very hard (making an effort to keep up)
9	Very, very hard
10	Maximum effort (cannot go any further)

The same heart rate zones cannot be used for every activity. The amount of muscle mass involved and technical proficiency at the activity can affect the heart rate response and metabolic intensity of the activity.

Adapted by permission from D.H. Fukuda and K.L. Kendall, "Fitness Evaluation Protocols and Norms," in NSCA's Essentials of Personal Training, 3rd ed., edited for the National Strength and Conditioning Association by B. J. Schoenfeld and R. L. Snarr (Champaign, IL: Human Kinetics, 2022), 204.

Session RPE (sRPE) is fundamentally different from using RPE to determine exercise intensity (Dantas et al. 2015). Session RPE is designed to measure internal load, representing the physiological stress that results from an external load after it has been applied; it is an aggregate perception of varying intensities throughout a training session. Acute RPE measures are used to determine the immediate effects of the external load and can be used to create cutoff points for training zones. Dantas and colleagues (2015) developed an equation to determine the RPE for a given level of blood lactate:

$$RPE = 1.092 \text{ BLC} + 2.143$$

Table 17.4 shows RPE values for several commonly used lactate values. To use the RPE scale effectively, proper instructions need to be used. Those using the scale are instructed to rate their exertion on the scale during the activity, combining all sensations and feelings of physical stress and fatigue and disregarding any single factor such as leg pain or shortness of breath. It is important to use a 1-10 RPE scale with the anchor words shown in table 17.3, which are critical to getting a valid and reliable measure (Dawes et al. 2005).

Table 17.4   Corresponding Blood Lactate Measures With RPE Values

Blood lactate (mmol/L)	RPE
1.5	3.8
2	4.3
2.5	4.9
3.5	6.0
4	6.5
6	8.7

Choosing an Intensity

Regardless of the method chosen to measure and monitor intensity, an appropriate intensity still needs to be applied during a training session. Cross-training can be used to improve aerobic fitness at any intensity, from low-intensity base work to high-intensity intervals (Chan, Ho, and Yung 2017; Flynn et al. 1998).

The intensity for cross-training depends on the goal of cross-training in the program. If it is used to increase training volume and build work capacity, lower intensity aerobic base work may be the best option. If cross-training is being used to relieve the boredom and monotony that comes with high volumes of sport-specific training, then lower intensity aerobic threshold work has been shown to be more enjoyable than high-intensity interval training (Foster et al. 2015). For some athletes a less structured approach to cross-training is even more enjoyable. A method like Fartlek training, traditionally used in running to mix periods of slow speeds with periods of faster speeds, can be applied across a variety of cross-training modalities.

High-intensity interval training (HIIT) provides a potent stimulus to increase both aerobic and anaerobic fitness and requires a fraction of the time of traditional long distance training (Engel et al. 2018), making it a good cross-training tool for rowers who have limited training time during the off-season. However, the highly technical nature of the rowing stroke and the need to develop timing with other crew members at race pace cannot be built through cross-training. Reserving cross-training for lower intensity activity is therefore likely better for rowers as the season progresses and developing rowing skills becomes a priority.

Conclusion

Cross-training is any type of training not done on the water or a rowing ergometer. It is a significant part of the program of many rowers, particularly those living in climates that do not allow them to be on water for a large portion of the year. It adds variety, helps decrease the risk of injury and mental burnout, and is an essential tool for maintaining fitness if a rower is injured. Although there is little research on the role of cross-training in a rowing program, experience suggests that a variety of activities that incorporate both the upper and lower body musculature are beneficial to rowers. The type, intensity, and total volume of cross-training needs to be as planned as rowing sessions. In some parts of the year, environmental conditions may make it necessary for more than 50% of total training to be cross-training, and having an understanding of cross-training allows safer and more effective programs to be developed.

Distance-Specific Pacing

Volker Nolte, PhD

The main goal in rowing a race over a certain distance is either to reach the finish line ahead of your competition or to achieve a certain time that satisfies a specific outcome. The first goal is typically associated with side-by-side racing, either during preliminary rounds when the results count for advancing to the next round or during a final. The second goal becomes a priority in so-called head races against the clock, in which the end time will be compared to competitors' times. This competition modus, which means that competitors start at a certain time interval from each other, is typically used in long distance races or in time trials that serve to rank all competitors. In all these cases, rowers have to make decisions about how much effort they exert at each stroke over the course of a race—or in short, how to pace themselves (Smits, Pepping, and Hettinga 2014). Ideally, they invest their energy in an optimal way to achieve their goal.

The following remarks refer to pacing strategies to achieve maximum rowing performance, or to complete the race distance in the fastest time possible. This goal invokes a preliminary template for a race strategy with the highest probability of success. Such a pacing strategy needs to meet the following criteria:

- Athletes will be able to use all their energy supply systems maximally to achieve the highest possible average power output over the course of the race.
- Athletes will be in the best position to achieve their highest competitive level without reaching early exhaustion.

However, the details of such a general template need to be logically adjusted to individual situations. For example, a 2,000 m race of a men's eight in tailwind conditions can take less than 5:20 min, whereas a race over the same distance can take a lightweight woman's single in headwind conditions more than 10 min. An optimal energy expenditure scheme under these circumstances therefore more closely resembles a sprint race for the men's eight, whereas it will look more like a long distance race for the lightweight woman.

Key Point

The ideal pacing strategy is mainly based on physiological considerations, but athletes also need to consider what their personal goals are and how intense they expect the race to be, then assess how the racing actions will influence their confidence.

Of course, rowers need to have the skill level to efficiently execute the required stroke rates and boat speeds at any part of the race. Furthermore, athletes have to anticipate external influences like the impact of weather, wind, and waves on how to best gauge their energy expenditure.

Factors That Affect Pacing

The ideal pacing strategy is mainly based on the athlete's physiology; however, other factors, both internal and external, need to be taken into account. Internal factors are of a psychological or biomechanical nature. As Smits, Pepping, and Hettinga (2014) point out, "the pacing strategy athletes adopt throughout the exercise bout is related to personal goals and knowledge of the likely demands of the bout" (763). The presence of other competitors, along with the perception of strength, assessment of the importance of the race, and personal objective for a placement have a definitive influence on how fast the athlete starts the race. De Koning and colleagues (2011) then argue that for the rest of the race "the athlete is continuously comparing how they feel at any moment in a competition with how they expected to feel at that moment" (1). The authors use the concept of the momentary rating of perceived exertion (RPE) together with the evaluation of how much longer the race will continue to explain how athletes will gauge their energy expenditure. "If their RPE is larger than expected for that point in the event, then power output (e.g., running speed) will decrease, even if it means giving up on the competition. If RPE is less than expected, then power output will increase" (1).

External factors that influence an ideal pacing plan include, for example, wind conditions or turns in the course. Athletes may adjust their level and length of energy expenditure at the start of the race depending on the expected effect of wind. Turns in the course of a long distance race may require energy bursts or breaks at a time when a constant exercise level would normally be preferable.

In rowing, races differ not only in the length of the course, but also in their organization. Side-by-side races, in which crews line up next to each other and start at the same time, and head races or time trials, in which crews race one after another without knowing how their opponents perform, are used depending on available physical space on the race course, when wind conditions require the usage of only one lane for fairness reasons, or when a ranking of a group of boats needs to be done at once. Race length and type will influence pacing strategies.

Many practical observations together with the previously mentioned studies lead to the following general statements:

- Athletes who set out to reach a maximal performance base their decisions about how and when to exert their energy on theoretical models, personal preferences, and experiences, as well as environmental situations.

- The presence of other participants increases the competitiveness of races and normally results in higher performance.

- Fast-starting crews make other competitors raise their efforts.

- Athletes must continue to make decisions throughout a race regarding how much energy to spend. They use information about the actual race situation (e.g., position within the race, rowing speed, weather and water conditions), their perceived exertion, and the estimation of how much distance remains.

- Proper assessment of fatigue leads to optimal performance. Athletes risk early exhaustion if they exert too much energy early in the race, but an overly conservative use of energy would not allow the achievement of maximum performance.

Energy Systems Involved in Pacing

As discussed in chapters 10 and 11, three energy systems work together to produce energy in humans: the anaerobic alactic system, the anaerobic lactic system, and the aerobic system. The energy produced by all these systems together at a given time signifies the work capacity that athletes have at their disposal. There is a time structure to each of the systems that dictates their best usage. The anaerobic alactic system is readily available because the high energy phosphates are stored right in the muscle. Humans can produce their highest energy throughput rate using this system, but it only lasts for 10 to 15 s. The anaerobic lactic system needs a short start-up time and is good for high power production, but in the process of breaking down glycogen to generate the necessary ATP, it produces lactic acid that lowers the pH value in the muscle. The aerobic system needs about 60 to 120 s to move from its basal metabolic rate to its full work capacity, but can then generate this energy output for a long time.

Mader and Hollmann (1977) presented a model that describes the interaction of the three energy supply systems to produce a large work output for an athlete in a rowing race over 7 min (figure 18.1). This model gives a very good overview of how the three energy supply systems work together and the course of the maximum overall energy that is available to rowers. It also shows how much lactate is produced at each minute time interval and how this manifests in the accumulation of lactate in the blood. This model is confirmed by other authors (e.g., Fox 1993; Foster et al. 2003; Hartmann and Mader 2005; Secher, Vollianitis, and Jürimäe 2007) and can be used to estimate the maximum possible energy production of a rower.

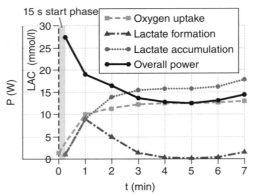

▶ **Figure 18.1** Typical power output of elite rowers during a simulated rowing race over 7 min.

Mader and Hollmann 1977, 20.

The course of oxygen uptake and its maximum is dependent on the rower's age, size, sex, genetic factors (e.g., distribution of muscle fiber types). and training (Fox 1993, 317ff) and is therefore not fixed. The anaerobic lactic contribution also depends mainly on training factors. The areas underneath the curves in figure 18.1 represent the total energy output that the rower achieves over the length of the race covered by the different energy supply systems. It is widely accepted that rowers produce about 80% to 85% of the overall energy of a 2,000 m race aerobically. The magnitude of the total power output is a measure of the speed that the rower achieves at that point of the race. This means that the shape of the power output and the boat speed curves are very similar.

Although there may be individual differences in the power outputs of each of the three systems for different rowers, they still follow the presented general courses. This means that an optimal power distribution over time is similar for all rowers and can be estimated for each individual athlete. The goal is to maximize the power output of all systems, all of which affect each other. A fast depletion of the ATP stores in the muscles and a high mechanical power output trigger a rapid increase of the anaerobic lactic system, and the magnitude of the acidosis in the muscle triggers the increase in oxygen consumption (Bailey et al. 2011). Of course, the generation of mechanical power needs to be controlled so that the lactate accumulation remains on a level that the rower can tolerate. This pacing strategy, in which "the athlete starts fast, slows down for a period in the middle portion of the event and increases speed towards the end of the event" (Thompson 2015, 16), is called *parabolic pacing*.

The marked areas (light and dark gray shaded) in figure 18.2*a* show the overall energy that the anaerobic and aerobic systems generate during a 7 min race. The total power at each point of the race is the summation of the output of all energy systems, and the rowing speed follows the same course. For example, studies have shown that it is possible—through specific training combined with an appropriate high power output—to accelerate the ramp-up of oxygen uptake at the beginning of a race, which in turn lets the rower achieve an increased energy output, which then translates into increased rowing speed (Bailey et al. 2011; Mader, Hartmann, and Hollmann 1988; Secher, Vollianitis, and Jürimäe 2007; Xu and Rhodes 1999). This is shown in figure 18.2*b*.

For races of shorter duration (tailwind conditions, big boats, sprint races) it is even more important to achieve a maximum oxygen uptake as early as possible. Under such circumstances the rower can also sustain a higher lactate accumulation earlier in the race, because it does not need to be carried for a long time. This means that shorter races can be attacked more aggressively to achieve the highest power output from athletes. Conversely, it is important for races of longer duration (headwind conditions, small boats, long distance races) to be more conservative about tapping into the anaerobic energy supply so that the oxidative capabilities can fully deploy for a longer time and so the associated fatigue does not set in.

The initial high power output at the start of a race helps with the energy demand that is necessary to generate the inertial forces to accelerate the rowing system. It also

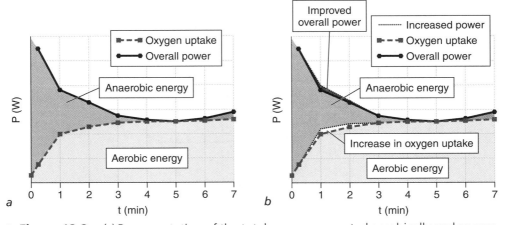

▶ **Figure 18.2** *(a)* Representation of the total energy generated aerobically and anaerobically. *(b)* Increase of the overall power through accelerated ramp-up of oxygen uptake and the energy gain thus achieved.

provides athletes with the opportunity to establish themselves favorably in the contest. This starting procedure requires high stroke rates, excellent sequencing of the power-generating body joints, and fine-tuned coordination within the crew, which are skills that correspondingly favor determined and experienced rowers.

Key Point

There are striking similarities of ideal pacing strategies for all endurance sport events. These can be summarized as follows:

- All races start with a power output that is much higher than the average energy expenditure of the event.
- Short races are started with maximum power output. This burst becomes more controlled and of shorter duration the longer the race is.
- Athletes need to adjust their efforts after the start phase so that they can quickly reach and then maintain their maximum aerobic output in races that last longer than 2 min.
- All remaining anaerobic energy supply capacities must be utilized at the end of a race to ensure maximum energy output for a complete race.
- An absolute best performance for races longer than 4 min can only be achieved when an athlete uses their maximum aerobic *and* anaerobic energy systems.
- The best pacing strategy for a specific race is then finalized by taking additional information into consideration: For example, is the race a heat, repechage, semifinal, or final? What are the progression rules? Does recovery time between races need to be observed?

Based on these considerations, general patterns of ideal pacing strategies can be identified for all distances of rowing races, from sprint races (200-1,000 m) to international races (2,000 m) to long distance races, which in fact are similar to other endurance sports like running or cross-country skiing. Figure 18.3 supports this assessment by presenting the pacing strategies used in world record performances in running.

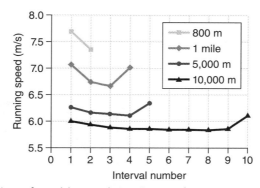

▶ **Figure 18.3** Pacing of world record running performances over different distances. Average running speeds are represented at 400 m intervals for the 800 m and 1 mi races and at 1,000 m intervals for the 5,000 m and 10,000 m races.

Tucker, Lambert, and Noakes 2006, 238.

Race Pace and Output

The recruitment and total contribution of the aerobic and anaerobic energy supply systems to the overall power output depends on the length of the race. As mentioned above, rowing literature is quite consistent in estimating the aerobic and anaerobic contributions for 2,000 m races at 80% to 85% and 15% to 20%, respectively. Unfortunately, studies on races of different distances are sparse, and specific energy distributions could not be found. However, energy contribution in other endurance sports like cross-country skiing or running should be comparable to that in rowing of equivalent duration. Spencer, Gastin, and Payne (1996, 61) presented data for 400, 800, and 1,500 m running and Duffield, Dawson, and Goodman (2005, 997) added data for 1,500 and 3,000 m running (figure 18.4). Such races last about 50 s, 2 min, 4 min, and 9 min for the mentioned distances, respectively. If these data are extrapolated to 6,000 m (about 20 min duration), all common rowing race times can be compared.

As figure 18.4a shows, the absolute amount of energy that can be generated by the anaerobic supply systems is almost the same for all exercise durations (Spencer, Gastin, and Payne 1996). The extra energy that longer distances require must be covered by the aerobic system, so that this system gains importance with the length of the race, which can be seen by the relative energy allocation in figure 18.4b. This link has clear implications for training for different race lengths. The training regimes for the different energy supply systems are discussed in the previous chapters.

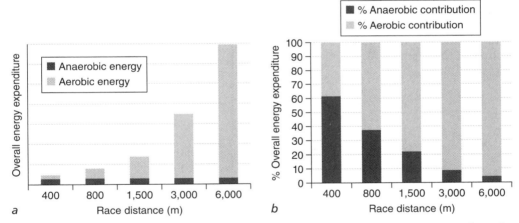

▶ **Figure 18.4** Aerobic and anaerobic systems' contribution to energy expenditure in running races of different distances: *(a)* absolute contribution, and *(b)* relative contribution in percent.

Data from Spencer, Gastin, and Payne 1996 and Duffield, Dawson, and Goodman 2005; data for 6,000 m distance extrapolated.

Pacing for Sprint Races

The Olympic race distance in rowing is currently 2,000 m, which is often called a sprint. However, in the context of this book, sprint races are those of distances shorter than 2,000 m. The shortest distance that is currently contested in international rowing events is 1,000 m, and it is only used in masters rowing. The subsequent discussion will therefore focus on this race length.

Key Point

Besides the physiological training, it is essential that rowers prepare for the exercise intensity and movement speeds that are used in races of different distances to improve the efficiency of the specific motions. Although race intensities and speeds can only be executed for short time periods, it is crucial that all stroke rates, power applications, and race actions are exercised as much as possible. It requires knowledge of physiology and prudent planning to optimize the time that rowers spend at high intensities without interference of their general performance improvements.

Athletes must also train variations in movement speeds and force applications at given intensities, because the external conditions of a race can vary greatly. For example, an explosive start, a high stroke rate sprint, and an efficient middle-of-the-race pace differ considerably in headwind compared to tailwind conditions. Executing a turn or maintaining an efficient pace at maximum aerobic energy output in waves also needs to be practiced so that the athletes do not inadvertently lose speed or overextend themselves, which could cause early exhaustion.

Positive Pacing

The ideal pacing pattern for a 1,000 m distance has some distinct differences from that for the 2,000 m. Based on the previously outlined parameters, the ideal pacing strategy for a 1,000 m race is called *positive pacing* (figure 18.5). As Thompson (2015) describes, "The athlete undertakes a fast start, which is not maximal but is at a high enough intensity that the athlete slows down as a result of developing fatigue over the course of the event" (16).

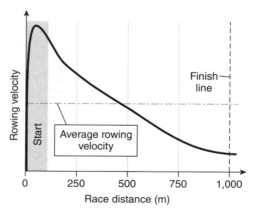

▶ **Figure 18.5** Positive pacing strategy for 1,000 m rowing races.

Practical experience supports the positive pacing strategy. The 1984 Olympic Games were the last international event in which women also rowed the 1,000 m distance. Figure 18.6, which shows the timing of the women's pair final at the 1984 Olympic Games, clearly supports the positive pacing strategy (unfortunately, there is not more detailed information available than 500 m split times, which provide the average rowing velocity for the two race halves). Rowers often call this race strategy "fly and die," which vividly describes how these athletes approach such a race. Crews begin the race with very high power output, trying to achieve the feeling of "flying" out of the starting gates at high speed for as long as possible, but feel like their efforts eventually "die." The winning time for this particular race was 3:32.6 and the difference between the first and second 500 m split time was an average of 6 s for all six boats in the final. All six crews in that final displayed the same general pacing strategy, and the same is true for all other women's boat classes.

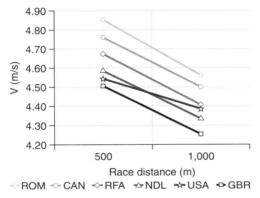

▶ **Figure 18.6**   Official timing of the 1,000 m women's pair final A at the 1984 Olympic Games.

World Rowing 2021b.

Measuring Output

Considering that these are average times and velocities for 500 m, it is expected that the difference between the absolute maximum and minimum rowing velocities on a stroke-by-stroke basis is actually substantially larger. Because the rowing velocity is a good indication of the power that the athletes generate, one can imagine the large difference in the magnitude of the power at the beginning and the end of the race.

In-boat equipment that could measure power during a race had not yet been developed at the time of the 1984 Olympic Games, so more detailed data is not available for these races. However, measurement technology has developed tremendously since then and can now be used in racing without performance impairment. It is therefore possible to present more detailed data from masters races that are held over the 1,000 m distance (figure 18.7). This equipment measures and stores data for every single stroke of the race averaged over each stroke cycle.

The analyses of masters races provide further proof of the ideal pacing strategy of races of that length. The presented examples from high level masters races show the same "fly and die" positive pacing pattern of the velocity and power data. The difference between the fastest and the slowest velocity is 1.4 m/s for the 2–, 0.9 m/s for the 2x, and 1.1 m/s for the 1x, which is 29.9%, 17.8%, and 24.7% of the average velocity of the respective boats. This shows the large variation in velocity that is displayed in sprint races.

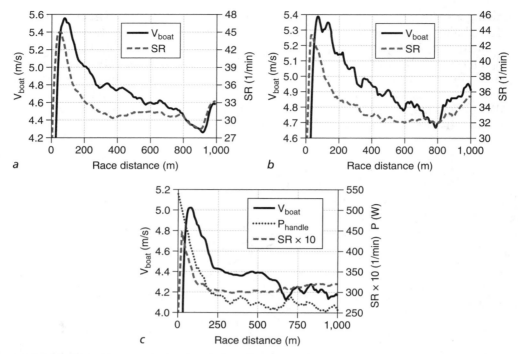

▶ **Figure 18.7** Boat velocity (v_{boat}), handle power (P_{handle}), and stroke rate (SR) data of 1,000 m races from first place masters crews at Canadian Henley Masters Regattas (all data smoothed with 5-point-moving-average). *(a)* 2015 men's 2–. *(b)* 2015 men's 2x. *(c)* 2017 men's 1x.

Data collected with NK SpeedCoach and NK EmPower Oarlock.

The maximum power in the masters 1x was measured at 522 W and the lowest power output at 232 W—a difference of 290 W. This comparison underlines the importance of the anaerobic energy supply system that is used in the beginning of the race.

The ideal tactics for race distances shorter than 1,000 m also follow the course outlined in figure 18.5, with the exception that the start and the first strokes are executed even more vigorously. There are currently no official races shorter than 1,000 m in international rowing. However, shorter distances are sometimes used to promote rowing (e.g., the Gold Cup in Philadelphia is 750 m) or in local settings (e.g., club regattas or so-called dash races). No detailed information about split times or power application is known to be recorded, but it is safe to expect that rowers follow the stated ideal pacing for such races.

2,000 m Races

The ideal parabolic pacing strategy for 2,000 m rowing races follows the model outlined by Mader and Hollmann (1977; figure 18.1), and is presented in figure 18.8a. It must be emphasized that this strategy is based on the rower's attempt for maximum energy utilization, which is not required in every race. Nevertheless, this pacing strategy does not only allow the optimum usage of all energy supply systems for a maximum output during the race time, it also allows the rowers to strive for their best psychological position in the race, whether they would like to lead the field, apply pressure on the leading crews, follow a preset course of speed or stroke rate, or simply achieve their best power output.

Early Sprint or Sprint to the Line?

If rowers are not required to use their maximum energy output, they can vary the ideal parabolic pacing strategy. Such considerations depend on the race situation—for example, whether the race is a heat or a final, whether the competition is strong or weak, or whether energy must be preserved for subsequent races.

Special attention should be put on the best approach for the finish sprint. On first view, one should think that the best approach would be "sprinting to the line" to reach the finish line at the highest rowing velocity. On closer examination, however, this is not the case. A crew reaches the finish line in a shorter time if they start their finish sprint early. The example in figure 18.8*b* explains this phenomenon.

It is assumed that two crews with exactly the same physical and technical abilities can start their finish sprint with the same rowing velocity and sprint for 1:45 min, increasing their rowing velocity during that time to the same maximum level. At the end of the 1:45 min sprint, they reach their maximum lactate level and from then on exert less power so that they have to slow down. One crew starts their sprint early, when they still have to row 2 min to the finish line. The second crew starts their sprint exactly 1:45 min before the finish line, so that this crew reaches the finish at their maximum rowing velocity.

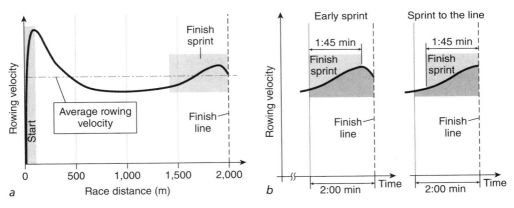

▶ **Figure 18.8** *(a)* Ideal pacing strategy for a 2,000 m race. *(b)* Comparison of "early sprint" and "sprint to the line" approaches.

Figure 18.8*b* shows the rowing velocities of the two crews during the last 2 min of their race. The area underneath the velocity curves represent the distances that the crews travel during that time, and it is obvious that the early sprint crew covers a larger distance in the 2 min. This means that if both crews had been exactly level in the race, the early sprint crew would move ahead. Although they would have to slow down 15 s before the line, the later sprinting crew would not be able to catch up.

The early sprinting strategy demands precise timing, because reaching the point of exhaustion too early would cause too large a drop in rowing velocity at the end of the race, and the advantage would be lost.

Key Point

The advantageous approach to start the finish sprint early (figure 18.8*b*) requires strong confidence of the athletes in their abilities and understanding of the concept. Proper timing is crucial and needs to be rehearsed.

It has been shown in several research papers that literally all crews in competitive 2,000 m races follow the ideal pacing strategy (Garland 2005; Kleshnev and Nolte 2011; Muehlbauer, Schindler, and Widmer 2010). Every year since the 2000 Olympic Games, Kleshnev has published an analysis of the respective World Championships or Olympic Games; he also presented a comprehensive overview (2016, 176) analyzing the data for all championship races between 1993 and 2014. He has always found—without exception—that finalists use strategy patterns that coincide with the presented ideal parabolic model presented in figure 18.8*a*. Muehlbauer, Schindler, and Widmer (2010) summarized: "Irrespective of race type, boat rank or boat type, our results show that, in both sexes, a parabolic-shaped pacing pattern (i.e. the first 500 m is performed faster than subsequent race quarters with a spurt at the end) is adopted during official rowing competitions" (295).

The Even-Splitting Debate

Despite this overwhelming theoretical and practical evidence, there is still considerable discussion about the value of the so-called *even-splitting strategy*, which means that the highest possible constant rowing velocity is maintained over the race distance. Klavora (1982) was probably the most prominent supporter of this strategy, and his arguments found wide distribution through his textbook for the Canadian National Coach Certification Program. The main evidence that he cites is the famous race between the two rowing giants Peter-Michael Kolbe (GER) and Pertti Karppinen (FIN) at the 1976 Olympic final. Being a race of such prominence and between two world-renowned athletes gave a lot of clout to the argument. Figure 18.9 shows the official split times from this race (World Rowing 2021a, 2021b, 2021c).

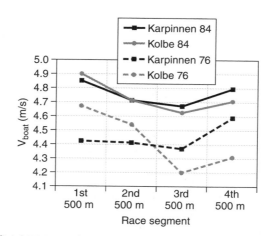

▶ **Figure 18.9** Official 500 m split times of Pertti Karppinen (Kar; 1st) and Peter-Michael Kolbe (Kol; 2nd) in the men's single at the 1976 Olympic finals and 1984 Olympic finals.

Klavora argues that Karpinnen's even-splitting approach, which can be seen for the first 1,500 m of the 1976 race (Kar 76 in figure 18.9), led to his success although Kolbe was the clear favorite going into the race. He adds a few more examples of successful crews that supposedly used similar race profiles and concludes that the even-splitting strategy is the superior method for success. This argument holds up stubbornly, although even Klavora (1982) admits "The fact is that in actual competition the great majority of races are certainly not rowed this way" (210).

A closer analysis, however, reveals that only very exceptional race circumstances produce such isolated results. A very strong headwind during the 1976 final elongated the race time considerably, and it is likely that Kolbe misjudged the wind influence and rowed the first 1,000 m far too fast, as the comparison of the split times in figure 18.9 (Kol 76) demonstrates. He seemed to use a strategy that would have been advantageous for a 1,000 m race and consequently fatigued early so that he could not maintain a high enough speed at the end of the 2,000 m race. Kolbe's failure to maintain his lead is more likely based on his own poor racing strategy than on Karpinnen's good one.

The two athletes faced each other again eight years later in the final of the 1984 Olympic Games, and the analysis of that race reveals that both rowers used the ideal parabolic race strategy when performing at the highest level under more normal weather conditions (figure 18.9, Kar 84 and Kol 84). Karpinnen rowed the first 500 m 3.8% faster than the third 500 m compared to the average race time, which conforms to the range of differences that are seen in long-term analyses (Kleshnev 2016).

A sprint-type athlete with high maximal strength will start faster than an athlete with enormous aerobic capacities. One would also start more carefully in headwind conditions on a wavy course. Nevertheless, the idea of an even-splitting race strategy is demonstrably inadvisable—as Lander, Butterly, and Edwards (2009) point out, "self-pacing exercise poses a reduced metabolic challenge when compared with matched intensity enforced constant paced submaximal exercise" (794).

Race Strategy of Bond and Murray, the Famous Kiwi Pair

Extraordinary weather conditions, differences in wind conditions along the race course, and possible errors in tactics can influence race split times and their outcome. Such singular events should not be used to argue an ideal pacing strategy. Also, putative observations of outstanding performances should not lead to deliberately suppress proper arguments. The New Zealand team of Hamish Bond and Eric Murray, arguably the most successful men's pair in the world, are frequently used for comparisons. They won many of their races with such ease that an exploitation of their maximum performance was not necessary and they were seldom in the lead after 500 m even in races that they would later win by large margins. This fact is often incorrectly interpreted as an even-splitting race strategy and used to bolster the argument of a supposedly superior pacing approach. A closer examination, however, will show that this argument not only misses the real particulars, but also shows the limitation of using only the official 500 m times as basis of a race analysis. One needs to be reminded that 500 m split times only give a very limited view on the actual power distribution for each of the approximately 60 strokes of that particular part of the race.

Kitch (2014), for example, proclaims that the New Zealand pair was superior because "they row even splits down the course" and "they don't care about high strokes coming out of the starting area." It is not clear which of the pair's races the author refers to and which data he was reviewing, but these statements are, generally speaking, completely inaccurate. Figure 18.10 will be used to refute the first statement.

Figure 18.10 presents the average 500 m velocities of two very significant races. The 2010 World Championship is arguably the race in which Bond and Murray were the most challenged in all their international championship victories, winning by only 0.32 s against Great Britain, who was leading the race for 1,950 m but never by more than 0.63 s. It should be noted that there was a headwind during this race, which had a greater impact during the first half of the course than toward the end. The second important race is the heat of the 2012 Olympic Games, where the New Zealand crew used very favorable conditions for an extremely fast race to set a world best time of 6:08.5, which still stands at the time of the publication of this book.

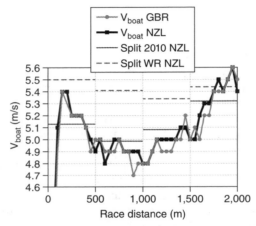

▶ **Figure 18.10**   Race data of the pairs from New Zealand (NZL; 1st) and Great Britain (GBR; 2nd) in the final of the 2010 World Championships (World Rowing 2021d), with additional data from the world record (WR) performance of the New Zealand pair in the heat of the 2012 Olympic Games (World Rowing 2021e). v_{boat} = 50 m average boat velocity taken by GPS. Split = average boat velocity for each 500 m section of the race.
All data from World Rowing 2021d, e.

The New Zealand pair was called out in both of these races to perform on their highest level and they could not allow themselves to play strategic games. To unleash their best performances, they followed the ideal parabolic pacing model, as figure 18.10 clearly depicts. In fact, a further analysis more firmly refutes the misleading opinion that the New Zealand pair's brilliance would come from an even-splitting approach.

Most authors only use the 500 m splits from official races when analyzing pacing strategies. Although this was the only race data available for a long time, World Rowing now also provides the average of all 50 m segments of international championships. These more detailed data in table 18.1 reveal that boat velocities vary in a much wider range than 500 m splits can display.

The comparison between 50 m GPS and 500 m split data reveals that the traditional split data vastly underrepresent the actual velocity variations of crews in highly competitive international races. In the presented case, the 500 m split data show the

Table 18.1 Comparison of 50 m and 500 m Pacing Data

		GPS		500 m	
		NZL	GBR	NZL	GBR
Max v_{boat}	m/s	5.6	5.6	5.32	5.27
Min v_{boat}		4.8	4.7	4.99	4.98
Diff		0.8	0.9	0.33	0.29
Min split	min/500 m	1:29.3	1:29.3	1:34.0	1:34.9
Max split		1:44.2	1:46.4	1:40.3	1:40.5
Diff		0:14.9	0:17.1	0:06.3	0:05.6

Note: Officially provided 50 m and 500 m pacing information presented in boat velocity v_{boat} (m/s) and splits (min/500 m) for the pairs from New Zealand (NZL) and Great Britain (GBR) in the final of the 2010 World Championships (figure 18.10).

All data from World Rowing 2021d.

difference between the fastest and the slowest 500 m part of the New Zealand pair's race to be 6.3 s, but it is actually at least 14.9 s—a difference of 15.3% of the fastest to the slowest average race splits.

The two pairs fighting for the first place also largely matched each other's parabolic pacing strategy to maximize energy output. If even splitting was indeed the ideal pacing model, crews would certainly use it in such important races. Based on the official data, it is therefore incorrect to state that the New Zealand pair used an even-split strategy.

Kitch's (2014) statement that the New Zealand pair did not use high stroke rates at the beginning of the race also does not stand up to scrutiny. During the first 50 m—or about the first 7 strokes of the final at the 2010 World Championships—their stroke rate was just 0.2 spm lower than the average of the other crews (40.9 spm to 41.1 spm). After that they were the highest stroking crew of all boats in the final for the next 450 m. Furthermore, the New Zealand crew stroked, on average, 1.7 spm higher than all other crews during the whole race (38.5 to 36.8 spm). Another comparison even more strongly contradicts the idea that the New Zealand pair could afford to row a lower stroke rate than their competition: The British pair led the New Zealanders at the 500 m mark by 0.55 s while rowing at a 1.3 spm lower stroke rate on average (39.4 to 40.7 spm). This shows that the New Zealand pair needed to use a higher stroke rate to keep up with the leader, let alone to win (World Rowing 2021d).

Pacing Strategy in Time Trial Racing

The discussion thus far refers to side-by-side 2,000 m races, as opposed to time trial races in which crews race on their own, so to speak. Although there is a profound difference between these two types of races from a psychological point of view, the optimal pacing strategy is generally the same, and preliminary results from international races support this. Although time trials are an option in international races in the case of certain weather conditions, they have never been used at a World Championship or Olympic Games. They are used frequently in national regattas to get a preliminary ranking of large entry fields or in the qualifying regatta for the famous Henley Royal Regatta. No pacing data exist from those regattas.

Key Point

World Rowing is very restrictive about the use of electronic measurement equipment in international races. For example, no force or power registering is allowed, so no such data are available from these races. However, boat velocity measurement is allowed and regularly used, and an example of such data is shown in figure 18.11. Such a recording is compared with the 50 m and 500 m average data provided by World Rowing and shows how much larger the actual range of velocity over a 2,000 m race is, especially in the starting portion of the race.

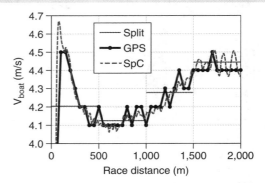

▶ **Figure 18.11** Comparison of three types of boat velocity measurements of the 1st place sculler in the women's single of the 2016 World Cup 1. Split = average 500 m; GPS = average 50 m; SpC = Nielsen-Kellerman SpeedCoach data of every stroke.

Time trials were used in international races only twice as a test for this race format: the heats in World Cup 1 in 2011 and World Cup 3 in 2019. A so-called "flying start" was used in 2011 whereby crews were given space to accelerate and time was started when their bow ball crossed the 100 m marker, meaning that the race was only 1,900 m. In 2019, crews were started from the normal fixed position to race the full 2,000 m. Therefore, data from this race are the only ones that can be compared to the standard 2,000 m side-by-side races. The following conclusions can be drawn based on the available 500 m split timing:

- Successful crews used the parabolic pacing strategy.
- The start sprint was shorter than in side-by-side races, based on the stroke rate data. The higher stroke rates were only used for a distance of about 250 m. (The GPS-based boat velocity data were unfortunately not reliable and can therefore not be interpreted.)

One interesting individual observation should be reported here. The German single sculler Oliver Zeidler raced in that 2019 time trial heat with a perfect even-split strategy (1:52.41, 1:52.25, 1:52.47, 1:52.09 min for the four 500 m race segments) and reached only the 16th fastest time out of 28 singles. However, he won the World Championships title two months later using the optimal race strategy (figure 18.12).

Oliver Zeidler's race results are compared to those of Sverri Nielsen. They were the top scullers in 2019, placing first and second in the World Championships final. The difference in the time trial results are striking, indicating that Nielsen was much better prepared for this type of racing. It should be emphasized that Oliver Zeidler was only competing in his second season of racing in 2019 and the time trial format was certainly unfamiliar to him. Therefore, this example should only indicate how important it is to learn the correct pacing strategy for both race formats.

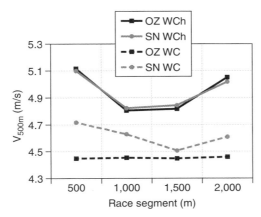

▶ **Figure 18.12** Analysis for two races in 2019 in which the two top scullers Oliver Zeidler (OZ) and Sverri Nielsen (SN) participated. WC = Heat of World Cup 3 (time trial), OZ 16th place, SN 2nd place. WCh = Final A of the World Championships (side-by-side), OZ 1st place, SN 2nd place.

Long Distance Races

Long distance races are usually organized in the time trial format, with very few exceptions. The Oxford–Cambridge Boat Race and the Harvard–Yale Boat Race are two rare examples where two university eights race side-by-side. In general, the same considerations as presented previously apply here, with the extension and higher prioritization of the elongated middle part of the race that is covered by the aerobic energy system.

The aerobic endurance system becomes more important as race distance increases. This means that the time increases during which a crew needs to maintain a constant work output on maximum aerobic energy supply compared to the shorter 1,000 m or 2,000 m races. Although the aerobic energy contribution for the total work of such a race increases, the anaerobic energy supply still plays an important role. Therefore, boat speeds that necessitate anaerobic energy contribution need to be included in long distance races and preliminarily performed at the beginning and the end of the race.

Flying Start Versus Standing Start Pacing in Long Distance Races

The timings of the start and the final sprints follow the same logic that is explained for the shorter time trials. Start efforts in a side-by-side race from a standstill have to be weighted carefully between optimal energy output and tactical considerations. These might include seeking an advantage psychologically (e.g., being in a position to observe and react to the competitors' actions or put pressure on them), exploiting specific race rules (e.g., that the leading crew can cross the path of competitors to affect them with their wake), or gaining the better position on the race course (e.g., attaining the inside of a turn or a favorable current on the river). Crews need to reach the best tactical position without exerting so much effort that their rowing velocity deteriorates dramatically.

Figure 18.13 exemplifies the optimal pacing strategy for a 3-mile (4.8 km) race in the time trial format without considerations of turns or tactical maneuvers. This race length is typical for long distance races in North America.

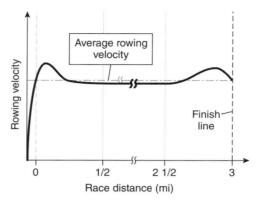

▶ **Figure 18.13** Ideal pacing strategy for a long-distance race over 3 miles (4.8 km) in time trial format.

This ideal pacing strategy is characterized by using the flying start to bring the boat speed up so that the start line is crossed at about the average boat speed of the race. The start sprint helps to kick all energy supply systems into full gear and to make use of anaerobic energy to reach a high boat speed. However, it needs to be managed and timed so that lactate levels do not inhibit maximal aerobic output or cause the athletes so much discomfort that their psychological energy is affected. After this initial sprint, which should last about 1 min, it is important to transition into a stroke rate and power output that is most efficient to let the athletes access their maximum aerobic energy while generating the highest possible boat speed at that work rate. Too low of a stroke rate would not serve this purpose, because the handle force would need to be relatively high, which in turn would generate more lactate. On the other hand, a too high a stroke rate costs unnecessary inertial energy to move the rowers' centers of mass. In the final stage of the race, the athletes need to use all energy systems at their disposal. The onset of the final sprint needs to be chosen with the same logic that is explained in figure 18.8*b*.

Adjusting to Wind and Directional Changes

These important elements of pacing for a long distance race require a lot of experience and need to be well rehearsed. Complicating matters further is the fact that most long distance race courses include turns, which require varying degrees of directional change, and sometimes require tactical overtaking maneuvers, which require spontaneous adjustments of effort and stroke rate. Additionally, changing wind direction and the influence of currents need to be taken into consideration.

Probably the most famous long distance head race is the annual Head of the Charles Regatta in Boston, Massachusetts, in which high-caliber international crews tend to compete. This regatta is known for its distinctive race course up the Charles River, which includes several sharp turns. Returning crews are seeded according to their results from the previous year, whereas crews that are entering for the first time receive random start numbers (e.g., in figure 18.14, Kallfelz started with bow number 18 in the W1x and Oxford Brookes started 27th in the M8+). This sometimes requires fast crews with high start numbers to overtake slower crews, which can be motivating but also can lead to holdups. Also, crews start in 10 to 15 s intervals, so that they can see competitors who start near them. Depending on experience level, they can estimate their distance to each other, albeit with limited accuracy. The influence of such special circumstances can only be speculated.

The regatta organizers provide official split times from four segments of the course. However, for practical reasons these segments have different lengths that are not officially provided. Therefore, the distances of the segments in figure 18.14 were determined through cross-referencing the official data with in-boat timing data from some competitors.

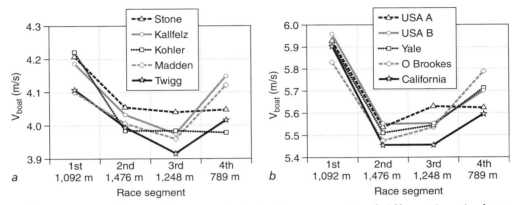

▶ **Figure 18.14** Average boat speeds during four segments of different lengths from championship category races of the 2019 Head of the Charles regatta. The order of the crews in the legend displays their placing in the race. *(a)* Women's championship singles placing 1-5. *(b)* Men's championship eights placing 1-5 (U.S. National Team A, U.S. National Team B, Yale University, Oxford Brookes University, University of California).

Here are some obvious assumptions that these data suggest:

- All crews show a higher average boat speed for the first race segment than any other segment, which indicates that they performed a start sprint.
- Most of the crews increased their rowing speed for the last segment of the race.
- Most of the crews maintained a similar boat speed during the two middle segments of the race, which together make up about 60% of the total race distance.
- The final ranking of the crews was established early in the race, and faster crews are faster in most if not all segments.
- None of the crews attempts an even-pacing strategy. In fact, the split times indicate that a crew cannot afford to start slowly without losing their position in the race and falling back in the final ranking.

There are no statistical data from a larger number of races, so these statements are not scientifically validated and their explanatory power is limited.

More detailed data were available from a masters race in which one can see quite well the influence of the turns, especially at the John W. Weeks Bridge (~2,300 m), at the Anderson Memorial Bridge (~2,700 m) and before the Eliot Bridge (~3,700 m).

Both analyses in figure 18.14 and figure 18.15 show that experienced crews try to follow the ideal pacing model while the peculiarities of the race course add interesting challenges. Although start and finish sprints seem shorter than in 2,000 m racing, crews certainly do not want to forgo tapping into their anaerobic energy supply.

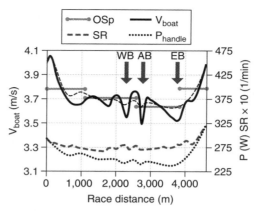

▶ **Figure 18.15** Detailed stroke-by-stroke data of boat speed (v_{boat}), stroke rate (SR), and handle power (P_{handle}) together with the official segment splits (OSp) of the third place masters M1x at the 2017 Head of the Charles Regatta. The dashed speed curve is an estimate of the boat speed based on the power data that theoretically eliminates the influence of the turns in the course and possible wind effects to receive a more realistic idea of the pacing strategy chosen by the athlete. The sharpest turns are indicated: John W. Weeks Bridge (WB), Anderson Bridge (AB), and before Eliot Bridge (EB).

Although the contribution of the anaerobic energy supply systems to the overall work becomes smaller the longer the exercise lasts, it still has a significant impact on the outcome of long distance races. Of course, rowers need to focus in their training first and foremost on improving aerobic capacity, the most important factor for success in long distance races, but pacing strategy must include parts of the race where the rowing speed is so high that anaerobic supply systems are used. Such planned high efforts need to be at the beginning and the end of the race to achieve the highest overall energy output. This approach is validated by world record performances in long distance running.

Pacing in Ergometer Races

Although there are several types of ergometers used for training, it is most common to compare ergometer race performances achieved on the stationary Concept2 ergometer. A monitor registers rotational data from the calibrated flywheel, from which it calculates the power that athletes spend for each stroke. This power data is then multiplied by a factor that results in a split time for 500 m, which rowers can relate to through their experience from on-water racing. The factor was chosen to resemble a measurement that seems to be similar to speeds that an athlete would experience rowing a 4-.

Every rower knows the training split times and even race records that they can achieve on this ergometer, because it is the most widely used and accessible system that exists. It is also the equipment that is used at the official World Rowing Indoor Championships, and record lists exist for nine distances (100-42,195 m) and four durations (1-60 min) for all official age categories. This makes it easy for any rower to compare themselves with any other rower. The most common race distance is 2,000 m in accordance with the Olympic on-water competition distance.

Ergometer rowing requires very little technical skill and there are no environmental influences, so consistent performances can be achieved. Consequently, every rower knows very well how it feels to row at a certain effort and which splits are realistic for various distances. This means that athletes striving for maximal performances can row more steadily right at their limit, which can be seen in pacing analyses of high-level ergometer competitions like World Rowing Indoor Championships or world record trials.

Although not statistically validated, a brief analysis of the stroke-by-stroke race profiles of the winners of the 2019, 2020, and 2021 World Rowing Indoor Championships reveals that athletes chose a strong start sprint limited to 30 to 60 s, followed by a very consistent effort for most of the race distance and a finish sprint of about 500 m. The pace vigor seems to be mainly driven by how hard the athlete has to go to finish the race successfully. Such a typical profile is presented in figure 18.16a. It is very interesting to see that almost all studied speed profiles end with a performance drop during the last 5 to 10 strokes. It is not clear whether athletes do this because they can afford to do so based on the race situation or because of an optimized pacing strategy that was discussed in figure 18.8b.

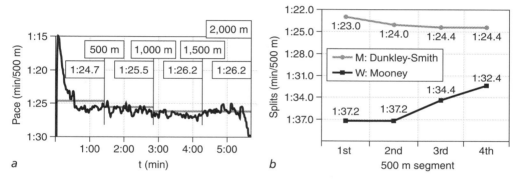

▶ **Figure 18.16** Pacing analyses from world class 2,000 m ergometer racing. *(a)* Stroke-by-stroke pace data and 500 m split times for the four segments of Oliver Zeidler's race at the 2019 World Rowing Indoor Championships (1st place; 5:42.6 min). *(b)* 500 m split times of the current 2,000 m world records for women (Brooke Mooney, 6:21.2 min) and men (Josh Dunkley-Smith, 5:35.8 min).

World Rowing 2021f

World record times are most often achieved outside of international competitions, so that stroke-by-stroke data is not available and one is limited to average split information for each of the four 500 m segments of a 2,000 m race. Figure 18.16b presents the pacing data of the current 2,000 m records. The men's record seems to have been achieved with the typical pacing strategy, whereas the women's world record row by Brooke Mooney shows a very unusual race profile. Comments made by Mooney after the trial indicate that she first attempted to row faster for the first 500 m, then tried to remain confident in her performance during the first part of the race only to realize how much faster she could row toward the end (World Rowing 2021a). It remains only a theory that Mooney can possibly row even faster following the optimal pacing strategy.

It remains to be seen but is highly probable that when data become available for other trial distances on ergometers that pacing profiles for maximal performances support the theoretical optimal approach for on-water races.

Conclusion

To achieve a truly maximal performance over any distance, rowers' pacing strategies must always use all of their three energy supply systems in the most appropriate way, with a fluid transition from a predominant use of the anaerobic system to the aerobic system as the race goes on. Psychological, technical, and environmental factors play a role in choosing a pacing strategy, but they simply require tweaking the physiology-based pacing profile to individual situations.

With regards to the ideal pacing strategy, it is advantageous to start with a high to very high effort in races of any distance. Of course, this strategy always needs to be fine-tuned to the individual abilities of the athletes and specific race conditions. Such an approach puts athletes in the best psychological position to remain confident in their actions.

PART
V

Practical Application

© Getty Images

19 CHAPTER

Designing Training Programs

Brett Smith, PhD

The goal of this chapter is to present steps for developing a successful on-water training program for a competitive rowing team. The TID, FITT, and progressive overload principles described in chapters 14 and 15 will now be used to construct the necessary aerobic and anaerobic conditioning elements of the training program. It is therefore strongly recommended to study the theoretical elements in those chapters before continuing with this chapter.

Constructing a training program is not accomplished only by applying scientific concepts; it also requires an understanding of the context (e.g., team goals, current athletes' abilities, seasonal influences, weather patterns, training water conditions) combined with the knowledge and experience of the coach and possibly the sport scientist. The first stage of developing a training program is therefore to study the training programs of as many different teams as possible and to learn the reasoning, context, and philosophies behind them. It is important to have a clear vision of the physiological adaptations the program was intended to achieve and the scientific strategies used to achieve these adaptations. Knowing why a program was constructed in a particular manner is probably more important than analyzing the actual program, so conversations with the coach or sport scientist behind it will be particularly helpful. Understanding the program and its underpinning scientific principles will allow you to then innovate more effectively.

The development of an effective training program requires robust preparation and the confidence to be an inquisitive lifelong learner with a growth mindset. Most importantly, a coach or sport scientist must effectively self-critique, as well as critique the information that is used to build a program. It is also recommended to include a trusted mentor who can aid in the positive critique of the training approach and its details.

Rather than presenting a theoretical training program, this chapter will present the construction of an actual rowing training program, developed by the author with Dick Tonks, that ran across three successful Olympic cycles with New Zealand's national rowing program. Scaled-down versions of this program template were also employed in the New Zealand's senior B and junior programs throughout this period. The application of this consistent training methodology was aimed to help the transition of rowers from the junior to senior A programs and support long-term performance gains.

Planning Phase

Before the construction steps for the program are introduced, the following background will help provide some context. When the training program was constructed, performances of Rowing New Zealand (RNZ) crews in international races from the junior to the senior A level were extremely poor, and the number of top-grade rowers eligible to represent the country at the senior A level was perhaps fewer than 40 in total. The challenge taken on by Dick Tonks when he took over the head coaching role in 2000 was to institute a training model that would engender success in the existing circumstances. The planned training model aimed to introduce not only a new training philosophy but also a unified approach to training. At the time, there was no centralized program in New Zealand. Therefore, Tonks made a strategic move during a preseason camp in 2000, surreptitiously inviting anyone interested to move to Lake Karapiro, where he committed to coaching them year-round. A group of 12 women took up the offer and started to train full time in a competitive environment supported primarily by family and friends. The success achieved by these remarkable women, culminating in an Olympic gold medal in the women's double at the 2004 Olympic Games, convinced RNZ to make Tonks' vision of a centralized program their own. Success led to increased financial support, and ultimately, not only the men joined the program, but the senior B and junior programs also became centralized in a new training facility at Lake Karapiro.

The very first stage of program development requires a comprehensive statement of the goals of the training group, as well as the inventory of the available support staff, funding, training facilities, and equipment. This gives the main frame of reference from which to evaluate the outcomes of the program. The team goals of winning win gold medals at the Olympics and World Championships were well established by RNZ. This meant that the rowers' goals became to physically train at the highest level and to row technically well.

Next, a preexercise screen for each rower was developed through a needs analysis, medical screen, testing protocol, and profiling inventory. Various expert support staff completed the screenings—including medical screening, psychological profiling, and nutrition and body composition analysis—so that the only remaining task for the planning team was to conduct various rowing-specific physiological tests to compare the athletes to preset targets and norms and determine any conditioning deficiencies that may require intervention. Most coaches will not have expert support staff on hand, so it is recommended to perform an extensive preexercise screen on all rowers before training begins.

Key Point

Determining the program goals and whether the resources are available to achieve those goals is an important first step in the development of a successful rowing program.

It is also important to understand each rower's goals, strengths and weaknesses, health status, training history, likes, dislikes, and any logistical limitations.

Organizing the Plan

Before the actual program construction started, there was an in-depth discussion with Tonks on which training methods should be employed. After much discussion, it was decided that the New Zealand rowing program would use predominantly a long slow distance (LSD) program. Specifically, this decision involved an extensive amount of U2 training; a smaller amount of zone 2 training, consisting primarily of AT intensity training; and an even smaller amount of zone 3 training, made up of a mixture of LaT and LaP work. Please note the T1 training zone was not part of the prescribed training zones during this period. While it may be argued that LSD programs are often polarized in nature, the greater amount of zone 2 than zone 3 training meant the program employed a pyramidal TID. The program construction process and training zones used are further described below.

Deciding on the Training Timeline

The program was constructed backwards from the major competitions: Olympics or World Championships, normally held in September (winter in New Zealand), and National Championships and team trials, normally held in February or March (at the end of summer in New Zealand). The year was consequently divided into two seasons with two extensive building stages: the first to a minor peak for the national rowing championships and national trials, and the second to a major peak for the world championships or Olympics. The world cup and domestic regattas were typically treated as training and not something to taper into and peak for.

Key Point

Once the training philosophy and methods are determined, it is recommended that the season program be constructed backwards from priority competition. The first step is determining macroelements, then meso- and microelements, and finally the session details to achieve peak conditioning for the ultimate event.

Developing the Mesocycles

The first training elements entered into the program were the specific training blocks (mesocycles) of 3 to 6 weeks duration, with each mesocycle having a specific conditioning focus (e.g., U2, AT, anaerobic). Working back from the major competition, the mesocycle blocks were constructed to fit around key events such as regattas and travel (see table 19.1). The mesocycles were as follows:

1. Taper and competition: One mesocycle of 2 to 3 weeks, which typically consisted of a 10-day taper and then the 6- to 8-day final regatta
2. Anaerobic: 1 mesocycle for the minor peak (national championships) and 1 to 2 mesocycles for the major peak (World Rowing Championships or Olympics)
3. AT: 1 mesocycle for the minor peak and 1 to 2 mesocycles for the major peak
4. U2: 1 to 3 mesocycles

The conditioning focus of each successive mesocycle followed a specific direction, with the early season focus being one or more U2 mesocycles to develop a good aerobic foundation before an AT mesocycle to add intensity but also maintain a large volume of U2 work. The next one or two mesocycles involved the AT training sessions being replaced by anaerobic sessions (LaT and LaP) to enhance anaerobic conditioning.

Table 19.1 Example Program Template (General outline of the NZ rowing team training program 2000-2010)

	September	October	November	December	January	February	March	April	May	June	July	August	September
Periodization	Transition	General Prep	General Prep	Specific Prep	Pre Comp	Comp	Taper	General Prep	Specific Prep	Specific Prep	Pre Comp	Comp	Comp
Competition				5,000 m ergs and races (selection)	2,000 m ergs and races (selection)		Nationals Trials		World Cup NZ	World Cup NZ	World Cup International		World Champs
Priority (1 highest – 3 lowest)				3rd	3rd		1st/2nd		3rd	3rd	2nd		1st
Priority component	Active recovery	U2	U2	U2	AT/U2	HIIT	Taper	U2	U2/AT	AT/U2	LaT: 1 session	LaP	Taper
Sessions per week	5	9	11	14	13	13		14	14	14	13	13	12
Aerobic cross-training sessions per week	5	2-4	2					1					
Row km/week		60-120	120-170	160-210	120-180	100-150	80-140	120-180	140-200	150-210	140-190	130-170	60-110
Approximate microcycle breakdown		U2: 3-5 sessions	U2: 6 sessions	AR: 2 sessions	AR: 1 session	AR: 1 session	AR: 2 sessions	AR: 1 session	AR: 2 sessions	AR: 2 sessions	AR: 1 session	AR: 1 session	AR: 1 session
				U2: 8 sessions	U2: 5 sessions	U2: 4 sessions	FP: 5 sessions	U2: 6 sessions	U2: 7 sessions	U2: 7 sessions	U2: 4 sessions	U2: 4 sessions	FP: 4 sessions
				U1: 1 session	U1: 1 session			U1: 1 session					
				PS: 1 session	PS: 1 session	PS: 1 session	AT (opt 1): 1 session	PS: 1 session	PS: 1 session	PS: 1 session	PS: 1 session	PS: 1 session	
					AT: 1 session	AT: 1 session		AT: 1 session	AT: 2 sessions	AT: 2 sessions	AT: 1 session	AT: 1 session	AT (opt 1): 1 session
						LaT: 1 session	LaT: 1 session				LaT: 1 session	LaT: 1 session	LaT: 1 session
			LaP (race): 1 session	LaP (race): 1 session	LaP (race): 1 session	LaP: 1 session	LaP (opt 2): 1 session		LaP (race): 1 session	LaP (race): 1 session	LaP (race): 1 session	LaP: 1 session	LaP: 1 session

(continued)

Table 19.1 *(continued)*

	September	October	November	December	January	February	March	April	May	June	July	August	September
AR (session and %)			1 and 10%	1 and 9%	1 and 14%	1 and 11%	2 and 20%	1 and 9%	2 and 17%	2 and 15%	1 and 10%	2 and 18%	2 and 20%
U2 (session and %)		4 and 100%	6 and 60%	6 and 55%	5 and 71%	4 and 44%	5 and 50%	7 and 64%	7 and 58%	7 and 54%	6 and 60%	6 and 55%	6 and 60%
AT (session and %)			2 and 20%	3 and 27%	1 and 14%	2 and 22%		3 and 27%	3 and 25%	3 and 23%	3 and 30%	2 and 18%	
Anaerobic (session and %)			1 and 10%	2 and 18%	0 and 0%	2 and 22%	1 and 10%		2 and 17%	3 and 23%	2 and 20%	2 and 18%	2 and 20%
AR (distance and %)			~50 km and 28%	~50 km and 23%	~50 km and 28%	~50 km and 33%	~60 km and 44%	~40 km and 22%	~35 km and 18%	~34 km and 16%	~50 km and 26%	~50 km and 29%	~40 km and 35%
U2 (distance and %)		~60 km and 100%	~110 km and 62%	~140 km and 65%	~100 km and 56%	~80 km and 53%	~70 km and 51%	~120 km and 67%	~140 km and 70%	~150 km and 70%	~120 km and 63%	~100 km and 58%	~70 km and 61%
AT (distance and %)			~15 km and 8%	~25 km and 12%	~25 km and 14%	~15 km and 10%		~20 km and 11%	~22 km and 11%	~25 km and 12%	~15 km and 8%	~15 km and 9%	
Anaerobic (distance and %)			~2 km and 1%	~2 km and 1%	~2 km and 1%	~5 km and 3%	~6 km and 4%		~3 km and 2%	~4 km and 2%	~5 km and 3%	~6 km and 4%	~4 km and 4%

Sessions per week for each intensity zone and the percentage calculated against the total sessions per week (session and %).

Distance per week for each intensity zone and the percentage calculated against the total distance per week (distance and %).

LaT = Lactate tolerance, LaP = Lactate production , AR = active recovery, AT = anaerobic threshold, U1 = utilization 1, U2 = utilization 2, FP = fast power, PS = power strokes.

Progressive overload was achieved within each mesocycle by increasing the distance rowed or intensity 5% to 15% for each successive microcycle, ending with an unloading (minimal distance) microcycle where testing or racing occurred. Significant distance changes were programmed early in the mesocycle (15%), with smaller distance increases (5%) occurring later when the athletes got closer to their maximum workload capacity. The challenge was to determine the maximum (and starting) microcycle distance for the priority training zone within each mesocycle.

Various international training programs were examined to establish this distance. The U2 maximal mileage was initially established as a weekly total of 220 to 240 km, but eventually, it became evident that anything above 160 km per week often meant intensity was compromised. The following reasoning was used to establish the final weekly distances:

1. One U2 mesocycle wasn't enough to move the rowers from the starting microcycle distance (e.g., 60 km) to the maximal (e.g., 160 km), so 2 to 3 mesocycles were used to achieve this change.

2. The total weekly mileage for each training zone can be deceiving. An AT session might be 20 km but only involve 8 km of AT-specific work, with the remainder a mixture of AR and U2. Likewise, an anaerobic session might only involve 3 km of LaP work in a 20 km row, with the remainder being warm-up, recovery intervals, and cooldown. The total distance programmed in each zone was therefore determined as well.

3. For some anaerobic microcycles, the distance remained the same throughout to help increase the session intensity. At some stages, the volume of successive LaP or LaT sessions would decrease with increasing rest intervals in an attempt to increase intensity.

The determination of the maximum distance for the final microcycle in each mesocycle was reliant on many factors, such as previous mesocycles and how the crew was tracking. There are no hard-and-fast rules here—experience will provide the best guidance. Note that the maximal weekly U2 mileage is not the same as the maximal weekly rowing mileage; the latter consists of on-water training across all intensity zones. Maximal weekly mileage did change slightly across boat classes.

Key Point

Each mesocycle should employ a progressive overload strategy, typically involving a 5% to 15% increase in distance per microcycle to develop one priority conditioning component. The mesocycle ends with an unloading microcycle that includes testing or competition.

At the time, the acute-to-chronic ratio (described in chapter 14) was not used to determine weekly changes in training load, but a modified version of this method was later successfully used to help improve the microcycle loading plan in other programs. Articles by Gabbett and Jenkins (2011) and Zouhal and colleagues (2021) are recommended to learn more about the acute-to-chronic ratio method and its applicability for managing training load.

The testing and racing results helped inform any possible training or crew modifications in the subsequent mesocycle. The mesocycles were constructed so the unloading week typically coincided with important regattas (e.g., World Cup regattas or North Island Rowing Championships), which are preparation competitions for the major and minor peaks of the year.

Developing the Microcycles

The structure of the microcycles was then determined for each mesocycle. A set order for the sessions within the microcycles was developed to accomplish the required TID and ensure the relevant FITT principles were followed. In the example in table 19.2, the structure of the microcycles was maintained throughout the mesocycle.

Table 19.2 Session Layout Within a Representative Microcycle for the Various Mesocycles

	Monday	Tuesday	Wednesday	Thursday	Friday	Saturday	Sunday
OFF-SEASON AND PRESEASON (U2 FOCUS)							
AM	U2: 16-30 km	U2: 16-30 km	U2: 16-30 km	U2: 16-30 km	Bungees or power strokes (LT)	U2: 16-30 km	
AM	Resistance training		Resistance training			AR 12 km	
PM	U2: 16-20 km	U2: 16-20 km		U2: 16-20 km	U2: 16-20 km		
EARLY COMPETITION SEASON (U2 AND AT FOCUS)							
AM	U2: 16-30 km	U2: 16-30 km	AT 5-16 km work	U2: 16-30 km	Bungees or power strokes (U1)	AT: 5-16 km work	
AM	Resistance training		Resistance training			AR 8-12 km	
PM	U2: 16-20 km	U2: 16-20 km		U2: 16-20 km	U2: 16-20 km		
LATE COMPETITION SEASON (ANAEROBIC FOCUS)							
AM	FP (U2): prerace 4-8 km	U2: 16-20 km	U2: 16-20 km, or bungees or power strokes (U1) 16-20 km	LaT: 6-10 km work	U2: 16-20 km, or bungees or power strokes (U1): 16-20 km	U1 or AT: 5-16 km work	
AM	LaP: 3-6 km work					AR: 8-12 km	
PM	AR: 12-20 km	U2: 12-20 km		AR: 12-20 km	U2: 12-20 km		
TAPER BLOCK INTO COMPETITION							
AM	FP, prerace 4-8 km	FP (U2): 8-16 km	Bungees or power strokes (U1): 16-20 km	FP, prerace 4-8 km	FP (U2): 8-16 km	FP (U2): 8-16 km	FP (U2): 8-16 km
AM	LaP: 1-2 km work			LaP: 1-2 km work			
PM	AR: 8-16 km	FP (U2): 8-16 km		AR: 8-16 km	FP (U2): 8-16 km		

LaT = Lactate tolerance, LaP = Lactate production, AR = active recovery, AT = anaerobic threshold, U1 = utilization 1, U2 = utilization 2, FP = fast power, PS = power strokes.

First, the priority conditioning component sessions were arranged within each microcycle (week). Special attention was paid to maintain the required rest periods between priority sessions. The remaining training sessions were then added. This involved some compromises to the FITT principles—for example, two anaerobic sessions three days apart meet the required recovery time, but when two U2 sessions are added in the two days between the anaerobic sessions, the recovery is compromised. This compromised state can be alleviated to some extent by reducing the volume of specific training sessions to lessen the overall stress and physiological strain on the rower, thereby reducing the required recovery period. This case shows that building an effective elite rowing program occasionally involves compromises, which we can only seek to minimize rather than remove completely.

Key Point

Each microcycle is constructed by utilizing the FITT principles relevant to the conditioning component being developed. Although some compromises are required when mixing multiple conditioning components, the priority component should be entered into the microcycle first and compromised the least.

Methods of Training Blocks

Once the structure and the total training distances for each microcycle were determined, the training methods (e.g., steady state, intervals) and distances for each session were entered. The following explanations help clarify the short descriptions of the training in the tables and provide more details about how the training sessions were performed. The data given here (e.g., length of training sessions, boat speeds, or stroke rates) refer to highly trained national team rowers who have been introduced to this program over a long period of time and must necessarily be adapted to the specific circumstances of the respective teams, including competition goals, age, training experience, and fitness.

The description of a session's intensity as U1, AT, LaP, FP, and so on identifies the intended focus of the session but does not refer to the entire content of the whole workout. Therefore, the percentage breakdowns of the training sessions performed at the various training intensities must be interpreted accordingly. For example, a session of 20 km with a designation of AT may only consist of 5 km at AT intensity (25%) within the total session, with the remainder of the distance rowed in the session (75%) being performed at a combination of AR or U2 intensity and the usual technical work.

- The training methods for the session were typically drawn from tables 19.3 through 19.12.
- The training method for the session was sometimes modified (e.g., a steady-state session may become an interval session), but training intensity and distance were maintained and only reduced if recovery was severely compromised or because of rough water. In the case of rough water, the same session was typically completed on a Concept2 rowing ergometer, sometimes with the crew's ergometers connected on sliders.

- Each training session had a specific distance and intensity goal, typically a target boat speed at a specific stroke rate based on the recommended intensities for each training zone.

- A half-day off on Wednesday afternoon was instituted after it was found that the athletes couldn't maintain the required intensities for all sessions throughout the week. This helped achieve the needed recovery so that Thursday's training intensity could be met. Saturday afternoons and Sundays were off to help the athlete recover sufficiently before the next microcycle.

- The U2 sessions were typically performed at continuous steady state, although long intervals were often used when training on a 2 km course (e.g., 2 km or 8 min on with 1-2 min off). Initially, the stroke rate was restricted during an AT session, but because different boats and crews had individual race rates, one set stroke rate (spm) did not work. For this reason, AT sessions were typically performed as long-distance races at open stroke rates. Such races were organized with the whole training squad to improve excitement and competitiveness within the crews. Therefore, these long-distance races were handicapped based on the results from the previous weeks to ensure competitive finishes, and crews were ranked according to the percentage of world best time pace they achieved. These measures stimulated a lot of competition among the varied boat classes in the team.

- When AT sessions were moved to Monday and Thursday for the AT mesocycle, greater boat speeds were generated during these sessions because the rowers were more recovered than usual. However, the U2 pace in the subsequent sessions became compromised, so the original schedule in table 19.2 was restored. The upshot was that training at U2 intensity was still an important focus within the AT mesocycle, which is why this mesocycle is often labeled as AT/U2. The benefits of training at AT intensity are sometimes doubted, but our practical experience suggests that it had some positive impact. The AT sessions added some intensive aerobic work in preparation for the upcoming anaerobic mesocycle and provided the athletes a different training stimulus that alleviated the boredom of the long frequent U2 training sessions.

- Blood lactate taken during specific bungee and power stroke sessions put this kind of training in the U1 or AT training zone. Although some training programs categorize these sessions as power or power-endurance, we categorized these sessions based on our findings into the intensity zone they fell within.

Table 19.3 AR (Active Recovery)

Aim	Facilitate recovery
Description	Moderate to easy rowing pace. Rowers should be able to converse freely.
Duration (min)	N/A
Boat speed (% of world best time)	<76%
Stroke rate (spm)	18-22
Lactate (mmol/L)	<1.0-1.5
Recovery between sessions	N/A
Example	40 min easy rowing

- Anaerobic sessions took the place of AT sessions during the transition to anaerobic mesocycles, but the structure of the microcycle was changed (see table 19.2). The anaerobic sessions were scheduled and performed after the rest days (or mid-week half-day rest, which were typically Wednesdays) to ensure the best quality anaerobic work when the rowers were more recuperated. Typically, the entire team participated in these sessions, which were completed as competitive, handicapped races over a 250 to 1,500 m distance. It was important that the rowers were well prepared, especially for the lactate production (LaP) anaerobic session, and they would often do a U2/AR prerace row similar to their race preparation. These LaP sessions enabled the rowers to practice their regatta day prerace and postrace regimens.

Table 19.4 U2 (Aerobic Base Development)

Aim	Develop aerobic base—this is the foundation of the presented training program
Description	"Hardish" steady state. Rowers should just be able to converse in short phrases.
Duration (min)	45-120[a]
Boat speed (% of world best time)	77%-82%
Stroke rate (spm)	18-22[b]
Lactate (mmol/L)	1.5
Recovery between sessions	6-12 h
Example	20 km steady-state row at 18 spm

[a]This does not include warm-up, exercises, and cool-down.

[b]Technically inefficient crews (e.g., juniors and U23 rowers) may have to row at a higher rate to achieve the required intensity and physiological training effect.

Table 19.5 U1 (Aerobic Intensity)

Aim	Expose rowers to higher aerobic intensities and stroke rates as an introduction to anaerobic threshold training
Description	Hard steady state. Conversation is difficult.
Duration (min)	30-90
Boat speed (% of world best time)	82%-88%
Stroke rate (spm)	~22-28
Lactate (mmol/L)	2-4
Recovery between sessions	36 h
Example	The session often involves pyramid work (see table 19.7); other options may include 3-4 pieces of 10-15 min at 20, 22, 24, and 26 spm.

Table 19.6 AT (Anaerobic Threshold)

Aim	Prepare rowers for more intensive conditioning and improve anaerobic threshold
Description	Hard intensity. A good method is to determine average pace for a 10-15 km race, which will provide a speed very close to AT pace.
Duration (min)	30-90
Boat speed (% of world best time)	88%-92%
Stroke rate (spm)	28-32
Lactate (mmol/L)	4
Recovery between sessions	48 h
Examples	Training can utilize a number of methods: • 60-90 min long distance race at open stroke rate • Competitive 5 km piece or series of pieces at open stroke rate • 2-3 × 20-30 min pieces at 26-32 spm

Table 19.7 AT: U2-U1, U1-AT, U2-AT Pyramids

Aim	Develop aerobic conditioning and stimulate neuromuscular coordination at a variety of different ratings
Description	These sessions are of alternating intensities with or without a short break between each new piece. The intensity alters within the various training zones.
Duration (min)	30-90
Boat speed (% of world best time)	Dependent on the intended intensity
Stroke rate (spm)	22-30
Lactate (mmol/L)	Dependent on the intended intensity
Recovery between sessions	36-48 h
Examples	In a pyramid fashion: • 10'-25', or 3 × 10' (4', 3', 2', 1') at 24, 26, 28, and 30 spm • or 2 × 15' (5', 4', 3', 2', 1') at 24, 26, 28, 30, 32 spm • Alternations, e.g., 2' @ 24 spm, 2' @ 28 spm, 3' @ 24 spm, 3' @ 28 spm, 4, 3, 2 etc. • AT pyramids, rating depends on boat class (single: 22-28 spm; eight: 22-30 spm), each piece lasts 7-30 min, with rating changes every 1-5 min, step rating up and then down. Other options include 2 km pieces with rating changes: • 4-8 × 500 m at 24 spm, 500 m at 26 spm, 500 m at 28 spm, 500 m at 30 spm, rest 2-5 mins between each repetition. • 4-8 × 1,000 m at 24 spm, 500 m at 26 spm, 500 m at 28 spm, rest 2-5 mins between each.

' = minutes

Table 19.8 Bungees

Aim	Focus on power endurance and improve drive time (i.e., rowing-specific power)
Description	Intensity is hard (U1 to AT). Wrap bungee cord around boat, tie a thin cord loosely under the boat, or tow a towel or bucket.
Duration (min)	10-60
Boat speed (% of world best time)	Depends on the braking system
Stroke rate (spm)	Don't push the stroke rate up; the strokes per minute come from the boat speed. 26-28 spm maximum
Lactate (mmol/L)	3-5
Recovery between sessions	48 h
Examples	• 2 × (15:10 × 10) strokes (i.e., 15 on and 10 off repeated 10 times up river, followed by a rest, then repeated down river) • 6-10 × 1-3 min on, 1-3 min off at 28-32 spm; take bungee off and repeat 1-2 times • 1-2 × 1 min on, 1 min off with bungee, 1-2 × 1 min on, 1 min off without bungee, repeat 2-4 times • 10 × 1 min on, 1-2 min off starting at 24 spm and moving up to approximately 32 spm

Table 19.9 PS (Power Strokes)

Aim	Focus on power endurance and improve drive time (i.e., rowing-specific power)
Description	Intensity is hard (U1 to AT). Half to quarter of the crew works, the remainder of the crew rests (not possible in single or pairs).
Duration (min)	10-60
Boat speed (% of world best time)	Depends on boat type and number of athletes working
Stroke rate (spm)	Don't push the stroke rate up; the strokes per minute come from the boat speed. 26-28 maximum spm
Lactate (mmol/L)	3-5
Recovery between sessions	~48 h
Examples	• 4-8 × 2-3 min on, 2-6 min off • With 1, 2, or 4 rowers: 3-6 × 1-3 min on, 1-6 min off

Table 19.10   FP (Fast Power)

Aim	Facilitate race pace neuromuscular power within the U2 training session
Description	Power endurance session (U2 to LaP intensity). This type of session usually only occurs during the taper period and is typically done on the 2 km regatta course.
Duration (min)	20-75
Boat speed (% of world best time)	Alternates between 77%-80% and 100%
Stroke rate (spm)	Alternates between 18-22 and race stroke rate (spm)
Lactate (mmol/L)	≤1.5
Recovery between sessions	6-12 h
Example	On the 2 km race course, 2 km warm-up and turn. The aim is to intersperse the 2 km U2 lap with 7-10 strokes at race pace every ~500 m, turn and repeat to achieve a total distance of 4-16 km.

Table 19.11   LaP (Lactate production)

Aim	Produce highest possible anaerobic lactic loading (lactic acid concentration and maximal performance) to enhance anaerobic capacity to develop maximal race intensity, which requires competition and speed targets.
Description	30 s to 3 min work interval, followed by a rest period 4 to 8 times as long as the work period. Usually performed as 500 or 1,000 m lengths, where the goal is to be above 2,000 m race pace.
Duration (min)	6-15
Boat speed (% of world best time)	>98%
Stroke rate (spm)	2,000 m race stroke rate (spm) or higher
Lactate (mmol/L)	Maximum
Recovery between sessions	72 h
Examples	• 6 × 500 m repeated every 6-8 min. The aim is to perform each at absolute maximal intensity. • 4 × 750 m repeated every 8-10 min. The aim is to perform each at absolute maximal intensity. • 8-10 × 250 m repeated every 4-5 min. The aim is to perform each at absolute maximal intensity. • Combinations of the above to simulate a particular stage of the race (e.g., first 500 m, middle 1,000 m, and last 250 m—total distance is equal to or less than 3,000 m).

Table 19.12 LaT (Lactate Tolerance)

Aim	Produce high average lactate for the session and therefore enhance anaerobic endurance so the muscle gets used to tolerating lactic acid.
Description	30 s to 3 min on, followed by a rest period 0.5 to 2 times as long as the work period. It is important to develop intensity above AT pace. Usually performed as 1-3 min pieces.
Duration (min)	10-30
Boat speed (% of world best time)	92%-96%
Stroke rate (spm)	Maximum
Lactate (mmol/L)	Maximum
Recovery between sessions	48-72 h
Examples	• 3 × (1 min on, 1 min off × 5) at race rate or 2-4 spm below race rate • 2 × (2 min on, 2 min off × 4) at race rate or 2-4 spm below race rate • 3 × (30 s on, 90 s off × 10) at maximum stroke rate

Using Boat Speed and Stroke Rate to Set and Monitor Training Load

The monitoring of intensity and recovery will be covered in chapter 20. However, it is worth noting that training intensities were set from boat speeds at specific stroke rates (with the speeds calculated as percentages of world best time paces for the different training intensity zones; see tables 19.3 through 19.12 for details). With technological advancements, the methods of measuring boat speed improved over time, which influenced the strategies employed by the coaches and crews to monitor the achievement of the required boat speed and stroke rate. During training, the crew would typically be provided feedback on whether they were achieving these targets. It was discovered very early on that those crews that could reach the set training speeds and stroke rates had a greater chance of success; thus, coaches and rowers generally bought into the need to meet the training speed goals.

Key Point

Although challenging, it is important to have some strategy for monitoring individual rowers' changes in conditioning, performance, and fatigue across training sessions to enable any required interventions to support effective recovery.

The decision to use a training model based on such a rigid prescription of boat speed and stroke rate—rather than, for example, specific heart rate training zones—has been reached through practical studies of champion crews from different nations in the late 1990s and early 2000s. Specifically, the determination of the large volume of weekly U2 intensity training by international champion crews at 80% of the world's best time paces at 18 to 20 spm was collected over years of observation initiated by Coach Tonks and supported by the author at various rowing venues. These observations eventually lead to an extensive library of data with which to build the intensity component (i.e., boat speed) of the training plan.

Lactate testing showed that top athletes could achieve their respective U2 boat speeds (~80% world best time pace) at 1.5 to 2.0 mmol/L, which fitted with the German Democratic Republic (GDR)'s LSD intensity recommendations (Körner 1993). In practice, however, many rowers struggled to maintain this pace throughout the microcycle. The introduction of competitive training groups, often employing handicapping in daily training sessions, was implemented to help motivate everyone to improve their respective training paces. Thus, fatigue management became an important part of supporting the whole training squad, and the rowers became highly receptive to good nutrition practices and effective recovery interventions. Heart rate data collected along with boat speed measures showed that the successful crews were typically those who could generate the prescribed boat speeds while working within their respective heart rate zones.

Training to specific speed zones could be considered an important factor in the success of the NZ rowing team under Tonks' leadership (47 world championship medals and 11 Olympic medals). It's unlikely that this type of approach would work outside an elite program with coaches and rowers tempered to this type of speed-specific training model and work ethic. But the fundamental drive to increase boat speed to some target during all facets of on-water training should arguably be an aspirational goal for all rowing coaches, because boat speed is the criterion measure for winning races. Ideally, the coach should have a target boat speed and stroke rate for each training zone that increases the chance of winning medals. However, coaches and sports scientists need to be aware of the danger of driving crews to achieve high training mileages at target boat speeds that are unattainable, which may lead to excessive fatigue and health problems.

Another factor to consider is that rowing has one unique feature compared to other endurance sports: The application of work and rest within the stroke cycle can be structured independently. During LSD training—more specifically during U2 intensity—a rower can maintain a speed of motion during the drive phase with a workload that is similar to that used in a 2000 m race while significantly increasing the duration of the recovery phase, thereby providing enough recuperation time to reduce the overall intensity per stroke. In this way, the intensity in the actual drive phase of the stroke can almost be at race pace while the rower maintains an U2 or AT intensity zone for the session by reducing the stroke rate. In contrast, if athletes of virtually any other endurance sport perform the propulsion phase of a stride, pedal, or stroke at competition intensity, the recovery phase has to meet the timing of the propulsion phase accordingly, automatically putting the exercise in the race-specific training intensity zone.

Many coaches, therefore, argue that employing a racelike drive phase at low stroke rates provides the ability to accrue the thousands of hours of training required to optimize aerobic conditioning as well as developing race-specific technique and crew synchronicity under fatigue. Whatever training method you choose, it is worthwhile to factor in the need to complete enough mileage to meet the crew's conditioning and technical requirements.

Monitoring Load and Fatigue

A wide variety of monitoring tools were explored with the NZ rowing team to manage training load and monitor fatigue. Measures such as training heart rates; heart rate variability; blood lactates; and recordings of athletes' mood, sleep, fatigue, soreness, and rate of perceived exertion; plus sampling key hormone, protein, and immune markers were implemented. Chapter 20 discusses many of these monitoring tools in more depth. Despite significant efforts, these tools lacked the accuracy to effectively monitor individuals' physical progress and fatigue. The coaches, therefore, preferred to monitor their rowers via a combination of achieved boat speed, observation of athletes' body language, communicated feedback from athletes, and their own intuition (Pope, Penney, and Smith 2018).

Key Point

Unfortunately, there is no single monitoring tool that predicts severe fatigue. Coaches are therefore recommended to constantly monitor their rowers' fatigue via changes in workload levels, observation of body language, effective communication, and intuition.

Assessing the Program

The presented training program, with its large amount of work at U2 intensity, was instituted during a period of phenomenal growth for RNZ. This success was all the more remarkable given the small senior rowing population and the performance achieved across a range of rowers and boat classes, including male and female, lightweight and heavyweight rowers.

However, some detractors, primarily from the sports science community, proposed various changes, arguing with the backing of good scientific evidence that HIIT was more effective than U2 training. The biggest critique focused on the rigid prescription of boat speed and rating for all U2 sessions. The logical argument was that setting training intensities based on boat speed alone meant some rowers were always working too hard and never fully recovered between sessions, limiting their physiological development. Many within the sports science community argued for training intensities prescribed by heart rate zones rather than boat speeds, similar to the training monitoring methods employed by the GDR. Although the U2 boat speeds were difficult to achieve, the centralized nature of the program, constant competitive training often completed in small boats, and the many successful outcomes seemed to keep everyone motivated to continue the original practice. Perhaps the physically demanding selection criteria ensured that only rowers were included who had the innate endurance capacity and aerobic conditioning to keep up with the prescribed training zones.

Although the training program underwent several minor modifications over the years as different approaches were examined, the fundamental TID were maintained. The only major change was an overall increase in U2 microcycles and a reduction in anaerobic microcycles.

The following questions still cannot be answered conclusively:

- Is a pyramidal TID model focusing on U2 intensity LSD training more effective than a polarized TID model focusing on HIIT?
- Are the benefits of one TID model over another so small that other factors (e.g., quality of athletes in a program, experience and intuition of a coach, good rowing technique) have a larger influence on final success?

- Training in individualized heart rate training zones is arguably the best method for managing each rower's training load. Taking this into account, how did the RNZ program become so successful by training primarily to set boat speeds?
- Are some rowers genetically gifted or so well trained that the standard FITT and progressive overload principles don't apply (i.e., do these athletes recover at substantially different rates from normal after completing heavy training workloads)?

Conclusion

This chapter outlines the processes used for developing an on-water rowing training program that generated successes at the world and Olympic levels for over a decade. This process was used to develop training programs not only for elite men's and women's heavyweight and lightweight crews, but also for internationally successful junior, under 21, and senior B rowing crews. Although some readers may disagree with the TID employed, the strategies and elements discussed here may add value to your programs.

The following steps are suggested as you develop an on-water training program:

- Critically examine successful rowing training programs relevant to your crew.
- Learn the science of exercise prescription, in particular the FITT and progressive overload principles.
- Determine the TID model you wish to use and how you will measure and implement it.
- Link the competition calendar to your training phases and mesocycles.
- Implement a microcycle structure within each mesocycle that achieves the required TID while respecting the requisite FITT principles.
- Ensure that effective progressive overload occurs across the majority of the microcycles within each mesocycle.
- Implement an unloading microcycle at the end of each mesocycle when testing (and racing) occurs to monitor progress.
- When possible, introduce competition into the various training sessions.
- Collect information from each training session to help monitor the progress of the crew and individual rowers.

An important element of any training program is regular and effective monitoring of the rowers to ensure any required program modifications occur in a timely manner (see chapter 20 for more detail). This requires a level of engagement and skill from the coach to first interpret the rower's mood, feedback, body language, and training load and then balance the need for hard training to promote optimal physical and mental conditioning with the requisite recovery periods.

CHAPTER 20

Monitoring Training

Brett Smith, PhD

Ensuring that the training workload is structured to consistently generate improved conditioning to enable the crew to reach their performance target is the ultimate goal of any competitive rowing program. It is therefore important that an effective monitoring regime is implemented to ensure that the training program is generating the planned improvements for every rower. Unfortunately, effective monitoring of conditioning and performance progress throughout a rowing season is very difficult. Some solutions to common monitoring problems will be described throughout this chapter.

Rowing is a physically demanding sport, and the frequent hard training required to succeed brings some risk of injuries, overreaching, or overtraining. As described in chapter 14, training stress is compounded by other nontraining stresses, genetics, and the psychological state of the rower. These combined factors generate a strain on the body. The magnitude of the training adaptation is dependent on the magnitude of the training-induced strain, with a larger strain generally stimulating a greater conditioning adaptation. Therefore, periods of hard training can generate the adaptations necessary for success in rowing, but this practice comes with a risk of injury, illness, or overtraining if the elevated strain is not balanced with the requisite recovery. The challenge when working with motivated rowers who are training hard is to regularly employ accurate monitoring tools to ensure adequate recovery and reduce extended periods of excessive fatigue.

Perhaps the simplest method of measuring effective recovery would be regular monitoring of fatigue: Once the rower's measure of fatigue has returned to "normal," they should be fully recovered and ready to train again. The use of a simple questionnaire or a rating of fatigue scale should suffice, which is why this method is employed by many teams. However, rowers' reported fatigue levels can be inaccurate, because some competitive rowers may not be willing to honestly report high fatigue levels and poor recovery if they perceive it will negatively impact their standing and selection opportunities in a crew. Furthermore, there are unanswered questions around what is "normal" versus "abnormal" fatigue and whether full recovery is required between training sessions to facilitate optimal adaptation. Thus, other more accurate measures of fatigue need to be considered as well.

One system of assessing a rower's fatigue level involves measures of competition or training performance. Such a system records the external load on the athlete or the physical work performed by the rower. Typical external load measures include time and stroke rate used to row a specific distance or the sets and repetitions of a weight lifted during resistance training. Changes in performance can provide insight into the

Key Point

Periods of hard training are an important element to optimize conditioning, but without adequate recovery it can lead to injury, illness, or overtraining. An effective training program should result in improved rowing performance, thus regular monitoring of changes in performance is an important method for managing rowers' conditioning.

rower's level of fatigue. Unfortunately, there are several major logistical and technical challenges to accurately measure and interpret an individual rower's on-water workload, especially in a crew boat, where achieved performance depends on the work rate of other crew members, stroke rate, water current, wind, temperature, technique, rig, and motivation. There are, however, new technologies involving force transducers that can measure an individual rower's power output on the water, which have the potential to revolutionize individual monitoring of external load in rowing.

As mentioned previously, it is the strain placed on the rower that stimulates the conditioning enhancement, so it is important to also monitor the internal load that the rower experiences in response to the external load. This is typically achieved by measuring the rower's physiological and psychological responses to the external load. Given that the strain is also affected by external stressors and psychological state of the rower, ideally these factors are monitored as well.

External Load Monitoring Tools

Best practice monitoring requires the measurement of the internal and external load together so that the internal load can be placed into context. Measuring the external load—or more specifically, the level of performance and changes in performance—is important for establishing the physical capacity of the rower and for monitoring their training progress throughout the season.

On-Water Rowing Tests

The ultimate criterion measure for rowing performance is the time to cover 2,000 m on water; however, environmental conditions can substantially modify 2,000 m speed, and without special instrumentation it is not possible to quantify an individual rower's performance in a crew boat. For this reason, testing is sometimes completed in singles or coxless pairs. However environmental conditions may affect particular athletes differently and performance improvements may occur as a result of changes in technique rather than conditioning. Testing of other conditioning components is also often completed via on-water time trials over a range of distances (e.g., 100 m for anaerobic alactic capacity, 500 m for anaerobic lactic endurance, and 20 km for aerobic endurance) but these tests suffer from the same limitations as the 2,000 m race. Performance in these tests is typically determined by boat speed expressed as a percentage of the crew's prognostic speed (i.e., the boat speed relative to the world best time or some other target speed of the particular boat class) to enable comparisons between different boat classes.

Despite their limitations, boat speed and calculated prognostic boat speed are often used for both testing and monitoring training performance, which has stimulated the development and use of various rowing speedometers that normally also measure stroke rate. The two common types of speedometers are impeller-based systems, which measure the "actual" boat speed relative to the water, or global positioning systems (GPS), which measure boat speed relative to land. If the boat is moving on a waterway that has a current—either through the flow of a river or through the influence of wind—the impeller system provides a more realistic measurement of the boat speed relative to the water, which is responsible for the main resistance that the rower has to overcome. If the boat is moving on a calm lake with no current, both systems provide the same measurements.

Key Point

On-water monitoring of boat speed and expressing the speed as a percentage of a prognostic target speed (e.g., world's best time for the boat class) is a common monitoring tool. However, boat speed is affected by environmental and water conditions, and this method isn't an effective workload measure of individual crew members.

Depending on the body of water, the impeller system provides more accurate feedback about the external work of the rower and more accurately measures stroke-by-stroke variances. However, GPS is very accurate at measuring land-based distances, such as in a 2,000 m race (Smith, Hopkins, and Lowe 2011). Despite the limitations of GPS, it is becoming more prevalent in rowing, possibly because of the ease of setup. There are a multitude of relatively cheap rowing speedometer apps that use a smartphone's built-in GPS and accelerometer to measure and display boat speed and stroke rate data. Some rowing-specific systems even let you transfer data directly to the coach's motorboat.

Regardless of which measurement system is used, the interpretation of the boat speed data needs to be done very carefully. Not only is boat speed affected by water currents and temperature, but also by wind speed, wind direction, and associated waves; thus changes may not accurately reflect the change in power output by individual members or the crew as a whole. Accounting for these environmental conditions is very difficult. Therefore, the inclusion of data from one or more on-water weather stations that measure current and wave height, as well as speed, direction, and temperature of the wind could provide some useful information. However, it is unlikely that even these data completely represent the specific environmental conditions each boat experiences throughout their row, and an equation that enables this environmental data to provide "corrected" boat speeds has yet to be validated.

Even with ideal environmental conditions, boat speed changes between tests or across a period of training are not a precise measure of changes in physical conditioning. Although many coaches argue that boat speed wins races and thus it is the most important measure to monitor during races, tests, and training, boat speed is not an absolutely accurate measure of physical conditioning. The challenge is therefore to find methods of precisely monitoring individual rowers' workloads.

The power output for each individual rower during on-water rowing can be calculated using various sensors in the oarlock or on the oar. Although there should be a strong correlation between power output and boat velocity in theory, the results are inconsistent. Greater understanding is required of the relationship between the power measured by these devices and the power propelling the boat forward as well as the possible errors. Despite these limitations, including the high costs of the often fragile hardware, these devices are becoming more popular, although they are typically used to provide feedback on technique rather than to monitor individual crew members' power outputs.

On-Water Monitoring of Rowing Training

The continued development of sensor technology combined with physiological assessment could potentially provide each rower with individualized data regarding power output at their training zones, as well as to monitor a rower's training load against these physiologically determined power training zones. The determination of physiological training zones will be discussed later in this chapter.

In lieu of physiological training zones, which are difficult and often expensive to monitor consistently, a common strategy is to set training zones based on prognostic boat speeds and stroke rates. An example of this type of training zone prescription is presented in table 20.1. An example of an on-water pace sheet for a men's heavyweight single sculler is presented in table 20.2.

Table 20.1 Example of Training Zone Prescriptions Based on FITT Principles Set by Stroke Rate and Boat Speed

Descriptors Sessions per week		FREQUENCY		Intensity	Type	Duration (time or distance) in training zone	Example methods
		Sessions per week	Session recovery				
Active recovery (AR)	AR	N/A	N/A	<75% WR pace for the boat class at 16-18 spm	Row or erg	N/A	8-12 km at 16-18 spm Warm-up, cool-down, recovery between intervals
Zone 1	T1	6-14	4-12 h	70%-77% WR pace for the boat class at 18-20 spm	Row or erg	10-120 min per interval 45-120 min per session	12-30 km steady state 2 km or 8 min at 18-20 spm, 1-2 min off × 6-12
	U2	6-12	6-12 h	77%-82% WR pace for the boat class at 18-20 spm		12-30 km per session 60-240 km per week	1-2 km at 16, 18, 20, 22 spm, 1-2 min off × 5-15 Pyramids, steps, ladders, W:R 1:0.25 or less
Zone 2	U1	3	36 h	82%-88% WR pace for the boat class at 22-28 spm	Row or erg	5-60 min per interval 20-60 min per session	10-15 min on, 3-10 min off × 3-4 at 28-34 spm Pyramids, steps, ladders, W:R 1:0.25 or less
	AT	3	48 h	88%-92% WR pace for the boat class at 28-32 spm		5-20 km per session 10-50 km per week	1 × 6-12 km at max sustainable spm (mspm) 2-3 × 4-5 km on, 5 min off at mspm
Zone 3	LaT	2	48-72 h	92%-98% WR pace for the boat class at ≥ 32 spm	Row or erg	10-20 min per session 3-5 min per session	1 min on, 1 min off × 5 × 3 at race pace spm 30 s on, 90 s off × 6 × 4 at max spm
	LaP	2	72 h	>98% WR pace for the boat class at ≥ max SR		20-60 min per week 6-12 km per week	500 m on, 8 min off × 6 at race spm 1,000 m on, 10 min off × 3 at race spm

mspm = maximal sustainable stroke rate for the specified duration; race spm = average strokes per minute for 2,000m race; spm = strokes per minute; session recovery = time between sessions; WR pace = world record pace for 2,000 m race, often expressed as percentage of world record pace e.g., 78-82% WR pace

Table 20.2 Example of Detailed Training Zones for a Men's Heavyweight Single Sculler Set by Various Metrics, Where 100% Boat Speed Is the Speed Required to Achieve the World's Best 2,000 m Time.

	Grade	Boat	
Grade and boat	Elite	M1x	(Enter grade and boat type)
2,000 m target race time	6:30.74		World's best 2,000 m time
Max heart rate	195		(Enter maximum heart rate)
Resting heart rate	42		(Enter resting heart rate)
Average race stroke rate	36		(Enter average race strokes per minute or target race strokes per minute)

Training zone	LaP		LaT		AT		U1		U2		T1	
Lactate levels	Peak		>6 mmol		3-5 mmol		2-3 mmol		1.5-2 mmol		1-1.5 mmol	
% 2,000 m target race speed	110%	98%	98%	92%	92%	88%	88%	82%	82%	77%	77%	70%
Strokes per min	43	36	36	33	31	29	27	25	22	18	20	16
Drive time (s)	0.67		0.68		0.71		0.73		0.76		0.78	
Heart rate reserve (HRR)	100%	97%	97%	95%	94%	89%	88%	85%	84%	81%	80%	77%
HR (bpm)	195	191	191	187	186	178	177	172	171	166	164	160
% race SR	120%		100%		85%		75%		~55%		~45%	
Speed (m/s)	5.63		5.02		4.71		4.50		4.20		3.94	
Seconds per stroke	1.39		1.67		1.96		2.22		2.73		3.00	
Distance per stroke (m)	7.82		8.36		9.23		10.01		11.45		11.82	
Recovery time (% of stroke)	52.0%		59.0%		64.0%		67.0%		72.0%		74.0%	
Recovery time (s)	0.72		0.98		1.25		1.49		1.96		2.22	

Note: The heart rate reserve training zones are different to those in the other training zone tables in this chapter. This is because this table was developed for elite senior A rowers, and it was found that these successful elite athletes were so well conditioned that their heart rate training zones had improved well beyond the recommendations for the normal rower.

There are many limitations to solely using prognostic boat speeds and stroke rates to set training zones, which revolve around the challenges of achieving the same desired physiological response for each member of the crew from one boat speed and stroke rate. For example, a crew's aerobic training pace may be set to 80% of their prognostic speed at 20 spm. However, during a 20 km training session intended to be at aerobic base speed, half of the crew may have to work above their physiological aerobic training zone to achieve the 80% pace, which would then require a longer recovery period for those rowers. Without this extended recovery period these rowers are likely to need to reduce the intensity of subsequent training sessions, and attempts to maintain this boat speed risks injury or overtraining. Despite the numerous limitations of this training method, it is still often used.

It is logical that the training speed that a crew is able to achieve consistently is a good indicator for the maximum speed that this crew can produce in a race, and experience supports this logic. Although there are always exceptions, most crews who are unable to progress to consistent high training and testing speeds are typically not able to achieve high 2,000 m racing speeds. Therefore, accurately determining a crew's boat speeds for the respective training zones based on their level of performance not only provides this crew with the appropriate training targets but also predicts the race speed that they can realistically expect to achieve. Thus, although training at a slow boat speed may provide the appropriate stress and physiological adaptations for an individual rower to improve their fitness, these improvements may still not be enough to achieve the high boat speeds required for success at 2,000 m.

The reality of elite programs are expectations to qualify for and perform well at events like University Championships or Olympic Games to maintain their funding. This requires high training, testing, and racing boat speeds, so a rower with poor physiological capacity may not be able to consistently generate the required workloads. Continued attempts of such an athlete to do so will likely result in overreaching, injuries, or eventual overtraining. The challenge for the program is not only to identify the performance level of the rowers, but also to monitor training and test output. If a rower does not meet the required performance levels it must be decided whether to replace the rower or to manage them by enhancing recovery or reducing workload. Both measures have possible significant impacts on the team dynamic, which underlines the importance of a proper monitoring process.

If circumstances allow, then the boat speed and stroke rate for every rowing session should be recorded alongside the normal session measures. This allows the training session to be analyzed to determine if the athlete's power output fell within the programmed boat speed and prognostic training zone. Any effective on-water rowing session monitoring tool should also record the environmental conditions, which will obviously influence boat speed. It is not always possible to accurately correct for environmental conditions, but noting how the wind, water, and current conditions could have affected the boat speed provides some insight into whether the speed was an accurate indicator of the crew's current capabilities.

Off-Water Rowing Tests

The challenges of accurately assessing the on-water performance of individual rowers has led rowing programs to typically employ rowing ergometers to monitor their rowers' off-water performance and conditioning levels.

Although the 2,000 m ergometer test is the most common test procedure, there are a wide range of other ergometer performance tests aimed to assess specific physical components of an athlete's performance. Examples of ergometer tests of anaerobic alactic capacity include peak power (single stroke peak power output during a 5-7 stroke maximal test), average peak power (highest average power output over 5 strokes in a test of 7-10 strokes) or maximal distance (or average power) over 10 s, 15 s, or 100 m. Ergometer tests of anaerobic lactic capacity include 30 s (modified Wingate test), 250 m, 500 m, or a repeated interval test (e.g., 4 rounds of 30 s maximal work followed by 30 s rest). The total distance or average power is determined for the various anaerobic tests.

If the measurements are available, other useful variables can be collected, such as peak power, occurrence of peak power (e.g., the time from the start of the test or stroke number that peak power occurred), and fatigue determined from the drop-off in power (e.g., the reduction in power output from the start of the test to the end of the test or from the peak power output to the minimal power output). There are various apps available that provide easy ways to collect all necessary data and generate different reports. These extra measures can provide useful information on how training program modifications need to be implemented to improve not only the overall power production but also the rate of acceleration (time to peak power) or anaerobic endurance.

Key Point

Rowing ergometry may be technically different from on-water rowing, but it is still a useful measure of individual rowing specific workload. If a reliable rowing ergometer is used, then consistent implementation of identical ergometer training sessions can help monitor whether training is effective.

A range of rowing ergometer performance tests for aerobic capacity are also available. The shorter tests, such as the 2,000 m, 4 min, and 6 min maximum tests, contain a significant anaerobic contribution. Longer aerobic endurance performance tests include maximal tests over 5,000 m, 30 min, maximal effort for 30 min restricted to 20 spm, and 60 min. Performance tests in which the stroke rate is restricted are common, but substantial variations in power output can occur if rowers fail to adhere to the set rating, which can create errors when comparing results between athletes and over time. One solution to this is to mechanically interconnect all ergometers for the participating rowers, which forces everyone to maintain the same stroke rate, but this requires a level of technical coordination that crews can struggle to attain, and some rowers claim it affects their power output. If the measurement tools are available, other variables can be measured, including power or fatigue rate determined from the drop-off in speed.

All these off-water rowing tests can be used to monitor the specific effects of the training program on the whole training group, as well as the progress and absolute performance of the individual rowers. The wide range of possible tests can make the decision of which to use difficult. Typically coaches use those tests they are familiar and comfortable with and that fit into their training approach at the given time in the season. Additionally, coaches need to carefully consider which specific tests need to be completed at predetermined times of the season for team and crew selection. For example, tests might need to be conducted whenever the organization decides they need to select or reselect a squad or a crew. Such test timing depends on the season, county, level, depth, athlete injuries, and regulations, among other factors.

A large challenge can occur if the selection measures set by the rowing organization (e.g., national body, club, or college) are different from those the coach wishes to incorporate in their training program. Unfortunately, there are no simple answers about which test battery is the best or most precise to monitor performance. However, as well as the 2,000 m maximal tests, you should also consider one test each for anaerobic alactic power, anaerobic lactic capacity, and aerobic endurance. The two anaerobic tests should ideally also provide measures of peak power and time to peak power, and all tests should assess the drop in power over the length of the trial to measure fatigue. The tests you choose are likely to be more useful and reliable if they always follow identical protocols and occur at the same relative time in the training micro- and mesocycle under the same environmental conditions. Also, the type of ergometer you use should be reliable and valid for all tests available.

Off-Water Monitoring of Rowing Training

Like for on-water training, the distance, average speed or power output, and stroke rate should be recorded for each ergometer training session. Although it is common to use set boat speeds and stroke rates for the whole crew for each training zone during on-water training, the ergometer training zones are more likely to be individualized. This individualization can be set as a percentage of the rower's average speed or power of their 2,000 m maximal ergometer test or from various physiological tests, which will be covered below.

It is easier to determine changes in individual performance through regular monitoring of performance on a rowing ergometer rather than in a crew boat. However, although ergometer training is a good surrogate for on-water rowing, the latter is essential for improving a crew's race performance, thus ergometer training is typically minimized, especially during the in-season. This unfortunately can limit the use of rowing ergometers as an effective and regular monitoring system of individual rowers. For those nations unable to row on the water year-round, or who wish to take an off-season break from on-water training, then rowing ergometry is often the only rowing-specific conditioning option available. The use of rowing ergometry through this period provides opportunities to individualize training zones and monitor progress by comparing session power output and stroke rate against RPE and various physiological measures such as heart rate and blood lactate.

Internal Load Monitoring Tools

Internal load is a measure of the physiological and psychological stresses placed on a rower, and it is common in high-performance rowing programs to measure specific psychological and physiological variables during training, testing, and recovery. General adaptation syndrome posits that the stress (strain) of training will eventually promote an anabolic adaptation and lead to increased conditioning, assuming adequate recovery occurs. The goal is to understand whether the stress of training was at the required level and whether the athlete recovered effectively between sessions. This can be ascertained through the rower's perception of their level of exertion and physiological measures of stress such as heart rate and lactate. Understanding whether the rowers perceive themselves to have recovered sufficiently between training sessions provides important insights into whether a positive training response will occur.

Maximal Physiological Tests

Different tests are used to assess various physiological components that predict rowers' conditioning levels. Presented here are those tests that have proven accurate for determining changes in conditioning, levels of conditioning against predetermined standards, and comparisons between rowers. These tests are typically performed on ergometers; a more comprehensive list of the accuracy of the various physiological tests are presented by Smith and Hopkins (2012). For the reasons outlined previously, the validity of a physiological test for predicting rowing performance is typically determined by the strength of the relationship between the physiological test and the 2,000 m ergometer test rather than the physiological test and 2,000 m on-water performance.

Arguably there are two types of rowing physiology tests: maximal tests, which measure peak capacity, and submaximal tests, which measure the effectiveness of the aerobic system. The most common maximal physiological test that has the required level of reliability and validity is the $\dot{V}O_2$max test, whereas the submaximal physiological tests with the required accuracy include some specific lactate tests (Smith and Hopkins 2012). The peak incremental power and the 30 s maximal tests are sometimes promoted as accurate physiological tests of rowing performance, and though these tests often include physiological measures such as heart rate (HR) and blood lactate (La), they are fundamentally measuring external workload, not internal load. Peak incremental power is typically the power output in the final step of the incremental stepwise test used to determine $\dot{V}O_2$max.

Key Point

The most common physiological tests that have the required level of reliability and validity for rowing at this time are the $\dot{V}O_2$max test and various submaximal lactate tests. Time trials on the Concept2 ergometer provide accurate estimates of a rower's physiological ability to produce power.

These tests typically provide a physiological measure that can be compared against rowing-specific normative values, individual or crew targets, and the rower's historical data, as well as individualized training zones. The $\dot{V}O_2$max test not only provides a maximal oxygen consumption value but can also be used to inform the rower of their appropriate values for workload (wattage or speed), HR, rate of perceived exertion (RPE), La, and oxygen saturation for HIIT or $\dot{V}O_2$max training sessions. The submaximal tests tend to focus on determining whether the various measures (e.g., HR, RPE, La) are lower for the respective rower than that recorded from the previous test for each workload level (speed or wattage), which signals improved conditioning. These

Table 20.3 Example of Training Zone Prescriptions Estimated From Various Internal and External Measures

Descriptors Sessions per week		FREQUENCY		Intensity	Type	Duration (time or distance) in zone	Example methods
		Sessions per week	Session recovery				
AR	AR	N/A	N/A	< Zone 1, very light RPE 8-9 <75% WR pace at 16-18 spm	Row or erg	N/A	8-12 km at 16-18 spm Warm-up, cool-down, recovery between intervals
Zone 1	T1	6-14	4-12 h	60% V̇O₂max to aerobic threshold 60%-70% HRR 1.2-1.5 mmol/L [La] ≤LT1 or ≤VT1 Light–moderate RPE 9-10, 70%-77% WR pace at 18-20 spm	Row or erg	10-120 min per interval 45-120 min per session 12-30 km per session 60-240 km per week	12-30 km steady state 2 km or 8 min at 18-20 spm, 1-2 min off × 6-12 1-2 km at 16, 18, 20, 22 spm, 1-2 min off × 5-15 Pyramids, steps, ladders, W:R 1:0.25 or less
	U2	6-12	6-12 h	Aerobic threshold 70% HRR 1.5 mmol/L [La] Equal to LT1 or VT1 Moderate RPE 11-12, 77%-82% WR pace at 18-20 spm			
Zone 2	U1	3	36 h	Aerobic to anaerobic thresholds 70%-80% HRR 2.0-4.0 mmol/L [La] LT1-LT2 or VT1-VT2 Somewhat hard RPE 13-15, 82%-88% WR pace at 22-28 spm	Row or erg	5-60 min per interval 20-60 min per session 5-20 km per session 10-50 km per week	10-15 min on, 3-10 min off × 3-4 at 28-34 spm Pyramids, steps, ladders, W:R 1:0.25 or less
	AT	3	48 h	Anaerobic threshold, 80%-85% HRR 4.0 mmol/L [La] LT2 or VT2 Hard RPE 16-17, 88%-92% WR pace at 28-32 spm			1 × 6-12 km at max sustainable spm (mspm) 2-3 × 4-5 km on, 5 min off at mspm
Zone 3	LaT	2	48-72 h	90%-100% HRR, >6.0 mmol/L [La] >LT2 and >VT2 Very hard to extremely hard RPE 18-19, 92%-98% WR pace at ≥32 spm	Row or erg	10-20 min per session 3-5 km per session 20-60 min per week 6-12 km per week	1 min on, 1 min off 5 × 3 at race spm 30 s on, 90 s off × 6 × 4 at max spm
	LaP	2	72 h	Maximal HR Maximal [La] Extremely hard to maximal RPE 19-20 >98% WR pace ≥ race spm			500 m on, 8 min off × 6 at race spm 1,000 m on, 10 min off × 3 at race spm

[La] = concentration of blood lactate; HRR = heart rate reserve; mM = blood lactate concentration in millimole per litre; LT1 = lactate threshold 1; LT2 = lactate threshold 2; LSD = long slow distance; mspm = maximal sustainable stroke rate for the specified duration; race spm = average strokes per minute for 2,000 m race; RPE = rate of perceived exertion (20 point scale); spm = strokes per minute; session recovery = time between sessions; VT1 = ventilatory threshold 1; VT2 = ventilatory threshold 2; WR pace = world record pace for 2000m race, often expressed as percentage of world record pace e.g., 78-82% WR pace tests are also often set up so that they provide physiological and workload values for the various training zones (see table 20.3).

The generally recommended testing method for $\dot{V}O_2$max is a stepwise incremental protocol called the *graded exercise test*, in which gas exchange measures are taken during a series of incremental steps with the load improvements chosen so that the test lasts no more than 8 to 12 min (Beltz et al. 2016). The rower continues to lift the wattage and stroke rate each minute until they can no longer make the stepwise increase. It is gauged that a $\dot{V}O_2$max has been reached if $\dot{V}O_2$ plateaus, the respiratory exchange ratio is ≥1.15, heart rate reaches >95% of maximum, and the rate of perceived exertion (RPE) is ≥very hard.

As described in previous chapters, $\dot{V}O_2$max is considered a strong physiological predictor of rowing performance and for this reason it is often recommended as an important physiological test. In rowing programs the maximal 2,000 m rowing ergometer test is typically used as the criterion measure of a rower's physical capacity, and its test result correlates extremely highly with the rower's $\dot{V}O_2$max (Smith and Hopkins 2012). Given the complexity and expense of the $\dot{V}O_2$max test, coaches may be better off employing the 2,000 m test as an effective surrogate. However, the $\dot{V}O_2$max test is still a useful diagnostic test in a high-performance program to specifically examine changes in maximal aerobic capacity, because the 2,000 m test can be influenced by other factors such as technique, pacing strategies, rowing-specific power, supplements, and motivation. Moreover, the $\dot{V}O_2$max test may be useful for talent identification because an athlete new to rowing may lack the specific conditioning to perform well in a maximal 2,000 m rowing ergometer test despite having an exceptional aerobic capacity.

Submaximal Physiological Tests

There are several submaximal physiological tests that aim to measure changes in aerobic conditioning and provide information on some or all of the submaximal training zones. The most common include the ventilatory threshold test, the Conconi heart rate test for anaerobic threshold identification, and various lactate tests. This section will focus on the lactate tests, which are considered to have the required accuracy. Although controversy exists about the efficacy of blood lactate testing from a physiological and biochemical standpoint, it is a common submaximal test for endurance athletes that correlates well to rowing performance (Smith and Hopkins 2012).

There are not only numerous lactate testing protocols, but also various measurement protocols, methods of interpretation, and lactate measurement tools. Stepwise incremental testing with lactate measures is often used to determine aerobic and anaerobic thresholds, but disagreements over which of the various lactate measures accurately determine these thresholds have led in many instances to these measures being relabeled. For example, although both are used to estimate anaerobic threshold, the 4 mmol/L lactate level is termed *onset of blood lactate accumulation* (OBLA) and the lactate turn-point or break-point is termed the *lactate threshold*. There are a plethora of lactate analyzers available, with many considered to have reasonable levels of accuracy (Bonaventura et al. 2015), so readers should follow best practice sampling methods and check the current published independent accuracy studies before purchase.

The testing protocols typically involve a discontinuous incremental stepwise exercise protocol, but unlike the $\dot{V}O_2$max test, the steps are usually 3 to 10 minutes in duration with short breaks between each step for lactate collection (Bourdon 2000; Janssen 1987; Maud and Foster 2006). The test protocol will influence the results, and care should be taken in selecting the starting workload and the workload increments. Durations of 6 to 10 min for each step should ideally be utilized so enough time elapses to reach aerobic steady state (Bourdon, Woolford, and Buckley 2018).

The main goals of lactate testing are to identify the rower's individual training zones and to monitor the rower's physiological progress over time with an accurate, consistent, and economical test procedure. An example of the lactate training zones can be found in table 20.3. Please note that workload, HR, RPE, and stroke rate data should be collected alongside the lactate values during testing so that the lactate-determined training zones have associated workload, HR, RPE and stroke rate training zones. This allows not only individualized wattage and stroke training zones to be set for rowing ergometer training but also HR and RPE training zones for both off- and on-water training. Although it is possible to complete an adapted form of lactate testing during on-water training, the logistical difficulties and potential environmental changes affecting boat speed limit its use.

Testing should ideally be performed at the start of a mesocycle in an unloading or minitaper week when the rowers are most recovered to reduce the effects of fatigue. Practical experience shows that if rowers are highly fatigued, they can present a false right shift of their lactate-performance curve through very low blood lactate levels (i.e., an apparent aerobic improvement). In these instances, the rowers also often finish the test prematurely due to fatigue while presenting very low lactate levels, high RPEs, and typically abnormally low or elevated HR. Although there is no final evidence on the causality of this rare phenomenon, it is often associated with low blood glucose levels (Smith unpublished findings). It can be debated whether the false right shift is due to glucose depletion, which lowers blood lactate, or whether autonomic fatigue is disturbing glucose and other internal regulatory mechanisms, which lower glucose and blood lactate. The bottom line is that it is important athletes are well rested, healthy, and replenished before and during any form of testing with blood lactate measurements.

Combining $\dot{V}O_2$max and lactate testing helps determine efficiency in that reduced lactate, HR, and RPE measures at specific stages can indicate improved aerobic conditioning, whereas reduced oxygen consumption at a specific work rate suggests an improvement in mechanical efficiency (i.e., improved rowing technique). However, tests that combine $\dot{V}O_2$max and aerobic or anaerobic threshold equivalent lactate measures should involve at least 3 min stages, making the test much longer than that recommended for a $\dot{V}O_2$max test and the steps too short to achieve steady-state lactate values. The measurement of oxygen consumption during lactate testing can provide useful information; however, the length of time and high cost make this option difficult, especially for large teams. One strategy to achieve both measures is to run a standard lactate test protocol with 6 to 10 min steps but only up until the athlete reaches 4 mmol/L lactate. This reduces fatigue levels, and after a short break the athletes can perform a maximal 3 to 4 min workload to achieve a $\dot{V}O_2$max measure. Combining ventilatory threshold and $\dot{V}O_2$max measures is somewhat easier because this test involves steps of 1 to 3 min duration, making the total test duration short enough to achieve maximal intensity. However, as mentioned previously, the ventilatory threshold test lacks the required accuracy and is expensive even though it can provide the benefit of combining $\dot{V}O_2$max and ventilatory threshold–determined training zones.

Some of the training zones intensities presented in this chapter are defined by the physiological measures previously mentioned in chapter 15 as lactate threshold (LT1 and LT2) and ventilatory threshold (VT1 and VT2), which are typically determined from graded exercise tests. Another measure used to determine training zones is heart rate reserve (HRR), which is calculated for each rower by adding their resting heart rate (RHR) to the percentage training zone intensity, multiplied by the difference between the maximal (MaxHR) and resting heart rates. For example, to calculate 60% training zone, HRR = RHR + (60% × (MaxHR-RHR)). Unfortunately, while the use of HRR training zones is very common, it can be extremely inaccurate. The reason is that this method typically applies the same percentage for each training zone across the whole squad and crew and therefore fails to account for individual differences and fitness levels.

Monitoring Training

The training zones generated from both the submaximal lactate test and the maximal test typically include active recovery, aerobic base, anaerobic intensity, anaerobic threshold, and $\dot{V}O_2$max (see table 20.3 for more details). These tests not only generate values for power output or speed for each training zone, but they can also provide measures of HR and RPE for the training zones as well (assuming these parameters were included and recorded in the testing protocol). Heart rate monitoring is considered a valid measure of exercise intensity for submaximal and continuous training, and resting morning HR is often used as a measure of health and recovery (Achten and Jeukendrup 2003). Heart rate monitoring systems are often promoted in rowing programs given the difficulties of accurately measuring individual on-water workloads. However, there are a number of limitations to this measure, which include cardiovascular drift, day-to-day variations, nutrition and hydration status, environmental effects, changes during menstruation, inconsistent modifications due to severe fatigue (i.e., increased or decreased HR response to a specific load) and, most importantly, inability to accurately monitor intensive or interval training (Juul and Jeukendrup 2003).

When setting training zones, it is important that steps are taken to validate these during training. A well-constructed test should provide values of power output in W, HR, RPE, and La for each training zone (see table 20.3). The ability to measure some or all of these metrics provides information on whether the performed workload is correct. For example, a rower working on an ergometer at their aerobic power output zone who returns a higher-than-prescribed La, HR, or RPE is either fatigued or deconditioned, or else the training zones are incorrectly set. Likewise, a rower training on water at their aerobic HR zone who returns a lower-than-expected RPE or La level has either improved their aerobic conditioning and needs to train at a higher boat speed or the training zone test was inaccurate.

Sometimes the monitoring of all these metrics causes more confusion than clarity when results are contradictory (e.g., power output is correct, but RPE and La levels are well below and HR is well above the respective training zone). Unfortunately, this is not uncommon and working through the possible causalities is the only way of addressing the issue (e.g., inaccurate testing values, measurement errors, health issues, poor nutritional or hydration status, technique changes, or menstrual cycle).

The most accurate method of monitoring rowing training is on the rowing ergometer, given the accurate measures of individual workload. However, most crews will tend to spend more time rowing on the water than on an ergometer. Monitoring HR and RPE during on-water training is common with many crews, although the challenges of training at HR zones during rowing has been discussed in chapter 13 and mentioned above. It is also possible to perform lactate testing on water to cross-check the relationship between La level, HR, and RPE. On-water lactate testing should be executed at the start of the week when the athlete is recovered and ideally in wind-still conditions.

With the development of gate forces, the on-water measurement of individual workload is now possible. Cost, necessary continuous calibration, the influence of rigging changes, and workload validation need to be considered when choosing a system. One interesting observation about ergometer versus on-water lactate testing should be presented here. We found instances when some members of a senior A eight could not generate above 1 mmol/L lactate levels at stroke rates of 18 to 22 spm, and their HR and RPE were also lower than expected. Force gates attached to the eight led to the discovery that these rowers were technically unable to perform the same work in the boat that they were able to perform on the ergometer as a result of technical limitations and the inability to generate the required power in the highly flexed catch position on water.

Key Point

On-water ergometry (e.g., force gates) has the potential to provide accurate measures of an individual rower's workload within a crew boat. This technology allows constant monitoring of training load, which is a major component of monitoring on-water rowing performance and conditioning.

Other HR-based measures to assess athletes' fitness include heart rate recovery, which is the rate at which heart rate decreases after the cessation of exercise. Higher levels of fitness are suggested to improve the rate of decrease, whereas fatigue has the opposite effect (Halson 2014). Despite heart rate recovery being a theoretically useful tool for managing fatigue, difficulties in standardizing the monitoring protocol during training and competition make this measure very difficult to perform in real-life situations.

Heart rate variability (HRV) refers to the inherent variability of the heart rate that occurs as the sympathetic and parasympathetic branches of the autonomic nervous system oscillate in their management of resting and postexercise heart rate. The reduction of this natural variability suggests a dysfunction in the autonomic nervous system's regulation mechanism, possibly caused by high levels of fatigue. Although the theory is sound, results of testing have been inconsistent and the use of HRV measures has both detractors and supporters (Halson 2014; Jimenez Morgan and Molina Mora 2017).

The training stress score (TSS) is a training workload management system that requires a power measurement device (TrainingPeaks 2021). When recording power is possible, the equation for TSS is:

$$TSS = (SDS \times NP \times IF) / (FTP \times 36)$$

where SDS is session duration in seconds; NP is normalized power (30 s rolling average of power calculated with a normalization algorithm); FTP is functional threshold power (average power from a 60 min maximal test); and IF is intensity factor (NP/FTP).

TSS is commonly used in cycling and may one day be relevant in rowing when power measuring devices become more common. Without power output monitoring, TSS can be estimated from heart rate (Plews and Laursen 2017). For TSS utilizing HR, FTP is replaced by average heart rate for a 60 min max test and NP is replaced by normalized heart rate. This complicated system also enables the quantification of training load for sessions with changing intensities by allowing calculation of the TSS for the different segments of the session, then the total session TSS can be calculated by summing the segment TSS. A steady-state session of 60 min maximal effort provides a score of 100.

The various advanced workload monitoring systems such as session RPE, TRIMP, T2minutes, and TSS may provide some value in quantifying training load, but their application is complex and requires a high level of expertise and resourcing. Additionally, users should be aware of the possible limitations to using both HR and RPE to monitor training intensity, especially in interval sessions (Tran et al. 2015).

Monitoring of endocrine, immune, or biochemical markers theoretically should enable the confirmation of positive training adaptations through measured increases in the body's anabolic responses, as well as warn of maladaptation through increases in catabolic responses caused by severe fatigue. Despite a large body of research in this area, no marker or combination of markers have shown the necessary accuracy to add value (Halson 2014). To make matters worse, these measures are normally extremely costly and their regular collection during training often provides a number of difficult logistical problems.

Psychometrics

There are various psychometric measures of internal load, the most common being RPE, which has already been introduced. There is a large body of work (Borg 1998; Marriott and Lamb 1996) supporting the notion that RPE is a valid measure of exercise intensity; however, the validity may not be as high as originally thought (Halson 2014). RPE is the rower's perception of the training intensity against a 10- or 20-point exertion scale (Borg 1998). Factors that may influence RPE include difficulty determining an average RPE level in a session of varying intensities and instances where rowers only remember the hardest or most recent element of training. Results can also be influenced by outside factors like fatigue, nutrition, environment, sociopsychological influences, health, and so forth.

As mentioned previously, combining workload (power output or speed), the physiological strain (HR or La level) and psychological perception of the effort (RPE) provides a very effective measure of training intensity that can be used to monitor training sessions over a longer time and against the individual's training zones. Other monitoring options include the HR-to-RPE ratio and HR-to-lactate ratio (Halson 2014).

As described in chapter 16, multiplying the time of the session in minutes with the RPE from the 10-point Borg scale provides the session RPE (sRPE), which is considered a simple and accurate measure for quantifying the training load of a session (Haddad et al. 2017). The limitations of RPE described above also apply to this measure. If the rowing program has access to heart rate monitoring, it is recommended that the HR-based training impulse (TRIMP) measure also be included (Borresen and Lambert 2009).

There have been numerous adaptations to the TRIMP measure; more recent ones divide the session into the segments of time spent in each HR training zone, with each zone having a different weighting factor (Borresen and Lambert 2009). Perhaps the most comprehensive rowing-specific TRIMP model, the T2minute method, was developed by Tran and colleagues (2015), who determined set weighting factors for each of the training zones as well as the various off-water training options. These weighting factors were scaled to on-water rowing workloads and enabled the determination of the impact of continuous and interval-type training sessions.

Perhaps the simplest and most insightful psychometric monitoring tool is a training diary. However, the ability to systematically evaluate conditioning improvements and manage fatigue is difficult with the largely unstructured subjective data typical of a diary. A common strategy to improve the usefulness of this data is to use athlete self-report monitoring (ASRM) questionnaires to evaluate areas such as stress, recovery, fatigue, soreness, sleep, body weight, and health. A questionnaire developed by McLean and colleagues (2010) addresses most of these areas and can be easily adapted to utilize colors, words, and facial expressions to provide responses on a 5 point scale from bad (5, red, sad face) to neutral (3, blue, neutral face) to good (1, green, happy face) (figure 20.1). Other more comprehensive questionnaires to examine each area in more detail include the Profile of Mood Scores (POMS), Positive and Negative Affect Score (PANAS), and the Recovery Stress Questionnaire of Athletes (REST-Q-Sport) (Halson 2014).

Sleep is an important component of the recovery process, and reduced quantity and quality of sleep is a sign of a maladapted or stressed athlete. Monitoring sleep can involve the addition of a simple question in the screening tool or the use of a more comprehensive sleep questionnaire such as the Athlete Sleep Screening Questionnaire (ASSQ) (Bender et al. 2018). Noninvasive sleep monitoring technology such as actigraphy is also an option (Halson 2019), although this requires the purchase of equipment and a level of expertise to accurately measure, analyze, and interpret the correct parameters. Nevertheless, good sleep is important for athletes, so finding some way to accurately monitor sleep can add value to training.

Although questionnaires are simple to employ and can be useful, it is always a challenge to get the whole crew to regularly fill them out. The often-stated reasons for nonadherence are that the rowers do not see any value in questionnaires because the information the athletes provide in them is often not acted on by the coaches (Akenhead and Nassis 2016). Elite rowing coaches may be hesitant to implement and use these types of questionnaires because they believe they can see and hear directly from the athletes when fatigue, soreness, or stress levels get too high. Interviews were conducted with a group of highly successful international elite rowing coaches to get information on how they monitored fatigue in rowers without collecting any questionnaire or diary data. It was found that these coaches monitored the rowers through a combination of direct communication, evaluation of each session's training load, and observation of how individual rowers approached training and how intensely they

Key Point

Daily monitoring of various well-being metrics provides important insights into whether the rower perceives themselves to have achieved adequate recovery. This monitoring can be performed informally or formally using morning wellness inventories.

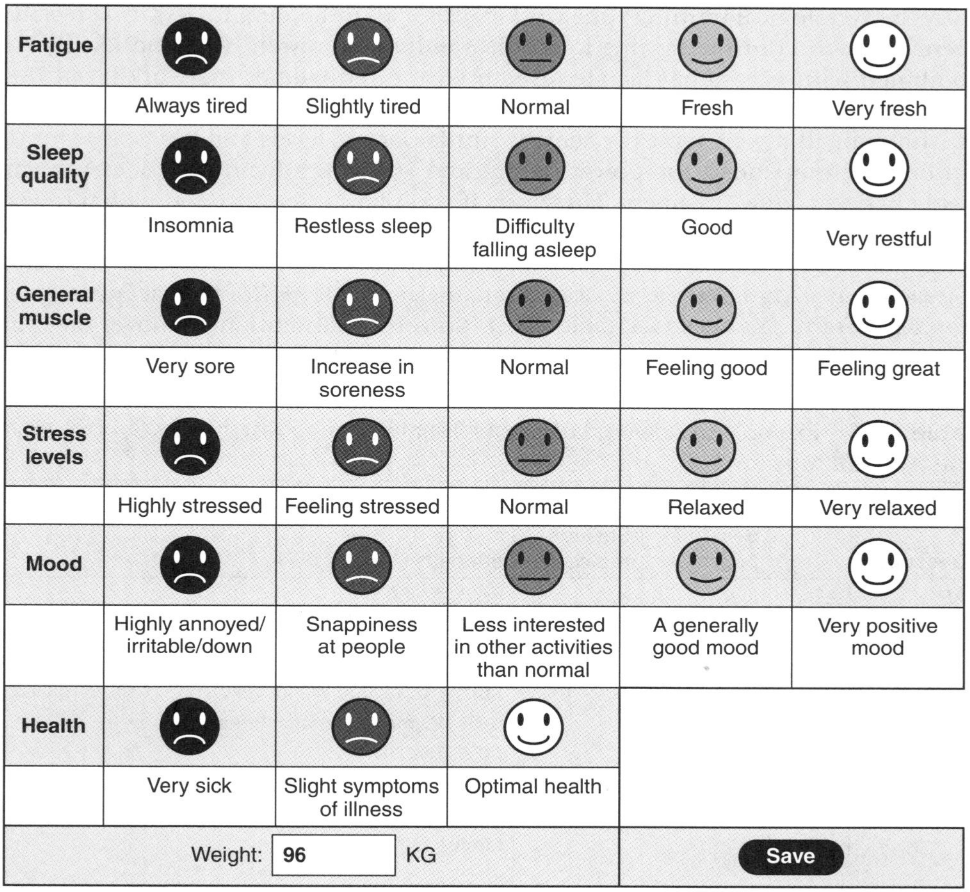

Fatigue					
	Always tired	Slightly tired	Normal	Fresh	Very fresh
Sleep quality					
	Insomnia	Restless sleep	Difficulty falling asleep	Good	Very restful
General muscle					
	Very sore	Increase in soreness	Normal	Feeling good	Feeling great
Stress levels					
	Highly stressed	Feeling stressed	Normal	Relaxed	Very relaxed
Mood					
	Highly annoyed/ irritable/down	Snappiness at people	Less interested in other activities than normal	A generally good mood	Very positive mood
Health					
	Very sick	Slight symptoms of illness	Optimal health		
	Weight: 96 KG				Save

▶ **Figure 20.1** Example of an interactive adapted version of the McLean et al. (2010) questionnaire.

Adapted by permission from B.D. McLean, A.J. Coutts, V. Kelly, et al., "Neuromuscular, Endocrine, and Perceptual Fatigue Responses During Different Length Between-Match Microcycles in Professional Rugby League Players," International Journal of Sports Physiology and Performance 5, no. 3 (2010): 367-383.

worked. The coach's intuition and experience helped them work through these various considerations to decide how to modify the team or individual training (Pope, Penney, and Smith 2018).

Training Zone Recommendations

The most common method of setting on-water training zones is to utilize set boat speeds and stroke rates for particular training zones (see table 20.1). There is a large range of accurate and inexpensive rowing speedometers and phone apps, although coaches should be aware of the limitations of these tools, especially on waterways with currents and in rough and windy conditions. Boat speed and stroke rate training zones are often set from aspirational targets and do not necessarily represent the correct physiological training zone workloads for all individual rowers in a crew. It is therefore useful during training to monitor individual rowers' RPE and ideally HR, combined with occasional lactate tests to ensure individuals are working in their correct training zones.

Although all rowers typically achieve similar lactate levels and RPE scores for the various training zones, the power output and HR values for these zones can vary vastly between crew members. Therefore, if you plan to monitor individual rowers' training HR and possibly power output (e.g., on rowing ergometer or via on-water force gates), then testing needs to be undertaken to accurately determine the values for each zone. Arguably the most accurate method is to perform a lactate step test to set the training zones (see table 20.3), however, as mentioned above, there are other possible options you may wish to explore. A simplified method was developed

Table 20.4 Example of Rowing Ergometer Training Zone Prescriptions Set by Stroke Rate and Wattage

Descriptors		FREQUENCY		Intensity
		Sessions per week	Session recovery	
AR	AR	N/A	N/A	≤60% 2,000 W Light RPE 8-9 16-20 spm
Zone 1	U2	6-12	12-24 h	~60%-70% 2,000 W, possibly ~55%-65% for males 60% $\dot{V}O_2$max to aerobic threshold 60%-70% HRR 1.2-1.5 mmol//L [La] ≤LT1 or ≤VT1 Moderate RPE 10-12 18-22 spm
Zone 2	AT	2- 3	48 h	~70%-80% 2,000 W, possibly ~65%-80% for males Anaerobic threshold 80%-85% HRR 4.0 mmol/L [La] LT2 or VT2 Hard RPE 16-17, 24-30 spm
Zone 3	LaT	1-2	48-72 h	~80%-95% 2,000 W 90%-100% HRR >6.0 mmol/L [La] >LT2 and >VT2 Very hard to extremely hard RPE 18-19 ≥30 spm
	LaP	1-2	72 h	~95%-105% 2,000 W Maximal HR Maximal [La] Extremely hard to maximal RPE 19-20 Max spm

100% W is the average wattage for the most current 2,000 m ergometer test of the rower.

These data were collected with the New Zealand Rowing team, who did not complete T1 or U1 ergometer training sessions.

using data from lactate testing, as well as 2,000 m and 60 min max ergometer tests collected over a period of 15 years. Average power and maximal heart rate measured during the various tests were compared to the maximal 2,000 m ergometer test data, which allowed a mathematical estimate of ergometer power and heart rate for all the training zones. Table 20.4 shows these rough training zone guidelines. It is interesting to note the difference between men and women—specifically, the women would train at a higher percentage of their 2,000 m ergometer power for aerobic base and sometime anaerobic threshold sessions compared to the men. One could argue that the women were of a higher standard than the men, but within the data set more men won Olympic medals, whereas World Championship senior A and senior B medal performance were approximately equal.

Monitoring Recommendations

An ideal rowing monitoring system should encompass several tools that fit within the program's resources and expertise. Best practice would be to have permanent calibrated force transducers attached to the footstretcher and oarlock or oar that enable the accurate measurement of force and power output for each rower during on-water rowing. Combined with measures of HR, RPE, and occasionally lactate, this would be a highly effective monitoring tool to compare external workload with internal physiological strain and perceived intensity. The combination of daily psychometric monitoring via questionnaire and regular end-of-mesocycle maximal performance or lactate testing to help monitor progress and evaluate training zones would round out the monitoring system. Furthermore, observing changes in HR, RPE, and lactate at set on-water training power output would enable best practice to monitor improved conditioning or excessive fatigue. The effectiveness of the system requires accounting for environmental conditions and other external factors that can affect these measures.

Key Point

The ideal monitoring tool involves combining performance, physiological, and psychological measures (e.g., increased workload with lesser or unchanged physiological and psychological strain suggests improved conditioning and vice versa).

It is not uncommon to find that the tests used to determine the training zones don't provide accurate zones for every member of the team. Rowers may struggle to achieve the calculated training zones' power outputs, HR, RPE, or lactate levels, or conversely the training zones may be too easy for them. Effective monitoring of all these metrics helps provide insights into individual differences and allow specific training modifications to support the rowers' progress. Unfortunately, large reductions in power output, La, and HR values below the training zone targets can be an indication of such diverse factors as laziness, incorrect training zones, ineffective technical application, or excessive fatigue. It remains a challenge for the coach to determine the cause while being aware of the dangers of making an incorrect diagnosis. For example, a rower who is unable to achieve the required training zones may be considered lazy, resulting in the coach working to motivate them, yet the rower may be suffering from low energy availability as a result of fatigue and stress-related appetite suppression, which inhibits recovery.

The reality is that most programs do not have the resources to use all these measures, but monitoring training is essential to inform any required training modifications. Therefore, effective monitoring should include end-of-mesocycle testing, regular monitoring of key training sessions, and possibly daily psychometrics. The end-of-mesocycle testing should consist of on-water performance measures to determine boat speed as well as individual rowing ergometer physiology and performance tests. The specific tests used depend on the stage of the season and should reflect the training component focus within each mesocycle. Examples of such tests could include lactate testing, strength and power testing, ergometer performance testing, and on-water racing.

Test protocols need to be tailored to the program's goals and resources. For example, if resources and time are limited, the following three maximal effort ergometer tests should cover most rowing specific conditioning aspects: 7 stroke test for maximum power, 500 m test for anaerobic capacity and endurance, and 30 to 60 min maximal ergometer test to estimate anaerobic threshold. As mentioned above, the results of a 30 min ergometer test with the stroke rate set at 20 spm have a very high correlation to the power output of the rower at 4 mmol/L lactate (note that they don't equal each other but do correlate strongly). This test is therefore a good surrogate for a lactate test as a measure of change in aerobic conditioning, and because the stroke rate is limited to 20 spm, this becomes a submaximal test, which is easier on the rowers than the 30 to 60 min maximal test at open stroke rate. Session monitoring could consist of recording on-water boat speed or ergometer output combined with RPE, HR, and possibly La measures. This would provide information on whether the rower's conditioning is progressing, enabling possible individualized interventions. Here, of course, the limitations of on-water workload measures of boat speed and stroke rate must be taken into account. If the requisite resources and expertise are available then perhaps a sRPE, TRIMP, or TSS monitoring system could be employed. Finally, a simple daily wellness questionnaire could be employed, ideally online or via an app to make the process simple for the rowers.

Conclusion

Many researchers have proposed that tracking changes in various physiological and psychological markers can be useful for monitoring performance and fatigue (Halson 2014; Smith, Hopkins, and Lowe 2011). For each training phase there is an optimum training load that could be defined by the apex of an inverted-U relationship between executed training and subsequent performance: Below the optimum load, the lower training stimulus results in smaller performance gain, whereas the stress of training above the optimum load results in severe fatigue, maladaptation, and decreased performance. Therefore, logic would suggest that training load should be reduced for rowers who suffer an extended bout of negative responses to an increased training load. Despite the large volume of research on monitoring athletes and the multitude of promoted metrics, especially in high-performance programs, there is unfortunately still no single valid and reliable method for monitoring training.

Research with the New Zealand rowing program found experimental and practical evidence that large increases in physiological and psychological stress markers may be more indicative of an effective training overload than impending maladaptation

(Smith, Hopkins, and Lowe 2011). It is possible that successful elite rowers may be hardened survivors who do not experience nonfunctional overreaching or overtraining syndromes, no matter how hard they train, as long as the additional stress of a chronic infection, overuse injury, or psychological trauma is avoided. The coaches of these athletes may well be sufficiently skilled to manage training load based on measures of boat speed and stroke rate, plus observation and communication. It is possible that this information combined with the coach's intuition, experience, and knowledge of their rowers may be a highly effective monitoring tool.

Although this approach may be effective for highly experienced, skilled, and successful elite rowing coaches, it is recommended that until a coach has reached that stage, they should consider a set of monitoring strategies that suit their expertise, resources, and the level of rowers they coach. Fundamentally, some regular measures of individual rowing performance need to be implemented along with strategies for understanding the rowers' training load, recovery, fatigue, stress, mood, soreness, sleep, and health. Whatever monitoring tools a coach decides on, they typically will only work if the rowers are engaged. A simple step to facilitate this is through effective communication with the rowers and collaborative solutions to any negative results.

Environmental Countermeasures

Stephen S. Cheung, PhD

Care is definitely required when exercising in extreme environments, but proper planning and precautions can still enable safe training and competition. Although performance will be reduced in hot weather, in polluted environments, and at altitude, the important aim is to treat it as a variable to adapt to rather than an obstacle to peak performance. A well-developed environmental countermeasures plan can also provide a psychological benefit by increasing athlete confidence, especially if rivals are not equally well prepared and confident in their ability to thrive in extreme conditions. This chapter complements the basic overview of extreme environments covered in chapter 13, providing practical strategies and advice for adapting training and competing to heat, pollution, and altitude, along with tips to use heat adaptation and altitude training to potentially enhance performance.

Cooling Strategies

The use of cooling protocols to improve performance or to counteract the risks of heat stress and hyperthermia has gained popularity among elite and even recreational athletes. Early adopters include the Australian rowing teams, who used vests containing ice packs during warm-ups before competing in the 1996 Atlanta Olympics. Since then, many elite athletes have used ice vests or cooling suits while warming up on stationary ergometers or on the water. Variations also include wearing lightweight cooling collars, dousing their heads with cool water, or using ice socks down their necks and backs to keep cool.

Precooling

Precooling is typically adopted to enhance athletic performance in hot environments rather than to increase the safety of exercising in such conditions. Precooling has regularly been shown to enhance endurance, exercise performance, and capacity in hot environmental conditions for exercise of moderate duration (e.g., 5 km run), though it may negatively impact strength and power-based efforts (Tyler, Sunderland, and Cheung 2015). An actual reduction in core temperature is not necessarily essential for precooling efficacy, which suggests that the benefit may also arise from reductions in skin temperature and the magnitude of perceived heat stress.

Ice vests are popular for precooling because they cover the important torso region and are relatively nonconstricting compared with wearing cooling pants. They also permit the legs to exercise and get the usual benefits of warming up before competition while keeping the torso as cool as possible. Precooling the legs may eliminate most of the benefits of warming up (refer to discussion in chapter 13 about the impaired capacity of cooled muscles). Cooling hoods are also common because they theoretically keep the brain cool, though direct evidence of this remains lacking. Regardless, the head and face play a major role in the overall perception of thermal stress and comfort, and cooling the head may achieve greater advantage by directly targeting the thermoregulatory centers in the brain and the high thermosensitivity associated with the head and neck. Head cooling may also protect some aspects of mental functioning when the extent of thermal strain is high, which is potentially a huge benefit in a sport with as many instantaneous decisions and technical adjustments as rowing. Possible methods of precooling and percooling (cooling during exercise) may therefore expand to include caps that have been wetted or frozen, sponges with cold water, or wetted towels draped over the torso.

Although head and neck cooling may make athletes feel better, it is unlikely to reduce the level of thermal or cardiovascular strain experienced, so this technique should not be used as a method to lower body temperature. When using these precooling methods, it is important for athletes to realize that the improved perceptual strain in the absence of physiological improvements may cause them to dangerously underestimate their degree of thermal strain. See chapter 13 for specific details on the symptoms of exertional heat illness.

Percooling has been studied less than precooling; however, the effects and mechanisms of action (reduced core and skin temperature, heart rate, thermal sensation, and perceived exertion) are likely similar. Although cooling during exercise can offer performance benefits, cooling jackets and vests can also increase the energy demands of exercise as a result of extra mass, create a microenvironment around the body that impairs evaporative heat dissipation, and cause discomfort and skin irritation.

Although some increase in body temperature during exercise is acceptable and even desirable, extreme temperatures impose extra stress on the body that diverts its focus from generating power at the muscles and delivering it to the oars. How can one apply some of the research on heat stress and cooling strategy to rowing?

- Exercise capacity is clearly reduced in both warm and hot environments. Therefore, it is important to anticipate this reduction when planning your training and racing. For example, when traveling to a hot environment to train or race, power or performance targets should be adjusted until full adaptation occurs.

- Although full adaptation in physiology and performance can occur within about 2 weeks, individual responses to heat and adaptation rate can differ greatly. It is therefore important to monitor individual responses to heat to make predictions—for example, by logging training and responses during the initial heat wave of the summer.

- Rowers should keep as cool as possible before an event. They should stay out of the sun and heat; every bit of heat exposure is unnecessary additional stress that detracts from training or recovery.

- Precooling can be useful when competing in hot environments, but it is not universally positive as an ergogenic aid. It appears to be most effective for events lasting 10 to 30 min, making it an ideal intervention for rowing. Cooling may also be effective in between competition heats. In contrast, if the goal is to maximize power output for brief periods during training, such as intervals simulating rowing starts, precooling may not be necessary or even desirable.

- Precooling or percooling the torso may strike the ideal balance between cooling the largest surface area without impeding the legs. Cooling the head and neck may improve perceptual sensations and performance despite only minimal impact on actual heat storage.

Heat Adaptation

Scientific research on heat stress, and specifically our physiological responses and adaptation to prolonged heat exposure, is quite well studied. In general, humans have a high ceiling for physiological adaptation to prolonged heat exposure. Some of the major adaptations include the following:

- A slight decrease in resting core temperature, theoretically permitting more heat storage before hyperthermia-induced exercise impairments occur and decreasing the risk of catastrophic exertional heat illness.

- An increase in plasma volume (the liquid component of blood), resulting in an elevated total blood volume. This decreases cardiovascular strain from pumping blood to both the muscle and skin, resulting in a lowered resting and exercise heart rate. Note that hemoglobin and red blood cells typically do not increase, so hematocrit generally decreases with heat adaptation. However, recent studies with very long (>5 week) heat adaptation protocols suggest an increase in total hemoglobin mass, possibly as a counterbalance to the reduced hematocrit.

- The beneficial sweat response adaptations include an earlier onset of sweating, a redistribution of the sweat response, and a conservation of sodium. Adapted individuals are able to dissipate heat more readily because they begin to sweat at a lower core temperature and sweat more from the limbs (the trunk is the main area of sweat loss for an unacclimatized individual), thus making better use of the skin surface area for evaporative heat loss. Of course, the disadvantage of enhanced sweating is that there is an increased rate of fluid loss from the body.

- Sweat becomes more diluted as the sweat glands become better at reabsorption of electrolytes. This helps to minimize overall electrolyte loss at a higher sweat rate.

- Both separately and in conjunction with these physiological changes, perceptual sensitivity to heat decreases, with athletes reporting a lower thermal discomfort and ratings of perceived exertion while resting or exercising in the heat.

Adaptation Timeline

Generally, the rate of heat adaptation follows an exponential path, initially increasing rapidly and then plateauing; however, the physiological adaptations to heat occur at differing rates. The most immediate adaptation is a reduction in heart rate, with most of the observed reduction occurring within 4 to 5 days and full acclimatization occurring after about 7 days of exposure, coinciding with the majority of the beneficial core and skin temperature reductions. Thermoregulatory adaptations take a little longer than cardiovascular ones, but when following a structured acclimatization protocol, full adaptation will often occur after 10 to 14 days of exposure. Maximal sweat response improvements may take a month and resistance to exertional heat illness may take twice that long.

Once heat adaptation is achieved and responses plateau, another important issue is the rate of decay of such adaptations, along with the reinduction of adaptation. Studies on heat adaptation decay are sparse compared to heat adaptation itself because of the difficulty of securing long-time commitment from participants and researchers. A meta-analysis on existing research suggests that, once fully heat adapted, decay is relatively prolonged and decreases roughly linearly, at 2.5% per day for heart rate and core temperature (Daanen, Racinais, and Périard 2018). No real research is currently available concerning the decay of sweating changes or actual performance. However, heat adaptation reinduction appears to occur quite rapidly even despite some state of decay. Overall, this suggests that heat adaptation can be periodized into a particular training cycle, and then maintained with periodic heat exposures (e.g., every 4-5 days).

Heat Acclimation Protocols

The devil is in the details for sport scientists when it comes to heat adaptation—specifically, what are the best and most efficient heat exposure protocols? How much daily exposure time or intensity is required for optimal adaptation? How do other individual factors (e.g., fitness, hydration) impact the rate of heat adaptation?

Core Body Temperature

The primary aim of heat adaptation protocols should be a consistent raising of core body temperature. The method by which this is achieved does not appear important, with similar magnitude and rate of physiological responses following 6 days of 1.5 °C core temperature elevations via water immersion, sauna, or exercise in humid conditions (Kissling et al. 2022). Similarly, specificity of the heat adaptation environment to the competition environment also appears irrelevant. Greifahn (1997) reported similar improvements in response to a heat stress test following 2 weeks of heat adaptation through exercise in either hot and dry, warm and humid, or high solar load environments at the same wet bulb globe temperature. Importantly, similar heat stress test responses were also found across heat adaptation environments (e.g., when the hot and dry group did the heat stress test in warm and humid conditions and vice versa).

Alternatives to Heat Facilities

If specialized heat facilities are not available and the additional time required for passive heat exposure is too restrictive, layering on heavy clothing and exercising indoors with reduced airflow may be a valid mode of heat adaptation. Similar physiological and performance gains were found with 10 days of moderate cycling in either 35 °C wearing normal training attire or in 19 °C but wearing heavy winter training attire (Lundby et al. 2021). Interestingly, no additional benefits were found with a third condition consisting of the clothing intervention with an additional 40 min of hot water immersion, suggesting that a ceiling of adaptation may exist in these already elite athletes. Therefore, the goal of heat adaptation should not be to blindly maximize heat stress.

Coordinate Adaptations With Training

Heat adaptation must be carefully scheduled and periodized into an annual training program, because it may not be possible to optimize both heat adaptation and training adaptation simultaneously. Slivka and colleagues (2021) reported that endurance exercise in 33 °C over 3 weeks blunted $\dot{V}O_2$max improvements compared to 20 °C endurance exercise. Furthermore, expression of the gene PGC-1α, a marker of mitochondrial development, was also blunted in the heat training group. This suggest that, when heat training, the focus on training adaptations needs to be deemphasized or scaled back.

Fitness Level and Gender Considerations

It remains unclear whether highly fit athletes acclimate to heat more quickly than less fit individuals, with no evidence of a fitness benefit observed across multiple physiological responses in a comprehensive meta-analysis (Tyler et al. 2016). In addition, relatively minimal research has been conducted specifically on female response to heat adaptation, but there is some evidence that, although the overall heat adaptation capacity remains similar across sexes, females may adapt at a slower rate. Notably, Mee and colleagues (2015) reported that male adaptation had largely plateaued after 5 days and was greater than females, but that the adaptation of females continued to increase over a further 5 days and matched the males after 10 days of heat adaptation.

Outlying Factors to Acclimatization

Factors such as alcohol consumption, sleep loss, and illness have all been linked to reductions in acclimatization-related benefits. Such factors should be carefully considered, especially when any acclimatization protocol causes significant disruption to the normal routine of the athlete (e.g., excessive travel and relocation associated with training camps).

Heat Adaptation and Temperate Performance

An interesting question is whether the adaptations caused by chronic heat exposure may lead to improved response and performance when returning to a more temperate environment. If this is the case, then heat adaptation protocols may serve a double benefit, enhancing performance across both temperate and hot environments. The first study testing this idea had trained cyclists heat adapt with 10 days of 1 h cycling at 50% $\dot{V}O_2$peak in 40 °C, then tested $\dot{V}O_2$peak and time trial performance in both cool (13 °C) and hot (38 °C) environments before and after. Time trial performance and lactate threshold all improved by approximately 5% to 8% in both cool and hot conditions, whereas no changes were reported in any variable in a control group performing 10 days of identical training in 13 °C (Lorenzo et al. 2010).

Despite these promising data, temperate benefits are not a universal finding. A logistically challenging field experiment on elite cyclists performed by a Qatari–Danish collaboration suggests that heat acclimatization can eventually restore performance to levels found in temperate conditions, but not exceed them. The second half of the field study tested whether the increased blood volume, higher sweat rate, and other heat adaptation responses helped the cyclists when they went back to Denmark and competed in a cool environment. The interesting answer is that no improvements in time trial performance were found compared to either the initial precamp test in Denmark or any of the time trials done in Qatar (Karlsen et al. 2015). This suggests that heat acclimatization is highly specific to a hot environment, and that it is not effective as an ergogenic tool for competitions in temperate environments.

Integrating the equivocal findings, it appears that heat adaptation is absolutely critical to optimize performance in the heat, requiring roughly 2 weeks for best effect.

In contrast, the physiological changes from heat adaptation may or may not actually improve performance in a temperate environment. However, there is no evidence that a state of heat adaptation is deleterious to temperate performance, so at worst there is no penalty except for the additional time cost.

Dehydration and Heat Adaptation

Although usually perceived as a negative health or performance risk, some research suggests that permitting a slight state of dehydration in conjunction with exercising in the heat may accelerate the rate of heat adaptation (Garrett et al. 2014). However, permissive dehydration should only be employed during the heat adaptation session itself, and it is important to ensure adequate rehydration after sessions to prevent chronic dehydration and maximize recovery.

Managing Air Pollution for Athletes

It is clear that air pollution, particularly acute exposure, can pose a challenge to the respiratory and circulatory systems and thus present a major obstacle for peak athletic performance. As long as logistics and marketing keep national and world championships—along with large multisport competitions—tied to major urban metropolises, air pollution is likely to remain an issue for elite athletes in the coming years. During smog alert days or periods when air quality is low, extra planning is required for both training and competition. The aim in this section is to outline some major considerations for planning and research.

Lessons From the Olympic Games in Beijing

The hosting of the 2008 Summer Olympics in Beijing, one of the world's most polluted megacities, instigated a thrust within the sport science community to understand the potential effects of air pollution on exercise. The pollution levels for ozone, carbon dioxide, sulfur dioxide, nitrogen oxides, and particulate matter were very close to or exceeded the standards set for long-term health in the general population by the U.S. Environmental Protection Agency, and the effects of this pollution would potentially be exacerbated by the high heat and humidity typical of Beijing in August.

The preparation and planning by sport agencies and athletes revolved primarily around avoiding arrival in Beijing until shortly prior to the actual competition times. For example, many teams traveled early to areas in or close to the same time zone as Beijing (e.g., Japan, South Korea, Singapore) for final training in the weeks before the Games, then arrived in Beijing very shortly (1-3 days) prior to their competition. Such an approach allowed athletes to adjust to the time change, temperature, and humidity conditions while avoiding prolonged pollution exposure. This practice was not universally adopted, however. The Swiss cyclist Fabian Cancellara arrived in Beijing a full 2 weeks before the road cycling events in order to adapt himself to the local environment, training for 4+ h/day outdoors in the Beijing area. Ultimately, Cancellara earned a bronze in the 6+ h cycling road race and gold in the time trial (~1 h duration). Such an accomplishment, with ventilation rates exceeding 100 L/

min, demonstrates the unique ability of humans to adapt to different environmental stressors.

The ultimate question posed by sport scientists is the effect of air pollution on actual sport performance. Judging from a survey of Olympic and world records, this impact is arguably mixed. Among indoor events, where there was some degree of air filtering along with climate control, multiple world records in both swimming and track cycling were shattered in Beijing. This would suggest that the continual improvements in training and technology were effective in improving and maximizing human capabilities. However, in outdoor running competitions, although Olympic records were broken in numerous events, it is perhaps notable that very few world records were broken. Olympic records were set by men in the 100, 200, 5,000, and 10,000 m events, along with the marathon and the 50 km race-walk. Of these, only the 100 and 200 m times were world records. On the women's side, Olympic records were set in the 3,000 m steeplechase, the 10,000 m run, and the 20 km race-walk, with only the steeplechase breaking a world record. It should be noted that world record performances are reliant on many factors, not the least of which are race dynamics. However, given the combination of multiple world records set indoors and relatively few outdoors, it can be argued that despite optimal preparation, the environmental conditions in Beijing may have limited performance capacity—only slightly, but just enough to minimize the potential for world record performances in outdoor events.

Preparing and Planning for Pollution

Sport scientists can plan ahead by performing sophisticated modeling of the pollution patterns of a competition site, as occurred prior to the Athens 2004 Olympics (Flouris 2006). This analysis, based on existing meteorological data for the greater Athens area from 1984 to 2003, was able to accurately predict O_3 and PM_{10} as the most problematic pollutants during the period before and throughout the Games. Furthermore, the model was able to break down pollution levels both throughout the 24 h cycle and for different regions of the city, including the northern region where the Olympic Village was located and the downtown area for many of the venues. Models of particulate matter concentrations, distribution, and emission sources were also developed prior to the Beijing 2008 Olympics. Such models can be used by athletes and teams to plan the timing, location, and intensity of training sessions or decide whether to train off-site completely and arrive shortly before competition.

To minimize pollutant exposure, athletes may consider moving some training sessions indoors, preferably to an air-conditioned facility in the summer so that temperature and humidity are controlled. Ideally, the incoming air is filtered to screen out particulates. This recommendation is obviously based on the assumption that the air quality of the indoor facility is adequate and does not present a different set of pollutants! However, research on the relative merits of exercise indoors versus outdoors in terms of total pollutant load during both smog alert and nonalert days remains lacking. Periods of high pollution levels or the need to exercise outdoors may necessitate the use of masks to filter out pollutants. These may range from simple gauze masks to sophisticated designs aimed at minimizing flow resistance or particular pollutants.

Although it may make little sense to unnecessarily expose athletes to air pollution long term, some short-term adaptation over 1 to 4 days prior to competition may help to alleviate some of the major inflammatory and respiratory responses with acute exposure to O_3 and other pollutants, along with psychologically habituating the athlete to the potential discomfort posed by the pollution. Keep in mind that any adaptation appears to be brief in duration, so such preexposure must happen immediately prior to competition. It should be possible to design this environmental acclimatization into an overall tapering regimen. For example, athletes might arrive on site 3 to 7 days prior to competition to begin their tapering. During this time, high-intensity training can be performed in a controlled environment, if possible. At the same time, passive exposure to the ambient environment during rest and recovery phases or active exposure during lower intensity training sessions may be used for acclimatization purposes. However, it must be noted that 3 days of 2 h passive exposure to 0.20 ppm of ozone did not provide any protective effect from acute exposure to higher levels of ozone (0.42 or 0.50 ppm) compared to no preexposure, with the high ozone doses eliciting similar levels of spirometric impairment (e.g., FEV_1) with or without preexposure (Gliner, Horvath, and Folinsbee 1983). Therefore, passive acclimatization to low effective doses may not ultimately translate to competition at high exercise intensities.

Secondhand Smoke and Exercise

Even with a nonsmoking lifestyle, athletes can become exposed to high levels of secondhand tobacco smoke (e.g., through travel or roommates), which could lead to acute decreases in functional capacity and performance. Direct research on the effects of passive smoking on exercise capacity in healthy nonsmoking athletes is nonexistent, though indirect evidence exists for a number of physiological changes with acute passive exposure that may relate to exercise capacity in athletes. Unknown are the effects of chronic passive smoke exposure on exercise capacity during growth and development in children and adolescents. Nonetheless, the copious literature on the effects of secondhand smoke makes it highly likely that the long-term potential for athletic development would be compromised in some fashion.

Antioxidant Supplementation

It is evident from chapter 13 that O_3 can impair pulmonary function and potentially exercise capacity. It may also appear that pollutants are a systemic problem whose effects can only be minimized rather than neutralized. However, besides the avoidance and management of exposure, one potential area of interest is the use of nutritional countermeasures such as vitamins and antioxidants. Because one of the proposed pathways for pollutant damage is through inflammation within the cells of the lungs and respiratory pathways, it has been suggested that antioxidants may minimize oxidative stress. The exact biochemical mechanism for antioxidant protection from pollution remains unclear, but may revolve around attenuating the ozone-induced production of arachidonic acid, which may in turn also decrease central neural inhibition of ventilation.

Grievink and colleagues (1998) studied the effects of 3 months of beta-carotene and vitamins C and E versus no supplementation on a group of amateur Dutch racing cyclists. Lung function measures were taken posttraining and postcompetition on 4 to 14 occasions per subject over this period, with the results regressed over the previous 8 h average ozone level, which in turn averaged 101 mg/m³ across the two groups. Pulmonary function, including FVC, FEV_1, and peak expiratory flow, decreased with increasing O_3 levels in the control group. This was significantly different from findings for the supplementation group, which experienced no reduction in pulmonary function with increasing O_3 levels. In a subsequent study, the same research group examined a placebo versus vitamin C and E supplementation (Grievink et al. 1999) in another cohort of amateur racing cyclists. Similar results were obtained, with progressive decrement in FEV_1 and FVC during exposure to O_3 levels of 100 mg/m³ in the placebo group but no decrements in the supplementation group. Subjects in both of these Dutch cycling studies stopped taking vitamin and mineral supplements prior to the study and abstained throughout the study; however, the typical dietary intake of the subjects was not reported, so existing diet could potentially have confounded the results. However, the magnitude of supplementation was relatively small, at 500 to 650 mg and 75 to 100 mg for vitamins C and E, respectively, and the utility of such conclusions is that these may be less than the amounts commonly available in many supplements. A more recent study testing 2 weeks of vitamin C and E or placebo supplementation found that, following an 8 km running time trial in a hot and humid (31 °C, 70% relative humidity) and polluted (0.1 ppm O_3) chamber, lung injury markers were lower in the vitamin group (Gomes et al. 2011). However, no differences were seen in 8 km running times.

Antioxidant supplementation may also prove beneficial as short-term protection for support staff exposed to high levels of ozone. Mexico City street workers, tested in a placebo-crossover study, took a supplement consisting of beta-carotene and vitamins C and E or a placebo (Romieu et al. 1998). Protective effects similar to those previously discussed were observed in the supplement group versus the placebo group. Interestingly, after crossing over into the second phase of the study, the group that had received the supplementation first showed lower lung function decrements than the group receiving the placebo first had shown during the first phase. This suggests that antioxidants have a washout period, resulting in a slight residual protective effect. Overall, it appears that moderate vitamin intake, either via alterations in diet or through supplementation, may prove valuable for athletes and support staff preparing for competition in polluted regions as well as for individuals chronically exposed to elevated ozone levels.

Applying Altitude Training

For athletes, coaches, and exercise scientists, the vast body of literature available on altitude training, along with the multiple modalities and tools available, makes it difficult to answer the simple question: How high and for how long should altitude or hypoxia be used to achieve performance benefits? The answer is obviously modulated by individual factors, such as individual responsiveness, competitive demands, competition altitude, and training status. Although the efficacy of altitude training does not appear to be universal for all individuals, it is nevertheless likely to remain popular among rowers and other athletes due to its relative accessibility, generally perceived efficacy, and legality.

Dose and Duration of Hypoxic Training

Findings with short-term exposures have prompted many investigators to suggest that athletes must reach a cumulative hypoxic threshold, which is a function of the living altitude and the number of hours per day spent there, in order to realize gains in hemoglobin mass and endurance performance. Indeed, successful studies incorporating simulated high altitude (normobaric hypoxia) have required over 14 h/day of hypoxic exposure above a simulated ~2,000 m altitude above sea level, suggesting that without access to terrestrial high altitude, prolonged confinement to a hypoxic facility is required to foster any benefit to this approach. When multiple studies from the same research group were collated, red blood cell volume was shown to be elevated similarly at 1,780, 2,085, 2,454, or 2,800 m. However, though $\dot{V}O_2$max is also elevated after sleeping at all altitudes, 3,000 m time trial was only improved after the intermediate altitude camps (2,085 and 2,454 m) (Chapman et al. 2016). Another meta-analysis suggests that hemoglobin mass increases by ~1.1% for every 100 h spent at altitude (ranging from 2,320 to 3,000 m) (Chapman et al. 2014). Ultimately, it seems that athletes need to spend over 14 h/day at altitudes ranging from 2,000 to 2,500 m for about 2 to 4 weeks in order to significantly increase hemoglobin mass, $\dot{V}O_2$max, and possibly performance.

Decay of Altitude Adaptations

Upon attainment of any adaptive response, another consideration for athletes training for competition is how long the improved response may be maintained after the cessation of training—or in this case, upon return to low altitude. There is minimal agreement or consensus on this given the high degree of individual variability in response and lack of a single defined mechanism of action. Chapman and colleagues (2016) concluded that, following an altitude camp, athletes should either aim to return to competition altitude and compete very shortly afterwards (e.g., 2-3 days) or else within a time range of 14 to 21 days. That advice largely comes from the experience of elite athletes, who often experience wide fluctuations in perceptual sensations and performance capacity in the first 2 weeks of return from altitude. This is balanced by eventual deacclimatization from altitude, with hemoglobin mass remaining high over the first 14 days and then contracting over time.

Similar to the marked variability in initial acclimatization to altitude, it is likely that these and other physiological responses to deacclimatization display large individual variation, and as such, careful measurements and individual responses should be considered to optimize performance. For example, those individuals who experience rapid loss of hemoglobin mass should return to low altitude closer to competition than those individuals who experience delayed loss of ventilatory acclimatization and require more time for these changes to dissipate. Other questions include whether periodic hypoxic exposures at less frequent intervals can maintain acclimatization following descent and what the time course is for reinduction of hematological and nonhematological responses. These questions have become especially relevant with the emerging prevalence of portable hypoxic facilities, such that athletes may be able to receive periodic doses to potentially "top up" their hypoxic responses even while traveling throughout the training year or during prolonged competitions.

Transition From Sea Level to Altitude

For competitions at altitude, it would appear that acclimatization should take place at levels as close as is reasonable or practical to the competition altitude. But when this is not possible, when is the best time to arrive at the competition venue? Should athletes arrive at altitude as long as possible beforehand to acclimatize and possibly suffer the consequences of lower training capacity and fitness, or should they attempt a "commando mission" approach and arrive at altitude as close to competition time as possible? A 2001 study by Weston and colleagues addressed this question by testing 15 native lowlander rugby players at sea level, then transporting them rapidly to a test center at 1,700 m (5,580 ft) altitude, where they underwent testing again at 6, 18, and 47 h after ascent. In this way, the timing of ascent simulated typical arrival times for a 3 p.m. competition. For example, the 6 hr trial simulated arriving at altitude at 9 a.m. for a 3 p.m. event, and the 47 h trial simulated arrival at 10 p.m. two nights before the event. The study therefore also provided information on the time course of performance upon the first few days of altitude exposure. No change to hematocrit or hemoglobin occurred with arrival to altitude. Heart rates were significantly higher during a submaximal cycle test at 6 h compared with sea level (182 vs. 177 bpm), but returned to "normal" at 18 and 47 h (177 and 176 bpm, respectively). Only five subjects could complete the test trial at the 6 h trial compared to nine at sea level. The same pattern in heart rates was found for the four trials with a shuttle run aerobic capacity test. The tolerance time for the shuttle test was 37% shorter at 6 h compared to sea level. Although it improved with the 18 and 47 h tests, tolerance times for both remained lower than at sea level. A similar pattern of initial impairment and some level of recovery with 45 h of short-term altitude acclimatization was reported with exposure to 3,200 m (10,500 ft) in 5 and 50 min cycling tests (Burtscher et al. 1996). Interestingly, no decrement was reported with a 30 s cycling test upon initial and short-term exposure, suggesting that anaerobic-based exercise is not affected by moderate altitude.

Overall, the results of these studies led to the conclusion that athletes should try to arrive as early as possible at the competition altitude to allow time to acclimatize to the hypoxia. Fortunately, even if logistics preclude early travel, the popularity of hypoxic tents among elite athletes makes acclimatization easier to achieve. However, potential problems from jet lag will still persist if athletes adapt at home and then have to cross many time zones to compete. Perhaps not surprisingly, giving the complexity of the topic, recent recommendations propose that altitude training in elite endurance athletes should involve both long- and short-term inclusion and periodization of hypoxic stimulus, integrating manipulation of exercise training and recovery, performance peaking, adaptation monitoring, nutritional approaches, and the use of normobaric hypoxia in conjunction with terrestrial altitude (Mujika, Sharma, and Stellingwerff 2019).

Living–Training Hypoxic Models

Over the years, a number of methods for exposing athletes to hypoxia have been identified, including living and training at high altitude (LHTH); living at high altitude and training at low altitude (LHTL); and living at low altitude and training at high altitude (LLTH). Various studies, with mixed findings, have been undertaken to investigate each of these training paradigms and are briefly summarized next.

Live High–Train High

The concept of LHTH has not received the same degree of scientific inquiry as the other paradigms, likely as a result of reduced training intensities at high altitude. Some studies suggest there may be benefits associated with the LHTH approach. For example, Daniels and Oldridge (1970) studied U.S. national team distance runners who completed two 14-day LHTH blocks at 2,300 m (7,545 ft) separated by a 5 day period during which the athletes competed in elite events. Competitions also occurred in the 5 days following the second 14-day LHTH block. Aerobic capacity testing following the initial and final LHTH blocks elicited a 4% and 5% increase, respectively, in $\dot{V}O_2$max compared to sea-level baseline values. Exercise performance also benefited, with a significant 3% improvement in 3 mi (4.8 km) race pace at the end of all LHTH blocks. From an applied perspective, the most important finding was that the majority of the athletes set and further bested their personal records in competition over the course of the study. However, caveats do need to be raised with this study, primarily the lack of a control group of elite athletes training at a sea-level camp.

College runners ($\dot{V}O_2$max ~65 mL/kg/min) can also see improvements in hemoglobin mass and sea-level $\dot{V}O_2$max after 4 weeks of high-altitude (~2,500 m) training (Levine and Stray-Gundersen 1997); however, 5,000 m distance running performance was not improved. Hemoglobin mass is also increased in Olympic swimmers after 3 weeks of living and training between 2,130 and 3,094 m, albeit with no improvements in swimming $\dot{V}O_2$peak and marginal improvement in some performance metrics (Bonne et al. 2014). Despite these positive studies, other LHTH studies have not shown evidence of performance benefits, especially when the athletes reside at altitudes below ~2,000 m. This is consistent with one of the early classic studies that, employing a repeated-measures crossover design following 3 training weeks at sea level or at 2,300 m (7,545 ft), concluded there was no effect of LHTH on $\dot{V}O_2$max or performance time in trained male distance runners (Adams et al. 1975).

Live High–Train Low

The late 1990s saw a new paradigm emerge in altitude training. In order to maximize the physiological adaptation from exposure to hypoxia yet minimize the reduction in exercise capacity typically observed at altitude, Levine and Stray-Gundersen (1997) suggested that if athletes were acclimatized to a moderate altitude (2,500 m), but trained at lower altitude (1,500 m) for 6 weeks, they could get the best of both worlds and improve their performance more than equivalent control groups at sea level and altitude who lived and trained at the same elevation. In addition to a variety of physiological measurements, a 5,000 m running time trial was the main measure of performance. Both altitude training groups improved hemoglobin mass and sea-level $\dot{V}O_2$max, but only the runners who "lived high and trained low" showed an increase in 5,000 m performance.

Live Low–Train High

To reduce the significant time and financial burden of the LHTL protocol on athletes, efforts have been made to generate similar physiologic benefits with shorter exposures to hypoxia. Moreover, the development of hypoxic facilities within the last two decades has prompted the implementation of the live low–train high (LLTH) methods, whereby normobaric hypoxia is achieved through either O_2 filtration or nitrogen dilution. While living at sea level, athletes receive intermittent exposure to hypoxia (IH) either at rest or during exercise training sessions. Different LLTH protocols exist, utilizing either physiologically systemic (e.g., intermittent hypoxic training, repeated sprint training in hypoxia, or resistance training in hypoxia) or local (e.g., blood flow restriction and ischemic preconditioning) hypoxia.

Initially, IH studies were designed based on observations from animal studies, with the general approach of exposing athletes to very short intermittent periods of severe hypoxia. Human studies in which athletes were exposed to hypoxia-to-normoxia ratios of 5:5 and 6:4 min once per day for 2 to 4 weeks showed little improvement in performance or physiological variables. Slightly longer exposures of a few hours each over several weeks have elicited increases in erythropoietin—the hormone that signals red blood cell production—but not actual markers of red cell production, submaximal economy, or performance.

Some investigators have attempted to utilize doses of hypoxia during training sessions to achieve a training advantage. However, high-intensity bouts of exercise with integrated exposures to simulated altitude seem to elicit no change in aerobic capacity, at least over training periods of about 6 weeks. In general, studies suggest that although short-term exposure to hypoxia during intense training may favorably alter skeletal muscle adaptations (e.g., glycolytic enzyme activity, mitochondrial function, mRNA level), there seems to be no discernible overlap of these benefits toward enhanced endurance performance, especially in well-trained athletes (Mujika, Sharma, and Stellingwerff 2019).

Performing repeated maximal effort sprints under hypoxic conditions (RSH) with the aim of maintaining training intensity and improving normoxic sprint performance has also been used to test the efficacy of the LLTH paradigm. The physiological underpinnings of this approach are not based on hematological adaptations, as the hypoxic exposure is too short, but is potentially multifactorial and similar to IH training. The first study in this area showed promise, with RSH conveying greater improvements in maximal repeated sprint performance and resistance to fatigue in normoxia (Faiss, Girard, and Millet 2013). Although other studies have also found improvements in fatigue resistance and sport-specific sprint training with RSH, like classic LHTL, the field of intermittent hypoxic training and RSH has been plagued with large individual variability and difficulty with repeatability between and within research groups. Thus, similarly to LHTL, a debate on the utility of the LLTH approach persists. More research is needed to provide information on the merits, if any, of newer approaches such as resistance training in hypoxia or local (blood flow restriction) and ischemic preconditioning.

Conclusions on the Benefits of Altitude Training

At present, the literature does not provide a definitive answer as to whether different forms of altitude training provide clear performance gains to all athletes. Full acclimatization to moderate altitude consistently increases hemoglobin mass, and training in hypoxia can promote advantageous adaptations in skeletal muscle, both of which should theoretically improve performance. However, when appropriate controls are included and the increased training load in participants of LHTL camps taken into account, the results have been variable and less impressive, particularly given the challenges of quantifying performance improvements with large between-subject variability. Finally, reproducibility is a challenge, because the individual response of both hemoglobin mass and performance to altitude camps is not consistent. It would seem that standardization of hypoxic dose metrics would help establish clear guidelines for altitude training prescription, which includes the potential for a targeted approach based on individual response patterns. This information would help provide a stronger framework for interpreting and comparing different training protocols employed in research and practice.

Hyperoxia and Performance?

A large body of evidence shows that maximal performance acutely increases during the breathing of supplemental oxygen (Mallette, Stewart, and Cheung 2018). A minimum threshold of 30% F_iO_2 appears to be required for benefit, with a moderate positive dose-dependent relationship with higher oxygen concentrations. The mechanism of benefit does not appear to lie with increases in central cardiopulmonary capacity, but possibly in peripheral extraction at the muscles. Only a limited number of studies have explored prolonged training with hyperoxia with unclear results. However, one key consideration is that the higher workload possible with hyperoxia needs to be balanced with adequate recovery to avoid risk of injury or overtraining.

Conclusion

Environmental factors such as temperature extremes, pollution, and altitude inarguably impact and impair performance, but they do not preclude the ability to achieve a peak performance on race day. Rather than view these stressors as a firm negative, it is important to optimize one's ability to compete as well as possible despite such challenges. The best method of preparation for competing in the heat is to incorporate a program of heat adaptation leading up to race day, along with performing race-day interventions such as pre- and percooling. Preparing for polluted environments largely involve avoiding exposure to pollution as much as possible beforehand. Finally, whether competing at altitude or sea level, altitude training may provide a physiological and performance benefit, although high interindividual variability in responses means that experimentation may be required to develop an optimized individual program. Using environmental stressors as an adaptive stimulus will provide a psychological advantage over competitors who do not properly prepare.

Recovery

Ed McNeely

Sport training programs are designed to create stress and subsequent adaptations in an athlete, leading to improved performance. Hans Selye (1936) was the first to describe the adaptive nature of a living organism in response to stress. As described in chapter 14, Selye's three-stage response to nocuous agents—general alarm reaction, resistance, and exhaustion, became known as the general adaptation syndrome (GAS) and has been used extensively in exercise science to form a central theory in the periodization of training (Bompa and Haff 2009; Haff 2016).

The accumulated exposure to various stressors results in fatigue. Although a certain level of fatigue that results in functional overreaching (i.e., a short-term decrement in performance that is not accompanied by negative health outcomes) is required for performance enhancement (Kellman et al. 2018), excessive fatigue leads to overtraining syndrome. The optimization of training adaptations and the prevention of overtraining syndrome are the goals of a comprehensive recovery program.

Key Point

Stress is a nonspecific response, meaning that there are some common responses to all forms of stressors. For athletes, this means that the stress of training, competition, school, exams, relationships, work, and money can all contribute to an overall stress load.

Monitoring Stress and Recovery

There are a variety of ways to monitor stress and recovery, including physiological, biochemical, perceptual, and performance measures (Saw, Main, and Gastin 2015a). Significant research has been done to determine physiological and biochemical markers of fatigue, including hormonal, hematological, inflammatory, and immune measures (Hooper et al. 1995; Hug et al. 2003; Lehman et al. 1998; Petibois et al. 2003; Robson 2003; Smith 2000; Urhausen, Gabriel, and Kindermann 1995). However, results have been mixed, with no single or combination of markers emerging as a clear and consistent indicator of training stress or fatigue. Physiological and biochemical measures also tend to be invasive, disruptive to training sessions, and expensive, putting them out of reach for most rowers and rowing programs.

Performance measures through competitive results, simulated competitions, or maximal physical capacity tests like vertical jump are often used to assess fatigue or staleness (Thorpe et al. 2017; Watkins et al. 2017). Although race results provide the clearest picture of whether a rower's performance has improved, the short and compressed competitive season that some rowers face makes them less useful for adjusting a program. Simulated competitions or performance tests like a 2,000 m or 6,000 m test—either on water or using an ergometer—are good alternatives if there is a standardized protocol to control the volume and intensity of training in the days leading up to the test.

Daily or weekly vertical jump measures on a force plate have been suggested as a method of measuring neuromuscular readiness and fatigue in team sports (Watkins et al. 2017) and is commonly used in many strength and conditioning settings. Because the daily vertical jump score is compared to a previous baseline or rolling average, there needs to be a high level of repeatability or reliability; otherwise it is hard to tell if the changes in jump score are from fatigue or inconsistent technique. Scores from a peak power ergometer test may provide similar data in a more rowing-specific manner, because many rowers do not jump enough to have a consistent jump technique.

Done at the start of the first training session of the day following a good warm-up, the peak power test involves a 10 s maximum effort at a stroke rate of 40 spm with a drag factor of 200 on the Concept2 ergometer. Rowers are required to row full slide and only wattages at 40 spm are counted. Perform 3 trials, with the highest wattage for the day recorded and used in the analysis. Table 22.1 shows sample data from a 21-day training period. The daily peak power score is compared to a 14-day rolling average (RA score). A z-score, which is a measure of how many standard deviations below or above the population mean the result lies, is calculated and any z-value below -2 on consecutive days requires attention and adjustment to the training program.

Key Point

Consistency is key to using peak power data for monitoring fatigue and recovery. It is important to emphasize that the goal of the peak power test is to use the technique and rhythm similar to what would be used in a normal training session, rather than pulling as hard as possible with no regard for technique.

Supplementing physiological and performance measures with athlete self-report monitoring (ASRM) questionnaires provides a more complete look at athletes' stress levels and has been shown to be better than physiological and performance measures for monitoring fatigue, staleness, and overtraining in athletes (Saw, Main, and Gastin 2016). ASRM questionnaires typically ask an athlete to rate their mood, stress, muscle soreness, fatigue, motivation, and sleep (McGuigan 2017). A variety of validated questionnaires are available, including mood state questionnaires like the Profile of Mood States (POMS) and Brunel Mood Scale (BRUMS), the Training Distress Scale (TDS), Hooper Index, Daily Analysis of Life Demands for Athletes (DALDA), and the Recovery Stress Questionnaire (REST-Q).

When choosing an ASRM questionnaire, consider the ease of use. Saw, Main, and Gastin (2015a, 2015b) found that the time to complete, question structure, mode of use, accessibility, and the user interface all play a role in how compliant athletes are with

Table 22.1 Peak Power Data Over a 21-Day Period

Daily score (W)	RA score (W)	Standard deviation (W)	Change in power (W)	z-score
598	584	16.3	13.9	0.86
553	581	18.8	−28.4	−1.51
604	584	20.0	20.5	1.03
572	581	20.0	−9.4	−0.47
575	583	19.0	−7.7	−0.40
552	582	20.3	−29.7	−1.46
560	581	21.2	−20.5	−0.97
553	577	22.6	−24.1	−1.07
588	577	22.7	10.6	0.47
578	573	18.0	4.7	0.26
597	573	17.9	23.8	1.33
618	580	20.9	38.3	1.83
618	581	22.9	36.9	1.61
602	584	23.4	17.9	0.76
609	588	24.3	21.5	0.88
580	590	21.5	−10.3	−0.48
588	593	19.1	−5.1	−0.27
609	599	14.1	10.3	0.73
595	599	13.7	−4.4	−0.32
515	593	28.5	−78.1	−2.74
495	583	40.9	−87.9	−2.15

an ASRM program. In some cases, you may not feel that published and validated questionnaires meet the needs of your athletes or sport. Survey data on high-performance programs suggests that this is quite common, with up to 80% of sport practitioners developing their own questionnaires (Taylor et al. 2012).

Many of the questionnaires that practitioners develop are a modified version of the work done by Hooper and colleagues (1995). Their work employed a variety of measures to assess staleness and recovery of swimmers throughout a season. Their work included measures of plasma lactate, creatine kinase, urinary protein, and erythrocyte and leukocyte counts, as well as performance trials, competitive performances, and a logbook that included subjective ratings of quality of sleep, fatigue, stress, and muscle soreness. Ratings used a 1 to 7 scale with 1 being very, very low or good and 7 being very, very bad or high. This was one of the first studies to demonstrate the usefulness of self-reported measures for reliably differentiating between stale and nonstale athletes—those athletes who were on the verge of overtraining—with the self-report measures outperforming heart rate, blood pressure, and blood lactate for differentiating between stale and nonstale athletes.

An example of a questionnaire can be seen in table 22.2. The ratings are on a 1 to 7 scale as in the original Hooper and colleagues (1995) study. Sleep duration (recorded to the nearest 15 min) is often collected as a supplement to the questionnaire.

Table 22.2 Self-Report Questionnaire

HOW FATIGUED DO YOU FEEL?						
Not at all fatigued		A little fatigued		Somewhat fatigued		Very fatigued
1	2	3	4	5	6	7
HOW STRESSED DO YOU FEEL?						
Not at all stressed		A little stressed		Somewhat stressed		Very stressed
1	2	3	4	5	6	7
HOW WELL ARE YOU SLEEPING?						
Very well		Well		Not very well		Very poorly
1	2	3	4	5	6	7
DO YOUR MUSCLES FEEL SORE?						
Not at all sore		A little sore		Somewhat sore		Very sore
1	2	3	4	5	6	7
ARE YOU ENJOYING TRAINING?						
Very much		A little		Not really		No
1	2	3	4	5	6	7
ARE YOU IRRITABLE?						
Not at all irritable		A little irritable		Somewhat irritable		Very irritable
1	2	3	4	5	6	7
DO YOU FEEL HEALTHY?						
Very healthy		A little		Not really		No
1	2	3	4	5	6	7
DO YOU FEEL RESTED?						
Very rested		A little		Not really		No
1	2	3	4	5	6	7

Ed McNeely

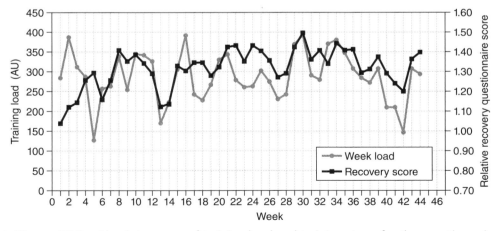

▶ **Figure 22.1** Absolute scores of training load and training stress for the questionnaire in table 22.2 in a group of international female rowers.

If a self-report questionnaire is developed, make sure that the results make sense. Plot the results of the recovery questionnaire against training load to see if the load and reported recovery or training stress trend as expected. Figure 22.1 shows a plot of training load and training stress for the questionnaire in table 22.2 in a group of international female rowers.

Using the Self-Report Monitoring Data

Given the growth in technology and the development of athlete monitoring apps, ASRM questionnaires would appear to be a relatively simple way to collect stress data. However, collection of the data is only part of the workflow required to make effective use of an ASRM tool. Data analysis and feedback can become time consuming if processes are not automated. The quality of the feedback and actionable insights that are delivered to both coaches and athletes will determine the acceptance and usefulness of an ASRM program.

Compliance is crucial for the results of an ASRM questionnaire to be meaningful and useful. Hopkins (1998) has suggested a compliance rate of at least 70% for questionnaire-based monitoring for analysis to provide meaningful information.

Compliance can vary widely depending on the level of play, sport context, and whether the monitoring program is supported by a coach. Saw, Main, and Gastin (2015b) examined the use of an ASRM questionnaire among 16- to 18-year-old athletes, finding that 53% chose to use the questionnaire. Of the 131 athletes in the study, 80% who were supported by a coach used the ASRM questionnaire, whereas only 50% of those who were self-directed did so. They found compliance rates of 83.6 ± 21.2% for team sport athletes who were supported by a coach, compared to an overall compliance rate of 42.5 ± 43.5%.

Key Point

ASRM tools can provide valuable data for monitoring recovery and training load and have become commonplace in many sports. Before adopting or developing an ASRM tool, understand that there is a time cost. Plan to spend 2 to 5 minutes per day per athlete to analyze each score, compare it to previous data, look for trends, provide feedback to the athlete, and plan adjustments to the program if needed. This may not sound like much, but with 12 athletes, as much as an hour per day would be required for ASRM data analysis.

Many of the apps and software commonly used to collect ASRM data use dashboards to automate some of this process, but they are no replacement for a thorough analysis of the data by someone who knows the athletes, training environment, and training plan.

Berglund and Safstrom (1994) used the POMS total mood disturbance scores to evaluate the training load and training stress of elite canoeists training for the 1992 Barcelona Olympics. Training programs were modified based on two criteria: Training was decreased if the POMS score was more than 50% above the off-season baseline; and training load was increased if the POMS score was less than 10% above the off-season baseline. They found that 12% of the POMS ratings suggested that the athletes were at risk of developing staleness, with 64% of the athletes reducing their training load at some point in the season because of an elevated POMS score. Changes in mood occurred within 3 to 4 days of decreasing training load and returned to normal in all but one case within a week of reducing training volume.

Although Berglund and Safstrom (1994) used the POMS scores to create a set of stress zones, the same concept can be applied to other practitioner-developed questionnaires like the one described in table 22.2. Establish a baseline during the transition phase between training years when the athlete is well recovered, rested, and not undergoing formal training. Use the average of the 10 lowest scores as the baseline. Note that individual baselines can vary from athlete to athlete and provide a better picture of accumulated fatigue and the recovery capacity of an athlete than raw scores. Table 22.3 shows baseline values for a group of rowers.

Table 22.3 Individual Baselines and Stress Zones

Athlete	Baseline	STD	1.1× baseline	1.5× baseline
1	25	2.63	27.5	37.5
2	21	4.03	23.1	31.5
3	23	2.56	25.3	34.5
4	18	3.15	19.8	27
5	19	1.56	20.9	28.5
6	22	1.2	24.2	33
7	19	2.16	20.9	28.5
8	14	3.2	15.4	21
9	31	2.59	34.1	46.5
10	17	2.37	18.7	25.5
11	29	3.28	31.9	43.5
12	18	4.77	19.8	27
13	19	3.07	20.9	28.5
14	14	3.14	15.4	21
15	16	2.44	17.6	24

Note: A maximum score is 56.

Key Point

Whether you decide to use individual baselines or rolling averages for comparison of daily scores to previous data depends on the purpose of the questionnaire or data. Individual baselines work better for recovery data, whereas rolling averages can be useful for load data.

From there, daily or weekly average scores can be converted to multiples of the baseline (weekly average relative scores) and plotted, as shown in figure 22.2. Three zones can be developed from this data: an overreaching zone (above 1.5× baseline), an adaptation zone (1.1×-1.5× baseline) and a recovery zone (below 1.1× baseline).

Short periods of overreaching are necessary to drive training adaptations, so individual days where a recovery questionnaire score exceeds 1.5× baseline are not concerning, but if the score remains high for 3 or more consecutive days it is worth considering an adjustment to the training program. Although there is very little published research on long-term recovery and adaptation in rowers, data collected over several years on a group of international rowers have shown that physiological adaptations as measured by a lactate step test are affected by the pattern of days with questionnaire totals above 1.5× individual baselines.

▶ **Figure 22.2** Weekly average relative scores from ASRM questionnaires with upper and lower stress zone borders.

Changes in wattage at 2, 4, and 6 mmol/L La from 185 step tests were examined over a period of 3 years. Using the criteria that a change occurred when there was a wattage difference of ±6 W at two of the three lactate points (anything less was considered no change), the following findings were established:

- Athletes who had 10% or more days between tests with a questionnaire score at or above 1.5× baseline showed a decrease in performance 54.7% of the time and no change in performance 40.9% of the time compared to their previous test. Only 4.4% of the time was there an improvement with this pattern of questionnaire score.

- Athletes who had less than 10% days between tests with a questionnaire score below 1.5× baseline resulted in an improvement in test scores 81% of the time. Of those that did not improve, 9.5% saw a decrease in performance and 9.5% saw no change.

- Athlete who switched their profile from having 10% of their training days above 1.5× baseline to less than 10% improved their scores on the next test 100% of the time.

Although there may be some variation based on training level and age in the percentage of days above 1.5× baseline that can occur before an athlete's performance is negatively affected, it is clear that an ASRM questionnaire that tracks individual baselines and stress zones can be useful in determining whether aerobic training adaptations will occur between testing periods.

Enhancing Recovery

There are many factors that play a role in recovery, but there are two crucial elements that need to be in place: nutrition and sleep.

Nutrition and Recovery

Nutritional interventions are crucial to a comprehensive recovery program and are built around the three Rs: rehydrate, replenish, and rebuild (Kim and Kim 2020).

Rehydrate

Dehydration increases the perception of fatigue and can impair performance. Dehydration of >2% body weight leads to compromised cognitive function and decreased aerobic exercise performance in hot weather. When dehydration rises to 3% to 5% of body weight, sport-specific technical skills, anaerobic performance, and higher intensity aerobic performance required for rowing are impaired.

Urine-specific gravity, a relatively simple and inexpensive method, can be used to monitor hydration status, with scores of <1.020 suggesting adequate hydration (Kenefick and Cheuvront 2012). An even simpler and more cost-effective method is to monitor hydration status through changes in body weight (Lee et al. 2017). Measure body weight without clothes 20 to 30 min before a training session. Immediately after the session, dry off with a towel to remove sweat and reweigh. The difference in weight is the amount of fluid lost (1 L fluid = 1 kg body weight). Aim to replace 1.25 to 1.5 times the weight lost over a period of about an hour (Thomas, Erdman, and Burke 2016).

Replenish

The volume and intensity of training places extreme demands on a rower's energy and carbohydrate stores and can result in depleted energy and carbohydrate levels (Koehler 2020). Keeping caloric intake high enough to meet these energy demands can be a challenge. General guidelines of 50 to 60 kcal/kg of body weight for men and 45 to 50 kcal/kg of body weight for women provides a reasonable estimate of daily energy requirements for most athletes in a high-performance rowing program (Economos, Bortz, and Nelson 1993).

Adequate energy intake is essential to rowing performance, and even short-term inadequate energy intake can decrease performance. In a study of 10 national-level Australian rowers (Woods et al. 2017), the rowers increased training volume by 20% to 50% over 4 weeks without increasing energy intake. The athletes lost weight (2.2 kg), decreased resting metabolic rate by 5%, and decreased rowing performance in a 5,000 m time trial by 3.5%.

Chronic inadequate energy intake can result in a condition called *relative energy deficiency in sport* (REDs), which may affect menstrual, endocrine, metabolic, and hematology function; growth and development; and bone health; as well as psychological, cardiovascular, gastrointestinal, and immunological systems. Performance effects include decreased endurance, increased injury risk, decreased training response, impaired judgment, decreased coordination, decreased concentration, irritability, depression, decreased glycogen stores, and decreased muscle strength (Mountjoy et al. 2014).

After ensuring adequate energy intake, carbohydrate (CHO) repletion is the next priority. It has long been known that a high CHO intake improves power output during rowing training compared to a lower CHO diet (Simonsen et al. 1985). The joint position statement of ACSM, Academy of Nutrition and Dietetics, and Dieticians of Canada (Thomas, Erdman, and Burke 2016) recommends consuming 1 to 1.2 g/kg/h of carbohydrate for the first 4 h following a demanding training session when there is less than 8 h before the next session. Kim and Kim (2020) have recommended that rowers establish an individual plan for total daily carbohydrate intake based on the duration and intensity of training. They suggest 6 to 10 g/kg/day for 1 to 3 h of training at a moderate to high intensity and 8 to 12 g/kg/day for 4 to 5 h of training at moderate to high intensity.

In the case of lightweight rowers trying to come down to weight or very large heavyweights, these general guidelines may not be appropriate. More precise measures of both resting and exercising metabolic rate and energy requirements can be made through indirect calorimetry, or the collection of expired gases during rest or exercise. Following a progressive incremental step test the expired gases, blood lactate, heart rate, and power data are combined to determine training zones or categories and the energy expenditure for each zone. Table 22.4 shows a sample data set from a lightweight male rower.

Table 22.4 Metabolic Data From a Step Test on a Rowing Ergometer for a Lightweight Male Rower

Stage	Power (W)	HR (bpm)	Lactate (mmol/L)	$\dot{V}O_2$ (L/min)	RQ	kcal/min	CHO (kcal/min)	CHO (g/min)
1	100	121	1.3	1.79	0.88	8.8	5.5	1.37
2	130	124	0.941	2.21	0.86	10.7	5.9	1.48
3	160	133	1.74	2.47	0.86	11.9	6.6	1.65
4	190	149	2.55	2.78	0.9	13.6	9.4	2.36
5	220	151	2.81	3.28	0.92	16.2	12.4	3.10
6	250	160	4.27	3.69	0.97	18.4	17.3	4.32
7	280	170	6.81	4.07	1.01	20.4	20.4	5.10
8	310	181	10.1	4.53	1.07	23.1	23.1	5.78

The respiratory quotient (RQ) is the ratio of expired CO_2 to O_2 and is used to determine the proportion of carbohydrate and fat used as fuel. Combined with the energy expenditure (kcal/min) the amount of carbohydrate used per minute (g/min) is determined. With this information, the training zones were developed for this particular athlete (table 22.5).

Table 22.5 Training Zones and the CHO Needs for Each Zone for a Lightweight Male Rower

Zone	Heart rate (bpm)	Power (W)	CHO (g/min)
1	115-135	105-165	1.38-1.77
2	136-155	165-235	1.77-3.71
3	156-161	235-250	3.71-4.32
4	162-181	250-280	4.32-5.1
5	182+	280+	5.1-5.78

These data can be now used to plan energy and CHO intake more precisely. For example, a 60 min ergometer workout at the high end of zone 1 (165 W) would burn 720 kcal and consume 106 g of CHO. Doing the same 60 min near the middle of zone 2 (220 W) would burn 972 kcal and consume 186 g of CHO. Assuming that this athlete is 70 kg, the general recommendation of 1 to 1.2 g/kg/h CHO for 4 h would have them taking in 336 g CHO—substantially more than they need, particularly when they are trying to come down to weight. For a lightweight rower, indirect calorimetry allows them to target appropriate levels of CHO and energy intake that will allow them to come down to weight while still getting adequate CHO and energy to prevent losses of muscle mass and performance.

For an elite heavyweight rower, on the other hand, the general guidelines are often not sufficient to cover their energy and CHO needs. Table 22.6 below shows the data from an elite heavyweight male rower.

Table 22.6 Metabolic Data From a Step Test on a Rowing Ergometer for a Heavyweight Male Rower

Stage	Power (W)	HR (bpm)	Lactate (mmol/L)	$\dot{V}O_2$ (L/min)	RQ	kcal/min	CHO (kcal/min)	CHO (g/min)
1	295	155	1.1	4.86	0.87	24.1	14.1	3.52
2	330	162	1.8	5.35	0.89	26.5	17.3	4.32
3	365	170	2.0	5.78	0.93	28.6	22.5	5.62
4	400	175	2.85	6.15	0.97	30.4	27.8	6.95
5	435	179	4.81	6.31	1.01	31.2	31.2	7.8
6	470	183	6.27	6.76	1.03	33.5	33.5	8.4
7	505	185	11.4	6.92	1.10	34.3	34.3	8.6

A typical training day for this athlete might involve a 90 min steady-state row (HR 170) in the early morning, during which they would burn 2,574 calories and consume about 500 g CHO, an amount that would likely fully deplete CHO stores. Assuming the athlete is 90 kg, following the recommended guideline of 1.2 g/kg/h CHO for 4 h would result in an intake of 432 g CHO, substantially less than what was used—and this is only in the first workout of the day.

Key Point

Individualizing nutritional recommendations based on physiology and fitness adds more precision to general recommendations, particularly for highly trained rowers and lightweights who are trying to come down to weight.

Rebuild

A breakdown of muscle tissue can occur because of mechanical stress or if energy demands are high enough that protein sources are used as energy, accounting for as much as 10% to 20% of total energy expenditure in endurance activities (Alghannam, Ghaith, and Alhussain 2021; Brooks 1987). The primary goal of protein intake during the recovery period is to stimulate muscle protein synthesis. Protein synthesis is optimized when high biological value protein is consumed within the first 2 h following training. Protein intake should ideally be 0.25 to 0.3 g/kg body weight and should provide at least 10 g of essential amino acids (Beelen et al. 2010; Philips 2012). Repeated consumption of this amount of protein every 3 to 5 h over multiple meals can further enhance protein synthesis.

Safe storage of protein-based foods is often difficult at rowing centers. Using protein or amino acid supplements from tested third-party sources is a quick and convenient way of getting the required protein when whole food sources are not available. If refrigeration is available, then dairy products may be superior to other types of protein because of their leucine content (Thomas, Erdman, and Burke 2016). However, there still needs to be more research on the efficacy of other high-quality protein sources.

Sleep and Recovery

With the advent of wearable sleep-tracking technology and smartphone apps, the importance of sleep is becoming more recognized in both general and athletic populations. This may be in response to the decrease in sleep time that has occurred over the past 60 years. In 1959 adults averaged 8 to 9 h of sleep per night, which dropped to 7 to 8 h by 1980 (Ferrara 2001). In 2013 a survey found that Americans averaged 6:51 h of sleep on weekdays and 7:37 h on weekends (National Sleep Foundation 2013). It is recommended that athletes get 9 to 10 h of sleep per night (Calder 2003), but this rarely seems to happen. A study of 890 elite South African athletes showed that three-quarters of athletes reported an average sleep duration of 6 to 8 h per night (Venter 2012). Leeder and colleagues (2012) used actigraphy to find that Olympic athletes, on average, slept for 6 h 55 min, compared to 7 h 11 min for control groups. A frequency distribution of hours of sleep per night over 8 months for a group of rowers can be seen in figure 22.3.

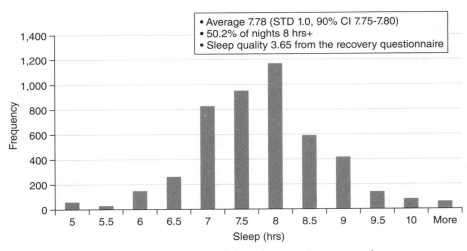

▶ **Figure 22.3** Frequency distribution of sleep hours of a group of rowers.

Sleep is broken into periods of rapid eye movement (REM) sleep and non-REM sleep, which can be divided into four phases by changes in brainwave activity. Non-REM sleep is associated with nervous system recovery and the release of anabolic hormones such as growth hormone, which play a role in recovery and adaptation to training stimuli (Weitzman 1976). Sleep also promotes the consolidation of memory and learning of motor skills in athletes (Walker et al. 2002). The impact of sleep on recovery can be seen in changes in ASRM questionnaires (Kölling et al. 2016). Using the questionnaire outlined earlier in the chapter, this author has found that there is a correlation of −0.8854 between the percentage of nights with 8+ hours of sleep and the percentage of overstress days where the questionnaire scores exceeded 1.5× baseline.

Improving Sleep

Although there is limited published research on it, increasing the number of hours of sleep per night has been shown to improve athletic performance, including tennis serve accuracy, free throw and 3-point accuracy, swim sprint times, swim turn and kick efficiency, half and full court sprints, and improved reaction time and mood (Mah 2008; Mah et al. 2011; Schwartz and Simon 2015; Waterhouse et al. 2007).

Basic sleep hygiene practices are the cornerstone of increasing sleep (Vitale et al. 2019) and include the following tips:

- Have regular bedtime rituals.
- Don't go to bed until you are sleepy.
- Have a consistent wake up time.
- Use the bed for sleep, not TV watching or computer or phone use.
- Avoid caffeine in the afternoon.
- Avoid alcohol.
- Make sure the bedroom is quiet, dark, and cool.
- Avoid blue-light-emitting screens in the 2 h before bed (phones, tablets, monitors), or use glasses or apps that block blue light.
- Get bright, natural light when waking.

Key Point

Lack of sleep is not just a problem that affects athletes or recovery from sports. It is a larger problem that affects that health and productivity of many people. Rowers and other athletes can implement a few changes to their training to increase sleep time.

Training Schedules

Early morning training times, typical of many rowing and swimming programs, have been shown to severely decrease sleep time. Sargent, Halson, and Roach (2014) found that on training days with a 6:00 a.m. start time, swimmers training for the 2008 Olympics only got 5.4 h of sleep per night compared to 7.1 h on nontraining days. Although early mornings often have the best water and many rowers need to train before work or school, even small changes in start time can have an effect on sleep. Table 22.7 shows the effects of beginning training 30 min later on the percentage of nights with 8+ h of sleep.

Table 22.7 Percentage of Nights with 8+ Hours of Sleep by Weeknight

Start time	Mon	Tues	Wed	Thurs	Fri	Sat
7:00	55.0%	49.2%	44.3%	47.2%	48.2%	51.2%
7:30	60.0%	54.0%	55.8%	54.0%	55.7%	63.0%

Consistency of training times also affects sleep duration and quality. Logistics and available start times often dictate rowing times during camps and competition. Figure 22.4 shows the effects of changing training times during a camp and racing on sleep duration and quality in rowers.

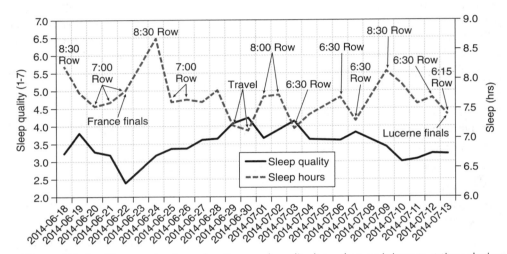

▶ **Figure 22.4**   Changes in sleep duration and quality based on training start time during a training camp.

Shifting high metabolic load sessions to earlier in the day may help with sleep. Performing high-intensity training sessions later in the day can negatively impact the ability to fall asleep. This may be due to increases in cortisol (Vitale et al. 2019), an increase in arousal levels, or an increase in body temperature (a drop in body temperature is a trigger for the onset of sleep) (Gilbert et al. 2004).

Nutrition and Sleep

Nutritional interventions not only rehydrate, replenish, and rebuild muscle tissue, they play a role in improving sleep. High glycemic index carbohydrate meals 2 to 4 h before bed, 20 g of whey protein supplements taken 1 h before bed, and tart cherry

Key Point

Tart cherry juice contains about 13 ng of melatonin, which can increase the production of exogenous melatonin. It also has anti-inflammatory properties, which can decrease the chronic pain and muscle soreness that many athletes experience. This chronic soreness is often cited by athletes as a reason for sleep difficulties.

juice have all been shown to increase total sleep time. Other foods like beetroot have been shown to improve subjective sleep quality, and two kiwi fruits 1 h before bed yielded a 55 min increase in total sleep time (Gratwicke et al. 2021). Part VII on rowing nutrition goes into more depth on fueling during training season.

Psychosocial Stress and Recovery

Although the original theory of general adaptation syndrome focused on environmental, physical, and drug-induced stressors (Selye 1936), emotional and psychological stressors can create a similar stress response (Selye 1950). Negative life events often result in prolonged periods of stress with no opportunity for recovery. People with anxiety disorders or excessive psychological stress have been found to have cortisol levels that exceed those seen following exercise (Boa, Meynen, and Swaab 2008). The combination of training stress and life stress can potentially impair training adaptations and performance. A study of college students who performed weight training found an average of 15% improvement in bench press strength in a low stress group versus an average of 12% improvement in a high stress group (Bartholomew et al. 2008). The smaller improvement in strength may be related to the negative effect that life stress has on recovery following exercise (Stults-Kolehmainen and Bartholomew 2012; Stults-Kolehmainen, Bartholomew, and Sinha 2014). Using the RESTQ-Sport questionnaire on a group of competitive runners, Otter and colleagues (2016) found that general well-being and social and physical recovery decreased following a period of negative life stress. As a result, running economy was impaired for 3 weeks after the negative life event.

A variety of interventions, including cognitive, behavioral, and mindfulness programs, have all been shown to be effective at reducing stress in university students (Regehr, Glancy, and Pitts 2013), decreasing both indicators of psychological and physiological stress (Dawson et al. 2014; Gaab et al. 2003). Coaches in educational institutions can take advantage of the programs offered to students to help their athletes deal with life stresses. The addition of 10 to 15 min of meditation or mindfulness training as part of a cool-down may help decrease psychosocial stress, as would counseling with a mental health professional.

Conclusion

Recovery is as crucial to performance as training. During the recovery process the body refuels and rebuilds and memory is consolidated, leading to improvements in skill and technique. Next to designing a training program with appropriate loading and rest periods, the most important elements of recovery are nutrition and sleep. Having adequate energy intake and sleeping for at least 8 hours most nights are key pillars of a recovery program. Rolling out an athlete self-report monitoring tool helps track recovery and the effectiveness of the recovery program. Planning recovery interventions and monitoring their success, though time consuming, is a worthwhile investment. These will ensure that a crew's hard work is rewarded with improvements in performance.

Tapering

Ed McNeely

Athletes and coaches are constantly looking for interventions that will help them gain the slight edge that is the often difference between winning and losing. Bringing together the physical, psychological, technical, and tactical elements of a performance is both an art and a science, requiring constant monitoring, tweaking, and input from both coach and athlete (Ritchie, Allen, and Kirkland 2017).

In chapter 22 the concept of general adaptation syndrome (GAS) and the role that stress plays in training adaptations and fatigue were discussed. Although GAS is an attractive model, it does not account for the varying rates of recovery and adaptation experienced by different body systems and tissues.

The fitness fatigue model of training response suggests that for each training session there are both fitness and fatigue aftereffects (Bannister 1991; Chiu and Barnes 2003). During stressful periods of training with inadequate recovery, fatigue accumulates over time, masking the full extent of the underlying physiological and performance adaptations. When the training stress is removed or decreased, there is a delayed training effect during which the body continues to adapt as fatigue dissipates, allowing the full fitness effect of the training period to be realized (Zatsiorsky 1995).

This phase of training is called a *taper* and has been defined as a period of progressively reduced training volume that lasts from 7 to 21 days prior to the year's important competitions (Costill et al. 1985; Houmard and Johns 1994). A careful training load balance must be established during a taper; too much of a decrease in training load can lead to detraining and a loss of fitness, whereas not enough will not allow the athlete's full ability to be expressed (Mujika 2010).

Performance Changes Following a Taper

The expected performance improvement following an effective taper is about 2% to 3%, ranging from 0% to 6% in trained athletes (Houmard 1994; Johns et al. 1992; Mujika and Padilla 2003; Mujika, Padilla, and Busso 2004; Neary, Bhambhani, and McKenzie 2003; Zarkadas, Carter, and Banister 1994). A worthwhile improvement in top-ranked athletes ranges from 0.5% to 3.0% from sprint to endurance events in sports like running, swimming, and cycling (Hopkins, Hawley, and Burke 1999). An analysis of the times from rowing finals for selected events at the Tokyo Olympics shows that the average difference between first and fourth is 0.88%, suggesting that the improvements in performance from a well-designed taper may have a significant impact on the outcome of a race. The amount of performance enhancement following a taper depends on the design of the taper, the level of the athlete, and the amount of adaptation that occurs.

Physiological Adaptations to a Taper

Various physiological adaptations contribute to the performance improvements during a taper, including changes in aerobic and anaerobic fitness.

Aerobic and Anaerobic Fitness

Aerobic fitness in endurance athletes is often measured with $\dot{V}O_2$max or submaximal lactate measures to determine anaerobic threshold. $\dot{V}O_2$max may increase or remain unchanged during a taper (Mujika, Padilla, and Busso 2004; Neary, McKenzie, and Bhambhani 2005), depending on the duration of the taper and the intensity of work prior to the taper. Of 13 studies reviewed by Mujika, Padilla, and Busso (2004), the five studies that employed tapers of more than 14 days found no increase in $\dot{V}O_2$max, whereas six of the eight studies that involved tapers of 14 days or less saw $\dot{V}O_2$max improvements. Rønnestad and Vikmoen (2019) examined the effects of a 5-day taper preceded by a 6-day high-intensity training period compared to a traditional taper without an overreaching period. They found $\dot{V}O_2$max increases of 4% in the high-intensity group compared to 0.8% in the traditional group. Effective monitoring of training load and recovery throughout the training year may allow rowers to better control accumulated fatigue and use a slightly shorter taper that will improve $\dot{V}O_2$max.

Endurance Capacity

Although maximum aerobic power may or may not be increased, other measures of endurance performance indicate that tapering improves endurance capacity. Hemoglobin and hematocrit values have been shown to increase by up to 14% and 2.6% respectively during the first 7 days of a taper, improving the oxygen-carrying capacity of the blood (Yamamoto and Mutoh 1988). Mujika and colleagues (1998) observed a significant correlation ($r = 0.83$) between posttaper red cell count and percentage improvement in swim performance during tapering, suggesting hematological changes are one of the primary factors contributing to the increase in endurance performance seen with tapering.

Blood Lactate Concentration

Peak blood lactate values are increased during tapering (Jeukendrup et al. 1992; Mujika et al. 2000). Percentage changes in race performance in middle distance runners have been correlated ($r = 0.87$) to changes in postrace peak lactate concentration (Mujika et al. 2000). Similar results have been seen in international-level swimmers and cyclists (Bonifazi, Sardella, and Luppo 2000; Jeukendrup et al. 1992). Changes in peak blood lactate values may be a result of an increase in muscle glycogen (Houmard and Johns 1994) or an increase in glycolytic enzyme activity (Neary et al. 1992). Increased storage of muscle glycogen provides more energy for anaerobic muscle fibers, allowing them to produce more power and thus more lactate.

Muscle Power Output

Sport-specific muscle power increases during a taper are greater than the improvement in aerobic fitness and account for most of the taper-induced performance improvement in endurance athletes (Johns et al. 1992). In rowers this can be seen as an increase in peak power as measured using the peak power test (described in chapter 22), shown in figure 23.1, or by the average power over a 60 s all-out effort on an ergometer. Peak power improvements are typically larger than 60 s average power improvements, with peak power typically increasing by about 18%, with a range of 4% to 28%, over a 6-week period that includes a 3-week taper. Average power on a 60 s test typically increases by 3.6%, with a range of 0.25% to 6.75%.

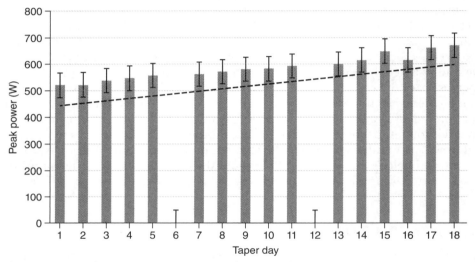

▶ **Figure 23.1** Changes in ergometer peak power during a taper.

Following a taper there are increases in the strength, speed of contraction, and power of both fast-twitch and slow-twitch muscle fibers (Luden et al. 2010; Trappe et al. 2000; Trinity et al. 2006). This can be seen in figure 23.2 as an increase in isometric peak handle force at catch position and handle force at 200 ms (milliseconds) using the isometric device described in chapter 16.

As discussed in chapter 12, there is evidence that high volumes of aerobic training and strength and power improvements are incompatible (Hickson 1980). Aerobic training inhibits nervous system mechanisms that are responsible for strength and power production and prevents the increases in muscle cross-sectional area needed to increase strength, possibly due to chronic muscle damage. Creatine kinase (CK), which has been used as a marker for muscle damage following endurance performance (Armstrong 1990; Romano-Ely et al. 2006) and eccentric exercise, is chronically elevated in endurance athletes during the training year. When training stress is reduced during a taper there is as much as a 70% reduction in circulating CK levels (Mujika, Padilla and Busso 2004; Yamamoto and Mutoh 1988). As the chronic damage dissipates there is a rapid period of adaptation and fiber hypertrophy, as seen by the 24% increase in type IIa fiber cross-sectional area in swimmers (Trappe et al. 2000); this increase is 14.2% in cyclists (Neary, Bhambhani, and McKenzie 2003) and 7% in distance run-

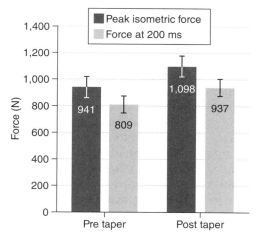

▶ **Figure 23.2** Peak isometric handle force and force at 200 ms before and after a simulated taper.

ners (Luden et al. 2010). This effect may not be as pronounced in athletes with lower training volume or frequency.

Designing a Taper

Not every athlete will benefit from a taper. Athletes who have limited training experience in technical endurance sports like kayak, canoe, rowing, and swimming will not see much improvement from a taper. Novices will probably benefit more from a continued higher volume of training leading into a race followed by 1 to 2 days off just prior to the race. Because many novices haven't mastered the technical skills of the sport to the point that they are going to be limited by their fitness, a higher volume of skill and tactical work leading into a race will probably pay bigger performance dividends than a taper.

Rowers who are training less than 4 hours per week will not benefit much from a true taper. These athletes can take a day or two off immediately before a race and be sufficiently recovered to race at their best.

Overload

An overload period of increased volume and intensity just before the start of a taper results in greater performance improvements than a taper alone (Rønnestad and Vikmoen 2019), provided that the overload is not so great to create an overreach state (Anael et al. 2014). In many cases the highest load of the year will occur in the 2 to 3 weeks before the start of the taper. During the overload, athletes should become fatigued and experience a slight decrement in performance, but they should still want to train and be sleeping well.

Intensity

Intensity is the key to performance improvements from a taper (Mujika 2010). Intensity increases throughout the taper as the training volume decreases. In a study that compared high-intensity and low-intensity tapers, Shepley and colleagues (1992) found that the physiological responses were similar but only the high-intensity taper group showed an increase in performance. Houmard and Johns (1994) suggested that training schedules that use intensities of less than 70% $\dot{V}O_2$max maintain or decrease performance during a taper, whereas tapers that use intensities of greater than 90% $\dot{V}O_2$max improve performance.

Intensity is one of the harder elements to quantify and plan in a rowing program. Employing an intensity-weighted volume calculation helps determine changes in planned intensity from week to week. The intensity-weighted volume is based on the T2minute from Tran and colleagues (2014) mentioned in chapter 17, which holds that not all training creates the same level of fatigue. For instance, a 45 min steady-state session is far less fatiguing than a $\dot{V}O_2$max level interval session of similar duration. If the power outputs at various key physiological points, aerobic threshold, anaerobic threshold, $\dot{V}O_2$max, and peak anaerobic power are known, time correction factors can be calculated. Table 23.1 provides an example.

Table 23.1 Sample Data for Calculating Volume Correction Factors

Physiological marker	Power (W)	Volume correction factor
Peak power	1,000	1.0
$\dot{V}O_2$max	465	0.465
Anaerobic threshold	390	0.39
Aerobic threshold	360	0.36

Key Point

Changes in intensity are often difficult to calculate in endurance sports. Weighted volume corrections allow for an intensity number to be calculated and used to ensure that intensity increases through the taper.

The power from the peak power test is used as 100%. The volume correction factors for the other variables are calculated by dividing their power values by the power value from the peak power test. The resulting number is then multiplied by the number of minutes spent in each training zone to arrive at an intensity-corrected volume. Table 23.2 shows an example of the distribution of training minutes over six training zones C6 through C1, with C6 being the lowest intensity and C1 being the highest intensity. To adjust the training minutes for intensity C6 minutes are multiplied by the 0.36 aerobic threshold correction factor from table 23.1, C4 minutes are multiplied by the 0.39 anaerobic threshold correction factor, and C2 minutes are multiplied by the 0.465 $\dot{V}O_2$max correction factor. The correction factors for C5 is halfway between the aerobic and anaerobic threshold correction factors, and the C3 Correction is halfway between anaerobic threshold and $\dot{V}O_2$max. When all the planned training minutes have been corrected for intensity, the average intensity for the week can be calculated by dividing the total adjusted training minutes by the total unadjusted minutes (table 23.2).

Figure 23.3 shows changes in intensity for the competitive phase of training for an international crew as measured by the intensity-weighted volume method. Week 12 is

Table 23.2 Developing a Taper by Correcting the Planned Training Volume From the Yearly Plan for Intensity

PLANNED TRAINING VOLUME FROM YEARLY PLAN							
Week	C6	C5	C4	C3	C2	C1	Weekly total minutes
1	714	42	42	13	25	4	840
2	672	42	42	55	25	4	840
3	647	42	42	55	42	13	840
4	816	48	48	14	29	5	960
5	672	42	0	84	34	8	840
6	420	30	18	60	54	18	600
INTENSITY-ADJUSTED VOLUME							
Week	C6	C5	C4	C3	C2	C1	Intensity-adjusted weekly total minutes	Average weekly intensity
1	257	16	16	6	12	4	310	0.370
2	242	16	16	24	12	4	313	0.373
3	233	16	16	24	20	13	320	0.381
4	294	18	19	6	13	5	355	0.370
5	242	16	0	36	16	8	317	0.378
6	151	11	7	26	25	18	238	0.397

a travel week, during which volume significantly decreases as a result of lost training days and the need to gradually rebuild volume following time zone changes. Week 7 is a racing week and weeks 6 and 5 are overload weeks before the start of a 28-day taper leading into the World Championships in week 1.

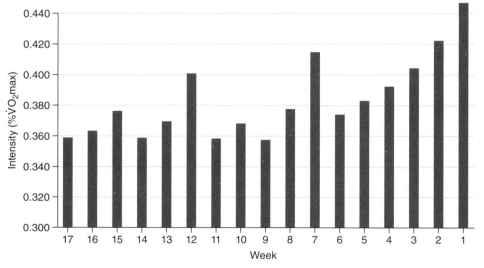

▶ **Figure 23.3** Changes in intensity during the competitive phase.

Using the intensity-adjusted volume method allows for an intensity number to be determined, and it is related to changes in fatigue as calculated through the relative scores from the recovery questionnaire (discussed in chapter 22).

Steady-state pieces are gradually replaced with shorter training sessions, including higher intensity intervals and short sprints. By the final week almost all the training will be done at or above anaerobic threshold. A final week of a taper may look something like the plan shown in table 23.3.

Table 23.3 Sample Final Week of a Taper

Monday	Tuesday	Wednesday	Thursday	Friday	Saturday	Sunday
40 min easy steady state	4 × 5 min above AT, 10 min rest	5 × 2 min, 30 min easy steady state	Off	4-6 × 250 m sprints with 10 min easy between sprints	4 × 2 min at race pace, 5 min rest	Race

The sprint work in the last 2 days is as much a psychological factor as it is a physiological factor. Sprints will give the athlete feelings of speed, power, and confidence that they can take with them into race day. This means it is important to have a good final training session that leaves the athletes energized, not fatigued. Ideally these final training days are done on the race course so that the athlete has time to familiarize themselves with the course.

Duration

Because the training stimulus is greatly reduced during a taper, the duration of the taper can have an impact on the magnitude of performance improvements. Within 1 to 4 weeks of stopping training highly trained athletes start to show decreases in some aspects of performance (Costill et al. 1985), possibly due to a "loss of feel" during training and competition (Mujika et al. 2002). Mujika and colleagues (1996) studied the effects of 21-, 28-, and 42-day tapers on performance in highly trained swimmers. They found significant improvements in the 21- and 28-day groups but not the 42-day taper group. Others who have measured performance and taper duration have found improvements in performance following tapers of 7 to 21 days (Costill et al. 1985; Houmard et al. 1994; Shepley et al. 1992). The number of days needed to taper may be affected by accumulated fatigue, training volume, and intensity going into the taper as well as fitness level of the athlete. Mathematical models have been developed to try to predict the optimal number of days needed to taper (Fitz-Clarke, Morton, and Banister 1991; Morton, Fitz-Clarke, and Banister 1990; Mujika et al. 1996). These models have been met with mixed results, causing many coaches to continue to rely on trial and error.

More recently, shorter tapers of 5 days following a 7-day overload period have been found to be effective in mountain bikers (Rønnestad et al. 2017) and elite cyclists (Rønnestad and Vikmoen 2019). This may be a good option for rowers who have a busy regatta schedule or who need to have a good performance in order to qualify for a later regatta.

For those who are training more than 4 hours per week, the taper needs to be planned according to work volume. Table 23.4 provides guidelines for the duration of a taper based on the number of hours per week of training.

Table 23.4 Weekly Training Hours and Taper Duration

Training h/wk	Overload	Taper
6-10	5 days	7 days
10-15	7 days	14 days
15+	14 days	21-30 days

Volume

A substantial decrease in training volume is one of the characteristics of a taper. Studies of distance runners (Houmard 1991; Houmard et al. 1990) have found that 800 m and 1,600 m running times were improved following a decrease in training volume of 70% over a 3-week period. Houmard and colleagues (1994) found an increase in running economy and a 3% improvement in 5 km run time following a 7-day 85% decrease in training volume. There is a relationship between the amount of volume decrease and performance improvements during a taper (Mujika 1995). Bosquet and colleagues (2007) conducted a meta-analysis of taper research and found that a reduction in volume of 41% to 60% yielded the greatest improvement, with an effect size (0.72) that was more than twice that of increasing intensity (0.33) or decreasing frequency (0.35).

Because an insufficient reduction in volume does not lead to performance improvement, shorter tapers may require a greater percentage reduction in training volume. Shepley and colleagues (1992) looked at the effects of a 7-day 62% reduction in volume and compared it to a 7-day 90% reduction in volume. They found the 62% scenario did not increase the time to exhaustion, whereas the 90% reduction resulted in an 22% increase in time to exhaustion.

Keep in mind that the decrease in volume for longer tapers should not be accomplished in one step; rather, volume is decreased progressively throughout the taper. Martin and colleagues (1994) found that performance improvements in cyclists peaked during the first week of a 2-week step taper. Zarkadas, Carter, and Banister (1994) found an 11.8% improvement in 5 km run times following a 10-day progressive taper but only a 3% improvement in performance using a step taper. Houmard and colleagues (1990) found no improvement in performance following a 3-week step taper.

Progressive tapers seem to have a greater impact on performance than step tapers (Mujika 1998). This is probably a result of detraining effects that occur when the rapid volume decrease used in step tapering is maintained for an extended period of time. Although a progressive taper is the obvious choice for the major competition of the year, a step taper may be better for minor and moderate tapers of less than 10 days.

Figure 23.4 shows a volume pattern over the competitive phase for an international crew, culminating in the World Championships in week 1.

Frequency

The reduction of training volume in a taper should not occur as the result of drastic changes in training frequency (Houmard and Johns 1994) but by decreasing the duration of each workout. Neufer and colleagues (1987) found that reducing training volume 80% to 90% through cutting frequency by 50% to 85% resulted in decreased swim power after only 7 days of tapering. Studies in which tapering has resulted in improved performance have typically decreased frequency by 20% to 50% (Houmard et al. 1989). The reasons why a reduction in frequency causes a decrease in performance

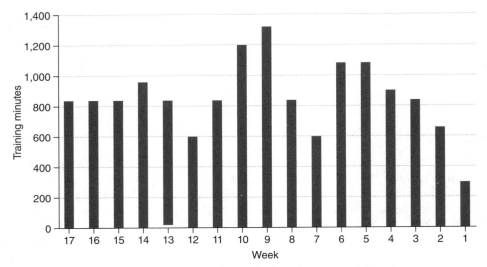

▶ **Figure 23.4**   Changes in training volume during the competitive phase.

are unclear, but may be related to decreased technical efficiency—that is, as frequency of technical work is decreased, there may be some loss in technique that ultimately affects performance.

Monitoring a Taper

A taper is a specialized period of recovery, and as such many of the tools and methods discussed in chapter 22 are applicable during a taper. Wellness scores from self-report questionnaires typically improve throughout a taper (Botonis, Toubekis, and Platanou 2019). Using the questionnaire outlined in chapter 20 (page 295), this shows up as a decrease in the number of overreach days where the relative score is above 1.5× the baseline.

Using minitapers with 2,000 m ergometer tests before and after the taper are a good way of gauging the effectiveness of the taper. A minitaper simulates the second or third week of a 3-week taper and should result in better scores after the taper. A 1% to 2% improvement would suggest the taper is effective. This is also a good time to practice the psychological aspects of racing that are so important to success.

Key Point

Practice the taper at least once before a major competition. The loss of training time from a practice taper is less important than knowing whether the taper works.

The Art of Tapering

Tapering is both an art and a science. The taper period can be a time of high psychological stress for both the coach and athlete. At this time of the year, it is important that the coach projects confidence both in what has been done during the season and in the taper. If the coach is openly worried about the athlete's preparation or starts making changes to a planned taper, the athletes may begin to question their preparedness and ability to win.

A taper should be practiced at least once before the major competition of the year. It is not necessary to practice a full 21-day taper, but the final week must be tried at least once during a less important competition. This will provide the opportunity to adjust the taper to individual needs and experiment with different combinations of intervals and sprints during the final week.

Key Point

Although often thought of in terms of physical preparation, having a plan to deal with the psychological and emotional stress for both coaches and athletes can make a difference in performance.

Athletes handle the decreased training volume differently. Many athletes will enjoy the feelings of speed, power, and renewed energy, whereas others may have difficulty dealing with the extra time as a result of the decreased volume and worry about detraining. A coach needs to be aware of the responses of each athlete and be prepared to deal with the worriers.

The primary purpose of a taper is to reduce fatigue and stress to allow physiological adaptations from training to be fully expressed as performance. The stress that needs to be eliminated or reduced during a taper is not only training stress. Other stressors can also affect the outcome of a taper.

Crew Selection

Crew selection can be a period of very high stress, particularly for those who are among the final picks or are deselected. Athletes who are deselected report feelings of anger, humiliation, anxiety, loss of athletic identity, and decreased academic performance (Barnett 2007; Brown and Potrac 2009; Grove, Fish, and Eklund 2004). Selection periods can vary widely from crew to crew and at different levels of competition. Coaches bring different approaches to conducting selection and informing players of selection decisions (Seifred and Casey 2012). Ideally crew selection is made several weeks before the start of the taper, but if there are last-minute selections coaches need to be flexible with their training plan to balance the stress and uncertainty with the need to make sure the athletes are physically prepared to perform in upcoming competitions. This is particularly important if final selections involve race-offs between a limited number of athletes who may require program adjustments while others who have made the team are ready for normal training.

Logistics

Although often not considered when designing a taper, the logistics around camps and competitions can impact stress and recovery and potentially affect the adaptations in the taper. Three categories of logistics to consider when designing a taper are travel, lodging, and food.

International travel, particularly across times zones, disrupts sleep, circadian rhythms, eating patterns, and performance (Forbes-Robertson et al. 2012), but even domestic travel can have negative effects that can undo the benefits of a taper. Long car or bus rides without regular breaks can cause discomfort and tightness that may inhibit performance (Lantoine et al. 2021). If travel to the race course takes more than 90 min, plan a short stretch stop or arrive at least 2 h before the race and include some extra mobility work into the warm-up.

Because it is a specialized period of recovery, sleep is an important part of the taper. When traveling to a camp or competition the quality of lodging affects the ability to sleep. When choosing a hotel or motel gather as much information as possible about the quality of the beds, room environment, and any noisy events such as concerts or festivals that may compromise the ability to sleep. A lot of this information can be found through web searches and posted reviews. When traveling internationally be aware that hotels in many countries are different from those in North America; air conditioning is not always available and, in many cases, small single beds are the norm, which may not be comfortable for tall heavyweight rowers.

At precompetition camps or competitions that last several days, eating can become an issue if not planned. Overreliance on fast food can have a negative impact as the regatta progresses, compromising energy levels and recovery. For lightweights the sodium content of most fast food leads to water retention and difficulty making weight. Book hotel rooms with refrigerators when possible, and try to find a grocery store near the hotel so that quality snacks and meals can be eaten and prepared in the room when possible. Most grocery stores have prepared meals and salads that are better than fast food options. Hiring a dietician to provide an education session to the crew on preparing nutritious meals with minimal equipment goes a long way to ensuring that poor nutrition does not sabotage the taper.

Lightweights

Lightweight rowers need to pay particular attention to their weight during a taper. One of the adaptations to a taper is an increase in muscle glycogen storage (Shepley et al. 1992). The muscles store 3 g of water for every 1 g of glycogen, which can result in a large increase in weight in a relatively short period of time. The increased glycogen storage not only feeds the muscles during training but is used as an energy source for other adaptations to occur. A certain amount of weight gain may therefore be necessary if the athlete is to see performance improvements as a result of the taper. Lightweight rowers must carefully balance the amount of glycogen supercompensation that will improve performance with the amount of weight they can gain and still compete.

Conclusion

During the course of a training year recovery between training sessions and microcycles is often incomplete, resulting in an accumulation of fatigue that masks true physiological adaptation. Tapering prior to an important competition is a specialized period of reduced training volume and increased intensity that reduces fatigue and allows the benefits of training to be fully realized. A well-designed taper can increase performance by 0.5% to 6% with typical rowing values in the 1% to 3% range; this equates to a 3 to 18 s improvement in performance. Decreasing volume is the key to an effective taper, with volume decreases of 40% to 70% over a 7-to-21-day period being the norm. This is accomplished by decreasing the duration but not frequency of training sessions so that technical skills are maintained.

Although there is a science to tapering, there is an art to it as well. Coaches and athletes need to be mentally prepared to deal with the anxiety of not constantly training and the stress of crew selection. Finally, the logistics of traveling to a competition can undo the benefits of a taper if not planned with an understanding of how changes in time zones, food, and lodging can create physical and mental stress.

PART
VI

Sports Medicine for Rowers

Principles of Rowing Injuries

Jane Thornton, MD, PhD

Rowing ranks among the most aerobically strenuous of all sports, with high training volumes and forces approaching 1,000 N (225 lbs) with every stroke executed. As a result, most rowing-related injuries are chronic in nature. Although most can be treated conservatively and debilitating injuries are less frequent, some do not resolve. In such cases athletes may be faced with early retirement or advanced medical treatment such as surgery.

Emerging concepts in the science of rowing injury include the optimization of prevention and management of low back pain and rib stress injury; low energy availability or relative energy deficiency in sport (REDs); and long-term impacts on athlete health (particularly cardiovascular). Other illnesses can occur, and health may be adversely affected by dermatologic conditions, infections due to water quality issues, relative energy deficiency in sport (REDs), and other conditions, which will be discussed in chapter 25. Fortunately, life-threatening or permanent injuries are rare.

The sport's rapidly changing demographics show significant growth in masters and para rowing populations. The World Rowing Federation has expanded beyond its traditional flat-water racing format to include the discipline of open-water or coastal rowing. Research into rowing injuries will undoubtedly recalibrate to meet the needs of these changes and increase in participation numbers. For the time being, however, traditional flat-water rowing and use of the stationary ergometer continue to account for the bulk of rowing injuries.

Key Point

Injury prevention strategies for rowing are still in their infancy, likely because the mechanisms and causes for many rowing injuries are still not fully understood.

Epidemiology

Epidemiology is the study of disease at the population level. From prevalence to incidence, distribution to possible control of diseases, it is an examination of all factors relating to health within a given group of people. Injury in rowing does not have a long history of in-depth epidemiological study.

There are several reasons for this. First is the research itself: Studies in rowing injury literature have traditionally been either descriptive (i.e., piecing together what happened postinjury) or theoretical in nature. The last decade has seen a shift toward a more objective analysis of risk factors and causes of injury, yet challenges remain, including differences in participant demographics, short periods of data collection, low sample size, differences in injury definitions, and bias due to retrospective analysis (Rumball et al. 2005).

Pinpointing the source of any given injury is a second complicating factor. From one stroke to the next, balance and timing issues within the crew, load on the blade, fatigue levels, and different muscular firing patterns make it difficult to determine the exact cause of an injury.

A third challenge is the capture of data specific to rowing. Rowers frequently engage in cross-training, therefore identifying injury as occurring during actual rowing as opposed to lifting weights or running can sometimes be difficult. Changes in equipment over time (e.g., use of dynamic ergometers vs. stationary) may lead to different injury patterns as well. Ergometer use has further facilitated rowing-specific year-round training that may increase the risk of overuse injuries.

Evolution in equipment and technology present a related fourth challenge: such changes can lead to adjustments in technique and body movements. For example, the shift from less rigid wooden boat and oar construction to stiffer materials, most notably carbon fiber, has led to increased boat speed. Stiffer materials may increase the forces placed on the rower's body as a result.

A fifth factor includes the rules of the sport: changes to the so-called "rules of racing" may exert an unexpected influence on the rate and type of injury. Perhaps the most significant of these rule changes was the introduction of Olympic-level women's rowing at the Montreal 1976 Games. Another significant rule change was the shift from 1,000 m racing to 2,000 m racing for female rowers in the mid-1980s. Para rowers similarly made their Games debut at the Beijing 2008 Paralympics racing 1,000 m, a distance that doubled by Tokyo 2020. These race distances utilize different energy systems and have the potential for different injury rates. Olympic lightweight rowing, which debuted at the Atlanta 1996 Games, has an added dynamic of weight-related health concerns. Although these factors make it difficult to develop a completely accurate overall picture, there continues to be a consistent pattern to injury onset, cause, and prognosis.

How Common Are Rowing Injuries?

One early injury study of athletes across 11 sports showed a reported injury rate of 1.4 per 10,000 person-hours for rowing (the highest rate was 36.5 for football). Unfortunately, the authors did not specify which injuries were rowing induced; for example, two rowers suffered ankle fractures. Either way, the authors concluded that rowing is "a very safe sport" (Weightman and Browne 1975).

Individual nations have also collected this data. A prospective study on the patterns of injury in elite South Korean rowers training for the Olympic Games recorded 514 injuries over a 10-year period, with an average of 2.86 injuries per athlete annually; among these, over half (57.8%) were mild (Kim and Park 2020). A prospective study of 153 Australian national team rowers found 4.1 to 6.4 injuries per 1,000 athlete days over eight seasons, with one athlete day representing a day of training or competition for an individual athlete (Trease et al. 2020). Researchers studying a sample of 29 German female rowers also found a high prevalence of musculoskeletal injuries, mainly resulting from overuse (Winzen et al. 2011). In a sample of 20 Irish international-level rowers, a mean injury rate of 3.67 per 1,000 exposure hours was reported, with a total of 44 injuries reported in a 12-month period (Wilson et al. 2010).

Who Is Affected by Injury?

Three studies involving Australian and Irish international-level rowers (Hickey, Fricker, and McDonald 1997; Reid et al. 1989; Trease et al. 2020) showed several similarities. One Australian study took a retrospective approach, using years of injury data that revealed 320 injuries in 172 elite rowers (Hickey, Fricker, and McDonald 1997). When it came to Irish rowers, 65% of those surveyed reported a history of injury (Reid et al. 1989). A recent prospective study involving 153 national team rowers over eight seasons observed 270 total injuries, with no differences in overall injury rate between men and women, scullers and sweepers, or lightweight and openweight rowers (Trease et al. 2020).

Work has been done to determine a correlation between injury rate and age. For senior international rowers, the mean injury rate per year was 0.92 injuries per rower (1.75 injuries per 1,000 training sessions per rower) (Smoljanović et al. 2015). In junior rowers, mean injury rate was not reported, but 73.8% of the 398 rower-reported injuries involved overuse, and 26.2% were related to a single traumatic event. In a study involving masters rowers, the mean injury rate per year was found to be 0.48 injuries per rower (2.25 injuries per 1,000 training sessions per rower). The majority of injuries were chronic and did not lead to the loss of training or competition time (Smoljanović et al. 2018).

How Does Injury Occur?

The evidence shows that injuries do not only occur during on-water rowing. Land-based training—including running, ergometer training, and weight training—has been linked to up to 50% of injuries in elite rowers (Hannafin 2000; Hickey 1997). Forty years ago, one researcher observed that all back pain in his sample of rowers could be attributed to weight lifting (Stallard 1980). A later study documented 54 rowing injuries, of which 65% occurred in the context of rowing and 28% in the weight room, the latter causing more incidents of lumbosacral injury (Wajswelner, Mosler, and Coburn 1995). Other researchers have noted a similar pattern in rowing injury in general (Karlson 2000; Warden et al. 2002). Interestingly, Trease and colleagues found that over eight seasons, on-water training comprised 68% of injuries reported in national team rowers and weight training only 8% (Trease et al. 2020). They found a disturbing trend that road cycling accounted for one-third of all acute injuries reported, with a mean loss of 31 athlete days per injury.

The potential for elevated risk in the weight room may be a result of the long levers (arms and legs) that typify a rower's physical build, especially at the elite level. Long limbs are pivotal to maximizing stroke length, but are not ideally suited to lifting heavy weights.

For those rowers without year-round access to water, the transition period between dry land and on-water training can be a source of higher rates of injury (Hannafin 2000), as can heavy training periods that emphasize a large volume of work coupled with high intensity. Data from Australian national teams collected in the late 1990s substantiate these findings with two peak times for injury presentation: the high-volume months and high-intensity months (summer racing) (Hickey 1997).

Where Does Injury Occur?

The main sites of rowing injury are the lumbar spine (2%-53%), followed by the chest wall (6.0%-22.6%) and the forearm and wrist (2.3%-15.5%) (Bahr et al. 2004; Devereaux and Lachman 1983; Rumball et al. 2005; Trease et al. 2020). Specific injuries are detailed in the next chapter.

What Is the Outcome?

From reduced time on the water or in the gym to missed competitions or, in more extreme cases, lost seasons, dealing with injury can have a major impact on elite rowers' training. A paper written 30 years ago documenting 54 rowing injuries over a 12-month period observed that only 20% of injuries kept rowers out of the boat for longer than 1 week (Coburn and Wajswelner 1993). Wilson and colleagues (2014) observed a time loss of 1 to 2 weeks for most. Recently, Trease and colleagues observed that 9% of training days were lost to illness and injury over 8 years in elite rowers selected to the Australian national team (Trease et al. 2020).

On an individual basis, time out of the boat or away from training can last much longer than the average and may be the reason rowers retire early or switch sports. Typically, this is caused by low back pain or rib stress fractures, although once again researchers are limited by a lack of good data—it is possible that many rowers retire early as a result of injury and never make it to the collegiate or elite level, where much of the research is done.

Rib stress fractures can result in time loss of up to 4 to 6 weeks (Warden et al. 2002), although these do not occur as often in recreational- or club-level rowers. In the elite population, research suggests that an estimated 10% to 15% of elite rowers will sustain a rib stress fracture at some point in their competitive careers (Hannafin 2000).

It's important to remember that a history of injury doesn't mean it will happen again. Preexisting back pain may be an indicator of more back pain in future, but counterintuitively, could lead to less time off from training. In collegiate rowers, O'Kane, Teitz, and Lind (2003) noted that preexisting back pain led to differences in time off sport. Of college rowers with a history of back pain prior to college, 79% missed one week and 6% missed one month. For athletes with no history of back pain, 62% missed one week and 18% missed one month. In other words, athletes with preexisting back pain were more likely to have back pain in college and to take short-term breaks from training, but less likely to experience significant time away or end their college rowing careers because of it. The authors postulated that athletes with no history of back pain may not have developed coping strategies, been exposed to treatment strategies, or gained a psychological benefit from prior recovery of symptoms.

Risk Factors

Understanding the risk factors for rowing injury can both improve prevention and help with successful management. Risk factors are generally considered intrinsic (characteristics or circumstances within the body) or extrinsic (factors outside of the athlete).

Intrinsic

Intrinsic factors include physical and motor characteristics, stroke mechanics, energy availability, sleep, and biopsychosocial elements.

Physical Characteristics

Rowers are typically tall and lean, with an average height approaching 6 ft (182 cm) for women and 6 ft 6 in. (198 cm) for men. Yet those very characteristics, an advantage in the sport, may themselves be risk factors for injury in the sport. One study of a group of 1,632 college rowers linked greater height and weight, as well as taking up rowing before the age of 16, with significantly increased risk for low back pain (Teitz et al. 2002).

Motor Characteristics

Regardless of how tall a rower is, success at the elite level requires technical mastery that must be honed over many years of dedicated training. Research is inconclusive whether or not hypomobility (relatively "stiff" joints) or hypermobility ("loose" joints) contribute to back pain. One study of 20 elite male rowers with and without low back pain observed that those with current or previous symptoms had variable ranges of motion (McGregor, Anderton, and Gedroyc 2002). Those with pain demonstrated hypomobility in their lumbar spines, although authors could not conclude whether these differences in mobility were a result or a cause of their pain. In a study of low back pain in 17 female elite lightweight rowers, a high positive correlation was found between hyperflexion (abnormally high range of motion with forward flexion) of the lumbar spine and low back pain, as well as a high negative correlation between adherence to a regular stretching program and low back pain (Howell 1984).

Key Point

Equally as significant as their contribution to an athlete's performance potential, technical elements such as motor coordination, balance, and flexibility may have a significant influence on injury development or its prevention.

In the broader injury literature, functional movement screens and tests such as the sit-and-reach test have been found unable to predict injury (Bahr 2016). What's more, better performance on the sit-and-reach test (for hamstring flexibility) shows an inverse relationship to running economy and potentially athletic performance as well (Nuzzo 2020). A good rule of thumb might be to avoid or at least address extremes of flexibility or mobility, and if injury happens, to specifically target areas of weakness.

Stroke Mechanics

When rowers are learning to row, there is a theoretical risk of injury because the boat may be continually off-balance and compromise effective (and protective) power application (McNally, Wilson, and Seiler 2005). More experienced rowers selectively recruit muscle groups to effectively move the boat (Yoshiga and Higuchi 2003).

Even in individual rowers, stroke mechanics may change over time, whether over the years or over the course of a race as the athlete becomes fatigued. Toward the end of a long training session, motor control of the muscles of the low back may be impaired (Caldwell, McNair, and Williams 2003; Holt et al. 2003). There is an increase in lumbar spine flexion with duration of stationary rowing ergometer use (Wilson et al. 2013).

A Danish study documented the effect of movement patterns with potential for injury risk. Rowers with a history of rib stress fractures had a higher velocity of the seat in the initial drive phase (corresponding to a sequential drive pattern), along with greater co-contraction of serratus anterior and trapezius muscles and a reduced leg-to-arm strength ratio (Vinther et al. 2006).

Energy Availability

Low energy availability means insufficient amounts of available energy relative to what the body needs to perform tasks and basic functioning. It is a result of either intentional or unintentional energy deficit caused by a higher energy output than calorie intake and may negatively impact bone health and performance. This in turn may lead to relative energy deficiency in sport (REDs), which results in impaired physiological function and performance, including metabolic rate, menstrual function, bone health, immune system status, protein synthesis and cardiovascular health. It is described in more detail in chapters 26 and 28.

Sleep

As discussed in chapter 22, our understanding of sleep's central role in athletic performance has grown in recent years. Adolescent athletes who get fewer than 8 hours of sleep per night have 1.7 times greater risk of sporting injury than their counterparts who sleep for 8 hours or more. Injury risk was doubled when an increased training intensity and volume was coupled with shorter sleep in elite adolescent athletes (Milewski et al. 2014).

Biopsychosocial Elements

The final intrinsic risk factor for potential injury is the subjective experience of how each of us registers pain. There has been an upsurge in research on elements of the injury experience unrelated to anatomical damage; specifically, with respect to pain. Pain is expressed differently from person to person (Gatchel et al. 2017). Everything from social supports, team culture, coping skills, family background, attitudes, and beliefs can all influence the intensity and duration of pain.

Extrinsic

Extrinsic factors of injury in rowing include equipment, type of rowing, the increased use of indoor ergometers, and weather conditions.

Equipment

There is no question that advances in equipment over the years have played a role in improved rowing performance. These same changes, however, have also been implicated in higher injury rates.

The greatest blame for injury has been leveled (possibly unfairly) against the so-called hatchet blade. Introduced in 1992, the hatchet blade's surface area was substantially larger than the standard symmetrical Macon or tulip blade. Unpublished observations from the Canadian national team at the time led some to believe that this resulted in increased incidence of injury (outlined in Thornton and Vinther 2018). However, the size of the blades may not have been as much a factor as their rapid adoption by coaches and athletes, who may not have adjusted their rig to account for the larger surface area.

Regardless of the type of boat or blades, setting the correct rig may play a central role in reducing the risk of injury. Even something as seemingly benign as improper foot angle or placement may contribute to knee injuries (Karlson 2000). As discussed in chapter 9, because the rowing oar is essentially a lever, length adjustments to one or both ends of the oar or changes to the length of the oarlock significantly increase or decrease the load experienced by the rower. Too much or too little load both reduce boat speed and increase risk of injury. In larger boats with more than one rower, attention must be paid to ensuring the correct rig so that rowers are not loaded differently and that the port and starboard oars are similarly loaded for each sculler.

Type of Rowing

Sculling is by definition—although not always in reality—a symmetrical motion in which the arms spread out to left and right at the catch while the body remains above the boat's center. In contrast, a sweeper's arms and body must follow the arc of a single oar handle as it sweeps around the oarlock like the hand of a clock out beyond the boats' gunwales.

Conventional wisdom holds that the innate symmetry of sculling makes it a safer choice when it comes to lowering the risk of injury. The assumption is that sweep rowing's asymmetrical movement of the trunk to varying degrees at the catch lends itself to higher rates of injury. The findings of early research in this area have done much to reinforce this general impression within the sport. Two studies in 1980 and 1993 suggested that because sweep rowers specialize on one side, this may lead to asymmetric muscle development and subsequent low back pain (Secher 1993; Stallard 1980). As research continues, however, opinions may be changing. Although studies through the 1980s and 1990s suggested a link between sweep rowing and increases in rib stress fracture incidence (Bojanić and Desnica 1998; Christiansen and Kanstrup 1997; Holden and Jackson 1985), more recent studies have observed no differences (Hannafin 2000; Trease et al. 2020).

Ergometers

Rowing ergometers are as ubiquitous as boats when it comes to training, testing, and crew selection. Many former rowers and even nonrowers also use ergometers for general fitness purposes. Because of the greater control over variables such as weather, temperature, and balance versus on-water rowing, the rowing ergometer is also the modality of choice for researchers investigating various aspects of the sport.

Along with the benefits of indoor rowing, using the ergometer is not without risk. In a study involving 1,632 U.S. college rowers, authors observed that using a stationary rowing ergometer for longer than 30 min at a time increased the risk of low back pain (Teitz et al. 2002; Wilson et al. 2014).

Traditional rowing ergometers are referred to as *stationary* or *static* because the movements are limited to the seat and a handle attached to the flywheel, usually by a bicycle chain. Dynamic ergometers, in contrast, have more moving parts, specifically allowing the flywheel to move in relation to the ground. Dynamic ergometers can be purpose-built machines or stationary ergometers that have been placed onto sliders (tracks with a rolling carriage system to allow a range of lateral movement).

The relative newcomer status of dynamic ergometers means that research into their differences from static machines is still in its infancy. Although it is still unclear how injury outcomes are influenced by ergometer type, some researchers postulate that dynamic ergometers may reduce the rate of rib stress injury (Thornton and Vinther 2018). A study of 153 Australian national team rowers over eight seasons highlighted an interesting observation: With a switch from stationary to dynamic ergometers and back again (as a result of changes in policy), the authors found a significant decrease in lumbar injury with dynamic ergometer use and a similar increase when the stationary ergometer once again became the standard (Trease et al. 2020).

Weather Conditions

When rowing on the water, participants are further exposed to a number of environmental risks. Besides the risk of collision into other watercraft or stationary objects such as moored boats or bridge abutments, these include exposure to heat and cold, poor water quality, wind and high waves, sudden changes in weather, and lightning. Illnesses and infections related to environmental issues are discussed in chapter 13. Rowing clubs, coaches, athletes, and other stakeholders must take environmental risks into consideration at all times.

Prevention

On the whole, injuries in rowing have not been as thoroughly studied as those in many high-profile or professional sports. Historically, rowing-specific injury prevention strategies have been based on expert opinion or consensus, small case studies, or anecdotes. Fortunately, this is changing and more solid evidence-based advice is becoming available.

Rowing-Specific Strategies

Addressing strength deficiencies is a promising place to start. In one study, researchers introduced a 6 to 8 month hamstring-strengthening program to 22 female rowers and observed a reduction in low back pain incidence (Koutedakis, Frischknecht, and Murthy 1997). Others have advocated for hamstring and gluteal muscle stretching and core stability work (McGregor, Anderton, and Gedroyc 2002) and maintaining anterior rotation of the pelvis (Caldwell, McNair, and Williams 2003) to prevent low back pain.

A more synchronous, flowing rowing stroke technique may be beneficial for prevention of rib stress injury (Vinther et al. 2006), compared with a sequential strategy of initiating the drive phase with only the legs (knee extension) followed by extension of the hip and back. Practical (but theoretical) strategies include modifying technique for longer rows (Karlson 2000) and switching sides for injured sweep rowers (McNally, Wilson, and Seiler 2005).

Workload

There has been much recent work investigating the influence of acute or chronic workload on injury. One intriguing concept emerging from this research is chronic workload acting as a "vaccine against injury." The premise is that acute spikes in workload increase the risk of injury, but striking the right balance of acute-to-chronic workload in any given month of training might reduce such risk. This research postulates a sweet spot of ≤1.5 where gains can be made while minimizing the injury risk (Gabbett 2016).

This is not a perfect model, as the author himself freely admits (Gabbett 2020). When it comes to the rate of actual injury, an important rule of thumb for clinicians and rowers alike to remember is that risk does not equal rate. In other words, "just because an athlete is at risk (even high risk), the event may not occur" (Gabbett 2020, 59). It is also important to keep in mind that too little training, or detraining, may also increase risk (i.e., a trough versus a spike).

Two other important concepts to keep in mind are those of monotony (low variability in training stimulus) and strain (the product of high training loads and high monotony), which have been associated with the greatest incidence of illness in athletes (Gabbett 2016).

Reasonable advice for coaches and sport scientists designing a training program might therefore include the following (Gabbett 2020):

1. Establish a moderate chronic training load.
2. Minimize week-to-week changes in training load.
3. Avoid exceeding the ceiling of safety for the sport.
4. Ensure a minimum training load is maintained.
5. Avoid inconsistent loading patterns.
6. Ensure training loads are proportionate to the demands of the sport.
7. Monitor the athlete throughout the latent period (i.e., following the application of load or spikes in load).

It would also be advisable to ensure a smooth and gradual increase or decrease in workload when transitioning between phases of the annual training plan (with respect to periodization and tapering).

Motor Variability

Motor variability is the range of movement patterns athletes use in undertaking specific tasks such as the rowing stroke. In the extreme, high motor variability means that an athlete rarely uses the same movement pattern while executing the same task: Imagine a beginner rower who does not take any two strokes in the same way. Low motor variability, on the other hand, means recruiting the same limited group of muscles to execute movements as similarly as possible from one repetition to the next. Moderately experienced rowers with a decent grasp of stroke mechanics, especially "fair weather" rowers, will generally have low motor variability. Interestingly, as a rower progresses to the point of mastery, motor variability becomes a U-shaped curve. Expertise seems to bring with it a return to high motor variability, yet this time it is not a result of lack of skill. Researchers believe that years of training teach the body to spread the load across different body regions, muscles, and soft tissue structures (Potvin-Gilbert 2018). Pain and fatigue cause adaptations to this variability. Acute pain may increase motor variability to avoid painful patterns, whereas chronic pain reduces variability to minimize pain. This decrease may remain after the injury has healed, which may increase further risk (Potvin-Gilbert 2018). Cross-training may also increase this variability or selective recruitment.

Injury Recovery and Management

Once an athlete is injured, there are various strategies to consider for management and prevention of recurrence. Removing an athlete from training completely is predictive of injury recurrence, because the rower must play catch-up upon return to sport. Maintaining normal training load and avoiding aggravating factors and complete (prolonged) rest is therefore important (Gabbett 2016). Using adequate chronic loads to prevent reinjury while also returning to sport as quickly and safely as possible can sometimes be a delicate art.

Research on pain management strategies is scarce in the elite sporting population and there is virtually none for elite athletes with a disability. Many questions have yet to be answered about the influence of preexisting, persistent pain on sports performance or the use of cognitive behavior therapy or other therapies as treatment.

Rowers can optimize factors within their control, such as diet, recovery, sleep, and maintaining a positive outlook. Although not yet confirmed in rowers, there is evidence for increased stress fracture prevention through supplementation with calcium and vitamin D in female military recruits.

Key Point

The following are some practical examples for injury prevention:

- Try not to exceed 30 min on a static ergometer if you are at risk for low back pain. Try switching it up by lowering the drag factor, changing the stroke rate or length, and using dynamic ergs or ergs on sliders.
- Cross-train to minimize injury risk. Cross-country skiing, cycling, running, elliptical use, and swimming can help decrease load on the joints or muscles at risk for injury in rowing.
- Static stretching right before activity may increase risk of injury. Stretching after may provide benefits for isolated injuries, but not for performance or overall risk of injury.
- Allow time for adequate recovery between ergometer and weight sessions (especially power cleans) (Wilson, Gissane, and McGregor 2014).
- Optimize nutrition.
- Get enough sleep (>8 hours).

Conclusion

Rowing is a sport with a relatively low risk of injury and illness. Reducing risk of injury through education and prevention can allow athletes at all levels to continue to enjoy the sport and perform to their potential. Even after an injury occurs, identification and modification of risk factors to prevent future injury is key. Specific strategies are outlined in the next chapter.

25 CHAPTER

Mechanisms and Management of Rowing Injuries

Jane Thornton, MD, PhD

Many rowers are familiar with being sidelined with an injury, and though most are short term in nature, some can be debilitating and even career-ending. Although many rowers report muscle soreness, blisters, and general aches and pains when getting back on the water or ergometer, there are a few injuries that don't fade as quickly as we would hope. The majority of injuries that sideline rowers for long periods of time include low back and chest wall injuries.

> "I remember being on the water, and it was like a tsunami of pain came through. It was overwhelming. I couldn't breathe, I couldn't do anything. . . . I got in to have an MRI. . . . The doctor said, 'The bad news is that you've got two discs that are extremely protruding, one is likely ruptured. And the really bad news is this isn't something that fixes in three weeks, like between now and the Olympics.' So then all the decision making went into withdrawing from the competition. . . . I was in such a lucky position in that I already had four Olympic medals at home and none of my decision-making had to be made on desperate measures. I could think, 'Well, I want to have a kid one day and I want to be able to play physically with my kid and I want to be able to continue to have a really physical lifestyle, so I don't want to try desperate measures, I don't want to try cortisone shots.'"
>
> Marnie McBean, three-time Olympic gold medalist (2020)

Low Back

As mentioned in the previous chapter, the lower back region accounts for most rowing injuries. However, prospective data is lacking, and most studies concentrate on elite or college rowers.

How Does It Happen?

Risk factors for low back pain in sport in general include a previous history of low back pain, high volumes of training and competition with poor load management, and years of exposure to sport (Wilson et al. 2020). Most low back pain is chronic in nature and is associated with higher training volume (total training hours and years rowing) (Newlands, Reid, and Parmar 2015) or biomechanical "errors." The strongest risk factors for future low back pain are a previous episode (Ng et al. 2014; Teitz, O'Kane, and Lind 2003) and amount of time spent on the rowing ergometer, especially sessions over 30 min in length (De Campus Mello et al. 2014, Ng et al. 2014; Teitz, O'Kane, and Lind 2003). Other factors include entering the sport of rowing prior to age 16, time of year (i.e., winter season), and improper weight lifting or core stability training technique.

Key Point

Risk factors for low back pain include the following:

- Previous low back pain episode
- Amount of time spent on the rowing ergometer
- Entering the sport of rowing prior to age 16
- Time of year (i.e., winter season)
- Improper weight lifting or core stability training technique

During the rowing stroke, flexion and twisting forces are most intense at the catch, where compressive loads on the spine at the initial movement of the blade are an estimated 4.6 times the rower's mass (Morris et al. 2000). As rowers get tired, especially during periods of high-volume or high-intensity training, muscle fiber contractibility and proprioception become increasingly impaired, which results in "spinal creep," or the reduced ability to load the spine (Solomonow et al. 1999; Wilson et al. 2010), as well as altered kinematics (Wilson et al. 2010; Wilson et al. 2012). Lumbar ligaments may become inflamed with such a high-magnitude cyclic load (King et al. 2009).

One frequently cited hypothesis suggests that maintaining hip range of motion will reduce this stress on the spine (Buckeridge 2012; Bull and McGregor 2003; Holt et al. 2003; McGregor, Anderton, and Gedroyc 2002). Researchers postulate that a posterior pelvic tilt (or backward pivot of the pelvis) may increase lumbar flexion and therefore the risk of low back pain (Caldwell, McNair, and Williams 2003; Mackenzie, Bull, and McGregor 2008; Wilson, Gissane, and McGregor 2014), but we do not have enough data to confirm these relationships yet. Novice rowers and those with a history of back injury use higher degrees of lumbar flexion along with limited pelvic rotation, particularly with increasing work intensity (McGregor, Bull, and Byng-Maddick 2004). To date, there is no definition of an ideal range of motion for rowing; it is likely individual.

Another protective mechanism may be through increased intra-abdominal pressure (IAP), mostly modulated through breathing patterns. These are linked mostly to prevention, although in one rare case, it has been associated with the development of an injury. One study examining the effect of breathing in during the drive versus breathing out noted that the latter increases IAP, which can offset the high levels of shear force and compression observed in the lumbar spine (Manning et al. 2000). A case study of a recreational rower with an existing diaphragmatic hernia observed a worsening of that hernia due to increased IAP (Shah et al. 2013).

Of course, not all rowers get low back pain, and some may in fact have incidental findings noted on imaging without any symptoms. For those who do experience low back pain, the cause is likely multifactorial—cumulative loading combined with other factors such as biomechanics, genetic predisposition, lifestyle, and work activities (figure 25.1). When the lumbar extensor muscles tire, this leads to impaired awareness of excessive lumbar flexion, which is associated with injury risk (Taimela, Kankaanpaa, and Luoto 1999).

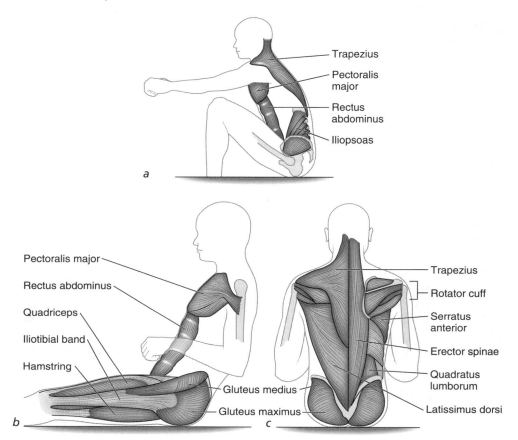

▶ **Figure 25.1** Muscles used in the rowing stroke: forward *(a)*, pull *(b)*, and rear *(c)* positions.

Courtesy of Genevieve Brysdon.

Specific Low Back Injuries

The low back injuries most frequently seen in rowers are spondylolysis and spondylolisthesis (O'Kane, Teitz, and Lind 2003), sacroiliac joint pain (Dolan and Adams 2001), and intervertebral disc dysfunction (Karlson 2000).

Spondylolysis and Spondylolisthesis

Spondylolysis is a stress fracture at a part of the vertebra called the pars interarticularis, part of each vertebra's interlocking winglike structure that protects the spinal cord. Spondylolysis is usually preceded by a stress reaction at the same site (figure 25.2).

Athletes in sports using high levels of lumbar extension and rotation are at higher risk of spondylolysis. It usually occurs only on one side of the spine (unilateral). Bilateral (on both sides) spondylolysis is rare and can lead to spondylolisthesis, or the forward displacement of one vertebra relative to another.

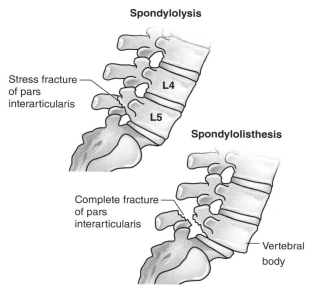

Spondylolysis

Stress fracture of pars interarticularis

L4

L5

Spondylolisthesis

Complete fracture of pars interarticularis

Vertebral body

▶ **Figure 25.2** Spondylolysis and spondylolisthesis in the lumbar spine.

Spondylolysis is more prevalent in rowers than in the general population; it is seen in 17% of adult rowers (O'Kane, Teitz, and Lind 2003) versus 11.5% of nonrowers (Hedman and Ferney 1997). This is particularly true of adolescent rowers, 22.7% of whom presented with a stress reaction and 4.5 with spondylolysis compared to 0% for both in nonrowing controls (Heuer et al. 2007). Young rowers' spines are still growing, and their exposure to repetitive hyperextension and rotation of the lumbar spine may make them susceptible to injury. Although rowers' spines may not reach full lumbar extension during the rowing stroke, the act of extension occurring through the drive on a loaded spine may contribute. There may also be an association with weight lifting (Callaghan and McGill 2001).

Sacroiliac Joint Pain

The sacroiliac (SI) joint is where the fused bottom portion of the spine (sacrum) fits between the two large hip bones (ilia). Pain in the region of the ligaments connecting the sacrum and one or both ilia can be an uncomfortable experience. Pain over the SI joint may be caused by several factors, including referred pain from the low back, irritation of the sacroiliac ligaments, leg length discrepancy, underlying hypermobility, or limited hip range of motion (Karlson 2000).

Data on SI joint pain caused by rowing are limited and there is some evidence that it may only present in sweep rowers (Dolan and Adams 2001). Bilateral SI joint pain could indicate an inflammatory condition known as ankylosing spondylitis and should be brought to the attention of a health care provider.

Intervertebral Disc Dysfunction

The third major source of low back pain in rowers comes from the connective tissues of the spine itself and the muscles supporting its function. A common way to think of the spine is as a column made up of small cylindrical drums (vertebrae) stacked one on top of another with a rubber-like cushion (intervertebral disc) between each. Ligaments attached to each vertebra hold the whole column in place as muscles contract to bend or extend the spine (flexion and extension).

The intervertebral disc is made up of several parts. The outside ring of tougher ligament material (annulus) and inner gelatinous section (nucleus) work together to sustain compressive loads (figure 25.3a) (Van Dieen 2002). High anterior (forward) compressive force is noted in high ranges of lumbar flexion (Brinjikji et al. 2015). As the spine bends, discs are compressed in the direction of flexion. When discs are compressed in one direction during repeated cyclical loading, such as the spinal flexion of the rowing motion, rowers can experience disc bulging (Soler and Calderon 2000), herniation (Kalichmman, Kim, and Hunter 2009), and facet joint capsule strain (figure 25.3b) (Maurer, Soder, and Baldisserotto 2011). Compression forces noted in the rowers' lumbar spine are comparable to those in repeated lifting, which has been reported to cause fracture of the vertebral end plates (Stallard 1980).

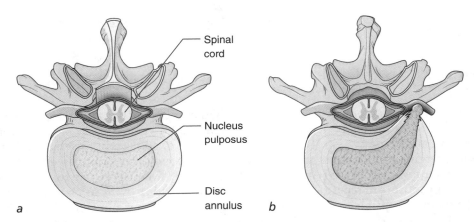

Spinal cord

Nucleus pulposus

Disc annulus

a　　　　　*b*

▶ **Figure 25.3**　The parts of *(a)* a normal spinal disc and *(b)* a herniated disc.

How Can We Treat It?

Conservative treatment should be considered first, including exercise and physiotherapy. Current research suggests that dynamic, endurance-based training is preferable to static core stability during regular training (Wilson 2016). That said, there is some suggestion that limited isometric trunk activity may reduce pain in the short term. Other strategies include using a lower load setting on the ergometer (Teitz 2003) and correcting any underlying hip range-of-motion or strength and flexibility deficiencies (Thornton 2016). Surgery may be considered in rare cases of significant nerve damage, progressive pain and disability, or nonresponse to treatment. Surgical repair has a good prognosis and return-to-sport rate (Little 2005). The routine use of imaging is not recommended by expert clinicians. There also isn't enough evidence regarding the value of manual therapy (massage, spinal manipulation) or biomechanical modifications alone (Thornton et al. 2021).

Treatment will differ across time. At initial presentation and during the acute phase of recovery, experts prioritize early identification of symptoms, pain control, remaining active with cross-training, and regaining rowing-specific movement patterns (Wilkie et al. 2021). During the subacute phase and throughout rehabilitation to return to sport, experts prioritize progressively increasing on-water training volume and intensity with concomitant reduction in cross-training, interdisciplinary involvement in the return-to-sport plan, and ensuring modifiable risk factors for rowing-related low back pain are addressed (Wilkie et al. 2021). There has also been a recent shift in attention to the biopsychosocial element in low back pain and the need to incorporate behavioral therapies into management (Hainline 2017).

It can also be helpful for coaches or other members of the support team to observe the rower's technique on the ergometer and in the boat (Nugent et al. 2021). It is common for rowers to have some asymmetry in their muscular development, which may or may not be related to their sweeping side preference (Reide et al. 2014). Rowers with current or prior low back pain may experience lower lumbar stiffness (McGregor, Anderton, and Gedroyc 2002; Ng et al. 2015) and compensate via the pelvis, upper lumbar, or lower thoracic spine to achieve desired length at the catch.

A natural curvature of the spine is desirable for even load distribution through the vertebrae and optimal load-bearing function (Mackenzie, Bull, and McGregor 2008). At the catch, it appears as an extended C shape with shins vertical while the hips are in full flexion (see figure 25.4). Moving through the stroke to the release sees the pelvis rotate posteriorly while the hips and the C shape of the spine extend (although never reach neutral). It used to be common guidance for rowers to maintain a very straight spine, but contemporary advice is usually to allow some flexion.

▶ **Figure 25.4** Lumbar curve of a successful Olympic rower, with the C shape at the catch position.

In sport in general, treatment using exercise approaches reduces pain and improves function, but the effect on return to sport is unknown (Thornton et al. 2021). When 25 rowers with low back pain were interviewed, they reported a culture of conceal-ment of pain from coaches and teammates and fear of being judged as weak because of the limitations caused by their pain (Wilson, Ng, et al. 2021). A recent consensus statement on treating low back pain in rowers recommended early recognition and management, as well as creating a training environment in which rowers are educated about the nature of low back pain and encouraged to disclose their pain early to improve outcomes (Wilson, Thornton, et al. 2021).

Chest Wall

The chest (thorax or thoracic region) by most anatomical definitions covers the part of the body between the neck and abdominal region. This includes the cavity enclosed by the ribs, sternum, and vertebrae, which contains the chief organs of circulation and respiration.

Chest wall injuries can be among the most debilitating in the sport of rowing, with overall time lost measured in weeks or even months. In rare cases, life-threatening cardiac or respiratory events can occur. Although the risk is low, the severity of these events necessitates first ruling out chest pain that is due to cardiac or respiratory origins. Most other types of chest wall injury are due to overuse and will ultimately self-resolve, although complications can include delayed or incomplete rehabilitation due to misdiagnosis, or in the case of rib stress fractures, concerns for nonunion (or arrest in the fracture repair process) where the bone has improperly healed.

How Does It Happen?

Pain in the chest wall region lends itself to a very broad differential diagnosis, especially among rowers, who use their upper bodies to simultaneously apply force, provide stability, and breathe. Furthermore, muscles, bones, nerves, and internal organs can all contribute to pain in the chest wall. Here again, data specific to the rowing population are sparse—the clear majority of the existing research is anecdotal or retrospective in nature. As such, early clinical diagnosis is key so that important measures can be taken as soon as possible. Such diagnoses may be verified by imaging such as ultrasound, bone scan, or magnetic resonance imaging (MRI).

Common Injuries

Common chest injuries include strained intercostal muscles, costochondritis, costovertebral joint pain and dysfunction, and rib stress injury (RSI), whereas much more rare conditions may include bone malignancy such as Ewing's sarcoma (Evans and Redgrave 2016a; Rumball et al. 2005; Smoljanovic and Bojanic 2007). Others are listed in table 25.1. Although the mechanisms of injury appear slightly different in each case, pain in the chest region should be taken as a signal for further investigation in order to pinpoint the likeliest site of injury and determine that best management strategy.

Table 25.1 Causes of Chest Wall Pain in the Rower

Common	Rare
Intercostal muscle strain	Intercostal nerve injury
Costochondritis	Serratus anterior avulsion
Rib stress reaction	Bone malignancy (e.g., Ewing's sarcoma)
Rib stress fracture	Thoracic outlet syndrome
Costovertebral joint pain or dysfunction	Referred pain from cardiac or respiratory origin

Intercostal Muscle Strain

This is often confused with rib stress injury at initial presentation. Intercostal muscle strains exhibit nonspecific tenderness on palpation, but instead of being a bony injury, the muscles in between the ribs are the structures involved.

Costochondritis

This is a poorly understood condition that can be very painful and debilitating to the athlete. It is most likely to occur because of excessive rotation in sweep rowing (Thornton et al. 2016) and is characterized by an slow onset of generalized chest wall pain aggravated by rowing, reaching, and even rolling over in bed. Costochondritis will exhibit pain and tenderness on costochondral joints without swelling.

Costovertebral Joint Pain or Dysfunction

Although not well understood, costovertebral joint pain or dysfunction is sometimes diagnosed when athletes present with a constant sharp pain in the interscapular region and spasm of the rhomboids and local paravertebral muscles. There is marked local tenderness in acute cases but may only be local muscle irritation in recurrent cases. Lateral flexion and thoracic rotation is limited at the affected level.

Rib Stress Injury

Rib stress injury is a spectrum ranging from mild stress reaction all the way to rib stress fracture and even severe (fortunately uncommon) complete facture. They result because of an imbalance between microdamage caused by continuous mechanical loading of the bone and its ability to remodel and repair itself (Warden 2002). Because there is no direct loading on the ribs during rowing, injuries are likely due to repeated high-force muscular contractions (McDonnell, Hume, and Nolte 2011; Warden 2002).

In the initial phase the pain is relatively localized and may mimic a simple intercostal strain or nerve irritation. Average incidence of rib stress fracture among rowers has been estimated at 9% (McDonnell, Hume, and Nolte 2011). Among specific populations, this equates to 8.1% to 16.4% of elite rowers, 2% of university rowers, and 1% of junior elite rowers. Injury occurrence is equal among sweep rowers and scullers, but the regional location of the injury differs.

Rib stress fracture pain tends not to resolve between training sessions. The point during the rowing stroke at which a rower feels pain can provide some clues to a fracture's location: Aggravation at the catch is associated with the more common anterolateral fractures, whereas pain at the finish is associated with the less common posterior fractures (see figure 25.5). When it comes to rib stress injury, ribs 5 to 9 are the most frequently involved.

Key Point

Rib stress injury is a spectrum ranging from mild stress reaction all the way to rib stress fracture and even severe complete facture. Injury occurrence is equal among sweep rowers and scullers, but the regional location of the injury differs. Grading severity of this injury as mild, moderate, or severe can guide rowers and coaches regarding time to return to full activity.

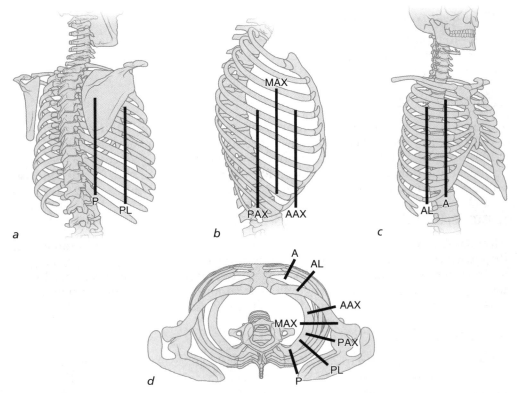

▶ **Figure 25.5** Regions where rib stress fractures occur: posterolateral view *(a)*, lateral view *(b)*, anterolateral view *(c)*, and transverse view *(d)*. A = anterior, AL =anterolateral; AAX = anterior axilla; MAX = mid-axilla; P = posterior; PL = posterolateral; PAX = posterior axilla.

Theories have been advanced as to the mechanism of rib stress fracture, which generally involve opposing forces between serratus anterior and external oblique muscles at the end of the drive phase, external obliques inducing excessive rib loading at the end of the drive phase when resisting layback (Wajswelner et al. 2000), or combined forces arising from transmission of force to the oar handle and the contraction of the shoulder retractors (latissimus dorsi and trapezius muscles) resulting in rib cage compression (Vinther et al. 2006; Warden 2002).

Rare Presentations of Chest Wall Pain

Rarely, chest wall pain may be evidence of something more serious. Particularly in masters athletes, chest pain that comes on with exertion, is crushing or retrosternal, radiates down the arm or up the neck, or is coupled with nausea, sweating, or palpitations could be cardiac. Similarly, a rower who is acutely short of breath or who has chest wall pain accompanied by fever or other systemic symptoms may be having referred pain arising from their lungs. Both should be promptly evaluated by a physician.

Intercostal nerve impingement can occur, and in severe cases, there may be radiation of burning pain along the dermatome, or area of skin that is mainly supplied by a single spinal nerve. Thoracic outlet syndrome can be related to overuse and occurs when blood vessels or nerves in the space between the clavicle and first rib are

Rib Stress Injury: Guidelines for Diagnosis and Management

Definition: Rib stress injury is the development of pain due to bone oedema caused by overload along the bone shaft.

Chest wall pain

GBROWINGTEAM

⬇

Diagnostic features for rib stress injury (and clinical markers*)

History	Examination
• Insidious sudden onset or crescendo pain over a few days or weeks • Pain on deep breathing* • Pain on pushing/pulling doors* • Difficulty rolling over in bed or sitting up from a lying position* • Unable to sleep on affected side* • Possible cough/sneeze pain*	• Tenderness — commonly midaxillary line of chest wall • Ribs 5–8 in particular • Tender spot over oedema and sometimes palpable callous • +ve spring/compression of ribcage (AP & lateral)* • Pain with press up or resisted serratus anterior testing* • Pain on initiating trunk flexion (sit up position including oblique bias)*

⬇

Severity of Injury

Mild	Moderate	Severe
• VAS score 2-3/10** • Rib pain towards end of activity • 'Can row through it' • 'Tightness or soreness' • Mild tenderness • Compression test may be negative • May only be stiff splinted rib cage without pain • Often not all clinical markers* present	• VAS score 4-6/10** • Rib pain on movements • Unable to complete training/ racing • Tender on palpation and compression test positive • Most clinical markers* will be present	• VAS score 7-10/10** • Rib pain at rest • Painful on deep inspiration/ coughing • Pain on simple movements/ lying/reaching • Unable to train or race • Compression test positive • All clinical markers* like to be present

**Interpret VAS score cautiously as can be highly subjective to individual

⬇

Early investigations may be normal and therefore not helpful

Investigations:
Usually CLINICAL DIAGNOSIS

Consider MRI or bone scan if unclear diagnosis. Bone oedema may be present beyond resolution of symptoms so imaging may be misleading

⬇

Management

Stage 1	Stage 2
• Offload rib — stop all rowing mechanics both in a boat and on the ergo • Initiate pain free cross training • Analgesia for comfort but not NSAIDs as impede recovery • Consider taping for comfort • Soft tissue work helpful to alleviate symptoms of protective mechanism • Ultrasound/laser treatment may shorten recovery period if available but not essential • Gradual return to activity ensuring load kept low and under supervision • Ensure resolution of all clinical markers* • Time frame 3–6 weeks	• Biomechanical assessment by physiotherapist and coach • Improvement of thoracic mobility and maintenance of mobility as load increases • Assess rowing technique and correct to reduce areas of overload if possible • Consider all intrinsic and extrinsic risk factors (see overleaf) • Consider implementing prevention program *N.B. Stage 2 may be started early in rehabilitation process and does not necessarily require completion of Stage 1*

See overleaf for intrinsic and extrinsic risk factors for rib stress injury
The GB Rowing Team is the High Performance Arm of British Rowing

▶ **Figure 25.6** Guideline for diagnosis and management of rib stress injuries.

compressed, causing neck and shoulder pain and numbness in the fingers or circulatory dysfunction in the arm. Finally, there is one case report in the literature of a 19-year-old female college rower who presented with right rib pain and was later diagnosed with a serratus anterior muscle avulsion (detachment from bone) (Carr et al. 2017). Another case report detailed the account of unremitting rib pain in a rower, later diagnosed with a bone malignancy known as Ewing's sarcoma (Smoljanovic and Bojanic 2007).

How Can We Treat It?

In general, avoidance of the aggravating activity and relative rest will suffice for many chest wall injuries. Figure 25.6 provides an overview of the hallmark features of rib stress injuries in rowers and their management (Evans and Redgrave 2016a, b).

Grading rib stress injury severity as mild, moderate, or severe can guide rowers and coaches regarding time to return to full activity. Management includes a symptom-dependent approach of initial rest and activity modification followed by a graded return to rowing over a period of approximately 3 to 6 weeks (Vinther and Thornton 2016). Complete rest may be initially necessary if deep breathing is painful during isolated lower extremity exercise. Nonsteroidal anti-inflammatory drugs (NSAIDs) should be avoided. Taping, soft tissue treatment, and thoracic spine mobilization can manage symptoms, and ultrasound and laser therapy can be attempted (Evans and Redgrave 2016a; Evans and Redgrave 2016b), although the latter are supported by conflicting or little evidence.

Upper Extremity

The upper extremity is the third most common region associated with injury in rowers. These injuries are generally caused by overuse. In one study of six sports, rowers had the longest-lasting shoulder pain, from 1 year to a "lifetime" (Mohseni-Bandpei et al. 2012).

How Does It Happen?

The two main sites of injury in the upper extremity are shoulder and forearm or wrist. Mechanisms of injury appear to be relatively straightforward for shoulder injury, whereas those for forearm and wrist injuries are more complex.

Shoulder Injuries

Chronic shoulder pain may ensue from a combination of an anteriorly placed glenohumeral head (the part of the upper arm that moves in the shoulder joint), a tight posterior shoulder capsule, tight latissimus dorsi, and weak rotator cuff muscles (Richardson and Jull 1995). This decentralized glenohumeral joint (Watson 1996) may lead to impingement and instability (Kibler et al. 2002). In the sweep rower, this position is exaggerated in the outside arm.

Forearm and Wrist Injuries

Overly tight grip, size of grip, and excessive wrist motion while feathering the oar are the primary causes of forearm and wrist injuries. These injuries include exertional compartment syndrome, lateral epicondylitis, de Quervain's tenosynovitis, and intersection syndrome.

Anatomists divide the upper (dorsal) side of the wrist into six compartments numbered from the thumb (first compartment) to the little finger (sixth compartment). de Quervain's tenosynovitis involves the wrist's first dorsal compartment, marked by inflammation of the two thumb-controlling tendons and their tendon sheaths, which can impact grip ability. "Sculler's thumb," or hypertrophy of the muscles running through the first dorsal compartment (Williams 1977), may be linked to overuse of the thumb in feathering, leading to swelling over the top of the forearm. Intersection syndrome (historically described as "oarsmen's wrist") involves inflammation at the point where the major wrist-controlling muscles running through both the first and second dorsal compartments intersect at the wrist end of the forearm (Hanlon and Luellen 1999).

Exertional compartment syndrome is marked by increased pressure inside a compartment or compartments and subsequent reduced circulation and function of tendons and muscles running through the affected area. In the forearm, this is attributed to initiating the drive phase of the rowing stroke with the elbow instead of the shoulder girdle (Williams 1977) or bending the arms too early. Poorly sized grips, poor rigging (blades digging too deeply into water due to improper pitch on the oarlock or blade), and wet or cold conditions can all exacerbate this problem (Vinther and Thornton 2016).

Pain with intersection syndrome is felt at the dorsal wrist and is made worse with extension. Lateral epicondylitis is characterized by pain over the lateral aspect of the elbow, especially with resisted wrist extension. If exertional compartment syndrome is suspected, intercompartmental pressure may be measured at rest and immediately after provoking activity. The diagnosis is confirmed if the pressure remains elevated for a prolonged time postactivity.

How Can We Treat It?

Treatment of shoulder or forearm and wrist injuries will vary depending on the nature of the injury.

Evaluation of the shoulder should include the neck, shoulder girdle, thoracic spine, and rib cage. One case study reported a clavicular stress fracture in a lightweight rower (Abbott and Hannafin 2001). In the masters athlete, degenerative rotator cuff tears may be more common, and osteoarthritis should be ruled out as well.

Treatment involves correcting muscle imbalances of the upper quadrant, including strengthening scapulothoracic stabilizers, stretching the neck muscles, and modifying technique (Thornton et al. 2017).

Management strategies for wrist injuries may involve the application of ice, stretching, deep tissue massage, myofascial release, acupuncture, NSAIDs, and bracing or taping. Relaxing the grip, training on the ergometer, or rowing on the square may help. When cold and damp weather is an issue, wearing fleece pogies (rowing mittens that cover the hand and handle) to keep the hands and wrists warm may also help. Cortisone injections may result in short-term pain relief, but there is a small risk of tendon damage or rupture and the procedure may need to be reported if the rower is subject to doping control. For these reasons injections are usually not helpful over the long term. Immobilization and surgical intervention are usually only required in severe or recalcitrant cases, but a recent study from Australia found encouraging results from early surgical intervention in elite rowers (Hoy, Trease, and Braybon 2019).

Lower Extremity

Most hip and knee injuries in rowing stem from overuse or improper biomechanics. Rowers can develop patellofemoral pain syndrome (PFPS), or iliotibial band syndrome (ITBS), as well as tendinopathy (Fairclough et al. 2006; Redgrave 1992; Waryaz and

McDermott 2008). One case report describes bilateral atraumatic meniscal tears in an adolescent female rower, likely caused by repetitive low-energy loading (Taylor, Frankovitch, and Rumball 2009).

How Does It Happen?

The majority of injuries in the lower extremity occur in and around the hip or knee, both of which move through large ranges of motion during the rowing stroke.

Femoroacetabular Impingement (FAI) and Labral Tear

Repetitive full flexion of the hips during the rowing stroke, along with anatomical variations or morphological changes to the femoral head neck junction or acetabulum, can result in femoroacetabular impingement (FAI). The mechanical stresses placed on the anterior chondrolabral junction of the hip may also cause labral tears. Both present as chronic progressions of pain as volume and intensity increase.

Patellofemoral Pain Syndrome (PFPS)

The knee joint moves though a full range of motion during the rowing stroke, resulting in high compressive forces between the posterior surface of the patella and the femur (Waryaz 2008). Abnormal tracking of the patella in the femoral groove may increase wear of the hyaline cartilage on the undersurface of the patella and result in PFPS. Rowers who appear knock-kneed or whose knees hyperextend through the drive phase may compound the problem, as can footstretcher angle or placement (Redgrave 1992).

The pain described is usually dull and located behind the patella. It can be aggravated by climbing stairs or sitting down, and there can be tenderness over the lateral and medial sides of the kneecap.

Iliotibial Band Syndrome (ITBS)

Rowers who appear bow-legged or who row with knees out to the side (versus straight up and down) may develop ITBS, which is irritation caused by the increase in compression of the iliotibial band over the outside of the knee (Fairclough et al. 2006). Leg length discrepancy should be ruled out. Often, running and cycling perpetuate the problem. Pain is located on the lateral aspect of the knee over what is known as the lateral femoral condyle.

How Can We Treat It?

Assessment of a rower with hip or knee pain should include gathering a history of previous injury and mechanical symptoms such as locking or clicking, swelling, or instability (particularly in the knee). Mechanical symptoms should be assessed by a health care provider.

Both FAI and labral tears are generally managed nonoperatively, but symptoms may return if the aggravating activity is restarted. Surgical results for FAI vary from 70% to 96% success rate in higher-level athletes (Thornton et al. 2016). It's important to advance the athlete slowly through a comprehensive rehabilitation protocol to prevent continued irritation or reinjury (Malloy, Malloy, and Draovitch 2013). A recent study in elite rowers showed positive effects (at least in the short term) of hip injections for pain relief for not only the hip but also the low back (Sharif et al. 2017).

For the knee, treatment consists of functional rehabilitation to strengthen hip and quadriceps musculature. Taping the patella in order to improve tracking within the patellofemoral groove can help in the short term for PFPS and allow for immediate resumption of activity. Ice and NSAIDs may be beneficial in the short term for pain relief. A change in the position of the footstretcher in the boat and the addition of heel wedges may help as well (Thornton et al. 2016).

Conclusion

Many injuries in rowing are minor and heal quickly, but some will become chronic and sometimes debilitating. Factors including training volume, rowing style, rigging, and preparing for environmental conditions and climate with appropriate clothing and gear. Addressing individual weaknesses and emphasizing education all make a profound difference in both prevention and treatment. Injuries do not need to be a given, and many rowers can experience the sport in full with solid preventative strategies in place.

Medical Aspects of Rowing and Special Populations

Jane Thornton, MD, PhD

Illness can plague the best rowers in the world at the worst possible times—such as the gastrointestinal illness that hampered New Zealander Mahé Drysdale during the 2008 Olympic Games, for example—but many are preventable. Some are chronic, some are acute, and some may require attention by support staff to achieve full return to sport. Just as there are specific medical aspects of rowing to consider, there are certain populations that require special attention when discussing health, including para rowers, junior rowers, and masters.

> "I kept falling ill during the summer after Lucerne (World Rowing Cup in July) and I missed a lot of training. The best decision was to let Paul [O'Donovan] race the single (at the World Rowing Championships). I was able to rest and recover at my own pace following that decision and the health has been good since."
>
> Gary O'Donovan, Ireland LM2x silver medalist, Rio 2016 (World Rowing 2020c)

Illness Prevention and Management

Illnesses can wreak havoc not only by affecting the rower, but in many cases spreading among a team and affecting global performance of a crew in training and competition. A study led by Australian clinicians and researchers found that illness represented 32% of all causes of lost training time in 153 rowers selected to the Australian national rowing team over eight seasons (Trease et al. 2020)—in fact, the incidence of illness was higher than chest wall or lumbar spine injuries. This section discusses illnesses and conditions common among rowers: respiratory, cardiovascular, dermatological, and other health aspects related to low energy availability, environmental exposure, travel, and antidoping.

Respiratory

Upper respiratory illness makes up the bulk of illness reporting in sport medicine literature and accounts for 35% to 65% of illness presentations to sport medicine clinics

(Gleeson and Pyne 2016). Although these are often acute and self-limited, recurrent symptoms can have a negative impact on rowers' health and performance. Many athletes suffer from respiratory symptoms resulting from chronic conditions such as asthma or allergies. The majority of cases are caused by common viruses, environmental allergies and exposures, and exercise-induced trauma to the epithelial lining of the airways.

Key Point

Asthma is the most common chronic condition, experienced by approximately 15% of Olympic athletes (Bonini et al. 2015). Elite athletes, particularly those in endurance sports, have a higher prevalence of asthma than the general population. There are several reasons for this, including the following:

1. High-intensity training coupled with high ventilation, causing damage to the lining of the airways and inflammation
2. Bronchial constriction caused high parasympathetic tone in athletes
3. Environmental exposures to cold or polluted air (Carlsen 2016)

It is important that athletes with symptoms of asthma (shortness of breath, chest tightness, wheezing, coughing) speak with their health care provider. Rowers with asthma should ensure they have their rescue or relieving inhaler and similar medication at hand at all times, include an appropriate warm-up and cool-down, and make relevant coaches and support staff aware of their condition and how best to manage an exacerbation. Importantly, elite athletes must ensure that their medications comply with national and international antidoping rules and follow the guidelines for reporting and therapeutic use exemption as needed.

Cardiovascular

Although life-threatening illnesses in rowing are rare, sudden deaths are usually attributed to undiagnosed cardiomyopathy or abnormal cardiac function (McNally et al. 2005). Although moderate- to vigorous-intensity exercise is associated with a marked reduction in cardiovascular morbidity and mortality in general, intense physical activity over years can result in cardiovascular conditions such as atrial fibrillation (i.e., irregular heartbeat).

There are limited recommendations and guidance for those who suffer a cardiac event and want to return to sport. Certain cardiac conditions confer a higher risk than others. The World Rowing Federation mandates precompetition cardiovascular screening in order to identify athletes at risk and advise them accordingly (World Rowing 2020d).

Cardiovascular screening usually consists of a medical questionnaire and a physical examination, which may be followed by 12-lead resting electrocardiogram (ECG). A personal history of cardiac issues, family history of inheritable cardiac disease, or positive physical or ECG result will require further evaluation by an age-appropriate cardiac specialist. The specialist may decide to do further investigations, including an exercise stress test (used to help diagnose and evaluate heart problems such as heart disease or heart failure), an echocardiogram (ultrasound of the heart to better understand the structure and function), or advanced imaging such as a cardiac MRI.

Not all heart problems can be detected by these investigations, but rapid advances are being made in the field of sport cardiology to determine the best way to diagnose and prevent heart conditions in athletes.

Key Point

Cardiovascular screening, as mandated by World Rowing, is highly recommended and usually consists of a medical questionnaire and a physical examination, which may be followed by further investigation. Not all heart problems can be detected by these investigations, but rapid advances are being made in the field of sport cardiology to determine the best way to diagnose and prevent heart conditions in athletes.

Dermatological Issues

Minor abrasions are common in rowing, and include hand and finger blisters caused by friction with oar handles, "sculler's knuckles" from banging handles together due to inexperience or inclement weather (Rumball et al. 2005), slide or track "bites" over the calf muscles, or abrasions on the buttocks from improperly fitted seats (Redgrave 1992; Tomecki and Mikesell 1987).

Keeping nails trimmed and using gloves that protect the knuckles but allow for continued grip of the oar can aid in prevention of sculler's knuckles, and high socks or long tights can cover the calves and protect against slide bites. Adjusting the position of slides or tracks or fitting a protective bumper over the end can also help mitigate slide bites. Properly fitted seats can prevent buttock abrasions. Open wounds should be cleaned with soap and water, with topical antibiotic ointment applied as needed.

As most rowers know from previous experience, blisters tend to occur or worsen during transition periods from land to water or with changes in equipment, humidity, and volume or intensity of training (Rumball et al. 2005). To reduce the occurrence of such abrasions, rowers should ensure handles are cleaned between users and that grip material is kept intact. The material and size of the grip itself can be changed to accommodate the rower's personal preference.

Blisters are common. Data collected from of a survey of 145 competitive and recreational rowers found that 69% had nonpainful calluses "most of the time," with blisters being less common and more painful. Participants demonstrated an acceptance of blisters and "even a sense of pride in what they represent" (Grima et al. 2022, 77). Blisters should be kept clean and intact. Open blisters in contact with handles and then shared among team members can increase risks for infection and even hand warts (Roach and Chretien 1995). Signs of infection include redness, pus, streaking, increased fevers, and malaise; these warrant urgent medical attention. If there is no infection, small blisters may be covered with bandages or athletic tape to prevent further damage.

Relative Energy Deficiency in Sport (REDs)

As mentioned in chapter 24, relative energy deficiency in sport (REDs) is a condition that can have negative effects on cardiovascular, musculoskeletal, hormonal, and gastrointestinal health as well as electrolyte balance and performance (Hoch et al. 2011; Mountjoy et al. 2014; Temme and Hoch 2013). The underlying pathology in REDs is reduced energy availability for physiological processes.

All rowers are at risk for REDs, whether lightweight or openweight, male or female. Low energy availability has been reported in males (Chapman and Woodman 2016; Tenforde et al. 2016), with disordered eating practices found in lightweight male rowers (Burke et al. 2018; Theil, Gottfried, and Hesse 1993), which negatively influences testosterone levels and bone mineral density (Talbott and Shapses 1998). In female athletes, low energy availability can cause disruption or cessation of menstrual cycle, with resultant negative impacts on bone health. Menstrual dysfunction may consist of:

- amenorrhea (no periods by age 15 or cessation of menstruation for three or more consecutive cycles),
- oligomenorrhea (cycle length is more than 45 days), or
- subtle changes such as light bleeding or midcycle spotting.

However, the long-term effects on reproduction are not yet known.

"Cutting weight" practices can lead to low energy availability, which in turn can negatively impact plasma and blood volume, stroke volume, cardiac output, endocrine function, and thermoregulation (Garthe et al. 2011; Sundgot-Borgen and Garthe 2011). These negative outcomes have been shown to be the same for both male and female rowers.

Risk Factors

Risk factors for developing REDs include starting sport-specific training at a young age, personality factors, frequent weight cycling to "make weight" in weight category sports, and certain coaching behaviors, including pressure to lose weight to improve performance or aesthetics (Mountjoy et al. 2014). A history of stress fracture; increases in frequency, volume, and intensity of training; use of medication or hormonal therapy; and nutritional habits, including dieting and history of weight fluctuations, can all play a role (Lebrun and Rumball 2002). There seems to be an individual response and susceptibility to REDs. In some, it can be a consequence of repeated intense or prolonged exercise and low energy intake or of psychological stress.

Although no rower is immune to energy availability issues, lightweight rowers are at increased risk (Karlson, Becker, and Merkur 2001; Sykora et al. 1993). Methods to shed weight can include so-called sweat runs, saunas, laxatives, and diuretics. Many rowers choose to focus on healthy diets to help performance, but sometimes what begins as a healthy choice can turn into a disordered eating pattern or develop into an eating disorder (such as anorexia or bulimia nervosa).

Disordered eating or low energy intake can be purposeful or inadvertent. In women, the term *female athlete triad* is used describe the interrelatedness of low energy availability, menstrual dysfunction, and altered bone mineral density (BMD), with each entity on a continuum from health to disease (Nattiv et al. 2007).

When energy deficits are prolonged, it can lead to harmful sequelae, including anemia, chronic fatigue, decreased immunity, endothelial dysfunction and cardiovascular effects, decreased protein synthesis, decreased base metabolic rate, psychological effects, and reduced performance. Low BMD has been associated with rib pain in both female (Mountjoy et al. 2014) and male rowers (Vinther et al. 2005).

Management

Many rowers are not concerned about long-term health when short-term performance is looming, but the little we know should prompt careful consideration and management—the long-term effects on bone health are not fully understood, and it is possible that it may never fully recover once bone microarchitecture is affected.

Key to treating low energy availability and REDs is to increase energy intake, reduce energy expenditure, or a combination of both, which can be more challenging than anticipated. Athletes should seek out help from a trusted health care provider. A calcium-rich diet with adequate vitamin D (600 IU daily for rowers aged 19-50) is key for bone health. This is, of course, in addition to ensuring adequate energy availability through sufficient calorie intake.

Resistance training for 2 to 3 days per week may help restore bone density as an adjunct to education, proper nutrition, and counseling, but this has to be balanced with the risk of causing or worsening stress fractures (Mountjoy et al. 2014).

Weight Loss Strategies

Taking an adequate amount of time to reduce weight is optimal. World Rowing's Sports Medicine Commission recommendations suggest that lightweight rowers enter the calendar year at no more than 3 kg heavier than their intended summer racing weight (World Rowing 2020e). They further recommend that the first kg should be lost over the course of a few months and the second between then and the race, leaving a maximum of 1 kg to be reduced within the final 24 h before weighing in for the race.

One study compared performance effects of 6 to 8 and 16 to 17 week periods of weight reduction among elite lightweight rowers, and found that the 16 to 17 week period was associated with improvements in nearly all physical performance parameters measured ($\dot{V}O_2$max, respiratory anaerobic threshold, upper body peak power, and knee flexor and extensor strength) (Koutedakis, Pacy, and Quevedo 1994). The shorter time period (6-8 weeks) was associated with a reduction in every performance parameter. As many rowers know, weight loss is often attempted in far shorter periods of time.

Key Point

Taking a longer time to reduce weight is optimal. A 16 to 17 week period of weight reduction was associated with improvements in nearly all physical performance parameters measured.

However, a maximum weekly weight loss rate of 0.7% in association with strength training has been shown to help athletes gain lean body mass and increase strength and power-related performance (Garthe et al. 2011).

Detailed management strategies for REDs are outlined in the most recent consensus statements of the Female Athlete Triad Coalition and the IOC (Mountjoy et al. 2014; Mountjoy et al. 2015).

Environmental Exposure

As an outdoor sport, many aspects of exposure to the environment cannot be avoided. Safety is of course of utmost importance, and the coach and rowers should be familiar with the environment and weather patterns. In some areas, weather can change rapidly, causing unforeseen thunderstorms or high winds. In general, a coach boat should be in proximity whenever possible and waves and weather patterns monitored closely. Chapters 13 and 21 go into more depth about the effects of extreme temperature and altitude in rowing, but the following are some other environmental factors to consider.

Cold and Hot Weather

As a sport increasingly done throughout all seasons of the year and pretty much wherever open water is available, temperature-related concerns for rowers range from hyperthermia (overheating) at the high end of the thermometer to hypothermia at the low end.

In colder months, it is important to wear appropriate warm layering, with wind barrier fabric if necessary, and to have cold water rules in place. Safety regulations can be found on the World Rowing website (World Rowing 2020b). If a rower tips the boat in frigid waters, it can be life-threatening, making a nearby safety boat even more important than in warm weather.

Lifejackets are often a local requirement for boaters in all weather conditions and should be stored in the shell or accompanying safety boat (as per regulations) in an easily accessible location.

In warmer climates and during the summer months, it is particularly important to monitor hydration status. Excess sweating can lead to dehydration and electrolyte loss. Prolonged exposure to hot conditions can also lead to various forms of hyperthermia, which include heat fatigue, heat exhaustion, and heatstroke. Sweating is a natural way the body copes with overheating. Although hydration and removal from the heat can mitigate the health impacts of low-grade hyperthermia, heatstroke can be life threatening. Heatstroke occurs when the body is no longer able to sweat in order to dissipate excess heat and internal temperatures rise above 40 °C (104 °F). Medical assistance should be sought immediately if heatstroke is suspected.

Sun Care

Sun care is an important consideration when it comes to long-term injury and illness prevention. Because reflection from the water causes sunlight exposure to be doubled, protection is even more important. Although overexposure to harmful ultraviolet (UV) rays are linked to a number of different conditions, melanoma is the most well known and fortunately one of the most preventable cancers. It is also one of the most easily treated, if caught early.

Prevention measures include limiting sun exposure, particularly avoiding outside activities between the hours of 10 a.m. and 2 p.m. (something more easily done during training than racing). When midday activity is unavoidable, seeking shade when possible or creating shade through the use of clothing that covers the body and head is important. Sunscreen with broad spectrum coverage (i.e., that protects against UVA and UVB light) and a minimum SPF of 30 should be applied to all exposed areas of skin and reapplied throughout the day. Generally, lighter skin is at greater risk of damage from UV light than darker skin, although no one is completely free from risk.

Water Quality

The World Rowing Federation outlines a range of possible contaminants that can affect water quality (World Rowing 2020a). Research on risk of illness from participation in recreational water activities involving contaminated waters is limited and inconclusive. A 1994 study by Fewtrell and colleagues reported no significant differences in health outcomes on canoeists and rowers exposed to water with varying levels of fecal contamination (e.g., E. coli) and those not exposed. To prevent illness, rowers should wash hands regularly before and after meals and after toilet use and avoid splashing, intentional or unintentional immersion, and ingesting water from contaminated sources and bodies of water. If a rower falls ill, they should report any symptoms of diarrhea (≥6 loose bowel movements in 24 hours), fever over 100.4 °F or 38°C, or severe abdominal pain to a health care provider.

Travel

Because rowing is practiced worldwide and events take place around the globe, it is important to take into account the usual precautions when traveling to foreign areas for camps or regattas. Be sure to consider endemic illness and requirements for vaccinations, access to potable water, and environmental considerations such as heat, humidity, and altitude.

Jet lag, a sleep disorder that occurs when an individual crosses multiple time zones, is another important consideration when travel planning for athletes. The condition is caused by the misalignment between the body's internal circadian rhythms and the time of day or night in their current physical location. The primary issues caused by jet lag include insomnia or daytime sleepiness, which usually persist for one day for every time zone passed through. Ultimately performance can be negatively affected, and individuals with jet lag may be at increased risk of injuries in general.

Although not always practical or within a rowing team's budget, the most effective travel plan will include adequate time for athletes to transition into the new time zone before having to compete. When this is not possible, strategies such as adjusting sleep patterns toward the destination time zone prior to departure (e.g., waking up progressively earlier before eastward travel) can help to shorten the duration of any jet lag symptoms. Although there is evidence to suggest that short 20 min naps may reduce daytime sleepiness, the best time for any kind of sleep (including naps) seems to be nighttime in the new time zone.

Special Populations

From a medical standpoint, para rowers, juniors, and masters can be considered "special populations" within the sport. Understanding the unique medical challenges frequently shared by members of these groups can help considerably in prevention, treatment, and management of illness and injury.

Para Rowing

The number of para rowers is on the rise, and as this population grows, so too will the incidence of para rowing injuries. Making the sport accessible to the various abilities of para rowers requires adjustments to standard rowing equipment, including ergometers, boats, and oars. These changes may present an increased injury risk in and of themselves, although it is not yet understood to what extent. One example is the use of a chest strap, mandated by the World Rowing Federation for one of the three official para rowing classifications, which some have suggested loads the ribs in a detrimental fashion (Smoljanovic et al. 2011). Athletes with spinal cord injury also lack skeletal loading, resulting in lower bone mineral density and a higher propensity for injury. Risk may also be increased by the necessary alterations in rowing mechanics, segmental sequencing, and force transmission to different areas of the body (Thornton et al. 2017).

Key Point

In line with other Paralympic sports, World Rowing has divided the range of international para rowing events into three ability-based classifications.

1. *PR1* (formerly known as AS or Arms and Shoulders) indicates the most restricted classification, in which rowers are effectively rowing with arms and shoulders alone.
2. *PR2* (formerly known as TA or Trunk and Arms) indicates the classification for rowers whose movements include use of arms, shoulders, and trunk.
3. *PR3* (formerly LTA or Legs, Trunk and Arms) is the classification for rowers with essentially full range of movement who possess restricted ability in areas such as vision or digit loss on the hand.

Additional classifications, including degrees between these three and some related to mental health, may be included in different national and regional jurisdictions.

Several considerations must be made when assessing risk, prevention, and management of injury in para rowers.

Prosthetics

Para rowers with prosthetics may experience phantom limb pain, stump swelling, and residual skin breakdown. Breakdown of skin in particular may require extended time away from rowing or time without wearing the prosthesis in question until the skin heals. Daily monitoring is the most effective prevention and mitigation strategy so that healing can take place in the least amount of time.

Isolated Force Generation and Transfer

Rowing in both the PR1 classification and to some extent the PR2 classification can put stress on isolated muscles or parts of the body as a result of limited range of motion or reduced or lost limb functionality. This means that forces may be generated and transferred in isolation rather than through a range of connected body movements into effective boat propulsion. This can put undue stress on affected areas of the body, which may be compounded by other factors, including boat rig and weight, stroke rate, level of exertion, and rowing session or race duration.

Spinal Cord Injuries

Preexisting spinal cord injuries are common in rowers in the PR1 classification and are also frequently found in rowers in the PR2 classification.

Care should be taken to create appropriate training sessions that maximize safety for this group of athletes. Autonomic hyperreflexia, bone fracture, or joint dislocations can be caused by trivial or imperceptible trauma as a result of bone demineralization and muscle spasticity, thermal dysregulation, and skin problems (e.g., pressure sores).

Pressure sores are a concern and can develop from the triad of shear forces, pressure, and moisture through exposure to water from sweating, waves, and backsplash. For athletes with restricted mobility or who spend extended time sitting (e.g., in a wheelchair), prevention of pressure sores from rowing is essential. Preventive solutions include adequate cushioning and padding for the buttocks, frequent pressure relief, good nutrition and hygiene, and moisture-wicking clothing. Given the life-threatening potential of infected pressure sores, any athlete with a pressure sore should not be allowed to row until healed.

Junior

Junior is a broad term to indicate any rowers training and competing who are aged 18 or younger. World Rowing recognizes one junior age category for international racing, Under 19, which restricts entry to those who are under 19 years of age. National and regional jurisdictions often recognize additional junior categories such as Under 17 and sometimes Under 15. Rowers who have turned 19 years old are usually classified as Under 23, whereas those who turn 23 in a given year enter the senior age category (also called *open* because any athlete 23 or older can race in a senior event).

One study demonstrated that junior rowers' annual aggregate injury rate is higher than that of seniors (2.1 vs. 1.75 injuries per 1,000 training sessions) (Smoljanovic et al. 2009), although research is limited. Lack of rowing experience or inappropriate training may be partly responsible for this difference, as well as a significantly higher incidence of traumatic low back injuries seen among junior sweep rowers who changed rowing side during the season. Risk of injury in junior rowers also appears to correlate strongly with training volume; more than seven training sessions per week during a rowing season showed increased rate of injury.

Because of the ongoing growth and maturation of junior rowers while engaged with the sport, certain aspects of their physical development are important to bear in mind when planning training and loading. Growth plates (or physes) are one such element. These, including the endplates of vertebral bodies, remain open in adolescents and their connective cartilage tissue is not able to withstand the additional stresses imposed by engaging in rowing training too frequently or at too high an intensity. Prevention and risk reduction through proper and regular stretching routines following practice sessions and races is recommended (Smoljanovic et al. 2009). Avoidance of complex cross-training is also suggested because proprioception problems and muscle weakening during the natural process of limb elongation increases teenage rowers' vulnerability to acute injuries.

Femoroacetabular impingement (FAI), described in the previous chapter, may be a source of pain in young adults and a cause of cartilage and labral damage that predisposes them to degenerative arthritis (figure 26.1a-c). Boykin and colleagues (2013) presented a review of 18 young rowers with a collective 21 hip labral tears. Of these, 15 hips showed evidence of the bony changes that are the hallmark of FAI (cam morphology, or bone shape) and only 10 of the rowers (56%) returned to rowing following arthroscopic treatment.

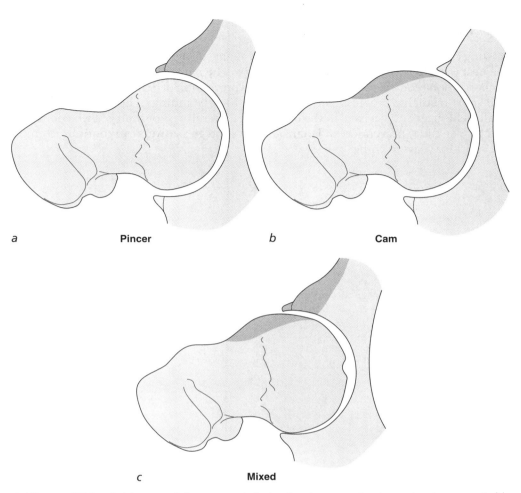

▶ **Figure 26.1** Subtypes of femoroacetabular impingement: pincer impingement *(a)*, cam impingement *(b)*, and mixed impingement *(c)*.

Masters

Masters is the broadest of rowing categories and includes rowers of almost all ages and abilities. Internationally, eligibility to compete in masters races begins the year an athlete turns 27, and age classes are grouped A through M. Regardless of age and prior experience in rowing or any other physical activity, all prospective masters rowers should begin with general conditioning to address lower extremity and abdominal strengthening, flexibility, and aerobic conditioning.

Older adults engaging in masters rowing should be evaluated by a physician before beginning training due to the strenuous nature of the sport. Competitively oriented masters in particular should undergo regular precompetition health screening. Masters with a history of aortic aneurysm or previous cardiovascular surgeries, such as repair of an abdominal aortic aneurysm, are strongly advised against participation.

Focusing on good technique and on-water safety is important for the masters rower to decrease the risk of injury and increase long-term involvement in the sport.

Conclusion

Rowing can be enjoyed by individuals across a range of ages and abilities and is one of the best ways to stay active and remain healthy. The nature of an outdoor sport lends itself to unique considerations about safety and prevention of ill health. As sport science and sport medicine progress, so too does our understanding of how rowers can stay healthier longer and get back in the boat sooner after illness or injury. With education and proper injury prevention and management strategies, rowers can continue to enjoy the sport for years to come.

Rowing Nutrition

Jeremy Ivey

Fueling Strategies

Susan Boegman

Nutrition plays a critical and continually evolving role in sport (Thomas, Erdman, and Burke 2016). Factors such as high training loads, large energy requirements (Mikulic and Bralic 2018; Tran et al. 2015; Winkert et al. 2022), and body mass management (particularly for lightweight rowers) means that nutrition has the potential to impact health, training adaptations, ability to make weight, and overall rowing performance.

The next three chapters will highlight important features of contemporary sport nutrition, including key nutrients for fueling and recovery; strategies for periodizing nutrition and hydration; optimizing energy availability; body composition management; and select micronutrients and health and performance supplements. Not all of the scientific data presented within the following chapters has been drawn from rowing-specific studies. However, the research and ideas described review key themes relevant to the metabolic and physiologic training needs of the rower. Although the majority of recommendations are evidence based, unpublished, anonymized data collected during the author's work with Rowing Canada will occasionally be presented. These recommendations are designed to be adapted by sport dietitians, athletes, and coaches to meet individual rowers' unique goals and needs. Indeed, rowers of all levels who look to improve performance can benefit from both the scientific and practical information provided in this chapter.

Fueling Foundations: Strategies and Key Considerations

When considering the fueling strategies used by rowers, it is critical to understand the physiological requirements for performance success. Rowing is a strength–endurance activity that requires the activation of almost all muscles in the body (Mikulic and Bralic 2018). To be successful over a 2,000 m race, rowers must develop precise stroke mechanics as well as muscular strength and endurance to achieve the high power outputs (450 to 550 W for elite openweight males) necessary to overcome water and wind resistance (Tran et al. 2015). Given the large contribution of aerobic metabolism during racing, high-volume, endurance-based training at various intensities makes up the majority of the rowing program (Maestu, Jurimae, and Jurimae 2005). Estimated training hours can vary considerably depending on the level of athlete. For example, masters may train anywhere from 2 to 12 hours and juniors from 5 to 18 hours per week. To achieve the extreme level of power, strength, and endurance required for international success, university or national team rowers may train two to three times per day 5 to 7 days a week, or up to 30 hours per week (Mikulic and Bralic 2018). This is primarily on-water, ergometer, or resistance training, but may include cross-training such as stationary cycling, particularly for the injured athlete (Tran et al. 2015).

This type of training stimulates both metabolic adaptation (such as mitochondrial biogenesis, capillarization, and increases in muscle fuel stores) and structural adaptation (such as contractile protein repair and synthesis) that will, over time, translate into increased performance (Moore 2015). Nutrition recommendations influence these specific adaptations, which are required to enhance rowing outcomes. The impact of nutrition on training adaptation is therefore critical.

Within the typical elite rowing program, athletes will ideally implement an individual, periodized nutrition plan that organizes practical nutrition strategies around training load (length, intensity, and frequency) within each training block over a year (table 27.1) (Stellingwerff, Maughan, and Burke 2011). It is also essential to consider the athlete's unique performance, health, and physiology (see table 27.2), as well as their body composition goals (Jeukendrup 2017a).

Table 27.1 Periodized Training Block Nutrition Strategy

	General preparation: Volume and endurance	Specific preparation: Intensity	Taper and competition	Regeneration
Training	1-3 sessions per day most days (primarily aerobic, technical, resistance; see chapter 14)	1-3 sessions per day most days (mix of aerobic, threshold, anaerobic, technical, resistance; see chapter 14)	Reduced volume, increased intensity, racing	Time off and gradually increasing load
Nutrition focuses	• Prevention of low energy availability (LEA), particularly when training multiple sessions per day • Fuel for the work required (i.e., match carbohydrate expenditure with intake) • Consideration of strategic low carbohydrate availability sessions for experienced, healthy athletes • Protein spread throughout the day • Increased attention to carbohydrate and protein recovery between daily training sessions • Increased attention to carbohydrate intake before endurance and hypertrophy sessions • Preparation of food on lighter days for higher volume days • Maintenance of good hydration practices	• Carbohydrate intake in advance of high-intensity sessions • Carbohydrate and protein recovery remains critical between daily training sessions • Protein intake spread throughout the day • Body composition management, if needed • Maintenance of good hydration practices • Practice of competition fueling strategies for upcoming regattas	• Nutrient vs. calorie dense foods • Mindful eating during taper for body composition management • Specific fat or weight loss strategies for lightweight athletes needing to make weight • Travel nutrition, illness prevention, and competition fueling strategies (see table 27.5) • High carbohydrate intake in advance of and during racing • Maintenance of good hydration practices	• Regular, high-quality meals (higher protein, vegetables vs. concentrated carbs) • Routines around menu planning and meal/snack preparation for the week • Cooked and frozen meals for large workload weeks • Maintenance of good hydration practices

(continued)

Table 27.1 *(continued)*

	General preparation: Volume and endurance	Specific preparation: Intensity	Taper and competition	Regeneration
Daily macronutrient and fluid recommendations	• Carbohydrate: ~6-12 g/kg body mass (BM) per day (~3-5 g/kg if training only once per day). Aim for higher end of the range on heavier training days, if energy needs are high, when struggling to maintain BM, or to prevent LEA. • Protein: ~1.6 g/kg BM per day or ~0.3-0.4 g/kg 4 or more times per day, including ~30-40 g before bed. Increase to ~2.0-2.5 g/kg BM if aiming for hypertrophy or fat loss. • Fat: As needed for body mass maintenance or lean mass gains. • Aim for lemonade-colored urine.	• Carbohydrate: ~6-12 g/kg BM per day. Aim for higher end of the range on high-intensity days, if energy needs are high, when struggling to maintain BM, or to prevent LEA. • Protein: ~1.6 g/kg BM per day or ~0.30-0.4 g/kg BM 4 or more times per day, including a protein-rich bedtime snack. Increase to ~2.0-2.5 g/kg BM if aiming for hypertrophy or fat loss. • Fat: As needed for body mass maintenance or lean mass gains. • Aim for lemonade-colored urine.	• Reduced intakes with focus on nutrient vs. energy-dense foods during taper. • Carbohydrate: ~6-10 g/kg BM 1-2 days before and during competition. Aim for the higher end of the range if racing more than once per day. • Sip on carbohydrate fluids during warm-up. • Protein: Maintain higher protein intake through the taper. • Ingest small amounts of protein during competition for meal satisfaction and comfort. • Fat: Limit fat to prevent weight gain and interference with carbohydrate intake. • Aim for lemonade-colored urine.	• Reduced intakes to match training reductions, with focus on nutrient vs. energy-dense foods • Carbohydrate: ~3-5+ g/kg BM unless growing, struggling to maintain weight, or active during time off • Protein: spread over the day to enhance meal satisfaction • Fat: minimize if excess weight gain is a concern during time off (some weight gain is expected and healthy)
Training and race recommendations	• ~40-60+ g/h carbohydrate during >60 min or higher intensity sessions; amount is dependent on energy needs • Minimum of ~40 g/h carbohydrate when sessions are 2 hours or longer or when >1 session/day • Water only (unless high energy needs) when training less than once per day	• ~30-60+ g/h carbohydrate during key/higher intensity sessions. • Carbohydrate mouth rinsing if gastrointestinal issues during high-intensity sessions.	• Water only during taper training sessions unless higher intensity or training undertaken in the 1-2 days prior to racing • No fueling during racing	

	General preparation: Volume and endurance	Specific preparation: Intensity	Taper and competition	Regeneration
Recovery	• Postsession recovery as soon as practical after training: * Endurance: Carbohydrate: ~0.8+ g/kg BM Protein: ~0.3-0.49 g/kg BM * Resistance: Carbohydrate: ~0.8 g/kg BM Protein: ~0.3-0.4 g/kg BM (use higher protein when more muscle groups are worked) • Follow-up snack or meal • Meals timed as recovery when training once per day or less	• Posttraining recovery as soon as practical when intensity session is very fatiguing, when training 2 or more times per day, when seat racing, if specific preparation phase maintains a relatively high level of endurance training, or if LEA is a concern. * Endurance: As per general preparation * Intensity: Carbohydrate: ~0.8-1.2 g/kg BM Protein: ~0.3–0.4 g/kg BM * Resistance: Carbohydrate: ~0.8 g/kg BM Protein: As per general preparation When less than 2 sessions per day meals can be timed as recovery.	• Posttraining: * Meals timed for recovery * High-quality carbohydrates and proteins • Postrace (as soon as practical, particularly if racing again): * Carbohydrate: ~0.8-1.2+ g/kg BM * Protein: ~0.30 g/kg BM	
	General preparation: Volume and endurance	Specific preparation: Intensity	Taper and competition	Regeneration
Notes	Higher illness risk during large volume training in particular if athlete underfuels on a regular basis	Risk of low appetite and poor recovery after high-intensity session	If racing several times over a day, liquids may be the preferred recovery option	

Table 27.2 Nutrition Considerations for Athlete Performance Gaps

Physiological gap (see chapter 14 for training explanations)	Nutrition strategy
Aerobic	Higher carbohydrate and energy availability for key training sessions, particularly when more than one long endurance session per day during high volume phase
	Lower carbohydrate availability for steady-state or technical sessions (may naturally occur as part of a back-to-back training day) if athlete is not at risk for LEA or REDs (see chapter 28)
Anaerobic	Higher carbohydrate availability prior to and during high-intensity sessions
Strength	Higher carbohydrate availability (glycogen stores) prior to session 20-40 g of protein consumed either before or after session

Note: A small number of performance supplements may also help the rower to address gaps (see chapter 29) but should only be considered once all other aspects of training, recovery, and nutrition are consistently well executed.

Fueling Foundations: The Macronutrients

Regardless of rowing level and nutritional periodization requirements, daily energy intakes should aim to match energy expenditure unless physique change is desired (see chapter 28). Considering specific macronutrients (see tables 27.1 and 27.3), general recommendations to support training are 3 to 12 g/kg of body mass (BM) of carbohydrate each day, with amounts depending on the length and intensity of the training session (Burke et al. 2011; Simonsen et al. 1991), approximately 0.4 g/kg BM of protein per meal spread over four or more meals per day (Huecker et al. 2019; Phillips and Van Loon 2011), and adequate fat and calories to prevent low energy availability (Thomas, Erdman, and Burke 2016) (see chapter 28 for further information on this topic).

Key Point

Not all rowers train like elite athletes. Youth and masters rowers will most likely undertake fewer training sessions each week than high-level rowers. Generally speaking, the lower the overall training volume or intensity, the lower the need for carbohydrate-rich foods. The number of daily sessions must also be considered. When training once per day, there is a greater likelihood of carbohydrate or glycogen replenishment to occur naturally in advance of each new session, especially if the training program does not deplete glycogen stores. A high-quality, mixed diet (grains, fruits, vegetables, and proteins) should suffice. In the case of long (~2 h) single daily sessions, deliberate consumption of a higher carbohydrate diet (i.e., >8 g/kg BM · day) may prevent gradual reductions in muscle glycogen stores over a training week (Moore 2015). Additionally, as young rowers progress to two or more training sessions per day, carbohydrate requirements will be similar to or—as a result of growth—possibly even higher than that of the U23 or national level rower (see table 27.4 for a sample meal plan).

Because carbohydrate use and absorption is not affected by aging, intake recommendations do not change for the trained masters athlete, and exercise quantity continues to be the primary determinant of daily carbohydrate need. On the other hand, masters athletes new to training store less glycogen while actually utilizing more during submaximal exercise. Consuming carbohydrates during training may help manage the potential glycogen shortfall and subsequent fatigue during a long row. Although not rowing-specific, research has also demonstrated that masters athletes may undereat carbohydrate during recovery from a training session (Doering et al. 2016), potentially increasing fatigue-related performance decrements. The masters athlete is advised to eat high-quality, carbohydrate-rich foods at each meal and snack when undertaking daily or more than once per day training. Finally, attention should be paid to overall energy needs when choosing carbohydrates, because total energy expenditure will decline due to age-related losses in lean mass, decreased resting metabolic rate, and reduced training volume.

Table 27.3 Macronutrients and Electrolytes: Considerations and Sources

Nutrient	Role	Considerations and sources
Energy/ calories	• Support training, manage body composition, and support growth	• Note that daily needs are dependent on RMR and training. Average amounts range from 2,600-7,000 kcal/day (some younger, larger male athletes who are still maturing may require up to 10,000 kcal/day when training volume is high). • Intakes should be spread across the day to meet within-day training energy needs.
Carbohydrates	• Supply primary fuel for working muscles and the central nervous system • Restore glycogen (a possible regulator for training adaptation) • Prevent overreaching or underrecovery and possibly REDs	• Consider training age and status, overall daily and weekly training load, energy needs, hunger, gastrointestinal tolerance, long-term body composition goals, and recovery management. • Choose nutrient-rich grains (oats, quinoa, rice, enriched or multigrain pasta), legumes (black, cannellini, kidney, and pinto beans; chickpeas; green and yellow split peas; red and green lentils), starchier vegetables (yams, potatoes, corn, peas, winter squash, carrots, beets). and fruits more often. • Include lower carbohydrate vegetables (asparagus, broccoli, cabbage, cauliflower, cucumbers, greens, green beans, mushrooms, onions, peppers, radish, summer squash) for additional nutrients at each meal and in particular during a taper, lower volume training, or if fat loss is a strategic goal. • Incorporate higher carbohydrate intakes around key sessions and if energy needs are high. Use sources such as juice, dried fruits, fruit sauces, bananas, honey, maple syrup, and sport foods and beverages. • Consider 1-2 low carbohydrate sessions per week during specific preparation phase for experienced, healthy adult athletes not prone to overreaching LEA. Lower carbohydrate training may naturally occur as a side effect of 2-3 training sessions per day, making strategic inclusion of low carbohydrate sessions unnecessary.
Protein	• Supports repair, maintenance, and growth of body tissues • Is a component of enzymes, hormones, and other chemicals • Building block of bones, muscles, cartilage, skin, and blood cells	• Obtain most protein from whole-food sources such as eggs, dairy, fish, seafood, meat, poultry, and legumes whenever possible, and evenly distribute throughout the day. • Plant-based athletes should obtain most of their protein from legumes, tofu, seeds, nuts, and higher protein dairy alternatives. • Choose protein supplements when adequate protein intake is otherwise a challenge. • Choose protein supplements that have undergone third-party testing for substances on the WADA list.
Fat	• Provides energy • Is a structural component of cell membranes • Is required for hormone production and fat-soluble vitamin absorption	• Obtain most fat from high-quality monounsaturated and polyunsaturated sources. Include avocados, olives, most nuts, seeds, and their oils as well as fatty fish, walnuts, and flax (sources of omega 3s). Limit highly processed foods such as chips, fried foods, and processed fatty meats. • Be aware that fats are calorie dense. A large fat intake may impact ability to consume adequate carbohydrate.
Fluids	• Deliver oxygen and nutrients and remove waste products • Dissipate heat	• Observe the combination of urine color, weight, and thirst; these are great indicators for overall hydration status. • Personalize fluid needs by weighing before and after a variety of training sessions and under differing environmental conditions to determine fluid losses (1 kg of body weight loss due to sweat is equivalent to 1 L of fluid). Aim to drink ~150% of losses.
Electrolytes	• Regulate nerve and muscle function • Maintain acid–base and water balance	• Salt food (if a salty sweater or have high sweat losses) and drink fluids with meals to improve fluid retention. • Incorporate electrolytes and carbohydrates during long training sessions if sweat sodium losses are high (salty sweat) and ≥70% or more of fluid losses are replenished (McCubbin 2022).

Carbohydrates: The Fueling King

Carbohydrate, the primary fuel source for working muscles and the central nervous system, is stored in limited amounts as liver and muscle glycogen. Muscle glycogen is both a fuel to support training as well as a possible regulator for training adaptation. Given the well-documented positive effects of carbohydrate on exercise performance, endurance athletes are typically advised to ensure they have high carbohydrate availability. This means they need well-stocked glycogen stores and should fuel before, during, and after high-intensity training and competition (Hearris et al. 2018). At the most basic level, rowers simply need to consume carbohydrate-rich foods throughout the day. However, recent research suggests that performing some endurance-based training with reduced carbohydrate or glycogen availability may augment training adaptation (Burke et al. 2018). There are many types of these so-called "train-low" strategies, including training "fasted" (i.e., after more than 6 h without carbohydrate intake), training with low glycogen stores as may naturally occur during a second daily session after deliberately limiting recovery carbohydrates and consuming only protein and vegetables, or training both fasted and with low glycogen stores (Burke et al. 2018).

One common and less stressful (Burke et al. 2018) train-low method for manipulating carbohydrate fueling involves an easy morning training session completed after an overnight fast. However, omitting a carbohydrate-rich breakfast has been shown to impair late afternoon performance during a 2,000 m rowing time trial despite a pretime trial meal (Cornford and Metcalfe 2019). Additionally, a demanding training schedule can limit the rowers' ability to consistently meet fueling requirements. Thus, rowers may naturally perform some portion of the week in a state of reduced carbohydrate availability (Boegman and Dziedzic 2016). In fact, a recent study in elite German rowers determined that glycogen is unlikely to be sufficiently restored between daily base endurance rowing sessions. Due to the potential high metabolic demand of this training, glycogen in working muscle will gradually decrease throughout the day and over consecutive days and may negatively impact training capacity (Winkert 2022).

Starting exercise with low muscle glycogen is likely to impair training intensity and muscle contractility. Over time, low carbohydrate availability may also increase susceptibility to illness (Impey et al. 2018), overreaching, and injury such as rib stress fracture (Thornton et al. 2017). Injury risk may be intensified when a poorly fueled, tired athlete alters their rowing stroke during training. Rowers should therefore aim to understand their carbohydrate requirements for day-to-day training effectiveness while also facilitating training adaptations (Impey et al. 2018). Within this framework of "fueling for the work required," (Impey et al. 2018, 2) total daily and even meal-to-meal carbohydrate intake can be adjusted to match training demands. The higher the training volume, the higher daily carbohydrate needs will be (see tables 27.1 and 27.4).

Table 27.4 Sample Meal Plan

	~3,000 calorie	~5,000 calorie	~7,000 calorie
Rower class and average training load	Lightweight athlete in a low volume or technical week Junior, club, or masters rower performing 0-1 session/day	Lightweight athlete in high volume performing 2-3 sessions/day Openweight athlete in moderate volume performing 1-2 sessions/day	Openweight male in moderate to high volume performing 2-3 sessions/day (a large or growing openweight male is likely to need higher calorie levels)

	~3,000 calorie	~5,000 calorie	~7,000 calorie
Carbohydrate (g)	404	684	948
Protein (g)	153	243	302
Fat (g)	100	174	240
	~3,000 calorie	**~5,000 calorie**	**~7,000 calorie**
FIRST BREAKFAST			
Overnight oats made with:			
Old-fashioned oats	N/A	250 mL (1 cup)	250 mL (1 cup)
2% milk	N/A	375 mL (1-1/2 cups)	375 mL (1-1/2 cups)
Fruit yogurt	N/A	125 mL (1/2 cup)	125 mL (1/2 cup)
Pumpkin seeds	N/A	2 tbsp	2 tbsp
Blueberries	N/A	250 mL (1 cup)	250 mL (1 cup)
Banana	N/A	N/A	1 large
DURING TRAINING			
Banana and/or sport drink	N/A	1 large *or* 500 mL (2 cups)	1 large *and* 500 mL (2 cups)
FIRST (IF NO AM TRAINING) OR SECOND BREAKFAST			
Smoothie made with:			
Mixed berries	250 mL (1 cup)	250 mL (1 cup)	250 mL (1 cup)
Flavored yogurt	125 mL (1/2 cup)	125 mL (1/2 cup)	125 mL (1/2 cup)
2% or chocolate milk	375 mL (1-1/2 cup)	375 mL (1-1/2 cups)	500 mL (2 cups)
Honey	15 mL (1 tbsp)	15 mL (1 tbsp)	15 mL (1 tbsp)
Banana	1/2 large	1 large	1 large
Whole wheat toast	2 slices	3 slices	4 slices
Jam	N/A	1 tbsp	2 tbsp
Scrambled eggs	2 large	3 large	4 large
Butter	10 mL (2 tsp)	15 mL (1 tbsp)	30 mL (2 tbsp)
	~3,000 calorie	**~5,000 calorie**	**~7,000 calorie**
FIRST (IF NO AM TRAINING) OR SECOND BREAKFAST (continued)			
Kale (can put in smoothie)	1 large handful	1 large handful	1 large handful
Onion	65 mL (1/4 cup)	65 mL (1/4 cup)	65 mL (1/4 cup)
LUNCH			
Wrap made with:			
Chicken thigh (skinless, boneless)	1 large	2 large	2 large
Power greens (kale, spinach)	1 large handful	2 large handfuls	2 large handfuls
Whole wheat tortilla	1-10 in.	2-10 in.	2-10 in.
Hummus	30 mL (2 tbsp)	60 mL (1/4 cup)	90 mL (1/3 cup)
Shredded cheddar	30 g (1/4 cup)	40 g (1/3 cup)	60 g (1/2 cup)
Apple	1 medium	1 medium	1 medium
Orange juice	N/A	N/A	500 mL (2 cups)
DURING TRAINING			
Banana and/or sport drink	1 large *or* 500 mL (2 cups)	1 large *or* 500 mL (2 cups)	1 large *and* 500 mL (2 cups)
	~3,000 calorie	**~5,000 calorie**	**~7,000 calorie**

(continued)

Table 27.4 *(continued)*

RECOVERY SNACK			
Greek yogurt pumpkin muffin	1 medium	1 medium	1 medium
2% milk	375 mL (1-1/2 cups)	375 mL (1-1/2 cups)	500 mL (2 cups)
Banana	1 large	1 large	1 large
DINNER			
Baked salmon fillet	120 g (4 oz)	150 g (5 oz)	180 g (6 oz)
Baked yam w/butter	500 mL (2 cups)	625 mL/750 mL (2.5-3 cups)	750 mL/1,000 mL (3-4 cups)
Vegetable medley or salad	500 mL (2 cups)	500 mL (2 cups)	500 mL (2 cups)
Dressing, oil and lemon	15 mL (1 tbsp)	15 mL (1 tbsp)	30 mL (2 tbsp)
Dark chocolate	25 g piece	25 g piece	50 g piece
BEDTIME SNACK			
Plain Greek yogurt	175 mL (3/4 cup)	175 mL (3/4 cup)	375 mL (1-1/2 cups)
Mixed berries	250 mL (1 cup)	250 mL (1 cup)	500 mL (2 cups)
Slivered almonds	15 mL (1 tbsp)	30 mL (2 tbsp)	30 mL (2 tbsp)

Notes: Vegan athletes can substitute tofu, legumes, seeds, and nuts for animal proteins. Dairy-intolerant athletes can substitute lactose-free or other milk and yogurt alternatives. Meals and snacks should be timed within the day based on training to prevent long gaps between feedings. This is a sample fueling plan only. Calorie requirements are estimates and should be determined based on height, weight, age, sex, and training hours. See chapter 28 for additional information. Increase portions if training session >90 minutes and substitute in additional sport drink or gels etc. if solid foods are not well tolerated during training. Increase pre-bed protein during hypertrophy phase.

Macronutrients are estimates only using the Food Processor Nutrition and Fitness Software Database by Esha Research Version 11.9.14.

Additionally, as exercise intensity increases, carbohydrate metabolism predominates (Hearris et al. 2018; Winkert 2022). With threshold and high-intensity work comprising approximately 15% to 20% of the rower's training, appropriate carbohydrate intake strategies are key. (See chapter 14 for rowing training descriptions.) (Maestu, Jurimae, and Jurimae 2005; Tran et al. 2015). High carbohydrate intakes (10 g/kg BM/day vs. 5 g/kg BM/day) have been shown to produce greater mean power outputs over a 4-week rowing training block, with the effect of carbohydrate on performance more pronounced the longer the high-carbohydrate diet and high-intensity training continued (Simonsen et al. 1991). An aggressive carbohydrate strategy is therefore particularly important for rowers before hypertrophy, high-volume or high-intensity sessions; during seat racing; or more generally during an intensified training block. If intentional low carbohydrate availability is desired for potential benefits to adaptation, it is best undertaken during a base aerobic training phase and never before high-intensity or quality work. Although training with low carbohydrate availability is an exciting strategy to consider, this approach is only recommended for very elite athletes supported by a sport nutrition professional and is not recommended for junior or developing athletes. Rowers at all levels should plan their daily carbohydrate intake with the entire week's training requirements and goals in mind.

Have a Plan

It is important for rowers to not only understand their carbohydrate needs but to also have a clear nutrition plan. When carbohydrate needs are high and the time for fueling between important exercise sessions is short, rowers must consider all opportunities for eating, such as a quick snack on the way to training, as well as during-session and recovery fueling. Advance meal planning and preparation during lighter days or days off increases the likelihood that a busy or tired rower will eat well-timed, high-quality, carbohydrate-rich meals when lack of time or energy is an issue (figure 27.1).

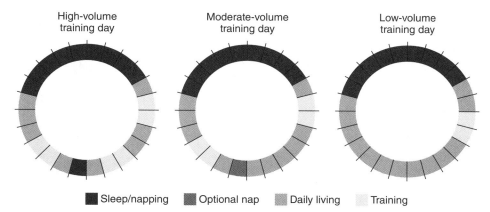

▶ **Figure 27.1** Typical training day for Canadian athletes, with each color block representing 1 hour: dark gray = sleep or napping; medium-dark gray = optional nap; medium gray = activities of daily living (e.g., travel to training, rigging and equipment maintenance, massage, treatment, meal preparation and eating, studying, work, socializing); light gray = training.

Susan Boegman and Sid Boegman (2021).

On the other hand, when training is lower in volume or intensity, athletes who do not struggle to maintain weight will need less carbohydrate (table 27.1) and may take a more relaxed approach to food planning. Considerations for daily carbohydrate requirements must therefore include training block objectives, number of training sessions per day, session intensity and goals, time available for fueling, and the number of years an athlete has been rowing. For specific meal planning strategies, see table 28.3 in the next chapter.

Before and During Session Fueling

At its most basic level, fueling before and during training should prevent hunger and provide hydration while avoiding gastrointestinal (GI) distress. More specifically, carbohydrate consumed before and during exercise has the potential to further benefit training performance in a variety of ways. When training is high intensity, prolonged (≥90 min), or frequent (more than once per day), carbohydrate consumed before and during each session will have a glycogen-sparing effect, provide additional fuel if glycogen stores are depleted, and prevent negative effects of low blood glucose in the latter stages of exercise (Burke et al. 2011). Studies have shown that a high carbohydrate meal in the hours before exercise improves performance (Kerksick et al. 2017). Additionally, although training diet was not controlled for, the distance covered in the final 12 min of a 30-min self-paced rowing time trial was improved when a 30 g carbohydrate solution was consumed 30 min before the start. Power output, rather than stroke rate, was the most likely reason for the improved performance (Bottoms et al. 2014). Rowers are encouraged to aim for preexercise carbohydrate intakes of 1 to 4 g/kg BM prior to key sessions when intensity, duration management, or performance is important (Kerksick et al. 2017).

Fueling during a session may also benefit future training performances. Although assessed in cycling studies, 20g carbohydrate ingestion every 30 or 45 min or 10 to 20 g every 15 min (approximately 40-60 g/h) during 2 h of cycling elevated blood glucose levels and enhanced subsequent time trial performances (Kozlowski, Ferrentino-DePriest, and Cerny 2020; Newell et al. 2015). Given that on-water or ergometer training sessions may be more than 2 h in length and involve the whole body, rowers are advised to consume approximately 40 to 60 g/h of carbohydrate when possible, with individual gut tolerance also considered. Easily digested foods and sport-specific products such as drinks, gels, and gummies can provide readily available carbohydrates for use by the working muscles in current and subsequent training sessions (figure 27.2) (Burke et al. 2011).

If an athlete experiences GI discomfort and struggles to fuel during training, carbohydrate mouth rinsing can be considered. Very simply, a sport drink or carbohydrate solution is swished in the mouth and typically not swallowed. However, because of the documented benefits of carbohydrate intake during a high-volume session (Burke et al. 2011), athletes who experience gastrointestinal discomfort are encouraged to practice in-session fueling rather than mouth rinsing. Over time, gradual increases in carbohydrate intake during training should enhance gastric emptying, gut carbohydrate absorptive capacity, and stomach comfort (Jeukendrup 2017b). The potential benefits are improved performance due to improved carbohydrate availability and decreased risk of relative energy deficiency in sport (REDs) (see chapter 28). Carbohydrate mouth rinsing, if considered, is best used as a possible strategy during fasted training, and protocols should be researched prior to consideration (Jeukendrup 2014).

On the other hand, when training is undertaken only once per day and lasts for less than 90 minutes, when sessions are shorter, or training is started in a fed state, fueling during a session is likely unnecessary (Burke et al. 2011; Kerksick et al. 2017). Drinking water should be sufficient. Individual athlete nutrition needs must always be considered, and athletes with higher energy needs may still benefit from fueling during shorter or once-a-day sessions if weight loss or underrecovery is a concern.

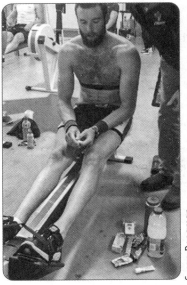

▶ **Figure 27.2** Conlin McCabe, Canadian national team member, Olympic silver medalist, Ergometer hour of power WR 2018 and ergometer half-marathon WR 2020, optimizing ready-to-use nutrition for long, intense training sessions.

Susan Boegman

Protein: The Repair and Regeneration Ruler

Although much of the focus on protein is how it relates to skeletal muscle synthesis and physical adaptation, protein has a much broader role within the human body, particularly for endurance athletes. Dietary protein is also necessary to optimize metabolic adaptations to training and is a key component of enzymes, hormones, blood cells, tissues, and mitochondria (see chapter 11). In fact, only an estimated 20% of consumed protein is taken up for use by skeletal muscle, with the rest used to maintain organs and other tissues (Groen et al. 2015). Given the importance of protein, general recommendations for most athletes have been set at approximately 1.6 g/kg BM per day, or twice

Key Point

Carbohydrate mouth rinsing is the practice of repeatedly swishing a 6% to 10% carbohydrate solution around the mouth for approximately 5 to 10 s and spitting out the drink. Receptors in the mouth detect carbohydrate energy and activate areas of the brain associated with reward. Although this strategy does not provide ingested carbohydrate energy, it may temporarily decrease fatigue, improve mood, and moderate performance decreases associated with lowered glycogen status. Importantly, artificially sweetened fluids do not have this effect, though both flavored and flavorless carbohydrate beverages do. Many, but not all, studies have demonstrated improved performance with carbohydrate mouth rinsing (Peart 2017). Nonetheless, a mouth rinse strategy may benefit the rower who struggles to complete a low carbohydrate availability session or fuel during a high-intensity training session.

what is recommended in a sedentary population, with safe daily targets in the range of 1.4 to 2.0 g/kg BM per day (Jager et al. 2017; Morton et al. 2018). There are circumstances in which higher protein intakes may be beneficial, including for athletes with high energy needs, in a hypertrophy phase, recovering from injury, or aiming to retain lean body mass during a fat loss phase (see table 27.1) (Jager et al. 2017; Huecker et al. 2019). See chapter 28 for additional information on body composition management.

Protein for Resistance Training

As power and endurance athletes, rowers train to improve strength, anaerobic, and aerobic energy systems (Tran et al. 2015). Resistance training, a typical component of a rowing exercise program, stimulates muscle protein synthesis (MPS). When synthesis exceeds breakdown, skeletal muscle gains will occur (Morton, McGlory, and Phillips 2015). Protein feeding also stimulates MPS, and the anabolic effect is greatest when food and training are paired (Morton, McGlory, and Phillips 2015). Although overall daily protein intake is likely the key nutritional factor in protein synthesis and remodeling, the timing, source, and per-meal quantity are also factors. Skeletal muscle appears most sensitive to the anabolic effect of protein intake in the first 5 to 6 h following exercise, and for approximately 24 h after a strength training session (Jager et al. 2017). Importantly, ingested protein provides essential amino acids—particularly leucine—which acts as both substrate and an anabolic signaling molecule (van Vliet, Burd, and van Loon 2015). High-quality, leucine-rich proteins such as whey, dairy, fish, and beef are highly effective sources to stimulate MPS. Rapidly digested, single-source, leucine-rich proteins (e.g., whey isolate) consumed shortly after resistance training are most anabolic in the early postexercise recovery phase (Burd et al. 2019), whereas whole foods such as dairy products (van Vliet et al. 2019) and eggs will stimulate muscle remodeling over a longer period after eating (Burd et al. 2019). When compared to leucine-rich protein supplements, whole foods contain a superior mix of nutrients and food components that may work synergistically to elevate anabolic signaling and postexercise protein synthesis (Burd et al. 2019) beyond the effect of protein-based amino acids alone.

Protein Needs Beyond the Gym

The typical rowing training program will include at least 3 to 12 on-water, ergometer, or cross-training sessions per week. These endurance sessions will stimulate nonhypertrophic adaptations such as increased mitochondrial density, capillary formation, and hemoglobin and myoglobin synthesis, which also require protein intake for optimization (Huecker et al. 2019). Even though whole-body protein turnover increases after an endurance session, protein intake beyond the daily targets recommended above does not appear to further enhance these nonhypertrophic adaptations.

On the other hand, skeletal muscle synthesis may benefit from greater postexercise protein intakes during recovery from an endurance session. Following endurance training an athlete may appropriately prioritize carbohydrates, forgetting to also include protein-rich foods. In fact, protein at this time is key to skeletal muscle synthesis. A recent study in young cyclists and triathletes demonstrated that after a 90 min cycle, skeletal MPS was maximally stimulated by a meal containing 30 g of protein, with further nonsignificant increases when 45 g of milk protein was eaten. The optimal dose was estimated to be 0.49 g/kg BM (Churchward-Venne et al. 2020), slightly larger than the recommended intakes when recovering from resistance training. Protein consumed during or after a high-volume endurance session may also suppress skeletal muscle damage and reduce muscle soreness (Jager et al. 2017). Additionally, higher daily protein intakes may "contribute to the considerable energy needs and meal satisfaction of the [typical] rower" (Boegman and Dziedzic 2016, 254).

Specific Protein Intake Protocols

In addition to the general per day protein intake recommendations outlined above, athletes will require specific intake protocols to support each aspect of training and performance. Consuming approximately 0.3 g/kg BM of protein, or 20 to 30 g for most athletes, appears to maximally stimulate MPS following resistance exercise (Morton, McGlory, and Phillips 2015; Stokes et al. 2018), with approximately 30 g to 50 g possibly needed after endurance training (Churchward-venne et al. 2020). However, total daily intake is even more important than this specific posttraining protein-intake strategy. To maximize whole-body protein anabolism, including lean mass gains, rowers are encouraged to consume approximately 0.3 to 0.4 g/kg BM of protein from whole food sources, evenly distributed over four or more meals across the day (see table 27.1). The higher per-meal protein recommendation is encouraged when fewer meals are consumed and when the training day includes a total body resistance session versus upper or lower body only (Burd et al. 2019; Huecker et al. 2019; Kerksick et al. 2017), because full body workouts stimulate higher levels of muscle protein breakdown. Unfortunately, a typical eating day for the busy athlete may skew toward a low-protein breakfast, a moderate-protein lunch, a very high-protein dinner once training has been completed, and then possibly a low-protein, high-sugar or -fat evening snack to satisfy cravings. This inadequate protein distribution throughout the day will prevent optimized protein-dependent training adaptations (Areta et al. 2013). Recommendations for lightweight female to openweight male athletes respectively are to consume approximately 25 to 40 g of protein per meal (see table 27.1). Finally, although a food-first approach is strongly recommended, when undertaking a busy, high-volume training program, a rower may benefit from a recovery fueling strategy that incorporates rapidly digesting, leucine-rich protein supplements followed by the ingestion of longer acting protein-rich whole foods.

Presleep Protein

When training load is high or lean mass gains are desired, protein should be included in a presleep snack. Casein or other whole-food proteins that digest more slowly than whey are particularly beneficial. Consuming approximately 30 to 40 g of protein prior to sleep is a practical strategy to sustain circulating amino acids into the night (Moore 2015), which may enhance overall MPS, recovery, and possibly strength (Jager et al. 2017). Anecdotally, some rowers undertaking high-volume training noted improved sleep and less morning fatigue when consuming a high-protein presleep snack.

Animal, Plant, or Both?

Debate on whether vegetable protein sources are a good choice for athletes aiming to maximize MPS has been informed by recent investigations. To date, however, most of the research has been on recreational athletes over 12 weeks or less and has typically only studied single-source vegetable proteins such as soy. More research into the effects of diverse proteins such as those found in a typical vegan whole-food diet is required.

In general, when compared to animal sources, the protein in plant foods such as legumes, oats, or quinoa is lower, less absorbable, and does not contain a full array of the essential amino acids (Nichele and Phillips 2022, Pinckaers et al. 2021). In addition, single-source vegetable protein supplements consumed in isolation result in lower levels of acute postexercise MPS than animal proteins. Overall lean mass and strength gains, however, appear similar, between some plant and whey supplements when adequate leucine was consumed and when assessed over time (Messina et al. 2018, Kerksick et al. 2021). Interestingly, a recent protein-matched plant versus omnivorous diet study in young adult males demonstrated no differences in muscle strength and lean mass gains over 12 weeks when daily protein recommendations of 1.6 g/kg BM were met (Hevia-Larraín et al. 2021). Among healthy females, however, lifelong vegetarianism has been linked to lower overall muscle mass. This may be a result of long-term low protein intake, a result of lower leucine intake, or because older individuals actually require more leucine to maximize MPS. With respect to posttraining muscle reconditioning, the athlete struggling to meet recommended daily protein targets may gain more lean mass following an omnivorous rather than a vegan eating pattern (van Vliet, Burd, and van Loon 2015).

For those who prefer a plant-only diet there are several approaches to minimize potential differences in lean mass gains. Strategies include increasing total per-meal protein (~30 g/meal), using supplements that contain multiple vegetable protein sources or added free leucine, and consuming a variety of whole foods that have been processed before consumption (Nichele and Phillips 2022; Pinckaers et al. 2021; van Vliet, Burd, and van Loon 2015). At-home food processing techniques such as soaking, fermenting, and cooking, as well as industry processing of proteins into isolates or concentrates will increase digestibility and absorption (Nichele and Phillips 2022). Based on the available evidence, rowers who choose a plant-only diet are encouraged to follow these strategies to ensure a daily protein intake of at least 1.6 g/kg BM. Additionally, given the high-fiber content of a vegan diet, athletes who find it difficult to meet energy needs are encouraged to consider adding egg, dairy, or fish to increase both high-quality proteins and calories to support training and adaptation (van Vliet, Burd, and van Loon 2015).

Fat: Friend or Foe?

The body has unlimited fat stores for use as an energy source. Even so, fat is a necessary component of a healthy diet. It provides insulation, protection for internal organs, energy, essential elements of cell membranes and nerve transmission, and it facilitates the absorption of fat-soluble vitamins (Thomas, Erdman, and Burke 2016). Fats are classified as saturated or unsaturated, with unsaturated further classified as polyunsaturated or monounsaturated. All fat sources contain varying levels of saturated, monounsaturated, and polyunsaturated fatty acids but are classified based on their predominant fatty acid profile. Of these fats, athletes are recommended to consume the majority as monounsaturated and the polyunsaturated, omega-3 fatty acids (see table 27.3) with lesser amounts as saturated fats. Omega-3 fatty acids cannot be made by the body, are therefore considered essential and, must be consumed in the diet.

The Omega 3s

Long-term intake of omega-3 rich foods (fish, seafood, walnuts) are cardioprotective and anti-inflammatory (Ritz et al. 2020; Witard and Davis 2021), and over time, the omega-3 fatty acids eicosapentaenoic acid (EPA) and docosahexaenoic acid (DHA) are incorporated into tissues such as heart, skeletal muscle, and brain. A recent meta-analysis of 32 research studies in athletes of all levels reported emerging findings that omegas in the form of fish oil supplements positively effect mood, reaction time and post exercise muscle recovery. The amount of omega 3s that were provided in some of the reviewed studies are achievable via fish intake several times per week (Lewis et al. 2020).

Unfortunately, most athletes struggle to meet the recommended intakes. A review of the dietary intakes of over 1,500 collegiate athletes found that only 6% met the recommended minimum omega-3 intakes of 500 mg per day (Ritz et al. 2020). To meet minimum requirements and improve omega-3 fatty acid status over time, athletes of all ages are urged to eat fish or seafood several times per week. Supplementation is an option for athletes who do not consume fish or seafood because of allergies, dietary preferences, or lack of access. For additional information, interested readers are directed to the excellent overview by Ritz and Rockwell (2021).

Fat as Fuel

Beyond essential nutrients such as fat-soluble vitamins, fat provides needed calories within a smaller food volume for the rower struggling to maintain or gain weight. As such, fat can increase an athlete's ability to achieve high energy intake goals and support training.

On the other hand, rowers aiming for weight loss may need to limit fat to decrease overall daily calories. In this situation, care must be taken to prevent excessive fat restriction, which may result in essential fatty acid and fat-soluble vitamin deficiencies. A small amount of fat from high-quality sources (see table 27.3) should be consumed at each meal and possibly at each snack. Rowers should be aware that excessive intake of fat calories—which are a component of high-fat protein sources, processed foods, and added fats—may replace some of the carbohydrates necessary to manage and recover from large training volumes. Finally, fats should be limited when immediate recovery is required.

Chronic Fat Adaptation

Current interest in high-fat, low-carbohydrate diets is high. A recent online search for high-fat, low-carbohydrate diet for athletes yielded over 41,600,000 results. One might wonder if this eating strategy may benefit rowing training adaptation. To date, there does not appear to be any published chronic, high-fat, low-carbohydrate research undertaken in the rowing population. Although fat is used as a fuel source for prolonged lower intensity endurance training, training intensity while on a high-fat diet will be compromised, possibly due to the downregulation of carbohydrate metabolism (Thomas, Erdman, and Burke 2016). High-intensity training is a mainstay of the rowing program; thus, high-fat, low carbohydrate diets are not recommended.

Recovery Fueling: Putting It All Together

Recovery nutrition should be a serious undertaking. Athletes that prolong the time between the end of an exercise session and refueling risk lower glycogen restoration and reduced remodeling of various body proteins. The posttraining hunger window may also pass, increasing risk for inadequate calorie intake.

Before planning a nutritional recovery strategy, several key questions must be considered:

- What type of session was undertaken?
- Is recovery meant to restore glycogen to optimize an upcoming training session or prolong training adaptation by purposefully limiting carbohydrate?
- How much time is available for recovery (1 hour, 1 day, 1 weekend)?
- What nutrients are needed? Which foods contain these nutrients?
- Where is this food coming from?

When rowers train 2 to 3 times per day with limited time between sessions, rapid recovery is required and aggressive postexercise carbohydrate and protein intake is recommended (figure 27.1). Because muscle glycogen resynthesis is greatest during the first hour after training (Kerksick et al. 2017), athletes should fuel as soon as is practical after training and will benefit from a recovery nutrition plan. Currently, there is insufficient research to recommend an optimal feeding pattern (i.e., many small carbohydrate intakes versus a larger single meal) (Moore 2015). Nevertheless, rowers should aim to have tasty, easy-to-digest foods and fluids readily available so that fueling can begin within 30 to 60 min of training. When time permits, a follow-up meal should also be consumed.

If a protein source is unavailable or an athlete prefers to eat carbohydrate-rich foods post exercise, approximately 1.2 g/kg BM of carbohydrate is optimal to maximize muscle glycogen resynthesis. Unfortunately, although carbohydrate intake will suppress muscle protein breakdown after exercise, in isolation, it has no effect on MPS (Moore 2015). Rather, carbohydrates and proteins work together. Consuming both in the recovery meal decreases the amount of carbohydrate required to replenish glycogen stores and supports whole body adaptation to training. Most athletes typically eat recovery meals that contain both nutrients, therefore 0.8 g/kg BM of carbohydrate is generally considered adequate unless energy needs are high. As discussed previously, recovery and reconditioning will be maximally stimulated as long as adequate amounts of high-quality, leucine-rich proteins are consumed after training and every 3 to 4 h, or four or more times throughout the day.

When training once per day, on lighter training days, or when there is more time for recovery (such as overnight or on a rest day), the pattern and timing of a carbohydrate-containing meal or snack can be much more flexible (Burke et al. 2011; Moore 2015), and main meals can be timed to act as recovery fuel. When an upcoming session is lower intensity, an athlete may wish to purposefully limit or withhold recovery carbohydrates to strategically train with low carbohydrate availability and potentially promote augmented adaptations to training (Hearris et al. 2018). Keep in mind that this recovery strategy should only be considered for healthy, experienced athletes, because the negative impact of unsupported training is substantial (Boegman and Dziedzic 2016; Impey et al. 2018). Generally speaking, fats contribute energy and nutrients as well as to overall meal enjoyment.

Regardless of the recovery strategy chosen, athletes should be knowledgeable about the foods that contain carbohydrates, proteins, and fats (see table 27.3) and the portion sizes required to meet recommended intakes. Finally, athletes are encouraged to create an achievable recovery plan.

Food Quality at Work

Although much of the prior discussion has revolved around specific macronutrients for performance (carbohydrates, proteins, fat), athletes eat food, not nutrients. A rower may eat 40 to 60 times over a standard training week, which translates to more than 2,000 times per year. Obviously, nutrition is important! High-quality, nutrient-dense whole foods are essential to minimize or prevent subclinical or overt nutrient deficiencies, as well as enhance the intake and positive health impacts of the over 26,000 distinct biochemicals present in unprocessed foods (Barabasi, Menichetti, and Loscalzo 2020).

Key Point

Food quality and composition are important considerations when energy needs are easily met, when body composition management is a goal or, conversely, when struggling to meet calorie needs during a high-volume training block.

A recent randomized control trial (Hall et al 2019) found that subjects consistently ate more calories over 2 weeks when provided with an unlimited amount of ultraprocessed foods versus unprocessed foods.

Subjects resided in a research unit for 28 days and were randomly assigned to 14 days of either an unprocessed diet or an ultraprocessed diet. Subjects were then switched to the alternate diet for the second 14 days. The researchers provided access to three meals plus snacks throughout the day, with calories and macronutrients matched for each group. Fiber was added to liquids in the ultraprocessed diet to match the fiber intake for both groups. The amount of available food was double that of estimated needs, and subjects were able to eat as much as they wished.

Ratings of palatability and food familiarity and measures of hunger, fullness, and meal satisfaction were not significantly different between the groups; however, participants ate faster when in the ultraprocessed diet group. Among the various study findings, energy intake was almost 500 calories a day higher and subjects gained weight when in the ultraprocessed diet group.

Although the researchers did not design the study to determine the cause of energy intake differences, they did find higher energy intakes from liquids, which are less satiating than solids, in the ultraprocessed diet group. They also saw increases in the appetite-suppressing hormone PYY and decreases in the hunger hormone ghrelin when participants were on the unprocessed diet, possibly contributing to lower energy intakes.

Athletes may struggle with feeding challenges such as dislikes, allergies, or intolerances, as well as a lack of time, food preparation skills, or nutrition knowledge. Left unaddressed, these challenges may negatively impact diet quality, especially if athletes limit food variety or choose nutrient-poor, prepackaged foods over fresh, unprocessed foods. Additionally, athletes who have high energy needs, are trying to gain lean body mass, struggle with GI issues, or experience limited appetite may forgo nutrient-rich plant foods for low-fiber, high-calorie foods. Finally, athletes who restrict energy intake, use extreme weight loss methods, limit vegetable and fruit intake, or eliminate entire food groups may end up consuming inadequate micronutrients (Thomas, Erdman, and Burke 2016). Interestingly, unpublished data from Canadian national rowing team athletes indicate that micronutrient requirements are generally achieved when fueling needs are met through a wide variety of foods. Exceptions are vitamin D, vitamin B12 and, for some athletes, omega-3 fatty acids, iron, and calcium (see chapter 29 for a broader discussion).

Staying Hydrated

Dehydration is the process of incurring a fluid deficit. Hypohydration, which is the actual fluid deficit, can impair endurance performance (Belval et al. 2019). Maximal aerobic power or $\dot{V}O_2$max is critical to rowing performance and a large cardiac output is key to high aerobic power. Dehydration decreases plasma, and therefore stroke volume, reducing cardiac output and significantly raising heart rate. Beyond cardiovascular strain, when hypohydration is severe rowers will also experience negative performance effects due to increases in core body temperature, glycogen use, and rates of perceived exertion. Although tolerance is highly individual, more than 2% to 3% fluid loss may impair aerobic and cognitive performance during endurance exercise in temperate, warm, or hot environments (American College of Sports Medicine et al. 2007). Dehydration is a real possibility when athletes undertake heavy training volumes combined with high sweat rates and limited drinking opportunities. Rowers should therefore understand how to assess their hydration status. Key indicators include changes in body mass, thirst, as well as urine color and volume. A poorly hydrated rower will experience significant thirst, produce small amounts of dark-colored urine, urinate infrequently, and experience morning body weight fluctuations greater than 1% from baseline (American College of Sports Medicine et al. 2007).

The Role of Sweat

Sweat rate is the largest contributor to body fluid losses. Consequently, rowers should be aware of their usual sweat loss patterns under various conditions. Sweat rates are highly individual. Many factors, including genetics, body size and muscle mass, training status, environment, clothing, training intensity, and duration will impact sweat rates and thus hydration status (American College of Sports Medicine et al. 2007). Approximately 1.0 to 3.0 L of sweat loss per hour is not uncommon in well-muscled, large rowers and can amount to significant total body fluid losses over several training hours per day (~4-12 L for a 4 h training day) (American College of Sports Medicine et al. 2007).

Hypohydration will occur when sweat rate exceeds fluid intake. Additionally, with gut fluid absorption at approximately 800 to 1,000 mL per hour it may be impossible for a rower with high sweat rates to keep session fluid losses under 2% to 3%. Hence, hydration strategies before, during, and between training sessions are critical. Unfortunately, when time between sessions is limited, posttraining rehydration may fall short. If athletes start their training poorly hydrated, carry a fluid deficit from one session to the next, or fail to adequately drink during exercise and throughout the posttraining recovery period, training intensity and quality will be negatively impacted. Thus, to maximize performance potential, rowers should develop a personalized hydration plan, particularly during warmer months and in hotter environments.

Replacing Electrolytes

When discussing sweat loss, electrolyte depletion must also be considered. Sweat, though approximately 99.9% water, also contains several key electrolytes, including potassium, chloride, and most importantly sodium (Maughan and Shirreffs 2010). Sodium has a role in fluid balance, blood pressure regulation, muscle contraction, and possibly performance. Although highly individual, average sweat sodium losses for endurance athletes are approximately 50 mmol/L or 1,150 mg/L (50 mmol/L x 23 mg/mmol) with daily variability (Barnes et al. 2019). Average sweat rates in endurance athletes are 1.3 L/h. This translates to 1,500 mg/h of sodium lost through sweat (1,150 × 1.3)—easily replaced within the normal diet for most athletes. Incredibly, several Rowing Canada national team athletes have been tested at sweat sodium losses over 80 mmol or 1800 mg/L (Canadian Sport Institute Pacific, unpublished data).

Thus, for those with both a high sweat sodium concentration and a high sweat rate, fluid and sodium replacement requires a deliberate rehydration strategy. Consider the very real example of a rower with an average daily sweat rate of approximately 8 L (2 L × 4 h training), and a potential sodium loss of 83 mmol or 1909 mg per L of sweat. Although sweat sodium loses decrease over a session, such an individual would need to replenish 8 to 12 L of fluids and potentially consume the equivalent of ~15,000 mg of sodium each day (83 mmol/L × 23 mg/mmol × 8 L). However, does sodium actually need to be replaced during exercise? The answer depends on how well one rehydrates. Because the body regulates sodium levels, intake during exercise is only necessary when replenishing 70% or more of sweat losses and when sweat sodium levels are higher than normal (McCubbin 2022).

Sweat sodium can be assessed with the help of a physiologist via sweat patch collection and analysis. If this is not available, athletes can look for clues to help understand sweat sodium losses. Signs of higher levels include salty tasting sweat, salt residue on skin, white salt stains on dark clothing, and possibly muscle cramping (Maughan and Shirreffs 2010). Any of these signs may indicate the need for a higher dietary sodium intake.

Lastly, there are many additional electrolytes in sweat such as potassium, magnesium, and calcium. Although these minerals perform key functions, losses during exercise are minimal compared to the amounts stored within the body, and replacement during training is currently deemed unnecessary (McCubbin 2022).

Considerations for Optimizing Hydration

To maximize performance potential, athletes should understand their individual fluid losses. Weighing before and after various training sessions and under diverse environmental conditions will allow rowers to estimate average sweat rate and develop a personalized hydration plan, particularly during warmer months and in hotter environments. The goal should be to start each session well-hydrated and limit losses to approximately 2% or less. A high sweat rate will necessitate regular drinking breaks during exercise. However, for an athlete with minimal sweat losses, fluids during a row may be unnecessary and drinking before and after exercise would be sufficient for the maintenance of good hydration. Regardless, carbohydrate-electrolyte beverages can be a valuable tool for rowers during training, because both carbohydrate and fluids improve performance (Maughan and Shirreffs 2010). Additionally, the electrolytes added to sport drinks improve palatability (which increases fluid intake), help replace sodium, and increase fluid retention. The added sodium may also prevent muscle cramps in susceptible athletes (Maughan and Shirreffs 2010). After training, drinking approximately 150% of lost fluids will account for ongoing losses in the postexercise period. Notably, improved fluid balance will occur at a faster rate when larger amounts are consumed within the first few hours of the recovery period (Kovacs et al. 2002) and in particular when fluids are consumed along with sodium-containing foods (Maughan and Shirreffs 2010). When hypohydration is significant and time for rehydration is limited, drinking larger volumes of fluid early in the recovery period is recommended. However, attention must be paid to what is physiologically and practically possible. For day-to-day hydration, athletes should aim to have most of their drinking completed a couple of hours before bed to minimize nighttime waking and sleep disturbances.

Key Point

Optimize hydration using the following simple steps:

- Monitor hydration status using sweat rate, first morning weight, urine color and quantity, and thirst.
- Set up a daily rehydration plan if sweat losses are high, including amounts and timing.
- Carry and sip fluids throughout the day. Aim for urine to be pale or lemonade-colored rather than clear.
- When possible, drink between training sessions and at turnaround points on the water if it is hot or you have a high sweat rate. Aim to limit weight loss during training to 2% to 3% of pretraining body mass. Fluids during a row may not be needed if you start training well hydrated, are performing a short, low-intensity session, have a low sweat rate, or if temperatures are cool.
- When time between sessions is short, replace approximately 100% of fluid losses within the first 2 h of recovery (Kovacs et al. 2002) and more if time permits.
- Drink with food to promote fluid intake and retention.
- Salty sweaters should salt meals and choose sodium-rich foods (such as soy sauce, seafood, pickles, olives, salted pretzels and nuts, canned legumes, tomatoes and soups, bread, packaged cereals, cheese) and fluids (such as tomato or vegetable juice, pickle juice, sport and electrolyte drinks, bouillon). When only fluids are consumed, they should contain sodium.

Table 27.5   Travel and Regatta Nutrition

Consideration	Potential issues	Strategies
Travel to regatta	• Unknown food availability • Altered meal timing • Gastrointestinal (GI) distress caused by jet lag • Increased risk of dehydration, constipation, and illness caused by dry airplane cabin air	• Research and plan for travel logistics (buffet, self-catered, restaurants, etc.) • Bring portable snacks. • Eat and drink based on the new time zone. • Bring two or more water bottles. Follow a hydration plan. • Travel with or purchase high-fiber foods on arrival. • Hydrate, aiming for pale-colored urine.
Health and hygiene	• Increased exposure to pathogens • Food or water contamination	• Educate athletes about risks. • Develop a team strategy and protocols for illness avoidance and management, including hand washing. • Use probiotics prior to and during travel (see chapter 29).
In camp and taper	• Reduced training energy expenditure (if tapering) • Boredom eating • Food monotony	• Use individualized nutrition plans for athletes who struggle to adjust intakes as training volume is reduced. • Practice mindful eating strategies. • Bring favorite snacks and comfort foods.
Food logistics	• Race not located near eateries or grocery stores • Limited availability of good quality carbohydrates and proteins • Unfamiliar foods at hotel buffet or restaurants	• Understand where meals and snacks are coming from. • Bring favorite and comfort foods from home if they will be difficult to locate in the host city. • Keep a small cooler with a ready supply of snacks close at hand.
Race day nutrition	• Altered appetite or GI issues caused by race anxiety • Meal plan impaired by race schedule or delays, leading to an athlete being hungry or overly full at the starting line • Timely fueling for the next race prevented by postrace distractions • Fueling challenges for lightweight athletes complicated by race scheduling and prerace weigh-in	• Use an individualized race-day nutrition plan. • Plan to have well-tolerated foods on hand. • Have top-up carbohydrates (sport drinks, gels, gummies) available as needed. • Eat 3-4 h before scheduled race time. Ensure that easy-to-digest, high-carbohydrate foods and fluids are available immediately before and after warm-up. Consider carbohydrate mouth rinsing and the use of slushies for pre-and-post race cooling and added carbohydrates. • Plan for recovery with carbohydrate-electrolyte beverages or foods such as granola or fig bars, bananas, or dried fruit. • Aim for 1-1.2 g/kg BM carbohydrate and 0.3 g/kg BM protein intake as soon as possible after racing. • A substantial meal should follow within 2-4 h of finishing for optimal recovery. • Lightweight athletes require an individualized plan (see chapter 28).
Hydration	• Increased fluid requirements caused by high heat or humidity • Fluid intake limited by distractions or lack of availability	• Use individualized hydration plans specific to the expected weather conditions. • Remind athletes to hydrate. • Perform event reconnaissance to understand fluid access.

Halson, Burke, and Pearce (2019).

Setting the Stage for Competition Success

A regatta is a series of races that usually occur over several days (including National Rowing Championships, various World Cups, and the Olympics). Depending on the regatta, rowers will race one to several times per day. The 2,000 m race, which occurs at a near-maximal effort over approximately 5.5 to 8 min (depending on boat class and competition level), will cause significant glycogen utilization and lactate production. Although a single race is unlikely to exhaust a rower's fuel stores (Martin and Tomescu 2017; Slater et al 2005), two or more races per day will deplete glycogen levels, particularly in explosive muscle fibers, and limit the time available for recovery fueling. A properly executed nutrition plan is therefore key to performance success over a regatta. Not only will it help manage glycogen levels, it will positively impact other factors such as travel fueling, jet lag symptoms, travel-related illness, and the logistics or distractions of an unfamiliar competition environment.

To optimize race results, potential nutrition issues and management strategies should be identified. Considerations include travel, taper, staging camp and regatta food and fluid logistics, race schedule, appetite, gastrointestinal (GI) comfort, health and hygiene, and race day nutrition and hydration. Table 27.5 includes some of these potential travel and regatta issues and solutions. For a complete review of travel and competition nutrition, the reader is directed to the excellent paper "Nutrition for Travel: From Jet Lag to Catering" by Halson, Burke, and Pearce (2019). In addition, refer to chapters 21, 22, and 26 for more discussion on traveling for competition.

Reconnaissance upon arrival at a regatta is important to adjust and finalize individual nutrition plans and team meals. Athletes should be able to confidently fuel a reduced training load as well as manage race preparation and recovery nutrition throughout the regatta. They should also know where their food supply will come from and, when appropriate, how to manage any relevant GI issues related to race day nerves.

In addition, athletes should be hydrated at the start line. It is well established that racing while dehydrated can increase physiological strain and decrease performance, particularly in the heat. Regattas often occur in the hotter summer months, increasing the risk of dehydration. A well-executed precompetition nutrition plan will minimize this risk.

Unfortunately, a lightweight rower may also miscalculate prerace fluid needs or be unable to replace extreme fluid losses as a result of "sweating down" prior to weigh-in. With weigh-in 2 h prior to racing, the time available for rehydration is short and requires careful strategic planning. See chapter 28 for a discussion on effective dehydration strategies for making weight. Finally, because of the short, near-maximal effort required, in-competition fueling and drinking does not occur.

Conclusion

This chapter highlights the importance of carbohydrate, protein, and fat, as well as fluid and electrolytes to support training and competition. Rowers must understand how to appropriately fuel for the work they are doing and how to recover wisely. They must also learn to choose and prepare a wide variety of high-quality whole foods, strategically incorporate convenience and sport foods into a busy training program, and manage the competition environment. To fully realize the impact of nutrition on optimizing health and performance, rowers are encouraged to develop a customized nutrition plan that reflects the numerous fueling and hydration strategies available, consulting with a sport nutrition professional for guidance when needed.

Optimizing Energy

Susan Boegman

For rowers at all levels, nutrition is key to maintaining health and driving performance throughout an athletic career. Ensuring good energy availability will insulate the athlete against a range of negative impacts, including illness or injury. Optimizing energy availability will also have a positive impact on performance.

Equally important to a rowers' performance is body composition management. Alterations in body composition can yield both fat loss and lean mass gains, which directly correlate with performance improvement. Although fundamental for lightweight rowers, who require effective strategies to make weight, it will likely be a focus for all athletes at some point in their athletic career. General guidelines exist; however, body mass manipulation should be an individualized part of a well-supported, holistic training, nutrition, and recovery program in which athlete health is the priority.

Rowers typically have intense training demands and extremely high energy requirements resulting in very large dietary energy intakes (EI). Unpublished data from elite Canadian national team and University of Victoria rowing team athletes suggest an approximate EI range of 3,500 to over 10,000 kcal per day may be necessary to support the considerable training volumes typically undertaken. An athlete's specific EI requirements are influenced by their total daily energy expenditure (TDEE), which includes individual resting metabolic rate (RMR) (affected by lean mass, sex, age, height, and weight); exercise energy expenditure (EEE); nonexercise activity thermogenesis (NEAT), which is the energy required to fuel all other activities of daily living; the thermic effect of food; and genetics (Bouchard et al. 1993).

Energy Availability

Not all rowers (e.g., club, masters) need to consume such a substantial amount. However, athletes at any stage may lack understanding of or struggle to meet total energy requirements, resulting in a situation of low energy availability (LEA). Energy availability (EA) is defined as the calories from dietary intake that are available for all non-exercise-related functions—such as digestion, circulation, thermoregulation, and activities of daily living—after the cost of exercise or exercise energy ependiture (EEE) is subtracted, then corrected for fat free mass (FFM). Essentially, the energy used by the body for exercise is unavailable to support anything else. EA is calculated using the equation EA = EI (kcal) – EEE (kcal)/FFM (kg). EA is assessed using an athlete's FFM versus total body mass because FFM is significantly more metabolically active than fat mass (Burke, Lundy, et al. 2018). Unlike lean body mass (LBM), which includes skeletal muscle only, FFM includes all components of the body apart from fat.

Although it is unclear what constitutes optimal EA in rowers, current overall intake targets to maximize health and performance appear to be at least 40 kcal/kg FFM for male athletes (Koehler et al. 2016), and 45 kcal/kg FFM for female athletes (Battista et al. 2007; Melin et al. 2015) respectively. For females, less than 30 kcal/kg FFM may indicate clinically LEA, whereas males may tolerate a slightly lower intake, experiencing negative effects of LEA at 20 to 25 kcal/kg FFM (Fagerberg 2018).

Importantly, each athlete's actual energy needs are highly individual; precise determination of EI, EEE, and subsequent EA is very challenging to calculate accurately in free-living athletes (Burke, Lundy, et al. 2018). There are currently no validated gold standard protocols for measuring EA as self-reports of EI lack accuracy, and EEE and activities of daily living energy expenditure assessments lack sensitivity (Heikura, et al. 2017, Mountjoy et al. 2018). Calculations may either over- or underestimate EA. Therefore, it is critical to monitor athletes for signs of LEA indicators (table 28.1) and use qualitative risk assessment tools (see section on prevention and early identification of LEA below) rather than relying on EA assessments. In fact, field-based EA evaluation is discouraged due to the high burden that reporting places on athletes and practitioners, as well as the possibility of inaccurate outcomes when assessments are external to research grade protocols.

Key Point

There is a lack of research on the specific energy requirements of junior or masters rowers. Regardless, RMR is usually the biggest determinant of overall energy expenditure and the best predictor of RMR is lean muscle mass.

Masters athletes may be at an age where muscle mass has begun to decline or losses have possibly accelerated. On the other hand, lifelong masters athletes have an attenuated decline in muscle mass, maintaining higher baseline energy needs.

Juniors tend to have a similar stature, but slightly lower lean body mass than adult openweight rowers. They will also be growing. Juniors will therefore need to fuel the high RMR associated with a younger body while also supporting growth and lean mass increases (Bourgois et al. 2000).

Beyond RMR, exercise energy requirements have the greatest influence on calorie needs (Desbrow et al. 2019) and should be individually evaluated due to large variability in training demands. Unfortunately, beyond formulas that use height, weight, and age to estimate RMR, energy recommendations are challenging to provide due to individual athlete body composition, metabolic variability, daily activities, and overall training demands. To effectively determine if energy needs are being met, review the quality and consistency of training, recovery, and sleep, as well as mood, health, and whether performance is progressing.

LEA and REDs

Consider the following analogy outlined by dietitian and sports nutritionist Jennifer Sygo (discussion, 2019). The cost of running a house is $3,000 per month, but you only

Table 28.1 Potential Health and Performance Effects of REDs

Physical	Psychological	Performance
• Endocrine dysfunction • Reproductive dysfunction (amenorrhea/low libido/low testosterone) • Impaired bone health including low bone-mineral density and stress injury • Metabolic alterations, reduced metabolic rate • Immune suppression • Cardiovascular dysfunction • Gastrointestinal changes • Sleep disturbances	• Disordered eating/eating disorders • Adverse mood outcomes • Irritability	• Decreased training response • Decreased endurance performance • Impaired recovery between training sessions • Decreased muscle mass and strength • Decreased glycogen storage • Increased injury risk (e.g., rib stress injury) • Impaired coordination, concentration, and judgement

Note: The severity of LEA and the presence of individual athlete moderating factors will impact if and when a negative outcome will occur, and each effect can occur for reasons other than LEA. Therefore, clinical assessment is essential. Moderating factors may include: female sex, young biological and training age, stressful lifestyle, training or training environment, genetic risk factors or inadequate nutrient intake or nutrient deficiencies; in particular low carbohydrate intake may exacerbate LEA-related negative health outcomes (Mountjoy et al. 2023).

have $2,000 to spend. You will need to decide what to cut because of this monetary shortfall. Perhaps you turn down the heat (e.g., decreased RMR), stop paying for yard maintenance (e.g., decreased muscle protein synthesis), and ignore a roof that needs repair (e.g., poor structural bone health). In the same manner, the body of an underfueled athlete will have reduced energy to expend on some of the body's less essential metabolic and reproductive hormone functions.

Occasional, short-term LEA that lasts for a few hours within a day—or for some athletes maybe even over a few weeks or months—is unlikely to cause significant, long-term problems. However, severe LEA that lasts over many hours within the same day, for many weeks to months, or protracted over years can have considerable negative health and performance consequences and is considered problematic. In fact, problematic LEA is the main factor triggering Relative Energy Deficiency in Sport (REDs) (Mountjoy et al. 2023). As discussed in previous chapters, REDs refers to impaired physiological and psychological function caused by energy deficiency and includes—but is not limited to—compromised metabolic regulation, menstrual function, libido, bone health, immunity, protein synthesis, growth, and cardiovascular health (table 28.1) (Logue et al. 2020; Mountjoy et al. 2018; Mountjoy et al. 2023; Wasserfurth et al. 2020). Although additional REDs research is required, there is mounting evidence linking underfueling with these negative outcomes; the more extreme the LEA, the faster or more severe the adverse effects (Mountjoy et al. 2023).

Recently, a questionnaire-based survey of 1,000 female athletes found that those with low EA had a higher prevalence of the proposed REDs health and performance consequences than athletes found to have adequate EA (table 28.1) (Ackerman et al. 2019). Athletes with low EA were more likely to be diagnosed with menstrual dysfunction; poor bone health; metabolic, hematological, and cardiovascular impairment; gastrointestinal (GI) dysfunction; and psychological disorders than those with adequate EA. Performance variables associated with LEA in this group included decreased training response, impaired judgement, decreased coordination, decreased concentration, irritability, depression, and decreased endurance. Since this survey was conducted, additional research has corroborated many of these negative health and performance effects (Mountjoy et al. 2023) including a REDs specific, qualitative study undertaken in 12 highly trained to international level lightweight female and male rowers. This study revealed that most of the symptoms detailed in table 28.1 were experienced by the participants who also admitted to deliberate food restriction for weight management (Gillbanks, Mountjoy, and Filbay 2022).

All potential negative effects of REDs are significant. However, of the possible consequences, four are worth additional discussion: rib stress injury, overreaching or overtraining, immune suppression, and disordered eating. These effects contribute to substantial long-term negative impacts on health, training quality and adaptation, and performance outcomes in rowers.

Key Point

The negative health consequences of energy deficiency or LEA were first identified in female athletes in the 1960s. In 1992, the term *female athlete triad* was introduced to refer to three related health problems: energy intake deficiency due to disordered eating leading to the abnormal absence of a menstrual cycle (amenorrhea) and subsequent low bone mineral density (osteoporosis). This concept was developed into an American College of Sports Medicine (ACSM) position stand in 1997 (Otis et al. 1997). In 2007 this definition was further updated when researchers demonstrated that these three related health factors exist along a continuum: optimal EA, eumenorrhea (healthy menstrual status), and optimal bone health versus LEA (with or without an eating disorder), functional hypothalamic amenorrhea, and osteoporosis (Nattiv et al. 2007). Depending on individual circumstances, an athlete's health could exist anywhere along each spectrum.

In 2014, the International Olympic Committee (IOC) introduced the more comprehensive concept of Relative Energy Deficiency in Sport (REDs, updated in 2023 to REDs), in part to recognize that LEA appears to be linked to additional negative outcomes. Importantly, REDs includes all aspects of the triad, as well as a broader scope of conceptual health and performance consequences beyond poor bone health, and recognizes males as well as females. This IOC publication stimulated research in the field of REDs and was updated in 2018 with the primary aims of increasing REDs awareness and further study (Mountjoy et al. 2014; Mountjoy et al. 2018). This has been a success. Since 2018, over 100 LEA and REDs related research studies have been published with ongoing research underway. In light of this research explosion, an updated consensus statement presenting a greater understanding of the physiological and psychological underpinnings of REDs was published in 2023 (Mountjoy et al. 2023). This paper also shares a newly validated clinical assessment tool to help with the identification of REDs and is recommended reading for all who support athletes.

Rib Stress Injury

Rib stress reactions or fractures, a relatively common rowing injury (further discussed in chapter 25), have a serious negative impact on training and performance. In fact, rib stress fractures have been reported as the number one reason rowers require training modifications or are unable to compete (Warden et al. 2002). There are many risk factors for this injury, including anatomical influences, technique, equipment, and accumulation of microdamage (McDonnell, Hume, and Nolte 2011). Underfueling, particularly carbohydrate restriction (Fensham et al. 2022), may also increase the possibility of rib injury.

For rowers, both short- and long-term underfueling may contribute to rib stress injury (Gillbanks, Mountjoy, and Filbay 2022; McDonnell, Hume, and Nolte 2011). Over the short term, inadvertent or deliberate underfueling and in-session energy restriction may exacerbate exercise-induced muscular fatigue, particularly during intense or prolonged training. This may lead to altered movement patterns and force distribution, resulting in increased rib injury risk (McDonnell, Hume, and Nolte 2011). Short-term low carbohydrate intake before, during, or after high-intensity exercise may also increase markers of bone tissue breakdown independent of EA (Hammond et al. 2019).

Over the long term, altered endocrine function (low testosterone in males and abnormal or absent menses in females), a consequence of ongoing LEA, is associated with reduced bone mineral density and decreases in the body's ability to repair loading-induced microdamage, again increasing rib injury risk (Burke et al. 2018; Mountjoy et al. 2018; Thornton, J.S. and A. Vinther 2018; Warden et al. 2002). Repetitive underfueling has specifically been demonstrated in lightweight rowers, who are known to engage in deliberate restrictive eating patterns to make weight for competition (Gillbanks, Mountjoy, and Filbay 2022; Slater, Rice, Sharpe, Mujika, et al. 2005). Lightweight rowers have higher rates of endocrine dysfunction, lower bone mineral density, and increased risk of rib pain or stress fracture than openweight rowers (Dimitriou et al. 2014; Vinther et al. 2008), although openweight rowers can still be diagnosed with low bone mineral density (Lundy et al. 2015) and experience rib injury.

In the previously mentioned Gillbanks study on lightweight rowers, all 12 athletes restricted calories to lose weight for competition and 10 of the rowers described recurrent injuries, including rib stress fractures (Gillbanks, Mountjoy, and Filbay 2022). In a nonrowing but very well-executed study, significant bone injury increases were demonstrated in national and world-class runners presenting with underfueling-related amenorrhea or lower testosterone levels (Heikura et al. 2017). In total, this research demonstrates an important relationship between LEA and bone injury risk in intermediate and elite athletes.

Overreaching

Overreaching, or overtraining, may also have a long-term negative impact on athlete health and performance. Functional overreaching is the desired outcome of planned training overload and is specifically designed to enhance performance when followed by a period of appropriate recovery. If adequate rest is not programmed into the athlete's training, underrecovery may lead to nonfunctional overreaching and eventual overtraining (Meeusen et al. 2013). Dietary inadequacy during periods of intensified training—whether intentional or accidental—is an ongoing stressor that may increase the risk of inadvertent underrecovery and overreaching, negatively impacting training and performance. In fact, overtraining and REDs share many symptoms and diagnostic similarities. A recent review of 19 overtraining studies where REDs symptoms occurred during the deliberate exercise overload versus the control period found overall underfueling in 12 studies and carbohydrate underfueling in 4 studies (Stellingwerff et al. 2021). Inadequate carbohydrate intake is emerging as a primary cause of underrecovery and, when sustained, eventual overtraining. Although not the only strategy to prevent overtraining, sustained LEA and low carbohydrate availability during training should be avoided. When prolonged, unintended overreaching may require weeks, months, or even years for full recovery (Birrer 2019) with resultant negative impact on rowing success.

Immune Suppression

Although there is limited research in this area, the immune system may also be compromised by long-term LEA and possibly even short-term low carbohydrate intake (McKay et al 2022), with chronically underfueled athletes at greater risk for upper respiratory tract infection (URI) (Raysmith and Drew 2016). The Gillbanks REDs study in lightweight rowers reported that 9 of the 12 athletes interviewed experienced recurrent colds and other health complaints (Gillbanks, Mountjoy, and Filbay 2022). Furthermore, a questionnaire-based study in Australian athletes preparing for the 2016 Rio Olympics found LEA to be one of the top reasons female athletes suffered upper respiratory, GI, or body-ache-related illnesses that subsequently led to training modifications (Raysmith and Drew 2016). Illness alters an athlete's ability to train effectively, and adjustments to training or time lost to illness or injury have been shown to negatively impact performance outcomes. Athletes who sustained fewer than two illnesses or injuries per season were three times more likely to achieve their competition goals than those who sustained two or more (Raysmith and Drew 2016). In fact, medal winners at major sporting events appear to complete more of their prescribed training hours and suffer fewer and shorter URIs than less successful national-level athletes (Walsh 2019).

Disordered Eating

Finally, dietary restriction or intentional LEA has been identified as a risk factor for disordered eating development in both males and females (Dimitriou et al. 2014; Gillbanks, Mountjoy, and Filbay 2022; Nattiv et al. 2007; Tenforde et al. 2016). Longer duration of sport participation and repeated dieting exacerbates this risk (Pietrowsky and Straub 2008). Adult elite athletes newly diagnosed with an eating disorder often report dieting and eating disorder development during puberty or adolescence. Disordered eating patterns in athletes may arise as a consequence of dieting in an attempt to optimize performance (Gillbanks, Mountjoy, and Filbay 2022) or may develop as a result of stress, anxiety, depression, or body weight or shape dissatisfaction (Logue et al. 2020; Martinsen and Sundgot-Borgen 2013). In fact, greater body dissatisfaction has been seen in male lightweight rowers when they were hungry than when they were satisfied (Pietrowsky and Straub 2008).

Although research specific to rowing athletes is limited, 5 of the 12 athletes in the Gillbanks study reported binge eating behaviors and all of the participants experienced a negative relationship with food (Gillbanks, Mountjoy, and Filbay 2022). Additionally, a study in collegiate rowers revealed that both male and female lightweights were more likely than openweight rowers to report behaviors consistent with an eating disorder (Gapin and Kearns 2013). Finally, intentional calorie restriction and weight loss coupled with significant training at a young age increases the potential for disordered eating in lightweight female rowers (Dimitriou et al. 2014). The effects of disordered eating are significant and can lead to athlete injury, emotional distress, negative health consequences, and the inability to reduce negative training loads that can linger well past the discontinuation of sport (Logue et al. 2020).

LEA and Negative Performance

Although less well studied, there also appear to be negative performance impacts related to LEA. Performance may be affected for a variety of reasons, including muscle and mitochondrial protein synthesis impairment (Wasserfurth et al. 2020) and, as noted above, inadequate recovery and training inconsistency due to increased illness and injury risk (Mountjoy et al. 2018). Performance impairment specific to inadequately fueled endurance training is real. Swimmers (who generally have similar training volumes to rowers) diagnosed with abnormal menstrual function and who underate during a 12-week block of intensified training experienced a 10% decline in swim velocity over a 400 m time trial. In contrast, the swimmers who maintained adequate intakes and normal menstrual function experienced an 8% swim velocity improvement (Vanheest et al. 2014).

A study in elite Australian rowers also demonstrated negative metabolic, wellness, and performance-related effects when the athletes failed to increase their calorie intake to match the higher energy demands during 4 weeks of intensified training. Over this block, weekly training increased by approximately 150 to 400 min. Body composition and resting metabolic rate (RMR) were measured before and after the 4-week block, with 3 day food records assessed prior to each RMR. Performance was evaluated via a 5 km time trial before and after the training block and a wellness questionnaire was administered each week. Over the course of the study, rowers did not naturally increase food intake to compensate for the higher training volume. Subsequent negative effects of this lower EA included weight loss, lowered RMR, substantial training fatigue, mood disturbances, and reduced 5 km time trial performance. In particular, velocity, stroke rate, and athlete pacing were negatively impacted during the follow up time trial (Woods et al. 2017).

Clearly, underfueling can have significant negative health and performance effects, and the potential for associated anxiety or loss of confidence can be disabling. For the majority of the year, rowers undertake high training loads to improve and excel at their sport. Prioritizing athlete nutrition support with the goal of matching food intake and energy expenditure is essential for both health maintenance and performance gains, particularly during periods of increased training.

Causes of LEA

A rower may experience LEA either on purpose or unintentionally. LEA may occur when an athlete deliberately restricts calories for overall physique management, for making weight in advance of competition, to manage the potential weight gain during injury or time off, or because of disordered eating, eating disorder, or highly disciplined eating, known as *orthorexia nervosa* (for more information, see www.nationaleating-disorders.org/learn/by-eating-disorder/other/orthorexia). LEA may also inadvertently occur even when an athlete consumes large meals or seems to eat frequently. Because of the high energy cost of training loads, as well as athlete size and muscularity, LEA can occur in openweight rowers despite the very large food volumes typically eaten (Burke, Close, et al. 2018).

Several barriers exist that may challenge a rower's ability to match energy expenditure with intake. Broadly, these include lack of time (see figure 28.1), gastrointestinal limits, appetite, money, knowledge, and skill. During higher volume base or winter training, a rower may struggle to find the time required to eat sufficient food throughout the day. Limits to the amount of food that an athlete can comfortably digest may also impact overall energy intake. Training intensity may cause appetite suppression, leading to limited food range and quantity. Abrupt training load increases without a change in intake, limited finances, poor understanding of energy needs, and minimal nutrition knowledge or food management ability may all lead to accidental underfueling (Burke, Close, et al. 2018). This is a particular risk for young or inexperienced rowers or when a rower moves from U23 to senior. Considering that an openweight male rower (junior through to senior) may need to eat the same amount of calories as a family of three or four, one begins to understand the financial and food management burden on the busy athlete. Finally, energy requirement prediction equations (which are easily found online) may not be an accurate estimate of an athlete's metabolic rate and daily energy needs. A rower relying on these equations may underestimate how much food they should eat, especially if they carry a high amount of lean body mass or have significant additional daily energy expenditure beyond training (Carlsohn et al. 2011). Consider an athlete who underfuels by a mere 300 to 400 kcal per day. Over the course of a year this would equate to approximately 3 to 4 weeks of not eating. When viewed in this light, it is easier to understand the significant negative health and performance ramifications of underfueling.

Timing of Fueling

Recent work has also demonstrated negative metabolic and hormonal effects when there is a mismatch between periodic calorie intake and energy expenditure within a day, particularly around training. Despite having adequate total energy intake over a 24-hour period, athletes who spent more hours during the day in a calorie deficit ($\geq$300 kcal for females and $\geq$400 kcal for males) experienced RMR suppression, elevation of the stress hormone cortisol (males and females), as well as menstrual dysfunction (females). The longer the period of energy deficit, the higher the level of stress hormones experienced (Fahrenholtz et al. 2018; Torstveit et al. 2018).

It is common for athletes to accidentally undereat in the middle of a busy day. This may occur when training sessions are back-to-back; when daily travel, school, or work obligations impact time available for fueling; or when snacks, rather than meals, make up the majority of the athlete's food intake. In fact, frequent nibbling on small amounts of food rather than eating fewer, more substantial meals each day is associated with impaired menstrual function in female athletes (Fahrenholtz et al. 2018). Given that altered metabolism and hormonal factors may interfere with recovery, training, and performance (Fahrenholtz et al. 2018; Torstveit et al. 2018), it is critical that athletes aim to match their overall daily energy needs and also ensure they consume adequate calories around training and throughout the day. Beyond an understanding of total daily energy and carbohydrate needs, both time and food management skills are key to the busy athlete's fueling success (table 28.2).

Table 28.2 Meal Planning Strategies and Tips

Meal planning strategies	Meal prep tips and suggestions	General tips and snack suggestions

• Use a spreadsheet to record typical weekly schedule.
• Menu plan, grocery shop, and organize meals on lighter days in preparation for busier or heavier training days when lack of time or fatigue may be an issue.
• Consider food supply, weekly grocery store bargains, and cooking skills.
• Prepare ingredients for easy meal prep later in the week.
• Use meals and recipes that freeze well.
• Buy and prepare foods that can be combined or transformed into a variety of nourishing meals with minimal effort.
• Prepare portable snacks that travel and keep well.
• Keep a selection of nonperishable foods and snacks close at hand (sport bag, locker, car, etc.).
	Weekly ingredient preparation:
	• Prepeel, chop, or grate carrots.
	• Prechop onions, kale, celery, and any other sturdy vegetables.
	• Pregrate and freeze cheese.
	• Hard boil a dozen eggs. Premix batches of trail mix, protein pancake mix, and spice mixes for favorite recipes.
	• Prepare a weekly sauce (grain bowl dressing or peanut sauce).
	Batch cook:
	• Roasted vegetables
	• Starches such as rice, quinoa, pasta, potatoes, and yams
	• Ground beef, chicken breasts and thighs
	• Lentils, tofu, or other legumes
	• Stews, casseroles, chili, pasta sauces (freeze half)
	• Muffins, recovery bars, rice bites, or energy bites
		• Prepare smoothie packets for the freezer (berries, banana, spinach, avocado) and add liquid ingredients when preparing.
		• Keep frozen vegetables and prepackaged greens on hand.
		• Buy rotisserie chickens for very busy days.
		• Prepare double batches of overnight oats for both breakfast and snack.
		• Nonperishable snack ideas:
		  * Bars
		  * Jerky
		  * Dried fruit
		  * GoGo fruit snacks
		  * Trail mix (pumpkin seeds, nuts, dried fruit, dry cereal)
		  * Tetra Paks of ready-to-drink meal replacements, juice, or soy milk

Prevention, Detection, and Intervention of LEA and REDs

REDs prevention, early detection, and intervention are essential to protect athletes' health and performance. All athletes, coaches, and other support staff should participate in education aimed at risk factor recognition and REDs outcome awareness. Although a single definitive and validated method remains to be established, athlete assessment and monitoring tools are available to help with early identification of LEA and REDs. These can include disordered eating questionnaires such as the Eating Disorder Examination Questionnaire (EDE-Q), the Periodic Health Examination, the Pre-Participation Physical Evaluation, and the Low Energy Availability in Females Questionnaire (LEAF-Q). Medical indicators such as low sex hormones and low sex drive (Lundy et al. 2022) are key elements that contribute to early identification of LEA and REDs, whereas repeated stress fractures and low bone mineral density (Mountjoy et al. 2018) would be factors in late identification. Athlete daily wellness (including monthly menstrual status), training load management ratings, and lack of performance improvement can be used to assist coaches, rowing support staff, athletes themselves, and possibly parents of young athletes with the early detection of underrecovery and LEA.

Athletes should also consult a qualified sport dietitian for guidance on optimizing EA throughout the yearly training program. Finally, given the REDs related health risks, foundational nutrition support and early detection at the beginning of the athlete's career should be a priority.

Body Composition Manipulation

Although a healthy athlete's body composition will change naturally over their career, there are specific occasions when targeted physique manipulation is desirable to achieve a performance advantage. At the senior level (and possibly at U23), it may be advantageous to alter power to weight for racing or, for a larger lightweight athlete, to make weight for international competition. A direct relationship exists between performance and physique: higher height, weight, and LBM and lower levels of body fat are linked to a greater probability of competitive success (Akca 2014; Ingham et al. 2002; Penichet-Tomas et al. 2021; Slater, Rice, Mujika, et al. 2005).

There are risks, however, with body mass manipulation, and any program must prioritize athlete health and safety. Attempts to alter fat mass or weight should only occur when an athlete has reached maturation. Further, because of the negative consequences associated with LEA, it is important to avoid long-term energy restriction in the pursuit of a leaner body. Rowers considering body mass manipulation should discuss realistic goals with their coach and support staff and undertake a risk–reward assessment. They should also seek the expertise of a performance nutrition professional who understands LEA, REDs, and body composition management science, as well as how to translate the science into optimal fueling strategies.

Additionally, athletes and coaches must be patient. Increasing lean mass and decreasing fat mass takes time. Both should be planned over the yearly training and competitive season and refined over an athletic career. Athletes who set unreasonable goals will undoubtedly be disappointed with their rate of lean mass development, as well as be at greater risk for REDs and related side effects if energy deficits are severe or long-term (Mountjoy et al. 2018).

Finally, junior athletes should not specifically alter body composition. Rather, when health, adequate energy intake to support training, and quality food are prioritized, body composition changes should naturally occur over a rower's transition from juniors, through U23s, to seniors. See figure 28.1 for an overview of body composition management.

Skeletal Muscle Hypertrophy

Rowing requires high levels of force production; therefore, in addition to an athlete's physiology and technique, a high amount of LBM is important for performance success (Slater et al. 2014; Slater, Rice, Mujika, et al. 2005). Many factors influence lean mass gains (skeletal muscle hypertrophy), including genetics, age, current body composition, resistance training stimulus, amount of overfeeding, timing of food intake, and diet composition (Aragon et al. 2017). As an athlete matures, skeletal muscle gains will naturally occur over years of consistent, well-fueled training involving moderate load and high repetition. This training must be underpinned by the critical basics of well-timed recovery, sleep, and nutrition. A rower may also attempt to accelerate these training related gains by calorie increases and strategic

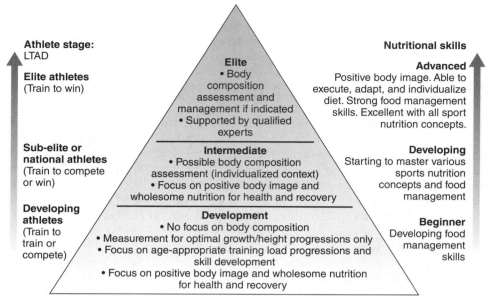

▶ **Figure 28.1** Framework for body composition management through Long Term Athlete Development (LTAD).

Reprinted by permission of T. Stellingwerff, "Case Study: Body Composition Periodization in an Olympic-Level Female Middle-Distance Runner Over a 9-Year Career," International Journal of Sport Nutrition and Exercise Metabolism 28, no. 4 (2018): 428-433.

macronutrient intakes. Overfeeding typically leads to both fat and lean mass gains with substantial variability in individual body composition changes (Aragon et al. 2017; Slater et al. 2019). Lean athletes are less susceptible to fat gains, and younger athletes will generally experience greater lean mass increases than older athletes (Slater et al. 2019).

Additionally, overfeeding triggers varying levels of energy expenditure adaptation. A small amount of the excess calories consumed are lost as heat (known as *diet-induced thermogenesis*) and some people increase random movement or NEAT when they eat more than required (Aragon et al. 2017; Slater et al. 2019). NEAT includes all movement not related to sleeping, eating, and training, such as walking a dog, gardening, house cleaning, and even fidgeting. Considered together, this means that not all of the extra calories eaten will go toward skeletal muscle gains. Food intake planning must therefore account for the athlete's resting energy needs, daily nonexercise activities, the increased energy expenditure that occurs when in energy surplus, and most importantly, overall training demands.

Rowers aiming for lean mass gains, or hypertrophy, will need to consistently consume more energy than they expend. A daily 350 to 500 calorie surplus is recommended as a starting point, adjusted as needed to facilitate weight gain (Slater et al. 2019). Aiming for five or six smaller main meals may minimize the potential gut discomfort of fewer large meals. Athletes are also encouraged to layer in extra calories as energy-dense beverages, spreads, and snacks (table 28.3). These simple energy manipulation strategies will help decrease the possible food intake fatigue associated with calorie excess. Finally, athletes and support staff need to appreciate that hypertrophy will be challenging for the rower to achieve during high-volume endurance training blocks.

High-Quality Weight Loss

Although optimal EA is crucial for health, temporary LEA may be strategically used by a rower to drive weight loss prior to the competitive season. On the other hand, long-term LEA will lead to metabolic adaptation by the body to prevent ongoing losses and promote survival (Areta, Taylor, and Koehler 2021). Weight loss strategies should therefore be undertaken over the short term and carefully managed within the rower's yearly training plan. To maintain health and reduce injury risk, rowers should aim for higher body weight and energy intakes during winter or base endurance training and restrict intakes in the competition preparation phase only. During this period of higher intensity, lower volume training, rowers commonly find fat loss easier. Unless temporary lean mass loss is required for making weight (not recommended), athletes should aim for *high-quality* weight loss during a period of energy restriction.

Several nutrition strategies for high-quality weight loss require consideration. They are flexible fueling, moderate weight loss (Garthe et al. 2011; Huovinen et al. 2015), and adjusted macronutrient intakes, with an emphasis on elevated protein (Hector and Phillips 2018). All three must be combined with a training stimulus to be effective. These strategies preserve lean mass and maximize fat loss while minimizing the risks associated with REDs.

Key Point

When an athlete loses weight, they typically lose both lean and fat mass. Although the goal is usually high-quality weight loss—defined as the preservation of or increase in lean mass while simultaneously losing fat mass—25% to 50% or more of lost weight may be from losses in lean mass. This is problematic because muscle is essential for healthy metabolic function, including postmeal fat oxidation and glucose storage. It is also a key component of a healthy RMR and functional strength. Athletes who engage in rapid and or frequent weight loss programs eventually struggle with future weight loss in part due to lean mass losses and metabolic suppression. Over time, this may lead to weight loss resistance and a cycle of increasing levels of underfueling and REDs consequences, including fat accrual, each time weight loss is attempted. Because muscle is also critical to athletic performance, lean mass losses will most likely have a negative impact on strength, speed, and power (Hector and Phillips 2018).

Flexible Fueling

A reduction in calorie intake is required for weight loss; however, if an athlete chooses severe dietary restraint, labels foods as "good" or "bad," has unrealistic weight loss goals, or expects perfection, weight loss will be stressful and the athlete may struggle. Generally speaking, highly rigid dietary rules and eating patterns during periods of weight loss are associated with a greater risk of disordered eating (Linardon and Mitchell 2017). Such eating patterns may lead to a higher body mass over time. Rather, athletes are more likely to be successful at fat loss when provided an individualized, flexible fueling approach they help design. Examples of techniques for healthy energy intake reduction include the following:

- Following a meal plan or menu
- Periodizing macronutrients
- Spreading food intake over several small meals and snacks
- Focusing larger meals around training while decreasing food portion sizes in the evening
- Increasing fiber-rich vegetables and minimizing fat intake
- Ensuring small amounts of favorite or discretionary foods are included each day or once a week

These are examples from a range of the possible fueling strategies that an athlete can choose when developing a healthy weight loss eating plan. Rowers who are aiming for fat loss are encouraged to experiment with flexible fueling in order to identify personal preferences and increase the probability for success.

Make It Moderate

The leaner the athlete, the greater the possibility that weight loss will come from lean mass versus fat mass (Hector and Phillips 2018). A moderate strategy minimizes this by targeting a slower weight loss rate. A loss of no more than 0.7% (0.5%-1%) body weight per week is recommended (Garthe et al. 2011) with energy restriction limited to about 300 to 400 kcal per day, depending on the size of the athlete (e.g., lightweight female vs. openweight male). If faster weight loss is required, short-term energy restriction up to a maximum of approximately 750 kcal per day may be considered. This should be limited to no more than a few weeks (Huovinen et al. 2015), minimizing the risk of unintentionally developing REDs consequences (table 28.1). Timing fueling (in particular carbohydrate intake) to occur around training while decreasing calories elsewhere in the day may help combat the negative effects of hormone suppression, metabolic adaptation, and REDs (Fahrenholtz et al. 2018; Torstveit et al. 2018).

Rowers and their coaches should also be aware that the rate of weight loss will slow over the weeks. This occurs as a result of decreasing body weight and the metabolic adaptation that arises with lower energy intakes (Aragon et al. 2017). Whenever fat loss is a desired outcome, athletes should be provided with a time limited, moderate calorie reduction plan with fueling guidelines that match personal preferences. They will also require a specific strategy to support their return to the nondieting intakes that are necessary for the preservation of long-term health (table 28.3). This strategic energy intake manipulation will help the rower reach optimal performance body composition while minimizing the health risks associated with reduced fueling (Stellingwerff 2018).

Manipulate Macronutrients for Weight Loss and Hypertrophy

In order to facilitate changes in body composition, rowers also need to appropriately fuel for, and recover from, all training sessions. As discussed in chapter 27, the three macronutrients—protein, carbohydrate, and fat—must be considered.

Table 28.3 Physique Manipulation Strategies

Nutrition intervention	Lean mass gains	Fat mass loss
Energy	• Aim for ~350-500 kcal surplus per day. • Prioritize fueling before, during, and after training • Review progress and adjust as needed.	• Reduce energy intake by ~300-400 kcal/day. • Prioritize fueling before, during, and after training. • Review progress and adjust as needed.
Protein	• Choose leucine-rich, whole-food sources (higher fat dairy, whole eggs vs. isolated proteins). • Aim for ~25-40 g/meal over 4 or more meals per day. • Consume before or after resistance training. • Add whole-food protein or casein before bed.	• Choose leucine-rich, whole-food sources (low-fat dairy, whole eggs vs. isolated proteins). • Aim for ~25-40 g/meal over 4 or more meals per day and up to 3 g/kg BM. • Consume before or after resistance training. • Add whole food lean protein or casein before bed.
Carbohydrate	• Increase carbohydrate amounts on higher load days. • Consume a higher carbohydrate meal in advance of a resistance training session. • Include carbohydrates in prebedtime snack. • Limit fiber-rich foods if poor appetite and struggling to add calories.	• Periodize carbohydrate intake to match training load. • Focus carbohydrate intake around higher intensity training and choose easily digested whole foods such as bananas rather than sport foods. • Choose higher fiber carbohydrates at meals and snacks.
Fat	• Daily intake of omega-3-rich fish or supplements. • Add visible fats at meals and snacks up to 35% of daily energy intake. • Choose higher fat dairy products. • Prioritize unsaturated fats such as nuts, seeds and their butters or oils, olives, olive oil.	• Daily intake of omega-3-rich fish or supplements. • Limit visible fat sources but prioritize unsaturated fats when consumed.
Meal size and timing	• Eat smaller and more frequent but substantial meals (6+/day) to minimize gut discomfort. • Time meals around training, and before bed to align intake with expenditure and support fueling and recovery goals.	• Eat larger and less frequent meals (4-5/day) for increased satiety. • Strategically time meals around training for recovery.
Food options	• Layer in extra calories with energy-dense foods and fluids such as dried fruits, nuts, coconut or whole milk, juice, and smoothies.	• Minimize liquid calories. • Minimize processed foods. • Choose lean protein, vegetables, and fiber-rich grains at each meal.

Note: Athletes should have a plan, be patient, and reach out to a knowledgeable nutrition practitioner for body composition management expertise and support.

Pay Attention to Protein and Carbs

Carbohydrate intake periodized relative to the work (see chapter 27) is particularly important when resistance training for lean mass maintenance or gains is part of a

Key Point

Junior athletes or those who have not yet reached maturation should not be manipulating body mass. Deliberate weight loss may delay puberty, negatively impact growth and bone health, negatively influence skeletal and mitochondrial protein synthesis and strength, and possibly increase disordered eating and eating disorder risk (Mountjoy et al. 2018; Wasserfurth et al. 2020). Additionally, long-term energy deficiency is more likely to occur if dieting behavior is started at a younger age. It is also associated with eventual higher body weight, which is likely related to metabolic adaptations over time (Fahrenholtz et al. 2018). Significantly, a healthy, performance-ready body composition will result when athletes adequately fuel throughout the course of a rowing career.

high-volume endurance program. The type of carbohydrates chosen may depend on the rowers' physique goals. For those athletes aiming to lose weight, higher fiber carbohydrates may assist with appetite management. Unfortunately, these same fiber-rich foods increase satiety and may cause gut discomfort, challenging an athlete's ability to eat the larger portions needed to support weight gain. Thus, depending on body composition goals, rowers must learn how to adjust the quantity and the types of carbohydrate-rich foods consumed (table 27.3).

Protein is also a key dietary component of both high-quality weight loss and hypertrophy. A higher protein intake will not only help to maintain lean mass and possibly minimize metabolic adaptation (Aragon et al. 2017), it may also decrease the stress and fatigue related to weight loss. Food restriction adherence can be difficult, especially if an athlete feels hungry or deprived. Protein may be the most filling of the macronutrients because it increases secretion of satiety-inducing hormones (Stokes et al. 2018). When consumed at each meal, whole-food protein sources may decrease between-meal hunger and overall daily food intake amounts. Rowers targeting high-quality weight loss are encouraged to aim for approximately 1.6 to 2.4 and possibly up to 3.0 g/kg BM of protein per day (Stokes et al. 2018). Unfortunately, the lower energy requirement during a weight loss phase may challenge the athlete's ability to achieve these higher protein recommendations while simultaneously ensuring adequate carbohydrate to support training. Rowers should therefore choose low-fat protein sources and minimize added fats so that both protein and carbohydrate needs can be met.

When it comes to hypertrophy, 25 to 40 g of leucine-rich protein sources spread over four (or more) meals each day, including before or after resistance training and before bed, should maximally stimulate lean mass gains. Higher quantities may contribute to meal satisfaction but are unlikely to trigger additional skeletal muscle synthesis. In fact, due to the potential satiating effect of protein-rich foods (Stokes et al. 2018), very large portions may limit hunger, reducing overall energy intake and thus compromising hypertrophy. Furthermore, extra protein should not be eaten at the expense of the carbohydrates needed to support training. Because meat, seafood, poultry, or protein supplements can be expensive, it may also be a financial burden for athletes. Therefore, once daily protein requirements are reached, rowers can manage their food budget by adding lower cost carbohydrates (potatoes, bananas) and mixed protein and carbohydrates (dairy, legumes) instead of eating excess high-priced protein. Combined with a resistance training stimulus, elevated protein intake is one of the best strategies to positively impact body composition during a fat loss (Slater et al. 2014) and hypertrophy phase.

Don't Forget Fat

Consideration of overall fat intake is important as well. Athletes aiming for weight gain often add calories in the form of butter, nut butter, ice cream, full-fat dairy, and fattier meats. Because 1 g of fat contains 9 calories, versus 4 calories for 1 g of carbohydrate or protein, adding fat can be an effective strategy. Higher fat foods will provide significantly more energy in a smaller portion. Consider that 1 cup of premium ice cream may contain approximately 550 calories. A rower would need to eat approximately 17 cups of broccoli, 3 cups of potato, or 450 g of boneless, skinless chicken breast to consume an equivalent number of calories. For the rower who already eats a large volume of food to prevent LEA, it makes sense to use high-fat, energy-dense foods for the additional fuel that gaining weight requires. Again, it is important that fat is not consumed at the expense of carbohydrate and protein.

Interestingly, the type of fat may also matter. Beyond the acknowledged health benefits, intake of omega-3 and monounsaturated fats as found in fish, olives, and olive oil may also result in enhanced muscle protein synthesis, mass, and function when compared with saturated fats (McGlory et al. 2019). Rowers who add fat calories for weight gain should be sure to choose unsaturated options more often. Finally, for rowers who are aiming to lose weight, it makes sense to also focus on monounsaturated options while minimizing overall fat intake (see tables 27.3 and 28.3).

As discussed, many factors influence weight loss and lean mass gains. Fundamental to success is a healthy athlete able to consistently engage in high-quality training. All rowers, regardless of their physique goals, should start the majority of sessions well-fueled, periodize carbohydrates, adjust fats to alter energy intake, and spread protein intake throughout the day. Adequate sleep is also essential. Finally, ongoing body composition review is recommended (Slater et al. 2019), with energy and macronutrient intakes and fueling strategies adjusted as required.

Body Composition Management in Lightweight Athletes

In preparation for the competitive season, lightweight rowers who do not naturally weigh 57 to 59 kg (female) or 70 to 72 kg (male) will need to decrease body weight in order to race. An assessment of lightweight rowing physique compared to competitive success undertaken at the 2003 Australian Rowing Championship regatta found that rowers with higher total body mass and muscle, as well as lower body fat, had faster heat times and superior regatta placing. This was more pronounced among the U23 rowers, where technical skill may be less developed (Slater, Rice, Mujika, et al. 2005). It is therefore reasonable that tall, muscular athletes who are not large enough to fit the openweight profile may consider rowing lightweight. In these circumstances, altering body composition to race lightweight may place an athlete at risk for disordered eating, as well as adverse effects on health and performance. Prior to a rower's selection to the lightweight category, they should undergo a multidisciplinary risk assessment that includes a professional with expertise in body composition, REDs, and eating disorders (e.g., RD or sports medicine physician). Athletes best suited to row lightweight are those who naturally weigh closer to boat average. If the required weight loss is deemed acceptable (≤6%), these athletes will then need to establish a healthy weight loss strategy, developed in collaboration with their coach and relevant support staff. In the months, weeks, and days leading up to racing, athletes may use both high-quality chronic weight loss and acute weight loss strategies (Slater, Rice, Sharpe, Mujika, et al. 2005).

It should be noted that a heavier lightweight athlete may struggle to make weight later in their career. This may be a result of increases in muscle mass or metabolic adaptation, particularly if the rower has engaged in a frequent cycle of unhealthy weight making over time. To minimize the amount of dieting an athlete is required to undertake each year, the number of events raced "at weight" should be considered, and where possible, priority given to key races only. Unfortunately, heavier athletes struggling to make weight may also engage in riskier weight loss behaviors such as extra training, low-carbohydrate intake, meal skipping, significant calorie restriction, disordered eating, or excessive dehydration in the lead-up to competition (Gillbanks, Mountjoy, and Filbay 2022). This should be avoided to minimize risk to both physical and mental well-being as well as long-term health. To reduce the amount of body composition change required, acute weight loss strategies may be useful in the days prior to competition.

Acute Weight Loss strategies

In cool to moderate temperatures, an athlete can use acute weight-loss and immediate post-weigh-in nutritional recovery strategies to make weight with minimal negative performance impact, including during repeat racing (i.e., heats, repechages, semifinals, and finals) over the course of a regatta (Slater, Rice, Sharpe, Tanner, et al. 2005). Several elements must be in place for success. Lightweight rowers employing acute interventions are advised to start this process fully hydrated and well nourished. Because weigh-in takes place 1 to 2 h before the start of a race, acute prerace body mass losses should never exceed 4%. Post-weigh-in recovery must also be extremely well executed to reverse physiological disturbances and optimize competition readiness (Slater, Rice, Sharpe, Tanner, et al. 2005). Moreover, postrace nutritional recovery in preparation for subsequent races must also be aggressive. Athletes should therefore have a fully individualized, well-rehearsed acute weight loss, post-weigh-in, and postrace recovery plan for the entire regatta. Acute weight loss and post-weigh-in strategies are shown in table 28.4.

Low-Residue Diet Low-residue dietary strategies can reduce total ingested food volume and body weight. Substituting high-fiber foods with smaller amounts of low-fiber, energy-dense foods will help the lightweight rower maintain macronutrient intake while decreasing GI contents and therefore body mass. Because of individual differences in gut transit times, athletes may need to start the low-residue diet anywhere between 24 and 96 h before racing. Decreases in fiber intake should be determined through experimentation; however, amounts are commonly limited to approximately 10 g or less per day. Typical weight reductions vary, but average 1.0 kg, with the amount of weight loss partially dependent on usual fiber intake (Reale, Slater, and Burke 2017).

Notably, a low-residue diet may become less effective over time and may increase the risk of constipation. Psychologically, it can be challenging to maintain over a long regatta. Therefore, this strategy should be tested well in advance and under similar conditions to upcoming racing. It is unlikely that a carbohydrate-based low-residue plan will negatively impact rowing performance. However, if an athlete following a low-residue diet also limits carbohydrates or increases training in the days before racing, glycogen

Table 28.4 Acute Weight Loss and Post-Weigh-In Recovery Nutrition

	Pre-weigh-in	Post-weigh-in	Females (total)	Males (total)	Sample foods and fluids
Fiber	• Decreases based on usual intakes but typical is ≤10 g/day • 24-96 h preregatta • Trial several times in advance to understand actual weight loss and timing • Read food labels for fiber content	≤10 g/day during regatta	N/A	N/A	• Refined cereals, breads, grains • Lower fiber vegetables and fruits such as potatoes, cucumbers, mushrooms, bananas, melon, canned fruit (no seeds or skins) • Pulp-free juices • Sweet spreads such as honey, maple syrup, jelly, Nutella • Animal-based proteins and dairy products
Fluid	• Hydrate well until the night before or morning of weigh-in • Consider a hot bath or shower and warm layers to start sweating during sleep • Plan to use active vs. passive sweating or a combination of both for fluid losses in the morning	~30 mL/kg BM	~1,700 mL	~2,100 mL	Higher sodium sport drinks[1]
Sodium	≤500 mg/day	~34 mg/kg BM	~1,940 mg	~2,380 mg	• Higher sodium sport drinks or juice with added salt[1] • Sodium-containing gels or sport chews • White bread • Pickles or pickle juice • Sodium bicarbonate[2]
Carbohydrate	• At least 6 g/kg BM 1-2 days before and during competiton, aiming for higher amounts if possible • Switch to low-fiber sources • Carbohydrate restriction to deliberately reduce glycogen stores is *not* recommended	2.3 g/kg BM	130 g	160 g	• Sport drinks • Juice • Gels • White bread • Honey or jam • Banana

[1]Carbohydrate- and sodium-rich fluids provide all three performance-enhancing nutrients.

[2]See chapter 29 for further discussion on sodium bicarbonate.

Carbohydrate, sodium, and fluid amounts are based on specific research undertaken in an elite Australian lightweight rowing population (Slater, Rice, Sharpe, Tanner, et al. 2005; Slater et al. 2014)

stores may become depleted. Although a moderate reduction in carbohydrate stores is unlikely to compromise a single 7 to 8 min event, limiting carbohydrate intake over an entire regatta may have a negative effect on performance and is not recommended (Slater et al. 2006).

Controlled and Monitored Dehydration To facilitate final, minor weight loss for weigh-in, some athletes restrict fluids and use their existing training and race warm-up plans for active sweating on the morning of weigh-in. To start the sweat-down process overnight, a hot bath or shower and wearing warm layers to bed can be considered as long as sleep is not negatively impacted (Reale, Slater, and Burke 2017). Rowers may find the sweat-down both physically and psychologically stressful (Russell et al. 2019). Thus, a light snack before starting may positively impact energy levels and cognitive function and provide psychological relief from the overnight fast. Rowers are recommended to limit sweating to no greater than 2 L (approximately 2 kg) of sweat loss (3%-4% body weight). They should also clearly understand their sweat rate under various environmental conditions to allow adequate time to sweat down. Weighing-in on time is critical to secure the entire 2 hour post weigh-in period necessary to optimize nutritional recovery. When rehydrating, the gut is able to absorb ~800 to 1,000 mL of fluids per hour. Therefore, with an effective plan, a lightweight rower should be able to replenish up to 2 L of lost body water within the 2 hour recovery window and race well hydrated (Slater et al. 2014).

Although racing hydrated is always important, it is essential when racing in the heat. 2,000 m ergometer performance was impaired by an average of 1.1% (4.1 s) when lightweight rowers dehydrated by 4% prior to time trialing in the heat (32.4 °C) even when they aggressively rehydrated prior to competition (Slater, Rice, Sharpe, Tanner, et al. 2005). Dehydration greater than 4% will be impossible to overcome during the 2 h between weigh-in and racing, leading to decreased performance outcomes. This level of dehydration should also be avoided because it creates a heath and safety risk for the athlete. Where possible, athletes are encouraged to minimize the need for prerace dehydration at regattas anticipated to take place during hot summer temperatures. Arrival at the regatta closer to race weight is therefore advised.

Heat acclimation and precooling strategies (discussed in chapter 20) should also be considered in advance of projected hot weather racing, and nutrition is an important aspect of both. Acclimation or training in the heat will elevate the body's carbohydrate, protein, fluid, and sodium needs. Heat increases glycolysis (the breakdown of glucose for energy), increasing carbohydrate use during exercise. Protein is vital for both albumin production and as a source of the amino acid L-glutamine. Additional albumin is essential for heat-related increases in plasma volume, and L-glutamine has a role in maintaining gut function during hot weather exercise. Last, due to the increased sweat response that occurs with heat acclimation, fluid and sodium intake should also increase to minimize the negative effects of hypohydration and any potential electrolyte losses.

Nutritional precooling strategies include slushie consumption prior to racing. Simply, ice consumed as a slushie functions as a "heat sink" whereby some of the body's extra heat energy is transferred from internal organs to the extremities via circulating blood as ingested ice is converted to water. Slushies may also decrease the sensation of heat by cooling thermoreceptors in the mouth and gut. The recommended protocol is to aim for approximately 7 mL/kg BM spaced out over 20 to 30 min. The drink should be consumed as close to racing as possible without interfering with the athlete's competition readiness plan. Due to the risk of GI issues from ice ingestion, as with all acute nutrition strategies aimed at enhancing performance, slushie intake should be trialed and refined in advance of competition. Finally, a slushie consumed postrace will also contribute to carbohydrate and fluid recovery needs.

Low Sodium Intake   Although less likely to produce significant body mass losses, avoidance of salt and high-sodium processed foods the day before racing may cause a temporary reduction in "bound water." A small increase in urine production, along with a corresponding weight loss, will occur before the body's tight control mechanisms respond to reduce urine output. See chapter 27 for a greater discussion of sodium loss and replacement.

Immediate Post Weigh-In Recovery

When acute weight loss strategies are used, aggressive, research-based rehydration and refueling strategies are needed immediately after weigh-in (table 28.4). If not, on-water performance will be negatively impacted (Slater et al. 2014), in part due to the negative effects of reduced plasma volume (decreased cardiac output, increased heart rate, and core temperature) caused by dehydration.

   Effective rehydration requires both liquids and sodium, particularly when time is short. Drinking without added sodium will limit intestinal absorption, increasing fluid excretion (i.e., more inconvenient trips to the bathroom). Rowers should drink a large amount (600-900 mL) as soon as possible after weigh-in to speed up gastric emptying and maximize plasma volume, continuing at regular intervals until they have consumed approximately 2 L of either sodium-rich fluids or low-sodium fluids alongside salty foods. Athletes who also limit food prior to weigh-in will likely be hungry or feel low energy and will need to replenish carbohydrate stores. Therefore, post-weigh-in intakes should include enough carbohydrate to minimize hunger, replenish immediate carbohydrate needs, and fuel racing. Food and liquids should be carefully selected to prevent GI distress during racing, particularly if the rower experiences prerace jitters. To minimize GI discomfort while ensuring both rehydration and refueling, athletes should focus on palatable, easily digested, carbohydrate-rich foods and beverages (table 28.4). Amounts and choices should be fully rehearsed well in advance.

Lightweight Postrace Recovery

Between the end of one race and weighing in for the next, the primary nutrition goal is recovery optimization, including full rehydration, carbohydrate restoration, and GI management. Athletes should aim for aggressive carbohydrate and fluid replenishment in the 12 to 16 h after racing to improve potential performances over a multiday regatta (Slater et al. 2006; Slater et al. 2014) (see chapter 27, table 27.1). Complete rehydration between races may also allow for an easier repeat sweat-down for subsequent races. Finally, as body mass reduction will most likely be required for subsequent weigh-ins, athletes should continue to limit fiber while being mindful of overall impact on bowel function.

Conclusion

This chapter highlighted the health and performance implications related to underfueling as well as various strategies for LEA and REDs prevention. Athletes, coaches, and supporters are encouraged to understand the signs and risks associated with LEA and

REDs to increase the likelihood of early intervention and improved athlete outcomes. Early education on fueling strategies and prevention of deliberate or inadvertent weight loss in young athletes will lay the foundation for long-term health, whether training at a club, national, or eventually a masters level.

Body composition management for rowing—including lean mass gains, fat mass losses, and making weight for racing—was also discussed as it relates to both long- and short-term physique manipulation. Given the inherent risks related to weight loss and the potential frustrations caused by unrealistic expectations, education and support that enables all athletes to make sound decisions is strongly encouraged. Nutritional management for performance should be strategic, science-based, and carefully planned to maintain athlete health over the yearly training program. A well-fueled, robust athlete is more likely to achieve competitive success and thrive throughout and beyond their athletic career.

CHAPTER 29

Supplements

Susan Boegman

This final nutrition chapter will discuss supplementation. Is it necessary? What are the potential risks and rewards? How should supplement decisions be made? Unfortunately, there is no single definition of *supplement* within health and scientific literature, making it very difficult to assess supplementation patterns among athlete populations. However, according to the IOC Consensus Statement on Dietary Supplements and the High-Performance Athlete, a supplement is "a food, food component, nutrient, or nonfood compound that is purposefully ingested in addition to the habitually-consumed diet with the aim of achieving a specific health and/or performance benefit" (Maughan et al. 2018, 439). As this definition suggests, a full review of supplements is well beyond the scope of this chapter. Rather, the focus will be on the primary supplements that may benefit the health and performance of a rower.

Supplements are highly desired—just look at the sales trends! In 2019, the global dietary supplements market was valued at 167.8 billion (USD) and is expected to reach 306.8 billion by 2026 (Grand View Research 2022b). Equally impressive, the 2022 global sports nutrition market was valued at 42.9 billion (USD) and is expected to reach 82.3 billion by 2030 (Grand View Research 2022b).

Why is there such a strong demand for supplements? Many factors contribute to this phenomenon, including an increased desire for health and well-being, fitness trends, concern over nutrient deficiencies, social media, a desire for convenience, and extreme product availability (Grand View Research 2022b). When considering elite athletes, additional reasons include desire for improved performance, training benefits, enhanced mood, optimized recovery, injury prevention, decreases in injury healing time, and support for physique manipulation (Maughan et al. 2018; Parnell, Wiens, and Erdman 2016). Finally, younger athletes may also be influenced by success-ful senior athletes who use supplements to augment performance. Coaches, parents, and support staff are encouraged to be aware of any product an athlete may be using beyond a healthy diet.

Notably, poor manufacturing practices are a key concern within the supplement industry. This is particularly important for elite athletes, who must ensure that anything they consume is free from World Antidoping Agency (WADA) banned substances. However, all athletes should be aware of what they are consuming, including any ingredient with the potential for short- or long-term health risks. Although Canada has procedures in place to ensure good manufacturing practices, there is significant evidence that the supplement industry does not always follow required regulations. Between 2017 and 2019, Health Canada inspected 46 supplement manufacturing facilities and found compliance issues for all companies (Health Canada 2021a,b). The resources required for comprehensive oversight of the supplement industry are enormous. Noncompliant products and manufacturing facilities may go unnoticed, increasing the risk that supplements may contain little to no active ingredient, undeclared ingredients, or WADA-banned substances (Mathews 2018; Outram and Stewart 2015; Temple et al. 2017). Supplementation is therefore an inherently risky activity for athletes.

Given the potential risks, are supplements even necessary? The answer is "possibly"—it depends on the specific context. Prior to supplementation, a medical, biochemical, nutrition, and training assessment should be undertaken, including the following considerations:

- Is there a clinical need?
- Is there a realistic food-based alternative?
- What is the athlete's age and stage of physical development?
- What is the athlete's stage of sport development?
- What is the amount of training undertaken during various stages of the yearly training plan?
- Is the athlete optimizing training, nutrition, and recovery strategies?
- Is the athlete at a competitive level where marginal gains may be required for performance enhancement?

If—after a fulsome needs assessment—supplementation is deemed appropriate, there are a wide variety of products that may be considered, depending on each rower's unique circumstances. The following sections review specific nutrients and supplements that support the health of all rowers, as well as those that may be used to enhance the performance of elite rowers.

Key Point

Athletes who follow a well-planned whole-food diet that includes a variety of protein-rich foods, vegetables, fruits, whole grains, and dairy or dairy alternatives, as well as adequate calories to support training, will likely ensure sufficient nutrient intake.

Health Supplements

Good health is critical to optimizing athlete performance. Healthy athletes are able to train more consistently, which is one of the main drivers of performance (Drew et al. 2018). This raises the question: Do athletes need supplements to be healthy? Athletes who follow a well-planned whole-food diet that includes a variety of protein-rich foods, vegetables, fruits, whole grains, and dairy or dairy alternatives, as well as adequate calories to support training, will likely ensure sufficient nutrient intake. In fact, overt nutrient deficiencies are rare in a healthy athlete (Larson-Meyer, Woolf, and Burke 2018). Although exercise and adaptation to training may stress the metabolic pathways and increase the amount of micronutrients an athlete requires (Thomas, Erdman, and Burke 2016), supplementation does not enhance performance in the absence of a deficiency (Williams 2005), and sport participation may improve overall diet quality compared to nonathletes (Lun, Erdman, and Reimer 2009; Parnell, Wiens, and Erdman 2016). Generally, when an athlete is in good energy availability (EA) there is less risk of nutrient deficiency (Mountjoy et al. 2014; Thomas, Erdman, and Burke 2016). Good EA should therefore be prioritized over supplementation.

Nevertheless, there are some groups with a higher likelihood of micronutrient deficiencies in part due to reduced food intake, declines in diet quality, or nutrient absorption impairments associated with aging. These athletes include lightweight rowers who frequently restrict energy intake (Thomas, Erdman, and Burke 2016, author observation), 14- to 18-year-old female athletes (Parnell, Wiens, and Erdman 2016), and older athletes with lower energy requirements (Campbell and Geik 2004). An assessment of younger and older athlete diets found that both groups may consume inadequate amounts of several vitamins and minerals. For adolescents, this was partially related to low vegetable, fruit, whole grain, and dairy product intake, as well as overconsumption of processed and fast foods (Parnell, Wiens, and Erdman 2016). For older athletes, this was primarily related to lower overall energy intake and altered nutrient absorption (Campbell and Geik 2004). In general, when adolescent and younger adult athletes meet energy needs with a wide variety of whole foods, they also appear to meet or exceed recommended intakes for most nutrients (Lun, Erdman, and Reimer 2009; Parnell, Wiens, and Erdman 2016). Older adult athletes should be considered individually (Campbell and Geik 2004).

Key Point

There are some notable exceptions to the rarity of nutrient deficiencies in healthy athletes. Any athlete who regularly underfuels, has a very high training volume, limits iron- or calcium-rich foods, or lives at latitudes where vitamin D production does not occur during winter months is more likely to be affected.

There are some notable exceptions to the rarity of nutrient deficiencies in healthy athletes. Any athlete who regularly underfuels in conjunction with a very high training volume, limits iron- or calcium-rich foods, or lives at latitudes where vitamin D production does not occur during winter months is more likely to be affected. Vegan and possibly masters athletes will also need supplemental vitamin B_{12} (Thomas, Erdman, and Burke 2016). A medical and nutrition assessment, including blood work, may help identify nutrient deficiencies before external symptoms appear. However, lack of accessibility to blood work and to well-established athlete reference norms for all nutrients makes definitive nutrient deficiency diagnoses a challenge (Larson-Meyer, Woolf, and Burke 2018).

Rowers of all ages will benefit from nutrition-specific support to prevent deficiencies. Early and ongoing education should be provided to all young athletes to lay a solid foundation and minimize the potential for future nutritional issues. Education for rowers who engage in very high-volume training, accidentally underfuel, or deliberately restrict calories or entire food groups should also be prioritized to minimize the negative consequences associated with LEA. Lastly, vegan and masters athletes are encouraged to consult a sport dietitian for comprehensive assessment and nutritional guidance.

Iron

Iron is a fundamental mineral involved in oxygen transport, energy metabolism, and immune response (Castell et al. 2019; DellaValle and Haas 2014). Stored as ferritin, it is mainly found in hemoglobin within red blood cells and myoglobin within the muscle tissue. Iron is one of the most common nutrient deficiencies in athletes and is classified in three stages: iron deficiency (ID), iron-deficient nonanemia (IDNA), or iron-deficient anemia (IDA) (table 29.1). ID affects approximately 15% to 35% of active females and approximately 3% to 11% of active males (Sim et al. 2019).

Given its role in the human body, it is not surprising that low iron may result in reduced work capacity, efficiency, training, and overall endurance performance (Castell et al. 2019; DellaValle and Haas 2014). For example, nonanemic but iron-depleted (stage 1 ID) female college rowers (serum ferritin ≤20μg/L) demonstrated poorer performance at the beginning of their season and had slower self-reported personal records from the previous season (DellaValle and Haas 2011). Of this group, a subsection of athletes with lower iron appeared unable to put in as many training minutes each day and were significantly slower over a 4 km ergometer test compared to rowers with normal iron status. Interestingly, both normal iron and ID groups had similar dietary iron intakes (DellaValle and Haas 2011). Given the significance of this mineral, it is important to appreciate the factors impacting iron levels, understand how to assess for iron status, and be familiar with treatment strategies for when iron reserves are low.

What Affects Iron Status?

Iron status is negatively affected by many things, including elevated losses due to menstruation and gastrointestinal (GI) disorders as well as inadequate dietary iron intake and poor bioavailability of plant-based iron sources. The leading factor, however, just might be training load. Training increases an athlete's energy metabolism and need for the red blood cells required to transport oxygen. Conversely, high activity levels also exacerbate iron loss in sweat and urine as well as exercise-induced red blood cell breakdown (Badenhorst, Black, and O'Brien 2019; McKay et al. 2020; Sim et al. 2019). Most importantly, the inflammation that occurs posttraining elevates hepcidin (McCormick et al. 2020; McKay et al. 2020).

A hormone that regulates both iron absorption and recycling (Sim et al. 2019), hepcidin may be one of the most important factors affecting iron status in endurance athletes. Postexercise inflammation transiently increases hepcidin for approximately 3 to 6 h, and training with low glycogen stores may exacerbate the elevation (McKay et al. 2020; Sim et al. 2019). Hepcidin negatively affects iron status by suppressing iron recycling from macrophages as well as iron absorption from the GI tract. This is particularly concerning for athletes with high training volumes and multiple sessions over a day (McCormick et al. 2020). Inadequate energy (Badenhorst, Black, and O'Brien 2019), and in particular low carbohydrate intake (McKay et al. 2020), is also linked to elevations in hepcidin. If an athlete is in a state of low energy or carbohydrate availability, either by accident or on purpose, iron intake, absorption, and status will be further compromised.

A study of Polish national team rowers demonstrated that a 2,000 m time trial caused increases in both inflammatory hormones and hepcidin and decreased serum iron, indicating that high-intensity exercise negatively impacts iron metabolism. Hence, during periods of deliberate training overload, rowers may therefore be at risk of ID (Skarpanska-Stejnborn et al. 2015). Furthermore, because of the high training loads typically undertaken in rowing, ID may occur over the season. Another study on elite rowers and professional soccer players found that 27% of all athletes and 25% of male

Table 29.1 Iron Deficiency: Stages, Assessment, and Treatment

STAGES (SIM ET AL. 2019)		
Stage 1: Iron deficiency (ID)	**Stage 2: Iron-deficient nonanemia (IDNA)**	**Stage 3: Iron-deficient anemia (IDA)**
Depleted iron stores, normal hemoglobin, and normal transferrin	Depleted iron stores, normal hemoglobin, abnormal transferrin	Severely depleted iron stores, decreased hemoglobin production, and abnormal transferrin
• Ferritin between 20-35 µg/L • Hemoglobin >115 g/L (females) or >135 g/L (males) • Transferrin saturation >16%	• Ferritin <20 µg/L • Hemoglobin >115 g/L (females) or >135 g/L males • Transferrin saturation <16%	• Ferritin <12 µg/L • Hemoglobin <115 g/L (females) or <135 g/L (males) • Transferrin saturation <16%
RISK FACTORS AND ASSESSMENT CRITERIA		
Low risk: Test yearly	**Moderate risk: Test biannually**	**High risk: Test as needed to monitor intervention success (every 3-4 months)**
• Healthy male or nonmenstruating female (due to contraception or menopause) • No previous iron status issues • Low to moderate training schedule • No longer growing • Good EA • Mixed diet with wide food variety • Good recovery from training • No underlying pathology	• Female • Regular menses, no iron status issues or ID in the past 2 years and intending to increase training load • Male with no previous iron status issues but intending to increase training load • Good EA • Mixed diet with wide food variety • Good recovery from training	• Female with regular, heavy menses or irregular menses due to LEA • Male or female with very high training loads (volume/intensity) • Current or recent history (<2 years) ID (any stage) or a significant drop in usual ferritin status even when ID not diagnosed • LEA • Low intake of iron-rich foods • Vegetarian or vegan • Poor recovery from training or prolonged fatigue, illness, hair loss • Unexplained poor athletic performance

Note: Iron status should be assessed at least 3 – 6 weeks prior to any hypoxic (altitude) training/competition (Sims et al. 2019)

TREATMENT	
Diet	**Supplement**
• If the athlete has experienced a significant change in their ferritin status, use diet changes first unless deficiency is severe or the need for iron status improvements are time sensitive • If no improvement after ~8 weeks, supplement	• 100 mg elemental iron (ferrous form) • If GI issues result or iron status does not improve, trial lower dose, alternating days, or chelated form

BLOOD COLLECTION PROTOCOLS (SIMS ET AL. 2019, CASTELL ET AL. 2019)

• No intense exercise 24 h prior to test
• No signs of illness or infection
• Athlete should be well hydrated
• Athlete should avoid iron for 2 days prior to test
• Blood draws should occur at the same time of day for each collection (i.e., first thing in the morning preferred)

rowers (5 of 20) had ID (ferritin <30µg/L) by the end of the season. The same study also found that 14% of all athletes and 20% of rowers (4 of 20) maintained their low iron status even after the postcompetition regeneration period (Reinke et al. 2012). Iron status should therefore be monitored at the start of each new training season to identify at-risk athletes and provide treatment strategies when needed. Biochemical assessment should include serum ferritin, hemoglobin concentration, and transferrin saturation measures. See table 29.1 for risk factors and assessment parameters.

Strategies to Address Iron Deficiency

There are three primary ways to address ID: diet, oral iron supplementation, or parenteral iron administration (Castell et al. 2019, Sim et al. 2019). Only diet and oral supplementation will be discussed in this chapter.

Because the body cannot synthesize iron, it must be consumed through food or as a supplement. Diet counseling for ID should therefore be the first consideration if an athlete has borderline rather than severely low levels of serum ferritin (the body's iron storage protein) and there is time in the training cycle to trial a food-first approach. Combating ID through diet counseling can be particularly effective if the athlete is in LEA, limits carbohydrates, or has iron intake habits that can be corrected. When deficiency is more severe, the athlete's ferritin drop precipitous, time for improving stores is limited, or a food-first approach has failed to maintain or improve iron status, then supplementation must be considered. Regardless of whether diet or supplementation is the chosen treatment option, an athlete's iron stores may actually be the primary physiological regulator of how much dietary iron is absorbed from the gut (Dainty et al. 2014; Fairweather et al. 2017; Hurrell and Egli 2010). Simply put, low serum ferritin stores elicit the greatest level of absorption. Nonetheless, athletes should be educated on all controllable strategies to maximize iron uptake.

Diet First: Iron Sources, Enhancers, and Inhibitors

Iron from food is absorbed at varying levels. Nonheme iron, found in both plant and animal sources, and which accounts for around 90% of iron intake in humans, is absorbed at 2% to 20%, whereas heme (animal only) sources are absorbed at 15% to 35% (Sim et al. 2019). Foods generally considered to be good sources of iron include red meat, legumes, fortified cereals, and leafy greens. However, even if the iron content of a food is relatively high, it may not be a good source due to poor bioavailability (Piskin et al. 2022).

Nonheme iron must be chelated prior to absorption. These chelators or dietary components will either inhibit or enhance iron absorption from the gut. Plant-based components such as the polyphenols in chocolate, coffee, and tea, as well as phytates (a storage form of phosphates and minerals) found in whole grains, nuts, and legumes will decrease nonheme iron absorption to varying degrees (Dainty et al. 2014; Piskin et al. 2022). Calcium-rich foods and supplements may also substantially decrease both heme and nonheme absorption (McCormick et al. 2020; Piskin et al. 2022). Conversely, vitamin C–rich foods or small amounts of animal proteins added to meals will have a small enhancing effect on nonheme iron absorption, and vitamin C may actually counteract the negative impact of phytates. This dietary landscape can present a challenge for athletes who struggle to maintain a healthy iron status, particularly when they eat a large amount of phytate-rich foods, limit or avoid animal proteins, drink coffee or tea with meals, or use dairy products at breakfast, in recovery from training, or as a protein-rich bedtime snack (tables 29.2-29.4).

Table 29.2 Iron Requirements

Population	Requirements
Adolescents aged 9-13, adult males, and postmenopausal women	8 mg/day
Premenopausal adult women	18 mg/day

Table 29.3 Iron Sources

Heme sources	Nonheme sources
Fish and seafood	Eggs, dairy, meat, fish, and poultry
Meat (game and domestic)	Fortified grains (cereal and pasta)
Poultry	Dried fruits (apricots, prunes, raisins)
	Legumes (beans, lentils, peas, soybeans)
	Nuts and seeds (pumpkin, sesame, chia, cashew, almond, hazelnuts, pistachio)
	Some vegetables (dark leafy greens, potato, tomato sauce/paste)
	Other foods (dark chocolate, blackstrap molasses, crystalized ginger root)
	Cast iron cookware

Table 29.4 Iron Inhibitors and Enhancers

Inhibitors*	Enhancers*
Calcium (see table 29.5)	Vitamin C–rich foods such as broccoli, citrus fruits and juices (orange, grapefruit, tangerine), kiwi, strawberries, sweet peppers
Phytates—found in fiber-rich foods such as bran, oats, raw nuts, raw seeds	Carotenoid-rich foods such as apricots, carrots, greens, tomatoes (paste, sauce, juice), cantaloupe
Polyphenols—found in tea, coffee, red wine, cocoa, chocolate, spinach, some herbs and spices	Meat, fish, or poultry (at least 50 g)
	Certain food preparation methods (fermentation, sprouting, soaking, cooking)

*Inhibitors and enhancers appear to have less impact in a varied, whole meal diet (Dainty et al. 2014) and are likely due to the body's compensatory mechanisms for iron homeostasis. They should not be eliminated, because they are a source of a wide variety of nutrients. Iron-enhancing factors and intake of heme sources of iron minimize dietary impact on absorption (Piskin et al. 2022).

Iron Supplementation

Given the negative consequences of iron deficiency, supplementation is the next logical treatment approach if an athlete does not respond to dietary changes. To date, there is no consensus on the ideal iron supplementation prescription. In general, recommended doses are approximately 60 to 100 mg elemental iron from iron salts (ferrous sulphate, gluconate, and fumarate) over at least a 2-month period (McCormick et al. 2020). Athlete responses to supplementation are usually positive, with approximately 100 mg of iron per day leading to 40% to 80% serum ferritin increases over 8 to 12 weeks (Sim et al. 2019). Although generally effective and the least expensive iron supplement, salts appear to cause the most GI complaints (McCormick et al. 2020). Taking iron either with food—a common strategy to reduce side effects—or in a lower dose may be better tolerated, increasing athlete compliance. Alternatively, athletes may consider supplementing with iron chelates (such as iron bisglycinates) which are available at lower dosages and may be easier on the gut. Additionally, when taken with food, they may promote greater absorption than iron salts, as chelates bind to and minimize the impact of dietary iron inhibitors. Finally, hepcidin levels increase during iron supplementation. For athletes who do not benefit from the traditional daily protocol, an alternate-day intake strategy may reduce the hepcidin response, leading to improved iron status (Sim et al. 2019).

Because of the large variability in athlete iron levels and the numerous reasons for deficiency, supplemental iron protocols should be individualized and overseen by an experienced medical and nutrition practitioner. Currently, athletes within the Canadian system receive a wide variety of recommendations based on their unique needs. Beyond dietary changes where appropriate, these individualization strategies include recommendations to take 25 to 100 mg of iron—daily, every second day, only during menses, or only on easy training or days off (author observation). Both iron salts and chelated products are used with success.

Iron Timing and Beyond

Recent research has demonstrated that iron absorption from a meal is better after morning versus afternoon training and even versus no training, possibly because hepcidin steadily increases over the day. There may be a 60 min window of opportunity after morning exercise during which iron absorption is maximized (McCormick et al. 2019). Because of postexercise hepcidin increases, once this window has passed iron is more likely to be poorly absorbed and metabolized for up to 5 or 6 h after high-intensity or prolonged exercise. To combat this, rowers should plan to eat iron-rich foods earlier in the day and supplement immediately after morning sessions or, when this is not realistic, more than 5 to 6 h after training and on days off. Rowers should add a small amount of red meat, fish, or poultry (if not vegan or vegetarian) and vitamin C–rich foods to each iron-containing meal, especially when the meal contains phytates. Soaking, sprouting, cooking, or fermenting plant-based foods should also be considered, particularly for vegan athletes. Rowers should also limit coffee and tea intake with food. Finally, rowers must also be knowledgeable about and able to maintain good EA and good carbohydrate status when training loads are high (see chapter 27).

Vitamin D

Vitamin D receives a great deal of media attention—for good reason. Vitamin D receptors have been found in almost all cells in the body, signifying its importance to metabolism and health (Bikle 2014). A steroid hormone, vitamin D plays a role in calcium absorption and bone health, gene expression, and cell growth (de la Puente Yague et al. 2020). Although more research is required, it may also have a positive impact on skeletal muscle remodeling as well as immune function, potentially decreasing risk of acute upper respiratory tract infection (URTI) (de la Puente Yague et al. 2020; Ksiazek, Zagrodna, and Slowinska-Lisowska 2019; Owens, Allison, and Close 2018). This is significant because illness has the potential to impair athlete performance (Drew et al. 2018). The role and overall importance of vitamin D cannot be overstated.

Bone Health

Vitamin D stimulates intestinal absorption of calcium, a key nutrient for normal bone growth and mineralization. A vitamin D deficiency (<30 nmol/L) lowers calcium absorption, increasing parathyroid hormone activity and leading to calcium release from the bone. Consequently, low plasma vitamin D has the potential to increase stress-related bone injuries (de la Puente Yague et al. 2020; McDonnell, Hume, and Nolte 2011). Bone injuries, and particularly rib stress injuries in rowers, will cause training modifications related to the severity of the injury. Although the causes of injury are multifactorial, prevention—and therefore, optimal vitamin D status—is critical to bone health (Lappe et al. 2008; McDonnell, Hume, and Nolte 2011) and performance (McDonnell, Hume, and Nolte 2011).

Key Point

Bone is dynamic. When athletes undertake mechanical loading or experience lean body mass increases from training, bone mineral density (BMD) in the working bone structures gradually increases (Owens, Allison, and Close 2018). Higher bone density is associated with decreased fracture risk. Athletes who participate in weight-bearing sports generally have higher BMD than those engaging in weight-supported sports. Loading the musculoskeletal system may compensate for the negative effects of vitamin D deficiency on bone integrity (Owens, Allison, and Close 2018).

What about rowers whose primary training is largely weight supported? Research undertaken in elite Australian rowers demonstrated that BMD is generally within optimal ranges and equal to or higher than the general population. Lightweight rowers tend to have lower BMD than openweight rowers (Lundy, Trease, and Michael 2015). However, this is possibly related to LEA rather than inadequate vitamin D status (Dimitriou et al. 2014). Collegiate rowers were reported to have higher spinal BMD, possibly related to the magnitude of force production during the rowing stroke (Lariviere, Robinson, and Snow 2003). Last but not least, male masters rowers with an average 9 years of competitive rowing experience prior to age 28 maintained higher BMD levels than age-matched nonathletic controls (Sliwicka et al. 2015). Overall, rowing appears to have beneficial effects on total and regional bone health.

Muscle and Immunity

Vitamin D is also involved in skeletal muscle remodeling, muscle function, and the immune system. Several trials suggest elevating vitamin D levels above 75 nmol/L may positively impact skeletal muscle remodeling after intense muscle-damaging exercise (Owens et al. 2015). It also appears that when vitamin D–deficient older adults improve their vitamin D status, they experience increases in muscular strength (Owens, Allison, and Close 2018). Conversely, there have been no studies linking vitamin D deficiency to muscle function in young endurance athletes such as rowers (Owens, Allison, and Close 2018). Clearly, additional research is required before irrefutable claims regarding vitamin D's role in muscle repair and strength can be made.

When considering immunity, vitamin D appears to have a role in both the innate and acquired immune system (Martens et al. 2020). A recent meta-analysis reveals that daily or weekly supplementation was protective against URTI. The effect was strongest on those who were the most deficient; however, protective effects were also seen in adults with higher plasma levels (Martineau et al. 2017). A few illness-related vitamin D studies have been undertaken in athletes. Very generally, during the winter months, college (Halliday et al. 2011), recreational, and elite endurance athletes (He et al. 2013) with lower vitamin D status experienced more URTIs, including a higher number of illness days and greater symptom severity (Owens, Allison, and Close 2018).

Key Point

Generally, nutrients do not work in isolation. As an example, over 17 key micro-nutrients work together to support bone health (Sale and Elliott-Sale 2019). Given the benefits related to healthy, functional aging, consider the specific relationship between vitamins D and K. Although limited, research in older populations supports a link between the combination of vitamin D and vitamin K on bone (Karpouzos et al. 2017) as well as cardiovascular health (Karpouzos et al. 2017; van Ballegooijen et al. 2017). There are two forms of vitamin K: K_1, or phylloquinone, which is primarily found in leafy greens and is critical to blood clotting, and K_2, or menaquinone, which is found in fermented dairy and soy and is also produced in the intestine by lactic acid bacteria. Vitamin K_2 helps regulate bone mineralization and vascular smooth muscle cell proteins. Insufficient vitamin K is associated with lower bone mineral density and increased fracture risk as well as increased blood pressure in older adults (van Ballegooijen et al. 2017). Although there is currently inadequate evidence to recommend combined vitamins D and K supplementation, given the potential bone and cardiovascular benefits, rowers of all ages are encouraged to eat a wide variety of nutrient dense foods including leafy greens and fermented dairy products. The bottom line: Whole foods typically contain the range of nutrients that work synergistically to support overal health.

Sources of Vitamin D

Known as the sunshine vitamin, vitamin D can be obtained from sun exposure, food, and supplements. Food sources are limited and include fatty fish (trout, salmon), cod liver oil, fortified milk, eggs, and mushrooms (in variable amounts). Depending on the circumstances, sunlight is recognized as the best source and exposure typically provides approximately 80% to 90% of requirements, as vitamin D is synthesized when skin is exposed to UVB rays (Owens, Allison, and Close 2018; van Ballegooijen et al. 2017). UVB intensity, sunscreen, and skin pigmentation alter the sun's efficacy, impacting the level of vitamin D formation within an individual. Geography also plays a role. At higher latitudes north or south of the equator the sun may be too weak to produce adequate vitamin D during winter months (October through April).

Risk Factors and Supplementation Recommendations

Rowers at risk of vitamin D deficiency are those that spend winter months where there is a short period of daylight, have highly pigmented skin, limit summer sunlight exposure to less than 20 min/day, or regularly wear sunscreen when training outside. In fact, insufficient vitamin D status over the winter months is not an uncommon occurrence for Canadian athletes (author observation). Further, the skin's ability to produce vitamin D decreases with aging, potentially increasing the risk of deficiency for the older masters athlete (Karpouzos et al. 2017).

Generally, there is lack of agreement regarding plasma vitamin D concentrations deemed optimal for health and in particular a lack of consensus between the U.S. Institute of Medicine and the Endocrine Society. The actual level of sufficiency is potentially linked to age, race, gender, weight, and individual hormone profiles (Ribbans et al. 2021). Although controversial, the following definition are often used:

- Vitamin D deficiency: <50 nmol/L
- Vitamin D insufficiency: 50-75 nmol/L
- Vitamin D sufficiency and ideal vitamin D range: 75-120 nmol/L

At-risk athletes should have serum vitamin D levels assessed. Supplementation is advised if values are lower than 75 nmol/L. Daily doses of 600 IU, 1,000 IU (Holick et al. 2011), 2,000 IU (Holick et al. 2011; Owens, Allison, and Close 2018), and up to 4,000 IU per day during the winter months have been recommended (Owens, Allison, and Close 2018), with higher doses resulting in faster elevation of serum levels (Martens et al. 2020). Supplemental sources appear best absorbed when coingested with a meal. A food-first approach is preferred whenever possible. However, due to the limited number of vitamin D sources, meeting winter needs through food intake alone is extremely challenging. For example, to obtain 2,000 IU from food, one would need to consume approximately 200-800 g of salmon (depending on the species), 4.75 L of milk, *or* 25 eggs each day (Canadian Nutrient File 2023).

Unfortunately, when it comes to supplementation, some people take a "more is better" approach. The tolerable upper intake level for vitamin D has been set at 4,000 IU per day to prevent excess intestinal calcium absorption and subsequent negative side effects. Additionally, a recent 3 year clinical trial in healthy 55- to 70-year-old adults with adequate (rather than deficient) vitamin D levels found a dose-dependent decrease in bone mineral density (BMD) when supplemented with 400, 4,000, or 10,000 IU per day. In short, the higher the dose, the greater the losses in BMD (Burt et al. 2019). Although further research is required, current research suggests that approximately 700 to 2,000 IU per day of vitamin D is sufficient, and more is definitely not better. Unless recommended by a medical practitioner, athletes are advised to supplement based on plasma concentrations and medical advice and against doses >4,000 IU per day.

Calcium

Calcium is an essential mineral, with 99% stored in bone and teeth and approximately 1% present in cells (Williams 2005). Although critical to bone remodeling, calcium is also key to many other metabolic functions, including muscle contraction and maintaining a regular heartbeat, energy metabolism, nerve impulse conduction, hormone secretion, water balance, immunity, and brain function. Because of its importance, calcium is very tightly regulated by the body (Sale and Elliott-Sale 2019). This means there are no blood tests that effectively measure calcium status (Larson-Meyer, Woolf, and Burke 2018). If intakes are inadequate, the body simply borrows from the bone (Sale and Elliott-Sale 2019). Additionally, calcium is excreted in sweat, therefore losses may increase with high-intensity or prolonged training (Williams 2005), possibly related to very high sweat rates (Sale and Elliott-Sale 2019). As such, along with high sweat loss, LEA, or poor vitamin D status, chronically low calcium intake or elevated losses is linked to poor bone mineralization and bone health over time.

Controversy exists regarding the effect of supplemental calcium on bone health (Karpouzos et al. 2017). Nonetheless, some research demonstrated a benefit. For example, calcium consumed prior to a lengthy or high-intensity training session decreased bone resorption and subsequent calcium losses (Sale and Elliott-Sale 2019). Additionally, calcium—along with vitamin D supplementation—decreased stress fractures in female naval recruits by 20% compared to a control group (Lappe et al. 2008). Calcium may also reduce age-related fracture (Kunstel 2005).

Although important across the life span, calcium needs are highest during adolescence and menopause. Inadequate intakes typically occur in those who restrict calories or avoid dairy or calcium-rich dairy alternates (Thomas, Erdman, and Burke 2016), particularly because dairy provides the most bioavailable form of calcium (Goolsby and Boniquit 2017). Supplementation may be necessary to minimize bone loss for those with chronically low intakes or elevated losses (Sale and Elliott-Sale 2019). Unfortunately, high calcium doses may increase the risk of both kidney stones and cardiovascular events. Supplemental calcium is therefore only advised after a thorough intake review determines that needs cannot be met through diet alone. See table 29.5 for calcium recommendations and sources.

Table 29.5 Calcium Intake Recommendations and Sources

Intake recommendations	Sources
• 1,300 mg/day for youth aged 9-18 • 1,000 mg/day for men aged 19 and older and women aged 19-50 • 1,200 mg/day for women aged 51-70 and rowers with rib stress injury • 1,500 mg/day for amenorrheic women*	• Dairy products • Dark green vegetables (kale, bok choy, broccoli) • Canned fish with edible bones (salmon, sardines) • Calcium-fortified foods (orange juice, milk alternates) • Tofu (check label) • Supplements (taken with meals to increase absorption)

*Resumption of menses is critical to support bone health (Mountjoy et al. 2014).

Probiotics

Although not considered an at-risk nutrient, probiotics are of great interest to the athletic community. A probiotic is defined as "live microorganisms, that when administered in adequate amounts, confer a health benefit on the host" (Hill et al. 2014, 507). The micro-organisms used in probiotic supplements also occur naturally in the human GI tract, with a diverse microbiota critical to overall gut health, nutrient production and absorption, immune function, and possibly mood and mental health (Jager et al. 2019). Because of the health benefits conferred by gut microbiota diversity, a probiotic supplement may indirectly improve training adaptations and athletic performance. Improved body composition, reduced stress hormones, and mitigation of age-related testosterone decline are also potential probiotic-related effects important to athletic performance (Jager et al. 2019).

Gut Diversity

Dietary patterns can begin to impact gut microbiota diversity within as little as 24 hours! Although this certainly is an exciting finding, it is more likely that an athlete's microbiome is effectively shaped over time through high-quality food intake and exercise (Jager et al. 2019). Years of training and large nutrient intakes increase gut microbiota diversity, leading to increases in metabolic pathways that improve both energy absorption from food and tissue repair (Jager et al. 2019; Wosinska et al. 2019). Very generally, fiber-rich carbohydrates, which provide prebiotics (non-digestible ingredients that benefit human health by positively influencing native beneficial microbes) (Guarner et al. 2017), appear to have the largest impact on diversity and should be the cornerstone of a food-first approach to gut health. Protein is also linked to healthy gut bacteria, as are probiotic-rich dairy and fermented food products (Wosinska et al. 2019). Less is known about the impact of fat. Although additional research is required to fully understand the influence of all nutrients (Clark and Mach 2016; Jager et al. 2019), consuming a highly varied array of vegetables, fruits, whole grains, fermented dairy, and plant-based proteins at each meal is recommended to promote gut microbiota abundance and diversity (Clark and Mach 2016).

What About a Probiotic Supplement?

The potential effects of probiotic supplementation on the athlete are wide ranging, multifactorial, and still mostly unknown. Unfortunately, athlete-specific research is limited and predominantly centered around immune function (Clark and Mach 2016), with only a small amount examining mood, gut cell health, nutrient metabolism, and exercise effects (Jager et al. 2019; Wosinska et al. 2019). Very generally, gut bacteria appear to impact mood and reduce anxiety through a complex system of anti-inflammatory actions within the hypothalamic–pituitary–adrenal (or gut-brain) axis. The few studies to examine probiotic supplementation on mood have demonstrated preliminary but positive effects (Jager et al. 2019). There is also evidence that multistrain probiotic supplements may provide symptom relief in irritable bowel syndrome (IBS)—which has been linked to low levels of the gut microbes that break down short-chain carbohydrates—as well as dysregulation of gut signaling and anxiety. Although fascinating, study sample sizes have been small and not fully conclusive (Dale et al. 2019).

Of specific relevance to athletes is research with the potential to impact both health and performance. Some strains improve the health of cells lining the GI tract, increasing nutrient absorption and protein digestibility (Jager et al. 2016). Probiotic bacteria also release metabolites known as postbiotics, including short-chain fatty acids, antioxidants, and organic acids. The improved nutrient absorption and additional nutrient production has the potential to augment recovery after intense exercise (Jager et al. 2019; Wosinska et al. 2019). Finally, though scarce, some performance-based research suggests probiotic supplementation may reduce oxidative stress caused by intense exercise (Wosinska et al. 2019), as well as increase aerobic power and endurance (Jager et al. 2019).

Immunity and Preventing Illness

Among probiotic research, immunity investigations are the most robust. Just over half of the current probiotic literature demonstrates a small but positive outcome of probiotic supplementation on immune markers or the incidence of URTIs (West et al. 2014).

Notably, the lining of the digestive tract is strongly linked to immunity. A healthy gut interacts with the immune system and inhibits pathogens from entering circulation. A poorly maintained digestive tract increases risk of pathogen entry into the body. Probiotics can help decrease this risk. Some strains enhance the ability of gut bacteria to upregulate the body's innate and acquired immune function, whereas other strains compete with pathogens to prevent their attachment to GI cells, minimizing risk of illness (Jager et al. 2019).

Beyond athlete research, there is a body of evidence linking probiotic supplementation in healthy individuals to improvements in traveler's diarrhea (TD) (Clinical Guide to Probiotic Products Available in Canada—www.probioticchart.ca). Given that approximately 70% of the immune system is located in the gut (Jager et al. 2019), if an athlete struggles with illness during high-volume training or foreign travel for competition, a multistrain probiotic could be considered as adjunct to good EA, a nutrient-dense diet, adequate sleep and recovery, and proper hygiene. Finally, if an athlete is planning to travel to an area where TD is common, they are encouraged to discuss strain-specific probiotic supplementation with their sport medicine practitioner.

Protocols

Many supplemental probiotic strains have been studied (Sivamaruthi, Kesika, and Chaiyasut 2019). Given the large numbers of strains and the wide variety of research protocols, recommended dosages are generally unknown. Confusing the situation is that probiotic supplementation may only be effective in colonizing a "dysregulated" gut versus a healthy one (Jager et al. 2019). However, 1×10^{10} CFU (colony-forming units) appears to be a common dosage, and the 2018 IOC consensus statement on dietary supplements indicates moderate support for probiotic supplementation at this level (Maughan et al. 2018). The best protocol for probiotic supplement timing is unknown; however, ingestion within 30 min of (or during) a meal may increase probiotic bacteria survival rate. If an athlete decides to use probiotics, they are recommended to start at least 14 days and up to 4 weeks before high-volume training, travel, or competition to allow the bacteria to colonize in the gut in time to potentially minimize the severity or incidence of illness (Sivamaruthi, Kesika, and Chaiyasut 2019). Athletes are also advised to take the probiotic throughout the entire high-risk time period, considering that probiotic bacteria are undetectable in the gut only 8 days after discontinuing the supplement (Jager et al. 2019).

It is important to understand that health benefits related to probiotics are strain specific. When determining whether a probiotic supplement may be beneficial, it is critical to look for the strain used in applicable research and then purchase a product that states the genus (*Lactobacillus*), species (*Lactobacillus rhamnosus*), and strain (*Lactobacillus rhamnosus GG*) as well as the number of CFUs clearly on the label. Interested readers are directed to the Health Canada probiotics guide (http://webprod.hc-sc.gc.ca/nhpid-bdipsn/atReq.do?atid=probio&lang=eng) and to the Clinical Guide to Probiotic Products Available in Canada (www.probioticchart.ca), which contain information related to probiotic strains, purpose, and evidence. In particular, the product guide site is updated annually with new evidence and product availability. This can support informed decision making regarding probiotic supplementation.

Overall, gut microbial diversity appears to be a key component for athlete health. A varied, high-fiber, plant-rich diet is necessary for this to occur and should be the priority over a supplement. However, where applicable, probiotic supplementation may further enhance gut microbiota, providing additional health and performance benefits (Jager et al. 2019; Sivamaruthi, Kesika, and Chaiyasut 2019; Wosinska et al. 2019).

Sport Foods, Protein Supplements, and Multivitamins

Finally, the health supplement section would be incomplete without discussing vitamins, minerals, sport foods and protein powders. Many athletes believe these products are an integral part of their nutrition tool kit (author observation). In fact, when broadly defined to include vitamins, minerals, sport bars and protein powders, supplement use in Canadian athletes aged 11 to 25 was found to be almost 100% (Parnell, Wiens, and Erdman 2016). Similar percentages exist for university, under 23, and national-level rowers (author observation) and evidence quantifying the use of these items in masters rowers is minimal. Although these supplements are not essential, there are circumstances where such items may support athlete health or performance.

Sport Foods

This category, which includes carbohydrate–electrolyte (sport) drinks, gels, gummies, and bars, can be an effective part of an athlete's fueling portfolio (Maughan et al. 2018). Easily digested sport foods and fluids can help an athlete meet their nutrition goals when consuming "real" food is impractical. Sport foods can fuel training, competition, and recovery or provide a quick snack to help the busy rower meet high energy or carbohydrate needs. They can also help hydration and electrolyte management, particularly for athletes with high sweat rates during hot weather training.

Powdered Proteins

This supplement group includes whey concentrates, isolates and hydrolysates, casein, beef, egg, cricket, and mixed and individual plant-based proteins. Although potentially valuable, rowers should be aware that these products typically do not contain the wide range of nutrients found in whole foods and may be less effective for long-term post-training muscle protein synthesis (Burd et al. 2019). Regardless, these products can augment a busy athlete's daily or recovery protein needs, either at home or on the road. Protein supplements may also assist masters athletes meet the elevated protein requirements needed to overcome anabolic resistance and minimize age-related reductions in lean mass. Athletes who choose a plant-based supplement should look for products that contain added leucine (Louis et al. 2019), and all athletes should look for products that have been third-party tested for WADA-banned substances.

Multivitamin and Mineral Supplements

Vitamins and minerals support a broad range of chemical reactions, including energy metabolism, muscle and nerve function, general cell protection, and growth and repair. It is important to note, however, that vitamins and minerals in supplement form lack important phytochemicals and are a poor replacement for food.

There is no evidence that a multivitamin and mineral supplement will improve performance unless an athlete has a demonstrated nutrient deficiency (Weight, Myburgh, and Noakes 1988). Fortunately, true deficiencies are the exception, particularly when athletes are in good EA (Mountjoy et al. 2014; Thomas, Erdman, and Burke 2016). Nonetheless, there are some circumstances where an athlete may benefit from daily multivitamin and mineral use. For example, athletes may limit food variety or intake for many reasons: dislikes, intolerances or allergies, body composition management, lack of availability while traveling, lack of time, or because of health issues such as celiac disease or an eating disorder. In these situations, daily multivitamin and mineral supplementation can be effective. Additionally, a masters athlete with reduced food intake may consume inadequate amounts of some vitamins and minerals (Campbell and Geik 2004). These athletes may benefit from a broad-spectrum, multinutrient supplement along with focusing their diet on nutrient-dense foods.

Keep in mind that the products discussed above are not usually essential for health and performance when an athlete has easy access to nutrient-dense foods and is in good EA. Even when training load is high, homemade sport drinks, bars or bites, smoothies, dairy products, bread and honey, dried fruit, bananas, and maple syrup are excellent, real food training support options. Regardless, most athletes will likely find one or more of these products beneficial under some circumstances.

Key Point

Overall, along with good sleep hygiene and well-structured recovery, a high-quality diet with adequate energy to support training and activities of daily living will reduce the risk of nutrient deficiencies that may impair health and performance. This should be prioritized over supplementation, particularly given the risks around WADA noncompliance.

The previous sections examined how supplementation can specifically be used to improve athlete health, which ultimately impacts performance. Supplements that may support health include, but are not limited to, iron, vitamin D, calcium, and probiotics. Nevertheless, supplements cannot make up for poor food choices and inadequate fueling. Overall, along with good sleep hygiene and well-structured recovery, a high-quality diet with adequate energy to support training and activities of daily living will reduce the risk of nutrient deficiencies that may impair health and performance. This should be prioritized over supplementation, particularly given the risks around WADA noncompliance (figure 29.1).

Performance Supplements

The rowing race requires continuous, high-intensity efforts, maximal stimulus of all energy systems, and a large production of lactate and hydrogen ions (Hagerman 1984). Additionally, rowers commonly drive themselves to optimize training adaptations—such as increased mitochondrial density, power output, and lean mass gains—with the aim of maximizing competitive success. A food-first approach should always be the foundation for supporting the rower's training and competition. However, performance supplements can be considered for the elite rower who has optimized both physical and mental training, as well as all aspects of health and recovery, including nutrition and sleep.

Beyond the considerations listed at the start of the chapter, coaches, support staff, and athletes should also ask the following questions whenever contemplating supplementation to enhance performance:

- Are the supplements banned by WADA (https://www.wada-ama.org/en)?
- Is there scientific evidence to support their use in rowing?
- Are there negative side effects or interactions when consumed, either alone or in combination with other products?

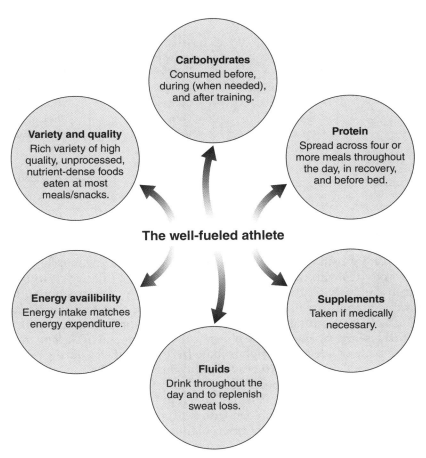

Carbohydrates
Consumed before,
during (when needed),
and after training.

Variety and quality
Rich variety of high
quality, unprocessed,
nutrient-dense foods
eaten at most
meals/snacks.

Protein
Spread across four or
more meals throughout
the day, in recovery,
and before bed.

The well-fueled athlete

Energy availibility
Energy intake matches
energy expenditure.

Supplements
Taken if medically
necessary.

Fluids
Drink throughout the
day and to replenish
sweat loss.

▶ **Figure 29.1** Nutrition foundations for a well-fueled athlete.

Susan Boegman and Sid Boegman.

- Is the supplement easy to use, avoiding distraction during training or competition?
- Can supplementation strategies be individualized given differences in athlete responses (Maughan, Greenhaff, and Hespel 2011)?
- Finally, does supplementation make sense for the individual rower (Halson and Martin 2013)?

See also table 29.6 and figure 29.2 for further supplement considerations.

There are certain performance supplements recognized by the IOC consensus statement as having good-to-strong evidence of efficacy (Maughan et al. 2018) that mechanistically apply to rowing. Interestingly, these same supplements were found to provide some level of efficacy in a study investigating the effects of preconditioning strategies on 2,000 m ergometer performance (Turnes et al. 2019). These supplements include creatine, caffeine, buffers, and nitrates.

Creatine

Creatine monohydrate is considered one of the most popular nutrition supplements (Kreider et al. 2017). It is a nonessential organic compound naturally found in skeletal muscle,

Table 29.6 Supplement Considerations

Supplements (assessment required before use)	Maximal aerobic capacity	Maximal anaerobic exercise capacity or peak power	Staying healthy
	• Iron, if indicated • Nitrates • Caffeine • Creatine • Sport foods	• Iron, if indicated • Caffeine • Creatine • Beta-alanine • Bicarbonate • Sports foods	• Iron, if indicated • Vitamin D • Calcium • Multivitamin and mineral • Probiotics • Sport foods

Note: Foundations before supplementation should include good EA, proper protein intake and timing throughout the day, periodized carbohydrate quantity and timing, fluids to prevent dehydration, overall high-quality food intake, and optimized training and recovery.

Maughan et al. 2018.

providing a readily available but very limited fuel supply during muscle contraction. The omnivorous diet will typically provide approximately 1 to 2 g of creatine each day (Butts, Jacobs, and Silvis 2018), with meat and fish as the primary sources. The body also synthesizes approximately 1 g of creatine per day, therefore muscle stores are naturally 60% to 80% saturated (Kreider et al. 2017). Supplementation with creatine increases fuel reserves by augmenting phosphocreatine content in skeletal muscle and increasing the rate of adenosine triphosphate (ATP) resynthesis during rest between high-intensity sets. This increases fuel availability during exercise and has the potential to decrease muscle acidosis in sports such as rowing (Kreider et al. 2017).

Creatine supplementation appears best suited to increase muscle strength, endurance, and hypertrophy when combined with resistance exercise (Kreider et al. 2017). It also supports the performance of brief, high-intensity exercise, including sprints embedded within or immediately following endurance training (Rawson 2018). This suggests that creatine may benefit rowing performance when used as a training aid in the gym or during high-intensity ergometer and on-water work. Notably, even a short period of creatine supplementation was found to improve lactate threshold and anaerobic performance in 16 elite male rowers (Chwalbinska-Moneta 2003).

Beyond its role as a fuel source during high-intensity exercise, elevating muscle creatine content enhances the expression of various genes that positively affect exercise performance (Rawson 2018). It also draws water into the muscle tissue, increasing glycogen and protein synthesis (Rawson 2018). Altogether, these functions may positively impact work capacity, training tolerance, and recovery, enhancing overall training adaptation (Kreider et al. 2017). These effects are possibly even more pronounced for vegans and aging athletes, two populations that typically have lower muscle creatine stores. When taking daily creatine along with resistance training, vegan athletes may achieve greater muscle creatine increases (Kreider et al. 2017), whereas older masters athletes may experience improved bone health, muscle mass, and strength (Candow et al. 2019; Kreider et al. 2017). Supplementation may therefore be particularly useful to these groups.

Creatine Protocols

Traditional creatine supplementation protocols include both a rapid and moderate loading regimen. A rapid loading protocol includes ingesting 20 g of creatine each day for 5 days, split into four 5 g doses. A moderate load is one 5 g dose per day over 1 month (Kreider et al. 2017; Rawson 2018). If a faster loading protocol is desired, two 5 g doses

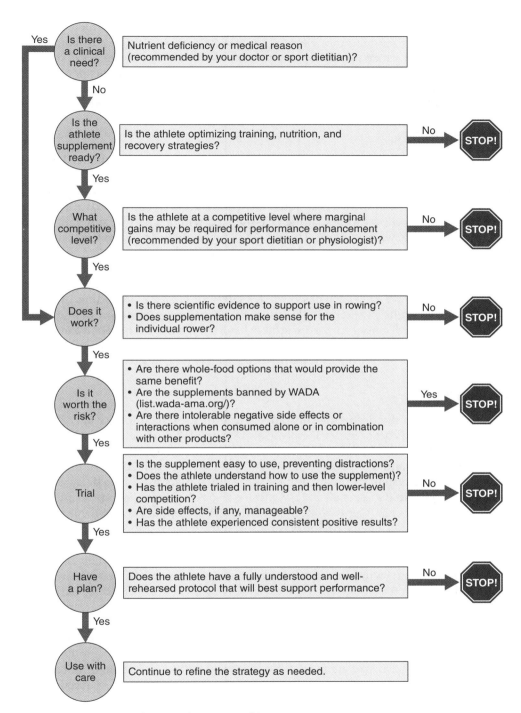

▶ **Figure 29.2** Supplement decision making.

Susan Boegman and Sid Boegman.

per day over 2 weeks is also easy to implement and well liked by most athletes. A daily 3 to 5 g dose will then maintain elevated muscle creatine levels. Once discontinued, creatine stores will return to presupplementation levels over 4 to 6 weeks (Kreider et al. 2017; Rawson 2018). Anecdotally, athletes report a preference for the 5 g per day protocol for ease of use and minimizing the potential "heavy" feeling or occasional bloating that some athletes experience with the rapid loading protocol (author observation).

Considerations

Creatine uptake into muscle tissue is insulin mediated and therefore enhanced by exercise and food intake. To maximize efficacy, it should be taken after exercise in a recovery shake or with a protein- and carbohydrate-based meal (Rawson 2018). Creatine quickly degrades into creatinine once it is in liquid form and should be consumed immediately after mixing. As well, creatine loading is associated with a small weight gain due to increases in muscle water content. This could be problematic for lightweight rowers if used in close proximity to racing and should be timed with this in mind. Adult rowers who decide to trial creatine are encouraged to time supplementation within their yearly training program in order to address specific physical or physiological gaps.

Finally, there have been debates over the safety of creatine, including its role in musculoskeletal injuries and renal dysfunction. Questioning the safety of any potential supplement is essential to ensure athlete health. However, more than 25 years of extensive research and athlete use demonstrate that concerns about creatine safety, particularly over short-term use, remain unfounded (Butts, Jacobs, and Silvis 2018).

Caffeine

Caffeine is a naturally occurring substance found in varying amounts in coffee, tea, guarana leaves, and cocoa (Burke, Desbrow, and Spriet 2013; Guest et al. 2021). Synthetic caffeine is also widely available and may be added to a variety of products, including sport foods, gum, and beverages (Guest et al. 2021; Temple et al. 2017). It functions as a central nervous system stimulant and for some individuals appears to decrease effort perception and pain (Guest et al. 2021). Caffeine also enhances mood, motivation, and focus, delaying fatigue (Guest et al. 2021). Analysis of doping control urine samples collected from 2004 (when caffeine was removed from the World Antidoping List) to 2015 indicates that rowers are among the highest caffeine users at international events (Aguilar-Navarro et al. 2019). And that's not just because rowers love their coffee!

Various 2,000 m rowing ergometer studies have demonstrated a performance benefit anywhere from 0.3% to 2.0% when caffeine is used (Bruce et al. 2000; Carr, Gore, and Dawson 2011), suggesting this may be related to reduced fatigue perception and improved pacing. As well, a recent systematic review of seven ergometer studies of good to excellent methodological quality, comprising 71 participants (46 competitive and 25 recreational rowers) examined the effects of caffeine ingestion on rowing performance. Caffeine dosing was anywhere from 1.3 to 9.0 mg/kg BM. Pooled data indicate that 2,000 m ergometer performances were an average of 4.3 s faster in caffeine trials (Grgic et al. 2020). A second review, which examined prerace strategies in rowers, found that caffeine ingestion at 6 mg/kg BM was the amount most likely to enhance performance (Turnes et al. 2019). Finally, another recent caffeine study in junior elite rowers found that caffeine at 6 mg/kg BM (vs. 3 mg or placebo) before a morning 2,000 m time trial mitigated more of the performance decrements that occurred during a 2,000 m time trial repeated 6 h later (Gharaat, Sheykhlouvand, and Eidi 2020).

In contrast, further research in a variety of sports—including rowing—have shown no improvement (Skinner et al. 2010) or slightly worse performance with caffeine intake (Southward et al. 2018). Although caffeine is likely to benefit performance for some rowers, it is apparent that there are significant differences in individual responses. Essentially, responses are complex and may be related to genetic factors, which are not yet completely understood (Guest et al. 2021; Pickering and Kiely 2018; Southward et al. 2018). Tolerance, ingestion timing, fasted versus fed intake (Christensen et al. 2014), training status, and possibly habituation to regular use may also impact the effect of caffeine on athlete performance (Guest et al., 2021; Pickering and Kiely 2018).

Caffeine Protocols

For healthy adults, moderate caffeine consumption is considered safe, but not without side effects (Guest et al. 2021; Temple et al. 2017). Given the numerous factors that influence caffeine's impact, athletes are recommended to adjust dosing based on responses to individual caffeine trials. Very generally, improvement may occur with as little as 1.3 mg and up to 9 mg of caffeine (not recommended due to likelihood of significant side effects), with the majority of rowing research using 3 to 6 mg/kg BM doses (Grgic et al. 2020). Additionally, caffeine may have a greater benefit earlier in the day, hinting at a temporal effect (Guest et al. 2021). Caffeine typically appears in the bloodstream within 15 min and peaks approximately 60 min after intake, thus the most common ingestion timing during a regatta is during the on-land warm-up. If a performance effect is not apparent, an increased caffeine dose or timing could be trialed. If negative side effects occur—such as restlessness, anxiety during competition, or poor sleep in the recovery period—athletes may wish to decrease their precompetition dose or avoid caffeine completely (Pickering and Kiely 2018), particularly if it interferes with sleep and recovery during a regatta.

Considerations

A final consideration is that caffeine can remain in the bloodstream for hours. Although highly individual, the average half-life (i.e., half of the caffeine remains in the system) is approximately 4 to 6 h (Guest et al. 2021), with a range of approximately 3 to 7 h

Key Point

In its purest form, caffeine is available as an over-the-counter supplement. It is also found in over-the-counter pain medications and many sport foods, gums, gels, and preworkout products. Coffee, tea, cola, and energy drinks also contain caffeine. Although colas, energy drinks, and sport foods will have the caffeine dose on the label and approximate caffeine amounts can be found online for coffee, coffee drinks, and tea, the caffeine content of commercial coffee (Desbrow, Hall, and Irwin 2019) and preworkout products will vary (Desbrow et al. 2019). This variability makes such products unreliable.

Energy drinks are also promoted to enhance mental alertness and physical performance and are one of the most popular dietary supplements consumed by North American teens and young adults. Due to potential heart and blood pressure related health risks associated with cumulative or rapid energy drink intake, these products are not recommended until more research can be undertaken (Wassef et al. 2017).

(Temple et al. 2017). Athletes who use caffeine must take all sources and ingestion timing into account because residual plasma caffeine can have an additive effect on newly ingested sources, increasing the risk of negative side effects. Overall, to prevent negative experiences with caffeine use during competition, athletes are advised to account for all ingested sources, practice and individualize dosing and timing, and then confirm caffeine protocols well in advance of competition.

Buffers

For competitive rowers, supplemental buffering agents may help manage fatigue during racing. Although fatigue is multifactorial, one of the primary reasons for exhaustion during high-intensity events (such as a 2,000 m event) is intramuscular acidosis, or the drop in pH caused by the accumulation of hydrogen ions (Lancha et al. 2015). The human body has many intrinsic mechanisms to buffer hydrogen and manage acidosis, including muscle carnosine and plasma bicarbonate. Augmenting this natural buffering has the potential to improve performance (Hobson et al. 2012; Lancha et al. 2015). Currently, there are two supplements a rower may consider for this purpose: beta-alanine and sodium bicarbonate (Stellingwerff, Maughan, and Burke 2011).

Beta-Alanine

Beta-alanine is a nonessential amino acid that occurs naturally in beef, pork, chicken, and fish. It is the rate-limiting amino acid needed by the body to produce muscle carnosine. Carnosine (beta-alanyl-L-histidine), which is synthesized and stored in muscle tissue, may improve performance through many physiological mechanisms, including calcium regulation, antioxidant, and antiglycation action. However, the most well-known function is its role as a natural intracellular buffer (Saunders, Elliott-Sale, et al. 2017). Acting like a sponge, carnosine accepts hydrogen ions released within contracting muscle during high-intensity exercise (Stellingwerff, Decombaz, et al. 2012). Baseline levels are both relatively stable and individual to each athlete, and rowers with high muscle carnosine appear to have a performance advantage. In fact, a study of nationally ranked Belgian rowers demonstrated that athletes with higher baseline muscle carnosine were faster in an ergometer time trial over 2,000 m than those with lower levels. A significant difference was found between the second and third 500 m splits (Baguet et al. 2010).

Why not simply consume carnosine? In fact, carnosine ingestion has minimal impact on muscle carnosine content. Although carnosine is also found in meat and fish, it is rapidly broken down to beta-alanine and L-histidine once it is absorbed into the bloodstream. The body has adequate L-histidine but limited beta-alanine supply; therefore, the only way to elevate muscle carnosine is to consume beta-alanine. Although a typical omnivorous diet will supply beta-alanine, one would need to consume approximately 800 g of chicken breast each day over 4 or more weeks to reach a level required to impact performance. Thus, beta-alanine supplementation is the most practical strategy to increase intramuscular carnosine.

Beta-alanine supplementation has been shown to improve exercise performance over high-intensity efforts of 30 s to 10 min (Matthews et al. 2019). Currently, pooled athlete data suggests smaller overall performance effect sizes in well-trained subjects (Saunders, Elliott-Sale, et al. 2017). A typical 2,000 m race is both under 10 min and maximally stresses the anaerobic energy systems, causing the accumulation of hydrogen ions. Competitive rowers may therefore benefit from beta-alanine supplementation. For example, the study on Belgian rowers also demonstrated that chronic supplemental beta-alanine elevated muscle carnosine content by 45%, with a range of 5% to 71%. Although the results did not reach significance, the athletes with the highest carnosine levels after 7 weeks of daily beta-alanine intake raced a 2,000 m ergometer time trial approximately 4.3 s faster (Baguet et al. 2010).

Beta-Alanine Protocols Optimal supplementation strategies are not yet fully understood, as the total amount of supplemental beta-alanine does not seem to impact efficacy (Saunders, Salles Painelli, et al. 2017). The most common beta-alanine ingestion protocols that demonstrated enhanced performance include 65 mg/kg BM (or 3.2-6.4 g) split into 1.6 g doses taken over the day over 4 or more weeks. Increases appear dose dependent, with larger doses decreasing the time required to elevate muscle carnosine content. Although evidence suggests it may take an average of 18 to 24 weeks to reach maximum levels (Saunders, Salles Painelli, et al. 2017), the greatest increases occur within the first 4 weeks (Matthews et al. 2019; Perim et al. 2019). Performance data from studies of larger beta-alanine doses is minimal, and to date, the resultant higher muscle carnosine has not been correlated with improved outcomes.

Considerations The harmless but uncomfortable side effect of paresthesia (a prickling or tingling sensation on the skin) (Perim et al. 2019) can be minimized by using a slow-release product or taking a powdered rapid-release version with a meal. Taking beta-alanine with food also significantly enhances carnosine loading efficiency and retention compared with beta-alanine taken between meals (Stegen et al. 2013). Washout rate from muscle tissue is linear—approximately 2% per week (Stellingwerff, Anwander, et al. 2012) or approximately 12-16 weeks for total washout with individual differences noted (Yamaguchi et al. 2021). Washout begins as soon as supplementation ceases; however, due to the relatively slow rate, 1.6 g per day should be sufficient if longer term maintenance is desired (Stellingwerff, Anwander, et al. 2012).

Because elevated carnosine is meant to enhance high-intensity endurance performance, adult elite athletes may consider starting supplemental beta-alanine 4 or more weeks before key competitions or periods where high-intensity training is the priority (Percival 2015). Finally, athletes should be aware that injury or overreaching are possible given the loading protocol length and the potential that supplementation may enhance sprint-interval training.

Sodium Bicarbonate

Bicarbonate, naturally present in the bloodstream, helps regulate blood pH (Hadzic, Eckstein, and Schugardt 2019). Oral ingestion of sodium bicarbonate ($NaHCO_3$)—or baking soda—will elevate plasma bicarbonate (HCO_3^-) levels (Boegman et al. 2020). This will increase blood buffering capacity and indirectly decrease the intramuscular acidity that leads to fatigue during high-intensity exercise (Lancha et al. 2015; Siegler et al. 2016). Performance benefits with $NaHCO_3$ supplementation are seen in repeat sprints (Percival et al. 2015) and high-intensity efforts of approximately 1 to 12 min (Grgic et al. 2021).

Although a meta-analysis on 2,000 m rowing outcomes post-$NaHCO_3$ supplementation estimated a 1.4% performance improvement (Turnes et al. 2019), rowing-specific research is not clear-cut (Carr et al. 2012; Carr, Gore, and Dawson 2011), possibly as a result of negative side effects (Carr, Gore, and Dawson 2011). A potential example of this involves a study on trained nonelite rowers. This research demonstrated a "very likely" beneficial effect of $NaHCO_3$ ingestion on the final 500 m of a 2,000 m rowing ergometer test when compared with placebo. For reasons unspecified, however, 7 of 20 participants were slower during the $NaHCO_3$ trial (Hobson et al. 2014). Evidence gathered during other sport-specific studies suggests these slower results could be related to side effects (Grgic et al. 2021).

Sodium Bicarbonate Protocols   Negative gastrointestinal side effects—such as bloating, nausea, vomiting, and diarrhea—are common with sodium bicarbonate supplementation (Carr et al. 2011; Grgic et al. 2021) and typically occur when ingestion protocols are mismanaged and when off-the-shelf baking soda is used. Supplementation usually involves acute doses of 0.2 to 0.4 g/kg BM of pharmaceutical grade $NaHCO_3$ taken approximately 60 to 180 min before competition (Grgic et al. 2021; Peeling et al. 2018). The optimal dose appears to be 0.3 g/kg BM (Grgic et al. 2021) and is the most common dosing strategy used in rowing. To improve the possibility of achieving a performance benefit, side effects must be minimized with a well-rehearsed protocol. For example, athletes are advised to have a small amount of food in the stomach before starting $NaHCO_3$ intake (author observation). Capsules are preferred over powder to allow for greater dosing control, to increase the likelihood the capsules dissolve in the intestine rather than the stomach, and because $NaHCO_3$ dissolved in liquid is extremely unpalatable. The pills should be coingested with approximately 7 to 10 mL fluid/kg BM to help minimize diarrhea and 1 to 1.5 g/kg BM of well-tolerated carbohydrates to further minimize GI distress and help maintain buffering. The capsules should be consumed over approximately 30 min (Boegman et al. 2020; Carr et al. 2011); however, athlete tolerance is individual.

Considerations   Beyond minimizing negative side effects, ingestion timing may also impact performance. An average 2 s performance benefit was seen in elite rowers when a 2,000 m ergometer time trial was timed to start at an athlete's HCO_3^- peak (Boegman et al. 2020). Specialized equipment is required to determine HCO_3^- peak and will likely be inaccessible to most athletes. Fortunately, athletes may have a post-ingestion time window where HCO_3^- levels are sufficiently elevated to enhance buffering during high-intensity events. Such a window would allow an athlete with a sensitive stomach to start taking $NaHCO_3$ further out from competition start time, even aiming for 2 to 4 h prior. Anecdotal experiences suggest that athletes need to practice multiple times before deciding whether to use $NaHCO_3$—in part to allow the body to adapt to the $NaHCO_3$, and also to determine an individualized ingestion protocol and an on-water pacing strategy (author observation).

Key Point

Theoretically, acute sodium bicarbonate supplementation layered over a beta-alanine loading protocol may confer an additive effect. This is because beta-alanine increases intracellular buffering, and sodium bicarbonate facilitates extracellular buffering. Both are distinct mechanisms that simultaneously regulate metabolic acidosis. Current evidence suggests that cosupplementation may elicit a small performance improvement beyond either supplement taken in isolation (Lancha et al. 2015), and a study in well-trained rowers showed a possibly beneficial effect (Hobson et al. 2013). As with most supplement research, evidence for a performance benefit is mixed. Not all studies demonstrate an additive benefit to beta-alanine and sodium bicarbonate despite the potential mechanistic rationale (Gilsanz et al. 2021). Side effects appear no different than when these products are taken as individual protocols (Lancha et al. 2015). Thus, adult athletes who have maximized other areas of performance preparation may wish to consider a cotrial of both products.

Because of the high sodium content of $NaHCO_3$, weight gain related to coingested fluid intake will occur (Boegman et al. 2020) and may be problematic for lightweight competitors. Additionally, repeat use over a regatta may exacerbate side effects and must be considered. Given the potential for negative side effects, interested athletes should establish an individualized $NaHCO_3$ supplementation strategy, including dosage, intake timing, and well-tolerated food and fluids. Finally, the increased risk of GI issues during high-stress competition environments necessitate that $NaHCO_3$ should be well rehearsed in training and low-level competition before implementing at a high-level event (Boegman et al. 2020; Hobson et al. 2014).

Nitrates

Nitrates are nitrogen- and oxygen-containing compounds that naturally form in the human body when the amino acid arginine is oxidized to generate nitric oxide (NO). Also found in many foods and a few supplements, nitrates may enhance both health and athletic performance. Beetroot, rhubarb, celery, and leafy greens (such as arugula, chard, and spinach) are the richest natural dietary sources of inorganic nitrates (Bond, Morton, and Braakhuis 2012; Hoon et al. 2014), with approximately 250 mg (4 mmol) of nitrate per 100 g of fresh produce. Once consumed, dietary nitrates are converted into nitrites by salivary bacteria, swallowed, and then either reduced to NO in the stomach or absorbed into the bloodstream where they are further reduced to NO in muscle tissue during exercise (Hoon et al. 2014; Wylie et al. 2013).

Notably, NO is an important signaling molecule involved in vasodilation and blood flow. It also facilitates skeletal muscle glucose uptake, skeletal muscle contraction, and neurotransmission (Bailey et al. 2012; Jones et al. 2018). Consequently, increasing endogenous NO may decrease the oxygen cost of exercise and enhance exercise performance during the sustained, whole-body, high-intensity efforts typical of a 2,000 m ergometer time trial or on-water race (Hoon et al. 2014; Wylie et al. 2013). It may also improve cardiovascular health (Jones et al. 2021).

Nitrate supplementation in rowing has been achieved with regular or concentrated beetroot juice, a safe, convenient, and easily accessible nitrate-rich product. A limited level of support exists for beetroot use in rowing. A 2012 study in trained junior rowers found that supplementation appeared to improve the final three (of six) supramaximal 500 m rowing efforts (Bond, Morton, and Braakhuis 2012), and a 2014 study found possibly beneficial performance effects in well-trained senior rowers when beetroot juice was consumed before a 2,000 m ergometer time trial (Hoon et al. 2014). Although these results are interesting, study numbers are small. Ongoing investigation is needed, particularly because research has also identified individuals who respond very well to nitrate supplementation (Jones et al. 2018; Jonvik et al. 2015). This is possibly related—at least partially—to the specific oral ecosystem (mouth bacteria) and primary muscle fiber type of these individuals (Jones et al. 2018; Jones et al. 2021). As well, newer research demonstrates potential performance benefits when oxygen demand exceeds supply (Jones et al. 2018), a likely occurrence during the very high-intensity start and finish of a 2,000 m event.

Nitrate Protocols

Plasma nitrite concentrations peak approximately 2.5 h after nitrate intake. Therefore, concentrated beetroot juice (the most practical strategy) should be consumed several hours prior to competition and nitrate-rich vegetables at least 3 h before (Jones et al.

2021). Aerobic fitness levels also influence the impact of dietary nitrate intake. Highly trained athletes ($\dot{V}O_2$max greater than 65 mL/kg/min) may have greater baseline plasma nitrate and nitrite levels and therefore either experience minimal to no performance benefits (Jonvik et al. 2015) or require a higher nitrate dose (Hoon et al. 2014).

To date, the most effective supplementation protocol for highly trained rowers used a 8.4 mmol (~500 mg) nitrate dose (Hoon et al. 2014). Other nonrowing research suggests doses above 300 mg (~5 mmol) (Jones et al. 2021). Both chronic (3-15 days) and single doses prior to exercise may improve performance (Jones et al. 2018). These recommended doses can be obtained through a focused nitrate-rich vegetable intake, beet juice, or concentrated rhubarb juice; however, most research has utilized beetroot juice concentrate. Note that concentrated beetroot can cause negative GI effects and antibacterial mouthwashes reduce the bacteria available for nitrate conversion. Athletes should avoid these mouthwashes if they wish to maximize plasma NO and its potential health and physiological effects.

A Food-First Approach

Even though the overall performance benefits of nitrate supplementation is unclear (Jones et al. 2018), a diet high in nitrate-rich vegetables has additional health benefits, including blood pressure reduction (Bailey et al. 2012; Kerley 2017) and improved antioxidant defenses (Menezes et al. 2019). Although dietary nitrates may potentially be harmful under certain circumstances, this is currently under debate and not the case when consumed in the form of antioxidant-rich vegetables and fruits. In fact, the body extracts dietary nitrates from these foods for storage in muscle tissue. This NO reservoir is essential to human health and physical exercise performance (Jones et al. 2021). As such, rowers at all levels are encouraged to consume a diet abundant in leafy greens, beetroot, and other nitrate-rich vegetables.

Interpreting Data: A Word of Caution

One cannot predict an individual athlete's response to supplementation based on cited research findings. Many factors, including the athlete's predominant muscle fiber type, fitness level, and usual eating patterns will impact individual responses and therefore the applicability of the research (Maughan et al. 2018). As well, not all research has been done on rowers. Where it has, all cited, rowing-specific research was undertaken on ergometers. Thus, even though the supplements reviewed are potentially relevant, ergometer performance is correlated to on-water performances in the small boats only (Mikulić, Smoljanović, Bojanić, Hannafin, and Matković 2009; Mikulić, Smoljanović, Bojanić, Hannafin, and Pediić 2009). One must therefore be wary of extrapolating ergometer data to all boat classes and race situations.

Additional considerations include blinding and placebo effect. Not all studies discussed employed questionnaires asking subjects to guess if they were in a placebo or supplement group. Correct supplement identification may positively impact performance, whereas correct placebo identification may negatively affect performance, impacting study outcomes (Saunders et al. 2016). Finally, consider that the magnitude of effect for both ergogenic aids and placebo is approximately 1% to 3%, with ingestion of two placebo pills providing a better result than one (Halson and Martin 2013). As such, performance-based research interpretation can be challenging.

Lastly, athletes may attempt to use more than one product over the course of a regatta. Unfortunately, in most cases research has not assessed multisupplement use.

Understanding the overall impact and potential interactions across a multiday event is crucial to prevent unforeseen negative side effects.

Key Point

This chapter only discusses IOC-supported supplements with evidence and relevance to the health and performance of rowers (Maughan et al. 2018). Some products popular in the athlete community, such as branched-chain amino acids (BCAAs), were deliberately left out due to disappointing research and the easy access to dietary BCAAs found in real food or supplemental protein options. However, nutrition research is continually evolving. Over the coming years, a little-known supplement may become backed by enough research to recommend its use for either health or performance. Some products not discussed in this chapter with emerging evidence for use in specific circumstances include tart cherry (for anti-inflammatory effects or management of delayed onset muscle soreness), omega-3 fatty acids (for brain health, anti-inflammatory effects, and to reduce physiological strain), and collagen (to manage injury). Although these products appear to be low risk and hold some promise of efficacy, more evidence is needed before they are universally recommended. Ultimately, the reader is encouraged to keep abreast of emerging research. Look for evidence from double-blind, randomized, crossover trials in which study participants received both treatment and placebo. The research should include rowers or similar athletes, conditions that mimic real-world supplement use, manageable ingestion protocols that would be likely to elicit an effect, performance protocols that make sense for rowing (time trial versus time to exhaustion), and appropriate statistical analysis and interpretation of results (Maughan et al. 2018). This is a considerable list, therefore readers are encouraged to consult field experts, including sport dietitians, physiologists, and sport medical practitioners, as applicable.

Conclusion

The desire for health benefits and the pressure to maximize performance may lead athletes to focus on supplements while mismanaging the foundations of a high-quality diet, adequate energy intake, sufficient fluids, and overall recovery practices. Supplements can be expensive, cause negative side effects, and be a distraction—particularly when an athlete has not maximized their training potential. Athletes are encouraged to remember that that a well-planned fueling strategy *will* impact each training session. In contrast, the potential of an unnecessary health or performance supplement is often unclear.

It is also important to consider that successful rowers require highly developed aerobic and anaerobic systems, as well as a significant level of strength and power. Given the demanding nature of rowing training loads, and the complexity of an individual's response to training and nutrition interventions, individualized performance supplement planning may be required. It can be assumed that research-informed, aggressive nutrition strategies are necessary to support the health and performance of open- and lightweight rowers. For many athletes, regardless of training level, health supplements will also be a part of the nutrition intervention. This foundation will assist in illness and injury prevention, as well as maximizing adaptation and recovery. For the high-level athlete, supplements known to enhance the energy systems that impact rowing performance should be thoughtfully considered for strategic use within both the daily training environment and competition settings. Although such interventions are exciting, the majority of rowers are discouraged from using performance supplements given the small effect sizes and potential side effects when protocols are poorly understood or executed. All athletes are encouraged to focus on prioritizing high-quality training, fueling, and recovery to maintain long-term health and performance.

Psychology
of Rowing

Motivation and Psychological Skills for Optimal Performance

Penny Werthner, PhD

Competing in sport at any level, whether at a national championships, World Championships, or Olympic Games, is challenging, and working toward the goal of winning or setting a personal best is even more difficult. An athlete or crew must work together with their coach to get everything right on a specific day and time, after many long hours on the water and in the gym. The pressure and expectations can be enormous. So, how can we ensure a best performance under such stressful and challenging conditions? First, with excellent physical and technical training; second, by implementing strategies to stay healthy, sleep well, and eat well; and third, by ensuring athletes are psychologically ready for both training and competition.

The purpose of this chapter is to discuss this third element—psychological readiness for training and competition—from two perspectives: first, by creating an environment that ensures a mentally and physically healthy career in sport, and second, by learning the critical psychological skills that must be developed to achieve an optimal performance at all levels of competitive sport. In order to ground our discussion of psychological skill development for optimal performance, we will begin with a brief exploration of the constructs of human motivation, psychological resilience, and growth mindset, and then discuss the specific psychological skills that, when well learned, will ensure best performances on a consistent basis.

Motivation

Human motivation is a topic that has been well researched in the literature. Within the sport literature we are often looking to understand what motivates young individuals to participate and continue in sport—or their reasons for getting discouraged and dropping out. Motivation, as a psychological construct, remains relevant for any level of competitive sport, but particularly at the current moment, because the COVID-19 global pandemic resulted in the cancelation and postponement of many competitions, which, in turn, very much altered the training plans of athletes, coaches, teams, and sport organizations.

Key Point

We understand motivation as the process that initiates, guides, and maintains goal- oriented behaviors, which can involve social, emotional, physiological, and cognitive aspects.

For example, an athlete may be motivated to work hard to make a national team with the help and support of their coach and parents.

Motivation and Self

Early research by Deci and Ryan (1985; 2008) and Roberts (2001) highlights some of the key aspects of how we understand motivation. One theory, Deci and Ryan's theory of self-determination, addresses the notion of extrinsic and intrinsic motivation as well as delineates three core needs that facilitate self-determined growth: a sense of autonomy, competence, and relatedness. *Autonomy* refers to the need of individuals to feel they have choices in their lives, *competence* refers to the need to learn and gain mastery, and *relatedness* refers to the need of an individual to feel a sense of belonging.

Key Point

You can develop autonomy, competence, and relatedness in your own athletes with the following tips:

- Encourage them to design a workout and debrief on its effectiveness (autonomy).
- Ensure they are asking questions and listening in order to understand technique as they become more technically skilled (competence).
- Create regular social occasions such as pizza or game night so the team can get to know each other outside of training (relatedness).

Another theory of motivation, achievement goal theory, has been researched by Roberts (2001), who wrote of two possible orientations that might be held by an individual—task and ego. *Task orientation* refers to a focus on mastery and *ego orientation* refers to a focus on one's performance primarily as it relates to that of others. Much of the early research encouraged an emphasis on a task orientation, through which one is more intrinsically motivated and focused on the mastery of, for example, rowing technically well. Over the years, our understanding of motivation has built on these concepts and become a bit more nuanced, as some research has shown that many successful athletes show both task and ego orientation and utilize what works well depending on the environment (Roberts, Treasure, and Kavussanu 1996).What this means is that many successful Olympic-level athletes have learned how to manage and motivate themselves both intrinsically ("let's see how strong and fast I can be") and extrinsically ("let's win the race," "let's be the best on the national team"). But to be clear, this is learned behavior over many years!

Key Point

You can grow motivation in young athletes with the following tips:

- Create an environment in which you individualize training whenever possible and provide regular feedback to each athlete on both what they are doing well and what needs correction.

- Encourage each athlete to focus primarily on their own boat skills or their crew, what their job in the boat is, and how to improve themselves technically. This keeps the focus and motivation on individual improvement.

- Understand that athletes will always compare themselves to their teammates— it is inevitable in competitive sport—but know that for most athletes, that comparison often leads to too much stress. Your job as a coach, certainly with young athletes, is to highlight personal improvement; that is what will keep your athletes loving their sport.

Resilience

More recently, Dweck (2006) and Duckworth (2016) have written about the mindset of success and the concept of grit, respectively. Dweck's *growth vs fixed mindset* comes from extensive research on how mindsets influence motivation and success in life. Her argument is that a mindset is simply a belief, and those individuals with a growth mindset believe they have choices and that they have an ability to learn and change. Angela Duckworth's work on the concept of *grit* defines grit as passion and sustained persistence, regardless of potential rewards. She writes of characteristics such as courage, conscientiousness, perseverance, resilience, and passion.

Key Point

The ability to develop and grow from adversity is truly exciting. Development occurs in our sport systems when athletes are encouraged to question, to struggle, to learn, and to train the key psychological skills necessary to develop a mindset that sees adversity as a challenge.

One final concept to consider is *psychological resilience*, defined as the ability to adapt positively in the face of stress and adversity. In sport it means that an athlete has a level of self-confidence and optimism that helps them persevere in the face of the ever-present stress of high-performance competition. The research on psychological resilience is extensive and has evolved from thinking of resilience as a trait—and therefore mostly unchangeable—to a group of characteristics that can be nurtured (Fletcher and Sarkar 2012; Fletcher and Sarkar 2013; Galli and Vealey 2008; Sarkar and Fletcher 2014). As of late, this includes an acknowledgement that social support plays a role in how one develops resilience (Ungar, Ghazinour, and Richter 2013).

Fletcher and Sarkar (2012) have done extensive research on resilience in the world of sport and note that competitive sport, by its very nature, is full of stress and adversity.

Athletes at all levels of competitive sport are exposed to a number of unique stressors, such as injuries, qualification processes, selection to teams, wins and losses, financial concerns, and coaching issues. These authors and others argue that the development of resilience in athletes will lead to improved sport performance. Fletcher and Sarkar (2016) developed a resilience training program for individuals performing in high-pressure domains that included individual evaluation of the stressor as a growth opportunity and the knowledge and practice of optimism, proactiveness, and intrinsic motivation. The authors also propose that an environment high in both challenge and support facilitates the development of resilience.

Developing Motivational Tools

What is critical, and at the same time exciting, about a discussion of motivation and resilience in sport is that the core needs of self-determination theory, orientation to goals and how we set and assess them, and psychological resilience can all be developed. Dweck, Duckworth, and Fletcher and Sarkar strongly emphasize this possibility of developing a challenge or growth mindset. Athletes are capable, as human beings, of altering beliefs and learning skills that will help them persevere and grow as they face the stresses of high-performance competition. This ability to develop and grow from adversity is truly exciting. However, what is needed to ensure that development occurs is for coaches and sport systems to foster an environment that encourages athletes to question, to struggle, to learn, and to train the key psychological skills necessary to develop a mindset that sees adversity as a challenge. This ensures both a healthy, competitive sport environment and great sport performances.

There has been extensive research in the field of sport psychology on the critical skills that ensure optimal performance. In 2007, Jones, Hanton, and Connaughton interviewed eight Olympic athletes, three coaches, and four sport psychologists to try to understand the attributes of an Olympic or world champion. Although this was a small study, the attributes identified fit well into what we know anecdotally is required to excel in Olympic-level sport. The attributes were categorized into four dimensions: *attitude* or *mindset*, which includes a belief in oneself and a clear focus; *training*, which includes goals as motivation, controlling the environment, and pushing hard; *competition*, which again included belief in oneself, focus, and controlling the environment as well as regulation, handling pressure, and awareness of thoughts and feelings; and finally *postcompetition*, which consists of handling both failure and success. These findings solidified the authors' definition of mental toughness as "having the natural or developed psychological edge that enables you to, generally, cope better than your opponents with the many demands (competition, training, lifestyle) that sport places on a performer and, specifically, be more consistent and better than your opponents in remaining determined, focused, confident, and in control under pressure" (247).

As the authors note, it is also critical to recognize that mental toughness may fluctuate throughout an athlete's competitive career and that all athletes must continually work on the various skills and attributes that make up the framework of mental toughness.

A more recent metastudy by Anthony, Gucciardi, and Gordon (2016) on the construct of mental toughness highlighted the need to expand our thinking to include a better understanding of how an athlete and their environment interact, how an athlete must proactively work to develop the attributes of mental toughness, how the environment (including coaches and teammates) may foster or hinder the development of these attributes, and how an athlete's mental toughness may indeed fluctuate over time due to adversity.

Psychological Skills for High Performance

Having now explored human motivation, psychological resilience, and mental tough-ness, let's look at the critical psychological skills that help athletes and coaches effec-tively manage the inherent stress of high-performance competition.

There are four key psychological skills, with a number of others that fit nicely within these four key skills:

1. The ability to develop a deep level of self-awareness of one's thoughts and emo-tions (what works in the stress of competition and what does not work)
2. The ability to focus on the correct cues at the correct time
3. The ability to physiologically, psychologically, and emotionally self-regulate
4. The ability to regularly reflect on and analyze training and competition results

The other skills that must be developed and fit within these four key skills are the following:

1. Designing training and racing plans
2. Setting effective long- and short-term goals
3. Using visualization
4. Effectively managing negative distractions

Developing Self-Awareness

The first step for an athlete to become psychologically well prepared for both training and competition is developing the ability to become deeply self-aware. The skill of coming to know who you are, what motivates you, what you love about your sport, what stresses you about competition, and what you need to work on technically, physi-cally, and psychologically is developed through regular reflection, both on your own and with your coach. Coaches should understand that although technical expertise is critical, they must also develop a strong working relationship with each athlete that includes providing critical feedback, setting appropriate challenges, and caring about the athlete as a human being. When such a relationship exists and this process of regular reflection is done well, self-awareness is built. This is the first step in ensuring consistently good performances at all levels of competition.

Developing the Ability to Focus

The skill of focus, sometimes called *concentration*, is one of the more important psy-chological skills. Moran (2004) states that "concentration refers to a person's ability to exert deliberate mental effort on what is most important in any given situation" (103). The state of full focus or selective attention allows us to be totally absorbed in what we have chosen to do. This is a skill that many do not fully understand. On one level, it is so simple—to just *be* in the moment, to choose to focus on one thing and ignore everything else. But this is often hard to do, especially with so many potential distractions in the world we live in. Yet this is what competitive sport demands for optimal performance.

When we ask athletes about what they were thinking and feeling in their best races, they often reply "I was not really thinking anything." This is not surprising. But what

Key Point

Critical psychological skills for high-performance athletes include the following:

- The ability to develop self-awareness
- The ability to focus effectively
- The ability to physiologically, psychologically, and emotionally self-regulate
- The ability to regularly reflect on and analyze training and competition
- The ability to design, evaluate, and adjust plans for training and racing
- The ability to set effective long- and short-term goals
- The ability to effectively visualize
- The ability to effectively manage negative distractions and fears

they really mean is that they were so absorbed in the execution of their race that there was no time for other thoughts. Csikszentmihalyi (2008) describes this state as *flow*. But how do we achieve that state consistently, particularly when the environment of high-performance sport is inherently stressful?

In terms of how much "thinking" is appropriate for an effective full focus, we need to understand how sport skills are learned. Fitts and Posner's (1967) human performance theory suggests that athletes are able to execute a performance in an effortless and automatic way once they have progressed in learning the motor skills. Hatfield and Kerick (2007) developed the psychomotor efficiency theory, which illuminates the processes that occur in an athlete's brain when performing. For example, when young novice athletes are learning a new skill, they must attend consciously and carefully and are rather inefficient in their physical movements—consider when you were learning to drive a car or ride a bike. With practice, less thinking about the step-to step components is required. Therefore, when an athlete becomes an expert in their sport, they process less, and the movement requires less attentional capacity.

Although optimal performance and a state of flow are what athletes strive for in racing, these elements are "often elusive, present themselves on rare occasions, and tend to be ephemeral" (Bortoli et al. 2012, 694). And because of this, athletes can underperform, or choke. Sian Beilock (2010) defines choking as occurring when we think too much about activities that are usually automatic—or conversely, think too little and do not devote enough attention to an activity. To be clear, when we use the term *choking*, we mean to perform "worse than expected given what you are capable of doing, and worse than what you have done before in the past" (6).

So how do we find that right combination of "correct thinking" about the "correct task"? It requires an understanding of the demands of the event and what fits for the individual athlete. It requires a plan for what to think about during a competition and a regular debrief after each competition to begin to solidify what works for this athlete. For example, rowing is highly technical, so starting with a focus on technical aspects of moving the boat smoothly through the water is an effective focus. Making a plan for what the athlete's technical cues will be and then having a conversation after training and competition allows a coach and athlete to begin to refine what works. It will most likely be a learning process over the course of a season. And, as you can start to see, this process fits closely with enabling an athlete to develop a deep sense of self-awareness of what works for them and what does not, facilitated by regular coaching conversations and feedback.

This discussion of what an effective full focus is—and what it is not—leads us to discuss the other components of psychological skills training that will ensure athletes can consistently find and sustain a full focus, and perhaps a flow state, in training and competition.

Effectively Managing Negative Distractions

In competitive sport, there are many distractions that can take an athlete away from their best full focus on race day. In rowing, there might be external distractions such as weather conditions that result in delays, wind that can create advantageous lanes, or changes in competition schedules.

There can also be negative thoughts that can distract from an effective focus. These distractions can be related to expectations, the need to make a final, the need to show the coaches that you are good enough for a crew boat, the need to qualify a boat for the Olympic Games, and fears that one might not be able to accomplish what one has trained and planned for over many years of hard training.

As an athlete, it is critical not to deny the reality of the wind or the fear of not being good enough. You want to acknowledge and accept the distractions, nerves, anxiety, and weather conditions, and then—critically—shift to recommitting to what *can* be done. Although it is easy to say, it is sometimes so very hard to do—and certainly much more difficult when the stakes are high and perhaps a place on a national team or an Olympic medal is on the line.

One way to prepare for any and all of these negative distractions is for an athlete and coach to work together to create a "what if" list—a list of all the possible distractions that might occur and then, equally important, a list of the solutions. It is important that each athlete understands they always have a *choice* in how they react to adversity. It is possible to train the mind to do this using the psychological skills of mental toughness, resiliency, and growth mindset: "I will rise above the wind, my fears, my doubts." Learning to effectively focus and refocus on the correct cues in the face of distractions and adversity is both possible and necessary for a best performance.

Setting Effective Goals

Creating a clear purpose or goal for *why and how* one wants to compete in high-performance sport is another psychological skill that is in many ways closely related to the skill of focus. When an athlete and coach create a goal, it provides an athlete with something very clear to focus on.

The research outlines three types of objective goals that an athlete can work with: outcome goals, performance goals, and process goals. An *outcome goal* emphasizes a focus on results (e.g., winning a race) and is most certainly dependent on other factors. A *performance goal* emphasizes achieving a standard based on the athlete's previous performance (e.g., to decrease 2,000 m time). A *process goal* emphasizes specific actions an athlete will engage in to execute or perform well (e.g., powerful catch, relaxed shoulders) as well as strategies (e.g., increase the number of training sessions per week, increase speed for certain training sessions).

All three types of goals are important and can be incredibly motivating at different times of the season. During the off-season, the big, long-term outcome goals of making the regional or national team, making a specific crew boat, or winning an

Olympic medal can motivate an athlete to train on those cold and dark winter days. But unfortunately, those goals more often than not become huge stressors on competition day—primarily because an athlete does not, in fact, have much control over the actual final result. What is best in the competitive season is to ground one's focus on process goals. For most athletes, this means that the best choice is to focus on their personal objective ("I will focus on the exact start sequence and hit the stroke rates that were best in training" "I will make it feel light at the 250 m mark" "I will find my race pace stroke rate with smooth movements"). How will you go about executing that fast and powerful race? Go back to those key cues that enable an athlete to be in the moment, in the race, and nowhere else, with confidence, strength, and power.

Visualization

Visualization is a final psychological skill that is critical for an athlete to practice. An athlete can visualize from an internal perspective (actually in one's boat executing the race) or an external perspective (where an athlete "watches" themselves executing a skill or a race, as if watching a video). There continues to be discussion in the research literature, but no definitive conclusions exist on which perspective is more effective. What is most important is that athletes understand this skill is closely linked to the skill of focus and their race plans—developing an ability to "see" and "feel" correct execution of skills, their role in a crew boat, and their plan for racing. Athletes and coaches can also plan and visualize how they want to feel in the boathouse prior to training and racing—happy to be there, relaxed and smiling, ready to provide clear instruction and encouragement, and ready to listen and ask questions for clarification.

Key Point

Visualization creates a sense of control and confidence by having an athlete learn to mentally see or feel how they want the race to unfold.

As the skill of visualization is developed, it can build confidence, enhance motivation, boost skill learning, and complement the actual physical practice of specific technical skills on the water. An athlete can begin by remembering a positive past performance or mentally re-creating a technical skill that they already do well. When the athlete has developed an ability to visualize past events, they can then work on visualizing a future event, such as next week's regional regatta or next month's World Championships: what the venue looks like, how they want to race, what they want to focus on. Most importantly, visualization should always be positive, because this skill is about creating a mental blueprint for optimal performance.

Developing the Ability to Self-Regulate

The third key psychological skill is learning how to regulate one's physiology and mind, and this skill requires finding the right level of intensity demanded by one's sport. We begin the discussion by distinguishing between the concepts of arousal, stress, and anxiety. *Arousal* is a blend of physiological and psychological activity and is not necessarily related to pleasant or unpleasant events. *Stress*, as defined by Selye in 1974, is "the nonspecific response of the body to any demand made upon it," and he emphasized that stress is not just nervous tension and it is not always to be avoided. *Anxiety* is a negative emotional state and has a cognitive component and a somatic component. With those concepts in mind, what does self-regulation mean in the sport of rowing?

Self-regulation for any athlete requires self-awareness (how one responds to the stress of competing and hard training) and awareness of the demands of the sport. Rowing is a technically precise sport, requiring focus and supreme physical effort for 6 to 8 minutes over 2,000 m. This event, whether in a single or a crew boat, requires a calm mind, simply but firmly focused on a plan for racing that enables the athlete to stay on task throughout the event (this plan will be discussed in a later section). Ultimately, managing arousal levels and focus is critical for optimal performance. Too much arousal and an athlete will have increased muscle tension, fatigue, and movement impairment; too little means an athlete is not effectively focused on the task and not physically prepared for the hard work to come. One tool that has shown to be helpful in enabling athletes to both learn about themselves and effectively manage the stress of training and competition is biofeedback and neurofeedback.

Biofeedback and neurofeedback training enable athletes to learn to self-regulate on multiple levels (psychologically, emotionally, and physiologically). The training involves developing self-awareness of one's own physiological and neurological activity and is designed to enhance an athlete's ability to create an optimal performance state on demand. The initial training is conducted in a lab setting, where an athlete is noninvasively connected to electrical sensors that enable them to receive information about how their body and mind react to various situations.

Specifically, biofeedback training focuses on the autonomic nervous system, which consists of the sympathetic nervous system, which activates the body's stress response (fight or flight) and the parasympathetic nervous system, which deactivates the stress response and activates the relaxation response (rest and regeneration). Biofeedback training allows an athlete to experience how they react physiologically to stress and then, most importantly, develop the skills necessary to shift to a recovery state at will.

Specifically, the modalities trained in biofeedback are muscle or electromyograph (EMG), skin conductance or electrodermal activity (EDA), respiration, heart rate and heart rate variability (HRV), and peripheral body temperature. The athlete first learns what each modality looks like, then trains the ability to shift that state as desired. For example, muscle feedback training enables an athlete to become aware of how they hold tension in the muscles under stress, then train those muscles to relax and release that tension—not dissimilar to progressive muscle relaxation but arguably more effective because visual feedback is provided on a computer screen. Skin conductance training allows an athlete to practice decreasing their arousal level when feeling anxious or overly stressed or to increase arousal or activation levels if feeling "flat" before a competition. Heart rate variability biofeedback training (HRVB), perhaps the most crucial modality, allows an athlete to learn how to induce greater parasympathetic nervous system activity and create a relaxation response, both to recover from hard training sessions and to attain the calm yet focused state prior to and during competition. An article by Lehrer and Gevirtz (2014) on HRVB explains this process very clearly.

Moving from the physiological to the neurological, neurofeedback training uses electroencephalography (EEG) feedback to provide information to an athlete about what is occurring in their brain. In the lab, feedback from the screen, which may be both visual and auditory, alerts the athlete to what their brain is doing (concentrating, daydreaming, ruminating, etc.), and they can then learn how to use this information in the sport setting. Goleman (2013), as well as many other researchers, have written about the importance of both a clear full focus and a more open awareness. Neurofeedback teaches the athlete what those two states (focus and recovery) feel like, how to be in each of those states at will, and how to shift in and out of each state depending on what is needed. With training, the athlete learns how to produce the brain waves that are associated with effective focus, staying in the present moment, and remaining calm. This training ensures an athlete is able to self-regulate their mental state, manage distractions, and sustain focus on the task at hand when desired.

This learning in the lab setting must then be transferred to the real world of training and competition. This is accomplished by working with a sport psychology expert who understands biofeedback and neurofeedback training and how to complement it with the psychological skills addressed in this chapter.

Analyzing Training and Competition

The process of regularly reflecting on training and race performances is the fourth key psychological skill and provides an opportunity for learning for both athletes and their coaches. The process of regular reflection and analysis of progress and results creates a learning culture, ensures a rower learns and grows as both a high-performance athlete and an individual, creates an increase in self-awareness and self-responsibility in terms of both training and competing, and greatly improves the possibility for optimal performance. If we think back to the earlier sections on motivation, challenge mindsets, and resilience, we can see how this also creates an environment that fosters a sense of autonomy for an athlete. At the conclusion of any reflection or analysis of a race, an athlete should be clear on what they need to do to continue to progress, where they are at in meeting their goals, and what next steps they need to take for the next phase of training and competing.

Importantly, this process requires time spent analyzing both good and poor training and racing. Athletes and coaches can learn a great deal from both, but often the tendency is to spend time on only aspects that are not going well. This is understandable; certainly coaches are trained to look critically at what needs improvement. But we can also learn a great deal from good performances. If the race was very good, we should consider what tactical, technical, and psychological aspects worked well (and if the race was not as successful as hoped, what needs to be adjusted and worked on). However, poor performances are usually much more difficult to talk about—they are often emotional, and athletes sometimes try to avoid these conversations or are reluctant to admit what may have happened. To ensure the process is effective, we need to recognize that the process of reflection and analysis is about learning, not about blame. A coach needs to be ready to ask questions, listen, and let emotions be expressed, remembering that the purpose is to ultimately enable the athlete to clearly understand the facts of what occurred, learn from any mistakes, let go of the emotions, and begin to create a new plan for the next competition. This work by the coach is analogous to creating what Fletcher and Sarkar (2016) called *the challenge mindset*.

Creating a regular process of reflection and analysis can be both informal and formal. Informally, coaches and athletes are always discussing how a daily training session went; checking in on fatigue, potential injuries, or illnesses; and determining adjustments to training. The more formal process includes planned meetings and analysis from a race weekend and the end-of-year review. Certainly, the end-of-year review should include everyone involved in the training program—the coach, the athlete, and other sport science individuals such as the sport psychology practitioner, exercise physiologist, biomechanist, or nutritionist.

One final comment regarding this process of learning, reflection, and analysis: It takes time to become effective. In the beginning, athletes and sometimes coaches may not know how to deeply self-reflect. Creating a useful and productive process requires a gathering of facts from training or performance and open and caring questions such as "Let's talk about today's race; tell me what you thought" and "Tell me how that second 500 m was. What were you thinking and feeling at that point?" What is most important is creating an environment where the athlete feels safe enough to reflect honestly on what occurred in the race—just know that it takes time.

Designing Training and Racing Plans

In order to focus effectively in training and competition, creating plans is an essential psychological skill. It is well accepted that coaches and athletes create yearly training and competition plans and adjust them according to changes in the competition schedule, weather, progression, injuries, and the like. However, because the high-performance environment is stressful and much is at stake, a plan for the competitive setting and for the actual race is also essential. These plans should be designed and individualized together by coach, athlete, and sport psychology practitioner.

Overall Competition Plan　From a broad perspective, let's look at two examples. First, for a regional regatta, you might want to create an overall plan for the week: what training will be done early in the week, what the taper will look like, what time to arrive at the boathouse for the first day of racing, what snacks to bring, when the warm-up will begin. The second example, for an Olympic Games, includes similar details but encompasses a greater time frame: a plan for the 3 to 4 weeks in a training camp and then in the Olympic Village, when training times will be, and when the taper will begin. Such competition plans at all levels of sport are critical and ensure an athlete and crew boat are organized, sleep and nutrition are managed well, boat rigging is factored into the program, healthy distractions are planned (movies or books, team dinners, time with family), training is well organized, and physiological and psychological recovery are taken into consideration.

Specific Plan for Racing　The primary purpose of a racing plan is to ensure that each athlete knows what cues to pay attention to and has practiced those cues. When the stakes are high, athletes tend to become distracted by negative thoughts and concerns: "What if I don't win regionals and then can't make the national team?" "What if the last 15 years of my life do not get me an Olympic medal?" "What if it hurts so much I can't do it?" "What if my partner is really not fit enough?" "What if I do my best and it is not good enough?" "What will my dad and my coach say if I do not win?" These are legitimate fears and the task is to recognize them, accept them, and then recommit to doing one's best (a cliché for sure)—but the best focus is a clear, well-practiced plan for racing, with specific cues to think about.

To create an effective plan for a race, and for a series of heats, repechage, semifinal, and final, use the following steps:

1. Develop an initial plan using best knowledge from previous races (or years) at the beginning of the season.
2. Practice parts of the plan and various tactics in training to ensure it makes sense for the athlete or crew boat.
3. Commit to execution in the first race of the season.

Evaluating and Adjusting Plans

This process of regularly refining competition and race plans creates an environment where the athletes and coach can systematically reflect on what works for them. Too many cues can be overwhelming and cause overthinking; too few cues increase the potential to be distracted by other competitors, the weather, spectators, and so forth.

The process of evaluating and adjusting throughout the racing season is an ongoing process. The coach, athlete, and sport psychology expert should meet after each race to reflect and analyze what went well and what needs to be improved. The athlete is encouraged to speak first, then the coach adds their observations and expertise. Decisions are then made to adjust the plan for the next competition as needed.

Conclusion

In summary, the continual development of all of these psychological skills, along with the use of biofeedback and neurofeedback when possible, ensures that each rower develops a deep sense of self-awareness, a solid level of self-confidence, and the psychological resilience necessary to effectively cope with the stress and demands of competitive sport. It is important to remember that each season of competition is different from the last, expectations change as an athlete progresses, sometimes time is lost to illness or injury, and just as physical training must continue throughout an athlete's career, so must work on psychological skills. It will always be a process of ongoing learning.

31 CHAPTER

Building an Effective Team Culture in Rowing

Penny Werthner, PhD

We know that great performances in sport often happen when an athlete feels a sense of belonging, a sense of "team." But what exactly is an effective team? Are there different kinds of teams? How do we go about creating an effective team culture? Can you build a sense of team in an individual sport? What is meant by a culture of excellence?

For most of us, when we think about the concept of a team, we think first of team sports, such as basketball, hockey, or soccer. This is not surprising, because to play well in these sports it is necessary for all team members to understand and embrace a common purpose and a common goal. We also know that in order to be successful, it is critical for each member to value being part of the team, work well together, and clearly understand and accept their role on the team.

Conversely, when we think of individual sports, we don't always think of a team, and it is not so easy to build a collective purpose. Yet we can indeed build effective and highly functioning teams in individual sports—and it is critical to do so. A terrific example of this is the Canadian rowing team, particularly in the years 1993 to 1996, during which Canada won the most medals at a world championship, a success that many team members attributed to an excellent "team culture" guided by strong and clear leadership (Nolte, personal communication, November 15, 2020).

When reflecting on how to build a strong team culture in individual sports, we must recognize their differences from team sports. Some sports such as athletics or swimming include multiple athletes in each event, whereas sports such as rowing allow only one individual per event. Importantly, both of these types of individual sports do have "teams" within them—for example, crew boats in rowing and relay teams in athletics and swimming. These sports also involve situations in which individuals might, for example, compete against each other for a place in a crew boat such as men's eight, do not get selected for that boat, but are then selected for the men's four. This can certainly create internal competition and conflict. All these nuances need to be taken into consideration when designing for an optimal team environment.

With those nuances in mind, the purpose of this chapter is to discuss how to build an effective team culture—what some individuals are now calling a *culture of excellence*—within the sport of rowing. When considering how to build an effective team culture, it is critical to do so in a psychologically safe way so that athletes and coaches not only perform optimally but thrive within that inherently competitive environment.

Over the years, there has been a great deal of research conducted on group dynamics and team cohesion, but quite a bit less research on the processes involved in creating and sustaining a high functioning team. We will begin by examining a few definitions of effective team culture, with a brief look at some of the historical and more recent research that underpins our understanding of the concept. We will then articulate the critical components that enable a coach and team members to create and sustain an optimally functioning team.

Definitions

It is useful to first define what we mean by various concepts such as group dynamics, team cohesion, team building, and culture of excellence. *Group dynamics* refers to actions, processes, and changes within and between groups (Forsyth 2010). *Team cohesion* is a well-researched concept defined by Carron, Brawley, and Widmeyer (1998) as a "dynamic process that is reflected in the tendency for a group to stick together and remain united in the pursuit of its instrumental objectives and/or for the satisfaction of member affective needs" (213). The *process of team building* usually refers to a method of helping a group of individuals work together and meet the needs of its members more effectively. These processes involve creating an effective team environment, creating a set of norms (such as roles, leadership, and behaviors), and developing accepted methods of effective, ongoing communication. When discussing how to go about developing a culture of excellence within a team, Fletcher and Arnold (2011) argue that the *creation of a team's culture* is central to building an effective team and involves "generating shared beliefs and expectations within the team via the development of role awareness and a team atmosphere" (235). They also note that it is important for everyone involved in the team to understand their roles, responsibilities, and boundaries and for each individual's contribution to be valued.

Group Development

Many theories explore the critical components of how a group of individuals can become an effective team. An early theory that helps us understand the processes involved in helping a group become a team is Tuckman's theory of group development (Tuckman 1965). He argued that groups and teams develop through different stages, which he called *forming*, *storming*, *norming*, and *performing* (*adjourning* was later added as a fifth stage). Briefly, in the forming stage, team members start to get to know each other, discover what the task is, and generally orient themselves within the group. In the storming stage, there is often conflict as team members work to see where and how they will fit within the team. As the group moves to the norming stage, members begin to accept their roles and positions, norms are discussed and established, and communication is frequent and effective. In the performing stage, team members relate well to each other and the focus is on successful execution of the task; this is ultimately where we want to be prior to major competitions. The adjourning stage is a critical but often neglected component of team functioning, ensuring there is some closure when the task or competitive season ends.

Key Point

Effective teams develop through different stages (Tuckman 1965):

- Forming: Hi, who are you? Where do I fit in? What is the task?
- Storming: I'm not sure I understand or agree. What if I want to be the singles scull?
- Norming: OK, I am happy where I am sitting in the boat. I understand our mission. I feel good about myself and my crewmates.
- Performing: We are here to work well together as a crew. We can win this championship or die trying. I will focus on my job in this seat.
- Adjourning: Whew, we did it. Glad we had that debrief. Now what? Do I go back to school, or do I commit again?

Dynamic Development

It can be argued that Tuckman's theory does hold up rather well, with the exception that the development of a group into an effectively performing team is often not quite so linear. Rather, the process can be dynamic, and teams might revisit a stage depending in large part on the introduction of new team members—for example, when new athletes join a well-functioning team, the team often goes back to storming until everyone again understands their roles and how they will fit within the new team environment. Certainly, when the processes are not in place and there is not effective leadership and communication, many teams do not move beyond the storming stage. Therefore, understanding these stages, the ongoing dynamics within a group, and the need for effective leadership and communication can help both athletes and coaches ensure a relatively smooth movement through the stages into a strong group.

Team Processes

A more applied framework that explicitly addresses team processes was developed by Carron and Spink (1993). The authors identified six team processes relevant to building cohesion and team functioning:

1. Identify team characteristics
2. Establish roles and norms
3. Establish leaders
4. Set goals
5. Cooperate
6. Communicate

These processes provide a framework that a coach and a sport psychology practitioner could utilize to build an effective, optimally functioning team. These processes emphasize the importance of involving all team members in all discussions and steps, the need for ongoing communication, and the critical importance of veteran team members in helping welcome and integrate new members.

Group Dynamics

A third useful theory that helps us understand the dynamics of a group explores personality and communication preferences (Beauchamp, Maclachlan, and Lothian 2005). The authors suggest that when members of a team understand themselves and others on the team (with the help of a sport psychology practitioner as needed), this can enable all members to effectively communicate, adapt, and connect their behaviors as necessary, which results in a better team culture and ultimately better performance. Beauchamp and colleagues suggest exploring the work of Jung (1971) for this process. Briefly, Jung saw individuals as active agents in their own development and theorized that individuals differ in how they see the world, how they make decisions, and how they take in information. He created the notion of four functions or mental processes (thinking, feeling, sensing, and intuition) and two personality attitudes (extroversion and introversion).

Two recent books, writing on an approach to leadership called *social identity* (Haslam, Fransen, and Boen 2020; Haslam, Reicher, and Platow 2020), emphasize the importance of leadership in creating a *we* and *us* rather than an *I* and *me*. Such an approach ensures a shared social identity among members of a team with leadership from both coaches and athletes within the team. These authors also argue that this kind of leadership increases confidence, effort, well-being, and resilience, which, in turn, can positively influence performance outcomes.

Importantly, a related article by Fransen, McEwan, and Sarkar (2020) argues that the construct of psychological safety may be what underpins the relevance of fostering a sense of *we* in order to ensure an effective team. The authors see psychological safety as the belief of an individual that the team is a safe place—for example, to ask questions, seek help, be vulnerable, and ask for feedback. Importantly, the authors also make a subtle but critical distinction between team cohesion, trust, and psychological safety. They argue that team cohesion is about a team that is united in pursuit of a goal, trust is about one's willingness to give another person a safe space, and psychological safety involves one's sense that others will give to them a safe space.

Key Point

Building a cohesive team involves understanding each team member's preferred mental processes and attitudes and what might conflict or complement other team members.

Developing an Optimal Team

With that brief literature review in mind, we turn now to a pathway for creating an effective team that encompasses the notion of both psychological safety and optimal performance. To be clear, this is possible—we can work within a highly competitive environment, create a culture of excellence, and ensure that culture is healthy and safe for all. To illustrate, figure 31.1 proposes a model that illustrates how the major components of that pathway fit together. Clarity of purpose and clear core values are the starting point, with ongoing work on specific skills that are required to build trust, create psychological safety, and ensure self-responsibility, accountability, and ultimately terrific sport performances, individually and as a team.

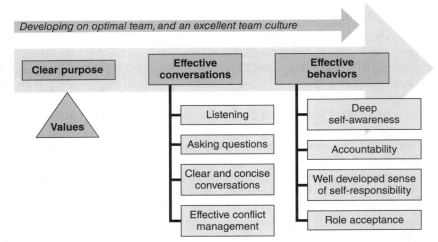

▶ **Figure 31.1** A model for developing an optimal team and an excellent team culture.

Clarity of Purpose and Core Values

It is critical that leaders, coaches, and the directors of competitive sport teams set the standards of thinking and acting that will result in excellent performance results within a healthy environment. The process begins by being clear about the purpose of the team, the values that underpin that purpose, and how and what the team will do.

When we think of establishing a clear purpose, it is about asking *why* we are doing what we are doing. In his book *Start With Why* (2009), Simon Sinek writes that *why* is about inspiring others, about knowing why you get out of bed each day—what is your purpose? We can think about the sport of rowing and reflect: What might that collective purpose be as a rowing team? It might be "we believe we are inspiring the next generation of young rowers," or "we believe in challenging the notion of excellence and going beyond what is thought possible," or "we believe in demonstrating intensity, power, and guts in the sport of rowing." Certainly, these are simply suggestions; what is critical in this first step is that the coach and the sport psychology practitioner facilitate a rich discussion with all the athletes on a team (whether a national, provincial, university, or club team) in creating a clear purpose. Once this is accomplished and everyone feels a part of the purpose, it sets the team up to be inspired by and committed to the collective purpose. A clear purpose will bring a group together as a team and create a strong sense of belonging within an individual sport like rowing.

Closely related to a clear purpose are the core values that underpin a team's beliefs and guide decisions and behaviors. As human beings, we hold many things in life as important, but core values are those that we will not compromise on and that will guide all our crucial decisions. Ultimately, they can be anything we choose, but when we talk about what will guide our team, our organization, and our decisions, these are more often than not values such as integrity, respect, honesty, authenticity, and humility. It is critical that we articulate exactly what we mean by such words. For example, if we want to be guided by integrity, a formal definition is "an uncompromising and predictably consistent commitment to honour moral, ethical, spiritual, and artistic values and principles" (Killinger 2007, 12). More simply, this can mean consistently doing what we say we will do and reliably doing the right thing. Again, what is critical is that the whole team engages in a discussion and final decisions about what values will guide the team. This is the team's choice. As Posner (2010) states, "Values provide the foundation for the purpose and goals of an enterprise. They silently give direction to the hundreds of decisions made at all levels of the organization every day. They are at the heart of the culture of an organization" (536).

We can also look at valuing as a process—for coaches to think about how they engage with the team and each athlete; how they talk about clear purpose with each part of the team; how they make difficult decisions with respect, fairness, and transparency; and how they listen and talk. Clear values, when clearly stated and consistently acted on, will positively influence the culture of any organization. As Posner (2010) notes, when we work to align personal values with organizational values, this benefits the well-being and safety of individuals and the team.

Effective Conversations

The second step in creating a high functioning team is ensuring we are continually demonstrating the core values and clear purpose through effective and ongoing conversations. Many of the best coaches and much of the research show that setting the purpose and core values for the team and then engaging in regular conversations is the key to building and maintaining a great team. In her book *Fierce Conversations*, Susan Scott (2002) argues that leaders must be willing to have "conversations that interrogate reality, provoke learning, tackle tough challenges and enrich relationships" (xix). By *leaders*, we mean both coaches and athletes, and indeed all team members, working to listen and talk on an ongoing basis.

The specific skills that enable such "fierce conversations" and create and maintain a high functioning team are:

- Understanding how to be assertive without being aggressive
- Knowing how to listen well
- Knowing when to ask questions
- Knowing how to speak clearly and concisely
- Providing and receiving feedback
- Effectively resolving conflict

To begin, it is important to first understand the difference between being aggressive, assertive, and passive within a conversation. Skillful conversations are about two individuals (or a group) being able to remain assertive as discussions are facilitated and decisions made. The danger, particularly when something emotional or difficult is being discussed, is that one of the individuals can fall into the trap of becoming either aggressive or passive.

What does it mean to be assertive rather than aggressive or passive? According to Webster's Dictionary, *assertive* means "to state positively, to affirm." *Aggressive* is defined as "to undertake an attack, to begin a quarrel," and *passive* is defined as "being the object of rather than the subject of action; unresisting, submissive." Being assertive in conversations means there is caring and respect for each person as an individual—that we are intentionally creating an environment where each individual knows they can have input into how the team culture will be crafted.

Actively Listen

If we break down the skills of effective conversations into manageable chunks, the first skill is *listening*, and listening well is one of the more difficult and least understood skills of effective conversations. When one is truly listening, one is listening to understand what the other person is thinking or feeling, not simply formulating a response.

It is imperative to note that listening and understanding what someone says does not necessarily mean agreement. But really listening first allows for a clear understanding of what the issue is in the conversation. So much conflict between individuals and within a team comes about because of incorrect assumptions—and incorrect assumptions often happen because we are eager to respond and solve too quickly. When coaches and team members are listening well, there is clear understanding of what others are thinking and feeling, and the right action can be taken.

Key Point

The following are some habits of good listening:

- Remind yourself that all team members have the same goal: to perform well, to bring visibility to the sport of rowing, to set an environment of excellence and respect.

- Look at who is speaking to you and focus on what they are saying—really listen to what they are saying, rather than immediately coming up with a response. You will get to a solution; you just want to first ensure you are solving the right issue!

- When listening well, you can ask questions to ensure you understand the issue. Inquiry questions might include "what do you mean by that?", "I understood . . ., is this correct?", or "can you explain a bit more?"

- If there is emotion, listen first, then acknowledge the feelings, and then try to guide them in finding their own solution. If the emotions are directed toward you, in the form of an attack or anger, be assertive and set a time to talk when things are calmer.

- Do your best to be empathetic and nonjudgmental. You may not agree with what is being said. You simply need to ensure that you are clear on what the issue or problem is before making any decisions!

Before we get to action, there are two more skills to be cultivated: *asking questions* and *delivering a clear message*. When we are engaging with others and listening to understand, we often need to ask questions for clarity. And when one works to clarify an issue, you ask a question, and then you listen again. The most common mistakes we make in conversation are presented in figure 31.2, along with some suggested solutions.

Speak With Clarity

The second key skill of effective conversations is *speaking clearly and concisely*. The coach, as the initial leader of any team, might begin by stating what they believe in.

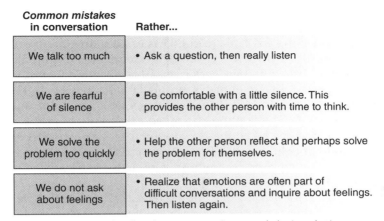

Common mistakes in conversation	Rather...
We talk too much	• Ask a question, then really listen
We are fearful of silence	• Be comfortable with a little silence. This provides the other person with time to think.
We solve the problem too quickly	• Help the other person reflect and perhaps solve the problem for themselves.
We do not ask about feelings	• Realize that emotions are often part of difficult conversations and inquire about feelings. Then listen again.

▶ **Figure 31.2** Common mistakes in conversations and their solutions.

For example, "I believe this team can make history at the next national championships" or "I believe we can all work toward a goal of every athlete and boat achieving personal bests at the national championships, and I want us to do that with great integrity." That statement of belief leads the team members from the *why* to the next step, which is engaging in a discussion about the *how*—how to go about accomplishing that purpose guided by agreed-upon values and ultimately behaviors that consistently align with those values.

Listening to the thoughts and concerns of all team members before moving to a decision point is critical. To build and maintain an effective team culture, all team members need to feel safe to express their thoughts, ideas, and concerns. As these discussions are enabled, each member begins to take responsibility for their training and actions on and off the water.

One way to think about the skill of speaking clearly and concisely—especially when there is conflict, as discussed later—is the *I* message: *I name the issue, I feel, I need.* For example, a team may decide that one of its core values is to show up for practice on time and with a good mindset, ready to train. One of the team members is often late for practice and is sometimes argumentative with fellow crew members. The clear and concise message could be: "I would like to speak with you about being late for practice these last few weeks" (naming the issue; dealing with only one issue at a time), "I am upset because we agreed as a team that being on time was an important value for us" (naming your emotions), and "I need us to meet and talk about this" or "I need to understand what is stopping you from being on time." These *I* messages are clear and concise and are particularly important when there is emotion. Name the issue in an even tone of voice, with no judgment or sarcasm. Name the emotion you are experiencing but stop there; do not go on and on, and do not raise other issues. Conclude by stating what you need, because only you know what that is. And it is key to do it all calmly.

A clear and concise message, interwoven with listening well, is critical and ensures there is both listening and speaking. It also helps to not put the other on the defensive because when we are on the defensive, we are busy thinking up excuses for our behavior rather than listening to what is being said and then working together to find solutions. Scott (2002) might call this "interrogating reality" and tackling the tough conversations (24). Scott would also add that we sometimes need to consider how we might be contributing to the issue.

Speak Constructively

Both listening and speaking well are critical parts of providing *constructive feedback*, and the ability to provide constructive feedback is essential to building a healthy and productive team culture. Providing feedback is certainly an important task of the coach, but it is equally important that teammates, particularly in crew boats, know how to provide effective feedback that builds the confidence of a teammate and addresses issues when necessary. As Scott (2009) has noted, the ability to create change and develop a culture of excellence "requires extraordinarily compelling feedback that is clear, insightful, well thought out, specific, and delivered face to face by someone who has observed us long enough and thoughtfully enough to tell us something about ourselves that gets our full attention" (31).

One critical word is *constructive*. What does that mean? It means that we go into any conversation with another team member with the intent to help. It means we meet face to face. It means feedback can be both appreciative and critical—an important point. We often do not spend enough time telling another what they are doing well. We should spend at least half our time looking for what an athlete or teammate is doing well, because this kind of feedback builds relationships. Positive feedback must be sincere and genuine; critical feedback must be specific. If you want or see a need for change in technique, be specific about what is not correct and what it should look like or how it should feel. Then check for understanding. Repeat.

Key Point

A terrific way to build a team that involves positive constructive feedback is an exercise of appreciation. The entire team (athletes, coaches, support staff) gathers as a group, each with a piece of paper. Each individual writes their name on the top of the page and circulates that paper to the right. Each individual then writes one thing they appreciate about the person and circulates the paper again to the right. This continues until the paper returns to its owner. At least three things occur in this simple exercise: First, each individual receives a list of what their teammates appreciate about them. Second, it demonstrates how feedback can be positive. Third, it builds a team culture where members notice and appreciate one another as teammates and as people, not just as competitors.

When we think about how a teammate or coach can provide critical yet constructive feedback, we need to circle back and utilize the clear message tool. The first step is to clearly state the problem or issue. If, for example, it is better execution of a specific skill, it helps to break the skill down into manageable chunks, both by using words and by demonstrating the technique or tactic physically, if possible. For example, if the coach is in the coach boat on the water, critique can be short and not much of a dialogue: "Remember to focus on your entry, quick and smooth. You want your hands loose, moving the blade quickly in the water with no splash, while you push horizontally on the footstretcher." If the athlete is experienced, ask them to think about what would work well.

When off the water, coach could first ask, "So how was that today?" This open-ended question allows the athlete to think about their performance, and the athlete's response is great information for a coach about how much the athlete does or does not understand. Then the coach can follow up with, for example, "Let's talk about that third interval. I saw that you fell off the pace and technique deteriorated. What do you think?" The athlete can respond, and the coach can then provide specific technical corrections. All of this encourages the athlete or crew to reflect, and the coach can still provide correction. This kind of conversation and process, although critiquing, develops a thoughtful, resourceful, and responsible athlete or crew boat. Asking questions, listening, and being willing to engage in conversation builds the coach and crew boat into a healthy and well-functioning team that can tackle any issue and come out better for it.

One quick reminder: The closer to competition, the more a coach needs to shift feedback to what the athlete or crew is doing well and away from what is not going well. First of all, at some point, it is too late to make corrections—further tasks should be left until after the competition. Second, and perhaps most important, this is a critical time for feedback because the confidence of most athletes is fragile, and that fragility increases as competition nears. Most athletes will begin to question their readiness, their skills, their technique, or their teammates. This is a natural reaction to stress. A coach should alleviate that stress and reassure the crew that they are well prepared. One should note that shifting feedback toward what is going well does not mean that there is no critique. It simply means doing less critiquing and more supporting at this point in time.

Be Receptive

Being able to receive both appreciative and critical feedback is another essential component for all team members to learn and practice in order to hold effective conversations and maintain a high functioning team. Many find it difficult to receive any kind of feedback, but critical feedback is often the most difficult, and developing the ability to receive criticism without getting defensive is a difficult but key skill to acquire.

One aspect of this skill—whether the feedback is coach to athlete, athlete to coach, or athlete to athlete—is to not take the criticism personally, step back a bit from the comment (certainly easier said than done), and consider it from the perspective of how the information might help the crew. For example, when you are being criticized, ask questions for clarification, so you clearly understand what is being asked of you. If one team member attacks another by saying "You are always finding what I do wrong," the individual being attacked needs to ask for an example of the behavior ("Can you give me an example of what you mean by that?"). It may be an unfair comment, but perhaps not. It is important to ensure you actually did something poorly or unfairly before taking ownership, apologizing, and considering how to change that behavior. Apologizing can be powerful in building the relationship with an individual teammate, but only if appropriate.

There are *problematic words* to avoid when providing feedback (Werthner and Taylor 2010). The way we speak (tone of voice) and the words we choose—assertive, clear, and precise language—influence the effectiveness of any message, which in turn influences the building of effective relationships and effective team culture. Here are a few words that may inhibit that process:

1. *You.* Be cautious about using this word. Saying "You are always the first to quit the workout" can sound like an accusation. Sometimes there is a tendency to avoid using *I* because it might appear conceited or vain; however, particularly in difficult conversations, using *I* means that you are taking responsibility for what

you say. It allows you to take ownership and hopefully avoids putting another team member on the defensive. (A clear directive such as "I want you to . . ." is not usually a problem.)

2. *They.* The use of *they* is an indirect way of speaking. If an athlete says, "They all feel this way" or "They all agreed we should take the day off training," it requires the following question: "Who are *they*?" Is it really the whole team, or just this athlete?

3. *But.* When a teammate says, "Yeah, but," it often means they are not listening well and have already made a decision about the issue or problem.

4. *Always* or *never.* Rarely is a situation *always* or *never.* For example, "You are always complaining about how hard the training is" and "You never help put the boat away and clean the boathouse" often escalate emotions and do not promote good conversations.

5. *Should* or *ought.* These are words that often cause conflict rather than build relationships. For example, "You should have known" causes most of us to become defensive. Then we are not listening well, and subsequently changing any behavior or action becomes much more difficult.

Resolve Conflict

A final component of effective conversations, which are vital to building and maintaining an optimal team culture, is the ability to *effectively resolve conflict.* As soon as a group of individuals begin working together, even before starting to develop as an effective team, there will be situations that could escalate to a conflict. Referring back to Tuckman's model earlier in the chapter, almost every team will need to work through a "storming" session that is connected with working through conflicts.

The very nature of conflict is often misunderstood. Conflict is inevitable whenever two or more individuals come together, and therefore it is important to develop the skills to prevent unnecessary conflict and learn to address it when it does occur. Importantly, conflict is *constructive* when we manage it well. It has the potential to open up discussion about issues of importance, which hopefully result in better conversations, shared solutions, and a psychologically safe environment for every team member. Conflict can be *destructive* when it diverts significant focus, time, and energy away from the critical aspects of the team, such as training and competition, and if it causes division among team members.

There are many ways that conflict can begin on a team. For example, when there is a misunderstanding, miscommunication, or lack of information, conflict often develops. DePree (1992), in his book on leadership, writes of the need for *lavish communication*, which he argues must be ongoing and checked for understanding. Conflict may also occur over team values (*how* a team will work together and *what* the team will do). For this reason, it is critical that the core values and team purpose are first discussed and agreed on, and then the *how* and *what* will be much easier to agree on and act on.

The good news is that by learning and utilizing all the skills that comprise effective conversations, it is possible to prevent a great deal of conflict within a team. When you listen well, speak clearly and concisely, and give and receive feedback well, and when these skills are shared and practiced by all team members, there is much less conflict—and when conflict inevitably does arise, you will be able to manage and resolve it effectively. Importantly, the more effectively you manage difficult conversations in a timely manner, the higher the probability for a high functioning team, greater satisfaction for all team members, and excellent performances and personal bests. What is most relevant in becoming skilled at effective conversations is that each team member takes the time to regularly reflect on what is working and what needs work.

Effective Behaviors

We turn now to the third step for developing an optimal team, *effective behaviors*. These behaviors—a deep self-awareness, accountability for one's actions, a well-developed sense of self-responsibility, and an understanding and acceptance of one's role within a team—are, in fact, a clear result of the first two steps. When time is spent as a team discussing a clear purpose and core values and working to develop all the facets of effective conversations, the behaviors and actions needed to sustain an effective and excellent team culture are a natural occurrence. It is simply important to understand that this is a flowing, ongoing process—the speaker, the listener, and the message are ever changing, among and even within conversations. Issues, concerns, and ideas will always arise. A team and members that are generous in sharing these skills, and themselves, will create a team culture that excels.

Conclusion

Allow me to conclude with a story about a rowing team preparing to go into an Olympic Games with a chance to win many medals. The team would be competing throughout much of the Games. We brought the whole team together—athletes, coaches, all medical and sport science staff, and the media individuals assigned to the team. We began by saying that we had athletes and teams who had the ability to win a medal on the first day of competition and on the last. This would be a long 10 days fraught with many potential issues. We asked three simple questions of each individual: How will you ensure you are at your best throughout the entire competition? What do you need to be your best? What will hurt your performance? The 3 hour conversation that ensued, facilitated by the head coach and the sport psychology practitioner, resulted in a terrific amount of dialogue, some surprising comments, and a deep understanding of both everyone's individual needs for optimal performance and their teammates' and the staff's needs and wants. The Games were a phenomenal result for this team: most medals were realized, and it was very much the best team results for Canada at that Games. But to be clear, issues still arose—again, that is inevitable. However, because we had this conversation as an entire team, we were able to refer back to it whenever we faced an issue ("remember we said we would . . . "). As a result, the issues were resolved in a timely way that enabled those involved to get back on track with a clear purpose: best performance by each athlete and team.

Building and sustaining an excellent team culture in competitive sport is an ongoing process. That is the bad news: The work is never completed. The good news is these foundational skills of effective conversations—listening well, asking questions, speaking clearly, providing constructive feedback, and developing an ability and willingness to confront conflict when it arises—can be learned by all team members, ensuring optimal performance and a healthy and safe culture for all.

Epilogue

The Future of Rowing

In general, science is understood as the knowledge of the physical and social aspects of the world based on evidence that is achieved through objective observation and measurement. Wikipedia (2021) defines it as "a systematic enterprise that builds and organizes knowledge in the form of testable explanations and predictions about the world." In the context of this book, it has been the goal to collect the best possible understanding of rowing as a sport with the help of outstanding scientists from around the globe. Ideally, scientific work is done collaboratively and shared freely, so that other researchers can discuss and scrutinize the findings. This process strengthens and supports the scientific findings and naturally leads to further discoveries that benefit everyone.

Institutional Innovations in Rowing

The science of rowing is used to find ways to make rowing ever faster, safer, and more efficient, so it is therefore no wonder that top competitive teams have always tried to engage scientists in their training. All contributors currently are or have been part of research teams and are connected to academic institutions, but also work or have worked directly with national rowing teams. The presented knowledge is therefore not only based on theories, but have found their way into practical applications that have helped to advance the sport.

When high-performance sports, and especially Olympic sports, gain national interest, governments and sponsors traditionally finance scientific research that will help their national teams improve performance. On one hand, this means increased opportunities for researchers to study the sport, but on the other, it creates a conflict of interest when it comes to maintaining scientific integrity, because the involved scientists are often not allowed to discuss and freely share their findings so as to not jeopardize the achieved advantage of the national team for which they work.

The consequences of this conflict become more pronounced through the complexity of the relevant scientific field and the costs associated with continuing such investigations. This means that only well-funded organizations can afford the highly educated scientific staff and necessary equipment to stay on top of these developments. Such organizations are mostly state-funded rowing associations or, occasionally, larger companies. However, the primary focus of such organizations is of course their own success, so that a general exchange of information is often limited or at least delayed. This puts smaller, less-funded rowing federations at a distinct disadvantage, which leaves them with little to no chance of success in international competitions. These circumstances could lead to a decline of interest in competing internationally, which in turn could have an impact on the universality of the sport of rowing.

Nevertheless, such attempts to handcuff science are often either short-lived or inhibit the success of the supported team, because coaches and scientists move from country to country to find the best working conditions. They then share their experience with the new employer and learn from the research that is done in that country. This way, a healthy exchange of knowledge and ideas is maintained.

Scientific progress is accelerated by the exchange of new ideas, the publication of knowledge, and the scrutinizing of theories and methods. Learning from each other accelerates everyone. One of the most successful and innovative international coaches of the last few decades, the Swedish coach Thor Nilsen, once answered when asked why he would so generously open his training camps to rowers and coaches from other countries to share and study his training and coaching methods: "You cannot grab anything with a closed fist!" While he was offering insight into his methods, he was always able to learn and get some new information from others that furthered his knowledge as well. By working with World Rowing and publishing his work on their website to be accessed worldwide, Nilsen served the whole rowing community with this approach while maintaining a competitive edge for his own coaches and rowers.

The Changing Faces of International Rowing

With the increasing logistical, financial, and political challenges that face the organization of Olympic Games, it is conceivable that the offered sport programs at the Games and how they are run will change in the future. The difficulty in finding hosts for the event has already put the International Olympic Committee (IOC) on alert, and it is trying to find ways to keep the Games relevant. There are different scenarios for how this may affect the sport of rowing.

Rowing has been a fixture in the Olympic sport program since the beginning of the modern Olympic Games and has remained committed to be part of the movement ever since. The International Rowing Federation, now called World Rowing, has always been open to listen to the IOC's requests for change. The inclusion of women's events, the recruiting of more national rowing federations to participate in international championships, the technical improvements of the regatta facilities (including the standardization of the course length for all age groups and boat classes), and equalizing the number of events for women and men are only a few examples. Most of these changes were well received by the international rowing community and led to overall positive developments in the sport. Facilities all over the world are of high quality, and international regattas are run professionally. More nations have taken part in international championships, the number of athletes participating in rowing races has been on a steady rise, and the overall performance level has increased steadily.

Although there have been many positive developments in rowing, there are concerning signs. Not all World Cup regattas are well attended—partly as a result of cost, but also the belief of some national team coaches that these events take away valuable training time, leading many associations to only partake in the last of the three World Cups. As a result, the number of international crews entered in the first two World

Cups has been small, so that some races do not have heats or even have no entries and must be canceled. These circumstances, in turn, diminish the interest of the media and potential spectators and sponsors, which then result in financial losses for the regatta organizer and World Rowing.

The Debate Over Lightweight

Another contentious issue in international rowing is the elimination of lightweight rowing at the Olympics after the 2024 Games. Although the introduction of lightweight boat classes to the Olympic rowing program was once seen as a savior of the sport by bringing more nations into the rowing family—as well as including large entries and more interesting races—they were successively taken out of the Olympic program. The rowing community is divided over whether this measure was necessary or wise. Although previous World Rowing leaderships have strongly supported lightweight rowing, the current leadership has with little resistance abandoned these boat classes as bargaining chips with the IOC.

These measures already show quite dire consequences at the national and international level. Since the removal of the lightweight four from the Olympic program after 2016, the number of entries from lightweight rowers at national regattas are clearly decreasing. Because financial and logistical support of the rowers from national federations is mostly limited to the Olympic boat classes, many lightweight junior athletes are deprived of future prospects. There are no identification mechanisms, development training camps, or financial support for lightweight rowers any more. However, as their chances of successfully racing against taller and more muscular opponents are limited, they turn away from rowing.

It is also conceivable that the general interest for lightweight rowing is negatively affected. At the international level, the same trend is emerging—federations do not support boat classes that are not included in the Olympic program. The number of entries for the lightweight four at the 2017 World Championships dropped to six, just one year after this boat class was contested for the last time at an Olympic Games, and by 2018 the lightweight four—once the most competitive boat class with hugely exciting races and large entries—disappeared from the World Championships program completely.

It remains to be seen what influence the decision to scrap lightweight rowing from the Olympic program has on rowing as a whole. The IOC developed a catalogue of criteria by which sports are evaluated for their inclusion in the Olympic program. Universality is a major criterion on this list, and international sport federations have to list how many countries are members of the federation, how many countries participate in international championships, Olympic qualifiers, and the Olympic Games; and how many medals are won by federations of each of the continents. Lightweight rowing has helped World Rowing to meet these criteria in the past, and it remains to be seen how the exclusion of lightweight rowing will affect them in the future.

World Rowing developed a qualifying system for the Olympic Games that secures the participation of crews from all continents by assigning fixed places to continental qualifiers. This means that, for example, South American crews are guaranteed a certain number of entries at the Games based on the results at their own qualifying regatta, although there may be faster crews on the other continents. This strategy assures the participation of crews from all continents, but in general waters down the competitiveness of the Olympic races, especially in the preliminary rounds where these guaranteed competitors participate, which garner little media attention. It is rare that crews from so-called smaller countries reach a place in the Olympic regatta, let alone reach the podium, if there are no guaranteed continental representation spaces. Lightweight crews were the exception to this rule in the past. For example, the only African crew to ever win a gold medal was the lightweight four from South Africa in 2012.

What is already clear today is that the elimination of lightweight rowing has had a significant negative effect for the smaller and lighter rowers around the world. Because the funding of most rowing associations is based on Olympic events, the support for lightweight rowing has been withdrawn worldwide, so that the lightweight boat classes that had previously large entry numbers are massively dwindling on the international and national level. A new push of interests at the national level is needed to invigorate lightweight rowing, and it remains to be seen if initiatives like U.S. collegiate rowing programs' pledge to strongly support their lightweight boat classes will ignite an excitement that allows high school programs and clubs to continue to offer and support lightweight rowing.

New Classifications of Rowing

World Rowing, on the other hand, has turned its focus and support to different types of rowing. The arguments to include indoor rowing, coastal rowing, and coastal sprints in the overall international rowing program are compelling. These activities certainly offer more people around the world the opportunity to participate in the sport.

Indoor Rowing

Indoor rowing has already been used for some time for training and physiological testing, yet it was not seen as a stand-alone sport category until recently (figure E.1*a*). Once Dick and Peter Dreissigacker started to produce the Concept2 rowing ergometer in 1981, which allowed athletes to kinematically and kinetically mimic the rowing stroke, indoor rowing took off. The machine was easy to maintain, did not take up a lot of room, and was quite inexpensive. Not only did this rowing machine became mainstream in boathouses around the world, many rowers obtained their own private equipment to be able to train more easily. Moreover, indoor rowing was discovered by fitness clubs as an excellent training method, and so rowing was introduced to people who would never be attracted to join a rowing club.

It is therefore not surprising that interest in ergometer competitions, which were initially held locally, quickly spread. There are now competitions held at the national and international level, all the way up to official World Rowing Indoor Championships. Additionally, because indoor machines are calibrated and not dependent on the weather, it is very easy to create rankings of results and even world records. These are available for age groups from 12 and under to 100+, from sprint distances of 100 m to marathon distances of 42,195 m, and durations from 1 min to 60 min or even longer.

The COVID-19 pandemic was used as an initial spark to develop and hold virtual competitions as well. The widespread interest in this indoor sport encouraged more equipment manufacturers to develop and market new rowing machines, and to make the activity more interesting and motivating. Feedback monitors became colorful displays with gamelike video training sessions and races in virtual environments of actual waterways. Despite its growing popularity and the ease of holding virtual competitions, it is hard to imagine that such competitions could be made interesting for spectators.

Coastal Rowing

Both long distance coastal rowing and sprints are executed on sea in more rugged boats than typical flatwater rowing shells (figure E.1*b, c*). Also known as *offshore* or *open-water rowing*, coastal rowing was already performed and contested in various forms before World Rowing discovered its appeal and started to regulate the sport in 2007. This sport development can be traced back from competitions between crews of larger ships anchored in harbors to make their idle time a little more entertaining or from the training of Coast Guard safety crews on ocean beaches. Some initial coastal rowing events showed World Rowing that there is some interest within and outside of existing rowing clubs, that such competition bears entertainment value, that athletes who have access to these open waterways could be attracted to get into rowing, and that staging such events is much less expensive than the current Olympic flat-water racing. Based on these factors, World Rowing now intends to have coastal rowing included in the Olympic program, and there are strong indications that the IOC will accept.

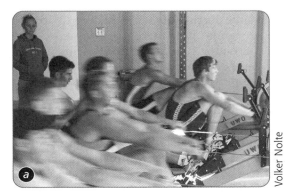

Volker Nolte

Courtesy of World Rowing/Benedict Tufnell

Courtesy of World Rowing/Ben Rodford

▶ **Figure E.1**   The new World Rowing events: *(a)* Indoor rowing; *(b)* coastal sprint rowing with a Le Mans beach start and a sprint race out to a buoy and back; and *(c)* coastal rowing with a minimum distance of 4,000 m.

However, it remains to be seen if these new types of rowing indeed will open new and exciting avenues for the sport. Coastal rowing is a new addition, and time will tell how it will develop. To be included into a national sport program, infrastructures and training facilities need to be developed and built so that athletes can properly train to elevate the national performance level. It also remains to be seen how this sport develops from an organizational point of view. Presumably, individuals could learn the basics of the sport in a short time in introductory courses, buy their own personal equipment, and continue on their own—similar to what we can see, for example, with stand-up paddling. Athletes could store their equipment at home and transport it to the next waterway to row individually without being a member of a club.

With new ways to exercise rowing, be it coastal or indoor, it is very likely that they will lead to completely different organizational structures than traditional club rowing. Professionally managed institutions are likely better able to run these new sports than the previous clubs, which are mostly based on volunteer work. However, this also means that higher-level organizations (such as national and international federations) will have to reorganize their structures.

Budgeting and Hosting Rowing

As long as rowing is part of the Olympic program, it can benefit from the financial support that comes with it. The IOC provides a large portion of the annual World Rowing budget, and it is therefore all the more understandable that World Rowing is working hard to remain within the Olympic family. Even the funding from governments and sponsors for high-performance programs on the national level is almost exclusively linked to participation and success at the Olympic Games, which underlines the sport's close reliance on the IOC.

With the dependence of rowing in the Olympics comes a significant influence of the IOC on the sport. This opens up two possible scenarios for the future of rowing: What happens if all efforts fail to keep rowing in the Olympics? Even more dramatically, what if the Olympic Games cease to exist because they become unmanageable to run and no new host cities can be found? Neither development can be ruled out. The IOC regularly reviews all sports regarding their continued inclusion in the Olympic program, and rowing has a few weaknesses: The costs of the large facilities and lack of plans for their continued use after the Games as well as the difficulties of televising the sport in an exciting way are a few examples of challenges that rowing faces.

It would be advisable for rowing to at least consider a future without the Olympics. Touring rowing, recreational rowing, and university or club rowing are the main pillars of the sport outside of the Olympics, and competitive lightweight rowing seems to be joining them soon. These areas need to be strengthened so they can continue to thrive as part of a sport that has a long history, wonderful opportunities for diverse experiences, exciting areas for science to study, high levels of health benefits, and excellent values.

The Scientific Outlook for New Rowing

Ergometers are already widely used in research. However, these studies are almost exclusively limited to the physiological and medical fields because it is easier to perform the required measurements in the laboratory and one has far more possibilities to control test settings and the environment. Ergometers are excellent instruments when it comes to investigating the influence of, for example, certain training methods, nutritional patterns, or environmental influences on the physiological performance of athletes. It is also possible to gain knowledge about certain injuries that can be attributed to fatigue, forms of loading, or body postures. Movements on the ergometer, on the other hand, offer little scope for research.

The subtleties of rowing technique discussed in this book are not important on the ergometer. These movements—to properly guide the blades, balance the boat, and coordinate the rower's movement to lose the least amount of speed—simply do not occur on the indoor rowing machine. In order to achieve a high competition performance on the ergometer, the only thing that counts is what physical power the athlete can achieve on the handle over the required duration of the race. This is why many diverse types of athletes perform well at indoor competitions using extreme elements of technique that work on the ergometer but would not work at all on the water. For example, some athletes pull the ergometer handle extremely high toward the neck to gain more stroke length, which is literally impossible to do in the boat. The technique of ergometer rowing is often self-taught among fitness athletes, and the focus is mainly on physiological training. In fact, many athletes competing in ergometer races have excellent fitness but cannot perform a single stroke in the boat.

A quick literature search for peer-reviewed articles pertaining to coastal rowing has so far yielded no results. This sport is still in its infancy and is therefore not yet discovered by research. Rowing associations all over the world are currently trying to gather validated knowledge about this sport in order to get useful information to properly educate and train their rowers and coaches. The physiological training and general motions for coastal long distance as well as sprint rowing are already very well covered by flat-water rowing research. However, the often rough water conditions in the wider, heavier boats; strategies for how to best navigate the race buoys; and study of how to handle waves, wind, and currents provide many new research questions. In addition, the start and finish of beach sprint races is completely different from flat-water racing. First, a rower must run a certain distance on the beach to get into the boat before rowing can begin. After the crew has rowed the set slalom course on the water, the boat must be returned to the beach, where again a rower must jump out of the boat to run a distance on the beach to the actual finish, where a button must be pressed that stops the race time. All this may be influenced by factors that need the consideration of specific techniques and tactics. It is therefore conceivable that we will see more scientific studies of these sports over time.

Conclusion

The two main goals of this publication have been to present the latest scientific findings from the sport of rowing and to stimulate discussions about and further investigations and studies into rowing.

The book is therefore designed for actively engaged rowers and coaches, as well as the scientists interested in this sport. Some rowers and coaches may find parts of the book to be a little challenging, but we assume that everyone should be fascinated by the idea of learning new and scientifically sound knowledge. In addition, let us note that most innovations in rowing come from practitioners—scientists often only prove what came from the ideas and intuitions of athletes and coaches who try to find ingenuous ways to row faster.

References

Introduction

Bourne, G.C. 1925. *A Textbook of Oarsmanship*. London: H. Milford.

Helfand, D.J. 2017. *A Survival Guide to the Misinformation Age*. New York: Columbia University Press.

Lefeuvre and Pailliotte. 1904. "Étude Graphique du Coup d'Aviron en Canoe." *Bulletin de l'Association Technique Maritime*, no. 15: 115-139.

Nolte V. 1981. "The Sliding Rigger Concept." *Rowing* (August/September): 10-16.

Nolte, V. 1984. *Die Effektivität des Ruderschlages: biomechanische Modelle, Analyse und Ergebnisse*. Berlin: Bartels & Wernitz.

Nolte V. 2009. "Shorter Oars Are More Effective." *Journal of Applied Biomechanics* 25 (1): 1-8.

University of California Berkeley. 2019. "Understanding Science 101." Accessed July 22, 2019. https://undsci.berkeley.edu/understanding-science-101/what-is-science/science-aims-to-explain-and-understand.

Woodgate. W.B. 1888. *Boating*. London: Longmans, Green and Co.

Chapter 1

Arbeit, E. 1997. *Practical Training Emphases in the First and Second Decades of Development*. Lecture from the XXth European Athletics Coaches Association (EACA) Conference, Belgrade.

Mallory, P.D. 2011. *The Sport of Rowing*. Henley-on-Thames: River and Rowing Museum.

Everett, H. 2016. "Helen Glover Feature." Harry Everett Sports Journalism. https://harryeverett-sportsjournalism.wordpress.com/2016/02/27/helen-glover-feature/

Roser, M., C. Appel, and H. Ritchie. 2013. "Human Height." Retrieved from https://ourworldin-data.org/human-height'

www.sports-reference.com/Olympics. https://www.olympedia.org/sport_groups/RO

Chapter 2

2000 Intersecondary School Sports Association Boys and Girls Athletics Championship. April 11-15, 2000. National Stadium, Kingston, Jamaica W.I. http://www.cfpitiming.com/class_1_boys_results.htm

Beunen, G., M. Ostyn, J. Simons, Roland Renson, Albrecht Claessens, Bavo Van en Eynde, J. Lefevre, Bart Vanreusel, Robert Malina, and M.A. van't Hof. 1997. "Development and Tracking in Fitness Components: Leuven Longitudinal Study on Lifestyle, Fitness and Health." *International Journal of Sports Medicine* 18 (Suppl. 3): S171-8. doi: 10.1055/s-2007-972710.

Beunen, G.P., and Malina, R.M. 2008. "Growth and Biological Maturation: Relevance to Athletic Performance." In *The Young Athlete*, edited by H. Hebestreit and O. Bar-Or, **8**, Oxford, UK: Blackwell Publishing.

Bourgois, J., A. Steyaert, and J. Boone. 2014. "Physiological and Anthropometric Progression in an International Oarsman: A 15-Year Case Study." *International Journal of Sports Physiology and Performance*, no. 9: 723-726.

Byers, J. 1998. "The Biology of Human Play." *Child Development* 69, no. 3 (June): 599-600.

Diamond, A. 2000. "Close Interrelation of Motor Development and Cognitive Development and of the Cerebellum and Prefrontal Cortex." *Child Development* 71 (1): 44-56.

James, T.E. 1960. "The Age of Majority." *The American Journal of Legal History* 4, no. 1 (January): 22-33.

Kaiser, J., and J.H. Gruzelier. 1996. "Timing of Puberty and EEG Coherence During Photic Stimulation." *International Journal of Psychophysiology* 21: 135-149.

Nybo, L., J.F. Schmidt, S. Fitzdorf, and N.B. Nordsborg. 2014. "Physiological Charactereistics of an Aging Olympic Athlete." *Medicine & Science in Sports & Exercise* 46, no. 11 (November): 2132-2138.

Saugstad, L.F. 1989. "Mental Illness and Cognition in Relation to Age at Puberty: A Hypothesis." *Clinical Genetics* 36 (3): 156-116.

Seidler, R.D. 2010. "Neural Correlates of Motor Learning, Transfer of Learning, and Learning to Learn." *Exercise and Sport Sciences Reviews* 38, no. 1 (January): 3-9.

Chapter 3

Buccino, G., and Riggio, L. 2006. "The Role of the Mirror Neuron System in Motor Learning." *Kinesiology* 38 (1): 1-13.

Fairbairn, S. 1990. *The Complete Steve Fairbairn on Rowing.* London: The Kingswood Press.

LeDoux, J. 1997. "Parallel Memories: Putting Emotions Back Into the Brain (A Talk With Joseph LeDoux)." www.edge.org/conversation/joseph_ledoux-parallel-memories-putting-emotions-back-into-the-brain.

Longman, D., J.T. Stock, and Wells, J.C.K. 2017. "A Trade-Off Between Cognitive and Physical Performance, With Relative Preservation of Brain Function." *Scientific Reports* 7: 13709.

Pessoa, L. 2010. "Emotion and Cognition and the Amygdala: From 'What Is It?' to 'What's to Be Done?'" *Neuropsychologia* 48 (12): 3416-3429.

Royal, K., D. Farrow, I. Mujika, S. Halson, D. Pyne, and B. Abernethy. 2006. "The Effects of Fatigue on Decision-Making and Technical Skill Performance in Water Polo Players." *Journal of Sports Sciences* 24 (8): 807-815.

Urgesi, C., M.M. Savonito, F. Fabbro, and S. Aglioti. 2012. "Long- and Short-Term Plastic Modelling of Action Prediction Abilities in Volleyball." *Psychological Research* 76: 542-560.

Chapter 4

Abernethy, B., D. Farrow, and J. Berry. 2003. "Constraints and Issues in the Development of a General Theory of Expert Perceptual-Motor Performance: A Critique of the Deliberate Practice Framework." In *Expert Performance in Sports: Advances in Research on Sport Expertise,* edited by J.L. Starkes and K.A. Ericsson, 345-369, 436-441. Champaign, IL: Human Kinetics.

Bengtsonn, S.L., Z. Nagy, S. Skare, L. Forsman, H. Forssberg, and F. Ulen. 2005. "Extensive Piano Practice Has Regionally Specific Effects on White Matter Development." *Nature Neuroscience* 8 (9): 1148-1150.

Black, J.E., K.R. Isaacs, B.J. Anderson, A.A. Alcantara, and W.T. Greenough. 1990. "Learning Causes Synaptogenesis Whereas Motor Activity Causes Angiogenesis in Cerebellar Cortex of Adult Rats." *Neurobiology* 87: 5568-5572.

Bompa, T.O. 2000. *Total Training for Young Champions.* Toronto: Human Kinetics.

Fairbairn, I., ed. 1990. *The Complete Steve Fairbairn on Rowing.* London: The Kingswood Press.

Herberger, E. 2004. *Rowing/Rudern: The GDR Text of Oarsmanship.* Toronto: Sport Book Publishers.

Proia, P., C.M. Di Liegro, G. Schiera, A. Fricano, and I. Di Liegro. 2016. "Lactate as a Metabolite and a Regulator in the Central Nervous System." *International Journal of Molecular Sciences* 17, no. 9 (September): 1450. doi: 10.3390/ijms17091450. PMID: 27598136. PMCID: PMC5037729.

Seidler, R.D., A. Purushotatham, S.G. Kim, et al. 2002. "Cerebellum Activation Associated with Performance Change but Not Motor Learning." *Science* 296: 2043-2046.

Seiler, K.S., and G.Ø. Kjerland. 2006. "Quantifying Training Intensity Distribution in Elite Endurance Athletes: Is There Evidence for an `Optimal' Distribution?" Scandinavian Journal of Medicine & Science in Sports 16 (1): 49-56.

Chapter 5

Affeld, K., K. Schichl, and A. Ziemann. 1993. "Assessment of Rowing Efficiency." *International Journal of Sports Medicine* 14 (Suppl. 1): S39-S41.

Filter, K. 2004. "The System Crew – Boat." Lecture. www.row2k.com/features/files/20160308ATBad dendumSystemCrewFilterPDF.pdf

Hamilton, G. 2016. *Sculling in a Nutshell*. Milton Keynes, UK: Lightning Source UK Ltd.

Herberger, E. 1970. *Rudern*. Sportverlag Berlin.

Klavora, P. 1982. *Rowing 3: National Coaching Certification Program*. Ottawa: Canadian Amateur Rowing Association.

Kleshnev, V. 2016a. *The Biomechanics of Rowing*. Ramsbury, Marlborough Wiltshire: The Crowood Press Ltd.

Kleshnev, V. 2019. "New Method of Kinetic Energy Evaluation." *Rowing Biomechanics Newsletter* no. 217.

Körner, T., and P. Schwanitz. 1985. *Rudern*. Sportverlag Berlin.

Nolte, V. 1984. *Die Effektivität des Ruderschlages: Biomechanische Modelle, Analyse und Ergebnisse*. Berlin, Germany: Bartels & Wernitz Druckerei und Verlag KG.

Sliasas, A., and S. Tullis. 2009. "A Hydrodynamics-Based Model of a Rowing Stroke Simulating Effects of Drag and Lift on Oar Blade Efficiency for Various Cant Angles." Procedia Engineering, 8th Conference of the International Sports Engineering Association (ISEA).

Williams, J., and A. Scott. 1967. *Rowing: A Scientific Approach*. Cranbury, NJ: Barnes & Co.

World Rowing. 2021. "FISA Rule Book 2019." https://worldrowing.com/2014/05/22/rule-book.

Chapter 6

Concept2. "Watts Calculator." Accessed July 2020. https://www.concept2.com/indoor-rowers/training/calculators/watts-calculator.

Grosser, M., and A. Neumaier. 1982. *Techniktraining. Theorie und Praxis aller Sportarten* (BLV Sportwissen, 406). München: BLV-Verl.-Ges.

Kleshnev, V. 2015. "Variation of the Boat Velocity." *Rowing Biomechanics Newsletter* no. 166 (January).

Martin, D. 1991. "Merkmale einer trainingswissenschaftlichen Theorie des Techniktrainings." In *Sportmotorisches Lernen und Techniktraining*. Internationales Symposium Motorik- und Bewegungsforschung 1989, Saarbrücken, Bd. 1 (53-77): Hofmann Verlag.

McGinnis, P.M. 2013. *Biomechanics of Sport and Exercise*. 3rd ed. Champaign, IL: Human Kinetics.

Meinel K. 1961. "Die Bewegungslehre unter pädagogischem Aspekt als Synthese und Grundlage." *Theorie und Praxis der Körperkultur* 10 (11/12): 1028-1038.

World Rowing. 2021. "FISA Rule Book 2019." https://worldrowing.com/2014/05/22/rule-book.

Chapter 7

Abbott, I., and A. Von Doenhoff. 1959. *Theory of Wing Sections*. New York: Dover Publications.

Affeld, K., and K. Schichl. 1985. *Untersuchungen der Kräfte am Ruderblatt mithilfe eines mechanischen Simulators*. Internal Report: Technische Universität Berlin.

Affeld, K., K. Schichl, and A. Ziemann. 1993. "Assessment of Rowing Efficiency." *International Journal of Sports Medicine* 14 (Suppl. 1): S39-S41.

Bogucki, B. 2008. "A Biomechanical Analysis of the Rowing Catch: Airstroke." Independent study project thesis. University of Western Ontario.

Cabrera, D., and A. Ruina. 2006. "Propulsive Efficiency of Rowing Oars." Report. Department of Theoretical and Applied Mechanics, Biorobotics and Locomotion Laboratory, Cornell University.

Föppl, O. 1912. "Die Windkräfte an Platten und anderen Versuchskörpern nach dem heutigen Stand von Theorie und Versuch." *Zeitschrift des Vereins Deutscher Ingenieure*, 56 (II): 1930-1936.

Hamilton, G. 2016. *Sculling in a Nutshell*. Milton Keynes, UK: Lightning Source UK Ltd.

Hill, A.V. 1938. "The Heat of Shortening and the Dynamic Constant of Muscle." Proceedings of the Royal Society B: Biological Sciences 126B: 136-195.

Hill, H., and S. Fahrig. 2009. "The Impact of Fluctuations in Boat Velocity During the Rowing Cycle on Race Time." *Scandinavian Journal of Medicine & Science in Sports* 19, 585-594.

Kleshnev, V. 1998. "Estimation of Biomechanical Parameters and Propulsive Efficiency of Rowing." Research report. Australian Institute of Sport.

Kleshnev, V. 2006. "Trampoline Effect." *Rowing Biomechanics Newsletter* 6 (2): February.

Kleshnev, V. 2016. *The Biomechanics of Rowing*. Ramsbury, Marlborough Wiltshire: The Crowood Press Ltd.

Kleshnev, V. 2019. "Review on Blade Propulsive Efficiency." *Rowing Biomechanics Newsletter* no. 225 (December).

Kleshnev, V. 2021. "Effect of Stroke Rate on Rowing Technique." *Rowing Biomechanics Newsletter* no. 239 (February).

Macrossan, M.N., and N.W. Macrossan. 2006. "Back-Splash in Rowing Shell Propulsion." Mechanical Engineering Report No. 2006/07. University of Queensland, Australia.

Nolte, V. 1981. "Über die Wissenschaft beim Rollausleger." *Rudersport* 30 (81): 639-642.

Nolte, V. 1984. *Die Effektivität des Ruderschlages: Biomechanische Modelle, Analyse und Ergebnisse.* Berlin, Germany: Bartels & Wernitz Druckerei und Verlag KG.

Nolte, V. 2010. "Hang Time. By Mastering the Art of Suspension You'll Be Adhering to the Most Important Biomechanical Principle of Our Sport." *Rowing News* 17 (October): 58.

Nolte, V., and S. McLaughlin. 2005. "The Balance of Crew Rowing Boats." *Malaysian Journal of Sport Science and Recreation* 1 (1): 51-64.

Spera, D. 2008. "Models of Lift and Drag Coefficients of Stalled and Unstalled Airfoils in Wind Turbines and Wind Tunnels." Technical Report NASA/CR–2008-215434.

Thompson, P. 2005. *Sculling.* Ramsbury, UK: Crowood Press Ltd.

Wegschneider, P. 2012. "Assessment of Airstroke Via a New Methodology Involving a Hull-Mounted Camera System." Independent study project thesis. University of Western Ontario.

Chapter 8

Barret, R.S., and J.M. Manning. 2004. "Relationships Between Rigging Set-Up, Anthropometry, Physical Capacity, Rowing Kinematics and Rowing Performance. *Sports Biomechanics* 3 (2): 221-235.

Brown, D.J. 2013. *The Boys in the Boat: Nine Americans and Their Epic Quest for Gold at the 1936 Berlin Olympics.* New York: Penguin Books.

Buckeridge, E.M., A.M. Bull, and A.H. McGregor. 2015. "Biomechanical Determinants of Elite Rowing Technique and Performance." *Scandinavian Journal of Medicine and Science in Sports,* 25: 176-183.

Buckeridge, E.M., R.A. Weinert-Aplin, A.M. Bull, and A.H. McGregor. 2016. "Influence of Foot-Stretcher Height on Rowing Technique and Performance." *Sports Biomechanics* 15 (4): 513-526.

Caplan, N., and T. Gardner. 2005. "The Influence of Stretcher Height on the Mechanical Effectiveness of Rowing." *Journal of Applied Biomechanics* 21: 286-296.

Caplan, N., and T. Gardner. 2008. "The Influence of a Three Week Familiarization Period of Rowing Mechanics at a New Stretcher Position." *International Journal of Sports Science and Engineering* 2 (1): 15-22.

Herberger, E. 1987. *Rowing/Rudern: The GDR Text of Oarsmanship.* Toronto: Sport Book Publishers.

Jensen K. 2007. "Performance Assessment." In *Handbook of Sport Medicine and Science: Rowing,* edited by N. Secher and S. Volianitis, 96-102. Malden, MA: Blackwell Publishing.

Lamb, D.H. 1989. "A Kinematic Comparison of Ergometer and On Water Rowing." *American Journal of Sports Medicine* 17 (3): 367-373.

Liu, Y., B. Gao, J. Li, Z. Ma, and Y. Sun. 2018. "Increasing Foot-Stretcher Height Improves Rowing Performance: Evidence From Biomechanical Perspectives on Water." *Sports Biomechanics* 19 (2): 168-179.

Navy, M. 2011. "Body-Seat Interface Pressure and Discomfort During Rowing." MSc diss., University of Western Ontario.

Nolte, V. 2011. "Rigging." In *Rowing Faster,* edited by V. Nolte, 125-140. Champaign, IL: Human Kinetics.

Nolte, V., and S. McLaughlin. 2005. "The Balance of Crew Rowing Boats." *Malaysian Journal of Sport Science and Recreation,* 58-59.

Soper, C., and P.A. Hume. 2005. "Ergometer Rowing Performance Improves Over 2000m When Using a Steeper Foot Stretcher Angle." 23rd International Society of Biomechanics in Sports, Beijing, China.

Thornton, J.S., A. Vinther, F. Wilson, M.L. Lebrun, M. Wilkinson, S.R. Di Ciacca, K. Orlando, and T. Smoljanovic. 2017. "Rowing Injuries: An Updated Review." *Sports Medicine* 47: 641-661.

Torres-Moreno, R., C. Tanaka, and K.L. Penney. 2000. "Joint Excursion, Handle Velocity, and Applied Force: A Biomechanical Analysis of Ergonometric Rowing." *International Journal of Sports Medicine* 21: 41-44.

World Rowing. 2020. "FISA Rule Book 2017." Accessed July 1, 2020. https://worldrowing.com/2014/05/22/rule-book.

Chapter 9

Affeld, K., and K. Schichl. 1985. *Untersuchungen der Kräfte am Ruderblatt mithilfe eines mechanischen Simulators.* Internal Report: Technische Universität Berlin.

Ashbourne, B. 2008. "Evaluation of Computational Fluid Dynamics as a Method for Evaluating Oar Blade Response in Rowing." Graduate thesis, Mechanical and Materials Engineering, University of Western Ontario.

Borrmann, H. 1941. *Ruder, Boot und Bootshaus.* Wassersport-Verlag, Berlin, Germany.

Bourne, G.C. 1925. *A Textbook of Oarsmanship.* London: H. Milford.

Braca Sport. 2021. "Shaft Stiffness." Accessed May 2021. https://rowing.braca-sport.com/oars/shafts/shaft-stiffness.html.

Caplan, N., and T.N. Gardner. 2007. "Optimization of Oar Blade Design for Improved Performance in Rowing." Journal of Sports Sciences 25: 1471-1478.

Concept2. 2019. "Oars and Sculls." Accessed July 2019. https://www.concept2.com/files/pdf/us/oars/Oar_Brochure.pdf.

Concept2. 2021a. "The Vortex Edge." Accessed April 2021. https://www.concept2.com/oars/how-made-and-tested/vortex-edge.

Concept2. 2021b. Accessed April 2021. "Smoothie2 Vortex Edge Blade." Accessed April 2021. https://www.concept2.com/oars/oar-options/blades/smoothie2-vortex-edge.

Concept2. 2021c. "The Typical Blade Path During the Drive." Accessed April 2021, https://www.concept2.com/oars/how-made-and-tested/blade-path.

Croker Oars. 2021. "Handles and Grips." Accessed April 2021. https://www.crokeroars.com/handles-grips.

Davenport, M. 2002. *The Nuts and Bolts Guide to Rigging.* 10th ed. Centreville, MD: SportWork.

Dreher–Durham Boat Company. 2021. "Oars." Accessed April 2021. https://www.durhamboat.com/oars.

Dreissigacker, D., and P. Dreissigacker. 1992. "New on the Scene – the Big Blade." *FISA Coach* 3 (2): 9-12.

Empacher Bootswerft. 2021. "Racing Scull Shaft." Accessed May 2021. https://www.empacher.com/en/products/sculls-oars/racing-scull/#c577.

Filter, K. 2009. "The System Crew – Boat." Lecture. www.row2k.com/features/files/20160308ATBaddendumSystemCrewFilterPDF.pdf

Haines, A., E. Palombi, K. Shipley, and V. Nolte. 2004. "A Sweeping Improvement – Wind Tunnel Experiment Report." Internal report for mechanical design project MME 499. Faculty of Engineering, University of Western Ontario.

Kleshnev, V. 2016. *The Biomechanics of Rowing.* Ramsbury, Marlborough Wiltshire: The Crowood Press Ltd.

Kleshnev, V., and V. Nolte. 2011. "Learning From Racing." In *Rowing Faster*, 2nd ed., edited by V. Nolte, 253-267. Champaign, IL: Human Kinetics.

Kong, Y., and B. Lowe. 2005. "Optimal Cylindrical Handle Diameter for Grip Force Tasks." *International Journal of Industrial Ergonomics* 35: 495-507.

Körner, T., and P. Schwanitz. 1985. *Rudern.* Sportverlag Berlin.

Kuyt, C., A, Greidanus, and J. Westerweel. 2016. "Drag Reduction by Applying Speedstrips on Rowing Oars." 11th Conference of the International Sports Engineering Association (ISEA). *Procedia Engineering* 147: 110-115.

Laschowski, B., C. Hopkins, J. de Bruyn, and V. Nolte. 2016. "Modelling the Deflection of Rowing Oar Shafts." *Sports Biomechanics* 16 (1): 76-86.

Laschowski, B., V. Nolte, M. Adamovsky, and R. Alexander. 2015. "The Effects of Oar Shaft Stiffness and Length on Rowing Biomechanics." Proceedings of the Institution of Mechanical Engineers, Part P. *Journal of Sports Engineering and Technology* 229: 239-247.

McGinnis, P. 2013. *Biomechanics of Sport and Exercise.* 3rd ed. Champaign, IL: Human Kinetics.

Nolte, V. 1984. *Die Effektivität des Ruderschlages: Biomechanische Modelle, Analyse und Ergebnisse.* Berlin, Germany: Bartels & Wernitz Druckerei und Verlag KG.

Nolte, V. 2005. "Rigging." In *Rowing Faster,* edited by V. Nolte, 125-140. Champaign, IL: Human Kinetics.

Nolte, V. 2009. "Shorter Oars Are More Effective." *Journal of Applied Biomechanics* 25: 1-8.

Nolte, V. 2011. "Using Equipment More Effectively." In *Rowing Faster,* 2nd ed, edited by V. Nolte, 125-144. Champaign, IL: Human Kinetics.

Nolte, V., and B. Ashbourne. 2006. "Dem Antrieb beim Rudern aufs Blatt geschaut." In *Sporttechnologie zwischen Theorie und Praxis,* edited by K. Witte, J. Edelmann-Nusser, E. Sabo, and E. Moritz, 329-338. Aachen, Germany: Shaker Verlag.

Nolte, V., and V. Kleshnev. 2011. "Facts. Do You Know That..." *Rowing Biomechanics Newsletter* 11, no. 126 (September).

Nolte, V. 2021a. "Rigging Numbers for Scullers. A Primer on Basic Measurements." *Rowing* 28, no. 1 (February): 62.

Nolte, V. 2021b. "A Primer on Sweep Rigging Numbers. Start With a Zero-Number and Tweak From There." *Rowing* 28, no. 2 (March): 62.

Nørstrud, H., and E. Meese. 2013. "On the Hydrodynamics of Rowing Oars and Blade Design." In *Sports Physics,* edited by C. Clanet, 115-122. École Polytechnique.

Ritchie, A. 2007. "Effect of Oar Design on the Efficiency of the Rowing Stroke." In *The Impact of Technology on Sport II,* edited by A. Subic, F.K. Fuss, and S. Ujihashi, 509-512. Abingdon: Taylor & Francis Group.

Secher, N. 1993. "Physiological and Biomechanical Aspects of Rowing." *Sports Medicine* 15 (1): 24-42.

Sliasas, A. 2012. "Understanding the Interaction of the Blade in the Water." Presentation at the 2012 Rowing Canada Coaches Conference. Toronto, Canada.

Sliasas, A., and S. Tullis. 2009. "A Hydrodynamics-Based Model of a Rowing Stroke Simulating Effects of Drag and Lift on Oar Blade Efficiency for Various Cant Angles." 8th Conference of the International Sports Engineering Association (ISEA). *Procedia Engineering* 2857-2862.

Sliasas, A., and S. Tullis. 2010. "The Dynamic Flow Behaviour of an Oar Blade in Motion using a Hydrodynamics-Based Shell-Velocity-Coupled Model of a Rowing Stroke." Proceedings of the Institution of Mechanical Engineers, Part P. *Journal of Sports Engineering and Technology* 224 (1): 9-24. doi: 10.1243/17543371JSET57.

Thompson, P. 2005. *Sculling.* Crowood Press Ltd., Ramsbury, UK.

Volianitis, S., and N. Secher. 2007. "History." In *Handbook of Sport Medicine and Science: Rowing,* edited by N. Secher and S. Volianitis, 1-21. Malden, MA: Blackwell Publishing.

Wolloner, L. 1983. Personal communication.

Woodgate, W.B. 1888. *Boating.* London: Longmans, Green & Co.

World Rowing. 2021. "FISA Rule Book 2019." Accessed April 2021. http://www.worldrowing.com/fisa/events-update/rule-book.

Chapter 10

Baggish, Aaron L., Kibar Yared, Rory B. Weiner, Francis Wang, Robert Demes, Michael H. Picard, Fredrick Hagerman, and Malissa J. Wood. 2010. "Differences in Cardiac Parameters Among Elite Rowers and Subelite Rowers." *Medicine & Science in Sports & Exercise* 42 (6): 1215-1220.

Baggish, A.L., F. Wang, R.B. Weiner, J.M. Elinoff, F. Tournoux, A. Boland, M.H. Picard, A.M. Hutter, and M.J. Wood. 2008. "Training-Specific Changes in Cardiac Structure and Function: A Prospective and Longitudinal Assessment of Competitive Athletes." *Journal of Applied Physiology (1985)* 104 (4): 1121-1128.

Bourdin, Muriel, Jean-Rene Lacour, Charles Imbert, and Laurent André Messonnier. 2017. "Factors of Rowing Ergometer Performance in High-Level Female Rowers." *International Journal of Sports Medicine* 38 (13): 1023-1028.

Dempsey, Jerome A., and Peter D. Wagner. 1999. "Exercise-Induced Arterial Hypoxemia." *Journal of Applied Physiology* 87 (6): 1997-2006.

Ekblom, B., and L. Hermansen. 1968. "Cardiac Output in Athletes." *Journal of Applied Physiology* 25 (5): 619-625.

Hagberg, James M., William K. Allen, Douglas R. Seals, B.F. Hurley, A.A. Ehsani, and J.O. Holloszy. 1985. "A Hemodynamic Comparison of Young and Older Endurance Athletes During Exercise." *Journal of Applied Physiology* 58 (6): 2041-2046.

Hartmann, Ulrich, and Alois Mader. 2005. "Rowing Physiology." In *Rowing Faster*, edited by Volker Nolte, 9-23. Champaign, IL: Human Kinetics.

Kerr, D.A, W.D. Ross, K. Norton, P. Hume, M. Kagawa, and T.R. Ackland. 2007. "Olympic Lightweight and Open-Class Rowers Possess Distinctive Physical and Proportionality Characteristics." *Journal of Sports Sciences* 25 (1): 43-53.

Larsson, L., and A. Forsberg. 1980. "Morphological Muscle Characteristics in Rowers." *Canadian Journal of Applied Sport Sciences* 5 (4): 239-244.

Levine, B.D. 2008. "VO2 Max: What Do We Know, and What Do We Still Need to Know?" *Journal of Physiology* 586: 25-33.

Levine, B.D., L.D. Lane, J.C. Buckey, D.B. Friedman, and C.G. Blomqvist. 1991. "Left Ventricular Pressure-Volume and Frank-Starling Relations in Endurance Athletes. Implications for Orthostatic Tolerance and Exercise Performance." *Circulation* 84 (3): 1016-1023.

Nielsen, H.B. 1999. "Ph After Competitive Rowing: The Lower Physiological Range?" *Acta Physiologica Scandinavica* 165 (1): 113-114.

Nielsen, H.B., and P.M. Christensen. 2020. "Rower With Danish Record in Maximal Oxygen Uptake." *Ugeskr Laeger* 182 (8).

Pripstein, L.P., E.C. Rhodes, D.C. McKenzie, and K.D. Coutts. 1999. "Aerobic and Anaerobic Energy During a 2-Km Race Simulation in Female Rowers." *European Journal of Applied Physiology* 79 (6): 491-494.

Roth, W., E. Hasart, W. Wolf, and B. Pansold. 1983. "Untersuchungen Zur Dynamik Der Energie-bereitstellung Während Maximaler Mittelzeitausdauerbelastung." *Med Sport (Berl)* 23: 107-114.

Roth, W., P. Schwanitz, P. Pas, and P. Bauer. 1993. "Force-Time Characteristics of the Rowing Stroke and Corresponding Physiological Muscle Adaptations." *International Journal of Sports Medicine* 14 (Suppl. 1): S32-S34.

Rowell, L.B. 1986. *Human Circulation Regulation During Physical Stress.* New York: Oxford University Press.

Schierbauer, Janis, Torben Hoffmeister, Gunnar Treff, Nadine B. Wachsmuth, and Walter F.J. Schmidt. 2021. "Effect of Exercise Induced Reductions in Blood Volume on Cardiac Output and Oxygen Transport Capacity." *Frontiers in Physiology* 12: 770.

Secher, N.H. 1993. "Physiological and Biomechanical Aspects of Rowing: Implications for Training." *Sports Medicine* 15 (1): 24–42.

Sousa, A., J. Ribeiro, M. Sousa, J.P. Vilas-Boas, and R.J. Fernandes. 2014. "Influence of Prior Exercise on Vo2 Kinetics Subsequent Exhaustive Rowing Performance." *PLOS One* 9 (1): e84208.

Steinacker, J.M., W. Lormes, M. Lehmann, and D. Altenburg. 1998. "Training of Rowers Before World Championships." *Medicine & Science in Sports & Exercise* 30 (7): 1158-1163.

Telford, R.D., J.C. Kovacic, S.L. Skinner, J.B. Hobbs, A.G. Hahn, and R.B. Cunningham. 1994. "Resting Whole Blood Viscosity of Elite Rowers is Related to Performance." *European Journal of Applied Physiology* 68 (6): 470-476.

Treff, G., W. Schmidt, N. Wachsmuth, C. Völzke, and J.M. Steinacker. 2013. "Total Haemoglobin Mass, Maximal and Submaximal Power in Elite Rowers." *International Journal of Sports Medicine* 35 (7): 571-574.

Volianitis, Stefanos, C.C. Yoshiga, and Niels H. Secher. 2020. "The Physiology of Rowing With Perspective on Training and Health." *European Journal of Applied Physiology* 120: 1943-1963.

Wasfy, M.M., R.B. Weiner, F. Wang, B. Berkstresser, G.D. Lewis, J.R. DeLuca, A,M. Hutter, M.H. Picard, and A.L. Baggish. 2015. "Endurance Exercise-Induced Cardiac Remodeling: Not All Sports Are Created Equal." *Journal of the American Society of Echocardiography* 28 (12): 1434-1440.

Winkert, Kay, Jürgen M. Steinacker, Katja Machus, Jens Dreyhaupt, and Gunnar Treff. 2019. "Anthropometric Profiles Are Associated With Long-Term Career Attainment in Elite Junior Rowers: A Retrospective Analysis Covering 23 Years." *European Journal of Sport Science* 19: 208-216.

Chapter 11

Allen, D., and H. Westerblad. 2004. "Physiology. Lactic Acid—the Latest Performance-Enhancing Drug." *Science* 305 (5687): 1112-1113.

Allen, D.G. 2020. "Human Muscle Performance." *Journal of Physiology* 598 (4): 613-614.

Allen, D.G., G.D. Lamb, and H. Westerblad. 2008. "Skeletal Muscle Fatigue: Cellular Mechanisms." *Physiological Reviews* 88 (1): 287-332.

Armstrong, R.B. 1988. "Muscle Fiber Recruitment Patterns and Their Metabolic Correlates." *Exercise, Nutrition and Energy Metabolism* 9-26.

Bangsbo, J., and C. Juel. 2006. "Counterpoint: Lactic Acid Accumulation Is a Disadvantage During Muscle Activity." *Journal of Applied Physiology (1985)* 100 (4): 1412-1413.

Bergman, B.C., E.E. Wolfel, G.E. Butterfield, G.D. Lopaschuk, G.A. Casazza, M.A. Horning, and G.A. Brooks. 1999a. "Active Muscle and Whole Body Lactate Kinetics After Endurance Training in Men." *Journal of Applied Physiology (1985)* 87 (5): 1684-1696.

Bergman, B.C., G.E. Butterfield, E.E. Wolfel, G.D. Lopaschuk, G.A. Casazza, M.A. Horning, and G.A. Brooks. 1999b. "Muscle Net Glucose Uptake and Glucose Kinetics After Endurance Training in Men." *American Journal of Physiology-Endocrinology and Metabolism* 277: E81-E92.

Bergman, B.C., M.A. Horning, G.A. Casazza, E.E. Wolfel, G.E. Butterfield, and G.A. Brooks. 2000. "Endurance Training Increases Gluconeogenesis During Rest and Exercise in Men." *American Journal of Physiology-Endocrinology and Metabolism* 278 (2): E244-E251.

Brooks, G.A. 1985. "Lactate: Glycolytic End Product and Oxidative Substrate During Sustained Exercise in Mammals—the 'Lactate Shuttle.'" In *Comparative Physiology and Biochemistry: Current Topics and Trends, Volume A, Respiration-Metabolism-Circulation*, edited by R. Gilles, 208-218. New York: Springer.

Brooks, G.A. 2020a. "Lactate as a Fulcrum of Metabolism." *Redox Biology* 35: 101454.

Brooks, G.A. 2020b. "The Tortuous Path of Lactate Shuttle Discovery: From Cinders and Boards to the Lab and ICU." *Journal of Sport and Health Science* 9 (5): 446-460.

Brooks, G.A., J.A. Arevalo, A.D. Osmond, R.G. Leija, C.C. Curl, and A.P. Tovar. 2021. "Lactate in Contemporary Biology: A Phoenix Risen." *Journal of Physiology*. https://doi.org/10.1113/JP280955.

Brooks, G.A., T.G. Brooks, and S. Brooks. 2008. "Lactate as a Metabolic Signal of Gene Expression." *German Journal of Sports Medicine* 59 (12): 280-286.

Brooks, G.A., and J. Mercier. 1994. "Balance of Carbohydrate and Lipid Utilization During Exercise: The 'Crossover' Concept." *Journal of Applied Physiology (1985)* 76 (6): 2253-2261.

Brooks, G.A., and J.K. Trimmer. 1996. "Glucose Kinetics During High-Intensity Exercise and the Crossover Concept." *Journal of Applied Physiology (1985)* 80 (3): 1073-1075.

Brooks, George A. 2018. "The Science and Translation of Lactate Shuttle Theory." *Cell Metabolism* 27 (4): 757-785.

Clanton, T.L., M.C. Hogan, and L.B. Gladden. 2013. "Regulation of Cellular Gas Exchange, Oxygen Sensing, and Metabolic Control." *Comprehensive Physiology* 3: 1135-1190.

Dubouchaud, H., G.E. Butterfield, E.E. Wolfel, B.C. Bergman, and G.A. Brooks. 2000. "Endurance Training, Expression, and Physiology of Ldh, Mct1, and Mct4 in Human Skeletal Muscle." *American Journal of PhysiologyEndocrinology and Metabolism* 278 (4): E571–9.

Fabiato, A., and F. Fabiato. 1978. "Effects of Ph on the Myofilaments and the Sarcoplasmic Reticulum of Skinned Cells From Cardiac and Skeletal Muscles." *Journal of Physiology* 276: 233-255.

Ferguson, Brian S., Matthew J. Rogatzki, Matthew L. Goodwin, Daniel A. Kane, Zachary Rightmire, and L. Bruce Gladden. 2018. "Lactate Metabolism: Historical Context, Prior Misinterpretations, and Current Understanding." *European Journal of Applied Physiology* 118 (4): 691-728.

Fiskerstrand, A., and K.S. Seiler. 2004. "Training and Performance Characteristics Among Norwegian International Rowers 1970-2001." *Scandinavian Journal of Medicine and Science in Sports* 14 (5): 303–10.

Fitts, R.H. 1994. "Cellular Mechanisms of Muscle Fatigue." *Physiological Reviews* 74 (1): 49-94.

Fitts, R.H. 2016. "The Role of Acidosis in Fatigue: Pro Perspective." *Medicine & Science in Sports & Exercise* 48 (11): 2335-2238.

Gaitanos, G.C., C. Williams, L.H. Boobis, and S. Brooks. 1993. "Human Muscle Metabolism During Intermittent Maximal Exercise." *Journal of Applied Physiology (1985)* 75 (2): 712-719.

Gertz, E.W., J.A. Wisneski, W.C. Stanley, and R.A. Neese. 1988. "Myocardial Substrate Utilization During Exercise in Humans. Dual Carbon-Labeled Carbohydrate Isotope Experiments." *Journal of Clinical Investigation* 82 (6): 2017-2025.

Gladden, L.B. 2016. "The Basic Science of Exercise Fatigue." *Medicine & Science in Sports & Exercise* 48 (11): 2222-2223.

Lamb, Graham D., and D. George Stephenson. 2006. "Point:Counterpoint: Lactic Acid Accumulation is an Advantage/Disadvantage During Muscle Activity." *Journal of Applied Physiology* 100 (4): 1410-1412.

Hargreaves, Mark, and Lawrence L. Spriet. 2020. "Skeletal Muscle Energy Metabolism During Exercise." *Nature Metabolism* 2 (9): 817-828.

Hogan, M.C., L.B. Gladden, S.S. Kurdak, and D.C. Poole. 1995. "Increased [Lactate] in Working Dog Muscle Reduces Tension Development Independent of Ph." *Medicine & Science in Sports & Exercise* 27 (3): 371-377.

Huxley, A F. 1974. "Muscular Contraction." *The Journal of Physiology* 243 (1): 1-43.

Kent-Braun, J.A., R.H. Fitts, and A. Christie. 2012. "Skeletal Muscle Fatigue." *Comprehensive Physiology* 2: 997-1044.

Maassen, N., and D. Boning. 2008. "Physiologische 'nebenwirkungen' Der Milchsaeure." *Deutsche Zeitschrift fur Sportmedizin* 59 (12): 292.

Maciejewski, H., M. Bourdin, L. Féasson, D. Hervé, and L.A. Messonnier. 2020. "Non-Oxidative Energy Supply Correlates With Lactate Transport and Removal in Trained Rowers." *International Journal of Sports Medicine.*

MacRae, H.S., Steven C. Dennis, Andrew N. Bosch, and Timothy D. Noakes. 1992. "Effects of Training on Lactate Production and Removal During Progressive Exercise in Humans." *Journal of Applied Physiology* 72 (5): 1649-1656.

Mader, A., and W. Hollmann. 1977. "Zur Bedeutung Der Stoffwechselleistungsfaehigkeit Des Eliteruderers Im Training Und Wettkampf." *Leistungssport* 9: 8-62.

Mazzeo, R.S., G.A. Brooks, D.A. Schoeller, and T.F. Budinger. 1986. "Disposal of Blood [1-13c] Lactate in Humans During Rest and Exercise." *Journal of Applied Physiology* 60 (1): 232-241.

Miller, B.F., J.A. Fattor, K.A. Jacobs, M.A. Horning, F. Navazio, M.I. Lindinger, and G.A. Brooks. 2002. "Lactate and Glucose Interactions During Rest and Exercise in Men: Effect of Exogenous Lactate Infusion." *Journal of Physiology* 544 (3): 963-975.

Mougios, V. 2007. "Reference Intervals for Serum Creatine Kinase in Athletes." *British Journal of Sports Medicine* 41 (10): 674-678.

Olsson, K., A.J. Cheng, M. Al-Ameri, V.L. Wyckelsma, E. Rullman, H. Westerblad, J.T. Lanner, T. Gustafsson, and J.D. Bruton. 2020. "Impaired Sarcoplasmic Reticulum Ca^{2+} Release is the Major Cause of Fatigue-Induced Force Loss in Intact Single Fibres From Human Intercostal Muscle." *Journal of Physiology* 598 (4): 773-787.

Pellerin, L., G. Pellegri, P.G. Bittar, Y. Charnay, C. Bouras, J.L. Martin, N. Stella, and P.J. Magistretti. 1998. "Evidence Supporting the Existence of an Activity-Dependent Astrocyte-Neuron Lactate Shuttle." *Developmental Neuroscience* 20 (4-5): 291–299.

Poole, David C., Harry B. Rossiter, George A. Brooks, and L. Bruce Gladden. 2021. "The Anaerobic Threshold: 50+ Years of Controversy." *The Journal of Physiology* 599 (3): 737-767.

Pripstein, L.P., E.C. Rhodes, D.C. McKenzie, and K.D. Coutts. 1999. "Aerobic and Anaerobic Energy During a 2-Km Race Simulation in Female Rowers." *European Journal of Applied Physiology* 79 (6): 491-494.

Romijn, J.A., E.F. Coyle, L.S. Sidossis, A. Gastaldelli, and J.F. Endert Horowitz, E. Wolfe, R.R. 1993. "Regulation of Endogenous Fat and Carbohydrate Metabolism in Relation to Exercise Intensity and Duration." *American Journal of Physiology-Endocrinology and Metabolism* 265: E380-E391.

Roth, W., E. Hasart, W. Wolf, and B. Pansold. 1983. "Untersuchungen Zur Dynamik Der Energiebereitstellung Während Maximaler Mittelzeitausdauerbelastung." *Med Sport (Berl)* 23: 107-114.

Secher, N.H., M. Espersen, and R.A. Binkhorst. 1982. "Aerobic Power At the Onset of Maximal Exercise." *Scandinavian Journal of Sports Science* 4: 12-16.

Spriet, L.L. 2014. "New Insights Into the Interaction of Carbohydrate and Fat Metabolism During Exercise." *Sports Medicine* 44 (Suppl. 1): S87-S96.

Stanley, W.C., E.W. Gertz, J.A. Wisneski, R.A. Neese, D.L. Morris, and G.A. Brooks. 1986. "Lactate Extraction During Net Lactate Release in Legs of Humans During Exercise." *Journal of Applied Physiology (1985)* 60 (4): 1116-1120.

Steinacker, Jürgen M. 1993. "Physiological Aspects of Training in Rowing." *International Journal of Sports Medicine* 14 (Suppl. 1): S3-S10.

Treff, G., K. Winkert, M. Sareban, J.M. Steinacker, M. Becker, and B. Sperlich. 2017. "Eleven-Week Preparation Involving Polarized Intensity Distribution is Not Superior to Pyramidal Distribution in National Elite Rowers." *Frontiers in Physiology* 8: 515.

Treff, Gunnar, R. Leppich, K. Winkert, J.M. Steinacker, B. Mayer, and B. Sperlich. 2021. "The Integration of Training and Off-Training Activities Substantially Alters Training Volume and Load Analysis in Elite Rowers." *Scientific Reports* 11 (1): 17218.

Volianitis, Stefanos, C.C. Yoshiga, and Niels H Secher. 2020. "The Physiology of Rowing With Perspective on Training and Health." *European Journal of Applied Physiology* 120: 1943-1963.

Wasserman, K, B.J. Whipp, S.N. Koyl, and W.L. Beaver. 1973. "Anaerobic Threshold and Respiratory Gas Exchange During Exercise." *Journal of Applied Physiology* 35 (2): 236-43.

Westerblad, H. 2016. "Acidosis is Not a Significant Cause of Skeletal Muscle Fatigue." *Medicine & Science in Sports & Exercise* 48 (11): 2339-2242.

Winkert, Kay, Juergen M. Steinacker, Karsten Koehler, and Gunnar Treff. 2022. "High Energetic Demand of Elite Rowing—Implications for Training and Nutrition." *Frontiers in Physiology* 13: 829757.

Chapter 12

Abe, Takashi, Senshi Fukashiro, Yasuhiro Harada, and Kazuhisa Kawamoto. 2001. "Relationship Between Sprint Performance and Muscle Fascicle Length in Female Sprinters." *Journal of Physiological Anthropology and Applied Human Science* 20 (2): 141-147.

Arsoniadis, Gavriil, Petros Botonis, Gregory C. Bogdanis, Gerasimos Terzis, and Argyris Toubekis. 2022. "Acute and Long-Term Effects of Concurrent Resistance and Swimming Training on Swimming Performance." *Sports* 10 (3): 29. https://doi.org/10.3390/sports10030029.

Bentley, D.J., P.A. Smith, A.J. Davie, S. Zhou. 2000. "Muscle Activation of the Knee Extensors Following High Intensity Endurance Exercise in Cyclists." *European Journal of Applied Physiology* 81, no. 4 (March): 297-302. doi: 10.1007/s004210050046. PMID: 10664088.

Bentley, D.J., S. Zhou, and A.J. Davie. 1998. "The Effect of Endurance Exercise on Muscle Force Generating Capacity of the Lower Limbs." *Journal of Science and Medicine in Sport* 1 (3): 179-188.

Craig, B., J. Lucas, R. Pohlman, and H. Stelling. 1991. "The Effects of Running, Weightlifting and a Combination of Both on Growth Hormone Release." *Journal of Strength and Conditioning Research* 5: 198-203.

Ellefsen, S., and K. Baar. 2019. "Proposed Mechanisms Underlying the Interference Effect." In *Concurrent Aerobic and Strength Training: Scientific Basics and Practical Applications*, edited by M. Schumann and B. Ronnestad, 89-99. Cham, Switzerland: Springer Nature.

Franchi, M.V., P.J. Atherton, C.N. Maganaris, and M.V. Narici. 2016. "Fascicle Length Does Increase in Response to Longitudinal Resistance Training and in a Contraction-Mode Specific Manner." *SpringerPlus* 5, no. 94 (January 28). doi: 10.1186/s40064-015-1548-8.

García-Pallarés, J., L. Sánchez-Medina, L. Carrasco, A. Díaz, and M. Izquierdo. 2009. "Endurance and Neuromuscular Changes in World-Class Level Kayakers During a Periodized Training Cycle." *European Journal of Applied Physiology* 106: 629-638.

Goldspink, G. 1992. "Cellular and Molecular Aspects of Adaptation in Skeletal Muscle." In *Strength and Power in Sport*, edited by P.V. Komi, 211229. London, England: Blackwell Scientific Publications.

Hakkinen, K. and P.V. Komi. 1983. "Electromyographic changes during strength training and detraining." *Medicine and Science in Sports Exercise* 15 (6): 455-460.

Hakkinen, K., P.V. Komi, and M. Alen, 1985. "Effect of Explosive Type Strength Training on Isometric Force and Relaxation Time, Electromyographic and Muscle Fibre Characteristics of Leg Extensor Muscles." *Acta Physiolica Scandinavica* 125: 587-600.

Hartmann, U., A. Mader, K. Wasser, and I. Klauer. 1993. "Peak Force, Velocity, and Power During Five and Ten Maximal Rowing Ergometer Strokes by World Class Female and Male rowers." *International Journal of Sports Medicine* 14 (Suppl. 1): S42-S45.

Henneman, E. 1957. "Relationship Between Size of Neurons and Their Susceptibility to Discharge." *Science* 1126: 1345-1347.

Hickson, R.C. 1980. "Interference of Strength Development by Simultaneously Training for Strength and Endurance." *European Journal of Applied Physiology and Occupational Physiology* 45 (2-3): 255-263. https://doi.org/10.1007/bf00421333.

Ingham, S.A., G.P. Whyte, K. Jones, and A.M. Nevill. 2002. "Determinants of 2,000 m Rowing Ergometer Performance in Elite Rowers." *European Journal of Applied Physiology* 88 (3): 243-6. doi: 10.1007/s00421-002-0699-9. Epub 2002 Oct 10. PMID: 12458367.

Kearns, Charles F., William F. Brechue, and Takashi Abe. 1998. "Training-Induced Changes in Fascicle Length: A Brief Review." *Advances in Exercise and Sports Physiology* 4 (3): 77-81.

Kim, J., and E.K. Kim. 2020. "Nutritional Strategies to Optimize Performance and Recovery in Rowing Athletes." *Nutrients* 12, no. 6 (June 5): 1685. doi: 10.3390/nu12061685.

Konrad, A., and M. Tilp. 2014. "Increased Range of Motion After Static Stretching Is Not Due to Changes in Muscle and Tendon Structures." *Clinical Biomechanics* 29: 636-642. doi: 10.1016/j.clinbiomech.2014.04.013.

Küüsmaa, M., M. Schumann, M. Sedliak, W.J. Kraemer, R.U. Newton, J.P. Malinen, K. Nyman, A. Häkkinen, and K. Häkkinen. 2016. "Effects of Morning Versus Evening Combined Strength and Endurance Training on Physical Performance, Muscle Hypertrophy, and Serum Hormone Concentrations." *Applied Physiology, Nutrition, and Metabolism* 41, no. 12 (December): 1285-1294. doi: 10.1139/apnm-2016-0271. PMID: 27863207.

Latorre-Román, P.Á., F. García-Pinillos, E.J. Martínez-López, and V.M. Soto-Hermoso. 2014. "Concurrent Fatigue and Postactivation Potentiation During Extended Interval Training in Long-Distance Runners." *Motriz: Revista de Educação Física* 20: 423-430.

Lawton, T., J.B. Cronin, and M.R. McGuigan. 2013. "Factors That Affect Selection of Elite Women's Sculling Crews." *International Journal of Sports Physiology and Performance* 8: 38-43.

Leveritt, M., and P.J. Abernethy. 1999. "Acute Effects of High-Intensity Endurance Exercise on Subsequent Resistance Activity." *Journal of Strength and Conditioning Research* 13: 47-51.

Lundberg, T. 2019. "Long Term Effects of Supplementary Aerobic Training on Muscle Hypertrophy." In *Concurrent Aerobic and Strength Training: Scientific Basics and Practical Applications*, edited by M. Schumann and B. Ronnestad, 167-180. Cham, Switzerland: Springer Nature.

McNeely, E. 2012. "Rowing Ergometer Physiological Tests Do Not Predict on Water Performance." *Sports Journal* (January).

Mikulic, P. 2009. "Anthropometric and Metabolic Determinants of 6000 m Rowing Ergometer Performance in Internationally Competitive Rowers." *Journal of Strength and Conditioning Research* 23 (6): 1851-1857.

Moritani, T. and H.A. DeVries. 1979. "Neural Factors Versus Hypertrophy in the Time Course of Muscle Strength Gain." *American Journal of Physical Medicine* 58 (3):115-130.

Panidi, I., G.C. Bogdanis, G. Terzis, A. Donti, A. Konrad, V. Gaspari, and O. Donti. 2021. "Muscle Architectural and Functional Adaptations Following 12-Weeks of Stretching in Adolescent Female Athletes." *Frontiers in Physiology* 12 (July 16): 701338. doi: 10.3389/fphys.2021.701338. PMID: 34335307. PMCID: PMC8322691.

Reed, J.P., B.K. Schilling, and Z. Murlasits. 2013. "Acute Neuromuscular and Metabolic Responses to Concurrent Endurance and Resistance Exercise." *Journal of Strength and Conditioning Research* 27: 793-801.

Riechman, S., R. Zoeller, G. Balasekaran, F. Goss, and R. Robertson. 2002. "Prediction of 2000m Indoor Rowing Performance Using a 30s Sprint and Maximal Oxygen Uptake." *Journal of Sport Sciences* 20: 681-687.

Russell, A.P., Rossignol, P.F., and Sparrow, W.A. 1998. "Prediction of Elite Schoolboy 2000m Rowing Ergometer Performance From Metabolic, Anthropometric, and Strength Variables." *Journal of Sport Sciences* 16: 749-754.

Rutherford, O.M., and D.A. Jones. 1986. "The role of learning and coordination in strength training." *European Journal of Applied Physiology* 55 (1):100-105.

Sale, D.G., J.D. MacDougall, A.R.M. Upton, and A.J. McComas. 1983. "Effect of strength training upon motoneuron excitability in man." *Medicine and Science in Sports and Exercise* 15 (1): 57-62.

Sale, D.G. 1992. "Neural Adaptations to Strength Training." In *Strength and Power in Sport*, edited by P.V. Komi, 249265. London, England: Blackwell Scientific Publications.

Sale, D.G., I. Jacobs, J.D. MacDougall, and S. Garner. 1990. "Comparison of Two Regimens of Concurrent Strength and Endurance Training." *Medicine & Science in Sports & Exercise* 22 (3): 348-356.

Secher, N. 1975. "Isometric Rowing Strength of Experienced and Inexperienced Oarsmen." *Medicine & Science in Sports & Exercise* 7: 280-283.

Slater, Gary J., Anthony J. Rice, Inigo Mujika, Allan G. Hahn, Ken Sharpe, and David G. Jenkins. 2005. "Physique Traits of Lightweight Rowers and Their Relationship to Competitive Success." *British Journal of Sports Medicine* 39 (10): 736-741.

Sporer, B.C., and H.A. Wenger. 2003. "Effects of Aerobic Exercise on Strength Performance Following Various Periods of Recovery." *Journal of Strength and Conditioning Research* 17: 638-644.

Steinacker, J.M. 1993. "Physiological Aspects of Training for Rowing." *International Journal of Sports Medicine* 14 (Suppl. 1): S3-S10.

Tachinaba, K., K. Yashiro, J. Miyazaki, Y. Ikegami, and M. Higuchi. 2007. "Muscle Cross Sectional Area and Performance Power of Limbs and Trunk in the Rowing Motion." *Sports Biomechanics* 6 (1): 44-58.

Tan, J.G., J.W. Coburn, L.E. Brown, and D.A. Judelson. 2014. "Effects of a Single Bout of Lower-Body Aerobic Exercise on Muscle Activation and Performance During Subsequent Lower- and Upper-Body Resistance Exercise Workouts." *Journal of Strength and Conditioning Research* 28: 1235-1240.

Thiele, Dirk, Olaf Prieske, Helmi Chaabene, and Urs Granacher. 2020. "Effects of Strength Training on Physical Fitness and Sport-Specific Performance in Recreational, Sub-Elite, and Elite Rowers: A Systematic Review With Meta-Analysis." *Journal of Sports Sciences* 38 (10): 1186-1195.

Timmins, Ryan G., Anthony J. Shield, Morgan D. Williams, Christian Lorenzen, and David A. Opar. 2016. "Architectural Adaptations of Muscle to Training and Injury: A Narrative Review Outlining the Contributions by Fascicle Length, Pennation Angle and Muscle Thickness." *British Journal of Sports Medicine* 50 (23): 1467-1472.

Thomas, D.T., K.A. Erdman, and L.M. Burke. 2016. "American College of Sports Medicine Joint Statement." *Nutrition and Athletic Performance* 48, no. 3 (March): 543-568. doi: 10.1249/MSS.0000000000000852.

van Wessel T, A. de Haan, W.J. van der Laarse, and R.T. Jaspers. 2010. "The Muscle Fiber Type-Fiber Size Paradox: Hypertrophy or Oxidative Metabolism?" *European Journal of Applied Physiology* 110, no. 4 (November): 665-694. doi: 10.1007/s00421-010-1545-0. Epub 2010 Jul 3. PMID: 20602111. PMCID: PMC2957584.

van der Zwaard, Stephan, Tommie F.P. Koppens, Guido Weide, Koen Levels, Mathijs J. Hofmijster, Jos J. De Koning, and Richard T. Jaspers. 2021. "Training-Induced Muscle Adaptations During Competitive Preparation in Elite Female Rowers." *Frontiers in Sports and Active Living* 3.

van der Zwaard, Stephan, Guido Weide, Koen Levels, Michelle R.I. Eikelboom, Dionne A. Noordhof, Mathijs J. Hofmijster, Willem J. van der Laarse, Jos J. de Koning, Cornelis J. de Ruiter, and Richard T. Jaspers. 2018. "Muscle Morphology of the Vastus Lateralis Is Strongly Related to Ergometer Performance, Sprint Capacity and Endurance Capacity in Olympic Rowers." *Journal of Sports Sciences* 36 (18): 2111-2120.

Wilson, J.M., P.J. Marin, M.R. Rhea, S.M. Wilson, J.P. Loenneke, and J.C. Anderson. 2012. "Concurrent Training: A Meta-Analysis Examining Interference of Aerobic and Resistance Exercises." *Journal of Strength and Conditioning Research* 26 (8): 2293-2307.

Yashiro, K., K. Tachibana, C. Usui, J. Miyazaki, T. Tani, and M. Higuchi. 2003. "2000 Meter Rowing Power and Muscle Cross Sectional Areas." *Medicine & Science in Sports & Exercise* 35 (5, Suppl. 1): S389.

Yoshiga, C.C., and M. Higuchi. 2003. "Bilateral Leg Extension Power and Fatfree Mass in Young Oarsmen." *Journal of Sports Sciences* 21: 905-909.

Chapter 13

Adams, W.C., W.M. Savin, and A.E. Christo. 1981. "Detection of Ozone Toxicity During Continuous Exercise via the Effective Dose Concept." *Journal of Applied Physiology* 51: 415-422. https://doi.org/10.1152/jappl.1981.51.2.415.

Cain, J.B., S.D. Livingstone, R.W. Nolan, and A.A. Keefe. 1990. "Respiratory Heat Loss During Work at Various Ambient Temperatures." *Respiration Physiology* 79: 145-150. https://doi.org/10.1016/0034-5687(90)90014-P.

Chapman, R.F., J. Stray-Gundersen, and B.D. Levine. 1998. "Individual Variation in Response to Altitude Training." *Journal of Applied Physiology* 85: 1448-1456. https://doi.org/10.1152/jappl.1998.85.4.1448.

Cheung, S.S., and G.G. Sleivert. 2004. "Multiple Triggers for Hyperthermic Fatigue and Exhaustion." *Exercise and Sport Sciences Reviews* 32: 100-106.

Ely, M.R., S.N. Cheuvront, W.O. Roberts, and S.J. Montain. 2007. "Impact of Weather on Marathon-Running Performance." *Medicine & Science in Sports & Exercise* 39: 487-493. https://doi.org/10.1249/mss.0b013e31802d3aba.

Ferguson, S.A.H., N.D. Eves, B.D. Roy, et al. 2018. "Effects of Mild Whole Body Hypothermia on Self-Paced Exercise Performance." *Journal of Applied Physiology* 125: 479-485. https://doi.org/10.1152/japplphysiol.01134.2017.

Galloway, S.D., and R.J. Maughan. 1997. "Effects of Ambient Temperature on the Capacity to Perform Prolonged Cycle Exercise in Man." *Medicine & Science in Sports & Exercise* 29: 1240-1249.

Giles, L.V., C. Carlsten, and M.S. Koehle. 2012. "The Effect of Pre-Exercise Diesel Exhaust Exposure on Cycling Performance and Cardio-Respiratory Variables." *Inhalation Toxicology* 24: 783-789. https://doi.org/10.3109/08958378.2012.717649.

Gore, C.J., A.G. Hahn, R.J. Aughey, et al. 2001. "Live High:Train Low Increases Muscle Buffer Capacity and Submaximal Cycling Efficiency." *Acta Physiologica Scandinavica* 173: 275-286. https://doi.org/10.1046/j.1365-201X.2001.00906.x.

Hartung, G.H., L.G. Myhre, and S.A. Nunneley. 1980. "Physiological Effects of Cold Air Inhalation During Exercise." *Aviation, Space, and Environmental Medicine* 51: 591-594.

Hazucha, M.J., L.J. Folinsbee, and E. Seal. 1992. "Effects of Steady-State and Variable Ozone Concentration Profiles on Pulmonary Function." *American Review of Respiratory Disease* 146: 1487-1493. https://doi.org/10.1164/ajrccm/146.6.1487.

Mallette, M.M., L.A. Green, D.A. Gabriel, and S.S. Cheung. 2018. "The Effects of Local Forearm Muscle Cooling on Motor Unit Properties." *European Journal of Applied Physiology* 118: 401-410. https://doi.org/10.1007/s00421-017-3782-y.

Maughan, R.J., H. Otani, and P. Watson. 2012. "Influence of Relative Humidity on Prolonged Exercise Capacity in a Warm Environment." *European Journal of Applied Physiology* 112: 2313-2321. https://doi.org/10.1007/s00421-011-2206-7.

Otani, H., M. Kaya, A. Tamaki, et al. 2019. "Exposure to High Solar Radiation Reduces Self-Regulated Exercise Intensity in the Heat Outdoors." *Physiology & Behavior* 199: 191-199. https://doi.org/10.1016/j.physbeh.2018.11.029.

Racinais, S., and J. Oksa. 2010. "Temperature and Neuromuscular Function." *Scandinavian Journal of Medicine & Science in Sports* 20: 1-18. https://doi.org/10.1111/j.1600-0838.2010.01204.x.

Shave, R., E. Dawson, G. Whyte, et al. 2004. "Altered Cardiac Function and Minimal Cardiac Damage During Prolonged Exercise." *Medicine & Science in Sports & Exercise* 36: 1098-1103. https://doi.org/10.1249/01.MSS.0000131958.18154.1E.

Siebenmann, C., P. Robach, R.A. Jacobs, et al. 2012. "'Live High–Train Low' Using Normobaric Hypoxia: A Double-Blinded, Placebo-Controlled Study." *Journal of Applied Physiology* 112: 106-117. https://doi.org/10.1152/japplphysiol.00388.2011.

Stellingwerff, T., P. Peeling, L.A. Garvican-Lewis, et al. 2019. "Nutrition and Altitude: Strategies to Enhance Adaptation, Improve Performance and Maintain Health: A Narrative Review." *Sports Medicine* 49: 169-184. https://doi.org/10.1007/s40279-019-01159-w.

Tucker, R., T. Marle, E.V. Lambert, and T.D. Noakes. 2006. "The Rate of Heat Storage Mediates an Anticipatory Reduction in Exercise Intensity During Cycling at a Fixed Rating of Perceived Exertion: Exercise Regulation in the Heat." *The Journal of Physiology* 574: 905-915. https://doi.org/10.1113/jphysiol.2005.101733.

Chapter 14

Barnett, A. 2006. "Using Recovery Modalities Between Training Sessions in Elite Athletes." *Sports Medicine* 36 (9): 781-796.

Bishop, P.A., E. Jones, and A.K. Woods. 2008. "Recovery from Training: A Brief Review." *The Journal of Strength & Conditioning Research* 22 (3): 1015-1024.

Bompa, T. 1999. *Periodization: Theory and Methodology of Training.* 4th ed. Champaign, IL: Human Kinetics.

Bompa, T.O., and C. Buzzichelli. 2018. *Periodization: Theory and Methodology of Training.* Champaign, IL: Human Kinetics.

Brown, D.J. 2014. *The Boys in the Boat.* Penguin Books.

Coffey, V.G., and J.A. Hawley. 2017. "Concurrent Exercise Training: Do Opposites Distract?" *The Journal of Physiology* 595 (9): 2883-2896.

Cotter, J.D. 2013. "Novel Stress Conditioning for Health and Performance." Paper presented at the 15th International Conference on Environmental Ergonomics, Queenstown, NZ, February 11-15.

Cunanan, A.J., B.H. DeWeese, J.P. Wagle, K.M. Carroll, R. Sausaman, W.G. Hornsby, et al. 2018. "The General Adaptation Syndrome: A Foundation for the Concept of Periodization." *Sports Medicine* 48 (4): 787-797.

Gabbett, T.J. 2020. "Debunking the Myths About Training Load, Injury and Performance: Empirical Evidence, Hot Topics and Recommendations for Practitioners." *British Journal of Sports Medicine* 54 (1): 58-66.

Garber, C.E., B. Blissmer, M.R. Deschenes, B.A. Franklin, M.J. Lamonte, I.-M. Lee, et al. 2011. "Quantity and Quality of Exercise for Developing and Maintaining Cardiorespiratory, Musculoskeletal, and Neuromotor Fitness in Apparently Healthy Adults: Guidance for Prescribing Exercise." *Medicine and Science in Sports and Exercise* 43 (7): 1334-1359.

Hagerman, F.C. 1984. "Applied Physiology of Rowing." *Sports Medicine* 1 (4): 303-326.

Halson, S.L. 2014. "Monitoring Training Load to Understand Fatigue in Athletes." *Sports Medicine* 44 (2): 139-147.

Issurin, V.B. 2010. "New Horizons for the Methodology and Physiology of Training Periodization." *Sports Medicine* 40 (3): 189-206.

Kellmann, M., M. Bertollo, L. Bosquet, M. Brink, A.J. Coutts, R. Duffield, et al. 2018. "Recovery and Performance in Sport: Consensus Statement." *International Journal of Sports Physiology and Performance* 13 (2): 240-245.

Kellmann, M., G. Bussmann, D. Anders, and S. Schulte. 2006. "Psychological Aspects of Rowing." In *The Sport Psychologist's Handbook: A Guide for Sport-Specific Performance Enhancement*, edited by J. Dosil, 479-501. John Wiley & Sons.

Kellmann, M., M. Pelka, and J. Beckmann. 2018. "Psychological Relaxation Techniques to Enhance Recovery in Sports." In *Sport, Recovery and Performance: Interdisciplinary Insights*, 247-259. Kellmann, M. and Beckmann, J., eds. London: Routledge, 247-259.

Kiely, J. 2012. "Periodization Paradigms in the 21st Century: Evidence-led or Tradition-Driven?" *International Journal of Sports Physiology and Performance* 7 (3): 242-250.

Kraemer, W.J., K. Adams, E. Cafarelli, G.A. Dudley, C. Dooly, M.S. Feigenbaum, et al. 2009. "American College of Sports Medicine Position Stand. Progression Models in Resistance Training for Healthy Adults." *Medicine & Science in Sports & Exercise* 41 (3): 687.

Kraemer, W. J., and N.A. Ratamess. 2004. "Fundamentals of Resistance Training: Progression and Exercise Prescription." *Medicine & Science in Sports & Exercise* 36 (4): 674-688.

Matveyev, L. 1964. *Problem of Periodization the Sport Training.* Moscow: Fizkultura i sport.

Maupin, D., B. Schram, E. Canetti, and R. Orr. 2020. "The Relationship Between Acute: Chronic Workload Ratios and Injury Risk in Sports: A Systematic Review." *Open Access Journal of Sports Medicine* 11: 51.

Pineau, T.R., C.R. Glass, K.A. Kaufman, and D.R. Bernal. 2014. "Self- and Team-Efficacy Beliefs of Rowers and Their Relation to Mindfulness and Flow." *Journal of Clinical Sport Psychology* 8 (2): 142-158.

Pope, C C., D. Penney, and T.B. Smith. 2018. "Overtraining and the Complexities of Coaches' Decision-Making: Managing Elite Athletes on the Training Cusp." *Reflective Practice* 19 (2): 145-166.

Selye, H. 1973. "The Evolution of the Stress Concept: The Originator of the Concept Traces Its Development From the Discovery in 1936 of the Alarm Reaction to Modern Therapeutic Applications of Syntoxic and Catatoxic Hormones." *American Scientist* 61 (6): 692-699.

Smith, T.B., and W.G. Hopkins. 2011. "Variability and Predictability of Finals Times of Elite Rowers." *Medicine & Science in Sports & Exercise* 43 (11): 2155-2160.

Smith, T.B., W.G. Hopkins, and T.E. Lowe. 2011. "Are There Useful Physiological or Psychological Markers for Monitoring Overload Training in Elite Rowers?" *International Journal of Sports Physiology and Performance* 6 (4): 469-484.

Swann, C. 2016. "Flow in Sport." In *Flow Experience*, 51-64. Flow Experience: Empirical Research and Applications, Harmat, L. et al., eds.: 51-64. Springer.

Yakovlev, N. 1967. *Sports Biochemistry.* Leipzig: Deutsche Hochschule für Körperkultur.

Zatsiorsky, V., and W. Kraemer. 2006. *Science and Practice of Strength Training.* 2nd ed. Champaign, IL: Human Kinetics.

Chapter 15

Arne, G., S. Stephen, and E. Eike, E. 2009. "Training Methods and Intensity Distribution of Young World-Class Rowers." *International Journal of Sports Physiology and Performance* 4 (4): 448-460.

Buchheit, M., and P.B. Laursen. 2013. "High-Intensity Interval Training, Solutions to the Programming Puzzle." *Sports Medicine* 43 (5): 313-338.

Cerezuela-Espejo, V., J. Courel-Ibáñez, R. Morán-Navarro, A. Martínez-Cava, and Pallarés, J. G. 2018. "The Relationship Between Lactate and Ventilatory Thresholds in Runners: Validity and Reliability of Exercise Test Performance Parameters. *Frontiers in Physiology* 9: 1320.

Driller, M.W., J.W. Fell, J.R. Gregory, C.M. Shing, and A.D. Williams. 2009. "The Effects of High-Intensity Interval Training in Well-Trained Rowers." *International Journal of Sports Physiology and Performance* 4 (1): 110-121.

Esteve-Lanao, J., C. Foster, S. Seiler, and A. Lucia. 2007. "Impact of Training Intensity Distribution on Performance in Endurance Athletes." *The Journal of Strength & Conditioning Research* 21 (3): 943-949.

Fiskerstrand, Å., and K. Seiler. 2004. "Training and Performance Characteristics Among Norwegian International Rowers 1970–2001." *Scandinavian Journal of Medicine & Science in Sports* 14 (5): 303-310.

Gullstrand, L. 1996. "Physiological Responses to Short-Duration High-Intensity Intermittent Rowing." *Canadian Journal of Applied Physiology* 21 (3): 197-208.

Ingham, S.A., H. Carter, G.P, Whyte, and J.H. Doust. 2008. "Physiological and Performance Effects of Low- Versus Mixed-Intensity Rowing Training." *Medicine & Science in Sports & Exercise* 40 (3): 579-584.

Jensen, K., N. Secher, and M. Smith. 1990. "Analysis of the Italian National Training Program for Rowing." *Fisa Coach* 1: 1-5.

Körner, T. 1993. "Background and Experience With Long-Term Build-Up Programmes for High Performance Rowers." *FISA Coach* 49 (3): 1-6.

MacInnis, M.J. and M.J. Gibala. 2017. "Physiological Adaptations to Interval Training and the Role of Exercise Intensity." *The Journal of Physiology* 595 (9): 2915-2930.

Mejuto, G., I. Arratibel, J. Cámara, A. Puente, G. Iturriaga, and J. Calleja-González. 2012. "The Effect of a 6-Week Individual Anaerobic Threshold Based Programme in a Traditional Rowing Crew." *Biology of Sport* 29 (4): 297.

Ní Chéilleachair, N.J., A.J. Harrison, and G.D. Warrington. 2017. "HIIT Enhances Endurance Performance and Aerobic Characteristics More Than High-Volume Training in Trained Rowers." *Journal of Sports Sciences* 35 (11): 1052-1058.

Plews, D.J., and P.B. Laursen. 2017. "Training Intensity Distribution Over a Four-Year Cycle in Olympic Champion Rowers: Different Roads Lead to Rio." *International Journal of Sports Physiology and Performance*, 1-24.

Plews, D.J., P.B. Laursen, Y. Le Meur, C. Hausswirth, A.E. Kilding, and M. Buchheit. 2014. "Monitoring Training With Heart-Rate Variability: How Much Compliance Is Needed for Valid Assessment?" *International Journal of Sports Physiology and Performance* 9 (5): 783-790.

Saltin, B., and P.O. Astrand. 1967. Maximal Oxygen Uptake in Athletes. *Journal of Applied Physiology* 23 (3): 353-358.

Seiler, K.S., and G.Ø. Kjerland. 2006. "Quantifying Training Intensity Distribution in Elite Endurance Athletes: Is There Evidence for an 'Optimal' Distribution?" *Scandinavian Journal of Medicine & Science in Sports* 16 (1): 49-56.

Seiler, S. 2010. "What Is Best Practice for Training Intensity and Duration Distribution in Endurance Athletes?" *International Journal of Sports Physiology and Performance* 5 (3): 276-291.

Seiler, S., and E. Tønnessen. 2009. "Intervals, Thresholds, and Long Slow Distance: The Role of Intensity and Duration in Endurance Training." *Sportscience* 13 (January): 32-53.

Steinacker, J.M., W. Lormes, M. Lehmann, and D. Altenburg. 1998. "Training of Rowers Before World Championships." *Medicine & Science in Sports & Exercise* 30 (7): 1158-1163.

Stöggl, T., and B. Sperlich. 2014. "Polarized Training Has Greater Impact on Key Endurance Variables Than Threshold, High Intensity, or High Volume Training. *Frontiers in Physiology* 5: 33.

Svedahl, K., and B.R. MacIntosh. 2003. "Anaerobic Threshold: The Concept and Methods of Measurement." *Canadian Journal of Applied Physiology* 28 (2): 299-323.

Tran, J., A.J. Rice, L.C. Main, and P.B. Gastin. 2015. "Profiling the Training Practices and Performance of Elite Rowers." *International Journal of Sports Physiology and Performance* 10 (5): 572-580.

Treff, G., K. Winkert, M. Sareban, J.M. Steinacker, M. Becker, and B. Sperlich. 2017. "Eleven-Week Preparation Involving Polarized Intensity Distribution Is Not Superior to Pyramidal Distribution in National Elite Rowers." *Frontiers in Physiology* 8: 515.

Treff, G., K. Winkert, M. Sareban, J.M. Steinacker, and B. Sperlich. 2019. "The Polarization-Index: A Simple Calculation to Distinguish Polarized from Non-Polarized Training Intensity Distributions." *Frontiers in Physiology* 10: 707.

Treff, G., K. Winkert, and J. Steinacker. 2021. "Olympic Rowing–Maximum Capacity Over 2000 Meters." *German Journal of Sports Medicine/Deutsche Zeitschrift fur Sportmedizin* 72: 203-211.

Chapter 16

American College of Sports Medicine. 2002. "Position Stand: Progression Models in Resistance Training for Healthy Adults." *Medicine & Science in Sports & Exercise* 34: 364-380.

Barber Foss, K.D., S. Thomas, J.C. Khoury, G.D. Myer, and T. Hewett. 2018. "A School-Based Neuromuscular Training Program and Sport-Related Injury Incidence: A Prospective Randomized Controlled Clinical Trial." *Journal of Athletic Training* 53 (1): 20-28.

Bartholomew, J.B., and D.E. Linder. 1998. "State Anxiety Following Resistance Exercise: The Role of Gender and Exercise Intensity." *Journal of Behavioral Medicine* 21: 205-219.

Brzycki, M. 1993. "Strength Testing: Predicting a One Rep Max From Reps to Fatigue." *Journal of Physical Education, Recreation, and Dance* 64: 88-90.

Cotter, J.A., M.J. Garver Dinyer, T.K. Fairman, C.M. Focht, and C. Brian. 2017. "Ratings of Perceived Exertion During Acute Resistance Exercise Performed at Imposed and Self-Selected Loads in Recreationally Trained Women." *Journal of Strength and Conditioning Research* 31 (8): 2313-2318, DOI: 10.1519/JSC.0000000000001782.

da Silva, L., P.F. de Almeida-Neto, D.G. de Matos, S.E. Riechman, V. de Queiros, J.B. de Jesus, V.M. Reis, et al. 2021. "Performance Prediction Equation for 2000 m Youth Indoor Rowing Using a 100 m Maximal Test." *Biology* 10 (11): 1082. https://doi.org/10.3390/biology10111082.

Davies, T., R. Orr, M. Halaki, and D. Hackett. 2016. "Effect of Training Leading to Repetition Failure on Muscular Strength: A Systematic Review and Meta-Analysis." *Sports Medicine* 46: 487-502.

Dias, M., R. Simao, F. Saavedra, C. Buzzachera, and S. Fleck. 2018. "Self Selected Training Loads and RPE During Resistance and Aerobic Training Among Recreational Exercisers." *Perceptual and Motor Skills* 125 (4): 769-787.

Ebben, William P., Alan G. Kindler, Kerri A. Chirdon, Nina C. Jenkins, Aaron J. Polichnowski, and Alexander V. Ng. 2004. "The Effect of High-Load vs. High-Repetition Training on Endurance Performance." *Journal of Strength and Conditioning Research* 18, no. 3 (August): 513-517.

Egan-Shuttler, J.D., R. Edmonds, C. Eddy, V. O'Neill, and S.J. Ives. 2017. "The Effect of Concurrent Plyometric Training Versus Submaximal Aerobic Cycling on Rowing Economy, Peak Power, and Performance in Male High School Rowers." *Sports Medicine Open* 3: 7.

Epley, B. 1985. "Poundage Chart." Boyd Epley workout. Lincoln, NE.

Feros, Simon, Warren Young, Anthony Rice, and Scott Talpey. 2012. "The Effect of Including a Series of Isometric Conditioning Contractions to the Rowing Warm-Up on 1,000-M Rowing Ergometer Time Trial Performance." *Journal of Strength and Conditioning Research* 26 (12): 3326-3334. doi: 10.1519/JSC.0b013e3182495025.

Focht, B.C. 2002. "Pre-Exercise Anxiety and the Anxiolytic Responses to Acute Bouts of Self-Selected and Prescribed Intensity Resistance Exercise." *Journal of Sports Medicine and Physical Fitness* 42: 217-223.

Folk, Amanda L., Christina A. Garcia, Samuel H. Whitney, and Sara J. Kovacs. 2020. "Relationship Between Strength and Conditioning Assessments and Rowing Performance in Female Collegiate Athletes." *Journal of Strength and Conditioning Research* 36, no. 6 (June 24): 1618-1621. doi: 10.1519/JSC.0000000000003698.

Fonseca, R.M., H. Roschel, V. Tricoli, E.O. de Souza, J.M. Wilson, G.C. Laurentino, A.Y. Aihara, A.R. de Souza Leão, and C. Ugrinowitsch. 2014. "Changes in Exercises Are More Effective Than in Loading Schemes to Improve Muscle Strength." *Journal of Strength and Conditioning Research* 28 (11): 3085-3092.

Gallagher, Dane, Loretta DiPietro, Amanda Visek, John Bancheri, and Todd Miller. 2010. "The Effects of Concurrent Endurance and Resistance Training on 2,000-m Rowing Ergometer Times in Collegiate Male Rowers." *Journal of Strength and Conditioning Research* 24, no. 5 (May): 1208-1214. doi: 10.1519/JSC.0b013e3181d8331e.

Glass, S.C., and D.R. Stanton. 2004. "Self-Selected Resistance Training Intensity in Novice Weightlifters." *Journal of Strength and Conditioning Research* 18 (2): 324-327.

Helms, E.R., J. Cronin, A. Storey, and M.C. Zourdos. 2016. "Application of the Repetitions in Reserve-Based Rating of Perceived Exertion Scale for Resistance Training." *Strength and Conditioning Journal* 38 (4): 42-49. doi: 10.1519/SSC.0000000000000218.

Keogh, J., P.A. Hume, and S. Pearson. 2006. "Retrospective Injury Epidemiology of One Hundred One Competitive Oceania Power Lifters: The Effects of Age, Body Mass, Competitive Standard, and Gender." *Journal of Strength and Conditioning Research* 20 (3): 672-681.

Kerr, Z., C. Collins, and R. Comstock. 2010. "Epidemiology of Weight Training Related Injuries Presenting at United States Emergency Departments, 1990-2007." *The American Journal of Sports Medicine* 38 (4): 765-771.

Kraemer, W.J., and N.A. Ratames. 2004. "Fundamentals of Resistance Training: Progression and Exercise Prescription." *Medicine & Science in Sports & Exercise* 36: 674-678.

Kramer, J.F., A. Morrow, and A. Leger. 1993. "Changes in Rowing Ergometer, Weight Lifting, Vertical Jump and Isokinetic Performance in Response to Standard and Standard Plus Plyometric Training Programs." *International Journal of Sports Medicine* 14, no. 8 (November): 449-454. doi: 10.1055/s-2007-1021209. PMID: 8300271.

Lander, J. 1985. "Maximums Based on Reps." *NSCA Journal* 6: 60-61.

Lawton, T.W., J.B. Cronin, and M.R. McGuigan. 2013a. "Does On-Water Resisted Rowing Increase or Maintain Lower-Body Strength?" *Journal of Strength and Conditioning Research* 27, no. 7 (July): 1958-1963. doi: 10.1519/JSC.0b013e3182736acb. PMID: 22996030.

Lawton, T.W., J.B. Cronin, and M.R. McGuigan. 2013b. "Strength, Power, and Muscular Endurance Exercise and Elite Rowing Ergometer Performance." *Journal of Strength and Conditioning Research* 27 (7): 1928-1935.

Leary, B.K., J. Statler, B. Hopkins, R. Fitzwater, T. Kesling, J. Lyon, B. Phillips, R.W. Bryner, P. Cormie, and G.G. Haff. 2012. "The Relationship Between Isometric Force-Time Curve Characteristics and Club Head Speed in Recreational Golfers." *Journal of Strength and Conditioning Research* 26 (10): 2685-2697.

Lombardi, V. 1989. *Beginning Weight Training.* Dubuque, IA: W.C. Brown.

Lum, D., and T.M. Barbosa. 2019. "Brief Review: Effects of Isometric Strength Training on Strength and Dynamic Performance." *International Journal of Sports Medicine* 40, no. 6 (May): 363-375. doi: 10.1055/a-0863-4539. Epub 2019 Apr 3. PMID: 30943568.

Mason, L., A. Kirkland, J. Steele, and J. Wright. 2021. "The Relationship Between Isometric Mid-Thigh Pull Variables and Athletic Performance Measures: Empirical Study of English Professional Soccer Players and Meta-Analysis of Extant Literature." *Journal of Sports Medicine and Physical Fitness* 61, no. 5 (May): 645-655. doi: 10.23736/S0022-4707.20.11205-2. PMID: 33146489.

Mayhew, J., T. Ball, M. Arnold, and J. Bowen. 1992. "Relative Muscular Endurance Performance as a Predictor of Bench Press Strength in College Men and Women." *Journal of Applied Sport Science Research* 6: 200-206.

Mazzetti, S.A., W.J. Kraemer, J.S. Volek, N.D. Duncan, N.A. Ratamess, A.L. Gomex, R.U. Newton, K. Hakkinen, and S.J. Fleck. 2000. "The Influence of Direct Supervision of Resistance Training on Strength Performance." *Medicine & Science in Sports & Exercise* 32 (6): 1175-1184.

McNeely, Ed, David Sandler, and Steve Bamel. 2005. "Strength and Power Goals for Competitive Rowers." *Strength and Conditioning Journal* 27 (3). doi: 10.1519/00126548-200506000-00001.

Mitchell, C.J., T.A. Churchward-Venne, D.W. West, N.A. Burd, L. Breen, S.K. Baker, and S.M. Phillips. 2012. "Resistance Exercise Load Does Not Determine Training-Mediated Hypertrophic Gains in Young Men." *Journal of Applied Physiology* 113: 71-77.

Morton, R.W., S.Y. Oikawa, C.G. Wavell, N. Mazara, C. McGlory, J. Quadrilatero, B.L. Baechler, S.K. Baker, and S.M. Phillips. 2016. "Neither Load Nor Systemic Hormones Determine Resistance Training-Mediated Hypertrophy or Strength Gains in Resistance-Trained Young Men." *Journal of Applied Physiology* 121: 129-138.

O'Conner, B., J. Simmons, and P. O'Shea. 1989. *Weight Training Today.* St. Paul, MN: West Publ.

Peterson, M.D., M.R. Rhea, and B.A. Alvar. 2004. "Maximizing Strength Development in Athletes: A Meta-Analysis to Determine the Dose-Response Relationship." *Journal of Strength and Conditioning Research* 18 (2): 377-382.

Rhea, M.R., B.A. Alvar, L.N. Burkett, and S.D. Ball. 2003. "A Meta-Analysis to Determine the Dose Response for Strength Development." *Medicine & Science in Sports & Exercise* 35 (3): 456-464.

Riechman, S.E., R.F. Zoeller, G. Balasekaran, F.L. Goss, and R.J. Robertson. 2002. "Prediction of 2000 m Indoor Rowing Performance Using a 30 s Sprint and Maximal Oxygen Uptake." *Journal of Sports Sciences* 20, no. 9 (September): 681-687. doi: 10.1080/026404102320219383. PMID: 12200919.

Schoenfeld, B.J., M.D. Peterson, D. Ogborn, B. Contreras, and G.T. Sonmez. 2015. "Effects of Low- vs. High-Load Resistance Training on Muscle Strength and Hypertrophy in Well-Trained Men." *Journal of Strength and Conditioning Research* 29: 2954-2963.

West, D.J., N.J. Owen, M.R. Jones, R.M. Bracken, C.J. Cook, D.J. Cunningham, D.A. Shearer, C.V. Finn, R.U. Newton, B.T. Crewther, and L.P. Kilduff. 2011. "Relationships Between Force–Time Characteristics of the Isometric Midthigh Pull and Dynamic Performance in Professional Rugby League Players." *Journal of Strength and Conditioning Research* 25 (11): 3070-3075.

Winwood P.W., P.A. Hume, J.B. Cronin, and J.W. Keogh. 2014. "Retrospective Injury Epidemiology of Strongman Athletes." *Journal of Strength and Conditioning Research* 28 (1): 28-42.

Zourdos, M.C., A. Klemp, C. Dolan, J.M. Quiles, K.A. Schau, E. Jo, E. Helms, et al. 2016. "Novel Resistance Training-Specific RPE Scale Measuring Repetitions in Reserve." *Journal of Strength and Conditioning Research* 30: 267-275.

Chapter 17

Boutcher, S.H., R.L. Seip, R.K. Hetzler, E.F. Pierce, D. Snead, and A. Weltman. 1989. "The Effects of Specificity of Training on Rating of Perceived Exertion at the Lactate Threshold." *European Journal of Applied Physiology and Occupational Physiology* 59: 365-369.

Chan, H.C., W.K. Ho, and P.S. Yung. 2017. "Sprint Cycling Training Improves Intermittent Run Performance." *Asia-Pacific Journal of Sports Medicine, Arthroscopy, and Rehabilitation, and Technology* 11 (December 1): 6-11. doi: 10.1016/j.asmart.2017.11.001. PMID: 29552503. PMCID: PMC5850992.

Dantas, J.L., C. Doria, H. Rossi, G. Rosa, T. Pietrangelo, G. Fanò-Illic, and F.Y. Nakamura. 2015. "Determination of Blood Lactate Training Zone Boundaries With Rating of Perceived Exertion in Runners." *Journal of Strength and Conditioning Research* 29 (2): 315-320.

Dawes, H.N., K.L. Barker, J. Cockburn, N. Roach, O. Scott, D. Wade. 2005. "Borg's Rating of Perceived Exertion Scales: Do the Verbal Anchors Mean the Same for Different Clinical Groups?" *Archives of Physical Medicine and Rehabilitation* 86: 912-916.

Engel, F.A., A. Ackermann, H. Chtourou, and B. Sperlich. 2018. "High-Intensity Interval Training Performed by Young Athletes: A Systematic Review and Meta-Analysis." *Frontiers in Physiology* 9: 1012. https://doi.org/10.3389/fphys.2018.01012

Fiskerstrand, A., and K.S. Seiler. 2004. "Training and Performance Characteristics Among Norwegian International Rowers 1970-2001." *Scandinavian Journal of Medicine & Science in Sports* 14, no. 5 (November): 303-310. doi: 10.1046/j.1600-0838.2003.370.x. PMID: 15387804.

Flynn, Michael G., Kathy K. Carroll, Heather L. Hall, Barbara A. Bushman, Gunnar P. Brolinson, and Carol A. Weideman. 1998. "Cross Training: Indices of Training Stress and Performance." *Medicine & Science in Sports & Exercise* 30, no. 2 (February): 294-300.

Foster, Carl, Lisa L. Hector, Ralph Welsh, Mathew Schrager, Megan A. Green, and Ann C. Snyder. 1995. "Effects of Specific Versus Cross-Training on Running Performance." *European Journal of Applied Physiology and Occupational Physiology* 70 (4): 367-372.

Foster, C., C.V. Farland, F. Guidotti, M. Harbin, B. Roberts, J. Schuette, A. Tuuri, S.T. Doberstein, and J.P. Porcari. 2015. "The Effects of High Intensity Interval Training vs Steady State Training on Aerobic and Anaerobic Capacity." *Journal of Sports Science & Medicine* 14 (4): 747-755.

Hosea, T.M., and J.A. Hannafin. 2012. "Rowing Injuries." *Sports Health* 4 (3): 236-245. doi: 10.1177/1941738112442484.

Issurin, V.B. 2013. "Training Transfer: Scientific Background and Insights for Practical Application." *Sports Medicine* 43, no. 8 (August): 675-694. doi: 10.1007/s40279-013-0049-6. PMID: 23633165.

Krause P. 2009. "The Benefits of Cross Training." *AMAA Journal* 22, no. 2 (Spring/Summer): 9, 16.

Kunz, P., F.A. Engel, H.C. Holmberg, and B. Sperlich. 2019. "A Meta-Comparison of the Effects of High-Intensity Interval Training to Those of Small-Sided Games and Other Training Protocols on Parameters Related to the Physiology and Performance of Youth Soccer Players." *Sports Medicine Open* 5, no. 1 (February 21): 7. doi: 10.1186/s40798-019-0180-5. PMID: 30790134. PMCID: PMC6384288.

Loy, S.F., G.J. Holland, D.J. Mutton, J. Snow, W.J. Vincent, J.J. Hoffmann, and S. Shaw. 1993. "Effects of Stairclimbing vs Run Training on Treadmill and Track Running Performance." *Medicine & Science in Sports & Exercise* 25: 1275-1278.

Mäestu, J., J. Jürimäe J, and T. Jürimäe. 2005. "Monitoring of Performance and Training in Rowing." *Sports Medicine* 35 (7): 597-617. doi: 10.2165/00007256-200535070-00005. PMID: 16026173.

McNeely, E. 2014. Cross Training. Rowing 360 1, no. 2 (Sept/Oct): 80. 2014.

Milanović, Z., S. Pantelić, N. Čović, G. Sporiš, and P. Krustrup. 2015. "Is Recreational Soccer Effective for Improving VO2max? A Systematic Review and Meta-Analysis." *Sports Medicine* 45, no. 9 (September): 1339-1353. doi: 10.1007/s40279-015-0361-4. PMID: 26210229. PMCID: PMC4536283.

Paquette, Max R., Shelby A. Peel, Ross E. Smith, Mark Temme, and Jeffrey N. Dwyer. 2018. "The Impact of Different Cross-Training Modalities on Performance and Injury-Related Variables in High School Cross Country Runners." *Journal of Strength and Conditioning Research* 32, no. 6 (June): 1745-1753. doi: 10.1519/JSC.0000000000002042.

Raglin, J.S., and W.P. Morgan. 1989. "Development of a Scale to Measure Training Induced Distress." *Medicine & Science in Sports & Exercise* 21: 60.

Tanaka, H. 1994. "Effects of Cross-Training: Transfer of Training Effects on VO2max Between Cycling, Running and Swimming." *Sports Medicine* 18 (5): 330-339.

Tran, J., A.J. Rice, L.C. Main, and P.B. Gastin. 2014. "Development and Implementation of a Novel Measure for Quantifying Training Loads in Rowing: The T2minute Method." *Journal of Strength and Conditioning Research* 28, no. 4 (April): 1172-1180. doi: 10.1519/JSC.0000000000000248. PMID: 24077376.

van der Zwaard, S., W.J. van der Laarse, G. Weide, F.W. Bloemers, M.J. Hofmijster, K. Levels, et al. 2018. "Critical Determinants of Combined Sprint and Endurance Performance: An Integrative Analysis From Muscle Fiber to the Human Body." *The FASEB Journal* 32: 2110-2123. doi: 10.1096/fj.201700827R.

Chapter 18

Bailey, S., A. Vanhatalo, D. Wilkerson, and A. Jones. 2011. "Fast-Start Strategy Improves VO_2 Kinetics and High-Intensity Exercise Performance." *Medicine & Science in Sports & Exercise* 43 (3): 457-467.

Concept2. 2021. "World Records." Accessed April 2022. https://www.concept2.com/indoor-rowers/racing/records/world.

de Koning, J., C. Foster, A. Bakkum, S. Kloppenburg, C. Thiel, T. Joseph, J. Cohen, and J. Porcari. 2011. "Regulation of Pacing Strategy During Athletic Competition." *PLOS One* 6 (1): e15863. doi:10.1371/journal.pone.0015863.

Duffield, R., B. Dawson, and C. Goodman. 2005. "Energy System Contribution to 1500- and 3000-metre Track Running." *Journal of Sports Sciences* 23 (10): 993-1002. doi: 10.1080/02640410400021963.

Foster, C., J. De Koning, F. Hettinga, J. Lampen, K. La Clair, C. Dodge, M. Bobbert, and J. Porcari. 2003. "Pattern of Energy Expenditure Furing Simulated Competition." *Medicine & Science in Sports & Exercise* 35, no. 5 (May): 826-831.

Fox, S. 1993. *Human Physiology.* 4th ed. Dubuque, IA: Wm. C. Brown Publishers.

Garland, S. 2005. "An Analysis of the Pacing Strategy Adopted by Elite Competitors in 2000 m Rowing." *British Journal of Sports Medicine* 39: 39-42. doi: 10.1136/bjsm.2003.010801.

Hartmann, U., and A. Mader. 2005. "Rowing Physiology." In *Rowing Faster*, edited by V. Nolte, 9-24. Champaign, IL: Human Kinetics.

Kitch, B. 2014. "No Fade for the Kiwis: Even-Splitting is the New Black." Downloaded July 2021. https://www.rowingrelated.com.

Klavora, P. 1982. "Racing Strategy." In *Rowing 2: National Coaching Certification Program*, edited by P. Klavora. Ottawa: Canadian Amateur Rowing Association.

Kleshnev, V. 2016. *The Biomechanics of Rowing.* Ramsbury, Marlborough Wiltshire: The Crowood Press Ltd.

Kleshnev, V., and V. Nolte. 2011. "Learning from Racing." In *Rowing Faster*, 2nd ed., edited by V. Nolte, 253-268. Champaign, IL: Human Kinetics.

Lander, P., R. Butterly, and A. Edwards. 2009. "Self-Paced Exercise Is Less Physically Challenging Than Enforced Constant Pace Exercise of the Same Intensity: Influence of Complex Central Metabolic." *British Journal of Sports Medicine* 43: 789-795.

Mader, A., U. Hartmann, and W. Hollmann. 1988. "Der Einfluss der Ausdauer auf 6minütige maximale anaerobe und aerobe Arbeitskapazität eines Eliteruderers." In *Rudern – Sportmedizinische und sportwissenschaftliche Aspekte*, edited by J. Steinacker, 62-78. Berlin, Germany: Springer Verlag.

Mader, A., and W. Hollmann. 1977. "Zur Bedeutung der Stoffwechselleistungsfähigkeit des Eliteruderers im Training und Wettkampf." *Leistungssport* 9: 8-62.

Muehlbauer, T., C. Schindler, and A. Widmer. 2010. "Pacing Pattern and Performance During the 2008 Olympic Rowing Regatta." *European Journal of Sport Science* 10 (5): 291-296. doi: 10.1080/17461390903426659.

Nolte, V. 2011. *Rowing Faster.* Champaign, IL: Human Kinetics.

Secher, N., S. Vollianitis, and J. Jürimäe. 2007. "Physiology." In *Handbook of Sport Medicine and Science: Rowing*, edited by N. Secher and S. Volianitis, 42-65. Malden, MA: Blackwell Publishing.

Smits, B., G. Pepping, and F. Hettinga, F. 2014. "Pacing and Decision Making in Sport and Exercise: The Roles of Perception and Action in the Regulation of Exercise Intensity." *Sports Medicine* 44: 763-775. doi: 10.1007/s40279-014-0163-0.

Spencer, M., P. Gastin, and W. Payne. 1996. "Energy System Contribution During 400 to 1500 Metres Running." *IAAF Quarterly—New Studies in Athletics* 11 (4).

Thompson, K. 2015. *Pacing: Individual Strategies for Optimal Performance.* Champaign, IL: Human Kinetics.

Tucker, R., M. Lambert, and T. Noakes. 2006. "An Analysis of Pacing Strategies During Men's World-Record Performances in Track Athletics." *International Journal of Sports Physiology and Performance* 1 (3): 233-245. doi: 10.1123/ijspp.1.3.233.

World Rowing. 2021a. "World's Fastest for Indoor Rowing 2k. Who Is Brooke Mooney?" https://worldrowing.com/2021/04/01/worlds-fastest-for-indoor-rowing-2k-who-is-brooke-mooney/.

World Rowing. 2021b. "1984 Olympic Games—Lake Casitas/Los Angeles, United States." https://worldrowing.com/event/1984-olympic-games-lake-casitas-los-angeles-united-states.

World Rowing. 2021c. https://worldrowing.com/event/1976-olympic-games-notre-dame-montreal-canada.

World Rowing. 2021d. https://worldrowing.com/event/2010-world-rowing-championships-lake-karapiro-new-zealand.

World Rowing. 2021e. https://worldrowing.com/event/2012-olympic-games-dorney-lake-eton-london-great-britain.

World Rowing. 2021f. https://worldrowing.com/event/2019-world-rowing-indoor-championships.

Xu, F., and E. Rhodes. 1999. "Oxygen Uptake Kinetics During Exercise." *Sports Medicine* 27 (5): 313-327.

Chapter 19

Gabbett, T.J., and D.G. Jenkins. 2011. "Relationship Between Training Load and Injury in Professional Rugby League Players." *Journal of Science and Medicine in Sport* 14 (3): 204-209.

Körner, T. 1993. "Background and Experience With Long-Term Build-Up Programmes for High Performance Rowers. *FISA Coach* 49 (3): 1-6.

Pope, C.C., D. Penney, and T.B. Smith. 2018. "Overtraining and the Complexities of Coaches' Decision-Making: Managing Elite Athletes on the Training Cusp." *Reflective Practice* 19 (2): 145-166.

Zouhal, H., D. Boullosa, R. Ramirez-Campillo, A. Ali, and U. Granacher. 2021. "Acute:Chronic Workload Ratio: Is There Scientific Evidence?" *Frontiers in Physiology* 12.

Chapter 20

Achten, J., and A.E. Jeukendrup. 2003. "Heart Rate Monitoring." *Sports Medicine* 33 (7): 517-538.

Akenhead, R., and G.P. Nassis. 2016. "Training Load and Player Monitoring in High-Level Football: Current Practice and Perceptions." *International Journal of Sports Physiology and Performance* 11 (5): 587-593.

Beltz, N.M., A.L. Gibson, J.M. Janot, L. Kravitz, C.M. Mermier, and L.C. Dalleck. 2016. "Graded Exercise Testing Protocols for the Determination of VO2max: Historical Perspectives, Progress, and Future Considerations." *Journal of Sports Medicine*. https://doi.org/10.1155/2016/3968393.

Bender, A.M., D. Lawson, P. Werthner, and C.H. Samuels. 2018. "The Clinical Validation of the Athlete Sleep Screening Questionnaire: An Instrument to Identify Athletes That Need Further Sleep Assessment." *Sports Medicine Open* 4 (1): 1-8.

Bonaventura, J.M., K. Sharpe, E. Knight, K.L. Fuller, R.K. Tanner, and C.J. Gore. 2015. "Reliability and Accuracy of Six Hand-Held Blood Lactate Analysers." *Journal of Sports Science and Medicine* 14 (1): 203.

Borg, G. 1998. *Borg's Perceived Exertion and Pain Scales*. Champaign, IL: Human Kinetics.

Borresen, J., and M.I. Lambert. 2009. "The Quantification of Training Load, the Training Response and the Effect on Performance." *Sports Medicine* 39 (9): 779-795.

Bourdon, P. 2000. "Blood Lactate Transition Thresholds: Concepts and Controversies." *Physiological Tests for Elite Athletes*. Australian Sports Commission. Champaign, IL: Human Kinetics, 50-65

Bourdon, P.C., S.M. Woolford, and J.D. Buckley. 2018. "Effects of Varying the Step Duration on the Determination of Lactate Thresholds in Elite Rowers." *International Journal of Sports Physiology and Performance* 13 (6): 687-693.

Cerezuela-Espejo, V., J. Courel-Ibáñez, R. Morán-Navarro, A. Martínez-Cava, and Pallarés, J. G. 2018. "The Relationship Between Lactate and Ventilatory Thresholds in Runners: Validity and Reliability of Exercise Test Performance Parameters. *Frontiers in Physiology* 9: 1320.

Haddad, M., G. Stylianides, L. Djaoui, A. Dellal, and K. Chamari. 2017. "Session-RPE Method for Training Load Monitoring: Validity, Ecological Usefulness, and Influencing Factors." *Frontiers in Neuroscience* 11: 612.

Halson, S.L. 2014. "Monitoring Training Load to Understand Fatigue in Athletes." *Sports Medicine* 44 (2): 139-147.

Halson, S.L. 2019. "Sleep Monitoring in Athletes: Motivation, Methods, Miscalculations and Why It Matters." *Sports Medicine* 49 (10): 1487-1497.

Janssen, P.G. 1987. *Training Lactate Pulse Rate*. Oule, Finland, Polar Electro Oy.

Jimenez Morgan, S., and J.A. Molina Mora. 2017. "Effect of Heart Rate Variability Biofeedback on Sport Performance: A Systematic Review." *Applied Psychophysiology and Biofeedback* 42 (3): 235-245.

Juul, A., and A. Jeukendrup. 2003. "Heart Rate Monitoring: Applications and Limitations." *Sports Medicine* 33 (7): 517-538.

Marriott, H.E., and K.R. Lamb. 1996. "The Use of Ratings of Perceived Exertion for Regulating Exercise Levels in Rowing Ergometry." *European Journal of Applied Physiology and Occupational Physiology* 72 (3): 267-271.

Maud, P.J., and C. Foster. 2006. *Physiological Assessment of Human Fitness*. Champaign, IL: Human Kinetics.

McLean, B.D., A.J. Coutts, V. Kelly, M.R. McGuigan, and S.J. Cormack. 2010. "Neuromuscular, Endocrine, and Perceptual Fatigue Responses During Different Length Between-Match Microcycles in Professional Rugby League Players." *International Journal of Sports Physiology and Performance* 5 (3): 367-383.

Plews, D.J., and P.B. Laursen. 2017. "Training Intensity Distribution Over a Four-Year Cycle in Olympic Champion Rowers: Different Roads Lead to Rio." *International Journal of Sports Physiology and Performance*, 1-24.

Pope, C.C., D. Penney, and T.B. Smith. 2018. "Overtraining and the Complexities of Coaches' Decision-Making: Managing Elite Athletes on the Training Cusp." *Reflective Practice* 19 (2): 145-166.

Smith, T.B., and W.G. Hopkins. 2012. "Measures of Rowing Performance." *Sports Medicine* 42 (4): 343-358.

Smith, T.B., W.G. Hopkins, and T.E. Lowe. 2011. "Are There Useful Physiological or Psychological Markers for Monitoring Overload Training in Elite Rowers?" *International Journal of Sports Physiology and Performance* 6 (4): 469-484.

Svedahl, K., and B.R. MacIntosh. 2003. "Anaerobic Threshold: The Concept and Methods of Measurement." *Canadian Journal of Applied Physiology* 28 (2): 299-323.

TrainingPeaks. 2021. "Training Stress Scores (TSS) Explained." https://help.trainingpeaks.com/hc/en-us/articles/204071944-Training-Stress-Scores-TSS-Explained.

Tran, J., A.J. Rice, L.C. Main, and P.B. Gastin. 2015. "Convergent Validity of a Novel Method for Quantifying Rowing Training Loads." *Journal of Sports Sciences* 33 (3): 268-276.

Chapter 21

Adams, W.C., E.M. Bernauer, D.B. Dill, and J.B. Bomar. 1975 "Effects of Equivalent Sea-Level and Altitude Training on VO2max and Running Performance." *Journal of Applied Physiology* 39: 262-266. https://doi.org/10.1152/jappl.1975.39.2.262.

Bonne, T.C., C. Lundby, S. Jørgensen, et al. 2014. "'Live High–Train High' Increases Hemoglobin Mass in Olympic Swimmers." *European Journal of Applied Physiology* 114: 1439-1449. https://doi.org/10.1007/s00421-014-2863-4.

Burtscher, M., W. Nachbauer, P. Baumgartl, and M. Philadelphy. 1996. "Benefits of Training at Moderate Altitude Versus Sea Level Rraining in Amateur Runners." *European Journal of Applied Physiology and Occupational Physiology* 74: 558-563.

Chapman, R.F., T. Karlsen, R.-L. Ge, et al. 2016. "Living Altitude Influences Endurance Exercise Performance Change Over Time at Altitude." *Journal of Applied Physiology* 120: 1151-1158. https://doi.org/10.1152/japplphysiol.00909.2015.

Chapman, R.F., T. Karlsen, G.K. Resaland, et al. 2014. "Defining the 'Dose' of Altitude Training: How High to Live for Optimal Sea Level Performance Enhancement. *Journal of Applied Physiology* 116: 595-603. https://doi.org/10.1152/japplphysiol.00634.2013.

Daanen, H.A.M., S. Racinais, and J.D. Périard. 2018. "Heat Acclimation Decay and Re-Induction: A Systematic Review and Meta-Analysis." *Sports Medicine* 48: 409-430. https://doi.org/10.1007/s40279-017-0808-x.

Daniels, J., and N. Oldridge. 1970. "The Effects of Alternate Exposure to Altitude and Sea Level on World-Class Middle-Distance Runners." *Medicine in Science and Sports* 2: 107-112.

Faiss, R., O. Girard, and G.P. Millet. 2013. "Advancing Hypoxic Training in Team Sports: From Intermittent Hypoxic Training to Repeated Sprint Training in Hypoxia." *British Journal of Sports Medicine* 47: i45-i50. https://doi.org/10.1136/bjsports-2013-092741.

Flouris, A.D. 2006. "Modelling Atmospheric Pollution During the Games of the XXVIII Olympiad: Effects on Elite Competitors." *International Journal of Sports Medicine* 27: 137-142. https://doi.org/10.1055/s-2005-837660.

Garrett, A.T., N.G. Goosens, N.J. Rehrer, et al. 2014. "Short-Term Heat Acclimation Is Effective and May Be Enhanced Rather Than Impaired by Dehydration." *American Journal of Human Biology* 26: 311-320. https://doi.org/10.1002/ajhb.22509.

Gliner, J.A., S.M. Horvath, and L.J. Folinsbee. 1983. "Preexposure to Low Ozone Concentrations Does Not Diminish the Pulmonary Function Response on Exposure to Higher Ozone Concentrations." *American Review of Respiratory Diseases* 127: 51-55. https://doi.org/10.1164/arrd.1983.127.1.51.

Gomes, E.C., J.E. Allgrove, G. Florida-James, and V. Stone. 2011. "Effect of Vitamin Supplementation on Lung Injury and Running Performance in a Hot, Humid, and Ozone-Polluted Environment." *Scandinavian Journal of Medicine in Science and Sports* 21: e452-e460. https://doi.org/10.1111/j.1600-0838.2011.01366.x.

Griefahn, B. 1997. "Acclimation to Three Different Hot Climates With Equivalent Wet Bulb Globe Temperatures." *Ergonomics* 40: 223-234. https://doi.org/10.1080/001401397188314.

Grievink, L., S.M. Jansen, P. van't Veer, and B. Brunekreef. 1998. "Acute Effects of Ozone on Pulmonary Function of Cyclists Receiving Antioxidant Supplements." *Occupational and Environmental Medicine* 55: 13-17. https://doi.org/10.1136/oem.55.1.13.

Grievink, L., A.G. Zijlstra, X. Ke, and B. Brunekreef. 1999. "Double-Blind Intervention Trial on Modulation of Ozone Effects on Pulmonary Function by Antioxidant Supplements." *American Journal of Epidemiology* 149: 306-314. https://doi.org/10.1093/oxfordjournals.aje.a009814.

Karlsen, A., S. Racinais, M.V. Jensen, et al. 2015. "Heat Acclimatization Does Not Improve VO2max or Cycling Performance in a Cool Climate in Trained Cyclists." *Scandinavian Journal of Medicine in Science and Sports* 25: 269-276. https://doi.org/10.1111/sms.12409.

Kissling, L.S., A.P. Akerman, H.A. Campbell, et al. 2022. "A Crossover Control Study of Three Methods of Heat Acclimation on the Magnitude and Kinetics of Adaptation." *Experimental Physiology.* https://doi.org/10.1113/EP089993.

Levine, B.D., and J. Stray-Gundersen. 1997. "'Living High-Training Low': Effect of Moderate-Altitude Acclimatization With Low-Altitude Training on Performance." *Journal of Applied Physiology* 83: 102-112. https://doi.org/10.1152/jappl.1997.83.1.102.

Lorenzo, S., J.R. Halliwill, M.N. Sawka, and C.T. Minson. 2010. "Heat Acclimation Improves Exercise Performance." *Journal of Applied Physiology* 109: 1140-1147. https://doi.org/10.1152/japplphysiol.00495.2010.

Lundby, C., I.S. Svendsen, T. Urianstad, et al. 2021. "Training Wearing Thermal Clothing and Training in Hot Ambient Conditions Are Equally Effective Methods of Heat Acclimation. *Journal of Science and Medicine in Sport* 24: 763-767. https://doi.org/10.1016/j.jsams.2021.06.005.

Mallette, M.M., D.G. Stewart, and S.S. Cheung. 2018. "The Effects of Hyperoxia on Sea-Level Exercise Performance, Training, and Recovery: A Meta-Analysis. *Sports Medicine* 48: 153-175. https://doi.org/10.1007/s40279-017-0791-2.

Mee, J.A., O.R. Gibson, J. Doust, and N.S. Maxwell. 2015. "A Comparison of Males and Females' Temporal Patterning to Short- and Long-Term Heat Acclimation: Sex Comparison of Temporal Patterning to HA." *Scandinavian Journal of Medicine & Science in Sports* 25: 250-258. https://doi.org/10.1111/sms.12417.

Mujika, I., A.P. Sharma, and T. Stellingwerff. 2019. "Contemporary Periodization of Altitude Training for Elite Endurance Athletes: A Narrative Review." *Sports Medicine* 49: 1651-1669. https://doi.org/10.1007/s40279-019-01165-y.

Romieu, I., F. Meneses, M. Ramirez, et al. 1998. "Antioxidant Supplementation and Respiratory Functions Among Workers Exposed to High Levels of Ozone." *American Journal of Respiratory and Critical Care Medicine* 158: 226-232. https://doi.org/10.1164/ajrccm.158.1.9712053.

Slivka, D., R. Shute, W. Hailes, et al. 2021. "Exercise in the Heat Blunts Improvements in Aerobic Power." *European Journal of Applied Physiology* 121: 1715-1723. https://doi.org/10.1007/s00421-021-04653-0.

Tyler, C.J., T. Reeve, G.J. Hodges, and S.S. Cheung. 2016. "The Effects of Heat Adaptation on Physiology, Perception and Exercise Performance in the Heat: A Meta-Analysis." *Sports Medicine* 46: 1699-1724. https://doi.org/10.1007/s40279-016-0538-5.

Tyler, C.J., C. Sunderland, and S.S. Cheung. 2015. "The Effect of Cooling Prior to and During Exercise on Exercise Performance and Capacity in the Heat: A Meta-Analysis." *British Journal of Sports Medicine* 49: 7-13. https://doi.org/10.1136/bjsports-2012-091739.

Weston, A.R., G. Mackenzie, M.A. Tufts, and M. Mars. 2001. "Optimal Time of Arrival for Performance at Moderate Altitude (1700 m)." *Medicine & Science in Sports & Exercise* 33 (2): 298-302. https://doi.org/10.1097/00005768-200102000-00020.

Chapter 22

Alghannam, A.F., M.M. Ghaith, and M.H. Alhussain. 2021. "Regulation of Energy Substrate Metabolism in Endurance Exercise." *International Journal of Environmental Research and Public Health* 18 (9): 4963. https://doi.org/10.3390/ijerph18094963.

Bartholomew, J.B., M.A. Stults-Kolehmainen, C.C. Elrod, and J.S. Todd. 2008. "Strength Gains After Resistance Training: The Effect of Stressful, Negative Life Events." *Journal of Strength and Conditioning Research* 22: 1215-1221.

Beelen, M., L.M. Burke, M.J. Gibala, and L.J. van Loon. 2010. "Nutritional Strategies to Promote Postexercise Recovery." *International Journal of Sport Nutrition and Exercise Metabolism* 20 (6): 515-532.

Berglund, B., and H. Säfström. 1994. "Psychological Monitoring and Modulation of Training Load of World-Class Canoeists." *Medicine & Science in Sports & Exercise* 26, no. 8 (August): 1036-1040. PMID: 7968421.

Boa, A.M., G. Meynen, and D.F. Swaab. 2008. "The Stress System in Depression and Neurodegenerative Focus on the Human Hypothalamus." *Brain Research Reviews* 57 (2): 531-553.

Bompa, T., and G. Haff. 2009. *Periodization: Theory and Methodology of Training.* 5th ed. Champaign, IL: Human Kinetics.

Calder A. 2003. "Recovery Strategies for Sports Performance." USOC Olympic Coach E-Magazine 2003 (cited 2013 December 15). http://coaching.usolympicteam.com/coaching/kpub.nsf/v/3Sept03.

Dawson, Michelle A., Jennifer Jordan Hamson-Utley, Rodney Hansen, and Michael Olpin. 2014. "Examining the Effectiveness of Psychological Strategies on Physiologic Markers: Evidence-Based Suggestions for Holistic Care of the Athlete." *Journal of Athletic Training* 49 (3): 331-337.

Economos, C.D., S.S. Bortz, and M.E. Nelson. 1993. "Nutritional Practices of Elite Athletes. Practical Recommendations." *Sports Medicine* 16, no. 6 (December): 381-399. doi: 10.2165/00007256-199316060-00004. PMID: 8303140.

Ferrara, M. 2001. "How Much Sleep Do We Need?" *Sleep Medicine Reviews* 5 (2): 155-179.

Gaab. J., N. Blättler, T. Menzi, B. Pabst, S. Stoyer, and U. Ehlert. 2003. "Randomized Controlled Evaluation of the Effects of Cognitive–Behavioral Stress Management on Cortisol Responses to Acute Stress in Healthy Subjects." *Psychoneuroendocrinology* 28: 767-779.

Gilbert, Saul S., Cameron J. van den Heuvel, Sally A. Ferguson, and Drew Dawson. 2004. "Thermoregulation as a Sleep Signalling System." *Sleep Medicine Reviews* 8, no. 2 (April): 81-93. ISSN 10870792. doi: 10.1016/S10870792(03)00023-6.

Haff, G. 2016. Periodization. In *Essentials of Strength and Conditioning*, 4th ed, edited by G. Haff and T. Triplett, 583-604. Champaign, IL: Human Kinetics.

Hooper, S.L., L.T. Mackinnon, A. Howard, R.D. Gordon, and A.W. Bachmann. 1995. "Markers for Monitoring Overtraining and Recovery." *Medicine & Science in Sports & Exercise* 27, no. 1 (January): 106-112. PMID: 7898325.

Hopkins, W.G. 1998. "Measurement of Training in Competitive Sports." *Sportscience* 2 (4). sportsci.org/jour/9804/wgh.html.

Hug, M., P.E. Mullis, M. Vogt, et al. 2003. "Training Modalities: Over-Reaching and Over-Training in Athletes, Including a Study of the Role of Hormones." *Best Practice & Research Clinical Endocrinology Metabolism* 17: 191-209.

Kellmann, M., Maurizio Bertollo, Laurent Bosquet, Michel Brink, Aaron J. Coutts, Rob Duffield, Daniel Erlacher, et al. 2018. "Recovery and Performance in Sport: Consensus Statement." *International Journal of Sports Physiology and Performance* 13 (2): 240-245.

Kenefick, R.W., and S.N. Cheuvront. 2012. "Hydration for Recreational Sport and Physical Activity." *Nutrition Reviews* 70 (Suppl. 2): S137-S142.

Kim, J., and E.K. Kim. 2020. "Nutritional Strategies to Optimize Performance and Recovery in Rowing Athletes." *Nutrients* 12, no. 6 (Jun 5): 1685. doi: 10.3390/nu12061685.

Koehler, K. 2020. "Energy Deficiency and Nutrition in Endurance Sports – Focus on Rowing." *German Journal of Sports Medicine* 71: 5-10.

Kölling, S., J.M. Steinacker, S. Endler, A. Ferrauti, T. Meyer, and M. Kellmann. 2016. "The Longer the Better: Sleep-Wake Patterns During Preparation of the World Rowing Junior Championships." *Chronobiology International* 33 (1): 73-84. doi: 10.3109/07420528.2015.1118384. Epub 2016 Jan 5. PMID: 26730643.

Lee, E.C., M.S. Fragala, S.A. Kavouras, R.M. Queen, J.L. Pryor, and D.J.J. Casa. 2017. "Biomarkers in Sports and Exercise: Tracking Health, Performance, and Recovery in Athletes." *Journal of Strength and Conditioning Research* 31, no. 10 (October): 2920-2937.

Leeder, J., M. Glaister, K. Pizzoferro, J. Dawson, and C. Pedlar. 2012. "Sleep Duration and Quality in Elite Athletes Measured Using Wristwatch Actigraphy." *Journal of Sports Sciences* 30 (6): 541-545. doi: 10.1080/02640414.2012.660188. Epub 2012 Feb 14. PMID: 22329779.

Lehmann, M., C. Foster, H.-H. Dickhuth, et al. 1998. "Autonomic Imbalance Hypothesis and Overtraining Syndrome." *Medicine & Science in Sports & Exercise* 30: 1140-1145.

Mah, C.D. 2008. "Extended Sleep and the Effects on Mood and Athletic Performance in Collegiate Swimmers." *Sleep* 3: A128.

Mah, C.D., K.E. Mah, E. Kezirian, and W.C. Dement. 2011. "The Effects of Sleep Extension on the Athletic Performance of Collegiate Basketball Players. *Sleep* 34: 943-950.

Mountjoy, M., J. Sundgot-Borgen, L. Burke, et al. 2014. "The IOC Consensus Statement: Beyond the Female Athlete Triad–Relative Energy Deficiency in Sport (RED-S)." *British Journal of Sports Medicine* 48 (7): 491-497.

National Sleep Foundation. 2013. "Sleep in America Poll: Exercise and Sleep." http://sleepfoundation.org/sites/default/files/RPT336%20Summary%20of%20Findings%2002%20-%20%202013.pdf.

Otter, R., M. Brinks, R. Diercks, and K. Lemmink. 2016. "A Negative Life Event Impairs Psychosocial Stress, Recovery and Running Economy in Runners." *International Journal of Sports Medicine* 37 (3): 224-229.

Petibois, C., G. Cazorla, J.-R. Poortmans, et al. 2003. "Biochemical Aspects of Overtraining in Endurance Sports." *Sports Medicine* 33: 83-94.

Phillips, S.M. 2012. "Dietary Protein Requirements and Adaptive Advantages in Athletes." *The British Journal of Nutrition* 108 (Suppl. 2): S158-167.

Regehr, C., D. Glancy, and A. Pitts. 2013. "Interventions to Reduce Stress in University Students: A Review and Meta Analysis." *Journal of Affective Disorders* 148 (1): 1-11. doi: 10.1016/j.jad.2012.11.026. Epub 2012 Dec 13.

Robson, P.J. 2003. "Elucidating the Unexplained Underperformance Syndrome in Endurance Athletes: The Interleukin-6 Hypothesis." *Sports Medicine* 33: 771-781.

Sargent, C., S. Halson, and G.D. Roach. 2014. "Sleep or Swim? Early-Morning Training Severely Restricts the Amount of Sleep Obtained by Elite Swimmers." *European Journal of Sport Science* 14 (Suppl. 1): S310-S315.

Saw, A.E., L.C. Main, and P.B. Gastin. 2015a. "Monitoring Athletes Through Self-Report: Factors Influencing Implementation." *Journal of Sports Science and Medicine* 14: 137-146.

Saw, A.E., L.C. Main, and P.B. Gastin. 2015b. "Impact of Sport Context and Support on the Use of a Self Report Measure for Athlete Monitoring." *Journal of Sports Science and Medicine* 14: 732-739.

Saw, Anna E., Luana C. Main, and Paul B. Gastin. 2016. "Monitoring the Athlete Training Response: Subjective Self-Reported Measures Trump Commonly Used Objective Measures: A Systematic Review." *British Journal of Sports Medicine* 50 (5): 281-291.

Schwartz, J., and R.D. Simon, Jr. 2015. "Sleep Extension Improves Serving Accuracy: A Study With College Varsity Tennis Players." *Physiology & Behavior* 151: 541-544.

Selye, H. 1936. "A Syndrome Produced by Diverse Nocuous Agents." *Nature* 138, no. 3479 (July 4): 32.

Selye, H. 1950. "The Physiology and Pathology of Exposure to Stress, a Treatise Based on the Concepts of the General-Adaptation Syndrome and the Diseases of Adaptation." Montreal: ACTA Medical Publishers.

Simonsen, J.C., W.M. Sherman, D.R. Lamb, A.R. Dernbach, J.A. Doyle, and R. Straus. 1991. "Dietary Carbohydrate, Muscle Glycogen, and Power Output During Rowing Training." *Journal of Applied Physiology (1985)* 70, no 4 (April): 1500-1505. doi: 10.1152/jappl.1991.70.4.1500. PMID: 2055827.

Smith, L.L. 2000. "Cytokine Hypothesis of Overtraining: A Physiological Adaptation to Excessive Stress?" *Medicine & Science in Sports & Exercise* 32: 317-331.

Stults-Kolehmainen, M.A., and J.B. Bartholomew. 2012. "Psychological Stress Impairs Short-Term Muscular Recovery From Resistance Exercise." *Medicine & Science in Sports & Exercise* 44: 2220-2227.

Stults-Kolehmainen, M.A., J.B. Bartholomew, and R. Sinha. 2014. "Chronic Psychological Stress Impairs Recovery of Muscular Function and Somatic Sensations Over a 96-Hour Period." *Journal of Strength and Conditioning Research* 28 (7): 2007-2017.

Taylor, K., D. Chapman, J. Cronin, M. Newton, and N. Gill. 2012. "Fatigue Monitoring in High Performance Sport: A Survey of Current Trends." *Journal of Australian Strength and Conditioning* 20, 12-23.

Thomas, D.T., K.A. Erdman, and L.M. Burke. 2016. "American College of Sports Medicine Joint Statement." *Nutrition and Athletic Performance* 48, no. 3 (March): 543-568. doi: 10.1249/MSS.0000000000000852.

Thorpe, R.T., A.J. Strudwick, M. Buchheit, G. Atkinson, B. Drust, W. Gregson. 2017. "The Influence of Changes in Acute Training Load on Daily Sensitivity of Morning-Measured Fatigue Variables in Elite Soccer Players." International Journal of Sports Physiology and Performance 12: 107-113.

Urhausen, A., H. Gabriel, and W. Kindermann. 1995. "Blood Hormones as Markers of Training Stress and Overtraining." *Sports Medicine* 20: 251-276.

Venter, R.E. 2012. "Role of Sleep in Performance and Recovery of Athletes: A Review Article." *South African Journal for Research in Sport, Physical Education, and Recreation* 34 (1): 167-184.

Vitale, K.C., R. Owens, S.R. Hopkins, and A. Malhotra. 2019. "Sleep Hygiene for Optimizing Recovery in Athletes: Review and Recommendations." *International Journal of Sports Medicine* 40 (8): 535-543. doi: 10.1055/a-0905-3103.

Walker, M.P., T. Brakefield, A. Morgan, et al. 2002. "Practice With Sleep Makes Perfect: Sleep-Dependent Motor Skill Learning." *Neuron* 35 (1): 205-211.

Waterhouse, J., G. Atkinson, B. Edwards, and T. Reilly. 2007. "The Role of a Short Post-Lunch Nap in Improving Cognitive, Motor, and Sprint Performance in Participants with Partial Sleep Deprivation." *Journal of Sports Sciences* 25: 1557-1566.

Watkins, C.M., S.R. Barillas, M.A. Wong, D.C. Archer, I.J. Dobbs, R.G. Lockie, J.W. Coburn, T.T. Tran, and L.E. Brown. 2017. "Determination of Vertical Jump as a Measure of Neuromuscular Readiness and Fatigue." *Journal of Strength and Conditioning Research* 31 (12): 3305-3310.

Weitzman, E.D. 1976. "Circadian Rhythms and Episodic Hormone Secretion in Man." *Annual Review of Medicine* 27: 225-243.

Woods, A.L., L.A. Garvican-Lewis, B. Lundy, A.J. Rice, and K.G. Thompson. 2017. "New Approaches to Determine Fatigue in Elite Athletes During Intensified Training: Resting Metabolic Rate and Pacing Profile." *PLOS One* 12 (3): e0173807.

Chapter 23

Aubry, A., C. Hausswirth, L. Julien, A.J. Coutts, and Y. Le Meur. 2014. "Functional Overreaching: The Key to Peak Performance During the Taper?" *Medicine & Science in Sports & Exercise* 46 (9): 1769-1777. doi: 10.1249/MSS.0000000000000301.hal-01561483.

Armstrong, R.B. 1990. "Initial Events in Exercise Induced Muscular Injury." *Medicine & Science in Sports & Exercise* 22: 429-435.

Bannister, E.W. 1991. Modelling Elite Athletic Performance." In *Physiological Testing of the High Performance Athlete*, edited by J.D. MacDougal, H.A. Wenger, and H.J. Green, 403-424. Champaign, IL: Human Kinetics.

Barnett, L. 2007. "'Winners' and 'losers': The effects of being allowed or denied entry into competitive extracurricular activities." *Journal of Leisure Research* 39: 316-344.

Bonifazi, M., F. Sardella, and C. Luppo. 2000. "Preparatory Versus Main Competitions: Differences in Performances, Lactate Responses and Pre-Competition Plasma Cortisol Concentrations in Elite Male Swimmers." *European Journal of Applied Physiology* 82: 368-373.

Bosquet, L., J. Montpetit, D. Arvisais, and I. Mujika. 2007. "Effects of Tapering on Performance: A Meta-Analysis." *Medicine & Science in Sports & Exercise* 39: 1358-1365.

Botonis, P.G., A.G. Toubekis, and T.I. Platanou. 2019. "Training Loads, Wellness and Performance Before and During Tapering for a Water-Polo Tournament." *Journal of Human Kinetics* 66 (March 27): 131-141. doi: 10.2478/hukin-2018-0053. PMID: 30988847. PMCID: PMC6458570.

Brown, G. and P. Potrac. 2009. "'You've not made the grade, son': De-Selection and Identity Disruption in Elite Level Youth Football." *Soccer and Society* 10 (2): 143-159, DOI: 10.1080/14660970802601613.

Chiu, L.Z.F., and J.L. Barnes. 2003. "The Fitness-Fatigue Model Revisited: Implications for Planning Short and Long-Term Training." *Strength and Conditioning Journal* 25: 42-52.

Costill, D.L., D.S. King, R. Thomas, and M. Hargreaves. 1985. "Effects of Reduced Training on Muscular Power in Swimmers." *Physician and Sports Medicine* 30: 94-101.

Fitz-Clarke, J., R.H. Morton, and E.W. Banister. 1991. "Optimizing Athletic Performance by Influence Curves." *Journal of Applied Physiology* 71: 1151-1158.

Forbes-Robertson, S., E. Dudley, P. Vadgama, C. Cook, S. Drawer, and L. Kilduff. 2012. "Circadian Disruption and Remedial Interventions: Effects and Interventions for Jet Lag for Athletic Peak Performance." *Sports Medicine* 42, no. 3 (March 1): 185-208. doi: 10.2165/11596850-000000000-00000. PMID: 22299812.

Grove, J., M. Fish, and R. Eklund. 2004. "Changes in Athletic Identity Following Team Selection: Self-Protection Versus Self-Enhancement." *Journal of Applied Sport Psychology* 16: 75-81. doi: 10.1080/10413200490260062.

Hickson, R. 1980. "Interference of Strength Development by Simultaneously Training for Strength and Endurance." *European Journal of Applied Physiology and Occupational Physiology* 45: 255-263.

Hopkins, W.G., J.A. Hawley, and L.M. Burke. 1999. "Design and Analysis of Research on Sport Performance Enhancement." *Medicine & Science in Sports & Exercise* 31: 472-485.

Houmard, J. 1991. "Impact of Reduced Training on Performance in Endurance Athletes." *Sports Medicine* 12: 380-393.

Houmard, J., J.P. Kirwan, M.G. Flynn, and J.B. Mitchell. 1989. "Effects of Reduced Training on Submaximal and Maximal Running Responses." *International Journal of Sports Medicine* 10: 30-33.

Houmard, J., D. Costill, J.B. Mitchell, S.H. Park, R.C. Hickner, and J.N. Roemmich. 1990. "Reduced Training Maintains Performance in Distance Runners." *International Journal of Sports Medicine* 11: 46-52. 1990.

Houmard, J., B.K. Scott, C.L. Justice, and T. Chenier. 1994. "The Effects of Taper on Performance in Distance Runners." *Medicine & Science in Sports & Exercise* 26: 624-631.

Houmard, J., and R. Johns. 1994. "Effects of Taper on Swim Performance: Practical Implications." *Sports Medicine* 17: 224-232.

Jeukendrup, A.E., M.K. Hesselink, A.C. Snyder, H. Kuipers, and H.A. Keizer. 1992. "Physiological Changes in Male Competitive Cyclists After Two Weeks of Intensified Training." *International Journal of Sports Medicine* 13: 534-541.

Johns, R., J. Houmard, R.W. Kobe, et al. 1992. "Effects of Taper on Swim Power, Stroke Distance and Performance." *Medicine & Science in Sports & Exercise* 24: 1141-1146.

Lantoine, P., M. Lecocq, C. Bougard, E. Dousset, T. Marqueste, C. Bourdin, J.M. Allègre, L. Bauvineau, and S. Mesure. 2021. "Car Seat Impact on Driver's Sitting Behavior and Perceived Discomfort During Prolonged Real Driving on Varied Road Types." *PLOS One* 16, no. 11 (November 16): e0259934. doi: 10.1371/journal.pone.0259934. PMID: 34784401. PMCID: PMC8594853.

Luden, N., E. Hayes, A. Galpin, K. Minchev, B. Jemiolo, U. Raue, T.A. Trappe, M.P. Harber, T. Bowers, S. Trappe. 2010. "Myocellular Basis for Tapering in Competitive Distance Runners." *Journal of Applied Physiology (1985)* 108, no. 6 (June): 1501-1509. doi: 10.1152/japplphysiol.00045.2010. Epub 2010 Mar 18. PMID: 20299622.

Martin, D., J.C. Scifres, S.D. Zimmerman, and J.G. Wilkinson. 1994. "Effects of Interval Training and Taper on Cycling Performance and Isokinetic Leg Strength." *International Journal of Sports Medicine* 15: 485-491.

Morton, R., J. Fitz-Clarke, and E. Banister. 1990. "Modeling Human Performance in Running." *Journal of Applied Physiology* 69: 1171-1177.

Mujika, I., J.C. Chartrand, T. Busso, A. Geyssant, F. Barale, and L. Lacoste. 1995. "Effects of Training on Performance in Competitive Swimmers." *Canadian Journal of Applied Physiology* 20: 395-406.

Mujika, I., T. Busso, A. Geyssant, F. Barale, L. Lacoste, and J.C. Chartrand. 1996. "Modeled Response to Training and Taper in Competitive Swimmers." *Medicine & Science in Sports & Exercise* 28: 251-258.

Mujika, I., S. Padilla, A. Geyssant, and J.C. Chartrand. 1998. "Hematological Responses to Training in Competitive Swimmers: Relationships With Performance." *Archives of Physiology and Biochemistry* 105: 379-385.

Mujika, I., A. Goya, S. Padillo, A. Grijalba, E. Gorostiaga, and J. Ibanez. 2000. "Physiological Responses to a 6-d Taper in Middle-Distance Runners: Influence of Training Volume and Intensity." *Medicine & Science in Sports & Exercise* 32: 511-517.

Mujika, I., A. Goya, E. Ruiz, A. Grijalba, J. Santisteban, and S. Padilla. 2002. "Physiological and Performance Responses to a 6-d Taper in Middle Distance Runners: Influence of Training Frequency." *International Journal of Sports Medicine* 23: 367-373.

Mujika, I., and S. Padilla. 2003. "Scientific Bases for Precompetition Tapering Strategies." *Medicine & Science in Sports & Exercise* 35: 1182-1187.

Mujika, I., S. Padilla, and T. Busso. 2004. "Physiological Changes Associated With Pre-Event Taper in Athletes." *Sports Medicine* 34: 891-927.

Mujika I. 2010. "Intense Training: The Key to Optimal Performance Before and During the Taper." *Scandinavian Journal of Medicine and Science in Sports* 20 (Suppl. 2): 24-31. doi: 10.1111/j.1600-0838.2010.01189.x. PMID: 20840559.

Neary, J.P., T.P. Martin, D.C. Reid, R. Burnham, and H.A. Quinney. 1992. "The Effects of a Reduced Exercise Duration Taper Programme on Performance and Muscle Enzymes of Endurance Cyclists." *European Journal of Applied Physiology and Occupational Physiology* 65: 30-36.

Neary, J.P., Y.N. Bhambhani, and D.C. McKenzie. 2003. "Effects of Different Stepwise Reduction Taper Protocols on Cycling Performance." *Canadian Journal of Applied Physiology* 28: 576-587.

Neary, J.P., D.C. McKenzie, and Y.N. Bhambhani. 2005. "Muscle Oxygenation Trends After Tapering in Trained Cyclists." *Dynamic Medicine* 1-9.

Neufer, P.D., D. Costill, R.A. Fielding, M.G. Flynn, and J.P. Kirwan. 1987. "Effect of Reduced Training on Muscular Strength and Endurance in Competitive Swimmers." *Medicine & Science in Sports & Exercise* 19: 486-490.

Ritchie, Darren, Justine Allen, and Andrew Kirkland. 2017. "Where Science Meets Practice: Olympic Coaches' Crafting of the Tapering Process." *Journal of Sports Sciences* 36: 1-10. doi: 10.1080/02640414.2017.1362717.

Romano-Ely, B.C., M.K. Todd, M.J. Saunders, and T. St. Laurent. 2006. "Effect of an Isocaloric Carbohydrate Protein Antioxidant Drink on Cycling Performance." *Medicine & Science in Sports & Exercise* 38: 1608-1616.

Rønnestad, B.R., J. Hansen, G. Vegge, and I. Mujika. 2017. "Short-Term Performance Peaking in an Elite Cross-Country Mountain Biker." *Journal of Sports Sciences* 35, no. 14 (July): 1392-1395. doi: 10.1080/02640414.2016.1215503.

Rønnestad, B.R., and O. Vikmoen. 2019. "A 11-day Compressed Overload and Taper Induces Larger Physiological Improvements Than a Normal Taper in Elite Cyclists." *Scandinavian Journal of Medicine and Science in Sports* 29, no. 12 (December): 1856-1865. doi: 10.1111/sms.13536. Epub 2019 Aug 29. PMID: 31410894.

Seifried, C., and T. Casey. 2012. "Managing the Selection of Highly Competitive Interscholastic Sport Teams: Recommendations From Coaches on Cutting Players." *Journal of Sport Administration & Supervision* 4 (1): 79-96.

Shepley, B., J.D. MacDougall, N. Cipriano, J.R. Sutton, M.A. Tarnopolsky, and G. Coates. 1992. "Physiological Effects of Tapering in Highly Trained Athletes." *Journal of Applied Physiology* 72: 706-711.

Tran, Jacqueline, Anthony J. Rice, Luana C. Main, Paul B. Gastin. 2014. "Development and Implementation of a Novel Measure for Quantifying Training Loads in Rowing." *Journal of Strength and Conditioning Research* 28, no. 4 (April): 1172-1180, doi: 10.1519/JSC.0000000000000248.

Trappe, S., D. Costill, and R. Thomas. 2000. "Effect of Swim Taper on Whole Muscle and Single Fiber Contractile Properties." *Medicine & Science in Sports & Exercise* 32: 48-56.

Trinity, J.D., M.D. Pahnke, E.C. Reese, and E. Coyle. 2006. "Maximal Mechanical Power During a Taper in Elite Swimmers." *Medicine & Science in Sports & Exercise* 38: 1643-1649.

Yamamoto, Y. and Y. Mutoh. 1988. "Hematological and Biochemical Indices During the Taper Period of Competitive Swimmers." In *Swimming Science V: International Series on Sports Sciences*, edited by B. Ungerects et al., 243-249. Champaign IL: Human Kinetics.

Zarkadas, P., J. Carter, and E. Banister. 1994. "Taper Increases Performance and Aerobic Power in Triathletes." *Medicine & Science in Sports & Exercise* 26: 34.

Zatsiorsky, V. 1995. *Science and Practice of Strength Training*. Champaign IL: Human Kinetics.

Chapter 24

Bahr, R. 2016. "Why Screening Tests to Predict Injury Do Not Work—and Probably Never Will…:A Critical Review." *British Journal of Sports Medicine* 50: 776-780.

Bahr, R., S. Andersen, S. Loken, et al. 2004. "Low Back Pain Among Endurance Athletes With and Without Specific Back Loading: A Cross-Sectional Survey of Cross-Country Skiers, Rowers, Orienteers and Athletic Controls." *Spine* 29: 449-454.

Bojani⬚, I., and N. Desnica. 1998. "Stress Fracture of the Sixth Rib in an Elite Athlete." *Croatian Medical Journal* 39 (4): 458-460.

Caldwell, J.S., P.J. McNair, and M. Williams. 2003. "The Effects of Repetitive Motion on Lumbar Flexion and Erector Spinae Muscle Activity in Rowers." *Clinical Biomechanics* 18: 704-711.

Christiansen, E., and I.L. Kanstrup. 1997. "Increased Risk of Stress Fractures in Elite Rowers." *Scandinavian Journal of Medicine and Science in Sports* 7: 49-52.

Coburn, P., H. Wajswelner, and K. Bennell. 1993. A Survey of 54 Consecutive Rowing Injuries. *Proceedings of Annual Scientific Conference in Sports Medicine*. Melbourne: 88.

Devereaux, M.D., and S.M. Lachman. 1983. "Athletes Attending a Sports Injury Clinic, a Review." *British Journal of Sports Medicine* 17: 137-142.

Gabbett, T.J. 2016. "The Training-Injury Prevention Paradox: Should Athletes Be Training Smarter and Harder?" *British Journal of Sports Medicine* 50: 273-280.

Gabbett, T.J. 2020. "Debunking the Myths About Training Load, Injury and Performance: Empirical Evidence, Hot Topics and Recommendations for Practitioners." *British Journal of Sports Medicine* 54 (1): 58-66. doi:10.1136/bjsports-2018-099784.

Gatchel, R.J., Y.B. Peng, M.L. Peters, P.N. Fuchs, and D.C. Turk. 2007. "The Biopsychosocial Approach to Chronic Pain: Scientific Advances and Future Directions." *Psychological Bulletin Journal* 133 (4): 581-624.

Hannafin, J.A. 2000. "Rowing." In *The Encyclopedia of Sports Medicine, Vol. 8: Women in Sport* 486-493. Oxford: Blackwell Science.

Hickey, G.J., P.A. Fricker, and W.A. McDonald. 1997. "Injuries to Elite Rowers Over a 10-Yr Period." *Medicine & Science in Sports & Exercise* 29 (12): 1567-1572.

Holden, D., and D.W. Jackson. 1985. "Stress Fracture of the Ribs in Female Rowers." *American Journal of Sports Medicine* 13: 342-348.

Holt, P., Bull, A., Cashman, P., et al. 2003. "Kinematics of Spinal Motion During Prolonged Rowing." *International Journal of Sports Medicine* 24: 597-602.

Howell, D.W. 1984. "Musculoskeletal Profile and Incidence of Musculoskeletal Injuries in Lightweight Women Rowers." *American Journal of Sports Medicine* 12 (4): 278-282.

Karlson, K.A. 2000. "Rowing Injuries." *The Physician and Sportsmedicine* 28: 40-50.

Kim, H.C., and K.J. Park. 2020. "Injuries in Female and Male Elite Korean Rowing Athletes: An Epidemiological Study." *Sportverletz Sportschaden* 34, no. 4 (December): 217-226. English. doi: 10.1055/a-1257-7676. Epub 2020 Dec 1. PMID: 33260241.

Koutedakis, Y., R. Frischknecht, and M. Murthy. 1997. "Knee Flexion to Extension Peak Torque Ratios and Low-Back Injuries in Highly Active Individuals." *International Journal of Sports Medicine* 18 (4): 290-295.

McGregor, A., L. Anderton, and W. Gedroyc. 2002. "The Assessment of Intersegmental Motion and Pelvic Tilt in Elite Oarsmen." *Medicine & Science in Sports & Exercise* 34: 1143-1149.

McNally, E., D. Wilson, and S. Seiler. 2005. "Rowing Injuries." *Seminars in Musculoskeletal Radiology* 9 (4): 379-396. doi:10.1055/s-2005-923381.

Milewski, M.D., D.L. Skaggs, G.A. Bishop, et al. 2014. "Chronic Lack of Sleep Is Associated with Increased Sports Injuries in Adolescent Athletes." *Journal of Pediatric Orthopedics* 34 (2): 129-133. doi: 10.1097/BPO.0000000000000151.

Nuzzo, J.L. 2020. "The Case for Retiring Flexibility as a Major Component of Physical Fitness." *Sports Medicine* 50 (5): 853-870. doi: 10.1007/s40279-019-01248-w.

O'Kane, J.W., C.C. Teitz, and B.K. Lind. "Effect of Preexisting Back Pain on the Incidence and Severity of Back Pain in Intercollegiate Rowers." *American Journal of Sports Medicine* 31 (1): 80-82.

Potvin-Gilbert, M. 2018. "Motor Variability in Rowing." Electronic Thesis and Dissertation Repository, 5597. https://ir.lib.uwo.ca/etd/5597

Reid, R., P.A. Fricker, O. Kestermann, and P. Shakespear. 1989. "A Profile of Female Rowers' Injuries and Illnesses at the Australian Institute of Sport." *ExcelS*: 17-20.

Rumball, J.S., C.M. Lebrun, S. Di Ciacca, and K. Orlando. 2005. "Rowing Injuries." *Sports Medicine* 35 (6): 537-555.

Secher, N.H. 1993. "Physiological and Biomechanical Aspects of Rowing: Implications for Training." *Sports Medicine* 15 (1): 24-42.

Smoljanovic, T., I. Bohacek, J. Hannafin, H.B. Nielsen, D. Hren, and I. Bojanic. 2018. "Sport Injuries in International Masters Rowers: A Cross-Sectional Study." *Croatian Medical Journal* 59, no. 5 (October 31): 258-266. doi: 10.3325/cmj.2018.59.258. PMID: 30394018. PMCID: PMC6240823.

Smoljanovic, T., I. Bohacek, J.A. Hannafin, O. Terborg, D. Hren, M. Pecina, and I. Bojanic. 2015. "Acute and Chronic Injuries Among Senior International Rowers: A Cross-Sectional Study." *International Orthopaedics* 39, no. 8 (August): 1623-1630. doi: 10.1007/s00264-014-2665-7. Epub 2015 Jan 22. PMID: 25603972.

Stallard, M.C. 1980. "Backache in Oarsmen." *British Journal of Sports Medicine* 14 (2-3): 105-108.

Teitz, C., J. O'Kane, B. Lind, and J.A. Hannafin. 2002. "Back Pain in Former Intercollegiate Rowers." *American Journal of Sports Medicine* 30: 674-679.

Thornton, J.S. and A. Vinther. 2018. "Prevention of Rib Stress Injury in Rowers: What Do We Know and Where Do We Need to Go?" *Sports Orthopaedics and Traumatology* 34 (3): 278-286. doi: 10.1016/j.orthtr.2018.05.001.

Trease, L., K. Wilkie, G. Lovell, M. Drew, and I. Hooper. 2020. "Epidemiology of Injury and Illness in 153 Australian International-Level Rowers over Eight International Seasons." *British Journal of Sports Medicine* 54 (21): 1288-1293. doi: 10.1136/bjsports-2019-101402.

Vinther, A., I.L. Kanstrup, E. Christiansen, et al. 2006. "Exercise-Induced Rib Stress Fractures: Potential Risk Factors Related to Thoracic Muscle Co-Contraction and Movement Pattern." *Scandinavian Journal of Medicine and Science in Sports* 16: 188-196.

Wajswelner, H., A. Mosler, and P. Coburn. 1995. "Musculoskeletal Injuries in Domestic and International Rowing." Proceedings of National Annual Scientific Conference in Science and Medicine in Sport. Hobart: Sports Medicine Australia, 90-91.

Warden, S.J., F.R. Gutschlag, H. Wajswelner, et al. 2002. "Aetiology of Rib Stress Fractures in Rowers." *Sports Medicine* 32: 819-836.

Weightman, D., and R.C. Browne. 1974. "Injuries in Association and Rugby Football." *British Journal of Sports Medicine* 8 (4): 183-187.

Wilson, F., C. Gissane, and A. McGregor. 2014. "Ergometer Training Volume and Previous Injury Predict Back Pain in Rowing: Strategies for Injury Prevention and Rehabilitation." *British Journal of Sports Medicine* 48: 1534-1537.

Wilson, F., C. Gissane, J. Gormley, and C. Simms. 2010. "A 12-Month Prospective Cohort Study of Injury in International Rowers." *British Journal of Sports Medicine* 44, no. 3 (February): 207-214. doi: 10.1136/bjsm.2008.048561. Epub 2008 Aug 21. PMID: 18718978.

Wilson, F., C. Gissane, J. Gormley, and C. Simms. 2013. "Sagittal Plane Motion of the Lumbar Spine During Ergometer and Single Scull Rowing." *Sports Biomechanics* 12 (2): 132-142. doi: 10.1080/14763141.2012.726640.

Winzen, M., H.F. Voigt, T. Hinrichs, and P. Platen. 2011. "Beschwerden des Bewegungsapparats bei deutschen Hochleistungsruderern [Injuries of the Musculoskeletal system in German elite rowers]." *Sportverletz Sportschaden* 25, no. 3 (September): 153-158. German. doi: 10.1055/s-0031-1273299.

Yoshiga, C.C., and M. Higuchi. 2003. "Oxygen Uptake and Ventilation During Rowing and Running in Females and Males." *Scandinavian Journal of Medicine and Science in Sports* 13 (6): 359-363. doi:10.1046/j.1600-0838.2003.00324.x.

Chapter 25

Abbott, A.E., and J.A. Hannafin. 2001. "Stress Fracture of the Clavicle in a Female Lightweight Rower." *American Journal of Sports Medicine* 29 (3): 370-372.

Brinjikji, W., B. Luetmer, B.W. Comstock, et al. 2015. "Systematic Review of Imaging Features of Spinal Degeneration in Asymptomatic Populations." *American Journal of Neuroradiology* 36: 811-816.

Buckeridge, E., S. Hislop, A. Bull, et al. 2012. "Kinematic Asymmetries of the Lower Limbs During Ergometer Rowing." *Medicine & Science in Sports & Exercise* 44: 2147-2153.

Bull, A., and A. McGregor. 2000. "Measuring Spinal Motion in Rowers: The Use of an Electromagnetic Device." *Clinical Biomechanics* 15: 72-76.

Caldwell, J.S., P.J. McNair, and M. Williams. 2003. "The Effects of Repetitive Motion on Lumbar Flexion and Erector Spinae Muscle Activity in Rowers." *Clinical Biomechanics* 18: 704-711.

Callaghan, M., and S. McGill. 2001. "Intervertebral Disc Herniation: Studies on a Porcine Model Exposed to Highly Repetitive Flexion/Extension Motion With Compressive Force." *Clinical Biomechanics* 16: 28-37.

Carr, JB II, Q.E. John, E. Rajadhyaksha, E.W. Carson, K.L. Turney. 2017. "Traumatic Avulsion of the Serratus Anterior Muscle in a Collegiate Rower: A Case Report." *Sports Health* 9 (1): 80-83. doi: 10.1177/1941738116670636.

De Campos Mello, F., R. Bertuzzi, E. Franchini, et al. 2014. "Rowing Ergometer With the Slide Is More Specific to Rowers' Physiological Evaluation." *Research in Sports Medicine* 22 (2): 136-146.

Dolan, P., and M.A. Adams. 2001. "Recent Advances in Lumbar Spinal Mechanics and Their Significance for Modelling." *Spine* 16: S8-S16.

Evans, G., and A. Redgrave. 2016a. "Great Britain Rowing Team Guideline for Diagnosis and Management of Rib Stress Injury: Part 1." *British Journal of Sports Medicine* 50 (5): 266-269.

Evans, G., and A. Redgrave. 2016b. "Great Britain Rowing Team Guideline for Diagnosis and Management of Rib Stress Injury: Part 2. The Guideline Itself." *British Journal of Sports Medicine* 50 (5): 270–272.

Fairclough, J., K. Hayashi, H. Toumi, et al. 2006. "The Functional Anatomy of the Iliotibial Band During Flexion and Extension of the Knee: Implications for Understanding Iliotibial Band Syndrome. *Journal of Anatomy* 208 (3): 309-316.

Hainline, B., J.A. Turner, J.P. Caneiro, M. Stewart, and G. Lorimer Moseley. 2017. "Pain in Elite Athletes-Neurophysiological, Biomechanical and Psychosocial Considerations: A Narrative Review." *British Journal of Sports Medicine* 51 (17): 1259-1264.

Hanlon, D.P., and J.R. Luellen. 1999. "Intersection Syndrome: A Case Report and Review of the Literature." *Journal of Emergency Medicine* 17 (6): 969-971.

Hedman, T., and G. Ferney. 1997. "Mechanical Response of the Lumbar Spine to Seated Postural Loads." *Spine* 22: 734-743.

Heuer, F., H. Schmitt, H. Schmidt, et al. 2007. "Creep Associated Changes in Intervertebral Disc Bulging Obtained With a Laser Scanning Device." *Clinical Biomechanics* 22: 737-744.

Holt, P., A. Bull, P. Cashman, et al. 2003. "Kinematics of Spinal Motion During Prolonged Rowing." *International Journal of Sports Medicine* 24: 597-602.

Hoy, G., L. Trease, W. Braybon. 2019. "Intersection Syndrome: An Acute Surgical Disease in Elite Rowers. *BMJ Open Sport and Exercise Medicine* 5, no. 1 (June 7): e000535. doi: 10.1136/bmjsem-2019-000535.

Kalichmman, P.T., D.H. Kim, and D.J. Hunter. 2009. "Spondylolisis and Spondylolisthesis: Prevalence and Association With Low Back Pain in the Adult Community Based Population." *Spine* 34 (2): 199-205.

Karlson, K.A. 2000. "Rowing Injuries." *The Physician and Sportsmedicine* 28: 40-50.

Kibler, W.B., T.L. Uhl, J.W. Maddox, et al. 2002. "Qualitative Clinical Evaluation of Scapular Dysfunction: A Reliable Study." *Journal of Shoulder and Elbow Surgery* 11: 550-556.

King, K., B. Davidson, B. Zhou, et al. 2009. "High Magnitude Cyclic Load Triggers Inflammatory Response in Lumbar Ligaments." *Clinical Biomechanics* 24: 792-798.

Kleshnev, V. 2010. *Rowing Biomechanics Newsletter* 107 (10). Accessed 1 August 2020. http://www.biorow.com.

Little, J., and P. Khalsa. 2005. "Human Lumbar Spine Creep During Cyclic and Static Flexion: Creep Rate, Biomechanics and Facet Joint Capsule Strain." *Annals of Biomedical Engineering* 33: 391-401.

Mackenzie, H, A. Bull, and A. McGregor. 2008. "Changes in Rowing Technique Over a Routine One Hour Low Intensity High Volume Training Session." *Journal of Sports Science and Medicine* 7: 486-491.

Malloy, P., M. Malloy, and P. Draovitch. 2013. "Guidelines and Pitfalls for the Rehabilitation Following Hip Arthroscopy." *Current Reviews in Musculoskeletal Medicine* 6: 235-241.

Manning, T.S., S.A. Plowman, G. Drake, et al. 2000. "Intra-abdominal Pressure and Rowing: The Effects of Inspiring Versus Expiring During the Drive." *Journal of Sports Medicine and Physical Fitness* 40 (3): 223-232.

Maurer, M., R.B. Soder, M. Baldisserotto. 2011. "Spine Abnormalities Depicted by Magnetic Resonance Imaging in Adolescent Rowers." *American Journal of Sports Medicine* 39 (2): 392-397.

McBean, M. 2020. "Interview in Her Role as Chef de Mission for Tokyo Games Team Canada." Accessed July 28, 2020. https://www.sportsnet.ca/olympics/marnie-mcbean-olympics-tokyo-chef-de-mission.

McDonnell, L.K., P.A. Hume, and V. Nolte. 2011. "Rib Stress Fractures Among Rowers: Definition, Epidemiology, Mechanisms, Risk Factors and Effectiveness of Injury Prevention Strategies." *Sports Medicine* 41: 883–901.

McGregor, A., L. Anderton, and W. Gedroyc. 2002. "The Assessment of Intersegmental Motion and Pelvic Tilt in Elite Oarsmen." *Medicine & Science in Sports & Exercise* 34: 1143-1149.

McGregor, A., A. Bull, and R. Byng-Maddick. 2004. "A Comparison of Rowing Technique at Different Stroke Rates; A Description of Sequencing, Force Production and Kinematics." *International Journal of Sports Medicine* 25: 465-470.

Mohseni-Bandpei, M., R. Keshavarz, H. Minoonejhad, et al. 2012. "Shoulder Pain in Iranian Elite Athletes: The Prevalence and Risk Factors." *Journal of Manipulative and Physiological Therapies* 35 (7): 541-548.

Morris, F.L., R.M. Smith, W.L. Payne, et al. 2000. "Compressive and Shear Force Generated in the Lumbar Spine of Female Rowers." *International Journal of Sports Medicine* 21: 518-523.

Newlands, C., D. Reid, and P. Parmar. 2015. "The Prevalence, Incidence and Severity of Low Back Pain Among International Level Rowers." *British Journal of Sports Medicine* 49 (14): 951-956.

Ng, L., D. Perich, A. Burnett, et al. 2014. "Self Reported Prevalence, Pain Intensity and Risk Factors for Low Back Pain in Adolescent Rowers." *Journal of Science and Medicine in Sport* 17: 266-270.

Ng, L., A. Burnett, A. Smith, et al. 2015. "Spinal Kinematics of Adolescent Male Rowers With Back Pain in Comparison With Matched Controls During Ergometer Rowing." *Journal of Applied Biomechanics* 31 (6): 459-468.

Nugent, F.J., A. Vinther, A. McGregor, J.S. Thornton, K. Wilkie, and F. Wilson. 2021. "The Relationship Between Rowing-Related Low Back Pain and Rowing Biomechanics: A Systematic Review." *British Journal of Sports Medicine* Jan 4:bjsports-2020-102533. doi: 10.1136/bjsports-2020-102533.

O'Kane, J.W., C.C. Teitz, and B.K. Lind. 2003. "Effect of Preexisting Back Pain on the Incidence and Severity of Back Pain in Intercollegiate Rowers." *American Journal of Sports Medicine* 31 (1): 80-82.

Redgrave, S. 1992. "Injuries: Prevention/Cure." In *Steven Redgrave's Complete Book of Rowing*, edited by S. Redgrave, 200-217. London: Partridge Press.

Reide, N., V. Rosso, A. Rainoldi, et al. 2014. "Do Sweep Rowers Activate Their Low Back Muscles During Ergometer Rowing?" *Scandinavian Journal of Medicine and Science in Sports* 25 (4): e339-e52.

Richardson, C., and G. Jull. 1995. "Muscle Control: What Exercises Would You Prescribe?" *Manual Therapy* 1 (1): 2-10.

Rumball, J.S., C.M. Lebrun, S. Di Ciacca, and K. Orlando. "Rowing Injuries." *Sports Medicine* 35 (6): 537-555.

Shah, N., R. Fernandes, A. Thakrar, et al. 2013. "Diaphragmatic Hernia: An Unusual Presentation." *BMJ Case Reports*. doi: 10.1136/bcr-2013-008699.

Sharif, B., A. Redgrave, L. Arnold, D. Shah, and D. Remedios. 2017. "Back and Hip Pain in Elite Rowers: A Hip Injection Strategy for Prelabral Capsulitis." *Skeletal Radiology* 46 (6): 850.

Smoljanović, T., I. Bohaček, J. Hannafin, H.B. Nielsen, D. Hren, and I. Bojanić. 2018. "Sport Injuries in International Masters Rowers: A Cross-Sectional Study." *Croatian Medical Journal* 59 (5): 258-266. doi: 10.3325/cmj.2018.59.258. PMID: 30394018. PMCID: PMC6240823.

Smoljanovic, T., and I. Bojanic. 2007. "Ewing Sarcoma of the Rib in a Rower: A Case Report." *Clinical Journal of Sport Medicine* 17 (6): 510-512. doi: 10.1097/JSM.0b013e31815887cc.

Soler, T., and C. Calderon. 2000. "The Prevalence of Spondylolysis in the Spanish Elite Athlete. *American Journal of Sports Medicine* 28 (1): 57-62.

Solomonow, M., B. Zhou, R. Baratta, et al. 1999. "Biomechanics of Increased Exposure to Lumbar Injury Caused by Cyclic Loading: Part 1. Loss of Reflexive Muscular Stablisation." *Spine* 24: 2426-2434.

Stallard, M.C. 1980. "Backache in Oarsmen." *British Journal of Sports Medicine* 14 (2-3): 105-108.

Taimela, S., M. Kankaanpaa, and S. Luoto. 1999. "The Effect of Lumbar Fatigue on the Ability to Sense a Change in Lumbar Position." *Spine* 13: 1322-1332.

Taylor, T., R. Frankovitch, and J.S. Rumball. 2009. "Bilateral Atraumatic Medial Meniscal Tears in a 17-Year-Old Rower." *BMJ Case Reports*. doi: 10.1136/bcr.11.2008.1258.

Teitz, C., J. O'Kane, and B. Lind. 2003. "Back Pain in Former Intercollegiate Rowers." *American Journal of Sports Medicine* 30: 674-679.

Thornton, J.S., A. Vinther, F. Wilson, et al. 2017. "Rowing Injuries: An Updated Review." *Sports Medicine* 47 (4): 641-661. doi: 10.1007/s40279-016-0613-y.

Thornton, J.S., J.P. Caneiro, J. Hartvigsen, et al. 2021. "Treating Low Back Pain in Athletes: A Systematic Review With Meta-Analysis." *British Journal of Sports Medicine* 55, no. 12 (June): 656-662. doi: 10.1136/bjsports-2020-102723.

Van Dieen, J., M. Hoozemans, A. Van Der Beek, et al. 2002. "Precision of Estimates of Mean and Peak Spinal Loads in Lifting." *Journal of Biomechanics* 35: 979-982.

Vinther, A., I.L. Kanstrup, E. Christiansen, et al. 2006. "Exercise-Induced Rib Stress Fractures: Potential Risk Factors Related to Thoracic Muscle Co-Contraction and Movement Pattern." *Scandinavian Journal of Medicine and Science in Sports* 16: 188-196.

Vinther, A., and J.S. Thornton. 2016. "Management of Rib Pain in Rowers: Emerging Issues." *British Journal of Sports Medicine* 50 (3): 141-142.

Wajswelner, H., K. Bennell, I. Story, et al. 2000. "Muscle Action and Stress Forces on the Ribs in Rowing." *Physical Therapy in Sport* 1: 75–84.

Warden, S.J., F.R. Gutschlag, H. Wajswelner, et al. 2002. "Aetiology of Rib Stress Fractures in Rowers." *Sports Medicine* 32: 819-836.

Waryasz, G., and A. McDermott. 2008. "Patellofemoral Pain Syndrome (PFPS): A Systematic Review of Anatomy and Potential Risk Factors." *Dynamic Medicine* 7: 9.

Watson, L. 1996. *The Shoulder*. Hawthorn: Australian Clinical Educators.

Wilkie, K., J.S. Thornton, A. Vinther, L. Trease, S.J. McDonnell, and F. Wilson. 2021. "Clinical Management of Acute Low Back Pain in Elite and Subelite Rowers: A Delphi Study of Experienced and Expert Clinicians." *British Journal of Sports Medicine* 55, no. 23 (December):1324-1334. doi: 10.1136/bjsports-2020-102520.

Williams, J.G.P. 1977. "Surgical Management of Traumatic Non-Infective Tenosynovitis of the Wrist Extensors." *Journal of Bone and Joint Surgery* 59-B (4): 408-410.

Wilson, F. 2015. "Low Back Pain in Rowing: An Evolution of Understanding." World Rowing Championships 2015 Medical Meeting, Aiguebelette, France, August 2015. doi: 10.13140/RG.2.1.3312.3924.

Wilson, F., C.L. Ardern, J. Hartvigsen, et al. 2020. "Prevalence and Risk Factors for Back Pain in

Sports: A Systematic Review With Meta-Analysis." *British Journal of Sports Medicine.* Oct 19;bjsports-2020-102537. doi: 10.1136/bjsports-2020-102537.

Wilson, F., C. Gissane, J. Gormley, and C. Simms. 2010. "A 12-Month Prospective Cohort Study of Injury in International Rowers." *British Journal of Sports Medicine* 44 (3): 207-214.

Wilson, F., C. Gissane, and A. McGrego. 2014. "Ergometer Training Volume and Previous Injury Predict Back Pain in Rowing: Strategies for Injury Prevention and Rehabilitation." *British Journal of Sports Medicine* 48: 1534-1537.

Wilson, F., J. Gormley, C. Gissane, et al. 2012. "The Effect of Rowing to Exhaustion on Frontal Plane Angular Changes in the Lumbar Spine of Elite Rowers." *Journal of Sports Sciences* 30: 481-489.

Wilson, F., L. Ng, K. O'Sullivan, J.P. Caneiro, P.P. O'Sullivan, A. Horgan, J.S. Thornton, et al. 2021. "'You're the Best Liar in the World': A Grounded Theory Study of Rowing Athletes' Experience of Low Back Pain." *British Journal of Sports Medicine* 55, no. 6 (March): 327-335. doi: 10.1136/bjsports-2020-102514.

Wilson, F., J.S. Thornton, K. Wilkie, J. Hartvigsen, A. Vinther, K.E. Ackerman, J.P. Caneiro, et al. 2021. "2021 Consensus Statement for Preventing and Managing Low Back Pain in Elite and Subelite Adult Rowers." *British Journal of Sports Medicine* 55, no. 16 (August): 893-899. doi: 10.1136/bjsports-2020-103385.

Chapter 26

Bonini, M., C. Gramiccioni, D. Fioretti, et al. 2015. "Asthma, Allergy and the Olympics: A 12-Year Survey in Elite Athletes." *Current Opinion in Allergy and Clinical Immunology* 15 (2): 184-192.

Boykin, R.E., E.D. McFeely, K.E. Ackerman, Y.M. Yen, A. Nasreddine, and M.S. Kocher. 2013. "Labral Injuries of the Hip in Rowers." *Clinical Orthopaedics and Related Research* 471 (8): 2517-2522. doi: 10.1007/s11999-013-3109-1.

Burke, L.M., G.L. Close, B. Lundy, M. Mooses, J.P. Morton, and A.S. Tenforde. 2018. "Relative Energy Deficiency in Sport in Male Athletes: A Commentary on Its Presentation Among Selected Groups of Male Athletes." *International Journal of Sport Nutrition and Exercise Metabolism* 28 (4): 364-374. doi: 10.1123/ijsnem.2018-0182.

Carlsen, K.H. 2016. "Asthma in Olympians." *Paediatric Respiratory Reviews* 17: 34-35. doi: 10.1016/j.prrv.2015.08.013.

Chapman, J., and T. Woodman. 2016. "Disordered Eating in Male Athletes: A Meta-Analysis." *Journal of Sports Sciences* 34 (2):101-109.

Fewtrell, L., D. Kay, R. Salmon, M. Wyer, G. Newman, and G. Bowering. 1994. "The Health Effects of Low Contact Water Activities in Fresh and Estuarine Waters." *Journal of the Institution of Water and Environmental Management* 8: 97-101.

Garthe, I., T. Raastad, P.E. Refsnes, et al. 2011. "Effect of Two Different Weight-Loss Rates on Body Composition and Strength and Power Related Performance in Elite Athletes." *International Journal of Sport Nutrition and Exercise Metabolism* 21 (2): 97-104.

Gleeson, M., and D.B. Pyne. 2016. "Respiratory Inflammation and Infections in High-Performance Athletes." *Immunology & Cell Biology* 94 (2): 124-131. doi:10.1038/icb.2015.100.

Grima, J.N., M. Vella Wood, N. Portelli, J.N. Grima-Cornish, A. Attard, A. Gatt, C. Formosa, and D. Cerasola. 2022. "Blisters and Calluses from Rowing: Prevalence, Perceptions and Pain Tolerance." *Medicina (Kaunas)* 58, no. 1 (January 5): 77. doi: 10.3390/medicina58010077.

Hoch, A.Z., P. Papanek, A. Szabo, et al. 2011. "Association Between the Female Athlete Triad and Endothelial Dysfunction in Dancers." *Clinical Journal of Sport Medicine* 21: 119-125.

Karlson, K.A., C.B. Becker, and A. Merkur. 2001. "Prevalence of Eating Disordered Behavior in Collegiate Lightweight Women Rowers and Distance Runners." *Clinical Journal of Sport Medicine* 11 (1): 32-37.

Koutedakis, Y., P.I. Pacy, and R.M. Quevedo. 1994. "The Effects of Two Different Periods of Weight-Reduction on Selected Performance Parameters in Elite Lightweight Oarswomen." *International Journal of Sports Medicine* 5 (8): 472-477.

Lebrun, C.M., and J.S. Rumball. 2002. "Female Athlete Triad." *Sports Medicine and Arthroscopy Review* 10 (1): 23-32.

McNally, E., D. Wilson, and S. Seiler. 2005. "Rowing Injuries." *Seminars in Musculoskeletal Radiology* 9 (4): 379-396. doi:10.1055/s-2005-923381.

Mountjoy, M., J. Sundgot-Borgen, L. Burke, et al. 2014. "The IOC Consensus Statement: Beyond the Female Athlete Triad–Relative Energy Deficiency in Sport (RED-S)." *British Journal of Sports Medicine* 48 (7): 491-497.

Mountjoy, M., J. Sundgot-Borgen, L. Burke, et al. 2015. "RED-S CAT. Relative Energy Deficiency in Sport (RED-S) Clinical Assessment Tool (CAT)." *British Journal of Sports Medicine* 49 (7): 421-423. doi: 10.1136/bjsports-2015-094873.

Nattiv, A., A.B. Loucks, M.M. Manore, et al. 2007. "American College of Sports Medicine Position Stand: The Female Athlete Triad." *Medicine & Science in Sports & Exercise* 39 (10): 1867-1882.

Redgrave, S. 1992. "Injuries: Prevention/Cure." In *Steven Redgrave's Complete Book of Rowing*, edited by S. Redgrave, 200-217. London: Partridge Press.

Roach, M.C., and J.H. Chretien. 1995. "Common Hand Warts in Athletes: Association With Trauma to the Hand." *Journal of American College Health* 44 (3): 125-126.

Rumball, J.S., and C.M. Lebrun. 2010. "Chapter 83: Rowing." In *Netter's Sports Medicine*, edited by C.C, Madden, M. Putukian, C.C. Young, and E.C. McCarty, 679-685. Philadelphia: Saunders (Elsevier).

Rumball J.S., C.M. Lebrun, S. DiCiacca, and K. Orlando. 2005. "Rowing Injuries." *Sports Medicine* 35 (6): 537-555.

Smoljanovic, T., I. Bojanic, C.L. Pollock, et al. 2011. "Rib Stress Fracture in a Male Adaptive Rower From the Arms and Shoulders Sport Class: Case Report." *Croatian Medical Journal* 52 (5): 644-647.

Smoljanovic, T, I. Bojanic, J.A. Hannafin, et al. 2009. "Traumatic and Overuse Injuries Among International Elite Junior Rowers." *American Journal of Sports Medicine* 37 (6): 1193-1199.

Sundgot-Borgen, J., and I. Garthe. 2011. "Elite Athletes in Aesthetic and Olympic Weight-Class Sports and the Challenge of Body Weight and Body Compositions." *Journal of Sports Sciences* 29 (Suppl. 1): S101-S114.

Sykora, C., C.M. Grilo, D.R. Wilfley, et al. 1993. "Eating, Weight, and Dieting Disturbances in Male and Female Lightweight and Heavyweight Rowers." *International Journal of Eating Disorders* 14 (2): 203-211.

Talbott, S.M., and S.A. Shapses. 1998. "Fasting and Energy Intake Influence Bone Turnover in Lightweight Male Rowers." *International Journal of Sport Nutrition* 8: 377-387.

Temme, K.E., and A.Z. Hoch. 2013. "Recognition and Rehabilitation of the Female Athlete Triad/Tetrad: A Multidisciplinary Approach." *Current Sports Medicine Reports* 12 (3): 190-199.

Tenforde, A.S., M.T. Barrack, A. Nattiv, et al. 2016. "Parallels With the Female Athlete Triad in Male Athletes." *Sports Medicine* 46: 171-182.

Thiel, A., H. Gottfried, and F.W. Hesse. 1993. "Subclinical Eating Disorders in Male Athletes: A Study of the Low Weight Category in Rowers and Wrestlers." *Acta Psychiatrica Scandinavia* 88 (4): 259-265.

Tomecki, K.J., and J.F. Mikesell. 1987. "Rower's Rump." *Journal of the American Academy of Dermatology* 16 (4): 890-891.

Trease, L., K. Wilkie, G. Lovell, M. Drew, and I. Hooper. 2020. "Epidemiology of Injury and Illness in 153 Australian International-Level Rowers Over Eight International Seasons." *British Journal of Sports Medicine* 54: 1288-1293. doi: 10.1136/bjsports-2019-101402.

Vinther, A., I.-L. Kanstrup, E. Christiansen, et al. 2005. "Exercise-Induced Rib Stress Fractures: Influence of Reduced Bone Mineral Density." *Scandinavian Journal of Medicine and Science in Sports* 15: 95-99.

World Rowing. 2020a. "FISA Medical Recommendations for the Rio 2016 Olympic Games." Accessed August 1, 2020. http://www.worldrowing.com/mm//Document/General/General/12/22/77/Rio-MedicalRecommendationsat220216_Neutral.pdf.

World Rowing. 2020b. "FISA Minimum Guidelines for the Safe Practice of Rowing." Accessed August 1, 2020. http://www.worldrowing.com/mm//Document/General/General/12/64/45/FISA%E2%80%99sMinimumGuidelinesfortheSafePracticeofRowing_Neutral.pdf.

World Rowing. 2020c. "Gary O'Donovan." Accessed July 28, 2020. https://worldrowing.com/2018/02/16/gary-donovan-irl/.

World Rowing. 2020d. "FISA Pre-Competition Health Screening." Accessed August 1, 2020. http://www.worldrowing.com/athletes/medical-and-antidoping/fisa-pre-competition-health-screening.

World Rowing. 2020e. "Weight Loss by Lightweight Rowers and Coxswains." Accessed August 1, 2020. http://www.worldrowing.com/mm//Document/General/General/10/89/37/FISA%E2%80%99s_position_on_weight_loss_by_lightweight_rowers_and_coxswains_English.pdf.

Chapter 27

American College of Sports Medicine, M.N. Sawka, L.M. Burke, E.R. Eichner, R.J. Maughan, S.J. Montain, and N.S. Stachenfeld. 2007. "American College of Sports Medicine Position Stand. Exercise and Fluid Replacement" *Medicine & Science in Sports & Exercise* 39 (2): 377-390. https://doi.org/10.1249/mss.0b013e31802ca597.

Areta, J.L., L.M. Burke, L.M. Ross, D.M. Camera, D.W. West, E.M. Broad, N.A Jeacocke, D.R. Moore, T. Stellingwerff, S.M. Phillips, J.A. Hawley, and V.G. Coffey. 2013. "Timing and distribution of protein ingestion during prolonged recovery from resistance exercise alters myofibrillar protein synthesis." *The Journal of Physiology* 591 (9): 2319–2331. https://doi.org/10.1113/jphysiol.2012.244897

Barabasi, A.L., G. Menichetti, and J. Loscalzo. 2020. "Publisher Correction: The Unmapped Chemical Complexity of Our Diet." *Nature Food* 1 (1): 33-37. https://doi.org/10.1038/s43016-020-0030-0.

Barnes, K.A., M.L. Anderson, J.R. Stofan, K.J. Dalrymple, A.J. Reimel, T.J. Roberts, R.K. Randell, C.T. Ungaro, and L.B. Baker. 2019. "Normative Data for Sweating Rate, Sweat Sodium Concentration, and Sweat Sodium Loss in Athletes: An Update and Analysis by Sport." *Journal of Sports Sciences* 37 (20): 2356-2366. https://doi.org/10.1080/02640414.2019.1633159.

Belval, L.N., Y. Hosokawa, D.J. Casa, W.M. Adams, L.E. Armstrong, L.B. Baker, L. Burke, et al. 2019. "Practical Hydration Solutions for Sports." *Nutrients* 11 (7): 1550. https://doi.org/10.3390/nu11071550.

Boegman, S., and C.E. Dziedzic. 2016. "Nutrition and Supplements for Elite Open-Weight Rowing." *Current Sports Medicine Reports* 15 (4): 252-261. https://doi.org/10.1249/JSR.0000000000000281.

Bottoms, L., R. Westhead, J. Evans, T. Sleet, and J. Sinclair. 2014. "The Effects of Carbohydrate Ingestion on 30 Minute Rowing Time Trial Performance." *Journal of Comparative Physiology B* 10 (4): 247-252. https://doi.org/10.3920/CEP140018.

Burd, N.A., J.W. Beals, I.G. Martinez, A.F. Salvador, and S.K. Skinner. 2019. "Food-First Approach to Enhance the Regulation of Post-Exercise Skeletal Muscle Protein Synthesis and Remodeling." *Sports Medicine* 49 (Suppl. 1): 59-68. https://doi.org/10.1007/s40279-018-1009-y.

Burke, L.M., J.A. Hawley, A. Jeukendrup, J.P. Morton, T. Stellingwerff, and R.J. Maughan. 2018. "Toward a Common Understanding of Diet-Exercise Strategies to Manipulate Fuel Availability for Training and Competition Preparation in Endurance Sport." *International Journal of Sport Nutrition and Exercise Metabolism* 28 (5): 451-463. https://doi.org/10.1123/ijsnem.2018-0289.

Burke, L.M., J.A. Hawley, S.H. Wong, and A.E. Jeukendrup. 2011. "Carbohydrates for Training and Competition." *Journal of Sports Sciences* 29 (Suppl. 1): S17-S27. https://doi.org/10.1080/02640414.2011.585473.

Churchward-Venne, T.A., P.J.M. Pinckaers, J.S.J. Smeets, M.W. Betz, J.M. Senden, J.P.B. Goessens, A.P. Gijsen, I. Rollo, L.B. Verdijk, and L.J.C. van Loon. 2020. "Dose-Response Effects of Dietary Protein on Muscle Protein Synthesis During Recovery From Endurance Exercise in Young Men: A Double-Blind Randomized Trial." *American Journal of Clinical Nutrition* 112 (2): 303-317. https://doi.org/10.1093/ajcn/nqaa073.

Cornford, E., and R. Metcalfe. 2019. "Omission of Carbohydrate-Rich Breakfast Impairs Evening 2000-m Rowing Time Trial Performance." *European Journal of Sport Science* 19 (1): 133-140. https://doi.org/10.1080/17461391.2018.1545052.

Doering, T.M., P.R. Reaburn, G. Cox, and D.G. Jenkins. 2016. "Comparison of Postexercise Nutrition Knowledge and Postexercise Carbohydrate and Protein Intake Between Australian Masters and Younger Triathletes." *International Journal of Sport Nutrition and Exercise Metabolism* 26 (4): 338-346. https://doi.org/10.1123/ijsnem.2015-0289.

Hall, K. D., A. Ayuketah, R. Brychta, H. Cai, T. Cassimatis, K.Y. Chen, S.T. Chung, E. Costa, A. Courville, V. Darcey, L.A. Fletcher, C.G. Forde, A.M. Gharib, J. Guo, R. Howard, P.V. Joseph, S. McGehee, R. Ouwerkerk, K. Raisinger, I Rozga, and M. Zhou. 2019. "Ultra-Processed Diets Cause Excess

Calorie Intake and Weight Gain: An Inpatient Randomized Controlled Trial of Ad Libitum Food Intake." *Cell metabolism*, 30 (1): 67-77.e3. https://doi.org/10.1016/j.cmet.2019.05.008.

Halson, S.L., L.M. Burke, and J. Pearce. 2019. "Nutrition for Travel: From Jet Lag To Catering." *International Journal of Sport Nutrition and Exercise Metabolism* 29 (2): 228-235. https://doi.org/10.1123/ijsnem.2018-0278.

Hearris, M.A., K.M. Hammond, J.M. Fell, and J.P. Morton. 2018. "Regulation of Muscle Glycogen Metabolism During Exercise: Implications for Endurance Performance and Training Adaptations." *Nutrients* 10 (3). https://doi.org/10.3390/nu10030298.

Hevia-Larraín, V., B. Gualano, I. Longobardi, S. Gil, A.L. Fernandes, L. Costa, R. Pereira, G.G. Artioli, S.M. Phillips, and H. Roschel. 2021. "High-Protein Plant-Based Diet Versus a Protein-Matched Omnivorous Diet to Support Resistance Training Adaptations: A Comparison Between Habitual Vegans and Omnivores." *Sports Medicine* 51 (6): 1317-1330. https://doi.org/10.1007/s40279-021-01434-9.

Huecker, M., M. Sarav, M. Pearlman, and J. Laster. 2019. "Protein Supplementation in Sport: Source, Timing, and Intended Benefits." *Current Nutrition Reports* 8 (4): 382-396. https://doi.org/10.1007/s13668-019-00293-1.

Impey, S.G., M.A. Hearris, K.M. Hammond, J.D. Bartlett, J. Louis, G.L. Close, and J.P. Morton. 2018. "Fuel for the Work Required: A Theoretical Framework for Carbohydrate Periodization and the Glycogen Threshold Hypothesis." *Sports Medicine* 48 (5): 1031-1048. https://doi.org/10.1007/s40279-018-0867-7.

Jager, R., C.M. Kerksick, B.I. Campbell, P.J. Cribb, S.D. Wells, T.M. Skwiat, M. Purpura, et al. 2017. "International Society of Sports Nutrition Position Stand: Protein and Exercise." *Journal of the International Society of Sports Nutrition* 14: 20. https://doi.org/10.1186/s12970-017-0177-8.

Jeukendrup, A. 2014. "A Step Towards Personalized Sports Nutrition: Carbohydrate Intake During Exercise." *Sports Medicine* 44 (Suppl. 1): S25-S33. https://doi.org/10.1007/s40279-014-0148-z.

Jeukendrup, A.E. 2017a. "Periodized Nutrition for Athletes." *Sports Medicine* 47 (Suppl. 1): 51-63. https://doi.org/10.1007/s40279-017-0694-2.

Jeukendrup, A.E. 2017b. "Training the Gut for Athletes." *Sports Medicine* 47 (Suppl. 1): 101-110. https://doi.org/10.1007/s40279-017-0690-6.

Kerksick, C.M., S. Arent, B.J. Schoenfeld, J.R. Stout, B. Campbell, C.D. Wilborn, L. Taylor, et al. 2017. "International Society of Sports Nutrition Position Stand: Nutrient Timing." *Journal of the International Society of Sports Nutrition* 14: 33. https://doi.org/10.1186/s12970-017-0189-4.

Kerksick, C. M., A. Jagim, A Hagele, and R. Jäger. 2021. "Plant Proteins and Exercise: What Role Can Plant Proteins Have in Promoting Adaptations to Exercise?" *Nutrients*, 13 (6): 1962. https://doi.org/10.3390/nu13061962.

Kovacs, E.M., R.M. Schmahl, J.M. Senden, and F. Brouns. 2002. "Effect of High and Low Rates of Fluid Intake on Post-Exercise Rehydration." *International Journal of Sport Nutrition and Exercise Metabolism* 12 (1): 14-23. https://doi.org/10.1123/ijsnem.12.1.14.

Kozlowski, K.F., A. Ferrentino-DePriest, and F. Cerny. 2020. "Effects of Energy Gel Ingestion on Blood Glucose, Lactate, and Performance Measures During Prolonged Cycling." *Journal of Strength and Conditioning Research* 35 (11): 3111-3119. https://doi.org/10.1519/JSC.0000000000003297.

Lewis, N.A., D. Daniels, P.C. Calder, L.M. Castell, and C.R. Pedlar. 2020. "Are There Benefits from the Use of Fish Oil Supplements in Athletes? A Systematic Review." *Advances in Nutrition* 11 (5): 1300-1314. https://doi.org/10.1093/advances.nmaa050.

Maestu, J., J. Jurimae, and T. Jurimae. 2005. "Monitoring of Performance and Training in Rowing." *Sports Medicine* 35 (7): 597-617.

Martin, S.A., and V. Tomescu. 2017. "Energy Systems Efficiency Influences the Results of 2,000 M Race Simulation Among Elite Rowers." *Clujul Medical* 90 (1): 60-65.

Maughan, R. J., and S. M. Shirreffs. 2010. "Dehydration and Rehydration in Competitive Sport." *Scandinavian Journal of Medicine and Science in Sports* 20 (Suppl 3): 40-47. https://doi.org/10.1111/j.1600-0838.2010.01207.x.

McCubbin, A.J. 2022. "Modelling Sodium Requirements of Athletes Across a Variety of Exercise Scenarios: Identifying When to Test and Target, or Season to Taste." *European Journal of Sport Science*, 1-9. Advance online publication. https://doi.org/10.1080/17461391.2022.2083526.

Messina, M., H. Lynch, J.M. Dickinson, and K.E. Reed. 2018. "No Difference Between the Effects of Supplementing With Soy Protein Versus Animal Protein on Gains in Muscle Mass and Strength in Response to Resistance Exercise." *International Journal of Sport Nutrition and Exercise Metabolism* 28 (6): 674-685. https://doi.org/10.1123/ijsnem.2018-0071.

Mikulic, P., and N. Bralic. 2018. "Elite Status Maintained: A 12-Year Physiological and Performance Follow-Up of Two Olympic Champion Rowers." *Journal of Sports Sciences* 36 (6): 660-665. https://doi.org/10.1080/02640414.2017.1329548.

Moore, D.R. 2015. "Nutrition to Support Recovery from Endurance Exercise: Optimal Carbohydrate and Protein Replacement." *Current Sports Medicine Reports* 14 (4): 294-300. https://doi.org/10.1249/JSR.0000000000000180.

Morton, R.W., C. McGlory, and S.M. Phillips. 2015. "Nutritional Interventions to Augment Resistance Training-Induced Skeletal Muscle Hypertrophy." *Frontiers in Physiology* 6: 245. https://doi.org/10.3389/fphys.2015.00245.

Morton, R.W., K.T. Murphy, S.R. McKellar, B.J. Schoenfeld, M. Henselmans, E. Helms, A.A. Aragon, et al. 2018. "A Systematic Review, Meta-Analysis and Meta-Regression of the Effect of Protein Supplementation on Resistance Training-Induced Gains in Muscle Mass and Strength in Healthy Adults." *British Journal of Sports Medicine* 52 (6): 376-384. https://doi.org/10.1136/bjsports-2017-097608.

Newell, M.L., A.M. Hunter, C. Lawrence, K.D. Tipton, and S.D.R. Galloway. 2015. "The Ingestion of 39 or 64 g·h⁻¹ of Carbohydrate is Equally Effective at Improving Endurance Exercise Performance in Cyclists." *International Journal of Sport Nutrition and Exercise Metabolism* 25 (3): 285-292. https://doi.org/10.1123/ijsnem.2014-0134.

Nichele, S., S.M. Phillips, & B.C.B Boaventura. 2022. "Plant-based food patterns to stimulate muscle protein synthesis and support muscle mass in humans: a narrative review." Applied Physiology, Nutrition, and Metabolism = Physiologie Appliquee, Nutrition et Metabolisme 47 (7): 700–710.

Peart, D.J. 2017. "Quantifying the Effect of Carbohydrate Mouth Rinsing on Exercise Performance." *Journal of Strength and Conditioning Research* 31 (6): 1737-1743. https://doi.org/10.1519/JSC.0000000000001741

Phillips, S.M., and L.J. Van Loon. 2011. "Dietary Protein for Athletes: From Requirements to Optimum Adaptation." *Journal of Sports Sciences* 29 (Suppl. 1): S29-S38. https://doi.org/10.1080/02640414.2011.619204.

Pinckaers, P.J.M., J. Trommelen, T. Snijders, and L.J.C. van Loon. 2021. "The Anabolic Response to Plant-Based Protein Ingestion." *Sports Medicine* 51 (Suppl. 1): 59-74. https://doi.org/10.1007/s40279-021-01540-8.

Ritz, P., and M. Rockwell. 2021. "Promoting Optimal Omega-3 Fatty Acid Status in Athletes." GSSI SSE #212. www.gssiweb.org/en/sports-science-exchange/Article/promoting-optimal-omega-3-fatty-acid-status-in-athletes.

Ritz, P.P., M.B. Rogers, J.S. Zabinsky, V.E. Hedrick, J.A. Rockwell, E.G. Rimer, S.B. Kostelnik, M.W. Hulver, and M.S. Rockwell. 2020. "Dietary and Biological Assessment of the Omega-3 Status of Collegiate Athletes: A Cross-Sectional Analysis." *PLOS One* 15: e0228834.

Sawka, M.N., L.M. Burke, E.R. Eichner, R.J. Maughan, S.J. Montain, and N.S. Stachenfeld. 2007. "American College of Sports Medicine Position Stand. Exercise and Fluid Replacement." *Medicine and Science in Sports and Exercise* 39 (2): 377-390. https://doi.org/10.1249/mss.0b013e31802ca597.

Simonsen, J.C., W.M. Sherman, D.R. Lamb, A.R. Dernbach, J.A. Doyle, and R. Strauss. 1991. "Dietary Carbohydrate, Muscle Glycogen, and Power Output During Rowing Training." *Journal of Applied Physiology* 70 (4): 1500-1505.

Slater, G.J., A.J. Rice, K. Sharpe, I. Mujika, D. Jenkins, and A.G. Hahn. 2005. "Body-Mass Management of Australian Lightweight Rowers Prior to and During Competition." *Medicine and Science in Sports and Exercise* 37 (5): 860-866. https://doi.org/10.1249/01.mss.0000162692.09091.7a.

Stellingwerff, T., R.J. Maughan, and L.M. Burke. 2011. "Nutrition for Power Sports: Middle-Distance Running, Track Cycling, Rowing, Canoeing/Kayaking, and Swimming." *Journal of Sports Sciences* 29 (Suppl. 1): S79-S89. https://doi.org/10.1080/02640414./JSS.2011.589469.

Stokes, T., A.J. Hector, R.W. Morton, C. McGlory, and S.M. Phillips. 2018. "Recent Perspectives Regarding the Role of Dietary Protein for the Promotion of Muscle Hypertrophy with Resistance Exercise Training." *Nutrients* 10 (2). https://doi.org/10.3390/nu10020180.

Thomas, D.T., K.A. Erdman, and L.M. Burke. 2016. "American College of Sports Medicine Joint Statement." *Nutrition and Athletic Performance* 48 (3): 543-568. https://doi.org/10.1249/MSS.0000000000000852.

Thornton, J.S., A. Vinther, F. Wilson, et al. 2017. "Rowing Injuries: An Updated Review." *Sports Medicine* 47 (4): 641-661. https://doi.org/10.1007/s40279-016-0613-y.

Tran, J., A.J. Rice, L.C. Main, and P.B. Gastin. 2015. "Profiling the Training Practices and Performance of Elite Rowers." *International Journal of Sports Physiology and Performance* 10 (5): 572-580. https://doi.org/10.1123/ijspp.2014-0295.

van Vliet, S., J.W. Beals, A.M. Holwerda, R.S. Emmons, J.P. Goessens, S.A. Paluska, M. De Lisio, L.J.C. van Loon, and N.A. Burd. 2019. "Time-Dependent Regulation of Postprandial Muscle Protein Synthesis Rates After Milk Protein Ingestion in Young Men." *Journal of Applied Physiology (1985)* 127 (6): 1792-1801. https://doi.org/10.1152/japplphysiol.00608.2019.

van Vliet, S., N.A. Burd, and L.J. van Loon. 2015. "The Skeletal Muscle Anabolic Response to Plant- Versus Animal-Based Protein Consumption." *Journal of Nutrition* 145 (9): 1981-1991. https://doi.org/10.3945/jn.114.204305.

Witard, O.C., and J.K. Davis. 2021. "Omega-3 Fatty Acids for Training Adaptation and Exercise Recovery: A Muscle-Centric Perspective in Athletes." SSE #211.

Chapter 28

Ackerman, K.E., B. Holtzman, K.M. Cooper, E.F. Flynn, G. Bruinvels, A.S. Tenforde, K.L. Popp, A.J. Simpkin, and A.L. Parziale. 2019. "Low Energy Availability Surrogates Correlate With Health and Performance Consequences of Relative Energy Deficiency in Sport." *British Journal of Sports Medicine* 53 (10): 628-633. https://doi.org/10.1136/bjsports-2017-098958.

Akca, F. 2014. "Prediction of Rowing Ergometer Performance From Functional Anaerobic Power, Strength and Anthropometric Components." *Journal of Human Kinetics* 41: 133-142. https://doi.org/10.2478/hukin-2014-0041.

Aragon, A.A., B.J. Schoenfeld, R. Wildman, S. Kleiner, T. VanDusseldorp, L. Taylor, C.P. Earnest, et al. 2017. "International Society of Sports Nutrition Position Stand: Diets and Body Composition." *Journal of the International Society of Sports Nutrition* 14: 16. https://doi.org/10.1186/s12970-017-0174-y.

Areta, J.L., H.L. Taylor, and K. Koehler. 2021. "Low Energy Availability: History, Definition and Evidence of Its Endocrine, Metabolic and Physiological Effects in Prospective Studies in Females and Males." *European Journal of Applied Physiology* 121 (1): 1-21. https://doi: 10.1007/s00421-020-04516-0.

Battista, R.A., J.M. Pivarnik, G.M. Dummer, N. Sauer, and R.M. Malina. 2007. "Comparisons of Physical Characteristics and Performances Among Female Collegiate Rowers." *Journal of Sports Science* 25 (6): 651-657. https://doi.org/10.1080/02640410600831781.

Birrer, Daniel. 2019. "Rowing Over the Edge: Nonfunctional Overreaching and Overtraining Syndrome as Maladjustment: Diagnosis and Treatment From a Psychological Perspective." *Case Studies in Sport and Exercise Psychology* 3 (1): 50-60. https://doi.org/10.1123/cssep.2019-0006.

Bouchard, C., L. Perusse, O. Deriaz, J.P. Despres, and A. Tremblay. 1993. "Genetic Influences on Energy Expenditure in Humans." *Critical Reviews in Food Science and Nutrition* 33 (4-5): 345-350. https://doi.org/10.1080/10408399309527631.

Bourgois, J., A.L. Claessens, J. Vrijens, R. Philippaerts, B. Van Renterghem, M. Thomis, M. Janssens, R. Loos, and J. Lefevre. 2000. "Anthropometric Characteristics of Elite Male Junior Rowers." *British Journal of Sports Medicine* 34 (3): 213-216; discussion 216-217. https://doi.org/10.1136/bjsm.34.3.213.

Burke, L.M., G.L. Close, B. Lundy, M. Mooses, J.P. Morton, and A.S. Tenforde. 2018. "Relative Energy Deficiency in Sport in Male Athletes: A Commentary on Its Presentation Among Selected Groups of Male Athletes." *International Journal of Sport Nutrition and Exercise Metabolism* 28 (4): 364-374. https://doi.org/10.1123/ijsnem.2018-0182.

Burke, L.M., B. Lundy, I.L. Fahrenholtz, and A.K. Melin. 2018. "Pitfalls of Conducting and Interpreting Estimates of Energy Availability in Free-Living Athletes." *International Journal of Sport Nutrition and Exercise Metabolism* 28 (4): 350-363. https://doi.org/10.1123/ijsnem.2018-0142.

Carlsohn, A., F. Scharhag-Rosenberger, M. Cassel, and F. Mayer. 2011. "Resting Metabolic Rate in Elite Rowers and Canoeists: Difference Between Indirect Calorimetry and Prediction." *Annals of Nutrition and Metabolism* 58 (3): 239-244. https://doi.org/10.1159/000330119.

Desbrow, B., N.A. Burd, M. Tarnopolsky, D.R. Moore, and K.J. Elliott-Sale. 2019. "Nutrition for Special Populations: Young, Female, and Masters Athletes." *International Journal of Sport Nutrition and Exercise Metabolism* 29 (2): 220-227. https://doi.org/10.1123/ijsnem.2018-0269.

Dimitriou, L., R. Weiler, R. Lloyd-Smith, A. Turner, L. Heath, N. James, and A. Reid. 2014. "Bone Mineral Density, Rib Pain and Other Features of the Female Athlete Triad in Elite Lightweight Rowers." *BMJ Open* 4 (2): e004369. https://doi.org/10.1136/bmjopen-2013-004369.

Fagerberg, P. 2018. "Negative Consequences of Low Energy Availability in Natural Male Bodybuilding: A Review." *International Journal of Sport Nutrition and Exercise Metabolism* 28 (4): 385-402. https://doi.org/10.1123/ijsnem.2016-0332.

Fahrenholtz, I.L., A. Sjodin, D. Benardot, A.B. Tornberg, S. Skouby, J. Faber, J.K. Sundgot-Borgen, and A.K. Melin. 2018. "Within-Day Energy Deficiency and Reproductive Function in Female Endurance Athletes." *Scandinavian Journal of Medicine & Science in Sports* 28 (3): 1139-1146. https://doi.org/10.1111/sms.13030.

Fensham, N.C., I.A. Heikura, A.K. McKay, N. Tee, K.E. Ackerman, and L.M. Burke. 2022. "Short-Term Carbohydrate Restriction Impairs Bone Formation at Rest and During Prolonged Exercise to a Greater Degree than Low Energy Availability." *Journal of Bone and Mineral Research* 37 (10): 1915-1925. doi: 10.1002/jbmr.4658.

Gapin, J. I., and B. Kearns. 2013. "Assessing Prevalence of Eating Disorders and Eating Disorder Symptoms Among Lightweight and Open Weight Collegiate Rowers." *Journal of Clinical Sport Psychology,* 7(3): 198-214.

Garthe, I., T. Raastad, P.E. Refsnes, A. Koivisto, and J. Sundgot-Borgen. 2011. "Effect of Two Different Weight-Loss Rates on Body Composition and Strength and Power-Related Performance in Elite Athletes." *International Journal of Sport Nutrition and Exercise Metabolism* 21 (2): 97-104. https://doi.org/10.1123/ijsnem.21.2.97.

Gillbanks, L., M. Mountjoy and S.R. Filbay. 2022. "Lightweight rowers' perspectives of living with Relative Energy Deficiency in Sport (RED-S)." *PloS one,* 17(3): e0265268. https://doi.org/10.1371/journal.pone.0265268

Hammond, K.M., C. Sale, W. Fraser, J. Tang, S.O. Shepherd, J.A. Strauss, G.L. Close, et al. 2019. Post-Exercise Carbohydrate and Energy Availability Induce Independent Effects on Skeletal Muscle Cell Signalling and Bone Turnover: Implications for Training Adaptation. *Journal of Physiology* 597 (18): 4779-4796. https://doi.org/10.1113/JP278209.

Hector, A.J., and S.M. Phillips. 2018. "Protein Recommendations for Weight Loss in Elite Athletes: A Focus on Body Composition and Performance." *International Journal of Sport Nutrition and Exercise Metabolism* 28 (2): 170-177. https://doi.org/10.1123/ijsnem.2017-0273.

Heikura, I., A. Uusitalo, T. Stellingwerff, D. Bergland, A. Mero, and L. Burke. 2017. "Low Energy Availability Is Difficult to Assess But Outcomes Have Large Impact on Bone Injury Rates in Elite Distance Athletes." *International Journal of Sport Nutrition and Exercise Metabolism* 28 (4): 1-30. https://doi.org/10.1123/ijsnem.2017-0313.

Huovinen, H.T., J.J. Hulmi, J. Isolehto, H. Kyrolainen, R. Puurtinen, T. Karila, K. Mackala, and A.A. Mero. 2015. "Body Composition and Power Performance Improved After Weight Reduction in Male Athletes Without Hampering Hormonal Balance." *Journal of Strength and Conditioning Research* 29 (1): 29-36. https://doi.org/10.1519/JSC.0000000000000619.

Ingham, S.A., G.P. Whyte, K. Jones, and A.M Nevill. 2002. "Determinants of 2,000 m Rowing Ergometer Performance in Elite Rowers." *European Journal of Applied Physiology* 88 (3): 243-246.

Koehler, K., N.R. Hoerner, J.C. Gibbs, C. Zinner, H. Braun, M.J. De Souza, and W. Schaenzer. 2016. "Low Energy Availability in Exercising Men Is Associated With Reduced Leptin and Insulin But Not With Changes in Other Metabolic Hormones." *Journal of Sports Science* 34 (20): 1921-1929. https://doi.org/10.1080/02640414.2016.1142109.

Larson-Meyer, D.E., K. Woolf, and L. Burke. 2018. "Assessment of Nutrient Status in Athletes and the Need for Supplementation." *International Journal of Sport Nutrition and Exercise Metabolism* 28 (2): 139-158. https://doi.org/10.1123/ijsnem.2017-0338.

Linardon, J., and S. Mitchell. 2017. "Rigid Dietary Control, Flexible Dietary Control, and Intuitive Eating: Evidence For Their Differential Relationship to Disordered Eating and Body Image Concerns." *Eating Behaviors* 26: 16-22. https://doi.org/10.1016/j.eatbeh.2017.01.008.

Logue, D.M., S.M. Madigan, A. Melin, E. Delahunt, M. Heinen, S.M. Donnell, and C.A. Corish. 2020. "Low Energy Availability in Athletes 2020: An Updated Narrative Review of Prevalence, Risk, Within-Day Energy Balance, Knowledge, and Impact on Sports Performance." *Nutrients* 12 (3). https://doi.org/10.3390/nu12030835.

Lundy, B., M. Torstveit, T. Stenqvist, L. Burke, I. Garthe, G. Slater, C. Ritz, and A. Melin. 2022. "Screening for Low Energy Availability in Male Athletes: Attempted Validation of LEAM-Q." *Nutrients* 14 (9). https://doi.org/10.3390/nu14091873.

Lundy, B., L. Trease and D. Michael. 2015. "Bone mineral density in elite rowers." *BMC Sports Science, Medicine and Rehabilitation*, 7(S1).

Martinsen, M., and J. Sundgot-Borgen. 2013. "Higher Prevalence of Eating Disorders Among Adolescent Elite Athletes Than Controls." *Medicine & Science in Sports & Exercise* 45 (6): 1188-1197. https://doi.org/10.1249/MSS.0b013e318281a939.

McDonnell, L.K., P.A. Hume, and V. Nolte. 2011. "Rib Stress Fractures Among Rowers: Definition, Epidemiology, Mechanisms, Risk Factors and Effectiveness of Injury Prevention Strategies." *Sports Medicine* 41 (11): 883-901. https://doi.org/10.2165/11593170-000000000-00000.

McGlory, C., S. van Vliet, T. Stokes, B. Mittendorfer, and S.M. Phillips. 2019. "The Impact of Exercise and Nutrition on the Regulation of Skeletal Muscle Mass." *Journal of Physiology* 597 (5): 1251-1258. https://doi.org/10.1113/JP275443.

Meeusen, R., M. Duclos, C. Foster, A. Fry, M. Gleeson, D. Nieman, J. Raglin, G. Rietjens, J. Steinacker, A. Urhausen, Science European College of Sport, and Medicine American College of Sports. 2013. "Prevention, Diagnosis, and Treatment of the Overtraining Syndrome: Joint Consensus Statement of the European College of Sport Science and the American College of Sports Medicine." *Medicine & Science in Sports & Exercise* 45 (1): 186-205. https://doi.org/10.1249/MSS.0b013e318279a10a.

Melin, A., A.B. Tornberg, S. Skouby, S.S. Moller, J. Sundgot-Borgen, J. Faber, J.J. Sidelmann, M. Aziz, and A. Sjodin. 2015. "Energy Availability and the Female Athlete Triad in Elite Endurance Athletes." *Scandinavian Journal of Medicine & Science in Sports* 25 (5): 610-622. https://doi.org/10.1111/sms.12261.

Mountjoy, M., J. Sundgot-Borgen, L. Burke, S. Carter, N. Constantini, C. Lebrun, N. Connie, at al. 2014. "The IOC Consensus Statement: Beyond the Female Athlete Triad-Relative Energy Deficiency in Sport (RED-S)." *British Journal of Sports Medicine* 48: 491-497. https://doi.org/10.1136/bjsports-2014-093502.

Mountjoy, M., J. Sundgot-Borgen, L. Burke, K.E. Ackerman, C. Blauwet, N. Constantini, C. Lebrun, et al. 2018. "International Olympic Committee (IOC) Consensus Statement on Relative Energy Deficiency in Sport (RED-S): 2018 Update." *International Journal of Sport Nutrition and Exercise Metabolism* 28 (4): 316-331. https://doi.org/10.1123/ijsnem.2018-0136.

Mountjoy M.L., K.E. Ackerman, D.M. Bailey, L.M. Burke, N. Constantini, A.C. Hackney, I.A. Heikura, A.K. Melin, A.M. Pensgaard, T. Stellingwerff, J. Sundgot-Borgen, M.K. Torstveit, A. Uhrenholdt Jacobsen, E. Verhagen, R. Budgett, L. Engebretsen, and U.Erdener. 2023. "The 2023 International Olympic Committee's (IOC) consensus statement on Relative Energy Deficiency in Sports (REDs)." *British Journal of Sports Medicine.*

Nattiv, A., A.B. Loucks, M.M. Manore, C.F. Sanborn, J. Sundgot-Borgen, M.P. Warren, and American College of Sports Medicine. 2007. "American College of Sports Medicine Position Stand. The Female Athlete Triad." *Medicine & Science in Sports & Exercise* 39 (10): 1867-1882. https://doi.org/10.1249/mss.0b013e318149f111.

Otis, C.L., B. Drinkwater, M. Johnson, A. Loucks, and J. Wilmore. 1997. "American College of Sports Medicine Position Stand. The Female Athlete Triad." *Medicine & Science in Sports & Exercise* 29 (5): i-ix. https://doi.org/10.1097/00005768-199705000-00037.

Penichet-Tomas, A., B. Pueo, S. Selles-Perez, and J.M. Jimenez-Olmedo. 2021. "Analysis of Anthropometric and Body Composition Profile in Male and Female Traditional Rowers. "*International Journal of Environmental Research and Public Health* 18 (15): 7826, https://doi.org/10.3390/ijerph18157826.

Pietrowsky, R., and K. Straub. 2008. "Body Dissatisfaction and Restrained Eating in Male Juvenile and Adult Athletes." *Eating and Weight Disorders* 13 (1): 14-21. https://doi.org/10.1007/BF03327780.

Raysmith, B.P., and M.K. Drew. 2016. "Performance Success or Failure Is Influenced by Weeks Lost to Injury and Illness in Elite Australian Track and Field Athletes: A 5-Year Prospective Study." *Journal of Science and Medicine in Sport* 19 (10): 778-783. https://doi.org/10.1016/j.jsams.2015.12.515.

Reale, R., G. Slater, and L.M. Burke. 2017. "Acute-Weight-Loss Strategies for Combat Sports and Applications to Olympic Success." *International Journal of Sports Physiology and Performance* 12 (2): 142-151. https://doi.org/10.1123/ijspp.2016-0211.

Russell, S., D. Jenkins, M. Smith, S. Halson, and V. Kelly. 2019. "The Application of Mental Fatigue Research to Elite Team Sport Performance: New Perspectives." *Journal of Science and Medicine in Sport* 22 (6): 723-728. https://doi.org/10.1016/j.jsams.2018.12.008.

Slater, G.J., B.P. Dieter, D.J. Marsh, E.R. Helms, G. Shaw, and J. Iraki. 2019. "Is an Energy Surplus Required to Maximize Skeletal Muscle Hypertrophy Associated With Resistance Training?" *Frontiers in Nutrition* 6: 131. https://doi.org/10.3389/fnut.2019.00131.

Slater, G.J., A.J. Rice, I. Mujika, A.G. Hahn, K. Sharpe, and D.G. Jenkins. 2005. "Physique Traits of Lightweight Rowers and Their Relationship to Competitive Success." *British Journal of Sports Medicine* 39 (10): 736-741. https://doi.org/10.1136/bjsm.2004.015990.

Slater, G.J., A.J. Rice, K. Sharpe, I. Mujika, D. Jenkins, and A.G. Hahn. 2005. "Body-Mass Management of Australian Lightweight Rowers Prior to and During Competition." *Medicine and Science in Sports and Exercise* 37 (5): 860-866. https://doi.org/10.1249/01.mss.0000162692.09091.7a.

Slater, G.J., A.J. Rice, K. Sharpe, R. Tanner, D. Jenkins, C.J. Gore, and A.G. Hahn. 2005. "Impact of Acute Weight Loss and/or Thermal Stress on Rowing Ergometer Performance." *Medicine and Science in Sports and Exercise* 37 (8): 1387-1394. https://doi.org/10.1249/01.mss.0000174900.13358.7e.

Slater, G.J., A.J. Rice, K. Sharpe, R. Tanner, D. Jenkins, C.J. Gore, and A.G. Hahn. 2005. "Impact of Acute Weight Loss and/or Thermal Stress on Rowing Ergometer Performance." *Medicine & Science in Sports & Exercise* 37 (8): 1387-1394. https://doi.org/10.1249/01.mss.0000174900.13358.7e.

Slater, G.J., A.J. Rice, R. Tanner, K. Sharpe, D. Jenkins, and A.G. Hahn. 2006. "Impact of Two Different Body Mass Management Strategies on Repeat Rowing Performance." *Medicine and Science in Sports and Exercise* 38 (1): 138-146. https://doi.org/10.1249/01.mss.0000179903.05365.7a.

Slater, G., A. Rice, D. Jenkins, and A. Hahn. 2014. "Body Mass Management of Lightweight Rowers: Nutritional Strategies and Performance Implications." *British Journal of Sports Medicine* 48 (21): 1529-1533. https://doi.org/10.1136/bjsports-2014-093918.

Stellingwerff, T. 2018. "Case Study: Body Composition Periodization in an Olympic-Level Female Middle-Distance Runner Over a 9-Year Career." *International Journal of Sport Nutrition and Exercise Metabolism* 28 (4): 428-433. https://doi.org/10.1123/ijsnem.2017-0312.

Stellingwerff, T., I.A. Heikura, R. Meeusen, S. Bermon, S. Seiler, M.L. Mountjoy, et al. 2021. "Overtraining Syndrome (OTS) and Relative Energy Deficiency in Sport (RED-S): Shared Pathways, Symptoms and Complexities." *Sports Medicine* 51 (11): 2251-2280.

Stokes, T., A.J. Hector, R.W. Morton, C. McGlory, and S.M. Phillips. 2018. "Recent Perspectives Regarding the Role of Dietary Protein for the Promotion of Muscle Hypertrophy With Resistance Exercise Training." *Nutrients* 10 (2). https://doi.org/10.3390/nu10020180.

Tenforde, A.S., M.T. Barrack, A. Nattiv, and M. Fredericson. 2016. "Parallels With the Female Athlete Triad in Male Athletes." *Sports Medicine* 46 (2): 171-182. https://doi.org/10.1007/s40279-015-0411-y.

Thornton, J.S. and A. Vinther. 2018. "Prevention of Rib Stress Injury in Rowers: What Do We Know and Where Do We Need to Go?" *Sports Orthopaedics and Traumatology* 34 (3): 278-286. doi: 10.1016/j.orthtr.2018.05.001.

Torstveit, M.K., I. Fahrenholtz, T.B. Stenqvist, O. Sylta, and A. Melin. 2018. "Within-Day Energy Deficiency and Metabolic Perturbation in Male Endurance Athletes." *International Journal of Sport Nutrition and Exercise Metabolism* 28 (4): 419-427. https://doi.org/10.1123/ijsnem.2017-0337.

Vanheest, J.L., C.D. Rodgers, C.E. Mahoney, and M.J. De Souza. 2014. "Ovarian Suppression Impairs Sport Performance in Junior Elite Female Swimmers." *Medicine and Science in Sports and Exercise* 46 (1): 156-66. https://doi.org/10.1249/MSS.0b013e3182a32b72.

Vinther, A., I.L. Kanstrup, E. Christiansen, C. Ekdahl, and P. Aagaard. 2008. "Testosterone and BMD in Elite Male Lightweight Rowers." *International Journal of Sports Medicine* 29 (10): 803-807. https://doi.org/10.1055/s-2008-1038430.

Walsh, N.P. 2019. "Nutrition and Athlete Immune Health: New Perspectives on an Old Paradigm." *Sports Medicine* 49 (Suppl. 2): 153-168. https://doi.org/10.1007/s40279-019-01160-3.

Warden, S.J., F.R. Gutschlag, H. Wajswelner, and K.M. Crossley. 2002. "Aetiology of Rib Stress Fractures in Rowers." *Sports Medicine* 32 (13): 819-836. https://doi.org/10.2165/00007256-200232130-00002.

Wasserfurth, P., J. Palmowski, A. Hahn, and K. Krüger. 2020. "Reasons For and Consequences of Low Energy Availability in Female and Male Athletes: Social Environment, Adaptations, and Prevention." *Sports Medicine—Open* 6 (44). https://doi.org/10.1186/s40798-020-00275-6.

Woods, A. L., L. A. Garvican-Lewis, B. Lundy, A. J. Rice, and K. G. Thompson. 2017. "New approaches to determine fatigue in elite athletes during intensified training: Resting metabolic rate and pacing profile." *PLOS One* 12 (3): e0173807. https://doi.org/10.1371/journal.pone.0173807.

Chapter 29

Aguilar-Navarro, M., G. Munoz, J.J. Salinero, J. Munoz-Guerra, M. Fernandez-Alvarez, M.D. M. Plata, and J. Del Coso. 2019. "Urine Caffeine Concentration in Doping Control Samples From 2004 to 2015." *Nutrients* 11 (2). https://doi.org/10.3390/nu11020286.

Badenhorst, C.E., K.E. Black, and W.J. O'Brien. 2019. "Hepcidin as a Prospective Individualized Biomarker for Individuals at Risk of Low Energy Availability." *International Journal of Sport Nutrition and Exercise Metabolism* 29 (6): 671-681. https://doi.org/10.1123/ijsnem.2019-0006.

Baguet, A., J. Bourgois, L. Vanhee, E. Achten, and W. Derave. 2010. "Important Role of Muscle Carnosine in Rowing Performance." *Journal of Applied Physiology (1985)* 109 (4): 1096-1101. https://doi.org/10.1152/japplphysiol.00141.2010.

Bailey, Stephen J., Anni Vanhatalo, Paul G. Winyard, and Andrew M. Jones. 2012. "The Nitrate-Nitrite-Nitric Oxide Pathway: Its Role in Human Exercise Physiology." *European Journal of Sport Science* 12 (4): 309-320. https://doi.org/10.1080/17461391.2011.635705.

Bikle, D.D. 2014. "Vitamin D Metabolism, Mechanism of Action, and Clinical Applications." *Chemistry and Biology* 21 (3): 319-29. https://doi.org/10.1016/j.chembiol.2013.12.016.

Boegman, S., T. Stellingwerff, G. Shaw, N. Clarke, K. Graham, R. Cross, and J.C. Siegler. 2020. "The Impact of Individualizing Sodium Bicarbonate Supplementation Strategies on World-Class Rowing Performance." *Frontiers in Nutrition* 7: 138. https://doi.org/10.3389/fnut.2020.00138.

Bond, H., L. Morton, and A.J. Braakhuis. 2012. "Dietary Nitrate Supplementation Improves Rowing Performance in Well-Trained Rowers." *International Journal of Sport Nutrition and Exercise Metabolism* 22 (4): 251-256.

Bruce, C.R., M.E. Anderson, S.F. Fraser, N.K. Stepto, R. Klein, W.G. Hopkins, and J.A. Hawley. 2000. "Enhancement of 2000-m Rowing Performance After Caffeine Ingestion." *Medicine and Science in Sports and Exercise* 32 (11): 1958-1963.

Burd, N.A., J.W. Beals, I.G. Martinez, A.F. Salvador, and S.K. Skinner. 2019. "Food-First Approach to Enhance the Regulation of Post-Exercise Skeletal Muscle Protein Synthesis and Remodeling." *Sports Medicine* 49 (Suppl. 1): 59-68. https://doi.org/10.1007/s40279-018-1009-y.

Burke, L., B. Desbrow, and L. Spriet. 2013. *Caffeine for Sports Performance. The Truths and Myths About the World's Most Popular Supplement.* Champaign, IL: Human Kinetics.

Burt, L.A., E.O. Billington, M.S. Rose, D.A. Raymond, D.A. Hanley, and S.K. Boyd. 2019. "Effect of High-Dose Vitamin D Supplementation on Volumetric Bone Density and Bone Strength: A Randomized Clinical Trial." *JAMA* 322 (8): 736-745. https://doi.org/10.1001/jama.2019.11889.

Butts, J., B. Jacobs, and M. Silvis. 2018. "Creatine Use in Sports." *Sports Health* 10 (1): 31-34. https://doi.org/10.1177/1941738117737248.

Campbell, W.W., and R.A. Geik. 2004. "Nutritional Considerations For the Older Athlete." *Nutrition* 20 (7-8): 603-608. https://doi.org/10.1016/j.nut.2004.04.004.

Canadian Nutrient File. Government of Canada 2023. Accessed Jan 22 2023. https://food-nutrition.canada.ca/cnf-fce/index-eng.jsp

Candow, D.G., S.C. Forbes, P.D. Chilibeck, S.M. Cornish, J. Antonio, and R.B. Kreider. 2019. "Variables Influencing the Effectiveness of Creatine Supplementation as a Therapeutic Intervention for Sarcopenia." *Frontiers in Nutrition* 6: 124. https://doi.org/10.3389/fnut.2019.00124.

Carr, A.J., C.J. Gore, and B. Dawson. 2011. "Induced Alkalosis and Caffeine Supplementation: Effects on 2,000-m Rowing Performance." *International Journal of Sport Nutrition and Exercise Metabolism* 21 (5): 357-364.

Carr, A.J., G.J. Slater, C.J. Gore, B. Dawson, and L.M. Burke. 2011. "Effect of Sodium Bicarbonate on [HCO3-], pH, and Gastrointestinal Symptoms." *International Journal of Sport Nutrition and Exercise Metabolism* 21 (3): 189-194. https://doi.org/10.1123/ijsnem.21.3.189.

Carr, A.J., G.J. Slater, C.J. Gore, B. Dawson, and L.M. Burke. 2012. "Reliability and Effect of Sodium Bicarbonate: Buffering and 2000-m Rowing Performance." *International Journal of Sports Physiology and Performance* 7 (2): 152-160.

Castell, L.M., D.C. Nieman, S. Bermon, and P. Peeling. 2019. "Exercise-Induced Illness and Inflammation: Can Immunonutrition and Iron Help?" *International Journal of Sport Nutrition and Exercise Metabolism* 29 (2): 181-188. https://doi.org/10.1123/ijsnem.2018-0288.

Christensen, P.M., M.H. Petersen, S.N. Friis, and J. Bangsbo. 2014. "Caffeine, But Not Bicarbonate, Improves 6 Min Maximal Performance in Elite Rowers." *Applied Physiology, Nutrition, and Metabolism* 39 (9): 1058-1063. https://doi.org/10.1139/apnm-2013-0577.

Chwalbinska-Moneta, J. 2003. "Effect of Creatine Supplementation on Aerobic Performance and Anaerobic Capacity in Elite Rowers in the Course of Endurance Training." *International Journal of Sport Nutrition and Exercise Metabolism* 13 (2): 173-183. https://doi.org/10.1123/ijsnem.13.2.173.

Clark, A., and N. Mach. 2016. "Exercise-Induced Stress Behavior, Gut-Microbiota-Brain Axis and Diet: A Systematic Review for Athletes." *Journal of the International Society of Sports Nutrition* 13: 43. https://doi.org/10.1186/s12970-016-0155-6.

Clinical Guide to Probiotic Products Available in Canada. www.probioticchart.ca.

Dainty, J.R., R. Berry, S.R. Lynch, L.J. Harvey, and S.J. Fairweather-Tait. 2014. "Estimation of Dietary Iron Bioavailability From Food Iron Intake and Iron Status." *PLOS One* 9 (10): e111824. https://doi.org/10.1371/journal.pone.0111824.

Dale, H.F., S.H. Rasmussen, O.O. Asiller, and G.A. Lied. 2019. "Probiotics in Irritable Bowel Syndrome: An Up-to-Date Systematic Review." *Nutrients* 11 (9). https://doi.org/10.3390/nu11092048.

de la Puente Yague, M., L. Collado Yurrita, M.J. Ciudad Cabanas, and M.A. Cuadrado Cenzual. 2020. "Role of Vitamin D in Athletes and Their Performance: Current Concepts and New Trends." *Nutrients* 12 (2). https://doi.org/10.3390/nu12020579.

DellaValle, D.M., and J.D. Haas. 2011. "Impact of Iron Depletion Without Anemia on Performance in Trained Endurance Athletes at the Beginning of a Training Season: A Study of Female Collegiate Rowers." *International Journal of Sport Nutrition and Exercise Metabolism* 21 (6): 501-506.

DellaValle, D.M., and J.D. Haas. 2014. "Iron Supplementation Improves Energetic Efficiency in Iron-Depleted Female Rowers." *Medicine and Science in Sports and Exercise* 46 (6): 1204-1215. https://doi.org/10.1249/MSS.0000000000000208.

Desbrow, B., S. Hall, and C. Irwin. 2019. "Caffeine Content of Nespresso(R) Pod Coffee." *Nutrition and Health* 25 (1): 3-7. https://doi.org/10.1177/0260106018810941.

Desbrow, B., S. Hall, H. O'Connor, G. Slater, K. Barnes, and G. Grant. 2019. "Caffeine Content of Pre-Workout Supplements Commonly Used by Australian Consumers." *Drug Testing and Analysis* 11 (3): 523-529. https://doi.org/10.1002/dta.2501.

Dimitriou, L., R. Weiler, R. Lloyd-Smith, A. Turner, L. Heath, N. James, and A. Reid. 2014. "Bone Mineral Density, Rib Pain and Other Features of the Female Athlete Triad in Elite Lightweight Rowers." *BMJ Open* 4 (2): e004369. https://doi.org/10.1136/bmjopen-2013-004369.

Drew, M., N. Vlahovich, D. Hughes, R. Appaneal, L.M. Burke, B. Lundy, M. Rogers, et al. 2018. "Prevalence of Illness, Poor Mental Health and Sleep Quality and Low Energy Availability Prior to the 2016 Summer Olympic Games." *British Journal of Sports Medicine* 52 (1): 47-53. https://doi.org/10.1136/bjsports-2017-098208.

Duiven, E., L.J.C. van Loon, L. Spruijt, W. Koert, and O.M. de Hon. 2021. "Undeclared Doping Substances Are Highly Prevalent in Commercial Sports Nutrition Supplements." *Journal of Sports Science and Medicine* (20), 328-338. https://doi.org/10.52082/jssm.2021.328.

Fairweather-Tait, S.J., A. Jennings, L.J. Harvey, R. Berry, J. Walton, and J.R. Dainty. 2017. "Modeling Tool for Calculating Dietary Iron Bioavailability in Iron-Sufficient Adults." *American Journal of Clinical Nutrition* 105 (6): 1408-1414. https://doi.org/10.3945/ajcn.116.147389.

Freund, M.A., B. Chen, and E.A. Decker. 2018. "The Inhibition of Advanced Glycation End Products by Carnosine and Other Natural Dipeptides to Reduce Diabetic and Age-Related Complications." *Comprehensive Reviews in Food Science and Food Safety* 17 (5): 1367-1378. https://doi.org/10.1111/1541-4337.12376.

Gharaat, M.A., M. Sheykhlouvand, and L.A. Eidi. 2020. "Performance and Recovery: Effects of Caffeine on a 2000-m Rowing Ergometer." *Sport Sciences for Health* 16: 531-542. https://doi.org/10.1007/s11332-020-00643-5.

Gilsanz, L., J. López-Seoane, S.L. Jiménez, and H. Pareja-Galeano. 2021. "Effect of β-Alanine and Sodium Bicarbonate Co-Supplementation on the Body's Buffering Capacity and Sports Performance: A Systematic Review. *Critical Reviews in Food Science and Nutrition.* (December 9) :1-14. https://doi.org/10.1080/10408398.2021.2012642. Epub ahead of print.

Goolsby, M.A., and N. Boniquit. 2017. "Bone Health in Athletes." *Sports Health* 9 (2): 108-117. https://doi.org/10.1177/1941738116677732.

Grand View Research. 2022a. "Dietary Supplements Market: Global Industry Outlook, Market Size, Business Intelligence, Consumer Preferences, Statistical Surveys, Comprehensive Analysis, Historical Developments, Current Trends, and Forecasts, 2023-2030."

Grand View Research. 2022b. "Sports Nutrition Market Size, Share and Trends Analysis Report By Product Type (Sports Supplements, Sports Drinks), By Application, By Formulation, By Consumer Group, By End-User, By Sales Channel, By Region, And Segment Forecasts, 2023-2030." Accessed November 20, 2022. https://www.grandviewresearch.com/industry-analysis/sports-nutrition-market.

Grgic, J., F.J. Diaz-Lara, J.D. Coso, M.J. Duncan, J. Tallis, C. Pickering, B.J. Schoenfeld, and P. Mikulic. 2020. "The Effects of Caffeine Ingestion on Measures of Rowing Performance: A Systematic Review and Meta-Analysis." *Nutrients* 12 (2). https://doi.org/10.3390/nu12020434.

Grgic J., Z. Pedisic, B. Saunders, G.G. Artioli, B.J. Schoenfeld, M.J. McKenna, D.J. Bishop, et al. 2021. "International Society of Sports Nutrition Position Stand: Sodium Bicarbonate and Exercise Performance." *Journal of the International Society of Sports Nutrition* 18 (1): 61. https://doi.org/10.1186/s12970-021-00458-w.

Guarner et al. World Gastroenterology Organisation Global Guidelines. Probiotics and Prebiotics https://www.worldgastroenterology.org/guidelines/probiotics-and-prebiotics/probiotics-and-prebiotics-english.

Guest, N. S., T.A. VanDusseldorp, M.T. Nelson, J. Grgic, B. J. Schoenfeld, N.D.M. Jenkins, S.M. Arent, J. Antonio, J.R. Stout, E.T. Trexler, A.E. Smith-Ryan, E.R. Goldstein, D.S. Kalman, and B.I Campbell. 2021. "International society of sports nutrition position stand: caffeine and exercise performance." *Journal of the International Society of Sports Nutrition,* 18(1): 1. https://doi.org/10.1186/s12970-020-00383-4.

Hadzic, M., M. . Eckstein, and M. Schugardt. 2019. "The Impact of Sodium Bicarbonate on Performance in Response to Exercise Duration in Athletes: A Systematic Review." *Journal of Sports Science and Medicine* 18 (2): 271-281.

Hagerman, F.C. 1984. "Applied Physiology of Rowing." *Sports Medicine* 1 (4): 303-326. https://doi.org/10.2165/00007256-198401040-00005.

Halliday, T.M., N.J. Peterson, J.J. Thomas, K. Kleppinger, B.W. Hollis, and D.E. Larson-Meyer. 2011. "Vitamin D Status Relative to Diet, Lifestyle, Injury, and Illness in College Athletes." *Medicine and Science in Sports and Exercise* 43 (2): 335-343. https://doi.org/10.1249/MSS.0b013e3181eb9d4d.

Halson, S.L., and D.T. Martin. 2013. "Lying to Win—Placebos and Sport Science." *International Journal of Sports Physiology and Performance* 8 (6): 597-599.

He, C.S., M. Handzlik, W.D. Fraser, A. Muhamad, H. Preston, A. Richardson, and M. Gleeson. 2013. "Influence of Vitamin D Status on Respiratory Infection Incidence and Immune Function During 4 Months of Winter Training in Endurance Sport Athletes." *Exercise Immunology Review* 19: 86-101.

Health Canada. 2021a. "2017 Report on Compliance Monitoring: Natural Health Products." https://www.canada.ca/en/health-canada/services/inspecting-monitoring-drug-health-products/compliance-monitoring-reports/2017-reporting-compliance-monitoring-natural-health-products.html.

Health Canada. 2021b. "2018-2019 Compliance Monitoring Project: Good Manufacturing Practices for Natural Health Products." Accessed April 25, 2021. https://www.canada.ca/en/health-canada/services/inspecting-monitoring-drug-health-products/compliance-monitoring-reports/2018-2019-good-manufacturing-practices-natural-health-products.html.

Health Canada. 2021c. "Calcium." Accessed April 2021. https://www.canada.ca/en/health-canada/services/nutrients/calcium.html.

Health Canada. 2021d. "Iron." Accessed March 28, 2021. https://www.canada.ca/en/health-canada/services/nutrients/iron.html.

Health Canada. 2021e. "Vitamin D and Calcium: Updated Dietary Reference Intakes." Accessed April 2021. https://www.canada.ca/en/health-canada/services/food-nutrition/healthy-eating/vitamins-minerals/vitamin-calcium-updated-dietary-reference-intakes-nutrition.html.

Hill C, F. Guarner, G. Reid, G.R. Gibson, D.J. Merenstein, B. Pot, L. Morelli, R.B. Canani, H.J. Flint, S. Salminen, P.C. Calder and M.E Sanders. 2014. "The International Scientific Association for Probiotics and Prebiotics consensus statement on the scope and appropriate use of the term probiotic." *Nature Rev Gastro Hepatol.* doi: 10.1038/nrgastro.2014.66.

Hobson, R.M., R.C. Harris, D. Martin, P. Smith, B. Macklin, K.J. Elliott-Sale, and C. Sale. 2014. "Effect of Sodium Bicarbonate Supplementation on 2000-m Rowing Performance." *International Journal of Sports Physiology and Performance* 9 (1): 139-144. https://doi.org/10.1123/ijspp.2013-0086.

Hobson, R.M., R.C. Harris, D. Martin, P. Smith, B. Macklin, B. Gualano, and C. Sale. 2013. "Effect of Beta-Alanine, With and Without Sodium Bicarbonate, on 2000-m Rowing Performance." *International Journal of Sport Nutrition and Exercise Metabolism* 23 (5): 480-487. https://doi.org/10.1123/ijsnem.23.5.480.

Hobson, R.M., B. Saunders, G. Ball, R.C. Harris, and C. Sale. 2012. "Effects of Beta-Alanine Supplementation on Exercise Performance: A Meta-Analysis." *Amino Acids* 43 (1): 25-37. https://doi.org/10.1007/s00726-011-1200-z.

Holick, M.F., N.C. Binkley, H.A. Bischoff-Ferrari, C.M. Gordon, D.A. Hanley, R.P. Heaney, M.H. Murad, C.M. Weaver, and Society Endocrine. 2011. "Evaluation, Treatment, and Prevention of Vitamin D Deficiency: An Endocrine Society Clinical Practice Guideline." *Journal of Clinical Endocrinology and Metabolism* 96 (7): 1911-1930. https://doi.org/10.1210/jc.2011-0385.

Hoon, M.W., A.M. Jones, N.A. Johnson, J.R. Blackwell, E.M. Broad, B. Lundy, A.J. Rice, and L.M. Burke. 2014. "The Effect of Variable Doses of Inorganic Nitrate-Rich Beetroot Juice on Simulated 2,000-m Rowing Performance in Trained Athletes." *International Journal of Sports Physiology and Performance* 9 (4): 615-20. https://doi.org/10.1123/ijspp.2013-0207.

Hurrell, R., and I. Egli. 2010. "Iron Bioavailability and Dietary Reference Values." *American Journal of Clinical Nutrition* 91 (5): 1461S-1467S. https://doi.org/10.3945/ajcn.2010.28674F.

Jager, R., A.E. Mohr, K.C. Carpenter, C.M. Kerksick, M. Purpura, A. Moussa, J.R. Townsend, et al. 2019. "International Society of Sports Nutrition Position Stand: Probiotics." *Journal of the International Society of Sports Nutrition* 16 (1): 62. https://doi.org/10.1186/s12970-019-0329-0.

Jager, R., M. Purpura, J.D. Stone, S.M. Turner, A.J. Anzalone, M.J. Eimerbrink, M. Pane, et al. 2016. "Probiotic Streptococcus Thermophilus FP4 and Bifidobacterium Breve BR03 Supplementation Attenuates Performance and Range-of-Motion Decrements Following Muscle Damaging Exercise." *Nutrients* 8 (10). https://doi.org/10.3390/nu8100642.

Jones, A.M., C. Thompson, L.J. Wylie, and A. Vanhatalo. 2018. "Dietary Nitrate and Physical Performance." *Annual Review of Nutrition* 38: 303-328. https://doi.org/10.1146/annurev-nutr-082117-051622.

Jones, A.M., A. Vanhatalo, D.R. Seals, M.J. Rossman, B. Piknova, and K.L. Jonvik. 2021. "Dietary Nitrate and Nitric Oxide Metabolism: Mouth, Circulation, Skeletal Muscle, and Exercise Performance." *Medicine and Science in Sports and Exercise* 53 (2): 280-294. https://doi.org/10.1249/MSS.0000000000002470.

Jonvik, K.L., J. Nyakayiru, L.J. van Loon, and L.B. Verdijk. 2015. "Can Elite Athletes Benefit from Dietary Nitrate Supplementation?" *Journal of Applied Physiology (1985)* 119 (6): 759-761. https://doi.org/10.1152/japplphysiol.00232.2015.

Karpouzos, A., E. Diamantis, P. Farmaki, S. Savvanis, and T. Troupis. 2017. "Nutritional Aspects of Bone Health and Fracture Healing." *Journal of Osteoporosis* no. 2017: 4218472. https://doi.org/10.1155/2017/4218472.

Kerley, C.P. 2017. "Dietary Nitrate as Modulator of Physical Performance and Cardiovascular Health." *Current Opinion in Clinical Nutrition and Metabolic Care* 20 (6): 440-446. https://doi.org/10.1097/MCO.0000000000000414.

Kreider, R.B., D.S. Kalman, J. Antonio, T.N. Ziegenfuss, R. Wildman, R. Collins, D.G. Candow, et al. 2017. "International Society of Sports Nutrition Position Stand: Safety and Efficacy of Creatine Supplementation in Exercise, Sport, and Medicine." *Journal of the International Society of Sports Nutrition* 14: 18. https://doi.org/10.1186/s12970-017-0173-z.

Ksiazek, A., A. Zagrodna, and M. Slowinska-Lisowska. 2019. "Vitamin D, Skeletal Muscle Function and Athletic Performance in Athletes—A Narrative Review." *Nutrients* 11 (8). https://doi.org/10.3390/nu11081800.

Kunstel, K. 2005. "Calcium Requirements for the Athlete." *Current Sports Medicine Reports* 4 (4): 203-6. https://doi.org/10.1097/01.csmr.0000306208.56939.01.

Lancha, A.H., Jr., V. de Salles Painelli, B. Saunders, and G.G. Artioli. 2015. "Nutritional Strategies to Modulate Intracellular and Extracellular Buffering Capacity During High-Intensity Exercise." *Sports Medicine* 45 (Suppl. 1): 71-81. https://doi.org/10.1007/s40279-015-0397-5.

Lappe, J., D. Cullen, G. Haynatzki, R. Recker, R. Ahlf, and K. Thompson. 2008. "Calcium and Vitamin D Supplementation Decreases Incidence of Stress Fractures in Female Navy Recruits." *Journal of Bone and Mineral Research* 23 (5): 741-749. https://doi.org/10.1359/jbmr.080102.

Lariviere, J.A., T.L. Robinson, and C.M. Snow. 2003. "Spine Bone Mineral Density Increases in Experienced But Not Novice Collegiate Female Rowers." *Medicine and Science in Sports and Exercise* 35 (10): 1740-1744. https://doi.org/10.1249/01.MSS.0000089250.86536.D8.

Larson-Meyer, D.E., K. Woolf, and L. Burke. 2018. "Assessment of Nutrient Status in Athletes and the Need for Supplementation." *International Journal of Sport Nutrition and Exercise Metabolism* 28 (2): 139-158. https://doi.org/10.1123/ijsnem.2017-0338.

Louis, J., F. Vercruyssen, O. Dupuy, and T. Bernard. 2019. "Nutrition for Master Athletes: Is There a Need for Specific Recommendations?" *Journal of Aging and Physical Activity* (November 17): 1-10. https://doi.org/10.1123/japa.2019-0190.

Lun, V., K.A. Erdman, and R.A. Reimer. 2009. "Evaluation of Nutritional Intake in Canadian High-Performance Athletes." *Clinical Journal of Sport Medicine* 19 (5): 405-411. https://doi.org/10.1097/JSM.0b013e3181b5413b.

Lundy, Bronwen, Larissa Trease, and Drew K. Michael. 2015. "Bone Mineral Density in Elite Rowers." *BMC Sports Science, Medicine and Rehabilitation* 7 (1): O6. https://doi.org/10.1186/2052-1847-7-S1-O6.

Martens, P.J., C. Gysemans, A. Verstuyf, and A.C. Mathieu. 2020. "Vitamin D's Effect on Immune Function." *Nutrients* 12 (5). https://doi.org/10.3390/nu12051248.

Martineau, A.R., D.A. Jolliffe, R.L. Hooper, L. Greenberg, J.F. Aloia, P. Bergman, G. Dubnov-Raz, et al. 2017. "Vitamin D Supplementation to Prevent Acute Respiratory Tract Infections: Systematic Review and Meta-Analysis of Individual Participant Data." *BMJ* 356: i6583. https://doi.org/10.1136/bmj.i6583.

Mathews, N.M. 2018. "Prohibited Contaminants in Dietary Supplements." *Sports Health* 10 (1): 19-30. https://doi.org/10.1177/1941738117727736.

Matthews, J.J., G.G. Artioli, M.D. Turner, and C. Sale. 2019. "The Physiological Roles of Carnosine and Beta-Alanine in Exercising Human Skeletal Muscle." *Medicine and Science in Sports and Exercise* 51 (10): 2098-2108. https://doi.org/10.1249/MSS.0000000000002033.

Maughan, R.J., L.M. Burke, J. Dvorak, D.E. Larson-Meyer, P. Peeling, S.M. Phillips, E.S. Rawson, et al. 2018. "IOC Consensus Statement: Dietary Supplements and the High-Performance Athlete." *International Journal of Sport Nutrition and Exercise Metabolism* 28 (2): 104-125. https://doi.org/10.1123/ijsnem.2018-0020.

Maughan, R. J., P.L. Greenhaff, and P. Hespel, P. 2011. "Dietary supplements for athletes: emerging trends and recurring themes." *Journal of sports sciences*, 29 Suppl 1, S57–S66. https://doi.org/10.1080/02640414.2011.587446.

McCormick, R., D. Moretti, A.K.A. McKay, C.M. Laarakkers, R. Vanswelm, D. Trinder, G.R. Cox, et al. 2019. "The Impact of Morning Versus Afternoon Exercise on Iron Absorption in Athletes." *Medicine and Science in Sports and Exercise* 51 (10): 2147-2155. https://doi.org/10.1249/MSS.0000000000002026.

McCormick, R., M. Sim, B. Dawson, and P. Peeling. 2020. "Refining Treatment Strategies for Iron Deficient Athletes." *Sports Medicine* 50 (12): 2111-2123. https://doi.org/10.1007/s40279-020-01360-2.

McDonnell, L.K., P.A. Hume, and V. Nolte. 2011. "Rib Stress Fractures Among Rowers: Definition, Epidemiology, Mechanisms, Risk Factors and Effectiveness of Injury Prevention Strategies." *Sports Medicine* 41 (11): 883-901. https://doi.org/10.2165/11593170-000000000-00000.

McKay, A.K.A., D.B. Pyne, L.M. Burke, and P. Peeling. 2020. "Iron Metabolism: Interactions With Energy and Carbohydrate Availability." *Nutrients* 12 (12): 3692. doi: 10.3390/nu12123692.

Menezes, E.F., L.G. Peixoto, R.R. Teixeira, A.B. Justino, G.M. Puga, and F.S. Espindola. 2019. "Potential Benefits of Nitrate Supplementation on Antioxidant Defense System and Blood Pressure Responses After Exercise Performance." *Oxidative Medicine and Cellular Longevity* 2019: 7218936. https://doi.org/10.1155/2019/7218936.

Mikulić, Pavle, Tomislav Smoljanović, Ivan Bojanić, Jo A. Hannafin, and Branka R. Matković. 2009. "Relationship Between 2000-m Rowing Ergometer Performance Times and World Rowing Championships Rankings in Elite-Standard Rowers." *Journal of Sports Sciences* 27 (9): 907-913. https://doi.org/10.1080/02640410902911950.

Mikulić, Pavle, Tomislav Smoljanović, Ivan Bojanić, Jo Hannafin, and Zeljko Pedisić. 2009. "Does 2000-m Rowing Ergometer Performance Time Correlate With Final Rankings at the World Junior Rowing Championship? A Case Study of 398 Elite Junior Rowers." *Journal of Sports Sciences* 27 (4): 361-366. https://doi.org/10.1080/02640410802600950.

Mountjoy, M., J. Sundgot-Borgen, L. Burke, et al. 2014. "The IOC Consensus Statement: Beyond the Female Athlete Triad–Relative Energy Deficiency in Sport (RED-S)." *British Journal of Sports Medicine* 48 (7): 491-497.

Outram, S., and B. Stewart. 2015. "Doping Through Supplement Use: A Review of the Available Empirical Data." *International Journal of Sport Nutrition and Exercise Metabolism* 25 (1): 54-59. https://doi.org/10.1123/ijsnem.2013-0174.

Owens, D.J., R. Allison, and G.L. Close. 2018. "Vitamin D and the Athlete: Current Perspectives and New Challenges." *Sports Medicine* 48 (Suppl. 1): 3-16. https://doi.org/10.1007/s40279-017-0841-9.

Owens, D.J., A.P. Sharples, I. Polydorou, N. Alwan, T. Donovan, J. Tang, W.D. Fraser, et al. 2015. "A Systems-Based Investigation Into Vitamin D and Skeletal Muscle Repair, Regeneration, and Hypertrophy." *American Journal of Physiology - Endocrinology and Metabolism* 309 (12): E1019-E1031. https://doi.org/10.1152/ajpendo.00375.2015.

Parnell, J.A., K.P. Wiens, and K.A. Erdman. 2016. "Dietary Intakes and Supplement Use in Pre-Adolescent and Adolescent Canadian Athletes." *Nutrients* 8 (9). https://doi.org/10.3390/nu8090526.

Peeling, P., M.J. Binnie, P.S.R. Goods, M. Sim, and L.M. Burke. 2018. "Evidence-Based Supplements for the Enhancement of Athletic Performance." *International Journal of Sport Nutrition and Exercise Metabolism* 28 (2): 178-187. https://doi.org/10.1123/ijsnem.2017-0343.

Percival, M.E., B.J. Martin, J.B. Gillen, L.E. Skelly, M.J. MacInnis, A.E. Green, M.A. Tarnopolsky, and M.J. Gibala. 2015. "Sodium Bicarbonate Ingestion Augments the Increase in PGC-1alpha mRNA Expression During Recovery From Intense Interval Exercise in Human Skeletal Muscle." *Journal of Applied Physiology (1985)* 119 (11): 1303-2312. https://doi.org/10.1152/japplphysiol.00048.2015.

Perim, P., F.M. Marticorena, F. Ribeiro, G. Barreto, N. Gobbi, C. Kerksick, E. Dolan, and B. Saunders. 2019. "Can the Skeletal Muscle Carnosine Response to Beta-Alanine Supplementation Be Optimized?" *Frontiers in Nutrition* 6: 135. https://doi.org/10.3389/fnut.2019.00135.

Pickering, C., and J. Kiely. 2018. "Are the Current Guidelines on Caffeine Use in Sport Optimal for Everyone? Inter-Individual Variation in Caffeine Ergogenicity, and a Move Towards Personalised Sports Nutrition." *Sports Medicine* 48 (1): 7-16. https://doi.org/10.1007/s40279-017-0776-1.

Piskin, E., D. Cianciosi, S. Gulec, M. Tomas, and E. Capanoglu. 2022. "Iron Absorption: Factors, Limitations, and Improvement Methods." *ACS Omega* 7 (24): 20441-20456. https://doi.org/10.1021/acsomega.2c01833.

Rawson, E.S. 2018. "The Safety and Efficacy of Creatine Monohydrate Supplementation: What Have We Learned From The Past 25 Years of Research." *Sports Science Exchange* 29 (186): 1-6.

Reinke, S., W.R. Taylor, G.N. Duda, S. von Haehling, P. Reinke, H.D. Volk, S.D. Anker, and W. Doehner. 2012. "Absolute and Functional Iron Deficiency in Professional Athletes During Training and Recovery." *International Journal of Cardiology* 156 (2): 186-191. https://doi.org/10.1016/j.ijcard.2010.10.139.

Ribbans, W.J., R. Aujla, S. Dalton, and J.A. Nunley. 2021. "Vitamin D and the Athlete–Patient: State of the Art." *Journal of ISAKOS* 6 (1): 46-60. doi: 10.1136/jisakos-2020-000435.

Sale, C., and K.J. Elliott-Sale. 2019. "Nutrition and Athlete Bone Health." *Sports Medicine* 49 (Suppl. 2): 139-151. https://doi.org/10.1007/s40279-019-01161-2.

Saunders, B., K. Elliott-Sale, G.G. Artioli, P.A. Swinton, E. Dolan, H. Roschel, C. Sale, and B. Gualano. 2017. "Beta-Alanine Supplementation to Improve Exercise Capacity and Performance: A Systematic Review and Meta-Analysis." *British Journal of Sports Medicine* 51 (8): 658-669. https://doi.org/10.1136/bjsports-2016-096396.

Saunders, B., V.D.E. Salles Painelli, L.F.D.E. Oliveira, V.D.A. Eira Silva, R.P.D.A. Silva, L. Riani, M. Franchi, et al. 2017. "Twenty-Four Weeks of Beta-Alanine Supplementation on Carnosine Content, Related Genes, and Exercise." *Medicine and Science in Sports and Exercise* 49 (5): 896-906. https://doi.org/10.1249/MSS.0000000000001173.

Saunders, Bryan, Luana Oliveira, R. Silva, Vitor Painelli, Lívia Gonçalves, Guilherme Yamaguchi, T. Mutti, et al. 2016. "Placebo in Sports Nutrition: A Proof-of-Principle Study Involving Caffeine Supplementation." *Scandinavian Journal of Medicine and Science in Sports* 27. https://doi.org/10.1111/sms.12793.

Siegler, J.C., P.W. Marshall, D. Bishop, G. Shaw, and S. Green. 2016. "Mechanistic Insights into the Efficacy of Sodium Bicarbonate Supplementation to Improve Athletic Performance." *Sports Medicine Open* 2 (1): 41. https://doi.org/10.1186/s40798-016-0065-9.

Sim, M., L.A. Garvican-Lewis, G.R. Cox, A. Govus, A.K.A. McKay, T. Stellingwerff, and P. Peeling. 2019. "Iron Considerations For the Athlete: A Narrative Review." *European Journal of Applied Physiology* 119 (7): 1463-1478. https://doi.org/10.1007/s00421-019-04157-y.

Sivamaruthi, B.S., P. Kesika, and C. Chaiyasut. 2019. "Effect of Probiotics Supplementations on Health Status of Athletes." *International Journal of Environmental Research and Public Health* 16 (22). https://doi.org/10.3390/ijerph16224469.

Skarpanska-Stejnborn, A., P. Basta, J. Trzeciak, and L. Szczesniak-Pilaczynska. 2015. "Effect of Intense Physical Exercise on Hepcidin Levels and Selected Parameters of Iron Metabolism in Rowing Athletes." *European Journal of Applied Physiology* 115 (2): 345-351. https://doi.org/10.1007/s00421-014-3018-3.

Skinner, T.L., D.G. Jenkins, J.S. Coombes, D.R. Taaffe, and M.D. Leveritt. 2010. "Dose Response of Caffeine on 2000-m Rowing Performance." *Medicine and Science in Sports and Exercise* 42 (3): 571-576. https://doi.org/10.1249/MSS.0b013e3181b6668b.

Sliwicka, E., A. Nowak, W. Zep, P. Leszczynski, and L. Pilaczynska-Szczesniak. 2015. "Bone Mass and Bone Metabolic Indices in Male Master Rowers." *Journal of Bone and Mineral Metabolism* 33 (5): 540-546. https://doi.org/10.1007/s00774-014-0619-1.

Southward, K., K. Rutherfurd-Markwick, C. Badenhorst, and A. Ali. 2018. "The Role of Genetics in Moderating the Inter-Individual Differences in the Ergogenicity of Caffeine." *Nutrients* 10 (10). https://doi.org/10.3390/nu10101352.

Stegen, S., L. Blancquaert, I. Everaert, T. Bex, Y. Taes, P. Calders, E. Achten, and W. Derave. 2013. "Meal and Beta-Alanine Coingestion Enhances Muscle Carnosine Loading." *Medicine and Science in Sports and Exercise* 45 (8): 1478-1485. https://doi.org/10.1249/MSS.0b013e31828ab073.

Stellingwerff, T., H. Anwander, A. Egger, T. Buehler, R. Kreis, J. Decombaz, and C. Boesch. 2012. "Effect of Two Beta-Alanine Dosing Protocols on Muscle Carnosine Synthesis and Washout." *Amino Acids* 42 (6): 2461-2472. https://doi.org/10.1007/s00726-011-1054-4.

Stellingwerff, T., J. Decombaz, R.C. Harris, and C. Boesch. 2012. "Optimizing Human in Vivo Dosing and Delivery of Beta-Alanine Supplements for Muscle Carnosine Synthesis." *Amino Acids* 43 (1): 57-65. https://doi.org/10.1007/s00726-012-1245-7.

Stellingwerff, T., R.J. Maughan, and L.M. Burke. 2011. "Nutrition for Power Sports: Middle-Distance Running, Track Cycling, Rowing, Canoeing/Kayaking, and Swimming." *Journal of Sports Sciences* 29 (Suppl. 1): S79-S89. https://doi.org/10.1080/02640414.2011.589469.

Temple, J.L., C. Bernard, S.E. Lipshultz, J.D. Czachor, J.A. Westphal, and M.A. Mestre. 2017. "The Safety of Ingested Caffeine: A Comprehensive Review." *Frontiers in Psychiatry* 8: 80. https://doi.org/10.3389/fpsyt.2017.00080.

Thomas, D.T., K.A. Erdman, and L.M. Burke. 2016. "American College of Sports Medicine Joint Statement." *Nutrition and Athletic Performance* 48, 3 (March): 543-568. https://doi.org/10.1249/MSS.0000000000000852.

Turnes, T., R.S.O. Cruz, F. Caputo, and R.A. De Aguiar. 2019. "The Impact of Preconditioning Strategies Designed to Improve 2000-m Rowing Ergometer Performance in Trained Rowers: A Systematic

Review and Meta-Analysis." *International Journal of Sports Physiology and Performance* 14 (7): 871-879. https://doi.org/10.1123/ijspp.2019-0247.

van Ballegooijen, A.J., S. Pilz, A. Tomaschitz, M.R. Grubler, and N. Verheyen. 2017. "The Synergistic Interplay Between Vitamins D and K for Bone and Cardiovascular Health: A Narrative Review." *International Journal of Endocrinology* 2017: 7454376. https://doi.org/10.1155/2017/7454376.

Wassef, B., M. Kohansieh, and A.N. Makaryus. 2017. "Effects of Energy Drinks on the Cardiovascular System." *World Journal of Cardiology* 9 (11): 796–806. https://doi.org/10.4330/wjc.v9.i11.796.

Weight, L.M., K.H. Myburgh, and T.D. Noakes. 1988. "Vitamin and Mineral Supplementation: Effect on the Running Performance of Trained Athletes." *American Journal of Clinical Nutrition* 47 (2): 192-195. https://doi.org/10.1093/ajcn/47.2.192.

West, N.P., P.L. Horn, D.B. Pyne, V.J. Gebski, S.J. Lahtinen, P.A. Fricker, and A.W. Cripps. 2014. "Probiotic Supplementation for Respiratory and Gastrointestinal Illness Symptoms in Healthy Physically Active Individuals." *Clinical Nutrition* 33 (4): 581-587. https://doi.org/10.1016/j.clnu.2013.10.002.

Williams, M.H. 2005. "Dietary Supplements and Sports Performance: Minerals." *Journal of the International Society of Sports Nutrition* 2: 43-49. https://doi.org/10.1186/1550-2783-2-1-43.

Wosinska, L., P.D. Cotter, O. O'Sullivan, and C. Guinane. 2019. "The Potential Impact of Probiotics on the Gut Microbiome of Athletes." *Nutrients* 11 (10). https://doi.org/10.3390/nu11102270.

Wylie, L.J., J. Kelly, S.J. Bailey, J.R. Blackwell, P.F. Skiba, P.G. Winyard, A.E. Jeukendrup, A. Vanhatalo, and A.M. Jones. 2013. "Beetroot Juice and Exercise: Pharmacodynamic and Dose-Response Relationships." *Journal of Applied Physiology (1985)* 115 (3): 325-336. https://doi.org/10.1152/japplphysiol.00372.2013.

Yamaguchi, G. C., K. Nemezio, M.L. Schulz, J. Natali, J.E. Cesar, L.A. Riani, L.S. Gonçalves, G.B. Möller, C. Sale, M.H.G. DE Medeiros, B. Gualano, and G.G. Artioli. 2021. "Kinetics of Muscle Carnosine Decay after β-Alanine Supplementation: A 16-wk Washout Study." *Medicine and science in sports and exercise.* 53(5): 1079–1088. https://doi.org/10.1249/MSS.0000000000002559.

Chapter 30

Anthony, D., D. Gucciardi, and S. Gordon. 2016. "A Meta-Study of Qualitative Research on Mental Toughness Development." *International Review of Sport and Exercise Psychology* 9 (1): 160-190. doi: 10.1080/1750984X.2016.1146787.

Beilock, S. 2010. *Choke: What the Secrets of the Brain Reveal About Getting It Right When You Have To.* New York: Atria.

Bortoli, L., M. Bertollo, Y.L. Hanin, and C. Robazza. 2012. "Striving for Excellence: A Multi-Action Plan Intervention Model for Shooters." *Psychology of Sport and Exercise* 13: 693-701. doi: 10.1016/j.psychsport.2012.04.006.

Csikszentmihalyi, M. 2008. *Flow: The Psychology of Optimal Performance.* New York: HarperCollins.

Deci, E.L., and R.M. Ryan. 1985. *Intrinsic Motivation and Self-Determination in Human Behavior.* New York: Plenum.

Deci, E.L., and R.M. Ryan. 2008. "Self-Determination Theory: A Macrotheory of Human Motivation, Development, and Health." *Canadian Psychology/Psychologie Canadienne* 49 (3): 182-185. doi: 10.1037/a0012801.

Duckworth, A. 2016. *Grit: The Power of Passion and Perseverance.* Toronto: HarperCollins Publishers.

Dweck, C. 2006. *Mindset: The New Psychology of Success.* New York: Ballantine Books.

Fitts, P.M., and M.I. Posner. 1967. *Human Performance.* Monterey, CA: Brooks/Cole.

Fletcher, D., and M. Sarkar. 2012. "A Grounded Theory of Psychological Resilience in Olympic Champions." *Psychology of Sport and Exercise* 13: 669-678. doi: 13.10.1016/j.psychsport.2012.04.007.

Fletcher, D., and M. Sarkar. 2013. "Psychological Resilience: A Review and Critique of Definitions, Concepts and Theory." *European Psychologist* 18: 12-23.

Fletcher, D., and M. Sarkar. 2016. "Mental Fortitude Training: An Evidence-Based Approach to Developing Psychological Resilience for Sustained Success." *Journal of Sport Psychology in Action* 7, no. 3 (December): 135-157. doi: 10.1080/21520704.2016.1255496.

Galli, N., and R.S. Vealey. 2008. "'Bouncing Back' From Adversity: Athletes' Experiences of Resilience." *The Sport Psychologist* 22: 316-335.

Goleman, D. 2013. *Focus: The Hidden Driver of Excellence*. New York: HarperCollins.

Hatfield, B.D., and S.E. Kerick. 2007. "The Psychology of Superior Performance: A Cognitive and Affective Neuroscience Perspective." In *Handbook of Sport Psychology*, 3rd ed., edited by G. Tenenbaum and R.C. Eklund, 84-109. Hoboken, NJ: Wiley. doi: 10.1002/9781118270011.ch4.

Jones, G., S. Hanton, and D. Connaughton. 2007. "A Framework of Mental Toughness in the World's Best Performers." *The Sport Psychologist* 21 (2): 243-264.

Lehrer, P., and R. Gevirtz. 2014. "Heart Rate Variability Biofeedback: How and Why Does It Work?" *Frontiers in Psychology*. doi: 10.3389/fpsyg.2014.00756.

Moran, A. 2004. *Sport and Exercise Psychology: A Critical Introduction*. London: Routledge.

Roberts, G.C., ed. 2001. *Advances in Motivation in Sport and Exercise*. Champaign, IL: Human Kinetics.

Roberts, G.C., D.C. Treasure, and M. Kavussanu. 1996. "Orthogonality of Achievement Goals and Its Relationship to Beliefs About Success and Satisfaction in Sport." *The Sport Psychologist* 10 (4): 398-408.

Sarkar, M., and D. Fletcher. 2014. "Psychological Resilience in Sport Performers: A Review of Stressors and Protective Factors." *Journal of Sports Sciences* 32 (15): 1419-1434. doi: 10.1080/02640414.2014.901551.

Selye, H. 1974. *The Stress of Life*. New York: McGraw-Hill.

Ungar, M., M. Ghazinour, and J. Richter. 2013. "What Is Resilience Within the Ecology of Human Development?" *Journal of Child Psychology and Psychiatry* 54 (4): 348-366. doi: 10.1111/jcpp.12025.

Chapter 31

Beauchamp, M.R., A. Maclachlan, and A.M. Lothian. 2005. "Communication Within Sport Teams: Jungian Preferences and Group Dynamics." *The Sport Psychologist* 19: 203-220.

Carron, A.V., L.R. Brawley, and W. Widmeyer. 1998. "The Measurement of Cohesiveness in Sport Groups." In *Advancements in Sport and Exercise Psychology Measurement*, edited by J.L. Duda, 213-266. Morgantown, WV: Fitness Information Technology.

Carron, A.V., and Spink, K.S. 1993. "Team Building in an Exercise Setting." *The Sport Psychologist* 7 (1): 8-18.

DePree, M. 1992. *Leadership Jazz*. New York: Dell Publishing.

Fletcher, D., and R. Arnold. 2011. "A Qualitative Study of Performance Leadership and Management in Elite Sport." *Journal of Applied Sport Psychology* 23 (2): 223-242. doi: 10.1080/10413200.2011.559184.

Forsyth, D.R. 2010. *Group Dynamics*. 5th ed. Belmont, CA: Wadsworth, Cengage Learning.

Fransen, K., D. McEwan, and M. Sarkar. 2020. "The Impact of Identity Leadership on Team Functioning and Well-Being in Team Sport: Is Psychological Safety the Missing Link?" *Psychology of Sport and Exercise* 51. doi: 10.1016/j.psychsport.2020.101763.

Haslam, S.A., K. Fransen, and F. Boen. 2020. *The New Psychology of Sport and Exercise: The Social Identity Approach*. Thousand Oaks, CA: Sage Publications Ltd.

Haslam, S.A., S.D. Reicher, and M.J. Platow. 2020. *The New Psychology of Leadership: Identity, Influence and Power*. 2nd ed. New York: Routledge.

Jung, C.G. 1971. *The Collected Works of C.G. Jung* (vol. 6.). Princeton, NJ: Princeton University Press.

Killinger, B. 2007. *Integrity: Doing the Right Thing for the Right Reason*. Montreal: McGill-Queen's University Press.

Posner, B. 2010. "Another Look at the Impact of Personal and Organizational Values Congruency." *Journal of Business Ethics* 97: 535-541. doi: 10.1007/s10551-010-0530-1.

Scott, S. 2002. *Fierce Conversations: Achieving Success at Work and in Life, One Conversation at a Time*. New York: Berkley Publishing Group.

Scott, S. 2009. *Fierce Leadership*. New York: Crown Publishing Group.

Sinek, Simon. 2009. *Start With Why: How Great Leaders Inspire Everyone to Take Action*. New York: Penguin Group.

Tuckman, B.W. 1965. "Developmental Sequences in Small Groups." *Psychological Bulletin* 63: 384-399.

Werthner, P., and S. Taylor. 2010. "Communicating With Clarity: Guidelines to Help Female Coaches Succeed." In *Taking the Lead: Strategies and Solutions from Women Coaches*, edited by S. Robertson, 101-115. Edmonton: University of Alberta Press.

Epilogue

Atkinson, E.C. 1896. "A Rowing Indicator." *Natural Science* VIII: 178-185.

Atkinson, E.C. 1898. "Some More Rowing Experiments." *Natural Science* XIII: 89-102.

International Olympic Committee. Accessed July 2021. https://olympics.com/ioc/world-rowing.

Kleshnev, V. 2020. "Trends of Rowing Speed." *Rowing Biomechanics Newsletter* no. 233 (August).

Kleshnev, V. 2021. "Analysis of Tokyo Olympics Results." *Rowing Biomechanics Newsletter* no. 244 (July).

Nolte, V. 1981. Über die Wissenschaft beim Rollausleger. In: Rudersport, 30/81, 639-642.

Nolte, V. 1984. *Die Effektivität des Ruderschlages: biomechanische Modelle, Analyse und Ergebnisse.* Berlin: Bartels & Wernitz.

Schneider, E., and F. Morell. 1977. "Leistungs- und stilbestimmende Parameter beim Rudern." *Medizintechnik in der Schweiz Medita*: 9a.

Wikipedia. n.d. "Science." Accessed September 2021. https://en.wikipedia.org/wiki/Science.

Index

About the Editor

Volker Nolte, PhD, is a professor emeritus of the University of Western Ontario, where he taught biomechanics and coaching (1993-2019) and also was the head rowing coach (1993-2017). Nolte's leadership has led Western University Mustangs men's rowing team to 14 Ontario University Athletics Championships and six Canadian University Rowing Championships. Since he took over the women's team in 2010, they have won five Ontario University Athletics Championships and four Canadian University Rowing Championships. In 2008, the men's eight won the German University Championships, the Temple Challenge Cup at the Henley Royal Regatta (against 74 other crews from around the world), and the Canadian University Rowing Championships. In 2013 and again in 2015, Nolte's Mustang teams swept all university events in Canada, winning the Ontario and Canadian Rowing Championships in the women's and men's divisions. In 2016, the Western University team not only won both Ontario University Athletics Championships (women's and men's), as well as the Canadian University Rowing Championships for women, but also won two gold medals at the Head of the Charles Regatta.

In addition, Nolte was the lightweight men's national team coach with the German Rowing Association from 1984 to 1990 and with Rowing Canada Aviron from 1992 to 2000. His crews won an Olympic silver medal at the 1996 Atlanta Games, two world championship titles in 1993 and 2000, and several more medals at world championships. His latest successes with the Canadian national team were bronze silver medals at the 2012 and 2013 U23 World Championships in the women's single. In 2015-2016 he again coached the Canadian women's single, this time to two Pan Am Games gold medals, a first place at the FISA World Cup in Italy, a sixth place at the World Championships 2015, and a 10th place at the Rio de Janeiro Olympic Games.

Nolte received undergraduate degrees in both physical education (1976) and civil engineering (1979) from the University of Saarbrücken and a PhD in biomechanics (1984) from the German Sport University in Cologne, Germany. He is an internationally acknowledged expert in biomechanics and coaching, and he presents frequently at scientific and coach education conferences worldwide. His research includes biomechanics of high-performance sport and coaching. He is also a distinguished researcher in the field of sport equipment, and his innovations range from special measurement tools to new boat designs. His research has produced many papers in refereed journals, articles in various publications, and several books.

For his work in coach education, he received the prestigious Queen Elizabeth II Diamond Jubilee Medal in January 2013. For his outstanding success as a coach, he was named Ontario Coach of the Year in 1993 and again in 2014. Finally, Row Ontario presented Nolte with the President's Award in 2017, and Rowing Canada Aviron honored him with the Lifetime Achievement Award in 2018 to recognize his achievements in many areas of rowing.

Nolte is an experienced rower, representing his home country of Germany at several world championships. He is still a keen competitor in the Masters events.

Nolte lives in London, Ontario.

About the Contributors

Susan Boegman, RD, has been facilitating sport excellence through innovative nutrition strategies and athlete-centered care within the high-level sport system over the past four Olympic quadrennials. Boegman is currently the nutrition lead for the Canadian Sport Institute Pacific. She has provided integrated nutrition support for many national teams—including swimming, rugby, triathlon, and soccer—and has been an integral part of the sport science and medicine team working with Rowing Canada Aviron since 2007. Prior to focusing on sport, Boegman spent 19 years working as a nutrition counselor within a highly specialized eating disorders program. This background provided her with unique insight into the importance of our relationships to food and the need for individualized nutrition considerations, laying the groundwork for her passion for the art and science of high-performance sport nutrition support. As an advocate of lifelong health and activity, her top priority is caring for the whole athlete to facilitate success both in competition and in life. Boegman holds the Registered Dietitian credential from the College of Dietitians of British Columbia as well as the High Performance Certified Senior Practitioner credential from Sport Scientist Canada. She has a bachelor of science degree from the University of Alberta, is a level 2 anthropometrist certified by the International Society for the Advancement of Kinanthropometry (ISAK), and is now a contributing lecturer for the prestigious International Olympic Committee sport nutrition diploma program.

Daniel Bechard is the head coach of the men's rowing program at Western University in London, Canada, and a researcher at Hudson Boat Works. He completed his doctorate studying biomechanics in health and rehabilitation sciences, and he has coached internationally through his career. Bechard also regularly presents at conferences and coaching education courses on the impact of technology on the advancement rowing.

Glen Burston is part owner and operation manager of Hudson Boat Works in London, Canada. He received a master of engineering degree from Western University and is a professional engineer. Burston is a regular contributor to business forums and a founding member of the Rowing Industry Trade Association. Burston focuses on precision in the manufacturing process, engaging new technologies and enhancing accessibility to rowing.

Stephen S. Cheung, PhD, is a professor and senior research fellow in the department of kinesiology at Brock University, where he directs the Environmental Ergonomics Lab. Dr. Cheung's research focus is the impact of environmental stressors on human physiology and performance, with more than 140 peer-reviewed publications and 2 books. He has worked extensively with elite athletes, including world champion cyclists and Canadian Olympic athletes. Dr. Cheung has also worked with many industrial partners to improve work and safety in extreme environments, including firefighting, search and rescue, military duty, ultra-deep mining, offshore oil drilling, and clothing manufacturing. His love of physiology and human performance grew from his passion for bike racing since the mid-1980s, and he coauthored *Cutting-Edge Cycling* (2012) and *Cycling Science* (2017). When not cycling, he can usually be found hanging on for dear life in his other favorite sport, rock climbing.

Paula Jardine is a rowing coach and high-performance athlete development consultant specializing in talent transfer. She established the Talent Lab Project at the Canadian Sport

Institute Calgary and ran it between 2012 and 2016. The Talent Lab Project developed four Olympic competitors in the sports of cycling, swimming, and rowing, including three Olympic medalists, one of whom was an Olympic rowing champion. She also managed the Southwest Talent Centre at the University of Bath, which was selected as a semifinalist in the 2011 U.K. National Lottery Awards (Best Sport Project).

Ed McNeely has spent more than 30 years working in high-performance sports, providing physiology, strength and conditioning, and nutrition services to 20 national sport organizations, including 24 years working with Rowing Canada. He has been a frequent speaker at rowing conferences in Canada and the United States and has been a contributor to many rowing publications.

Brett (Tiaki) Smith, PhD, is a senior lecturer in the School of Health at Te Huataki Waiora (University of Waikato), New Zealand. Dr. Smith is a member of the Ngati Rakaipaaka iwi (tribe) from Tahaenui, Hawke's Bay. His wife, Connie, is a senior manager with Kainga Ora, and together they have two adult daughters. The eldest is married and now lives in British Columbia, while the youngest is completing postgraduate studies on concussions among freestyle skiers. Dr. Smith worked closely with Harry Mahon and then Dick Tonks in the New Zealand rowing program for over 15 years before working with Ian Wright in both the Swiss and Australian rowing programs. After the London Olympics, he branched out into professional rugby union, with a multitude of teams across the world, including the All Blacks and Black Ferns Sevens teams, the Chiefs and Blues Super Rugby teams, Kobe Steelers, Rugby New York, and Italian Rugby Federation. Despite competing a PhD in endocrine physiology and immunology, Dr. Smith's current research interests are more closely aligned with data science.

Jane Thornton, MD, PhD, is a sports medicine physician and clinician scientist specializing in long-term athlete health, female athlete health, and physical activity in the prevention and treatment of chronic disease. She is an assistant professor in the department of family medicine at the Schulich School of Medicine and Dentistry at Western University in London, Canada, with cross-appointments in the department of epidemiology and biostatistics and department of kinesiology. Dr. Thornton represented Canada for over a decade in the sport of elite rowing, becoming both a world champion (2006) and an Olympian (2008).

Gunnar Treff, PhD, is an exercise physiologist and a senior researcher at the Paracelsus Medical University in Salzburg, Austria. Until 2021 Dr. Treff worked at Jürgen Steinacker's lab at the University of Ulm, where he led several rowing research projects with high scientific and practical impact. Dr. Treff worked for the German Rowing Federation as a training scientist and physiologist for 16 years and was part of the successful scull teams during the London and Rio de Janeiro Olympics. In addition, he was the national scientific coordinator of the German Rowing Federation from 2012 to 2022.

Penny Werthner, PhD, is currently interim provost and vice president (academic) at University of Calgary, and served from 2012 to 2022 as dean of the faculty of kinesiology at University of Calgary, which is currently ranked number 1 for sport science schools in North America for the fourth time and is ranked number 11 globally. Her own research is in the area of lifelong and social learning, particularly in the area of high-performance coaches; leadership, particularly women's leadership experiences and learning; psychological health and wellness; and heart rate variability biofeedback and neurofeedback for optimal performance in high-performance sport. Dr. Werthner is a former Olympic athlete; she represented Canada at the 1976 Summer Olympics in the women's 1,500 m (and would have been in the 1980 Olympics in Moscow, if Canada had not boycotted the Games). She won medals in two Pan American Games and one Commonwealth Games in the 800 m and 1,500 m. Dr. Werthner is also recognized as one of Canada's most distinguished practitioners in the field of sport psychology and leadership behavior. She has worked with many Olympic-level athletes, coaches, and teams (Summer and Winter Games) from 1996 to the present.